Saskia Limbach

Government Use of Print

Official Publications in the Holy Roman Empire, 1500–1600

Studien zur
europäischen Rechtsgeschichte

Veröffentlichungen des
Max-Planck-Instituts
für Rechtsgeschichte und Rechtstheorie
Frankfurt am Main

Band 326

Vittorio Klostermann
Frankfurt am Main
2021

Saskia Limbach

Government Use of Print

Official Publications in the Holy Roman Empire, 1500–1600

Vittorio Klostermann
Frankfurt am Main
2021

Umschlagbild:
„Der Buchdrücker", Holzschnitt von Jost Amman aus:
Hans Sachs, Eygentliche Beschreibung aller Stände auff Erden, hoher und nidriger, geistlicher und weltlicher, aller Künsten, Handwercken und Händeln, Frankfurt am Main 1568, p. 24,
http://www.digitalis.uni-koeln.de/Amman/amman_index.html

Bibliographische Information der Deutschen Nationalbibliothek
Die Deutsche Nationalbibliothek verzeichnet diese Publikation in der Deutschen Nationalbibliographie; detaillierte bibliographische Daten sind im Internet über *http://dnb.dnb.de* abrufbar.

Druck und Bindung: docupoint GmbH, Barleben
Typographie: Elmar Lixenfeld, Frankfurt am Main

Gedruckt auf Eos Werkdruck.
Alterungsbeständig ∞ ISO 9706 und PEFC-zertifiziert

Printed in Germany
ISSN 1610-6040
ISBN 978-3-465-04425-3

Table of Contents

Acknowledgements

A great many people have contributed to the production of this study, which I submitted as a PhD thesis at the University of St Andrews in 2017 and then progressively extended and updated, and I am forever in their debt. Without them this work would not have taken the shape it has now, and they have helped make my graduate experience one that I will always cherish.

My deepest gratitude goes to my supervisor, Andrew Pettegree. He gave me the freedom to explore my own ideas and at the same time the guidance to recover when my steps faltered. Andrew's patience and support helped me to overcome obstacles, and his assistance in writing grant proposals and scholarship applications helped me to secure the financial means to conduct my research. His maddening attention to detail drove me to abandon split infinitives and see the beauty of short, succinct sentences.

A very special thanks goes to Falk Eisermann, without whose motivation and encouragement my work with broadsheet material would have been much harder. His extensive publications have provided me with a clear guideline, and I am deeply grateful to him for the long discussions that enabled me to sort out various details of my work. Falk never failed to answer my many questions and his *Lesefrüchte* were a particular treat to read.

My two examiners, Bridget Heal and Beat Kümin, have provided me with constructive criticism as well as excellent feedback. Their observations have helped me to see the impact of my work much more clearly, which enabled me to write more confidently about the results of my research. I would like to thank them wholeheartedly for engaging so thoroughly with my work and supporting me in my post-doc years.

Over the past years I had the privilege to meet aspiring historians at guest lectures, workshops or conferences. It was a particular joy to discuss aspects of my work with Natalie Zemon Davis, Sheilagh Ogilvie, Geoffrey Parker and Barbara Stollberg-Rilinger as my project took shape. I would like to thank them for their helpful suggestions and their encouraging words.

I would also like to thank the wonderful staff at the *Hauptstaatsarchiv Stuttgart*, especially Peter Rückert, who repeatedly helped me to unearth material essential to my research and provided me with valuable knowledge on early modern Württemberg. Erwin Frauenknecht was very kind in furnishing me with insights into watermarks and papermaking. The reading room staff, including Frau Deckert, Frau Kremser and Frau Heck, have always given me quick and uncomplicated access to various documents.

After the building collapse of the Historical Archive of the City of Cologne in 2009, it would have been extremely difficult to conduct my research if it had not been for the gracious help of various people. Although a tragedy, it also showed how fruitful collaboration can be in the face of adversity. First and foremost, I would like to thank Gerd Schwerhoff for his generous support and advice in the last year of my PhD. Klaus Militzer, although retired, has also helped me during my stay in Cologne and gave me much food for thought. Matthias Miller from the Deutsches Historisches Museum has pointed me to the many surviving Cologne broadsheets in the collection of the DHM which were very valuable for this study. Wolfgang Schmitz has always been approachable and helped me to discover hitherto unknown broadsheet editions. He also put me in touch with Frau Wagner from the *Stadtmuseum*, which houses more singe-sheet treasures. Lastly, Max Plassmann and Björn Raffelsiefen in the Cologne archive have provided me with much support on multiple occasions.

I am very grateful for the financial support I received from the AHRC, the St Andrews School of History, the Royal Historical Society, the German Historical Institute London and the Bibliographical Society. I owe special thanks to the German History Society, which not only offered generous financial assistance but also facilitated thought-provoking conferences and workshops. These events have enabled me to formulate ideas, discuss my research with experts and build a network of professional contacts. I would also like to thank Erk Volkmar Heyen for sponsoring a research fellowship in the field of European Administrative History, which helped me to finance the last stages of my PhD. Finally, I am thankful for the research stipend of the Max Planck Institute for European Legal History which allowed me to stay at the institute in late 2016. The institute's members have welcomed me warmly during my stay in Frankfurt, and I have received valuable advice from them, especially from Karl Härter and Michael Stolleis, who introduced me to new ideas on early modern *policey.* I had many interesting discussions with Manuela Bragagnolo about the common ground shared by book historians and legal historians, and I am looking forward to working with the members of the institute on building bridges between the two disciplines.

During my PhD I was fortunate to present my research at various events and universities. I am particularly grateful to Wolfgang Behringer, Renate Dürr, Gerd Schwerhoff and Susanna Burghartz for their cordial invitations. Their generous feedback has been of great use to me, particularly in understanding the meaning and value of some of my findings. The annual book history conferences organised by the USTC team have been very invigorating, and I would like to thank the entire team for their collegiality and support. This includes especially Jamie Cumby, Alex Hill and Arthur der Weduwen, who offered me great advice and the opportunity to discuss and further formulate my thoughts.

I greatly enjoyed my time in St Andrews as a member of a wonderful research community. The activities of the School of History were inspiring and created a stimulating environment. I would like to thank the entire student body and staff members, including those who left 'the bubble' before me: Flavia Bruni, Nik Funke, Nadja Pentzlin, Miriam Schneider, Abaigéal Warfield and Róisín Watson. Last, but certainly not least, I would like to thank Nikolaus Weichselbaumer for his generous support in the final stage of the publication of this book and Lena Hinrichsen for her helpful suggestions.

I am particularly grateful to the editors of the 'Studien zur europäischen Rechtsgeschichte' for accepting my proposal and the kind help I received afterwards from Otto Danwerth, James Thompson and Beate Jaeger. Finally, I would like to thank the Vittorio Klostermann Verlag for seeing this book through to publication.

Abbreviations and Editorial Conventions

Archives and libraries

DHM	Deutsches Historisches Museum Berlin
HAStK	Historisches Archiv der Stadt Köln
HStASt	Hauptstaatsarchiv Stuttgart
KSM	Kölnisches Stadtmuseum
UAT	Universitätsarchiv Tübingen
USBK	Universitäts- und Stadtbibliothek Köln
WLB	Württembergische Landesbibliothek Stuttgart

Collected source editions and bibliographies

BC	Borchling, Conrad and Bruno Claussen (eds.) (1976), *Niederdeutsche Bibliographie. Gesamtverzeichnis der niederdeutschen Drucke bis zum Jahre 1800*, 3 vols, Utrecht: Hes Publishers
Briefwechsel	Ernst, Victor (ed.) (1899–1907), *Briefwechsel des Herzogs Christoph von Wirtemberg*, 4 vols, Stuttgart: Kohlhammer
GW	Gesamtkatalog der Wiegendrucke, http://www.gesamtkatalogderwiegendrucke.de
Policey K	Militzer, Klaus (ed.) (2005), *Repertorium der Policeyordnungen der Frühen Neuzeit. Reichsstädte 2: Köln*, 2 vols, Frankfurt am Main: Klostermann
Policey W	Landwehr, Achim and Thomas Simon (eds.) (2011), *Repertorium der Policeyordnungen der Frühen Neuzeit.* Vol. 4: *Baden und Württemberg*, Frankfurt am Main: Klostermann
RB	Groten, Manfred and Manfred Huiskes (eds.) (1988–2003), *Beschlüsse des Rates der Stadt Köln, 1320–1550. Die Ratsmemoriale und ergänzende Überlieferung, 1320–1543*, 6 vols, Düsseldorf: Droste
Reske	Reske, Christoph (ed.) (2015), *Die Buchdrucker des 16. und 17. Jahrhunderts im deutschen Sprachgebiet*, 2nd ed, Wiesbaden: Harrassowitz
Reyscher	Reyscher, August Ludwig (ed.) (1828–1851), *Vollständige, historisch und kritisch bearbeitete Sammlung der württembergischen Gese[t]ze*, 19 vols, Stuttgart / Tübingen: Cotta/Fues

VD16	Verzeichnis der im deutschen Sprachbereich erschienenen Drucke des 16. Jahrhunderts, www.vd16.de
VD17	Verzeichnis der im deutschen Sprachbereich erschienenen Drucke des 17. Jahrhunderts, www.vd17.de
VE15	Eisermann, Falk (ed.) (2004), *Verzeichnis der typographischen Einblattdrucke des 15. Jahrhunderts im Heiligen Römischen Reich Deutscher Nation*, Wiesbaden: Reichert
USTC	Universal Short Title Catalogue, www.ustc.ac.uk

The spelling of sixteenth-century German was not standardised except to improve legibility. Contractions, such as 'ā', 'ē', 'ī', 'ō', 'ū', were replaced with the correct omission; abbreviations were resolved wherever possible.

When an early modern edition is cited, the USTC reference is given, supplemented by VD16 and VD17 references for German editions. This permits the use of a uniform reference system for all early modern books and limits verbose descriptions unless required by the context.

Unless otherwise stated, dates are given in the New Style. First names and place names appear (as far as possible) in Anglicised versions with standardised spelling. German quotes from primary and secondary sources have been translated into modern English by the author. All World Wide Web addresses were last accessed on January 31, 2021.

List of Illustrations

Chapter One

Chapter Two

Chapter Three

Chapter Four

Introduction

The 1540s were crucial years for John Frederick I, Elector of Saxony: his endorsement of Protestantism as well as his involvement with the Schmalkaldic League placed him in an extremely vulnerable position. He knew that, in order to seek support in these dangerous times, it was of utmost importance to communicate effectively. Therefore, when John Frederick rode into battle throughout these years, he not only took with him the usual supplies like ammunition, armour, and food, but also a printing press, several assistants to work it, as well as type, paper, and ink.[1] With this, the Elector was able to reproduce important letters and announcements on the spot without having to send them to a distant printing house first. This saved him extremely valuable time and enabled him to reach out to his subjects and ask for support as quickly as possible. When the Schmalkaldic War broke out in 1546, the technical innovation proved especially useful, and John Frederick employed the press to order his soldiers to reinforce his army and to instruct his vassals about the new taxes to support the defence of his territory.[2]

The press was not only useful on the battlefield; it also offered great possibilities for governments throughout the entire empire, and rulers seized the opportunities offered by typography almost from the very beginning. Duke Maximilian of Austria made ample use of the new medium from 1478 onwards, especially when he succeeded to the royal throne in the 1490s.[3] Alongside oral communication, Maximilian used printed documents to inform his subjects about recent events, provide war reports, and broadcast victories.[4] The emperor even smuggled pamphlets over the borders to undermine the authority of the

1 Volz (1963), 'Zur Geschichte des Wittenberger Buchdrucks, 1544–57', p. 116.

2 *Ibid.*, p. 117.

3 Eisermann (2002), 'Buchdruck und Politische Kommunikation', pp. 76–83; see also most recently Limbach (2021), 'New perspectives on broadsheets and political communication at the time of Maximilian I'.

4 Füssel (2005), *Gutenberg and the Impact of Printing*, p. 154; Müller (2004), 'Publizistik unter Maximilian I.', pp. 95–122; Tischer (2012), *Offizielle Kriegsbegründungen in der Frühen Neuzeit. Herrscherkommunikation in Europa zwischen Souveränität und korporativem Selbstverständnis*, pp. 108 ff.

Signoria in Venice.[5] His ambitions did not stop there; the emperor also embarked on numerous costly print projects covering a range of genres. Besides an autobiography, Maximilian had an epic poem published as well as his *Honour Arch*, a series of over 100 printed woodcuts. These many publications helped the emperor to solidify his political position and to establish himself as a memorable example for posterity.[6]

The use of the press was not confined to the imperial government; other authorities in the Holy Roman Empire quickly realised the advantages of the new technical communication and followed Maximilian's example.[7] The multiplicity of jurisdictions in the Holy Roman Empire created a surge of publications from official bodies. The USTC currently lists some 700 official publications printed in fifteenth-century Europe.[8] Whereas 138 of these editions were printed in Spain and 83 in France, the overwhelming majority of official publications, some 450 items, were printed in Germany. Among them are publications from the city magistrates in Nuremberg, Augsburg, and Cologne; the territorial rulers of Saxony, Bavaria, and Württemberg; and religious authorities such as the bishops of Bamberg and Würzburg. With the expansion of government activities in the sixteenth century, this already high number of publications increased exponentially. Many rulers perceived the printing press as the ideal means to spread announcements, invitations, and instructions and, above all, to implement law and order. As a result, Germany was flooded with official publications which were commonly posted on walls and on the doors of town halls and churches.

For many rulers in the sixteenth century, the printing press played a central role in their government activities. Despite the importance of this new technology, however, there are very few studies that focus on government use of print. This is especially surprising since the production of single-sheet items was an essential component of sixteenth-century publishing. In many parts of Europe, the printing of forms, official orders, and proclamations underpinned the economics of the industry. A recent survey on publishing in the Low Countries reveals that more than 10 % of the total output was made up by broadsheets.[9] These single-sheet items generated healthy profits for printers, and many were

5 Füssel (2005), *Gutenberg and the Impact of Printing*, p. 156; Lutter (2002), 'Propaganda Maximilians I. in Venedig', pp. 235–254.

6 Silver (2008), *Marketing Maximilian.*

7 Honemann, Griese and Eisermann (1999), 'Zu Wesen und Bedeutung des textierten Einblattdrucks', p. 341; Seggern (2009), 'Gedruckte Urkunden', pp. 129–144.

8 USTC search: Subject - Ordinances and Edicts, Date - 1450–1500.

9 Pettegree and Walsby (eds.) (2010), *Netherlandish Books*, I, p. xvii.

keen to secure these lucrative deals. Even Gutenberg paused the production of his famous Bible to print indulgences for religious authorities.[10] This way, he could generate more money for his ambitious project.

This study will address this research deficiency and investigate government use of print through two case studies: official publications printed in the Duchy of Württemberg and in the Imperial City of Cologne. These two contrasting jurisdictions – one a major princely state, the other, one of the greatest of the commercial cities – used print for a variety of different purposes, most importantly for publishing new legislation.[11] In this context, it is important to stress the interplay of various media in the sixteenth century. During that time, oral proclamations remained an essential means for authorities to communicate with their subjects. Comparing and contrasting Württemberg and Cologne will show us how various factors influenced the use of different media and enable us to trace the tentative beginnings of collaboration between rulers and printers in the Holy Roman Empire.

By focussing on governments and the use of media in the sixteenth century, this study will contribute to three different fields:

Book history

Already in the early days of print history, researchers had emphasised the economic side of the book business. Lucien Febvre and Henri-Jean Martin pointed out that in the printing industry, just like in any other industry, the producers faced two key problems: finance and costing.[12] Similarly, Rudolf Hirsch argued in his influential study on printing, selling, and reading that printers not only need the necessary skills to produce books but also business sense, intelligence, and a good understanding of the market.[13] These traits were vital to overcome the problems of selling printed books since the trade differed so decisively from the manuscript trade.

Although considered important from the very beginning, the financial aspect of the book business remained elusive for decades. When Elizabeth Eisenstein depicted the press as an agent of change and portrayed the printing house as a place where ambitious intellectuals did their best to democratise knowledge, she was criticised for paying far too little attention to the economic realities of the

10 Ing (1983), 'The Mainz Indulgences', pp. 14–31.

11 The Cologne council issued a very high number of police ordinances in contrast to other magistrates, such as those in Ulm, Frankfurt and Nördlingen, see Härter (2010b), 'Statut und Policeyordnung', p. 132.

12 Febvre and Martin (1958), *L'apparition du livre*, p. 204.

13 Hirsch (1974), *Printing, Selling and Reading*, p. 27.

early modern print industry.[14] In the following years, however, scholars did little to correct this mistake. We can only rely on a handful of studies which offer us glimpses into the finances of the trade, the sale of books, or their prices.[15] Sources are either scarce or fragmented, like the account book of Peter Drach, or so abundant that they have not yet been analysed with regard to production and sales, such as the Amerbach correspondence.[16]

Only recently did the economics of the industry attract more attention from international scholars. The book trade in particular became a focal point of many studies, with a special emphasis on the national and local trade as well as individual print shops.[17] Two large projects are particularly noteworthy: Christina Dondi and her research team currently investigate the book trade in the fifteenth century.[18] One of the focal points of the project is a bookshop's ledger recording nearly 7,000 sales between 1484–1488.[19] The second project, led by Angela Nuovo, reconstructs the economic and juridical framework of the European book market.[20]

For the German-speaking areas, only a small number of scholars have tried to address this omission more generally. Our knowledge of the financial transactions of printers, especially in the early age of print, rests only on a few studies.[21] Recently, Lucas Burkart has shown how quickly a successful printer in

14 Eisenstein (1979), *The Printing Press as an Agent of Change*; Grafton (1980), 'The Importance of Being Printed', pp. 265–286.

15 For instance, Krieg (1953), *Materialien zu einer Entwicklungsgeschichte der Bücher-Preise*; Widmann, Kliemann and Wendt (eds.) (1965), *Der deutsche Buchhandel in Urkunden und Quellen*. Also the new edition of Christoph Reske's standard work includes many references to singular payments, tax records, housing costs, and business transactions, see Reske.

16 Geldner (1964), 'Das Rechnungsbuch', col. 1–196; *Die Amerbachkorrespondenz*, ed. Hartmann and Jenny; Duntze highlights this lacuna of the Amerbach correspondence in his 'Verlagsbuchhandel und verbreitender Buchhandel', pp. 201–256.

17 For Germany, one of the standard works is Künast (1997), *'Getruckt zu Augspurg'*. Also, more recently, Bangert (2019), *Buchhandelssystem und Wissensraum in der Frühen Neuzeit*. For England, see for instance, Raven (2007), *The Business of Books*. For the Low Countries, see for instance, Bowen and Imhof (2008), *Christopher Plantin and Engraved Book Illustrations*. For a European perspective, see for instance the results of the USTC conference, Graheli (ed.) (2019), *Buying and Selling. The Business of Books in Early Modern Europe*.

18 http://15cbooktrade.ox.ac.uk/

19 Dondi and Harris (2014), 'Exporting Books from Milan to Venice', p. 121.

20 http://emobooktrade.unimi.it

21 See, amongst others: Keunecke (2015), 'Wirtschaftlicher Erfolg und Wohlstand bei deutschen Inkunabelndruckern', p. 64; Künast (1997), *'Getruckt zu Augspurg'*.

Basel could run into debt.[22] This reminds us, once again, that printers were businessmen and their first and foremost aim was to run a viable business that would yield enough profit to support the printer and his family. Many did not succeed in the new business and, as Andrew Pettegree argues convincingly, due to the economic hardship of the trade, it was not even certain that print would continue to exist in the sixteenth century.[23]

One way to survive in this cut-throat business was to seek the patronage of the state. Governments usually ordered an exact amount of copies and paid for the entire edition upon delivery. Printers, therefore, did not have to judge the size of the market and risk ending up with unsold stock. Many official publications were also short so that the production would only take a few days. This quick cash return offered printers much needed security and allowed them to embark on larger, more ambitious projects. Although present-day historians consider these smaller print jobs 'ephemera' or 'cheap print', they were, at the time, sought after by respected producers in the print industry. The celebrated typographer and publisher Christopher Plantin in Antwerp and his heirs printed hundreds of ordinances for the authorities and kept a file copy of almost every publication for posterity.[24] The high number of official broadsheets was not confined to Antwerp. In many parts of Europe, these publications formed an integral part of political life. We have ample evidence for the publishing activities of local governments in Bologna, Florence, Venice, Rome as well as the rulers in England and Ireland.[25] Just like in Antwerp, the producers of these documents were in many cases prolific printers. So, for example, Antonio Blado in Rome ran a successful and long-lasting business and also produced many ordinances for the popes.[26]

This plausible business strategy of early modern printers has long been overlooked by historians of print. When examining the interaction between authorities and printers, scholars have traditionally focussed on aspects of

22 See for instance, Burkart (2019), 'Early Book Printing and Venture Capital', pp. 23–54.

23 Pettegree (2010), *The Book in the Renaissance*, p. 53.

24 Voet (ed.) (1980–1983), *The Plantin Press (1555–1589)*; Imhof (2014), *Jan Moretus and the Continuation of the Plantin Press*; Cockx-Indestege, Glorieux and Beeck (eds.) (1968–1994), *Belgica typographica*.

25 Zanardi (ed.) (1996–2014), *Bononia Manifesta*; Grillo (2014), *Leggi e bandi di antico regime*; Hughes and Larkin (eds.) (1964–1969), *Tudor Royal Proclamations*; Salzberg (2014), *The Ephemeral City*, p. 63; Milner (2013), 'Town Criers and the Information Economy of Renaissance Florence', p. 113; Kelly and Lyons (eds.) (2014), *The Proclamations of Ireland 1660–1820*.

26 Bruni (2017b), 'In the Name of God', pp. 143–161. Santoro (2013), *Die Geschichte des Buchhandels in Italien*, p. 77.

regulation, censorship, and control.[27] To be sure, some studies emphasise that the regulation of the print industry was not simply a top-down imposition of order, but rather a dynamic process.[28] But only in recent years have historians concentrated on the common interests of rulers and printers. In France, officials and printers developed a mutually beneficial relationship.[29] Similarly, in England, the king's printers enjoyed a number of benefits and, in turn, ensured that the Crown's business went on smoothly.[30] In Spain, the printers worked closely with the Castilian Crown to edit, produce, and market legislation.[31]

It is, therefore, a more than welcome change that book historians are now dedicating more attention to the importance of ephemera and job printing. Although 'popular print' (or 'cheap print') has been the subject of study for decades (see, for instance, Margaret Spufford's work), the significance of these inexpensively-produced texts for their producers remained understudied.[32] Recently, Peter Stallybrass pointed to the importance of the 'little jobs' which kept the presses running.[33] In many cases, these were broadsheets produced for public display to reach as large an audience as possible. Additionally, new in-depth studies illuminate the production, distribution, and reception of cheap print as well as how it contributed to the creation of a public sphere.[34]

This study will contribute to these new research trends and present the first systematic examination of official print in sixteenth-century Germany. For this, I unearthed hundreds of broadsheet editions which were hitherto unknown to

27 GRENDLER (1981), *Culture and Censorship in Late Renaissance Italy and France*; PATTERSON (1984), *Censorship and Interpretation*; TODD (1991), *Political Bias, Censorship and the Dissolution of the 'Official' Press in Eighteenth Century France*. A notable exception is Karl Schottenloher whose work is cited throughout this study.

28 CREASMAN (2012), *Censorship and Civic Order in Reformation Germany*.

29 MCLEOD (2011), *Licensing Loyalty*.

30 REES and WAKELY (2009), *Publishing, Politics, and Culture. The King's Printers in the Age of James I and VI*.

31 RIAL COSTAS (2017), 'Marketing a New Legal Code in Fifteenth-Century Castile', pp. 87–108.

32 SPUFFORD (1981), *Small Books and Pleasant Histories*. For an overview of this area of research as well as new research trends, see ROSPOCHER, SALMAN and SALMI (eds.) (2019), *Crossing Borders, Crossing Cultures*.

33 STALLYBRASS (2007), '"Little Jobs": Broadsides and the Printing Revolution', pp. 315–341.

34 RAYMOND (ed.) (2011), *Cheap Print in Britain and Ireland to 1600*; SALZBERG (2014), *The Ephemeral City*; PETTEGREE (ed.) (2017), *Broadsheets. Single-Sheet Publishing in the First Age of Print*; WEDUWEN (2018), *State Communication*; BELLINGRADT (2011), *Flugpublizistik und Öffentlichkeit um 1700*, for more on the public sphere, see subchapter 'political culture' below.

book historians.[35] This new material provides a comprehensive overview of the official broadsheets published in Cologne and Württemberg over the space of 100 years. The study will not only analyse this rich material but also take into consideration lost editions, which have not survived until the present day, and larger publications financed by the authorities. The study also draws on extensive manuscript sources, such as drafts of ordinances, distribution lists, and instructions for circulation. An unparalleled source is the account book of the Württemberg government detailing over 300 individual payments to printers. Taken together, these sources provide invaluable insights into the composition, financing, printing, and distribution of government publications. These findings will be compared and contrasted with evidence from other territories and cities in the Holy Roman Empire, such as Nuremberg and Augsburg, as well as the Low Countries, France, and England. This way, I hope to provide a much more nuanced picture of the interaction between rulers and printers in the sixteenth century.

Legal history

Although bibliographers have paid little attention to official publications, the student of early modern ordinances can rely on some fruitful studies from other historical fields. Since the 1990s, legal historians have focussed increasingly on ordinances that were issued in the name of the *Gute Policey*. This expression does not refer to our modern day police forces – armed forces that ensure law and order – but to an altogether different concept: the 'common good' (*gemein Wohl*).[36] To contribute to the common good, authorities progressively intervened in nearly all spheres of public life; there were few areas of life left untouched by regulation.

This research has led to the publication of a formidable research tool: a repertory of early modern police ordinances issued in the Holy Roman Empire, Denmark, Sweden, and the Swiss Confederation. Since 1996, the project team at the Max Planck Institute for European Legal History has collected data on ordinances for some thirty jurisdictions, including secular and religious territories as well as imperial cities.[37] The repertories are based on printed compen-

35 See appendix. I am grateful to Andrew Pettegree, who supervised the first development of this study during my time at the University of St Andrews and generously agreed to integrate the broadsheets I found into the USTC online.

36 Härter (2010a), 'Security and 'Gute Policey' in Early Modern Europe', p. 42.

37 Twelve repertories have been published so far. A full list of the repertories is available at https://www.rg.mpg.de/publikationen/repertorium_der_policeyordnungen. In addition, see Weber (ed.) (2002), *Die Reichspolizeiordnungen von 1530, 1548 und 1577*.

dia, such as Reyscher's collection of ordinances passed in Württemberg, and complemented by archival records.[38] The volumes provide their readers with a basic overview of the ordinances: their issue date, a few key points concerning their subject matter, as well as the call number of the document and/or a reference to literature. This has been an on-going project; the latest volume was published in 2017. It has also inspired similar ventures in other countries, such as Poland.[39]

The repertories have provided the essential data for a number of in-depth studies addressing different aspects of criminal history and conflict regulation.[40] Achim Landwehr has investigated the effects of police ordinances on Leonberg, a district in Württemberg. Based on court records, Landwehr's study shows, among many other things, that the dukes did not simply impose new regulations onto the inhabitants of Württemberg; instead, they negotiated the implementation of new legislation with their officials and subjects.[41]

This important point was also observed for other territories and countries. The fruitful research on early modern ordinances showed that these texts were much more than just norms composed by governments;[42] they also fulfilled a symbolic function.[43] The publications were testimonies to the fact that rulers wanted to appear as if they were actively trying to improve the lives of their subjects. According to their view, the new legislation would make it safer and more secure to live in the territory.

This focus on media and its importance can also be observed in other areas. In the past decades, early modern media became an important focal point for legal historians investigating crime and justice.[44] It also became increasingly clear that the material aspects of law books played an important role in the contemporary

38 Reyscher.

39 Zapnik (ed.) (2016), *Repertorium der Policeyordnungen der pommerschen Städte*; Kotkas (2014), *Royal Police Ordinances in Early Modern Sweden*. Although the Kings of France also passed many police ordinances, scholars have not paid much attention to this aspect, see Kropf (2003), 'Der Begriff aus der politischen Theorie – das Konzept aus der administrativen Praxis. Zum Entstehen der *police* im frühneuzeitlichen Frankreich'; Kim (2008), *French Royal Acts printed before 1601*. This thesis includes an overview of some 6,000 royal acts published in sixteenth-century France.

40 Up until 2020, the series included 26 titles, see: https://www.rg.mpg.de/publikationen/policey-und-policeywissenschaft.

41 Landwehr (2000), *Policey im Alltag*, p. 315.

42 See for instance Schilling (2002), 'Gesetzgebung als Kommunikation', pp. 133–165.

43 Weber (2006), '"Bekennen und thun hiemit kunth und offentlich"', pp. 281–311.

44 For a comprehensive overview, see Härter (2018), *Strafrechts- und Kriminalitätsgeschichte der Frühen Neuzeit*, chapter six.

interpretation of their texts. The creation of knowledge remains elusive if one only concentrates on the authors and disregards the context of legal books.[45] To understand the conditions that shaped the production and dissemination of legal knowledge, historians of the law need to consider the material aspects of books, the limitations of local markets, the censorship legislation, and the printer's role in the production.[46]

This study will contribute to these new research trends by analysing the formats of legal publications, their design, their print runs, as well as instructions for circulation. These important aspects of police ordinances have largely been overlooked. Only a handful of studies address the dissemination of ordinances.[47] In these studies, however, the production of official documents remained opaque and important points have gone unnoticed. One of these points includes the sometimes quite significant time difference between issue date and actual publication date, which only becomes obvious when looking for sources beyond the printed text. It also remained opaque when and why the production of printed ordinances increased, as previous studies mostly focussed on material drawn from the seventeenth and eighteenth centuries.[48] Through the bibliographical approach adopted in this study, however, we can gain more insights into the mechanisms of early modern administration in the sixteenth century. We can trace the process from the urge to pass a new law, the decision-making process of rulers and their councils, the creation of a draft announcement, its production in print, and finally its distribution.

Such a bibliographical approach can reveal interesting facts. For instance, in some cases, ordinances were distributed weeks and even months after the date shown in the text. A bibliographical analysis also allows us to see that some ordinances were distributed for free by the authorities, whereas other publications had to be bought. These are important points to keep in mind for further studies on the implementation of new legislation.

This analysis further sheds light on the immense scope of government print. In many cases rulers sought not only to inform their subjects, but also to explain their policies, seek support, and shape public opinion well beyond the boundaries of their territories. This becomes especially clear in 1534 when Duke Ulrich tried to win back his duchy and widely distributed publications that depicted

45 Hespanha (2008), 'Form and Content in Early Modern Legal Books', p. 38.
46 Beck Varela (2016), 'The Diffusion of Law Books in Early Modern Europe. A Methodological Approach', p. 221.
47 Schennach (2008), 'Zuschreiben von Bedeutung: Publikation und Normintensität frühneuzeitlicher Gesetze', pp. 133–180; Härter (2002), 'Gesetzgebungsprozess und gute Policey', pp. 1–32.
48 See chapter three.

him as the rightful ruler. By broadening the scope of inquiry beyond police ordinances and considering other official publications as well, we can gain a more complete picture of the publishing activities of early modern governments.

In addition, the chapters that follow will bring into focus the printers who worked for governments at a time when the position of an official printer was not yet institutionalised. The study will reconstruct the printers' production of official publications, consider their overall production, and, most importantly, their relationship with the authorities. In many cases, the interaction was mutually beneficial, but there were also various problems associated with publishing official documents. Indeed, it was not always straight forward to have an important publication printed. For some authorities, finding a suitable printer was rather difficult; printers needed to be reliable, produce the documents quickly, keep the government's secrets, and resist the temptation to move to a far-off city with better economic opportunities. By focussing on these difficulties, I hope to present a more nuanced picture of the relationship between rulers and printers.

Political culture

Apart from legal history, this study both benefits from and contributes to another historical field that recently experienced a surge of interest: political culture.[49] The field witnessed a paradigm shift in the past century when the attention of scholars moved away from studying the political elites and instead gave centre stage to actors from the lower end of the social spectrum.[50] This turn in attention has shown that, in many parts of Europe, political power rested on negotiation between rulers and subjects conducted often within the context of established rituals and processions.[51] A key element of these negotiations was

49 For a comprehensive overview of the field, see KÜMIN (2009), 'Political Culture in the Holy Roman Empire', pp. 131–144.

50 See, for example, Peter Blickle's numerous studies such as BLICKLE (1973), *Landschaften im Alten Reich*; BLICKLE (2004), *Die Revolution von 1525*; HARRIS (ed.) (2001), *The Politics of the Excluded*; TE BRAKE (1998), *Shaping History: Ordinary People in European Politics*; PETTEGREE (2005), *Reformation and the Culture of Persuasion*; BEIK (1997), *Urban Protest in Seventeenth-Century France*.

51 For instance, BLOCKMANS, HOLENSTEIN and MATHIEU (eds.) (2009), *Empowering Interactions* and more recently, HARDY (2018) *Associative Political Culture in the Holy Roman Empire. Upper Germany, 1346–1521*. See also the work of the SFB 496 *Symbolische Kommunikation und gesellschaftliche Wertesysteme vom Mittelalter bis zur Französischen Revolution*, such as STOLLBERG-RILINGER, NEU and BRAUNER (eds.) (2013), *Alles nur symbolisch?*. For Württemberg in particular, see RUBLACK (1997), 'Frühneuzeitliche Staatlichkeit und lokale Herrschaftspraxis in Württemberg', pp. 347–376.

communication, and early modern authorities went to great lengths to try and influence as well as persuade their subjects.[52]

The question about the existence of a 'public sphere' before the eighteenth century remains hotly debated. Ever since its publication in 1962, and particularly since its English translation in 1989, Jürgen Habermas' work on the public sphere has been challenged by numerous historians.[53] Among many other aspects, critics have questioned the homogeneity of the involved actors and pointed to the decisive role of developing infrastructure (especially post courses and networks of correspondence) as well as emerging newspapers.[54] A consensus seems to have been reached that both the rulers and ruled employed a variety of media in various places to make their opinion known.[55]

This extensive communication leaves modern day historians with an abundance of sources such as petitions, grievances, paintings, material records, letters, and plays.[56] Although print and script became more and more important in these negotiation processes, the interaction between rulers and subjects, especially in the cities, took place largely in face-to-face settings employing oral means of communication.[57] In the case of Cologne, for example, numerous studies exist that investigate political communication within the context of the

52 For England, see Doig (1998), 'Political Propaganda and Royal Proclamations in Late Medieval England'; Dooley and Baron (eds.) (2001), *The Politics of Information in Early Modern Europe*; Peacey (2004), *Politicians and Pamphleteers*; Raymond (2003), *Pamphlets and Pamphleteering in Early Modern Britain*; for Italy, see De Vivo (2007), *Information and Communication in Venice*; for France, see Beik (1997), *Urban Protest in Seventeenth-Century France*; for Germany, see Pettegree (2005), *Reformation and the Culture of Persuasion.*

53 Habermas (1962), *Strukturwandel der Öffentlichkeit*; Habermas (1989), *The Structural Transformation of the Public Sphere*; Raymond (1999), 'The Newspaper, Public Opinion, and the Public Sphere in the Seventeenth Century'; Lake and Pincus (2006), 'Rethinking the Public Sphere in Early Modern England'; Helmers (2015), *The Royalist Republic: Literature, Politics, and Religion in the Anglo-Dutch Public Sphere*, pp. 22–24; Deen (2015), *Publiek debat en propaganda in Amsterdam tijdens de Nederlandse Opstand*, pp. 12–13. Schwerhoff (ed.) (2011), *Stadt und Öffentlichkeit in der Frühen Neuzeit.*

54 For an overview, see Gestrich (2006), 'The Public Sphere and the Habermas Debate'.

55 Dumolyn et al. (eds.) (2014), *The Voices of the People in Late Medieval Europe. Communication and Popular Politics*; Freist (1997), *Governed by Opinion*; Zaret (2000), *Origins of Democratic Culture*; Rospocher (ed.) (2012), *Beyond the Public Sphere*; Bellingradt (2012) 'The Early Modern City as a Resonating Box'.

56 See, amongst others: Kümin and Würgler (1997), 'Petitions, Gravamina and the Early Modern State'.

57 Schlögl (2008), 'Politik beobachten. Öffentlichkeit und Medien in der Frühen Neuzeit'; and his more extensive Schlögl (2014), *Anwesende und Abwesende. Grundriss für eine Gesellschaftsgeschichte der Frühen Neuzeit.*

large imperial city. Among them are the various surveys of Gerd Schwerhoff in which he establishes Cologne as a communication centre.[58]

Yet, in the communication process that took place in the sixteenth century, the use of print has been misunderstood. Focussing on the different media available, Robert Giel offers great insights into the interaction between council and inhabitants in Cologne.[59] However, it has been argued that the magistrates in Cologne progressively used printed ordinances from the early 1520s onwards; from then on, print became the dominant medium to spread information.[60] This argument requires significant refinement. As we will see in chapter three, the council only used print to a very limited degree until the 1560s. Special circumstances, such as the influx of migrants and looming war, forced the magistracy to change their practice of communication with their subjects, relying more on the technical innovation.

The rulers in Württemberg, on the other hand, employed the new technology to a much larger degree. Sixteenth-century Württemberg has recently gained much attention due to various anniversaries and celebrations. The 500th anniversary of Luther's Reformation movement spurred various publications focussing on the rapid adoption of the new faith in the southern duchy. In addition, in 2009, scholars celebrated the 450th anniversary of the Great Church Order, one of the most influential ordinances in the sixteenth century, which served as the impetus for a number of recent publications.[61] Duke Christoph in particular was a focal point in these studies, as historians see him as an illustrious Renaissance ruler who introduced long-lasting legal change.[62] To commemorate his achievements, the duke was celebrated with a large exhibition in 2015.[63]

In these studies, however, the importance of the printing press for introducing such long-lasting legal change has not been extensively treated. It was especially under Christoph that the press became an indispensable tool for the ducal administration. This study provides new insights into the creation of ordinances, the finances of the print production, and the distribution of official work in Württemberg. It shows that Duke Christoph invested a significant

58 See, for example, Schwerhoff and Mölich (eds.) (1999), *Köln als Kommunikationszentrum*.

59 Giel (1998), *Politische Öffentlichkeit im spätmittelalterlich-frühneuzeitlichen Köln*.

60 *Ibid.*, p. 95.

61 Arend and Dörner (eds.) (2015), *Ordnung für die Kirche*; Arend, Haag and Holtz (eds.) (2013), *Die württembergische Kirchenordnung von 1559*.

62 See, for instance, Langensteiner (2008), *Für Land und Lutherthum*.

63 The exhibition was shown in the Landesmuseum Württemberg from October 2015 – April 2016, see https://www.landesmuseum-stuttgart.de/ausstellungen/rueckblick/Christoph.

amount of money in the production of books, which he then circulated widely beyond the territory. In this way, print helped him to convey the picture we have of him today: the picture of an illustrious ruler.

Method and sources

The sixteenth century presents a very interesting period for official publications. At that time, administrations faced great challenges. Rulers had to react quickly to profound religious change, revolts, riots, plagues, famine, and harvest failure, to name but a few. To establish and maintain good order in these turbulent times, governments issued an increasing number of ordinances and announcements. It was essential that these official orders were communicated effectively and thus many rulers turned to the press. Yet, the enthusiasm and speed with which governments all over Europe embraced the new technical innovation varied considerably from place to place.[64]

One of the main reasons for this, as this study shows, is the fact that in the sixteenth century, having ordinances printed was not always straight forward. The position of an official printer who received an annual salary was not yet established widely, either in the cities as *Ratsdrucker* or in the territories as *Hofdrucker*. Only around 1600 did more authorities create such a position. Prior to this, most men and women working for the local authorities produced publications on the basis of individual orders. This meant that governments had only limited power over the press and that the publication of announcements and new legislation was determined by the economics of the industry. The ideal arrangements between rulers and printers were often negotiated over a considerable span of time. The sixteenth century was a period of experimentation, as governments attempted to find the most suitable printer for their work; in many parts of the empire, this period of trial and error lasted until the very end of the century.

To evaluate what factors influenced the use of the press in the sixteenth century, this study investigates government use of print through two case studies: official publications printed in an imperial city and in a territorial state. The different aspects of power exercised by a hereditary ruler and an elected council have prompted a number of scholars to study territories and cities in a comparative way.[65] This is especially true for legal historians, who have

64 Pettegree (2017b), 'Broadsheets: Single-Sheet Publishing in the First Age of Print. Typology and Typography', p. 17.

65 See, for instance, Chittolini and Willoweit (eds.) (1992), *Statuten, Städte und Territorien zwischen Mittelalter und Neuzeit in Italien und Deutschland.*

employed this approach to evaluate police ordinances, as the introduction of these ordinances developed in a parallel way in cities and territorial states.[66]

For a case study on official print in an imperial city, any number of cities with an abundence of evidence from the sixteenth century could have been selected. This includes most notably the three big trading centres of Cologne, Nuremberg, and Augsburg. In the course of the century, the councils of all three cities issued hundreds of ordinances with a great number of them in printed form. Many of the documents were later put together in extensive collections in the respective local archives. The Nuremberg city archive, for instance, holds some 400 ordinances from the sixteenth century gathered under the classmark 'Rep. A6'. Yet, these collections are far from complete, and it would require extensive research before one could even begin with an analysis of the evidence.

In the case of Cologne, the abundance of ordinances was edited by the project team at the Max Planck Institute for Legal History. The two published volumes on police ordinances in Cologne list no fewer than 2,000 police ordinances for the sixteenth century.[67] Many of these ordinances were produced in print to be posted on walls, boards, and gates. The repertory, therefore, presents an excellent starting point for a study on official print and allows us to contextualise the material in other large collections of Cologne ordinances housed in the University Library of Cologne, the City Museum of Cologne, and the German Historical Museum in Berlin. The extensive council minutes offer further evidence for the communication practices of the magistrates. In them, we can find information on how exactly the decision of the council was communicated and when.

Another interesting focal point is the religious element. In contrast to the large trading centres in the south, Cologne remained the only major Catholic city in the empire. The Reformation presented a fundamental disruption of tradition and brought with it extensive legal challenges that could, therefore, be avoided in Cologne. So this study will also show how such a radical break with tradition, like the introduction of the Reformation, influenced the use of the new technical innovation in other cities, such as Nuremberg and Augsburg. On top of that, the study will consider other special circumstances which had a similar effect.

To investigate this disruption of tradition the findings for Catholic Cologne will be compared and contrasted with those for a Protestant territory. Again, there are many Protestant territories to choose from. As with the cities, however,

66 See, for instance, KISSLING (2003), 'Reichsstädtische und territoriale Policeyen. Ein Vergleich der Reichsstadt und der Grafschaft Kempten im 16. Jahrhundert'.

67 Policey K, pp. 284–603, lists 2,571 police ordinances issued by the magistrates in Cologne between 1500–1600.

there are only a number of secular territories for which early modern ordinances have been systematically edited in a repertory. Among them, Württemberg is particularly interesting, since it integrated the new faith very early, and successfully, in its legal framework. The many ordinances addressing religious matters offer a splendid contrast to those issued in the Catholic bulwark in the north. A close analysis of these two contrasting governments allows us to shed light on the factors that determined the adoption of the new medium and establish why some rulers may have preferred other, more traditional means of communication.

The greatest obstacle to this study, a bibliographical analysis of all government publications, is the fact that many items survived in archives rather than libraries, the metier of book historians.[68] In libraries scholars can rely on (more or less) accurate catalogues providing information on the printer, the place of production, and the date of the book. By contrast, printed documents in archives are much more difficult to trace. They are often bundled together with manuscripts and not specifically mentioned in the archival finding aids (*Findmittel*). Additional information on the printer is often not provided since many government publications lack imprints. It is, therefore, extremely time-consuming to discover government publications in archives and recreate their production.

Tracing the beginnings of the collaboration between governments and printers is further complicated by the fact that many official publications were produced as broadsheets (or broadsides), single sheets that were printed on one side only to allow for public display.[69] Such broadsheets are difficult to identify, especially as they were excluded from the national bibliography of sixteenth-century Germany, the *VD16*. The decision to exclude single-sheet material was both unconventional and baffling, and a deviation from the practice of other major bibliographical projects, such as the cognat project, *VD17*, the English *STC* or the various components of the bibliography of the Low Countries now brought together in *Netherlandish Books*.[70] The absence of broadsheets from the

68 Eisermann (2006), 'Archivgut und chronikalische Überlieferung als vernachlässigte Quelle der Frühdruckforschung'. This holds also true for the Netherlands, see Le Bailly (2021), '"Na de publicatie van den niewe ordonnantie". The publication and printing of ordinances for the Court of Holland'.

69 'Broadside' is a synonym of 'broadsheet', see the discussion of terminology in Bruni (2017a), 'Early Modern Broadsheets between Archives and Libraries: Toward a Possible Integration', p. 43. See also Rautenberg (2000), 'Warum Einblattdrucke einseitig bedruckt sind. Zum Zusammenhang von Druckverfahren und medialem Typus'.

70 Pollard and Redgrave (eds.) (1976–1991), *A Short-title Catalogue*; Pettegree and Walsby (eds.) (2010), *Netherlandish Books*. The components are: Nijhoff and

VD16 presents a major obstacle and means that a vital aspect of the sixteenth-century print world is entirely missing from the German national bibliography. The scholar of official print, insofar as broadsheets are concerned, has therefore to fall back on their own resources.

To be sure, German broadsheets attracted much attention in the past, and here we have especially to thank Falk Eisermann for several illustrious studies.[71] These studies concentrate on the well-documented incunabula age (1450–1500), as broadsheets were included in the standard bibliographies of that period: the *Gesamtkatalog der Wiegendrucke* and the *ISTC*.[72] Falk Eisermann has gathered together information on all fifteenth-century broadsheets printed in Germany into a separate bibliography, *VE 15*.[73] It is an extremely rich source, including much additional information about the creation of the broadsheets, their print runs, and sometimes even their use.

Scholars investigating broadsheets produced in the sixteenth century cannot rely on such comprehensive surveys, despite the abundance of the material in archives, libraries, and museums. Due to the very different cataloguing practices in these institutions, it is rather difficult to create a census of sixteenth-century broadsheets.[74] With regard to printed bibliographies, scholarly interest has focussed almost exclusively on illustrated broadsheets.[75] Such publications show the diversity of German broadsheet production: polemical lampoons, portraits, reports of battles, strange and unusual events, and natural disasters. However, we must not lose sight of the fact that by far the largest proportion of broadsheets printed were not illustrated. This was the case even in Germany, which had a rich illustrative tradition. These more mundane publications include calendars as well as almanacs, indulgences, academic disputations, and, arguably the largest group of generally unillustrated broadsheets, legal records such as ordinances.

Kronenberg (eds.) (1923–1971), *Nederlandsche bibliographie van 1500 tot 1540*; Valkema Blouw (ed.) (1998), *Typographia Batava 1541–1600*; Cockx-Indestege, Glorieux and Beeck (eds.) (1968–1994), *Belgica typographica*.

71 See, for instance, his recent publication Eisermann (2017), 'Die Einblattdrucke Peter Schöffers'. For a comprehensive overview of the many broadsheet genres, their use and their reception in the first 70 years of print, see Honemann (2016), 'Neue Medien für die Stadt. Einblattdrucke, Flugblätter und Flugschriften 1450–1520'.

72 http://www.gesamtkatalogderwiegendrucke.de; http://www.bl.uk/catalogues/istc.

73 VE15.

74 Odenbreit (2014), *Einblattdrucke des 16. Jahrhunderts in Gedächtnisorganisationen*.

75 See, for instance, Geisberg (ed.) (1984), *The German Single-Leaf Woodcut 1500–1550*; Harms and Schilling (eds.) (1985–1997), *Deutsche Illustrierte Flugblätter des 16. und 17. Jahrhunderts*; Faust, Barthelmess and Stopp (eds.) (1998–2010). *Zoologische Einblattdrucke und Flugschriften vor 1800*.

The very low survival rate of such items further obstructs the compilation of a comprehensive corpus. Much of this material was simply not intended to be collected: single sheets were usually discarded after having been read and those exhibited for public view were destroyed by the weather. Roger Paas, the creator of an extremely lavish bibliography of political broadsheets in the seventeenth century, estimates that less than 1 % of all copies have survived to the present day.[76] For broadsheets printed a century earlier, the rates of survival may well have been even lower.

Fortunately, scholars working on official publications do not face such a daunting situation. Although many copies of ordinances were posted in public and thus destroyed by the elements, they were, nevertheless, legal records and a file copy was often kept for administrative purposes. These broadsheets would not necessarily have made their way into libraries; most of the documents survived in large collections in state or city archives.[77]

To accumulate my data for this study, the repertory of police ordinances provided a very good starting point, giving me an estimate of the material that is preserved in Cologne and Württemberg. Yet, as helpful as this splendid research tool is, it has its limitations for a bibliographical study like this one. Unfortunately, the books do not refer to standard bibliographies, such as the *VD16*, to facilitate the identification of the printed document. Some volumes helpfully include a note indicating that the ordinances existed in printed form, but as the separate volumes were handed over to different editors with diverging approaches, most volumes of the repertory omit this fact.[78]

This study, therefore, necessarily began with an extensive period of research leading me to libraries, archives, and museums in many parts of Germany. The repertory of police ordinances enabled me to find promising collections of ordinances in the State Archive of Württemberg where I could also find edited

76 Paas (ed.) (1985–2017), *The German Political Broadsheet, 1600–1700*, I, p. 25.

77 In the Landesarchiv Nordrhein-Westfalen (Rheinland), for instance, we can find over 100 official broadsheets, mostly issued by the dukes of Jülich-Cleves-Berg (call number: Handschriften L II 7, Handschriften L II 8); Another example is the large collection of official publications referred to as *Churfürstliche Mandate in Polizeisachen, Landfriedensbrecher und Plagen bis 1723* in the Wittenberg city archive. The Hauptstaatsarchiv in Dresden houses hundreds of official publications (call number 12883 Mandate [year]) as does the Niedersächsisches Landesarchiv (NLA) with its collection of publications issued by the dukes of Braunschweig-Wolfenbüttel (call number: NLA WO 40 Slg). The latter collection is currently the subject of investigation by Philip Haas of the NLA, who is working on an extensive survey of official publications printed between 1500–1806.

78 This is luckily the case for the volume on Cologne. The editor included the abbreviation 'Dr.' for the German word 'Druck' (English 'Print').

drafts, administrative notes, and instructions for the print production of many items. I was able to add a significant number of documents to this corpus by examining the holdings of the State Library of Württemberg, which had not been integrated into the repertory.[79] Here, I also found new evidence for other publications Duke Ulrich had printed, such as invitations to horse races and his print-intensive campaigns to win support in difficult times, especially in 1514 and 1534. This material offers an intriguing portrait of the ducal publishing activities.

In addition, I was able to establish, through careful analysis of the printed copies, that ordinances were often printed in more than one edition. It was above all the larger ordinances, such as the Landesordnungen, church ordinances, or others, that often appeared in two editions: one was produced for the duke to be distributed among his officials and the other was produced for a commercial market.[80] This included noblemen who needed to know when and how they were allowed to hunt or students of law who used the ordinance for their studies.

A hitherto unexplored source for the reconstruction of the publishing activities of the dukes is the account book of the General Church Fund (*Generelle Kirchenkasten*). It was established after the implementation of the new faith and lists revenues of church goods as well as expenditures occurring during the Reformation.[81] This included the many costs associated with the Council of Trent as well as payments for metalworkers, carpenters, singers, and – most interesting in this context – for religious books. In this account book, we find hundreds of payments to printers, book sellers, binders, and messengers who delivered books to Stuttgart. This account is unparalleled in its richness listing many details of the individual orders, such as titles, number of copies, number of printed sheets of the total order, costs for binding and delivery dates. It allows us to see just how ambitiously the dukes used the printing press, especially in the second half of the sixteenth century.

In contrast to Württemberg, the compilation of a census for Cologne was much more difficult. The riches of the Stuttgart archive would undoubtedly have been overshadowed by the treasures in the Cologne archive had not a fateful and fatal accident occurred in 2009. During construction work for an

79 The WLB and the HStASt recently digitised many of their broadsheets, and I was able to include the links to these digital copies in the appendix.

80 The *Landesordnung* (territorial statutes) is a collection of many police ordinances, see Härter and Stolleis (eds.) (1996), *Repertorium der Policeyordnungen*, p. 12.

81 HStASt, A 282 Kirchenkastenverwaltungsrechnungen. The archive offers a great overview of this particular source online: http://www.landesarchiv-bw.de/plink/?f=1-1166

underground system, the building hosting the city archive collapsed into its foundations, which had been undermined by the tunnelling below. This was a tremendous blow to the research community: the Cologne archive housed one of the most important collections of archivalia north of the Alps and it just disappeared into the rubble. And as if that were not enough, poor weather obstructed the rescue work, which I experienced firsthand as a volunteer on the rescue effort.

Recognising that a case study of government use of print in Cologne would be a splendid contrast to Württemberg, I embarked on a long and testing journey to compile a corpus for Cologne. When I contacted the archive in 2013, I was told that some of the collections were microfilmed, such as the collection on trades and guilds, but that the extensive 24 volumes of police ordinances were not preserved in this way. Although the microfilms of the other collections contained numerous ordinances, I repeatedly lamented the loss of the incredible volumes that would have revealed many more aspects of the publishing of Cologne ordinances in the sixteenth century. Then, in 2015, I met Klaus Militzer, the former director of the archive, who had worked repeatedly with the ordinance collection and edited the repertory of police ordinances for Cologne. When I informed him that I was told the 24 volumes were not microfilmed, he disagreed and encouraged me to ask the archivists again. As it turned out, the ordinances had indeed been microfilmed; however, the films had been misplaced after the collapse of the building. So, in the third year of my PhD, I was finally able to lay my eyes on the 24 volumes. In the intervening two years, the loss of the physical copies encouraged me to look beyond the borders of the city archive, and I was gratified to find that other institutions such as the city museum and the university library in Cologne as well as the German Historical Museum in Berlin possess a large number of sixteenth-century ordinances printed in Cologne.[82] I incorporated these findings into my survey, adding a large number of hitherto unknown publications not included in the major collection of the Cologne archive and the repertory. The hundreds of documents that I found were later integrated into the USTC to make the data, including many links to online copies, easily accessible to scholars worldwide. For the readers of this study, I have also created the appendix at the end of the book, which offers an overview of my many findings.

As almost all broadsheet ordinances do not include an imprint revealing the printer's name, I tracked down payment records, such as invoices and account books, that showed which printers were entrusted with the production of official publications. For Württemberg, with its small print industry, it was

82 Limbach (2016), 'Tracing Lost Broadsheet Ordinances Printed in Sixteenth-Century Cologne', p. 495.

relatively straightforward to uncover who published the many works financed by the dukes. However, with over 100 printers active in the sixteenth century, Cologne's thriving book business posed more challenges. Here, the key research strategy was the comparison of the woodcut initials included on the broadsheets with other publications that eventually revealed the printers who most likely produced the majority, if not all, official broadsheets in Cologne. To illuminate the world of these printers, I was able to rely on Christoph Reske's standard work on German printers.[83] It provides a short introduction to every printer focussing on his or her working world, such as family background, financial situation, relations to the authorities, printing equipment, and workmen.

Outline

To determine which factors influenced government use of print, the first chapter will assess how the rulers of Württemberg employed the new technical innovation. The dukes as well as the Habsburg authorities that ruled Württemberg for several years realised the great potential that the printing press had to offer. Therefore, they used the 'black art', as some contemporaries called it, to advertise the duchy, justify their political agendas, and aid the process of state formation. As a result, the authorities in Württemberg had a large quantity of documents printed in the sixteenth century that circulated widely beyond the duchy's border.

In the second chapter, I will introduce the printers who supplied these many documents. At the beginning, when the authorities only placed a few orders per year, producers were reluctant to settle in the duchy. Nearby print centres such as Basel or Nuremberg were much more appealing with their potentially large groups of buyers. Only when the orders increased could a printer be induced to set up his shop permanently in Württemberg, where he could cater for both the authorities and the recently founded University of Tübingen. Over the course of several decades, the printer Ulrich Morhart and his family made a decent living by producing for the dukes of Württemberg. Yet, this arrangement was not always ideal for the dukes. The printer's busy production schedule as well as the financial difficulties that the printer endured in his later life could seriously prolong the publication of official work.

The two subsequent chapters will introduce the case study of Cologne. Chapter three will show that the council only embraced print very slowly. The magistrates found it more effective to continue passing on new regulations

83 Reske.

orally. Due to the dense settlement of the city, the council viewed such oral proclamations as both more efficient and less expensive. The council had ordinances printed only if regulations were particularly complex or had implications for outsiders. Examples include coin regulations, which often stipulated specific values for a variety of coins. The printed documents thus facilitated the interaction of inhabitants and the many tradesmen that paid in foreign coins.

The final chapter will present the printers of official publications in Cologne. During the entire sixteenth century, the council did not have a designated printer who produced ordinances in return for an annual salary. Instead, the magistrates relied on a variety of publishers who shared the market for official publications between them. The few ordinances issued in the first two decades of the sixteenth century were exclusively produced in small print shops. Yet, as the council made progressively greater use of print in the second half of the century, production moved from the hands of the small producers to those of the big publishing businesses. For the council this was a great advantage since the publishers with their deep pockets allowed the council some leeway with its payment.

Information on nearly 400 printed broadsheets issued by the rulers of Württemberg and Cologne in the sixteenth century is included in the appendix. It gives a short overview of the title, date, and producer and provides references, information on surviving copies, and in many cases links to digital copies. The large majority of these broadsheets were hitherto unknown to book historians and are discussed and analysed here for the first time. As this data provides the evidential basis for parts of this study, especially chapters three and four, the appendix gives an overview of these newly discovered publications.

Terminology

The chosen title requires a short excursion on what constitutes a 'government'. The early modern period witnessed an expansion of governments, which comprised an ever-increasing number of officials. The government in Württemberg consisted not only of ducal councillors and those at both the court and the chancellery in Stuttgart but also of a significant number of officials at the local level, such as district governors, local courts, and *Schultheiße*. In Cologne, the city council exercised its power in collaboration with advisory bodies and other officials, for instance, the *Marktmeister*, who oversaw the markets. They all formed part of the local government. However, in this study the term 'government' will be used in its strictest sense, namely that it only refers to those who were at the highest level of political power: those who implemented new legislation and were in charge of publishing official announcements.

The second term that needs clarification is 'official print'. It is a loose translation of the German word *Amtsdrucke*, a category that comprises documents issued by authorities. Besides ordinances, official print includes invitations (e. g. to horse races or shooting contests), justifications (e. g. reports on revolts), and general announcements (e. g. bans). In contrast to other publications, these official documents are visually distinct as they are often signed and sealed to authenticate the text. On top of that, official broadsheets usually begin with a particular formula such as 'We, the Council of Cologne' or 'We, the Duke of Württemberg'.

In this context, it is also important to include a few words on the term 'broadsheet' (*Einblattdruck*). Generally speaking, a broadsheet is a publication printed on one side only. It is, therefore, the ideal medium to be posted on walls or boards. Just like books, broadsheets have different formats: full sheets, half-sheets, quarter-sheets, or even smaller fractions of a sheet.[84] The broadsheets discussed in this study range from small snippets with only a few lines to large placards consisting of several sheets glued together.

84 Needham (2014), 'The Formats of Incunable Broadsides', p. 128.

Chapter One: Governing the German Duchy

When Ulrich became Duke of Württemberg in the early sixteenth century, he ruled over one of the largest and most urbanised territories in the Holy Roman Empire with some 200,000 inhabitants.[1] Many of Ulrich's subjects made a living from agriculture, especially wine, which found a particular fertile environment in this part of Germany.[2] The duchy was situated in the south of the empire, between the important trading centres of Strasbourg, Basel, Augsburg, and Nuremberg, and surrounded by various other territories, such as Palatine-Neuburg and Baden-Pforzheim. The territory itself was fragmented and encompassed several imperial cities, such as Reutlingen – which lay outside ducal control, a fact that became particularly relevant in 1514 – within its territorial borders.

The invention of print offered great opportunities for the rulers of Württemberg. Moveable type made it possible to spread official news widely and quickly. The time-consuming and laborious process of composing letters for a large audience could now be significantly shortened. The dukes of Württemberg were among the many authorities who quickly realised the great potential of Gutenberg's invention, and in the 1470s, Count Eberhard im Bart had already entrusted printers in Reutlingen with official publications.[3] This enabled the count, for instance, to circulate information widely on his dispute with Hermann von Eptingen, a knight from Swabia.[4]

1 Mocker (1991), 'Quellen zur historischen Statistik des Herzogtums Württemberg vom 15./16. bis zum 18./19. Jahrhundert', p. 131.

2 Boelcke (1987), *Wirtschaftsgeschichte Baden-Württembergs von den Römern bis heute*, p. 98.

3 See, for example, USTC 744536.

4 USTC 744538.

Eberhard soon realised that print could also serve to enhance the prestige and status of Württemberg. After he had founded the University of Tübingen in 1477, he used a broadsheet to announce its opening.[5] This broadsheet – completely written in Latin – represents the first announcement of a German university to ever appear in print.[6] Eberhard had good reasons to break with more traditional means of communication: he wanted to reach as large an audience as possible in order to direct their attention to the new university. Future scholars as well as students needed to be drawn to this designated institution to further enhance the status of Eberhard's territory.

When Ulrich succeeded Eberhard in 1503, he followed the example of his predecessor and relied on print to communicate the magnificence of Württemberg far beyond the borders of the duchy. The young duke – who was only 16 years old when he succeeded his uncle – was eager to prove that Württemberg thrived under his rule, not least because its elevation from county to duchy had occurred only a few years before Ulrich came to power. So from the very beginning of his reign, Ulrich perceived the need to match the wealth and splendour of other ruling houses. He relentlessly tried to show off his wealth, and when Philip the Handsome was travelling through Württemberg, Ulrich managed to impress the emperor's son with his fine silver and gold treasures as well as his 700 antlers.[7]

Ulrich tried to impress on a large scale. To this end, he organised splendid events, such as a horse race on 11 May 1512, to which Ulrich invited a great number of guests. He even hoped that one or more of the seven electors would attend and addressed the invitation to them as well. The duke lured participants with attractive prizes: the winner of the race would receive the handsome sum of 32 Gulden and a silver tankard. Second and third places were also richly rewarded: the contestants were to receive a crossbow and a sword respectively.

To inform everyone about the race and ensure a great turn out, the duke printed broadsheet invitations six months before the race took place.[8] This already indicates that Ulrich not only invited guests from around Württemberg, but also those from far away, allowing them enough time to organise their

5 USTC 744537 (VE15 E-2).

6 See the additional information for the entry in VE15 (E-2).

7 Decker-Hauff (ed.) (1966), *Geschichte der Stadt Stuttgart. Von der Frühzeit bis zur Reformation*, p. 310.

8 The broadsheet was issued on 21 December 1511 and invited to the race on 11 May 1512, appendix no. 1. See Ostermann (2000), 'Zu den gedruckten Schützenbriefen des 15. Jahrhunderts', p. 409.

journey to the duchy.[9] The broadsheets did not address individuals (there was no line to fill in names by hand); instead, Ulrich sent his greetings to every elector, high feudal lord, secular and spiritual prince, count, knight, servant, official, mayor, and burghers. They were all invited to his race. Adorned with a fine woodcut initial, the document encouraged the guests to gather at eight o'clock in the morning in the meadow between Neckarweihingen and Benningen.

Ulrich advertised such events on a frequent basis, for example, a similar race within only a week of the other taking place.[10] These two surviving broadsheet invitations represent numerous documents that the duke had printed for noblemen and burghers in and around Württemberg. Even if they did not attend the races, the great number of invitations sent a clear message: the Duke of Württemberg must have great wealth.

The invention of moveable type helped Ulrich to evoke this impression. Moreover, the production of such broadsheets did not require him to invest much time or money. These small invitations were swiftly produced; as they consisted only of some 20 lines, the typesetting was straightforward. The printer could easily use a previous invitation as a template, changing only a few details like time and place. Once the type was set, hundreds of copies of such an invitation could be produced in less than a day.

Ulrich's need to impress, together with his extravagant lifestyle, soon brought him serious problems. During these times of trouble, the printing press continued to be a reliable partner. The duke understood very well that by letting his view on recent events be disseminated widely, he was able to shape public opinion – at least to a certain degree. Thus from the very start of his reign, Ulrich had a powerful tool at hand and he needed it desperately. As we will see in what follows, Ulrich used print to explain his policies as well as to appeal for support, both during the uprising of the Poor Conrad and his struggle to regain the duchy after his long exile.

The publications issued in the course of the former provide us with invaluable insights into the immense scope such government print could achieve. The uprising presented a serious threat to the duke's authority, and Ulrich found himself in a precarious situation. He vividly remembered how his uncle Eberhard II had been chased away from Württemberg after being declared unfit to rule. Ulrich had to root out any opposition if he was to avoid the same fate as his uncle. Thus, when numerous peasants opposed his new

9 Invitations to shooting contests could also be produced several months in advance to allow foreign guests to participate, see Ostermann (2000), 'Zu den gedruckten Schützenbriefen des 15. Jahrhunderts', p. 409.

10 Steiff (1881), *Der erste Buchdruck in Tübingen (1498–1534)*, p. 84.

taxes, he had several of the ringleaders brutally executed and their heads displayed on the city walls.[11]

Shortly after these drastic acts, Ulrich issued a report to warn other rulers. It was a lengthy account of the uprising, in which the duke explained in detail what had happened. As the uprising in 1514 was part of a wave of popular unrest in the German lands on the eve of the Reformation, many rulers in the Holy Roman Empire were troubled by unruly subjects who opposed their rule.[12] Thus detailed information about what had happened was keenly sought after in other territories. Ulrich's lengthy explanation served to satisfy this appetite for news.

The account of the uprising also helped to explain Ulrich's drastic measures and to persuade his audience that his actions were inevitable. *The true notification of the revolt and uprising in the Duchy of Württemberg* (*Warhafftig Underrichtung*) contained a long narrative of the beginnings of the uprising. It described in detail the meeting between the duke and the enraged rebels. According to the *Warhafftig Underrichtung*, the duke tried everything possible to calm the mob down, but the peasants refused to listen, disregarded their oaths, and treacherously attacked the duke and his officials.[13]

This long justification was a remarkable document, but its wide circulation served a further purpose: to track down the many fugitives that were able to escape his punishment. Despite the imprisonment of several hundred rebels, many were still missing and successfully avoided the duke's wrath. A great number of these rebels found refuge in the numerous imperial cities in the southern part of the Holy Roman Empire, far away from the duke's jurisdiction.[14] They did not even have to travel very far: as we have seen above, the free cities of Reutlingen, Esslingen, and Weil der Stadt lay within the territory of Württemberg. Zell, Gengenbach, Offenburg, Hagenau, and Weißenburg were only a short journey to the west, and Heilbronn, Wimpfen, Schwäbisch Hall a short journey to the north.

With the *Warhafftig Underrichtung*, the duke asked other rulers for help. He appealed to his audience to let his officials know immediately of the whereabouts of a fugitive. To identify the wanted rebels, the *Warhafftig Underrichtung*

11 Scheck (2014), 'Herzog Ulrich und der "Arme Konrad"', p. 73.

12 Scott (2002), *Society and Economy in Germany, 1300–1600*, pp. 16–19.

13 For more details about the content of the *Warhafftig Underrichtung*, see Limbach (2014), 'Propaganda im Druck – Politische Kommunikation beim 'Armen Konrad'', pp. 40–42.

14 Scheck (2014), 'Herzog Ulrich und der "Arme Konrad"', p. 73. For the political and administrative situation of cities in south-western Germany, see Quarthal (1991), 'Verfassung und Verwaltung in südwestdeutschen Städten der Frühen Neuzeit', pp. 217–239.

contained some 100 names of those believed to be affiliated with the uprising. The names were arranged by place of origin, listing among others people from Schorndorff, Winterbach, Bilderhausen, Großheppach, Kleinheppach, and Beutelsbach.

The *Warhafftig Underrichtung* was produced as a quarto pamphlet covering a total of 12 leaves (fig. 1.1.).[15] The simple design and lack of visual adornment suggest that this publication was produced in a hurry. The duke was determined to find the fugitives as quickly as possible. The title page comprises only the title itself, with no author, printer, or date mentioned. The rest of the pamphlet was very simple: The text was introduced with a rather small woodcut initial and the first line of text was printed in a larger font. Apart from that, the reader could not rely on any other visual aid or guidance to structure the text. The wordy explanation and the list of names were crammed into the 12 folios without any headings or line breaks.

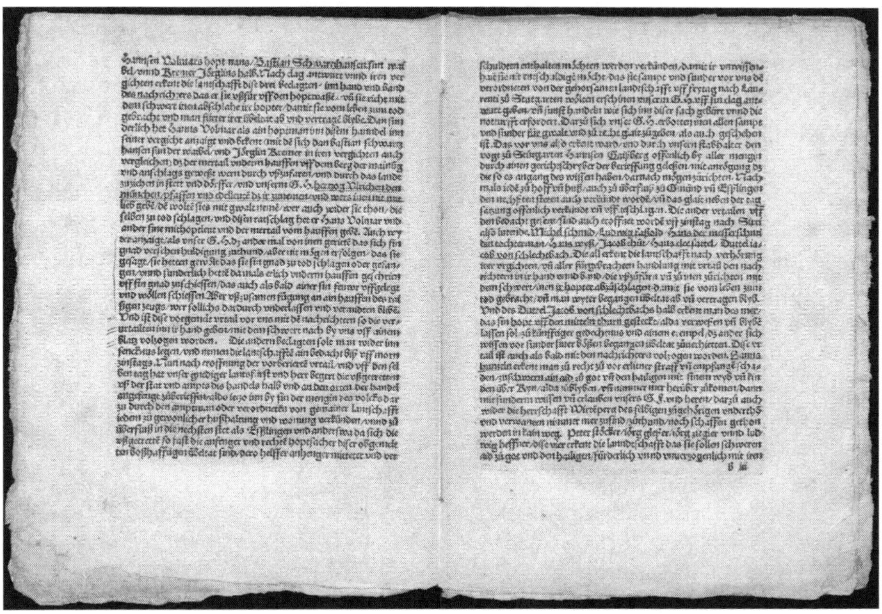

Fig. 1.1. *Warhafftig Underrichtung*, USTC 705112.

To authenticate the text, several seals were included on the last leaf of the pamphlet underneath the text. That of the duke was accompanied by the seals of Tübingen and Stuttgart, which served as representatives of the estates.

15 USTC 705112 (VD16 W 4458).

The pamphlet was issued in two editions – a simple edition and a more elaborate one including a woodcut of the duke's coat of arms on the title page.[16]

These pamphlets were intended for an astonishingly large audience. Ulrich sought to reach as many notables as possible, not only within the surrounding areas of his duchy, but within the entire Holy Roman Empire. Thus he sent the *Warhafftig Underrichtung* to archbishops and bishops, as well as abbots, princes, counts, *Freiherren*, cities, and lastly, of course, to his officials. To pay the necessary respect to the different ranks addressed, Ulrich had covering letters printed that contained the appropriate address.[17]

In principle these covering letters contained the same content and in most cases also the same woodcut initial.[18] What changed, however, was the tone of the address, ranging from humble greetings to respectful addresses and orders to the officials. Not surprisingly, the archbishops and bishops received the most humble address. Their letter opened with the words 'please receive our friendly and subservient willing service, venerable to God, beloved friend and reverend prince gracious lord'.[19] In contrast, the abbots received a less extravagant but still respectful greeting: 'Please receive our favourable greetings and willing service, worthy and devoutly beloved special and favourable lord.'[20] The text that followed was more or less the same: The recipient was asked to pay attention to this account (despite its length) and to show mercy on the duke.

These different letters were produced in dozens of copies. The covering letter for the abbots probably appeared in 100 copies to inform the many religious houses in and around Württemberg. At the beginning of the sixteenth century, the south-western part of the empire was studded with religious houses. There were 35 houses of the Franciscan Order, 22 houses of the Augustinian Order, 18 of the Dominican Order, and 12 houses of the Carmelite Order.[21] Presum-

16 USTC 705111 (VD16 W 4457), USTC 705112 (VD16 W 4458).

17 Appendix nos. 4–9. The practice of printing various editions with the appropriate addresses for the different ranks was already common in the fifteenth century, see, for instance, VE15, M-72, M-73, M-74, M-75, M-76, M-77, M-78, which addressed secular and religious princes, cities, and abbesses. The practice was still used in the late sixteenth century, for instance, in the composite duchy of Jülich-Cleves-Berg. There is even a manuscript note from a chancellery scribe on one broadsheet detailing the address for four different editions: 'Lieber Diener/ du', 'Lieber Rhat und getrewer/du', 'Lieber Rhat und getrewer/Ihr', 'Lieber getrewer/Ihr', Landesarchiv Nordrhein-Westfalen (Rheinland), Handschriften L II 7, Band 1.

18 The only broadsheet edition without a woodcut is the one for the officials.

19 Appendix no. 3.

20 Appendix no. 4.

21 Schaab, Schwarzmaier and Taddey (eds.) (2000), *Handbuch der Baden-Württembergischen Geschichte* (Vol. 1,2), p. 199.

ably, Ulrich sent a letter to each house trying to persuade them not to shelter fugitives but instead to cooperate with his officials. The covering letter for the princes probably had an equally high print run. After all, one of these letters was intended for Duke Albrecht of Mecklenburg, as the address on the back of the covering letter reveals.[22] If Ulrich was so ambitious that he informed the ruler in Mecklenburg on the Baltic Sea, far away from Württemberg, he probably also sent numerous copies of the *Warhafftig Underrichtung* to rulers in more proximate territories.

Once the broadsheet letters were out of the print shop, they were folded, sealed, and addressed. Some of these letters still bear the original handwritten address on their back, just like the one intended for Duke Albrecht of Mecklenburg. Among the letters for the bishops was one addressed to Reinhard, Prince-Bishop of Worms.[23] We may safely assume that Lorenz von Bibra in Würzburg and Christoph von Stadion in Augsburg, as well as the bishops and archbishops in Mainz, Speyer, Strasbourg, Basel, and Konstanz also received copies of the same covering letter.

Ulrich also found a way to capture the attention of those who possessed only limited reading skills. Two covering letters addressed the imperial cities as well as the duke's officials. However, these two addressees did not receive a pamphlet; instead, they received the entire text of the 12-leaf pamphlet on a single broadside. This impressive placard consists of four sheets of paper pasted together, which gives it a total length of over one metre (see fig. 1.2.). As in the pamphlet editions, it contained Ulrich's seal as well as those of Tübingen and Stuttgart.

In the covering letters, the duke asked his representatives as well as the city councils to read out the entire text to their subjects. This alone must have been a memorable event. The official would stand, with an unusually long paper in his hands, reading out the text for the better part of an hour. Once he had finished, he pinned the long placard on the wall of the town hall (the officials in the imperial cities were asked to find 'an appropriate place').[24]

One can easily imagine that this long broadsheet with three shiny seals at the bottom attracted a fair amount of attention. It presented a striking contrast to those publications that were usually hung up on walls, such as official orders or proclamations. Although such publications could also comprise a considerable amount of text, they usually did not consist of more than two sheets. The *Warhafftig Underrichtung* was meant to stand out clearly, with its

22 Appendix no. 7; HStASt, A 45 Bü 10.

23 Steiff (1881), *Der erste Buchdruck in Tübingen (1498–1534)*, p. 113, no. 62a, appendix no. 3, HStASt, A 45 Bü 10 Umschlag a, Nr. 3.

24 The original German text reads: 'vnnd als dann an ain gelegen ort euch gefellig vffschlagen'.

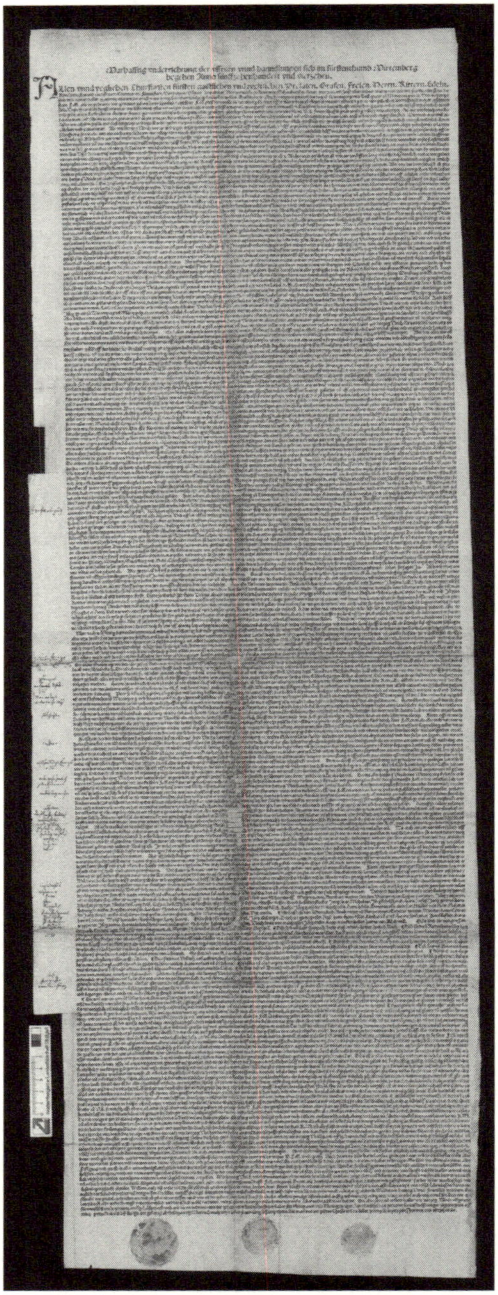

Fig. 1.2. *Warhafftig Underrichtung* (broadsheet), appendix no. 2.

four sheets and its impressive 220 lines of densely printed text. This broadsheet sent a strong message: the duke condemned the uprising along with everyone who was involved. Even to those who could not read the entire text, this message was clear.

Twenty years later, Ulrich again used the help of an impressively long broadsheet to inform, persuade, and seek support. Ulrich was on the verge of winning back his duchy from Habsburg hands after he had been in exile for 15 years. Finally, in 1534, after several failed attempts, Ulrich's fortune was about to turn in his favour. With the help of his cousin Philip, Landgrave of Hesse, leader of the Schmalkaldic League, and the financial support of France, Ulrich was able to raise an army and threaten the prince regnant Ferdinand. His timing was excellent: The Habsburgs were occupied with the Turks, and the Swabian League, the military association of smaller territories in Swabia that expelled Ulrich in 1519, had dissolved due to religious difficulties.

The campaign to recover the duchy was fought as much with words as with swords. The military conquest was accompanied by a number of publications. The initial announcement of war was produced as an impressive broadsheet, similar to the *Warhafftig Underrichtung*.[25] This time, however, Ulrich addressed an even larger audience. In the *Warhafftig Underrichtung*, the duke had taken great care to define his audience by opening with the words: 'To every elector, prince, prelate, count, *Freiherr*, lord, knight, free and imperial city, community, provost, principality, bailiff, official, mayor, councillor, court, and everyone whom we have given a title.'[26] In contrast, the broadsheet produced to announce the restoration only included the words: 'To each and everyone who sees this letter.' In the following, Ulrich and Philip explained in detail why they were driven to arms. They argued that Ulrich was the God-given Duke of Württemberg and his expulsion in 1519 was against the law of the Holy Roman Empire. So Ulrich announced his restoration to Charles V as well as his brother Ferdinand and asked them not to hinder his conquest. This 'open letter' to the public was then accompanied by the two letters that Ulrich sent to Charles and Ferdinand respectively.

With this broadsheet, printed in Marburg, the capital of Philip's landgraviate, Ulrich again demonstrated his faith in visual display to put his message across.[27] Similar to the *Warhafftig Underrichtung*, the broadsheet was made up

25 Appendix no. 19.
26 Appendix no. 2, lines 3–5.
27 Although the broadsheet has no imprint, the two elaborate woodcuts introducing the letters to Charles and Ferdinand point us to the producer. These woodcuts were also used to produce USTC 633121 (VD16 W 4440), a pamphlet printed by Franz Rhode in Marburg.

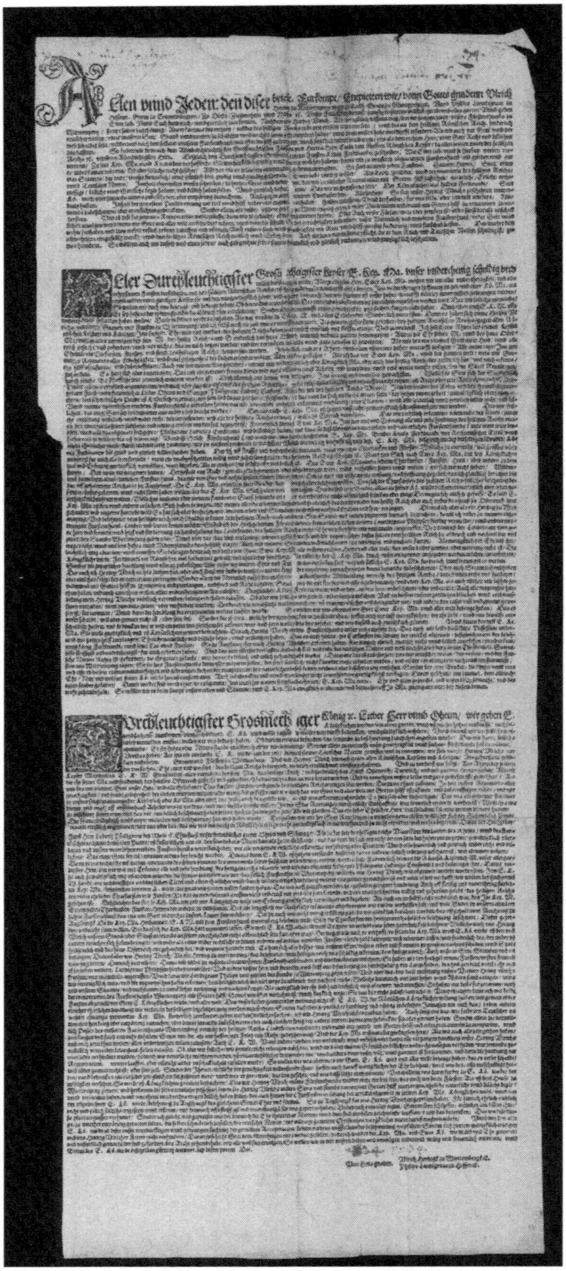

Fig. 1.3. *Ausschreiben, die vorgenommene Rekuperation und Eroberung des Herzogtums Württemberg betreffend*, appendix no. 19.

of several sheets of paper comprising an impressive length of over 80 centimetres. However, in contrast to the previous broadsheet, this publication now contained visual aids that helped the readers to find their way through the 150 lines of densely printed text. The three letters – to the public, Charles, and Ferdinand – were each set apart with generous spacing. Each section was, furthermore, introduced with elaborate woodcut initials as well as larger type for the first line of text.

This publication surely caught the eyes of many passers-by. With its unusual length, the elaborate woodcut initials as well as the duke's seal at the bottom, it clearly stood out from the other public proclamations of that time. Although no covering letters for this broadsheet have survived, we may assume that this publication was intended for the same recipients that received the broadsheet about the Poor Conrad uprising. Thus a considerable number of bishops, abbots, counts, *Freiherren*, and city councillors were informed about Ulrich's plans to win back his duchy.

The duke's conquest received much support from Protestants throughout the empire. In vain, numerous princes had previously tried to convince Charles V that Ulrich was the legitimate ruler of Württemberg and should be restored as duke.[28] Now that Ulrich took up arms, many rulers in the south welcomed his vigorous actions. Thus his three letters concerning the restoration were quickly reprinted in the nearby printing centres of Frankfurt, Basel, Strasbourg, and Marburg, the capital of Hesse, – all places that, just like Ulrich, embraced the new faith.[29] Ulrich's justification was even printed in far-off Wittenberg, where the Elector of Saxony supported the restoration.[30] All told, we can count 23 surviving copies, published in nine different places.

These numerous publications included the whole text of the restoration broadsheet. To allow for easier reading, though, the text was produced in pamphlet form. In Strasbourg there were even two editions – including a 'newe zeytung' title page intended for the emerging news-hungry public.[31] During the course of April, the content of the pamphlet grew by including a letter to the

28 Among the supporters were six of the seven electors as well as numerous princes who wrote a petition to Charles V asking him to restore Ulrich as duke. The emperor, however, did not react to this petition at the imperial diet in Augsburg 1530, see Schäfer (ed.) (1984), *Reformation in Württemberg*, p. 92.

29 USTC 633140 (VD16 ZV 15612), USTC 611791 (VD16 W 4441), USTC 633121 (VD16 W 4440), USTC 660971 (VD16 W 4452), USTC 611790 (VD16 W 4439), USTC 611795 (VD16 W 4437), USTC 707151 (VD16 W 4438), USTC 2214008 (VD16 ZV 29013), USTC 2214137 (VD16 ZV 29014); one edition even appeared in Latin: USTC 668887 (VD16 W 4443).

30 USTC 611789 (VD16 W 4442).

31 USTC 677827 (VD16 ZV 15613); Schäfer (ed.) (1984), *Reformation in Württemberg*, p. 95.

vassals, in which Ulrich promised to be a loyal duke. It was a truly print-intensive campaign that helped to spread Ulrich's message and explained his military conquest. In the end, his efforts paid off, and he triumphantly entered the capital, Stuttgart, in May 1534, where his return was celebrated with the first Protestant church service in Württemberg.

'For the common good': ruling Württemberg

Apart from advertising the magnificence of Württemberg and justifying their political agendas, the rulers of the duchy increasingly used print to aid the process of state-formation. The circulation of printed texts formed an essential part in maintaining corporate society and regulating its behaviour. As printing allowed for a quick and wide dissemination, the 'black art' presented a great opportunity to improve administration of the entire territory with its many districts. Inhabitants in the remote district of Böblingen could be informed nearly as quickly as the inhabitants of Stuttgart, the seat of the government, by means of a printed ordinance sent to every district governor, which would be read out loud.

Thanks to the invention of printing, Württemberg saw an unprecedented number of printed ordinances in the sixteenth century, many of which claimed to serve the common good.[32] These numerous printed regulations fall into three main categories.[33] The first category comprises the *Landesordnungen*, a collection of various police ordinances.[34] The explanation of the imperial police ordinance that Ulrich issued in 1549 falls into the same category.[35] It explained in detail the ordinance of the previous year that Charles V had issued for the entire Holy Roman Empire. The second category comprises ordinances that concerned one particular institution or issue, such as the church, the chancellery, or the forest.[36] Finally, the last group of printed ordinances is made up of mandates intended to regulate immediate issues.

32 About the 'common good', see Isenmann (2010), 'The Notion of the Common Good, the Concept of Politics, and Practical Policies in Late Medieval and Early Modern German Cities'.

33 Härter and Stolleis (eds.) (1996), *Repertorium der Policeyordnungen*, pp. 12–14. Härter and Stolleis list a fourth category that comprises rescripts intended for one or several officials. Throughout the sixteenth century, these rescripts were usually produced as manuscripts in Württemberg.

34 For a definition of *Landesordnungen*, see Winter (2014), 'Für gute Ordnung und Policey. Die Landesordnungen in der Frühen Neuzeit'.

35 During the sixteenth century, the emperors issued three imperial police ordinances, see Weber (ed.) (2002), *Die Reichspolizeiordnungen von 1530, 1548 und 1577.*

36 Forest ordinances addressing the use of wood became increasingly important in the sixteenth century, see Fuhrmann (2013), 'Holzversorgung, Waldentwicklung,

Von Gottes gnaden/Wir Ulrich Hertzog zů Wirtemberg vnd zů Teckh/Grave zů Mümppelgart rc.

Fig. 1.4. Typical mandate issued in sixteenth-century Württemberg. This particular broadsheet addressed the use of firearms, appendix no 20.

During the sixteenth century, mandates appeared in two formats: broadsheets and pamphlets. Broadsheets were ideal for public display. When Duke Ulrich sent the *Warhafftig Underrichtung* to his officials, he instructed them to attach copies to the town halls and the local churches.[37] At this time, the text of the mandates was usually printed as a solid block adorned with a woodcut initial at the top of the broadsheet.

Pamphlets, on the other hand, usually consisted of one sheet of paper that was folded once to create four pages.[38] This way the text stretched over numerous lines making the text more accessible and easier to read. The document could be easily folded again to fit into a pocket or bag. Thus, the officials could carry it with them and consult it whenever necessary. This was common practice in Saxony where the duke informed his officials, with an extra slip

Umweltveränderungen und wirtschaftliche Tendenzen in Spätmittelalter und beginnender Neuzeit', p. 318.

37 Appendix no. 6.

38 See, for instance, an ordinance regarding Jews, issued on 20 March 1536, http://digital.wlb-stuttgart.de/purl/bsz444417729; not in Policey W.

of paper, that he had sent them an ordinance printed in 'book form' (i. e. a pamphlet) and instructed them 'to have it with them at all times'.[39]

Württemberg rulers were not the only authorities who relied on print. Following Maximilian's early endorsement of the technology, many territorial rulers used the new medium for a variety of purposes.[40] Among them was Württemberg's neighbour Bavaria. The USTC currently lists over 90 documents, including announcements, invitations, official letters, and mandates, all issued and printed by the dukes of Bavaria before 1600.[41] Similarly, the dukes of Saxony used printed publications from the early sixteenth century onwards.[42]

As far as ordinances are concerned, however, the dukes of Württemberg were among the forerunners. Over the course of the sixteenth century, the rulers issued hundreds of ordinances – considerably more than their neighbours. This holds especially true for the Electorate of Mainz. Until 1601, the Electors issued about 150 ordinances in the name of the common good.[43] In contrast, the rulers of Württemberg produced 300 ordinances – in other words, twice as many.[44] This is especially surprising since Württemberg was only half the size of the Elector's territory.[45]

The dukes of Württemberg used these many ordinances not only to regulate the behaviour of their subjects; they also employed them to strengthen the position of the duchy within the empire. After Duke Ulrich's turbulent rule and expulsion at the beginning of the sixteenth century, the prince and his successors had to assert themselves as the rulers of Württemberg. Trying to avoid another banishment at all costs, the dukes had to communicate that Württemberg was a well-ordered, exemplary part of the empire.

The dukes used printed ordinances to establish Württemberg as the prototype of a Protestant territory. As soon as Duke Ulrich had introduced the Reformation, he called for help to craft a variety of new regulations. Only two months after his restoration as duke, Ulrich recruited several experts on church matters, including the distinguished Erhard Schnepf and Ambrosius Blarer. One year later, in 1535, the team of reformers was joined by Johannes Brenz,

39 Aurich (2000), *Die Anfänge des Buchdrucks in Dresden*, pp. 44–45, no. 4. The original German text reads: 'Wir schicken euch auch hiepey eyn Edict buchweys gedruckt, das yr stetigs bey euch haben vnd darnach richten moget'.

40 Eisermann (1998), '"Darnach wisset euch zu richten"', pp. 198–215. USTC search: Region - Holy Roman Empire, Subject - Ordinances and Edicts.

41 USTC search: Any field - Bayern, Subject - Ordinances and Edicts.

42 See, for instance, Claus (ed.) (1987), *Das Leipziger Druckschaffen der Jahre 1518–1539*, p. 94, no. 22.

43 Härter and Stolleis (eds.) (1996), *Repertorium der Policeyordnungen*, pp. 107–422.

44 Policey W, pp. 579–616.

45 I would like to thank Karl Härter for pointing this out to me.

after one of his relatives, who worked for Ulrich, had recommended Brenz's outstanding work.[46]

Together the three reformers worked diligently on new regulations and produced a variety of new ordinances. By 1536, three major ordinances had already appeared in print. Among them, most notably, was the first printed marriage regulation.[47] No other Protestant community had at that point agreed on regulations for marriage and had them printed.[48] The Württemberg ordinance was rather short, comprising only five leaves, but it regulated crucial matters that determined the new faith, such as divorce and re-marriage. In addition, the team of reformers presented an ordinance regulating charity as well as a church ordinance, both of which were issued in March 1536. With these ordinances, the duke aimed to regulate church services, baptisms, communions, care for the sick, and funerals.[49] Württemberg progressively became a Lutheran stronghold.[50]

These many legal publications were not only intended for the duke's representatives; they addressed a much larger audience comprising rulers throughout the Holy Roman Empire who intended to implement the Reformation into their legal system. Many copies were sent to princes who needed a guideline for their own church ordinances. Under Christoph, Württemberg underwent significant legal changes, and the ducal court received many requests for legal advice in religious matters. The duke participated in empire-wide discussions, such as the one on what was essential to worship, and rulers asked for the duke's opinion on particular ordinances as well as for guidance in drafting regulations similar to those in Württemberg.[51] Christoph and his councillors readily offered support and sent their ordinances as soon as they left the printing shop. Many of these ordinances were adopted by other rulers, not only in nearby territories such as Palatine-Neuburg and Baden-Pforzheim, but also in more distant principalities, such as the Electorate of Saxony, or the

46 Johann Gailing, who was the first preacher of the new faith in Württemberg and also worked at Ulrich's court, recommended his relative Brenz in a letter from early June 1534. Ulrich appointed Blarer and Schnepf in summer 1534, but called for Brenz already one year later on 15 July 1535, see Schäfer (ed.) (1984), *Reformation in Württemberg*, p. 104.

47 USTC 681575 (VD16 ZV 27244), USTC 681576 (VD16 W 4518); Hirsch (1953), 'The first printed Protestant "Eheordnung"', pp. 96 f.

48 Schäfer (ed.) (1984), *Reformation in Württemberg*, p. 116.

49 *Ibid.*, p. 117.

50 Dixon (2002), *The Reformation in Germany*, p. 116.

51 Watson (2015), *Lutheran Piety and Visual Culture in the Duchy of Württemberg, 1534–c.1700*, p. 67; Briefwechsel, IV, p. 650; Schäfer (ed.) (1984), *Reformation in Württemberg*, p. 315.

Kingdom of Sweden.[52] In some cases the Württemberg text was adopted word for word.[53]

This different audience brought with it a change in the design and the production of ordinances. To conform to the new design of imperial recesses, ordinances were published not in quarto but in folio format and contained a clearer structure, which made the works easily accessible.[54] In these instances, the print run was significantly higher. An ordinance that was just intended for the duke's officials, such as the explanation of the imperial police ordinance in 1549, was produced in 250 copies.[55] In contrast, ordinances addressing aspects of the Reformation had print-runs that were several times higher. The Great Church Order of 1559 appeared in 700 copies and (since there were no copies left) had to be reprinted in 1582.[56] The *Landesordnung* of 1567 was printed in 1,000 copies.[57] The second edition of the marriage ordinance issued in the 1550s was produced in no fewer than 2,000 copies.[58]

To fully understand these different print runs, let us trace the development of Württemberg ordinances in more detail. The *Landesordnungen* were the manifestos of the slowly emerging early modern state; they determined the regimen of control and formed the legal framework of the duchy. Responding to demographic growth, the expansion of market networks and above all religious divisions meant that Württemberg's *Landesordnungen* were progressively extended in the course of the sixteenth century. On each occasion, the publication closely followed a major turning point in Württemberg's history. As a result, by 1600, the *Landesordnung* had been reissued five times.

The *Landesordnung* were first issued in 1495 for mainly three reasons: to stabilise the recently unified Württemberg, to structure the duchy by giving it a law code, and to strengthen princely power. Their publication marked the final stage of Duke Eberhard's relentless efforts to increase Württemberg's power and status within the Holy Roman Empire.[59] The publication was preceded by the Diet of Worms a few months earlier, where King Maximilian had raised Württemberg from a county to a duchy. With the publication of the *Landesordnung*, Eberhard gave his new duchy a legal framework and was

52 Arend (2014), '"Lasset alles züchtiglich vnd ordentlich zugehen"', p. 39.

53 Schaab, Schwarzmaier and Taddey (eds.) (2000), *Handbuch der Baden-Württembergischen Geschichte* (Vol. 1,2), p. 225.

54 Weber (2006), '"Bekennen und thun hiemit kunth und offentlich"', p. 293.

55 See subchapter '"A humble request": appeals and law-making processes' for more information about Ulrich's explanation of the imperial police ordinance.

56 HStASt, A 282 Bd 1315.

57 Briefwechsel, IV, p. 650; HStASt, A 38 Bü 3.

58 HStASt, A 282 Bd 1291.

59 Policey W, p. 556.

thus one of the first rulers in Germany who embarked on such an important project.[60]

The first *Landesordnung* was rather short.[61] The edition comprised several regulations providing for the peaceful coexistence of the duchy's inhabitants and the prevention of future turmoil. The officials were instructed to maintain roads and bridges, to erect granaries for desperate times, and to ensure buildings were of a certain standard. At the heart of the *Landesordnung*, however, was social control. As of 1495, gambling, blasphemy, and dancing were restricted or even forbidden altogether.[62] In addition, the duke forbade the pledging of health, a traditional German drinking practice in which participants drank rounds in competition.[63] While the aim of this particular restriction was certainly to curb immoderate drinking, it primarily addressed the custom claiming it would lead to 'blasphemy, dishonour and other severe damage, and complaints'.[64]

In his opening words, Eberhard declared that the law code had been sent to every official, who in turn had to announce it to every subject. The address 'to every official' suggests that the *Landesordnung* appeared in print, despite the fact that only manuscript copies can be located today.[65] After all, the order to send an ordinance to every official justified a print run of 250 copies in the mid-sixteenth century. Although the duchy consisted of fewer districts in 1495, it is still plausible that the first *Landesordnung* was issued in a similar edition.

Twenty years after its initial publication in 1495, the *Landesordnung* was reissued.[66] By that time, Eberhard's successor Ulrich had undergone the traumatic experience of the Poor Conrad uprising. To prevent a recurrence in the future, he extended the *Landesordnung* by including several regulations that were almost exclusively aimed at the prevention of unrest. Thus from 1515 onwards, people were not allowed to gather in groups unless instructed to do so. Additionally, no Württemberg inhabitant was to carry either firearms or crossbows when walking in the fields.[67]

60 Franz (2003), *Die Landesordnung von 1516/1520*, p. 13*.

61 Molitor (ed.) (1995), *1495: Württemberg wird Herzogtum*, p. 109.

62 Blasphemy was a subject often addressed in early modern police ordinances, see Rox (2012), *Schutz religiöser Gefühle im freiheitlichen Verfassungsstaat*, p. 20. For an overview on blasphemy in Europe, see Schwerhoff (2005b), *Zungen wie Schwerter*.

63 Tlusty (2001), *Bacchus and Civic Order*, p. 91.

64 The original German text reads: 'Dieweyl gotteslesterung, uner und mercklich schaden und beschwerd von dem zutrincken khomen.'

65 Schmelzeisen (1955), *Polizeiordnungen und Privatrecht*, pp. 559f, 564.

66 USTC 701569 (VD16 W 4455).

67 The regulations for firearms and crossbow are discussed on fol. 9v.

Fortunately, this printed edition of the *Landesordnung* survived in two copies.[68] Produced in quarto format, the pamphlet's design was very simple. The publication comprised 14 leaves without a title page at the beginning. In contrast to the first *Landesordnung*, it contained a longer introduction covering the better part of the first leaf. This introduction provided more details about the actual publication of the rules: the district officials were instructed to read out the entire text of the *Landesordnung* at the local courts (*Vogtgerichte*).

When the Austrians took over Württemberg, the cities and districts decided that the *Landesordnung* needed to be reissued to include legislation on matchmaking, alms, and Jews.[69] Social control still featured prominently in these new versions and numerous laws, addressing issues such as blasphemy, were tightened and extended. These regulations now included specific details about the offences and the punishments that awaited the offender. Whereas the previous *Landesordnung* only referred to a fine for blasphemous behaviour, the new *Landesordnung* foresaw a penalty of several days in prison for this crime.[70] Furthermore, the publication procedure was enhanced to ensure that those subject to the regulations did not forget them. To this end, the officials were instructed to read out the Landesordnung at the courts every year.[71]

After Ulrich had succeeded in his attempt to win back his duchy, he published a new edition of the *Landesordnung* in 1536.[72] Moreover, as he strove to implement the new faith, the *Landesordnung* encompassed numerous regulations addressing religious issues; so, for instance, they forbade adultery and the celebration of carnival and prescribed care for the poor. Accordingly, the *Landesordnung* grew in size, now including a total of 49 leaves. Religious matters featured prominently among the many matters discussed. The first five issues dealt with in the previous 1521 edition were blasphemy, pledging health, homicide, violation of the peace, and the punishments to be carried out by the district officers. In contrast, Ulrich's 1536 edition placed more emphasis on pious behaviour. The first five issues comprised hearing the word of God, and tightened the regulations for blasphemy, pledging health, gambling, and prostitution.

Apart from this stress on pious behaviour, Ulrich's edition featured more economic regulations. It included, for instance, regulations for fishing in the Neckar and prescribed the acceptable size of fish to be sold (smaller fish should

68 One is in WLB, HBF 2751, and the other in HStASt, A 38 Bü 1.

69 Reyscher, XII, pp. 36ff; SCHÄFER (ed.) (1984), *Reformation in Württemberg*, p. 58.

70 To meet the need for more copies, the *Landesordnung* was reprinted without any changes in the content in 1576 and 1585, see Reyscher, XII, p. 38.

71 *Ibid.*, XII, p. 37.

72 USTC 635178 (VD16 W 4453).

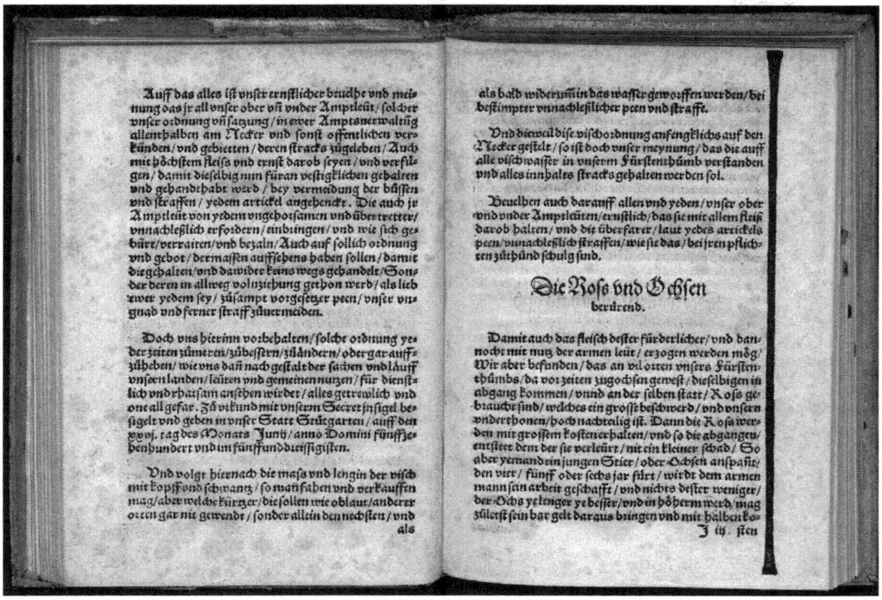

Die Roß vnd Ochsen berürend.

Fig. 1.5. Fish ordinance with reference line in the *Landesordnung* of 1536, USTC 635178.

be thrown back into the river).[73] As it was not until much later that sizes like cubits were determined by law, the *Landesordnung* from 1536 included a long printed line in the margin next to the regulation (see fig. 1.5.).[74] This line represented the minimal length a fish ought to have from head to tail. This way the officials had a frame of reference and could, in cases of dispute, take the *Landesordnung* to measure the fish.

With the introduction of the Reformation, Württemberg was in desperate need of a large variety of new regulations. How should the poor be treated? How should students of the new faith be educated in Württemberg? What was to happen to the many goods of the church? And how could the duke be sure that his new church regulations were actually followed? An enormous bureaucratic effort was required to address all these questions. To support this change financially, the dukes of Württemberg – like other major Protestant princes – secularised church goods on a massive scale.[75] These new revenues were used for

73 *Ibid.*, fol. 35r.

74 Measurements were not regulated in the *Landesordnung* before 1552, see USTC 635179 (VD16 W 4509).

75 Cohn (1987), 'Church Property in the German Protestant Principalities', p. 170.

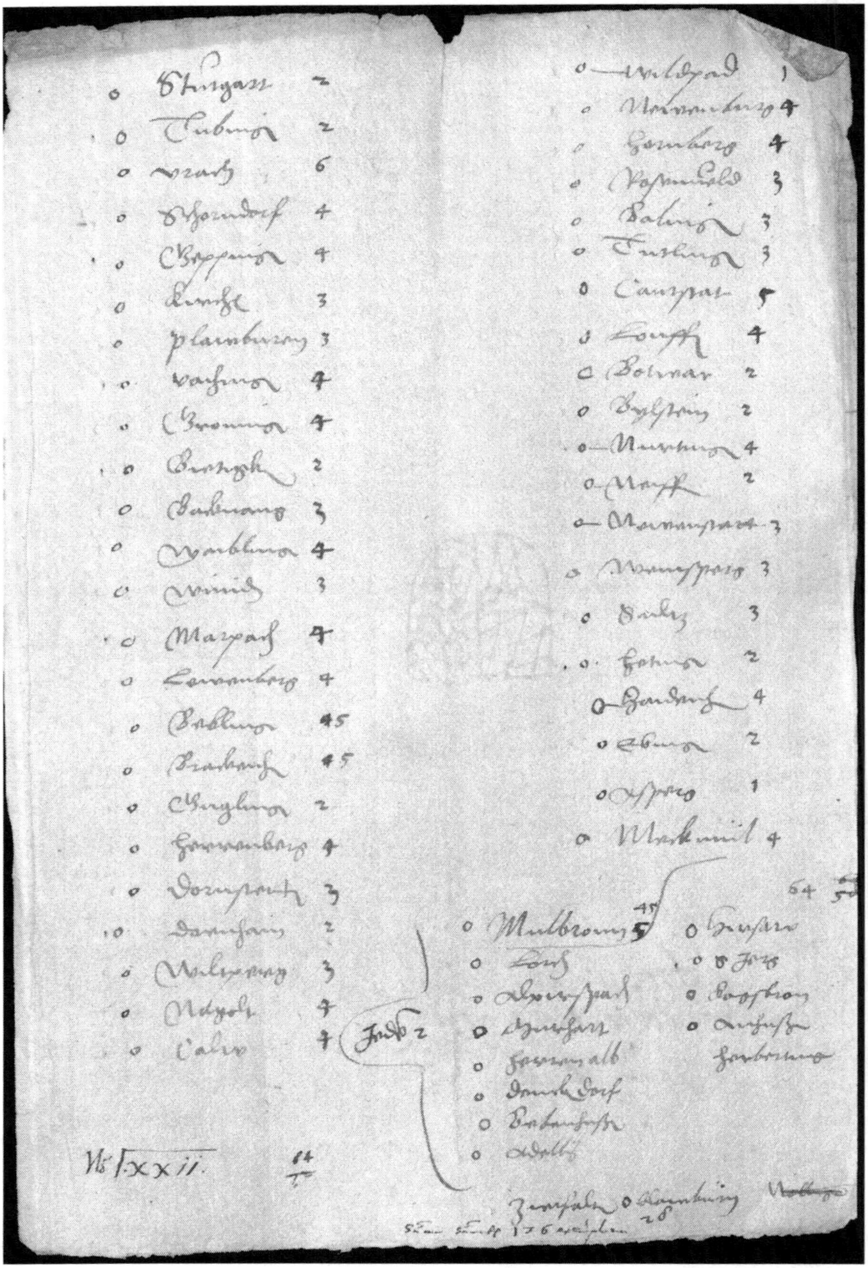

Fig. 1.6. List showing how many copies of the explanation of the new imperial police ordinance were distributed to each district in Württemberg [1549].

a variety of tasks, such as supporting the poor and introducing a new school system as well as a scholarship system to educate loyal Lutheran clerics.[76] It was also used to print a flood of additional ordinances that existed alongside the *Landesordnung*. These ordinances regulated the chancellery, the university, and – most importantly – the church.[77]

Towards the end of his reign, Ulrich also published an explanation of the new imperial police ordinance (*Reichspoliceyordnung*).[78] This explanation was to be sent to 'every official' and appeared in 250 copies. Thanks to a carefully created list, we know exactly where these copies went (fig. 1.6.). A number of the copies were kept at the court in Stuttgart for the chancellery as well as for the duke himself. But the majority of the copies – 176 – were sent out to the 56 districts in Württemberg. Smaller districts, such as Bietigheim and Beilstein, received only two or three copies.[79] More densely populated districts, such as Cannstatt, Vaihingen, and Böblingen, were sent four to five copies. Finally, the district with the most inhabitants, Urach, received six copies. This way not only the district governor but also other high-ranking officials had one copy to themselves, which could be consulted if need be.

When Ulrich's son Christoph began to rule, he worked relentlessly on new reforms. During his reign, Württemberg became the prototype of a Protestant territory and the printing press was an indispensible tool to make this possible. Christoph was keen to communicate his changes and the work of his reformers widely. He even hoped that he could help the Protestant movement in France.[80] To this end, he tried to talk to the Catholic leaders and also prepared a gift for the king. The gift included three important books, all printed in Württemberg: Johannes Brenz's *Catechism* (in French), Valentin Wanner's *De missa* (in Latin), and an account of the Council of Trent, probably the one compiled by Jacob Andreä.[81] Similarly, he sent theological books to England to win the favour of Queen Elizabeth.[82]

76 Stolleis (2014), *History of Social Law in Germany*, p. 13; Methuen (1994), 'Securing the Reformation Through Education', p. 841.

77 These ordinances were drafted in Stuttgart's new chancellery building erected in the 1540s, see Sommer (ed.) (1971), *Die Chronik des Stuttgarter Ratsherrn Sebastian Küng*, p. 146.

78 USTC 2214584 (VD16 ZV 30767). Apart from the copies in Vienna and Leipzig, there are further copies in HStASt (A 38 Bü 2) and WLB (HBF 2774).

79 For the size of Württemberg's districts, see Trugenberger (1994), 'Die württembergische Amtsstadt im 15. und 16. Jahrhundert', p. 136.

80 Schäfer (ed.) (1984), *Reformation in Württemberg*, pp. 299–300.

81 Bossert (1898), 'Zur Geschichte des Buchhandels in Stuttgart', p. 251; USTC 16488 (VD16 B 7575), USTC 630510 (VD16 W 1195), USTC 621820 (VD16 A 2552).

82 Schäfer (ed.) (1984), *Reformation in Württemberg*, p. 300.

The press also helped to multiply the many new legal works. From the very beginning of his rule, Christoph issued a number of new regulations and had them printed. In 1552, the duke compiled a new edition of the *Landesordnung*. By that point, the *Landesordnung* comprised a total of 150 leaves.[83] Christoph also extended the other ordinances his father had issued. The new charity ordinance appeared in 1552; the new marriage ordinance and a church ordinance followed a year later.[84]

Christoph's thorough reforms were eagerly observed by other rulers in the empire. In early February 1553, Count Palatine Otto-Henry, a neighbouring ruler, asked Christoph to send him a copy of the church ordinance once it was printed.[85] He did not have to wait long for a positive answer; Christoph responded within only a couple of days. The duke stated that he would be happy to send a copy as soon as it left the print shop.[86] Additionally, Christoph wrote, he would include the recently completed chancellery ordinance as it might also be of interest. After all, the new chancellery ordinance defined the church council. In the following years, Otto-Henry created his own church ordinance according to the Württemberg model. When it was published in 1556, it was nearly a word for word reprint of the Württemberg ordinance.[87] Similarly, the church ordinance for the Margraviate Baden-Durlach was strikingly similar to the Württemberg model, as were those of Braunschweig-Wolfenbüttel and the Electorate of Saxony.[88]

In 1559, Christoph orchestrated the publication of the Great Church Order, which represented the culmination of all significant regulations addressing religious matters.[89] This ordinance gave the new church its institutional character. It included a large variety of different regulations and thus comprised an astonishing 260 leaves. With a table of contents at the beginning, the Great Church Order was easily navigable. Now the reader had every ordinance regarding issues such as marriage, church service, education, visitation, and censorship in one single book.

The Great Church Order from 1559 had an astonishingly high print run: the voluminous compendium appeared in 700 copies.[90] This presented a stark

83 USTC 635179 (VD16 W 4509).

84 USTC 681576 (VD16 W 4518); the church ordinance even appeared in two editions: USTC 669885 (VD16 W 4491) and USTC 669964 (VD16 W 4492).

85 Briefwechsel, II, p. 40.

86 *Ibid.*, II, p. 43.

87 Schäfer (ed.) (1984), *Reformation in Württemberg*, pp. 315–317.

88 *Ibid.*, p. 317; Schaab, Schwarzmaier and Taddey (eds.) (2000), *Handbuch der Baden-Württembergischen Geschichte* (Vol. 1,2), p. 225.

89 USTC 703883 (VD16 W 4527). Sehling et al. (ed.) (1902–2015), *Die evangelischen Kirchenordnungen des XVI. Jahrhunderts*, XVI, pp. 54–61.

90 Briefwechsel IV, p. 650.

contrast to the 250 copies of the explanation of the imperial police ordinance just ten years earlier. In these ten years, Württemberg had not acquired any new territories or districts. Thus, as before, something in the region of 176 copies of the ordinance were probably sent out to the districts. On top of that, several dozen copies were given to religious personnel. This left a significant number of remaining copies, which could have been given to important allies outside Württemberg. We know that Duke Christoph sent copies to important Protestant rulers including Frederick III, Elector Palatine, and Wolfgang, Count Palatine of Zweibrücken.[91]

Finally, towards the end of his reign, Christoph issued the sixth and last edition of the *Landesordnung* in the sixteenth century. He had previously been urged by the estates to integrate the recently agreed *Landrecht* from two years earlier and to change the legislation accordingly.[92] This sixth edition of the *Landesordnung* remained unchanged until the mid-seventeenth century when the Thirty Years' War cast its shadow over the southern parts of the Holy Roman Empire.[93] This final edition of the *Landesordnung* marked the fulminant finale of Christoph's many reforms and changes during his reign. It touched on a large variety of issues that are explained in great detail over 250 pages. As the *Landesordnung* was so extensive, the table of contents now covered six leaves alone, listing each individual regulation. These issues range from church matters to economic issues and also include specific regulations for measurements. Compared to the 14-leave edition of the *Landesordnung* in 1515, only some 50 years earlier, it shows how quickly and extensively the rulers of Württemberg sought to extend their control into many areas of everyday life.

This development is echoed in the elaborate design of the *Landesordnung*. Whereas the *Landesordnung* from 1515 was solely an accumulation of different regulations without any visual aid to help the reader, the 1567 edition had clear, visible distinctions of issues. Thus the headings of each regulation were set apart, allowing for ease of reading. Moreover, an additional introduction now preceded the table of contents. This introduction is printed with red ink and adorned with a beautiful woodcut initial to add a highlight to the text. The margins on either side of the printed text are much larger than in previous editions, allowing for extensive notes. One contemporary owner

91 *Ibid.*, p. 650, these were probably handwritten copies, since the manuscript was only sent to the printer ten days before the letter was sent.

92 Schäfer (ed.) (1984), *Reformation in Württemberg*, pp. 258–259. The *Landrecht* (law of the territory) defined a variety of different legal areas, see Laufs and Schroeder (2014), 'Landrecht'.

93 Reyscher, XII, p. 344.

used this generous space to write little summaries next to the detailed regulations.[94]

In contrast to the 1515 edition, the *Landesordnung* from 1567 was clearly addressing a different audience. This is further underlined by the change of formats. Up until Christoph's reforms, the *Landesordnungen* had been published as quarto pamphlets. This way, the officials could carry the publication with them wherever they went. If they needed to refer to the *Landesordnung*, for instance, when asked about the acceptable size of fish, the officials could just draw the pamphlet out of their pockets and look at the relevant pages. Once Christoph had begun to reign, the two *Landesordnungen* – printed in 1552 and 1567 respectively – were published in folio format. They were big bulky books comprising over 140 and 250 pages respectively. These books could not be carried around as easily as their predecessors; they were designed to be studied at a desk.

The carefully crafted edition from 1567 was meant to be disseminated widely beyond the borders of the duchy. This can be seen from one of the concerns that marked the process of the compilation. After several months of consultation, a small committee consisting of ducal councillors and provosts finally presented a draft of the *Landesordnung* to the duke. In their draft, the committee pointed out that numerous clauses in the previous *Landesordnung* started by saying that many subjects as well as officials were not doing their duty: they offended others with blasphemous language, used magic, committed homicide, had sex outside their marriage, practised usury, and cheated. The committee was concerned that these introductions would create a certain – distorted – picture of the duchy. Württemberg, they argued, would appear to foreigners who read or heard the *Landesordnung* as a land of impious sinful people, who had no honour whatsoever.[95] It is another clear indicator that although many of the regulations only applied to the inhabitants of Württemberg, the *Landesordnung* was also intended to be read outside the duchy.

With respect to dissemination, the *Landesordnung* from 1567 was similar to the church ordinance from 1559. In contrast to the church ordinance, however, the *Landesordnung* from 1567 had an even higher print run and was produced in no fewer than 1,000 copies.[96] A considerable number of these many copies certainly found their way into the hands of other rulers, who could then, if they wished, use the *Landesordnung* as a role model for their own legal systems. Furthermore, they could inform their subjects about recent legislation in Württemberg. This was of particular interest to merchants and travellers who

94 See the digital copy in the Universitäts- und Landesbibliothek Sachsen-Anhalt, http://digitale.bibliothek.uni-halle.de/vd16/content/titleinfo/995743.

95 Sattler (1769–1783), *Geschichte des Herzogthums Würtenberg*, IV, p. 230.

96 HStASt, A 38 Bü 3.

had commercial dealings with, or needed to pass through, the duchy. They needed to know what was forbidden in Württemberg if they wanted to avoid a fine or corporal punishment.

Once printed, the *Landesordnung* was still not ready to be disseminated. Thanks to written exchanges between the duke and his councillors in Stuttgart, we get a glimpse of what exactly needed to be done after the production.[97] Although the issue date at the end of the *Landesordnung* mentioned 17 August, the copies did not leave the print shop before the end of the month. On 23 August, the printer paid a visit to the councillors in Stuttgart, bringing with him one complete copy of the *Landesordnung* and announcing that the remaining 999 copies were to follow within one week. When the councillors had received all 1,000 copies, they separated the last gatherings of 65 copies and sent them to the duke to sign. After only a few days, Christoph sent the signed gatherings back and instructed his councillors to send the *Landesordnung* out to every district. Presumably, the 65 authenticated copies were given to the most important officials in the duchy. The other officials and those outside the duchy received an unsigned copy of the *Landesordnung*.

Addressing immediate concerns

In addition to these large compilations of regulations, Württemberg's rulers often had smaller regulations printed that addressed one issue in particular. Contemporaries referred to these publications as 'open letters' (*offene briefe*) or 'mandates' (*mandate*). These smaller publications were vital, as the compilation of the *Landesordnung* or institutional ordinances could take several months. In some cases, such as the *Landesordnung* of 1567 and the marriage ordinance from 1536, this process took the better part of a whole year.[98] In the meantime, the authorities in Württemberg needed to address immediate concerns; so they issued mandates often in the form of broadsheets.[99] These publications could be easily produced. Once the ordinance existed in draft form, it could be printed in a single day. To this end, a chancellery scribe produced a draft manuscript, which was then sent to the printer. It was penned on one sheet of paper that

97 HStASt, A 38 Bü 3.

98 Schäfer (ed.) (1984), *Reformation in Württemberg*, p. 116.

99 Towards the end of the sixteenth century, the dukes of Württemberg tended to produce folio pamphlets, which were usually just one sheet of paper folded once; similar to the dukes of Jülich-Cleves-Berg, see Landesarchiv Nordrhein-Westfalen (Rheinland), Handschriften L II 7, Band 2 and Handschriften L II 8, Band 1. Some of the Württemberg pamphlets were folded and addressed in the same way as broadsheets.

was folded to create a pamphlet, a common practice in letter writing.[100] The text itself was only written on the right half of the leaf to allow a spacious margin for annotations and corrections.

One such mandate draft was compiled on 24 June 1551, shortly after Christoph had begun to reign and before he published a new edition of the *Landesordnung*. The draft manuscript, with its many corrections and instructions concerning the print run, fortunately survives in the Stuttgart archive alongside the printed broadsheet.[101] The mandate addressed firearms, a subject that was often discussed and from 1515 formed an integral part of the *Landesordnung*. The use and possession of guns was frequently regulated with mandates, not only in the Holy Roman Empire, but throughout Europe as well. Firearms were a major concern for rulers in the sixteenth century, as guns would often go off unexpectedly and presented a fire hazard.[102] Yet, many early modern authorities, including those in England, France, and Italy, were still not able to limit the use of firearms.[103]

Although the use of weapons was already regulated from 1515 onwards, Christoph again addressed the matter with this mandate from 1551. In order to print this mandate and disseminate it widely, Christoph's chancellery first created a manuscript draft. As this mandate comprised a significant amount of text, two sheets of paper were used, thus creating a total of four leaves in pamphlet format. For his draft, the scribe who composed the manuscript relied on the text of a previous mandate that had been issued under Ulrich some ten years earlier.[104] When the scribe copied Ulrich's mandate, he had already updated several details such as the name of the ruler and the issue date at the end. Apart from that, he copied most parts of the previous mandate word for word.

The draft started with a greeting from the duke (now Christoph and not Ulrich) to all who should be made aware of the new legislation: all bailiffs and district governors, mayors, courts, councillors, and visitors to the duchy. The wordy greeting was followed by an even wordier explanation of why it was necessary to issue this new regulation. Narrowed down to the gist, the duke argued that his subjects had recently suffered increasingly from assaults and attacks, many carried out with firearms. Finally, halfway through the long text, the new legislation is described in detail. At the very end of the text, the scribe included the issue date and place, leaving a small gap for the day to be filled in at a later point when this was established.

100 Daybell (2012), *The Material Letter in Early Modern England*, p. 2.
101 HStASt, A 39 Bü 2.
102 Tlusty (2011), *The Martial Ethic in Early Modern Germany*, p. 81.
103 Ruff (2001), *Violence in Early Modern Europe 1500–1800*, pp. 50–52.
104 Appendix no. 21.

After he had created his draft, the scribe gave the manuscript to another official to correct and amend. This official corrected superfluous expressions, as well as grammar and smaller issues of content: these included for instance a wrong date. When the scribe referred to the earlier mandate concerning firearms, previously issued by Ulrich, he inserted the year [15]22. However, this was incorrect; the mandate was actually published in 1543. So the chancellor changed it to the correct year: [15]43.

Most significantly, the new draft made important changes to the details of the legislation. Ulrich had originally intended the ban on carrying firearms to apply to every traveller – specifically mentioning merchants, burghers, members of the aristocracy, and visitors from the imperial cities. This presented a rather harsh restriction. Even if one only thinks of the many merchants that tried to protect their goods from thieves and robbers, it meant they had no choice but to avoid the Duchy of Württemberg if they did not want to pay the fine. That might result in many extra days of travel and high additional costs.

His son, Christoph, took a more liberal approach and significantly amended this very stringent regulation. The scribe who compiled the mandate for Christoph copied Ulrich's original passage in his draft, which was then amended to limit the ban only to the last two groups of people: the aristocracy and those from imperial cities. According to the new regulations, merchants and burghers were now allowed to carry their firearms with them when travelling through Württemberg. In addition, the revising official added a small phrase that helped to explain the legislation. The aristocracy and inhabitants of imperial cities were ordered to obey the firearms ban 'to prevent any disputes and conflict among neighbours'.[105]

The new mandate was also more liberal towards foreigners. Unlike the travellers, this group is not further specified, but it might be assumed that Ulrich meant immigrants, possibly religious refugees, who came to Württemberg with all their belongings to start a new life. In 1543, Ulrich banned every foreigner from bringing their weapons with them. Instead, they were to leave their weapons at the borders. To ensure that this legislation was followed, Ulrich had specifically instructed every porter as well as those officials working at the borders of Württemberg to communicate the ban to every individual that crossed into the territory. The revising official of Christoph's mandate cut out the entire paragraph. Thus the mandate did not mention foreigners at all. From 1551 onwards, they were no longer asked to leave their weapons behind. Finally, the corrector inserted the correct date in the free space left in the last line: it now read '24 June'. Additionally, he wrote instructions concerning the

105 The original German text reads: 'allerlei unnachperschafft, und widerwille zu verhüten'.

print production on the back of the manuscript. This particular mandate issued in June 1551 received the note '300 copies should be printed' and was produced as a broadsheet.[106]

This represents a slightly higher print run than the 250 copies of the explanation of the imperial police ordinance issued two years earlier. But this higher print run is easily explained: Duke Christoph wanted this mandate to be sent not only to every district official, but also to every forester.[107] Thus we may assume that again around 176 copies went out to the different districts and two dozen were kept in the chancellery and at the ducal court. In addition, several copies were sent to the officials in charge of the 16 forestry sectors.[108] Finally, as this mandate not only addressed the inhabitants of the principality but also travellers, it was exhibited at the borders of the territory to be read out by the officials stationed there. This was common practice in the not so distant Tyrol, where officials at the guardhouses and tollhouses were in charge of reading out mandates addressing vagabonds, beggars, or demobilised soldiers, as well as regulations for the use of firearms.[109] The Württemberg mandate that addressed a similar group of people was most likely proclaimed in the same way. Such a procedure would ensure that all people affected by such a mandate would hear it and be warned.

Depending on the contents, early modern mandates could be produced in very large numbers. The account book of the Elector of Saxony reveals that he had mandates printed in rather different quantities.[110] The amount of copies depended on the target audience: ordinances that primarily addressed the inhabitants of Saxony were usually produced in 200 copies. This included ordinances that addressed taxes as well as regulations for guilds.[111] In contrast, mandates banning inhabitants from joining foreign military service appeared in 600 or even 1,400 copies. These publications were undoubtedly intended for wide circulation beyond the border to prevent foreign rulers from recruiting in Saxony. Once foreign authorities heard that the rulers of Saxony banned their

106 The original German text reads: 'Es sollen 300 Exemplaria getruckt werd[en].'

107 HStASt, A 39 Bü 2.

108 Trugenberger (1994), 'Die württembergische Amtsstadt im 15. und 16. Jahrhundert', p. 137.

109 Schennach (2010), *Gesetz und Herrschaft. Die Entstehung des Gesetzgebungsstaates am Beispiel Tirols*, p. 627. Vagabonds and beggars were a particular problem in the mid-1580s, see Tolley (1995), *Pastors and Parishioners in Württemberg during the late Reformation*, p. 3 & p. 137, the inhabitants of Bodelshausen complained that they were overrun by beggars.

110 Buchwald (1934), 'Kleine Notizen aus Rechnungsbüchern des Thüringischen Staatsarchivs (Weimar)', p. 210.

111 *Ibid.*, p. 212.

subjects from taking up military service elsewhere, they might give up their efforts and recruit somewhere else.

Printed mandates, such as the one created in June 1551, bore a close physical resemblance to medieval charters.[112] The structure of the mandate followed a long-established tradition. It opened with the usual elements of *intitulatio*, *inscriptio*, and *salutatio*. Then the motive for the creation of the document was given as well as an exposition of the content (*arenga*, *promulgatio*). Finally, the broadsheet would describe the punishments in detail and remind its reader that with this mandate everyone was informed and could not claim to be unaware.

Mandates were often printed in horizontal format leaving large blank spaces around the text. This lent both the text and its author a sense of authority.[113] In a time when paper was still a costly commodity, such lavish consumption was a marker for social status.[114] The duke's subjects who encountered a broadsheet with ample space around the printed text readily understood that this message was of importance; even if they could not read the entire text and had to rely on officials to read the text out aloud.

Once a mandate was produced, it was given back to the chancellery in order to be signed and sealed. Ultimately, early modern mandates still functioned as charters that required authentication. In this fashion, royal and imperial mandates were often signed by the king or emperor himself. Maximilian I, however, who used print to a large degree, grew increasingly tired of signing countless documents by hand. Thus, in 1507, he had a stamp made with the formula 'per regem, per se'.[115] His successors Charles V and Ferdinand would follow this practice and employ stamps with their respective names. Just like the Habsburg emperors, the Habsburg governors of Württemberg did not sign all mandates by hand either. Instead, their signature formed part of the printed text. Thus, when in August 1521 the governor of Württemberg sent out new regulations on blasphemy and pledging health, his covering letter that accompanied the ordinance included 'Ro[e]mischer K. M. Stathalter und Regenten ir M. Fürstenthumbs Wirtemberg' in the printed text.[116] Yet, this did not render manuscript signatures redundant. Throughout the sixteenth century, mandates were still signed by hand, especially in Württemberg. When the Habsburgs issued the ban on Luther's works in 1522, the governor signed the ordinance by

112 Honemann (2000), 'Vorformen des Einblattdruckes. Urkunden – Schrifttafeln – Textierte Tafelbilder – Anschläge – Einblatthandschriften', p. 5.

113 Ordinances in the Low Countries were also printed with generous margins around the printed text, see Weduwen (2018), *State Communication*, p. 95.

114 Daybell (2012), *The Material Letter in Early Modern England*, p. 93.

115 Sybel and Sickel (1880/1891), *Kaiserurkunden in Abbildungen*, I, p. 479.

116 HStASt, A 238 Bü 1.

hand.[117] Moreover, once the dukes of Württemberg ruled the duchy again, they authenticated their mandates by hand until the end of the century.

In most cases, the responsibility of authenticating the mandates in Württemberg would fall to the *Landhofmeister*. He presided over the chancellery and was one of the highest officials in the duke's council.[118] After Christoph started to reign in 1550, Balthasar von Gültlingen accompanied the new duke as *Landhofmeister* in the first few years.[119] Hence, many ordinances that were issued during this time bear the signature of Balthasar, who signed a broadsheet mandate concerning poaching in January 1554, another concerning the sale of crops in March 1554, as well as one regulating winegrowing in June 1554.[120] In all three cases, his signature was accompanied by the signature of Johann Cnoder, a member of the duke's senior council.

During the century, there seems to have been no clear guideline as to which officials were responsible for signing mandates. The decision seems to have been made on the basis of who was available to sign it. It also appears that there was even some room for change while a particular mandate was being signed. After all, it was time-consuming work to sign several hundred copies. Thus it is hardly surprising that there are two copies of the same mandate signed by different officials.[121] Both mandates bore the signature of the governor, Heinrich von Castell, but the second signature varied: one copy was signed by Johann Brastberger, the vice chancellor, the other by Kilian Bertsch, a member of the duke's senior council.[122]

The procedure seems to have been slightly different when Württemberg was under Habsburg rule. As we have seen already in some official publications, the signature formed part of the written text. Other mandates were usually signed by the secretary Josef Münsinger von Frundeck as well as the governor.[123] When in 1533 Ferdinand ordered his officials to regulate fishing in the Neckar, this mandate was signed by Münsinger, and Philip, Duke of Palatinate-Neuburg, who was governor from 1532 until Ulrich returned. During Ferdinand's regency, mandates could be signed by up to three officials, not only by the governor and the secretary, but also by the chancellor. When Ferdinand instructed his officials in 1522 to ban Luther's books, a broadsheet mandate

117 Appendix no. 16.

118 Bernhardt (1972), *Die Zentralbehörden des Herzogtums Württemberg und ihre Beamten*, pp. 24–25.

119 *Ibid.*, p. 752.

120 Appendix nos. 24, 25, 26.

121 Appendix no. 27, both copies are in HStASt, A 238 Bü 2.

122 HStASt, A 238 Bü 2. For more information on both officials, see Bernhardt (1972), *Die Zentralbehörden des Herzogtums Württemberg und ihre Beamten*, p. 754.

123 *Ibid.*, pp. 742–743.

was created to address this issue.[124] It was signed by the governor, Truchseß Wilhelm of Waldburg, the chancellor, Heinrich Winckelhofer, and finally Münsinger as secretary.

Once the mandates were signed, they were sealed and addressed. The duke's red wax seal thus provided a highlight to the printed text. This meant that all who saw the mandate knew it was something important. When it was authenticated, a scribe folded the mandate just like a manuscript letter and wrote the address on its back. Pamphlets were sent in similar fashion – the text they contained usually only filled the first three pages. Thus the last page was empty and could be used for the address.[125]

However, not every copy was authenticated. Of the two surviving copies of the mandate banning firearms in 1551, only one was signed and sealed as described above.[126] The other copy remained unsigned. As this particular copy was meant to stay with the duke's official in the chancellery, there was no need for it to be authenticated. It was extremely useful to have a copy of a previous mandate at the ready for future reference. Thus, if a new mandate was needed, it could be drafted with the help of the previous one; just as the 1551 firearms mandate was created from a previous mandate of 1543.

Once the mandates were printed, they could still be changed. As soon as they had left the printing shop, they were carefully read. If the proofreader spotted a mistake, such as a typo, this mistake was crossed out by hand. Similarly, if the proofreader became aware of a missing word, it was added in the margin. This procedure was followed for every single copy of the many mandates. The two copies of the mandate addressing the ban on firearms from 1551 were both annotated in this way. Evidently, when the chancellor read the phrase 'the mercy we [the duke] showed', he considered it to be not as strong an expression as he intended. So he wrote the word 'great' (German: 'sondere') in the margin, which made the text 'the great mercy we [the duke] showed'. This addition was made in both copies, the one that was sealed and signed as well as the copy that was intended to stay in the chancellery.

One might think that these manuscript corrections only occurred on proof sheets. The printer could have produced a few copies to be proofread before he actually started to produce hundreds of mandates. This, however, does not seem to have been the case in Württemberg. After all, many mandates with manuscript corrections were signed and sealed. If it was only a proof copy, the officials would certainly not have wasted time and wax for a mandate that was not meant

124 Appendix no. 16, HStASt, A 63 Bü 2/6.

125 A pamphlet mandate from 30 August 1564 was folded and addressed to the officials in Nagold, see HStASt, A 39 Bü 3.

126 HStASt, A 39 Bü 3.

to leave the chancellery. Moreover, if the typo only became obvious after the mandate had been authenticated and the chancellery had decided not to send the broadsheet, the scribe would certainly not have made the effort to correct the mistake.

There were a number of Württemberg mandates that were corrected by hand.[127] One of them is an unusually long ordinance addressing the collection of a tax to fight the Turks. It included a printing mistake at the very end of the 114 lines of text.[128] Instead of 'werck' the typesetter had wrongly assembled the letters 'wreck'. Two copies of this particular mandate have survived, both of which were signed, received a seal, and the same typo was corrected by hand.

The interplay of ordinances

In the course of the sixteenth century, hundreds of such mandates were drafted, printed, and disseminated widely in this fashion. In many cases these mandates were later integrated into the new edition of the *Landesordnung*. The firearms mandate from 1551 found its way into the new *Landesordnung* that was released one year later.[129] It was provided with a title and was introduced with a short paragraph giving an overview of the regulation, that is, no one was allowed to have firearms in their house. If someone needed to practise, they should only carry their weapons on the main streets (not in the fields). Then the entire ordinance followed word for word, including the greetings, the lengthy explanation, the punishments, and even the issue date at the very end of the text. Another example of the integration of a broadsheet mandate into the *Landesordnung* is the fish ordinance that first appeared in the *Landesordnung* of 1536. It was this fish regulation that was accompanied by a long printed line to indicate the measurements fish ought to have in order to be sold (fig. 1.5.). This ordinance had already been issued four years earlier, in 1532, by Ferdinand during his time as governor in Württemberg. Although no copy has survived, we know that it existed in broadsheet form, as, according to the text, it was 'displayed openly'.[130]

As the regulations prescribed with this ordinance were not followed, they were renewed with another mandate in October 1533.[131] This detailed ordi-

127 For example, appendix no. 20, HStASt J 17 Bü 14.

128 Appendix no. 22, copies are in HStASt, J 17 Bü 14 and A 238 Bü 1.

129 USTC 635179 (VD16 W 4509), fol. 55r–57r.

130 In a successive ordinance from October 1533, Ferdinand referred to the printed ordinance issued from the previous year, appendix no. 17. The original German text reads: '[unser mandate des] nechstverschines jars [welches wir] in getruck außgeen, öffentlich verkönden und anschlagen lassen haben'.

131 Appendix no. 17.

nance comprised 59 lines of text in which regulations for fishing and use of the river Neckar were defined. So, for example, Ferdinand forbade anyone from bathing in the river if there was a dam nearby. This behaviour would scare away the fish and crabs that lived in these places. Ferdinand also ordered that the fish caught in the Neckar needed to be of a certain length in order to be sold. If a fish was too small, it should be thrown back into the river. To measure the fish, the mandate included a printed line at the bottom of the broadsheet.

When Ulrich regained his duchy only a few months after the publication of this mandate, he reissued the ordinance. For this, he adopted most parts of Ferdinand's mandate: the regulations for bathing and fishing still applied and the fines detailed in Ferdinand's ordinance were of the same level. So if someone was caught fishing at night, he still had to pay 8 Heller, just as he would have done one year earlier. A few parts, however, were amended. The lengthy explanation at the beginning was shortened from 12 to three lines of text, leaving space only for Ulrich to record that this legislation had been agreed on by his councillors and was intended for the common good. Additionally, the regulation for fish that did not meet the minimum size required was tightened. Ulrich expected not only the person who sold the fish but also the person who bought it to pay the fine of 3 Heller.[132] To make the regulation widely known, he inserted a paragraph that claimed the ordinance was to be read out not only in close proximity to the river Neckar but in the entire duchy. This way he could ensure that everyone would hear about the recent changes. Finally, Ulrich tried to achieve more efficiency by involving the public. He promised a reward for anyone who helped the officials to catch an offender: in case of a successful prosecution, they were to receive 5 Schilling.

The fact that the fish ordinance explicitly mentions a reward for people who denounced others is unusual for Württemberg mandates. In theory, the inhabitants were always required to denounce offenders. This duty was explicitly described at the end of the *Landesordnung* of 1515.[133] Yet, it is rarely repeated in mandates. What is even more interesting is that the fish ordinance is one of the very few mandates that promises a reward to those who denounced offenders.[134] This insertion of the clause probably indicates that the regulation was particularly difficult to implement, so the officials had to resort to other means to prompt cooperation.

132 Line 25, the original German text reads: 'nit allein der so die [Fische] gefangen, verkaufft, oder hingeschenckt hat, sonder auch der, so die kauffs oder anderer weis von jme annimt zubezaln'.

133 USTC 701569 (VD16 W 4455), fol. 12v.

134 The mandate banning Luther's work from 1522 is another ordinance which promises a reward to denouncers, appendix no. 16.

The fish mandate was taken over into Ulrich's new *Landesordnung* of 1536. Like the ban on firearms that Christoph would integrate later in 1552, the mandate was provided with a title 'fish ordinance' and a short introductory paragraph. It explained that fish were very rare at the moment in Württemberg and that this ordinance aimed to address the deficiency. Due to its length, the ordinances covered several folios in the *Landesordnung*, of which the last folio includes the printed line to measure the fish. Finally, two extra paragraphs were added at the end, one of which urged the officials to obey the legislation and punish the offenders accordingly. The other paragraph extended the scope of the ordinance, which was now applicable to every river, not only the Neckar.

These two broadsheet ordinances, the ban on firearms and the regulation for the river Neckar, were both issued shortly after Christoph came to power. Such a change of rulers always inspired a whole flood of short publications. There were a number of important issues that needed to be addressed straight away and could not wait for the new edition of the *Landesordnung* to be published. When the Habsburgs took over Württemberg in 1520, two mandates were sent – in June and July respectively – to every district official banning any support for the expelled duke.[135] In the first mandate from June, the govenor pointed out that previous orders had not been followed, so we may assume that these two mandates were not the only ones printed at that time to prohibit support for Ulrich.

As the conflict with Ulrich went on for a couple of months, banning support for him was not enough. The Habsburgs also tried to discourage any armed resistance by enforcing stricter gun legislation. With the help of a broadsheet, they ordered all district officials not to allow anyone to carry their firearms with them. Should the inhabitants need to practise shooting, they were to keep their arms close to the practice field and not take them home.[136]

Apart from banning support for the previous ruler, the Habsburgs had other immediate concerns on their minds once they were the overlords of Württemberg. The new governor needed to establish his feudal ties with his Württemberg subjects. To this end, only a few days after the ban on firearms, Charles issued a broadsheet asking his subjects to renew their feudal ties in Stuttgart.[137] This broadsheet was hung up in every town in and around the duchy to ensure great attention. It did not give a specific date, as more information was to follow. And, in fact, detailed information followed several months later. This time the broadsheet mentioned the exact date the vassals were expected to come to Stuttgart, namely 13 February.[138] So the broadsheet was issued, printed, and sent

135 Sattler (1769–1783), *Geschichte des Herzogthums Würtenberg*, II, pp. 158–159.
136 *Ibid.*, p. 157.
137 *Ibid.*, pp. 157–158.
138 Appendix no. 14.

out one month in advance to ensure that the vassals could make it to Stuttgart in time.

The Habsburgs also tried to lay their hands on the region of Reichenweier to the west of the duchy. They published a similar broadsheet that invited every vassal to the city of Reichenweier to renew their feudal ties.[139] This, again, did not contain the specific day; it was just an announcement that was to be followed up with another publication. The broadsheet itself was designed as a form: spaces were left so the name of the vassal and the issue date could be filled in by hand. Whereas the other two broadsheets fulfilled their purposes and brought Württemberg's vassals under Habsburg control, this broadsheet failed to have any effect. The small district of Reichenweier remained firmly in the hands of Stuttgart.[140]

When Duke Ulrich's efforts finally paid off and he regained his duchy, he had a number of documents printed. We have already looked at the impressively long broadsheet that Ulrich and Philip issued to announce their military conquest. In his quest to win back his duchy, the Duke of Württemberg also issued several other broadsheets that were to be disseminated widely. In one of these broadsheets, Ulrich asked every vassal, burgher, and peasant not to hinder his conquest; after all, Württemberg was Ulrich's God-given possession. In return, Ulrich promised to be a gracious lord once he was restored as duke.[141]

Apart from these print-intensive changes of rulers, and the mandates that preceded the new edition of the *Landesordnung*, broadsheets were also often issued *after* the publication of the law code. They were meant to amend and change a regulation previously presented in the *Landesordnung*. The publication of the law code in 1515, with its ban on firearms and crossbows, inspired the publication of several broadsheets in the following months. With the new edition of the *Landesordnung*, Ulrich reacted to the Poor Conrad uprising. It included several regulations that were intended to prevent any similar turmoil in the future. Among these regulations was a strict ban on firearms and crossbows. According to this law, no one was allowed to carry their weapons in the fields.

This strict law, however, provoked discontent. There were groups of people who relied on carrying firearms for protection or because they had the privilege to hunt. It is likely that many protests and appeals to change the legislation followed. Finally, a few months after the publication of the *Landesordnung*, the

139 Appendix no. 15.

140 Schaab, Schwarzmaier and Taddey (eds.) (2000), *Handbuch der Baden-Württembergischen Geschichte* (Vol. 1,2), p. 680.

141 Appendix no. 18, HStASt, A 84 Bü 29. Sattler dated this document 1 May 1534. Thus it appeared after Ulrich's invasion in April, Sattler (1769–1783), *Geschichte des Herzogthums Würtenberg*, III, pp. 95f. This date also appears in Schäfer (ed.) (1984), *Reformation in Württemberg*, p. 97.

law code was indeed changed. Issued by the council and governor of Stuttgart, the broadsheet addressed every forester in Württemberg and stated that firearms were allowed on official roads.[142] Additionally, those who were allowed to hunt could do so without risking the punishment of 2 Gulden prescribed in the *Landesordnung.*

By 1517, however, two years after the publication of the *Landesordnung* with the strict gun laws, Ulrich prescribed even harsher regulations for weapons in Württemberg. In July, he published a mandate addressing every bailiff and district governor.[143] In this mandate, Ulrich reminded them to do their job properly and to take everyone who tried to poach in Württemberg straight to court. The punishment was increased from an already significant fine of 2 Gulden to a much more serious corporal punishment: both the offender's eyes were to be put out.

In a similar fashion, a broadsheet was printed after the publication of the *Landesordnung* in 1521 by the Austrian government. Although the law code was issued years after Luther's first appearance on the German stage, it did not include any regulations concerning the reformer's teaching, the dissemination of his ideas or the question of how to deal with his followers. This was about to change in November 1522, when Ferdinand sent two letters to his governor in Stuttgart. The content of these two letters was published on one single broadsheet at the end of the month.[144] With this broadsheet the governor of Württemberg forbade everyone to obtain, read, print, or sell Luther's works. They were also forbidden to gather together, presumably to discuss the evangelical teachings. If the officials caught a wrongdoer, they were to be taken to prison straight away. The mandate is one of the few ordinances that mention a reward for informers, just like the fish ordinance. In the case that subjects became aware of anyone infringing the new regulations, they were rewarded if they informed the officials. In return the informer would be handsomely rewarded – they received half of the goods of anyone convicted.

Broadsheets could also serve to supplement the *Landesordnung*. In the 1515 edition of the law code, Ulrich ordered every priest in Württemberg to read out the legislation on blasphemy and pledging health on the four most significant holidays: Easter, Whitsunday, the Assumption of Mary, and Christmas. As a reminder, he had the two regulations published on a broadsheet comprising a total of 72 lines.[145] This broadsheet was then given to every priest. Thus they

142 Steiff (1881), *Der erste Buchdruck in Tübingen (1498–1534)*, pp. 123–124.

143 Policey W, p. 581, no. 21.

144 HStASt, A 63 Bü 2/7; Sattler (1769–1783), *Geschichte des Herzogthums Würtenberg*, III, pp. 226–229; appendix no. 12.

145 Appendix no. 12.

could take the broadsheet with them to church and read it out to their congregation. Although they were not explicitly required to do so, it nevertheless seems very likely that the broadsheet was used in this way.

As this particular broadsheet was sent to every single priest in the duchy, it must have been printed in a very high print run. Usually no more than three copies found their way into the ducal archives. However, there are no fewer than ten copies of this particular broadsheet.[146] Their various watermarks reveal that these broadsheets were produced from three different stocks of paper. One watermark, a lily, differs radically from the other two that show a bull's head.[147] This suggests that the printer had to use several stocks of paper to produce the many copies required.

The *Landesordnung* of 1521 was also accompanied by an additional publication. This document included the legislation for blasphemy and pledging health and was to be sent to every priest. This time, however, the publication was produced as a pamphlet.[148] In contrast to the previous publication, we are fortunate that a printed covering letter has survived, which provides us with more details about the intended publication.[149] In this letter, the duke asked rather more of the recipient than simply to read it out to his congregation. From 1521 onwards, the priests were no longer expected to read out the legislation only on the four holidays; instead, the duke expected them to remind their congregation to be pious and orderly throughout the entire year.[150]

As we have seen above, ordinances and mandates were often sent with covering letters.[151] In some cases, such as the *Warhafftig Underrichtung*, the duke even had several different texts produced to correspond to different addressees. This was, however, more the exception than the rule. In most cases, the rulers used one that addressed every official with 'loyal subject'. In this fashion, the officials received a covering letter in 1549 that instructed them exactly how to proceed with the explanation of the imperial police ordinance; similarly, they received a notification with the *Landesordnung* of 1567.[152] The firearms mandate from 1551 was sent with a letter to every bailiff and district governor as well as every forester. In this letter, Christoph ordered his representatives to have the

146 HStASt: one copy in A 38 Bü 12, two copies in A 39 Bü 1, seven copies in A 238 Bü 1.

147 I would like to express my gratitude to Erwin Frauenknecht at the Hauptstaatsarchiv in Stuttgart, who kindly helped me to identify the different watermarks.

148 HStASt, A 38 Bü 3.

149 Appendix no. 13.

150 The original German text reads: 'durch die iar offtermals'.

151 Philip Haas at the Niedersächsisches Landesarchiv has found various covering letters issued by dukes in northern Germany (call number: NLA WO 40 Slg).

152 HStASt, A 38 Bü 3.

mandate read out by the district scribe or the *Schultheiß* in every part of the district. Once they were finished with this task, they had to post the broadsheet in their towns as well as the 'special places'.[153] This probably referred to central places in the community, such as churches.

During the sixteenth century, the content of covering letters does not seem to have changed much. The officials were usually instructed to make the ordinance known and, in the case of a mandate, exhibit it at the designated places. Despite this fact, however, covering letters did not become obsolete. Rulers frequently issued them even though the content was similar to previous covering letters.[154] With this in mind, we might have to think of early modern ordinances as, in fact, two publications: the ordinance itself, in broadsheet or pamphlet form, and the accompanying letter. Thus it was even more lucrative for a printer to produce official documents for local authorities. The additional broadsheet letters meant valuable extra income for the printer.

'A humble request': appeals and law-making processes

During the sixteenth century, the dukes received many appeals from their subjects. These supplications were written as humble requests in which an individual or a group of individuals asked for a variety of favours – financial reimbursements, more time to pay taxes, or the postponement of a ducal hunt until the crop was harvested.[155] Some of these appeals also sought to encourage the duke to issue new legislation, often to cater for particular economic interests. One such appeal stood behind Ulrich's explanation of the imperial police ordinance in 1549.[156] With the imperial police ordinance, Emperor Charles V tried to establish a legal framework for each and every territory in the heavily fragmented Holy Roman Empire. Among other issues, it tackled economic matters and prescribed regulations for shipping wine, for price monopolies, the sale of crops, and the sale of cloths.

It was this last legislation that presented problems to the cloth traders in Württemberg. After all, the cloth traders frequently sold their goods outside the

153 HStASt, A 39 Bü 2, no. 9. The original German text reads: 'In d[er] Stat u[n]d den furne[m]lich Pleck[en].'

154 The *Kirchenordnung* from 1553 was for instance accompanied by such a letter. It was meant 'for all priests to send them the church ordinance' and was printed in 800 copies (a slightly higher print run that the church ordinance itself which was produced in 700 copies), HStASt, A 282 Bd. 1291.

155 Landwehr (2000), *Policey im Alltag*, pp. 280f.

156 HStASt, A 38 Bü 2. One copy of the explanation is in HStASt, A 38 Bü 2, another copy is in WLB, HBF 2774; the original Reichspoliceyordnung from 1548 - USTC 634336 (VD16 D 1058).

duchy.[157] Their products enjoyed a particularly high reputation in the Imperial City of Strasbourg.[158] However, after the publication of the imperial police ordinance in 1548, Strasbourg was quick to adopt the new legislation. As a result, traders who had previously sold their cloths dry now sold them slightly damp. Since cloths of inferior quality would tear when damp, the buyers could now easily judge the quality of the cloth.

Although Charles V instructed every ruler in the Holy Roman Empire to make the imperial police ordinance known in their territories as soon as possible, it was not published in Württemberg. Ulrich was not the only ruler who disregarded the emperor's order in this respect.[159] One fact that helps to explain this circumstance is that it had to be bought. One or maybe a few copies were made available to every imperial estate, so we may assume that Ulrich received a free copy from the emperor.[160] But if he wanted to make it known in Württemberg, the duke had to meet the costs for publication or instruct his officials to buy a copy. They had to do so in Mainz, as Ivo Schöffer was the only printer entrusted with an imperial privilege to produce this work.[161] There, they could choose if they wanted to buy the whole compendium or just individual regulations.

Initially, Ulrich chose to publish only the part of the imperial police ordinance that was most relevant for Württemberg. From the duke's perspective, this was the legislation on blasphemy and pledging health. As we have seen, these issues were often addressed in the *Landesordnungen* together with other ordinances. In 1548, blasphemous subjects and those that pledged health were still a thorn in the duke's flesh. So in November 1548, he published a mandate with a short introduction.[162] In his introductory words, the duke informed the audience that the emperor had recently issued the following regulation concerning blasphemy and pledging health. This was followed by a word for word repetition of the two sections from the imperial police ordinance. At the end of the text, the duke ordered his officials to instruct priests to read out this ordinance in church every Sunday. Thus the duke could ensure that every subject in his duchy would hear about this new legislation.

157 Boelcke (1987), *Wirtschaftsgeschichte Baden-Württembergs von den Römern bis heute*, p. 74.

158 Trugenberger (1994), 'Die württembergische Amtsstadt im 15. und 16. Jahrhundert', p. 148.

159 Holzborn (2003), *Die Geschichte der Gesetzespublikation*, p. 42.

160 This was the case with *Reichsabschieden*, see Weber (2006), '"Bekennen und thun hiemit kunth und offentlich"', p. 286.

161 Weber (ed.) (2002), *Die Reichspolizeiordnungen von 1530, 1548 und 1577*, p. 59.

162 Appendix no. 23.

Yet, Ulrich's refusal to publish the whole imperial police ordinance caused severe problems for cloth traders. In a letter to the duke, the cloth traders of the Württemberg district Göppingen explained their predicament in detail. When they had recently tried to sell their goods, they became aware of a new law passed by the emperor. The cloth traders were surprised, as they were completely unaware of the new regulations; there had not been any notification from the duke or the emperor. To avoid further complications, the cloth traders asked the duke to explain the current legal situation – how were they supposed to sell their cloths?[163]

The cloth traders in Göppingen were not the only cloth traders to complain about the current legal confusion. In a letter to the duke, the council in Stuttgart informed their ruler that quite a number of tradesmen had come to Stuttgart to address this difficult legal situation.[164] The traders wanted to follow the practice described in the imperial ordinance, but they had encountered problems when other traders in Württemberg were not acting accordingly. In addition, the councillors referred to other regulations in the imperial ordinance that had to be implemented within a certain amount of time; among them were regulations on clothing, measurements, weights, and day labourers. Thus the councillors strongly encouraged the duke to pass new regulations for Württemberg that would correspond to the imperial police ordinance.

The duke took this advice and, after several months of consultation, published a pamphlet comprising 38 pages that bore the title *Explanation of several issues in the imperial police ordinance for the Duchy of Württemberg.*[165] This was sent to every official with a covering letter to make it known in their districts. Additionally, the officials were instructed to buy a copy of the imperial police ordinance to have it for comparison if need be. The printer Ivo Schöffer must have been very happy about this order, as it meant that he could potentially sell 250 copies to the Württemberg officials (if they, in fact, followed the duke's orders).

One peculiar thing about the publication of the explanation is the discrepancy between issue date and print date. A discrepancy of several days was by no means unusual, as we have seen above with the publication of the *Landesordnung*. The ordinance was issued on 17 August 1567, but the printer did not deliver all 1,000 copies before the end of the month. Similarly, we can see from the printer's invoice in Cologne that the ordinances in the mid-1570s were produced within a few days after the council's meeting.[166] In the case of the

163 HStASt, A 38 Bü 2, 10.

164 HStASt, A 38 Bü 2, 1. The original German text reads: 'etlich gewerbsleutt'.

165 Reyscher, XII, pp. 149–167.

166 Limbach (2016), 'Tracing Lost Broadsheet Ordinances Printed in Sixteenth-Century Cologne', p. 496.

explanation, however, the dates are over five months apart: the issue date reads 30 June 1549, and the copies were sent to the court on 7 December.[167]

A first draft of the explanation was indeed finished by the end of June, but the revision took until 16 November. Only then was the manuscript sent off with a letter in which the duke specified that 200 copies should be printed.[168] The letter includes a small piece of paper, glued in, which was also written on the same day in mid-November. On this piece of paper, the duke specified that the printer was allowed to produce copies for himself to sell in his shop and that the 'date [of the ordinance] should not be adjusted, but kept just the way it is in the manuscript'.[169]

This significant discrepancy between issue date and publication date can also be found in other cases. Falk Eisermann has shown that an imperial mandate regulating blasphemy in the late fifteenth century was actually printed 18 months after it had been issued.[170] In this instance, the delay was caused by the imperial estates who refused to accept the ordinance at first. Only after everything was resolved could the publication be circulated within the empire and be locally reprinted, for instance, in Oppenheim and Cologne. On the document, however, the earlier date, 7 August 1495, is shown and is, therefore, easily confused with the print date.

Another interesting example occurred in Württemberg in the mid-1550s. During this time, Duke Christoph had a selection of important documents printed: a total of 16 privileges were produced in which kings and emperors grant the rulers of Württemberg exemption from foreign courts.[171] While the copies of the Württemberg privileges do not include the exact dates of their production, they do bear the date of issue. The earliest document displays the year 1361. However, all copies were printed on the same paper, as all of them reveal the exact same watermark (shield with arrow inside). Gerhard Piccard, the reknown watermark specialist, identified the watermark on one of the copies,

167 USTC 2214584 (VD16 ZV 30767). Apart from the copies in Vienna and Leipzig, there are further copies in HStASt (A 38 Bü 2) and WLB (HBF 2774); The *Untervogt* of Tübingen wrote on 7 December that he had received the copies of the printer and would send them to the court, HStASt, A 38 Bü 2, 23.

168 HStASt, A 38 Bü 2, 19.

169 The original German text reads: 'Wellennd auch das datum nit ennderen, sonder wie es Im Concept der erklärung gestellt, beleiben lassen'.

170 VE 15 M-41 and M-42.

171 Between 1–5 copies of each document are in HStASt A 251 Bd. 107 and A 238 Bü 1. Further copies are in WLB, HBFC 58, 59, 60, 61, 61a, 62, 62a, 63, 63a, 64, 65, 65a, 66, 67, 68, 69, 70, 105. I would like to thank Peter Rückert for helping me to contextualise my findings.

stating that the paper was either produced in Kirchheim or Göppingen between 1554 and 1555.[172]

These examples show that it is vital to look beyond the issue date in the printed text and investigate when the copies were actually produced. Orders, letters, and watermarks can often help to establish when a document was produced in print. Only then can we estimate when the texts were circulated. This has many implications for historical research, especially for studies on the implementation of police ordinances. In many cases, offenders pleaded that they did not know of the ordinance. Often this defence strategy was not entirely true, but there might be cases where the actual publication of the ordinance was much later than the printed text suggests so that the offender may have actually told the truth.

The example of the cloth traders asking for the publication of new regulation shows vividly that legislation in the early modern period was not just imposed on subjects; instead, subjects were often actively involved in the law-making process, influencing decisions and asking for new regulations. Through complaints as well as supplications, those subject to legislation were able to exercise influence on its enforcement. The inhabitants of early modern Württemberg frequently sent supplications as well as complaints to their rulers. During the Poor Conrad uprising, Duke Ulrich received no fewer than 330 complaints.[173] The authorities perceived the need to regulate the issue of supplications from an early stage. In 1515, the duke issued a mandate and included regulations for the correct way of delivering supplications in the *Landesordnung* of the same year.[174] The inhabitants continued this practice until 1646, when the duke forbade people to hand him supplications while he was travelling through the duchy.[175]

The Württemberg authorities were not the only rulers who negotiated law in such a way in early modern Europe. The practice of passing new laws based on subjects' appeals was widespread in other parts of the empire. There is ample evidence that politics in Bavaria as well as Tyrol were similarly influenced by the written statements of the common man.[176] In addition, Englishmen had

172 A handwritten note from Gerhard Piccard, dated 7 December 1962, is in HStASt A 238 Bü 1. For more information on the production of these privileges, see below.

173 Blickle (2003), 'Beschwerde und Polizeien. Die Legitimation des modernen Staates durch Verfahren und Normen', p. 552.

174 Appendix no. 7; USTC 701569 (VD16 W 4455).

175 Landwehr (2000), *Policey im Alltag*, p. 278.

176 Blickle (2003), 'Beschwerde und Polizeien. Die Legitimation des modernen Staates durch Verfahren und Normen', pp. 552–560.

ways to channel their discontent to the monarch and thus help shape future legislation.[177]

In sixteenth-century Württemberg, however, it was not only the subjects who appealed to the duke. In some particularly troublesome months, the duke also appealed to his subjects and implored them to follow his legislation. Two mandates were issued during that time in which Duke Ulrich expressed increasing anxiety.[178] These two mandates differ significantly from the other mandates that were published in the course of the century. Whereas the rulers usually ordered and commanded, now the duke actually begged.

The two mandates from 1534 and 1535 addressed the ban on firearms. This is not particularly unusual, as we have seen that guns presented many problems to early modern rulers in the Holy Roman Empire. What is unusual, however, is Ulrich's argument. In contrast to other mandates that legitimised the ban on firearms with the common good, Ulrich gave personal reasons: he feared assassination. Thus, his motivation is not based on his alleged concern for the life of his subjects. In fact, Ulrich was solely concerned with his own well-being and does not mention his subjects at all.

A little background helps illuminate this rather curious turn of events. When Duke Ulrich returned to his duchy in 1534, he had been in exile for over 20 years. Württemberg was ruled by the Habsburgs during this period, and when Ulrich finally defeated King Ferdinand's army, his victory created much discontent. The Bavarians were dissatisfied because they wanted to see Christoph, Ulrich's son, rule Württemberg. As Christoph was the nephew of the Bavarian Duke Wilhelm IV, the Bavarians hoped to extend their rule and counterbalance the power of the Habsburgs.

But the Bavarians were not the only ones who resented Ulrich's restoration. The Habsburgs were equally dissatisfied with Ulrich being back in Württemberg. Although they could not fight back initially, they succeeded in making the reluctant duke agree to the treaty of Kaaden, which stated that Ulrich only held the duchy as an Austrian fief. The treaty stipulated that, with the extinction of the line of the house Württemberg – that is, with the death of both Ulrich and Christoph – the duchy should fall back into Habsburgs' hands. Lastly, Ulrich's mercenaries were upset since he had not paid their salaries.[179]

In other words, Ulrich was acutely aware that his victory was not the end of his struggles. He knew very well that in the eyes of the Bavarians and the Habsburgs, Württemberg should have another duke, namely Christoph. On top of that,

177 Kümin and Würgler (1997), 'Petitions, Gravamina and the Early Modern State', p. 42.

178 Policey W, no. 585, no. 58; appendix no. 20.

179 Scott (2005b), 'From the Bundschuh to the Peasants' War', p. 145.

Ulrich's mercenaries demanded their pay. The restored duke was constantly reminded of this discontent in the form of utterances and ballads directed against him.[180] Ulrich quite rightly feared for his life and did not hesitate to communicate his fears to his subjects. Thus he legitimised his ban on firearms not with the usual arguments found in previous mandates. Ulrich instead expressed his genuine fears and tried to rouse compassion and pity among his subjects.

By the time he published the second mandate, Ulrich was more anxious than ever. In this ordinance Ulrich explained that he had discovered more details of the murder plot against him. In the past months he had learned that his enemies had paid quite a number of people to shoot him. Then the duke expressed his regret about this sad news and appealed to his 'honour-loving subjects' to take this news to heart.[181] In addition, Ulrich extended his appeal in asking everyone able to speak German to refrain from murderous or rebellious plans. This way, Ulrich not only appealed to his subjects, but also to those beyond Württemberg who may have heard about – or were even hired for – the plot against the duke.

With this mandate, Ulrich defined an even stricter regulation for firearms in Württemberg. His subjects were not only forbidden to carry guns, but everybody who did not need firearms for his duties should not even possess them. Indeed, they had to dispose of their weapons within four weeks. Ulrich also strengthened the harsh legislation for travellers. Whereas in the previous ordinance travellers were requested only to carry firearms on the official roads in the duchy, they were now required to leave all firearms behind before they crossed the borders into Württemberg. This harsh legislation remained active until 1551, when Ulrich's son took a more liberal approach to travellers and foreigners carrying firearms.

To print or not to print: the dissemination of official announcements

Sixteenth-century rulers in Württemberg relied increasingly on the new medium of print to communicate their orders to their subjects. However, this is not to say that print in any way superseded the importance of traditional means of notifying the public. The overwhelming majority of Württemberg ordinances were addressed to the duke's representatives, who were responsible for making the content of the regulation known. Officials had to proclaim mandates orally in every part of their jurisdiction. In addition, the *Landesordnung*

180 Scribner (1987), 'Police and the Territorial State in Sixteenth-Century Württemberg', p. 116.

181 Appendix no. 20, the original German text reads: 'Wo[e]lliches dann uns zu[e]ho[e]ren hochbeschwa[e]rlich und billich all Eerliebhabenden behertzigen'.

was, from its first publication in 1495, intended to be read aloud at the local courts. Over the course of the century, this procedure did not change. Quite the contrary, from 1515 onwards, the order to read out the law code was amended and now included the addition that it had to be done on a yearly basis. Furthermore, priests were notified separately to remind their congregation of the legislation on blasphemy and pledging health.

When a letter or order was only intended to reach a small audience consisting of a few officials, the duke relied on manuscripts to notify them. Thus, when Ulrich died in 1550, Christoph informed several rulers about this sad news and asked them to honour his deceased father according to Christian tradition.[182] This letter was intended for 15 rulers who were listed at the end of the manuscript draft, among them the Bishop of Salzburg, Count Palatine Friedrich, and Albrecht, Duke of Prussia. Similarly, in 1594, Duke Friedrich sent a manuscript mandate about silverware in religious houses to only 12 recipients.[183] Among them were the religious houses in Maulbronn, Blaubeuren, and Lorch.

But if a mandate or ordinances addressed a larger audience, such as every bailiff and district official, it was much more efficient to have them printed. With the help of moveable type, the rulers of Württemberg could ensure that their orders were disseminated widely and quickly. As many printed ordinances were not only addressed to the district officials, but also mentioned others, such as foresters, mayors, and *Schultheisse*, ordinances were necessarily produced in higher numbers. Once the type was set, it was easy for the printer to produce not only the usual 250 copies, but many more. He just needed to make sure that he had enough paper if he wanted to produce a mandate for every priest in Württemberg.

Conclusion

In 1554, Duke Christoph learned that the printing press offered security. In the previous year, Christoph had witnessed the misery of Georg Frederick of Brandenburg-Ansbach, whose legacy was in grave danger. During the Second Margrave War, the castle of Plassenburg was besieged, which caused Georg Frederick much distress as all the important documents of his dynasty – charters, privileges, and rights – were stored in the castle's vault.[184] Making matters worse, Georg Frederick did not know exactly which documents were kept in the castle.

At the time, Duke Christoph mediated between the fighting parties in Brandenburg and made the decision never to find himself in such a precarious

182 HStASt, G 41 Bü 11.
183 WLB, Cod. iur. 2° 308 Bd. 3.
184 Briefwechsel, II, pp. 183–184.

situation as Georg Frederick. As a result, Christoph turned to the printer in Tübingen and had a selection of privileges of his predecessors recorded in print: a total of 16 documents.[185] As we have already seen above, these documents dated back as far as 1361, when Charles IV had granted Eberhard II the privilege that he and his subjects were exempted from courts outside Württemberg. Now that he had a number of copies of each important document, Duke Christoph could keep copies of the documents in different places, such as in the chancellery and in various castles. This was a strategic step. Duke Christoph was now prepared for any eventual threat. As Christoph's father, Ulrich, had breached the Treaty of Kaaden, the Habsburgs were in a position to seize Württemberg. In case this were to happen, Christoph and his councillors could easily lay their hands on the documents to justify the duke's claims over the duchy.

The publication of the privileges also offered security on another level. The documents granted sovereignty to the rulers of Württemberg and were thus a central element in the process of state building.[186] This helped to solidify the power of the dukes against the claims of the many neighbouring rulers as well as the claims of the Habsburgs. It included security of religious courts at a particularly difficult time in which there was no clear line between religious and secular courts.[187] With the production in print, the privileges could be circulated widely within the territory and beyond and thus be recognised by a much larger audience than ever before.

But the printing press could be of much more use. The dukes of Württemberg used print for a variety of purposes: to spread explanations of riots, advertise their duchy, circulate orders, influence religious behaviour, and, as we have seen above, to ensure the continuation of their rule. These many official publications addressed not only the inhabitants of Württemberg, but were often distributed widely beyond the borders of the duchy. The wide circulation of the marriage ordinance, the Great Church Order, and the *Landesordnungen* enabled the dukes to establish the duchy as a role model for a Protestant territory. These ordinances created great resonance. The Great Church Order, for instance, was introduced by other rulers in their territories closely following the Württemberg model. In some cases, the ordinances were even adopted word for word, as for instance in Saxony and Braunschweig-Wolfenbüttel. This shows just how important Württemberg had become once again after the turbulent first half of the sixteenth century and how the printed law helped to re-establish power.

185 See above.

186 I would like to express my gratitude to Christoph Volkmar for pointing this out to me and helping me to contextualise my findings.

187 Volkmar (2008), *Reform statt Reformation*, p. 227.

Chapter Two: The Dukes' Printers

This chapter aims to shed light on the interaction between the government in Württemberg and the printers that produced the many official publications discussed in the first chapter. Printing for the authorities in Württemberg was a lucrative job. The government in Stuttgart paid their printers extraordinarily well for their production. As we will see, these payments were nearly twice as high as payments from private clients. Spurred by the Reformation and the dukes' ambition to elevate Württemberg's status within the empire, Württemberg witnessed an unprecedented output of official publications. This was very much to the delight of the printers, as they anticipated easy profits from printing for the authorities.

Some printers, however, were not as lucky when they worked for the government. The relationship between printers and authorities could also be problematic. In the sixteenth century, the office of the *Hofdrucker* – a printer who primarily produced for the government in return for an annual salary, often including housing and equipment – was not yet institutionalised in many parts of the empire. There were only very few governments who employed a *Hofdrucker*, and then often only for a few years. It was not until the seventeenth century that German governments increasingly employed *Hofdrucker*. This is not surprising, as in the sixteenth century the salary of a *Hofdrucker* in Germany often did not provide enough income for a printer, as the following discussion will make clear. The few *Hofdrucker* active in the sixteenth century often found that what they were paid was not enough to support their families. However, in contrast to other printers, they could not easily produce other books in addition to the government's publications. Firstly, they had to prioritise government orders. Secondly, they often needed to buy their own material from their already scarce income to produce books for sale. Lastly, pirated or unauthorised editions, which often brought a quick income, were almost impossible to produce under the watchful eyes of the authorities. If a *Hofdrucker* was caught acting against the authorities' will, it could mean the end of his career.

Instead of appointing a *Hofdrucker*, many authorities in the sixteenth century engaged with independent printers. These were men and women who produced books in their own print shop, used their own equipment, and were paid for every individual order. In principle, this was for the benefit of both governments and printers. However, it also caused some friction. As we will see, relying on a busy printer whose presses were already occupied with other work could seriously delay the publication of official work. Thus the authorities sometimes had to face very long waiting times for their proclamations and ordinances to appear in print. The reprint of the Great Church Order of 1582 should only have taken a few weeks production time. In fact, however, the government had to wait a whole nine months before the printed copies reached the chancellery in Stuttgart.

Furthermore, the finances of the independent printer played an important role. An extensive publication such as the *Landrecht* from 1555, which counts over 300 pages and was produced in 1,000 copies, required enormous investment from the start, unlike the many shorter mandates. The printer had to pay his workmen wages, pay for the equipment, and most importantly the paper. He had to meet all of these costs long before he received his payment, since the government only paid once all printed copies had arrived safely in the capital. Moreover, if the printer then struggled with bankruptcy, the production of the official work would take an extra few months and sometimes even several years. So, for example, a new edition of the *Landrecht* was issued in early 1606, yet the printed copies did not reach the chancellery before 1610, a whole four years later.

The case study of Württemberg illustrates very well the advantages and disadvantages of printers working for the government, as well as the difficulties for the ruling body. This chapter will trace the impact of publishing for the duke on the local print industry in Württemberg. To provide context, the chapter will first introduce three printers – Georg Erlinger, Ruprecht Höller and Georg Rhau – who were employed by their respective authorities in the Bishopric of Bamberg, the County of Tyrol, and Electoral Saxony. Then it will focus on the printers in Württemberg, tracing the modest beginnings in the early sixteenth century. Slowly, by trial and error, the authorities found a printing house that would serve them until the end of the century. As the press increasingly became an important part of the ducal government, the Morhart-Gruppenbach press in Tübingen steadily rose to become one of the most important presses in the German south-west. Throughout this period, the Morhart-Gruppenbach press remained an independent print shop, paid for every individual official order. It was not until 1597 that the ducal administration in Württemberg employed a *Hofdrucker*, Max Fürster, who printed in the capital in return for an annual salary.

Printing for the government

One of the printers who benefitted from a healthy relationship with his rulers was Georg Erlinger in Bamberg. He printed on a regular basis for the local bishop.[1] Between 1522 and 1543, the printer produced no fewer than 79 editions for the prince-bishop. These official publications were almost exclusively produced as broadsheets of different sizes, ranging from full sheets for mandates to be exhibited in public, to half-sheets and quarter-sheets for missives and instructions to vassals. Thus Erlinger produced an ordinance that prescribed taxes for the campaign against the Turks on 9 May 1522 as a full sheet.[2] The ordinance started by referring to the advances of the Turkish troops, who had raided a town near Kärnten close to the bishopric. This news and the details about the tax were supposed to be known to everyone in the bishopric. To this end the ordinance was produced on a full sheet to be hung up in public places. A few months later, Erlinger printed the bishop's request to his vassals to arm themselves.[3] In contrast to the ordinance, this order was to inform the vassals only; so each of them received their own copy. The order was not intended to be spread widely, and thus it was produced on a quarter-sheet, which meant very low costs in comparison to a full sheet. This particular broadsheet survives in no fewer than 19 copies, each bearing the receiver's name on the back, just like the *Warhafftig Unterrichtung* from Duke Ulrich, encountered in the first chapter.

Such regular publications provided a healthy income for Erlinger. Thanks to surviving payment records, we can see exactly how much the printer received for producing official orders for the bishop. On 9 July 1525, he received 5 Gulden for printing two editions: a contract between the knights and the bishop concerning the damage caused by the peasants' revolt, and an ordinance regarding the fugitives' property.[4] One month later, Erlinger again received 5 Gulden to produce a mandate for the reimbursement of the aristocracy as well as for publishing a contract with them.[5]

Although we cannot trace the payments for every single edition, the bishop's account book offers us a good grasp of how much money Erlinger actually received for his publications. Over the 20 years he worked for the bishop, i. e.

1 Schottenloher (1907), *Die Buchdruckertätigkeit Georg Erlingers in Bamberg.*

2 *Ibid.*, pp. 126–127.

3 *Ibid.*, p. 128.

4 Erlinger actually produced two editions of the contract: one was presumably a proof copy and was only produced in a small number for corrections. The other edition includes a printed phrase that the contract has been accepted. The payment probably refers to this second edition. Schottenloher (1907), *Die Buchdruckertätigkeit Georg Erlingers in Bamberg*, pp. 139–142.

5 *Ibid.*, pp. 142–144.

between 1522 and 1543, Erlinger earned more than 200 Gulden for these official publications. To be sure, some years were more profitable than others. In 1528, Erlinger printed the bishop's response to the accusation of the Duke of Saxony and the Landgrave of Hessen. For this order alone, the printer earned 16 Gulden.[6] In contrast, for the years 1538 and 1539 no payment records have survived. These records may have been lost over the past five centuries. The absence of these records could also suggest, however, that in 1538 and 1539 it was not Erlinger but another printer who produced for the bishop. After all, he was not a *Hofdrucker* but an independent printer.

In addition to printing ordinances and contracts, Erlinger was also frequently ordered to produce letters of passage. With such a letter a traveller obtained the right to travel through the Bishopric of Bamberg. A merchant from Nuremberg who wanted to sell his goods in the Electorate of Saxony was thereby able to use the short cut via the bishopric instead of taking the long way around the territory.[7] This saved him valuable time and costs. Such letters were very short; they only consisted of 12 printed lines in which the name of the recipient could be added by hand. The letters were produced on a frequent basis providing a recurring income for the printer. Over the course of 20 years, the Bishop of Bamberg regularly ordered hundreds of copies. In 1525 alone, Erlinger produced 4,250 letters of passage.[8] For Erlinger, this was an easy job: As the letters contained very little text, they could be produced swiftly. And since the small text fitted easily onto a quarter-sheet, Erlinger just set up the type for four letters producing four copies with each impression. After the ink had dried, he could then easily cut up the sheets. Thus to provide the bishop with 4,250 letters in 1525, Erlinger only needed 1,062 sheets in total.

At the beginning, the rate for such an order of letter of passage varied slightly. In 1524 and 1525, the bishop ordered Erlinger to produce 1,500 letters, for which he received 1 Gulden for each order.[9] In May and July 1525, Erlinger produced two batches of letters – 750 and 500 respectively – and each time received a ½ Gulden. One might have expected him to receive more money for the production of 750 letters, but this was not the case. Then, from 1526, the number of letters stabilised and so did the payments: for 1,000 letters the printer

6 *Ibid.*, p. 160.

7 On letters of passage in the Holy Roman Empire, see Scholz (2020), *Borders and Freedom of Movement in the Holy Roman Empire*, pp. 141 ff. I would like to express my gratitude to Luca Scholz for sharing the manuscript with me before publication.

8 Schottenloher (1907), *Die Buchdruckertätigkeit Georg Erlingers in Bamberg*, p. 131.

9 The following is taken from: Schottenloher (1907), *Die Buchdruckertätigkeit Georg Erlingers in Bamberg*, p. 131.

received 1 Gulden. Finally, 15 years later, Erlinger secured a price increase of 50 %. On 21 January 1541, Erlinger received 1 ½ Gulden for his usual 1,000 printed letters of passage. When Erlinger died later that year, his widow took over his shop and continued producing official documents for her overlord. In August 1541, she delivered another 1,000 letters of passage for which she received the new tariff of 1 ½ Gulden. She continued to earn this sum until 1543 when she was paid on 5 May for the last batch of 1,000 letters of passage. Later that year, Erlinger's widow not only stopped producing for the bishop but stopped printing altogether. She sold the press to the government for the handsome sum of 125 Gulden.[10]

These were secure payments in a business as competitive as printing. However, this does not imply that a printer could make a living solely from these official orders. The printer Ruprecht Höller learnt this bitter lesson when he produced exclusively for the Count of Tyrol.[11] He was one of the first *Hofdrucker* in the Holy Roman Empire, i. e. printers producing solely for the government in return for an annual salary. In the course of the sixteenth century, there were a number of rulers who tried to integrate the printing press into their government apparatus. What followed was a long period of trial and error spreading over the course of the entire century. When printers were employed by local rulers, many found the working conditions unsatisfactory. Höller's case shows us just how much the priorities of printers and governments diverged.

The salary of *Hofdrucker* varied significantly. When the government bought the press from Erlinger's widow, it appointed a *Hofdrucker* to produce official documents. He received only 6 Gulden per annum.[12] As we have seen, this was a sum of money Erlinger sometimes received for one single order. To be sure, Erlinger had to meet the costs for producing the documents, but it, nevertheless, shows that the annual salary of the first *Hofdrucker* in Bamberg was very low.

Hofdrucker who worked for territorial princes usually received annual payments that were comparable to those of clerks of the church council in Württemberg, who received 40 Gulden per year in the 1550s.[13] The lower end of a printer's salary seems to have been 20 Gulden per year, which Zacharias

10 Reske, p. 61.

11 The following is taken from: Schottenloher (1944/1949), 'Der Frühdruck im Dienste der öffentlichen Verwaltung', pp. 144–145.

12 Hans Müller, Erlinger's successor, printed until 1556. When the print shop was destroyed in 1553, a new press and type cost 118 Gulden, Reske, p. 61.

13 Bernhardt (1972), *Die Zentralbehörden des Herzogtums Württemberg und ihre Beamten*, p. 99. A notable exception is Johann Schönsperger in Augsburg who worked for the imperial government and allegedly earned 100 Gulden per year, see Künast (1997) *'Getruckt zu Augspurg'*, p. 96. It is, however, unclear if he actually received this money, given that Maximilian's coffers were chronically empty.

Bartsch earned in Graz, the capital of the Duchy of Styria.[14] His colleague in Hanau also received 20 Gulden; however, this was in addition to an annual allotment of wood and grain.[15] The *Hofdrucker* in Zweibrücken was much better off, earning twice as much with 45 Gulden.[16] Among the highest salaries were those paid to the *Hofdrucker* in Herborn and Marburg, who each earned 50 Gulden.[17]

Although this salary may have been enough for officials in Württemberg, it did not suffice for printers who operated in remote areas. The *Hofdrucker* in Lauingen, Emanuel Saltzer, experienced this firsthand while working for the Duke of Palatinate-Neuburg.[18] When in 1572 the printer produced a news report from the Netherlands, much disproved of by the duke, he was interrogated and eventually dismissed.[19] After his dismissal, Saltzer faced financial hardship, which eventually led him to steal 200 kilograms worth of printing material from his former work place, material he undoubtedly wanted to use or sell to make a living. When the duke found out about the theft, he decided not to punish the man further as he, the printer, had no financial means.

Although the *Hofdrucker* Ruprecht Höller in Tyrol received an above average annual salary starting in 1554 – 52 Gulden plus another 10 Gulden for housing and 3 Gulden for wood – he still encountered similar financial problems.[20] For that sum, he was supposed to keep the press tidy, source the necessary type himself, and keep all the secrets of the government. Ink and paper were provided as well as other supplies. Höller's press was in Innsbruck, the residential seat of the Habsburgs. This was much more convenient for the government than any previous arrangements. During the early sixteenth century, the Habsburgs had relied on Silvan Otmar's press in Augsburg, yet this caused significant delays and additional costs as the sheets had to be transported through the entire Duchy of Bavaria, a journey of some 200 kilometres. The government first had to send the manuscript to Augsburg, which took several days, and then the printed sheets needed to be transported back to the chancellery, which took another couple of days. Further time was probably spent on producing proof sheets and correcting them. The production of official documents in Electoral Saxony illustrates this very well: since 1514, the chancellary scribe had to travel several times a year from Torgau to the print shop in Wittenberg, which caused significant

14 Reske, p. 332.
15 *Ibid.*, p. 373.
16 *Ibid.*, p. 1141.
17 *Ibid.*, pp. 401, 654.
18 *Ibid.*, pp. 552–553.
19 USTC 677756 (VD16 N 688).
20 The following is taken from: Schottenloher (1944/1949), 'Der Frühdruck im Dienste der öffentlichen Verwaltung', p. 144.

costs for the chancellery. In one instance the scribe even had to stay 5 days in Wittenberg to supervise the print production of books and the government reimbursed the costs for his food and his lodgings during this time.[21] Thus for the authorities in Innsbruck, Höller's press in the same city offered a significant advantage. As it was close to the seat of the government, the chancellery could probably receive an order of 300 broadsheet ordinances on the same day they completed the manuscript.

Nevertheless, during the 20 years Höller worked for the government, he had to ask his employer for more money on several occasions. Already four years after his appointment, Höller was not able to cover his expenses with his annual salary. Thus he asked for another official job that would earn him some extra money. In 1558 the authorities complied with Höller's request and he was appointed *Kesselrichter*, supervising the guild of boilermakers.[22] This office would bring him several extra Gulden per year. Two years later, in 1560, Höller was delighted to receive an extra 8 Gulden for the production of 2,000 mandates. Some of these mandates were large, probably consisting of several sheets that needed to be glued together, just like the *Warhafftig Unterrichtung* issued by Duke Ulrich in 1514. For this, Höller had to employ an assistant, which naturally eroded his profit.

In June 1566, Höller asked Archduke Ferdinand to reissue the *Landesordnung*. Since there were no copies left of this particular edition, Höller hoped to make some income by selling a new edition. When Höller was permitted to do so, he hastily produced a second edition in 1568, followed closely by a third edition in 1570. He sold a bound copy of the latter for 1 Gulden and 12 Kreuzer. But although these two new editions must have provided some income, Höller was still not able to support himself and his family of four. In 1570, the year in which he produced the third edition of the *Landesordnung*, he asked for extra money to visit a bathhouse to improve his health. His income did not suffice to cover such a luxury. After 20 years of working for the authorities, Höller was eventually replaced by a younger printer in 1573. Although he received a charity payment of 24 Kreuzer a week, he continued to live in poverty until his death in 1580.

The fate of both Saltzer in Lauingen and Höller in Tyrol show that printing for the government did not necessarily equal financial security. To make a living, both printers had to produce other publications in addition to the books and mandates commissioned by the authorities. Since it was forbidden for Höller to use the equipment provided by the government for other purposes, the materials

21 Lang (2015), 'Simprecht Reinhart: Formschneider, Maler, Drucker, Bettmeister – Spuren eines Lebens im Schatten von Lucas Cranach d. Ä.', pp. 122–123.

22 For the duties of a *Kesselrichter*, see Deutsches Rechtswörterbuch, http://www.rzuser.uni-heidelberg.de/~cd2/drw/e/ke/ssel/rich/kesselrichter.html.

required for such printing jobs meant additional expenses. As Höller's cash was limited, he tried to use the official material despite the prohibition. However, this did not escape the government's attention. The government accused Höller of having worn out the equipment and of having lost parts of it.[23] No doubt he had to replace the material at his own cost.

Furthermore, Höller was limited in his choice of repertoire. Although a reprint of the *Landesordnung* promised valuable income, the printer had to ask for permission first. Fortunately, he was granted the reprint. But if his plea had been denied, it would have been impossible for Höller to produce a pirated edition. After all, he was under close observation by the watchful eye of the government and his fraudulent use of the equipment had already been detected. Even if Höller managed to produce an edition without being caught during its production, the misconduct would have certainly become obvious when he tried to sell the publication. In this case the printer would probably have faced dismissal, just like Saltzer in Lauingen.

It is clear that in the sixteenth century many printers chose to be paid for individual orders by the government rather than to be employed for an annual salary. This was especially true during the turbulent years following Luther's break with the church. In Wittenberg, the printer producing for the Elector of Saxony must have been delighted by the frequent orders of the Elector who, as we have already seen, valued the printing press so much that he took one with him to the battlefield. Between 1538 and 1545, in the course of only six years, John Frederick I., Elector of Saxony, ordered Georg Rhau to print no fewer than 65 official documents.[24] The exact payments of these orders have luckily all survived to the present day. The account book detailing the payments, unfortunately, does not provide any information on the format of the ordinances, but most of them were probably broadsheets, just like the ordinances in Bamberg.

Depending on the year, Rhau in Wittenberg made much more money than the *Hofdrucker* Höller in Tyrol. The income of the printer in Saxony, who earned 11 and 12 Gulden respectively in the late 1530s, rose significantly to 78 Gulden in 1541 (fig. 2.1.). In this exceptional year, the printer supplied various publications, including not only the usual mandates but also an announcement addressing the conflict with Braunschweig, for which the duke paid 42 Gulden alone.[25] As Rhau had to provide type, paper, and ink himself, some of the differences in contrast to Höller's payments can be explained. According to the

23 Schottenloher (1944/1949), 'Der Frühdruck im Dienste der öffentlichen Verwaltung', p. 144.

24 Buchwald (1934), 'Kleine Notizen aus Rechnungsbüchern des Thüringischen Staatsarchivs (Weimar)', pp. 209–214.

25 *Ibid.*, p. 211.

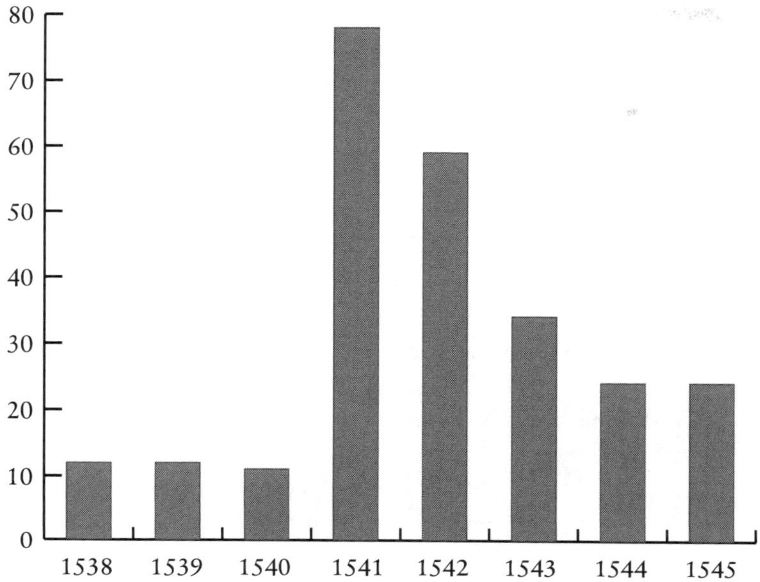

Fig. 2.1. Payments Georg Rhau received from the Elector of Saxony to produce official documents (in Gulden).

account book, Rhau did not receive special payments for this necessary equipment. Only on one occasion was the printer reimbursed when he accidentally destroyed some paper as a result of printing an ordinance hastily. So the duke gave him 4 Gulden to cover the cost of the damaged six reams of paper as well as double wages to the printer and typesetter to produce the ordinance quickly.[26] Despite the fact that Rhau had to provide most of his supplies, the high payments still suggest that he made more money from individual orders for the duke than by earning a constant but low yearly income.

As Rhau was not a *Hofdrucker*, he was not limited to official work only; he received these payments on top of his already thriving business. When he started to work in Wittenberg, the printer soon became one of the most important publishers of Reformed works producing biblical exegesis, sermons, and catechisms. He also printed music for the Reformed church, an endeavour only few printers embarked on, as such publications presented particular challenges

26 The original German text reads: 'iiij gulden Idem Jeorgen Rauhen zu steuer, das ime in eilenden drucken disses ausschreibens vj Riß verderbet worden und das ehr seinen setzern und druckern duppel besoldung zu geben vertrostung gethan, domit der druck dester ehr gefertigt wurd', BUCHWALD (1934), 'Kleine Notizen aus Rechnungsbüchern des Thüringischen Staatsarchivs (Weimar)', p. 211.

with their requirement for special type for musical notations.[27] Rhau had a close professional relationship with Martin Agricola, a cantor at a Protestant school, and produced his various books.[28] Undoubtedly, the high payments from the elector provided Rhau with the necessary financial means to embark on such capital-intense projects.

Trial and error in Württemberg

At first sight, printers who produced for the authorities in Württemberg seemed to have been destined to suffer the same fate as Höller in Tyrol. A printer who wanted to set up his press in the duchy had to expect strong competition. The duchy was surrounded by the large printing centres of Strasbourg, Augsburg, and Basel. Additionally, books could easily be imported from Frankfurt – another close print centre with a biannual book fair. The smooth connections via the Rhine and the Neckar facilitated transport. Together, these centres produced a large variety of different books – theological, literary, medical – that quickly found their way into the duchy. Unlike Austria, where the nearest printing centre, Augsburg, was quite distant, there was no urgent need for a printer in Württemberg. The government in Stuttgart could easily employ printers in one of these centres to produce official publications. In this way, the resolution of the *Landtag* in 1498 was produced in Strasbourg and sent to the court in Stuttgart.[29]

In addition to the big printing centres, the south-west part of the empire was studded with imperial cities. In general, a large imperial city offered a printer much better sales opportunities than a small territorial city, due to a constant flow of visitors and travelling merchants. In addition, a large imperial city offered printers more liberal conditions to produce books. Printers were often associated with one of the guilds and thus had a certain degree of freedom and influence on the city's politics. It was no accident that many printers set up their press in imperial cities. This situation was very convenient for the government in Württemberg. The costs and time for the transportation would be considerably reduced if a printer produced in an imperial city close-by instead of in Strasbourg. Thus in the fifteenth century, the authorities of Württemberg also had official print produced in Reutlingen and Ulm.[30]

27 Wetzel and Heitmeyer (eds.) (2013), *Johan Leisentrit's Geistliche Lieder und Psalmen*, p. 32.

28 *The 'Musica instrumentalis deudsch' of Martin Agricola. A treatise on musical instruments, 1529 and 1545*, ed. and trans. William Hettrick, p. xiii.

29 USTC 749932.

30 See, for example, USTC 744542, USTC 744536, USTC 744543, USTC 744544.

For a printer who wanted to work in the Duchy of Württemberg, it was quite difficult to compete in such an environment. Neither Tübingen nor Stuttgart were international trading centres. Printers could not easily sell books to a large readership since many potential buyers were already catered for. Hence, the first printers who set up a press in the Duchy of Württemberg managed to sustain their businesses only for a short period of time. Johannes Otmar, Thomas Anshelm, and Hans Wehrlich all left Württemberg after a few unproductive years. In what follows we will see why they left – or in the case of Hans Wehrlich, even had to leave the duchy.

Let us examine this trial and error period in Württemberg in the first decades of the sixteenth century. The first printer in Tübingen was Johannes Otmar. As a learned printer, he had obtained his *Magister* in Ingolstadt and started to print in Reutlingen (his birthplace) in 1481.[31] In 1497 he moved to Tübingen and his son took up studying at the university.[32] During his time in Tübingen, Otmar produced mostly religious pamphlets and academic works.[33] However, he did not stay long in the duchy. After only a few years, in early 1502, he and his family moved to Augsburg to extend their business and to flee from the Black Death.[34] After Otmar left, the duchy was without a printer for a whole decade.

Otmar printed for the authorities on only two occasions. One of the publications was the imperial confirmation of Eberhard II's removal from power (1499); the other was an announcement of the Swabian League (1500).[35] Other official documents continued to be produced in Reutlingen or in Pforzheim.[36] Otmar's press does not seem to have been of much use for the Swabian League, Duke Eberhard II, or the estates of Württemberg, who ruled after Eberhard II's removal from power. One reason for this may have been the fact that Otmar lacked the appropriate equipment. Another reason may have been that the authorities were just keen to maintain their good relations with other printers. Whatever the reason, for a few orders per year, the government in Stuttgart was happy to entrust a printer outside the duchy, even if that meant extra waiting time and additional costs.

The next printer who came to Württemberg was Thomas Anshelm. In contrast to Otmar, Anshelm printed for the authorities on a regular basis. Anshelm had learned the black art in Basel and had printed in Strasbourg and Pforzheim before he came to Württemberg.[37] By the time his first book appeared in the

31 Reske, p. 1004.

32 Steiff (1881), *Der erste Buchdruck in Tübingen (1498–1534)*, p. 6.

33 Reske, p. 1004.

34 Steiff (1881), *Der erste Buchdruck in Tübingen (1498–1534)*, p. 8.

35 USTC 746967 (VE15 M-139), USTC 748837 (VE15 S-30).

36 See, for example, USTC 749566.

37 Reske, p. 843.

duchy, in July 1511, he had already published quite extensively, having produced over 90 publications.[38] Just like his predecessor in the duchy, Anshelm settled in the university town of Tübingen. His good relationship with the scholars at the university probably convinced him to set up a press close to the institution. Here Anshelm could rely on professors and students, who would help him with the correction of his works.[39] As Anshelm had not attended a university himself, this was invaluable help for him, especially when it came to Greek and Hebrew works.

In his Württemberg period, Anshelm was even more productive than before. The USTC lists 91 publications for his Württemberg period of only five years (1511–1516).[40] This includes the many broadsheets he produced for the duke, especially during the times of trouble of the Poor Conrad uprising. When the duke ordered his official statement on what exactly happened during the revolt, Anshelm not only published both pamphlets but also the long broadsheet and every cover letter to the bishops, abbots, princes, counts, *Freiherren*, cities, and officials.[41] Anshelm also produced the *Landesordnung* of 1515, with the harsh ban on firearms as well as the restriction of the ban for foresters.[42]

Despite this official work, Anshelm's main business was the production of humanist works. He was highly appreciated by contemporary humanists, especially by Johannes Reuchlin. It was Reuchlin in particular who had every single one of his works printed in Anshelm's shop. Furthermore, he recommended Anshelm to his friends not only in the empire, but also beyond its borders, even in far-off Rome.[43]

But just like his predecessor, Johannes Otmar, Anshelm did not stay in the Duchy of Württemberg for long. In July 1516, he published Jakob Heinrichmann's *Grammaticae Institutiones* and then left for the imperial city of Hagenau.[44] What caused Anshelm to leave Tübingen after only five years is not clear. We can speculate that the heated atmosphere in Württemberg and Duke Ulrich's eccentric and oppressive behaviour drove the printer to a more peaceful area of the empire.[45] Another possibility could be that the imperial city offered the printer more liberty in his publications.

38 USTC search: Printer - Anshelm, Date - 1510–1516.

39 Steiff (1881), *Der erste Buchdruck in Tübingen (1498–1534)*, p. 21.

40 USTC search: Place - Tübingen, Printer - Anshelm.

41 Steiff (1881), *Der erste Buchdruck in Tübingen (1498–1534)*, pp. 111–114; see subchapter 'The discovery of print'.

42 *Ibid.*, pp. 119 and 123–124.

43 *Ibid.*, pp. 14–15.

44 USTC 668695 (VD16 H 2025).

45 Widmann (1971b), *Tübingen als Verlagsstadt*, p. 42.

Despite his move, Anshelm continued to produce for the scholars at the University of Tübingen.[46] Anshelm also printed advertisements for the university that he distributed to potential new teachers and students. As a frequent visitor to the Frankfurt Fair, Anshelm had very good connections.[47] In 1522, long after he had left Württemberg, the university ordered Anshelm to produce the announcement that the university offered courses for free.[48] In his letter to the university, the printer informed the senate that he had produced 1,000 advertisements both in Latin and in German. As both texts would not fit on one single sheet of paper, the printer produced them on two, creating a total of 2,000 sheets. Anshelm pointed out that these sheets could be glued together if required. The production required four reams of paper, each comprising 500 sheets. For each ream he charged 2 Gulden, so this would amount to a total of 8 Gulden for the whole task. However, Anshelm gave the university a reduction, and they only had to pay a total of 6 Gulden. The printer probably gave the university this cheaper rate since they had assumed that the production would be less expensive as the Latin and German texts would both fit on only one sheet.

Although Anshelm continued to print for the university, the government in Tübingen had to entrust other printers with their official documents from 1516 onwards. When Duke Ulrich murdered his stable master, Hans von Hutten, and his cousin Ulrich von Hutten attacked Ulrich in writing, the duke released an official statement in print. For this job, he relied on Jacob Stadelberger in Heidelberg, who published the small quarto pamphlet of 11 leaves.[49] When the Habsburgs took over the duchy, they employed Johannes Grüner in Ulm to print instructions to their new vassals.[50]

Only once did Anshelm produce for the Württemberg authorities again. This was in 1521 when the duchy had fallen to the Habsburgs and the new overlords reissued the *Landesordnung*.[51] Perhaps the Austrian government turned to Anshelm for issuing such an important document because of the superior quality of his work. After all, he had produced the previous *Landesordnung* of 1515. However, the collaboration between the Habsburgs and the former Württemberg printer did not flourish. Presumably the government was discouraged by the long journey from Hagenau to Stuttgart and the associated costs.

46 Steiff (1881), *Der erste Buchdruck in Tübingen (1498–1534)*, p. 26.

47 *Ibid.*, p. 18.

48 The following is taken from: Schott (1879), 'Zur Geschichte des Buchhandels in Tübingen', p. 241.

49 USTC 614124 (VD16 W 4445).

50 WLB HBFC 83. Printer identified by the librarians in Stuttgart.

51 This book is not in USTC or VD16; WLB HBF 2751. The WLB assigns this book to Anshelm.

Hans Wehrlich von Erfurt in Stuttgart (1522–1524)

When Württemberg fell into Habsburg hands, the Austrian government made great efforts to upgrade bureaucratic efficiency as they needed to find an effective way to foster communication between Vienna and every district official in their new fief.[52] Setting up a printing press close to the seat of the government was an important means to achieve this goal. To this end, in 1522, the Austrian government encouraged Hans Wehrlich from Erfurt to set up a press in the capital of Württemberg, Stuttgart.[53] At that time, Wehrlich had been a printer for only four years. He started his business in Augsburg where he produced a few smaller publications, including a cure against syphilis.[54] After only two years there, he decided to go to Worms. With no printer in that city but one of the most important imperial diets taking place, Wehrlich assumed that Worms would be in need of a printing press very soon.[55]

Wehrlich was not mistaken. In 1521 the printer's output reached an unprecedented peak. He published several pamphlets concerning the imperial diet, including an overview of the attendees.[56] In addition, he produced numerous Lutheran works, such as the reformer's justification against Eck, his reaction to the papal bull, and an address to the pope – books that were keenly sought after as events unfolded.[57] Most notably, Wehrlich's press was responsible for Charles V's ordinance against Luther: *The Edict of Worms*. In March, it appeared as a broadsheet to be hung up in public and as a 12-leaf pamphlet for those who wanted to purchase a copy. Two months later, in May, Wehrlich produced Charles V's explanation of how the edict should be executed. Both edict and announcement were sent to every ruler in the empire, and we know from a surviving copy that Otto-Henry, Elector Palatine, received his copy in mid-August.[58]

As the Habsburgs were looking for a suitable printer to take up the work in Stuttgart, Charles V probably recommended Wehrlich to his brother Ferdinand, the ruler of Württemberg. The Austrian government invited the printer to move to Württemberg, where they had arranged for his housing.[59] For Wehrlich, this

52 Lorenz (2010), 'Vom herrschaftlichen Rat zu den Landständen in Württemberg. Die Entwicklung vom 13. bis zum 16. Jahrhundert', p. 24.

53 Reske, p. 990.

54 Schottenloher (1927a), 'Hans Wehrlich, genannt Hans von Erfurt, der Drucker des Wormser Edikts', p. 60.

55 *Ibid.*, p. 54.

56 USTC 609665 (VD16 A 3019).

57 Schottenloher (1927a), 'Hans Wehrlich, genannt Hans von Erfurt, der Drucker des Wormser Edikts', pp. 60–66.

58 *Ibid.*, p. 62.

59 Reske, p. 990.

was an easy decision to make. Although the imperial diet had kept him busy in 1521 and brought him welcome income, once the diet was over, there remained little work for a printer.

In April 1522, the printer left for Stuttgart and started producing for the Habsburgs. By May he had already produced the pamphlet *Triumph und Victoria* in honour of Archduke Ferdinand's visit to Stuttgart, followed by a welcoming poem by Johannes Brassicanus.[60] In November, he published the *Freedom of Württemberg*, confirming the freedom of the estates from the Habsburg government.[61] This was a pamphlet consisting of several legal documents such as the *Tübinger Vertrag* with the imperial authentication, Charles' assignment of Württemberg to Ferdinand, and Ferdinand's approval. This publication was produced in 150 copies.[62] These copies presumably found their way to every nobleman in Württemberg. In addition to the *Freedom of Württemberg*, Wehrlich produced another important legal document in November 1522: the ban on Luther's books. It was published as a broadsheet, authenticated with signatures and seal, to be sent to every district and hung up in public.[63] According to this ordinance, it was forbidden to 'buy, sell, read, possess, print, copy, or have printed' books of Luther or his followers.[64]

Despite producing this clear prohibition, Hans Wehrlich himself neglected it. His salary of 20 Gulden did not suffice and, apart from official work, his press did not receive very many orders.[65] Just like Höller in Tyrol, Wehrlich soon realised that most printers in the sixteenth century could not live solely from producing for the government. However, he could not enter the market for university books, since Anshelm was still producing all the books that the university needed. So Wehrlich, who had made a good profit with selling Luther's works in Worms, decided to print Protestant works again. As this would be very much disapproved of by the Catholic Habsburgs, Wehrlich tried to conceal his identity by publishing the works anonymously, without imprint.

Yet, the authorities eventually found out. The Catholic Austrian government was clearly displeased that its very own printer, entrusted with official work, was

60 USTC 699455 (VD16 T 2013), USTC 665745 (VD16 B 7150).

61 USTC 633889 (VD16 ZV 15615).

62 Schottenloher (1927a), 'Hans Wehrlich, genannt Hans von Erfurt, der Drucker des Wormser Edikts', p. 56.

63 Appendix no. 16.

64 The original German text reads: 'Ewr kainer: des obgenanten Martin Luthers: und seiner anhenger: schrifften: bißher gemacht/oder die hinfür gemacht werden/oder außgeen mögen, kaufen, verkauffen, lessen, behalten, trucken, abschreiben, oder trucken lassen'.

65 In the ducal account book from 1524, it was noted that Wehrlich received 20 Gulden 'Jahressold'. The first part of the word ('Jahres') was erased, probably because Wehrlich did not finish one year's work, HStASt, A 256 Bd. 12.

not following the legislation he printed.[66] This was a serious offence, much more serious than Höller's use of official equipment for private use. For Wehrlich this had serious consequences and he had to leave Stuttgart in 1524. In June, he published his last (official) work, Johann Cochlaeus' response to Luther, accompanied by an introduction by Ferdinand.[67] When Wehrlich left Stuttgart, he had only printed in the capital of Württemberg for two years.

Ulrich Morhart – the loyal servant

After this short interlude with Hans Wehrlich, the authorities in Württemberg were once again looking for a suitable printer to produce official publications. They finally found the right candidate in Ulrich Morhart. The printer had come from Strasbourg to Tübingen in early 1523. As he was one of Anshelm's friends, Morhart was probably encouraged by Anshelm to set up a press in Tübingen to cater for the university's needs. Morhart matriculated at the university in May 1523 and married Anna Zorn from Bulach.[68] Her dowry allowed Morhart to buy a house and set up a print shop.[69] The press was up and running in July, and within the first couple of months, he published nine books: the works of both professors Johannes Stöffler and Kaspar Churrer, three works by Melanchthon, two small pamphlets by Johann Eberlin von Günzburg and Johannes Reninger, Pope Hadrian's letter to Frederick the Wise against Luther, and finally Erasmus' translation of the New Testament.[70] This was a very productive first six months for a printer, especially since the New Testament comprised over 350 leaves.

Morhart himself was a Protestant, but he strictly separated his beliefs from his work.[71] He did not make the mistake of reprinting the lucrative Luther books in Württemberg and endanger his good relations with the authorities. As soon as he started producing works for the Catholic government in Stuttgart in 1524, he only printed books against Protestantism. In 1524 alone, he produced Tuberinus' work against Luther's theses, Johannes Cochlaeus' *Warning*, and Johannes Dietenberger's work against Luther's *Confession*.[72] Over

66 Reske, p. 990.
67 USTC 690857 (VD16 C 4376).
68 Steiff (1881), *Der erste Buchdruck in Tübingen (1498–1534)*, p. 27 and pp. 137–138; Haller Haus-Chronik (1962), p. 11.
69 Reske, p. 1005; Haller Haus-Chronik (1962), p. 69.
70 USTC 667966 (VD16 S 9203), USTC 608786 (VD16 F 1839), USTC 662638 (VD16 M 3461), USTC 665690 (VD16 M 2480), USTC 611675 (VD16 M 2494), USTC 632970 (VD16 E 129), USTC 707773 (VD16 ZV 4300), USTC 617061 (VD16 ZV 8861), USTC 676054 (VD16 B 4241).
71 Steiff (1881), *Der erste Buchdruck in Tübingen (1498–1534)*, pp. 140–141.
72 Widmann (1971b), *Tübingen als Verlagsstadt*, p. 48.

the following years, Morhart published the works of many opponents of Luther, including Kaspar Schatzgeyer, Johannes Eck, Johann Fabir, Melchior Vattlin, and Georg Neudorffer.[73] Between 1524 and 1534, Morhart's press became a centre 'against the new movement coming from both North and South', as Karl Steiff so elegantly put it.[74]

Over the ten years, when he worked under the watchful eye of the Austrian government, Morhart produced only four Lutheran pamphlets, including *Admonition to Peace* (1525).[75] Since the government had moved to Tübingen during the turbulent time of the Peasants' War, it would have been impossible for Morhart to produce this pamphlet on his own without being noticed by the authorities.[76] Instead, the government actually ordered Morhart to produce the short pamphlet as it could be of very good use: it could help to calm down the rebellious peasants. If it failed to do so, the government could still use the pamphlet to attack Luther's authority. Probably for the same reason, the government ordered the publication of the other pamphlets, such as *Against the Murderous, Thieving Hordes of Peasants*.[77]

Apart from responses against the new faith, Morhart printed numerous ordinances for the government such as an ordinance that instructed noblemen to come to Stuttgart in full armour to defend the capital during the Peasants' War; an ordinance that regulated the levy of the clergy from January 1526; and an ordinance which renewed the ban on firearms in March 1526.[78] During their 15 years in Württemberg, the Habsburgs tended not to publish larger ordinances, apart from the *Landesordnung* of 1521. Only in 1530 did they have an ordinance printed, addressing the issue of how to help the poor and how to discourage beggars.[79] This ordinance appeared as a small pamphlet in quarto, comprising eight leaves.

With the steady income from these official orders, Morhart could extend his business and invest in new equipment. In 1534 he bought expensive Hebrew type.[80] But since Morhart knew that he, as the only printer in and around Tübingen, could sell his Hebrew books to the students and professors at the university, this investment would soon pay off. Later he also acquired equally costly Greek type. Again, this was a considerable but at the same time secure

73 *Ibid.*, p. 49.
74 Steiff (1881), *Der erste Buchdruck in Tübingen (1498–1534)*, p. 46.
75 USTC 653520 (VD16 L 4689).
76 Steiff (1881), *Der erste Buchdruck in Tübingen (1498–1534)*, p. 150.
77 USTC 706700 (VD16 L 7498).
78 HStASt, H 54 Bü 50 (not in Policey W); HStASt, A 63 Bü 3/5 (not in Policey W); Policey W, p. 583.
79 USTC 681631 (VD16 W 4463).
80 Steiff (1881), *Der erste Buchdruck in Tübingen (1498–1534)*, p. 28.

investment.[81] Since Hans von Wehrlich had left Stuttgart in 1524, Morhart had no competition in the duchy. The scholars at the university would undoubtedly have asked Morhart for specific books first, before they undertook the journey to larger print centres such as Augsburg and Nuremberg.

When Duke Ulrich's military and public campaign had ended successfully in 1534 and the duke had returned to Württemberg, the many official documents that followed were all produced by Morhart. From that point on, Morhart was the unofficial printer for the duke – all he lacked was a proper title and an annual salary.[82] Instead, he was paid for every individual order separately. With the help of a capable printer who ran a successful business, Duke Ulrich could rely on a steady output of the printed works he commissioned. Within the first couple of months after his return, Ulrich ordered Morhart to produce several publications: Ulrich's promise to his vassals to be a good lord, a ban on firearms, regulations for the sale of crops, and, of course, several ordinances concerning the new faith and against the Anabaptists.[83] Within the next few years, longer ordinances followed that regulated marriage, the *Armenkasten*, and the church.[84]

In addition, Morhart produced church ordinances for surrounding areas like the County of Montbéliard.[85] The county was part of the Duchy of Württemberg and Ulrich started to reform it in 1535.[86] In 1542 Ulrich appointed his son Christoph as governor of Montbéliard and ordered him to adopt the Württemberg church ordinance. However, since many members of the clergy were not able to read German, the government could not simply use the German church ordinance. Instead, Erhard Schnepf had to translate the church ordinance into Latin to make it accessible to every cleric. This Latin edition was published by Morhart in 1553 and was then distributed in Montbéliard.

In addition to these ordinances, Morhart also produced other official publications. The production of these books is sometimes only evidenced through archival sources, as some books have not survived the past centuries. The account book of the ducal *Landschreiberei* (the office responsible for the administration of finances) reveals such a lost edition when it lists the following entry:

81 Widmann (1971b), *Tübingen als Verlagsstadt*, p. 52.
82 *Ibid.*, p. 56.
83 Appendix no. 18; Steiff (1881), *Der erste Buchdruck in Tübingen (1498–1534)*, pp. 156–157; Policey W, pp. 585–586.
84 USTC 681575 (VD16 ZV 27244), USTC 681571 (VD16 W 4454), USTC 659058 (VD16 W 4451).
85 The edition cannot be found in USTC or VD16; WLB HBF 206.
86 Schäfer (ed.) (1984), *Reformation in Württemberg*, pp. 116–117.

> LXXXVI Gulden XX Kreuzer to Ulrich Morhart, printer in Tübingen, for 2,000 [...] books from the announcement of the Elector in Saxony and the Landgrave of Hesse, and Luther's warning.[87]

This entry refers to two publications: one is Luther's *Warning*, which has survived in the State and City Library in Augsburg.[88] The other publication refers to an announcement from the Elector of Saxony and the Landgrave of Hesse. During the Schmalkadic War in 1546, Duke Ulrich sought to circulate this announcement widely, ordering Morhart to produce 2,000 copies. Unfortunately, the account book does not give us any details about the content of this announcement. According to *VD16*, between 1546 and 1547 Morhart did not print any books that were written by either the Elector of Saxony or the Landgrave of Hesse. However, we can assume that the publication was a reprint of Johann Friedrich and Philip's refutation of the imperial ban. This particular pamphlet appeared in no fewer than ten editions, printed in Magdeburg, Ulm, Nuremberg, Augsburg, Marburg, and Erfurt.[89] We can safely assume that Duke Ulrich was also keen on circulating this popular statement in his duchy.

The production of these two pamphlets brought Morhart over 80 Gulden, a good sum of money. It was equivalent to the annual salary of a bookkeeper who oversaw the duke's finances.[90] Such income helped Morhart not only to sustain his press but also to become progressively one of the most important printers in the Reformation era: first for the Catholics, and after Duke Ulrich regained his duchy in 1534, for the Protestants. By the time Ulrich Morhart died in March 1554, he had produced over 230 books.[91]

A large proportion of his output are legal works. In many cases, Morhart was paid for one edition produced for the government officials and then the printer took the opportunity to produce extra copies or even a new edition to sell on the

87 HStASt, A 256 Bd. 31, the original German text reads: 'Item Lxxxvi guld[en] xx cr Ulrichen Morhart Buchtruckeren zu Tuvingen fur ii M Druck oder buechlin des Churfürst von Sachsen, und Landtgraven zu Hessen usschreyben unnd des Lutthers Ermanung lut quite thut Lxxxvi gl'.

88 USTC 706039 (VD16 L 7349).

89 USTC 633083 (VD16 S 995), USTC 2212481 (VD16 ZV 30277), USTC 633132 (VD16 S 997), USTC 633112 (VD16 S 1071), USTC 633136 (VD16 S 1075), USTC 633113 (VD16 S 1072), USTC 2214459 (VD16 ZV 29142), USTC 633114 (VD16 S 1079), USTC 633078 (VD16 S 1076), USTC 633133 (VD16 ZV 13618). Three of these publications do not have an imprint, but it is unlikely that Morhart produced one of them as he produced most of his publications with imprint.

90 The *Rentkammerbuchhalter* earned 80 Gulden yearly between 1550–1628, in addition to an annual allotment of spelt and wine, see BERNHARDT (1972), *Die Zentralbehörden des Herzogtums Württemberg und ihre Beamten*, p. 98.

91 According to a search in the USTC: Printer - Morhart, Place of Printing - Tübingen, Date - 1522–1553 (result: 236 books).

market. Since these were important legal publications, Morhart had to have permission for this undertaking from the government. Such a permission can be found among the documents about the explanation of the new imperial police ordinance (*Reichspoliceyordnung*). One of these documents, as was seen in the previous chapter, reveals that a total of 176 copies were sent out to the various districts in Württemberg. With another document the government ordered the production and specified (on a separate piece of paper) that the printer 'may produce more copies for himself which he can offer for sale'.[92] In this instance, Morhart probably sold the extra copies to the cloth traders and the many other tradesmen who had previously prompted the ducal government to explain the imperial police ordinance.[93] In other instances, reprints of official works were sold to lawyers who needed to be familiar with the latest legislation and merchants who hoped to use the new information for their advantage.[94]

Another group of buyers for legal publications comprised officials who did not receive their own copy from the government. As the list of copies of the explanation shows, very few officials in the districts received a free copy: on average three officials in each district. Other print runs for ordinances to be distributed in the duchy, as we have seen in the previous chapter, were equally low. When an ordinance addressed procedures in court, however, such a small production run would not suffice to inform every member of the local courts. The members of the courts would then welcome the opportunity to buy their own copy from Morhart's shop in Tübingen. The ordinance regulating how to keep accounts and make calculations (published in 1551) appeared in different editions: one for the district officials, one for the foresters, one for the clerics, and one for the burgomasters and courts.[95] This last one, for the burgomasters and courts, was reprinted in the same year with only slight variations in the typesetting.[96] Morhart certainly could have sold a number of copies of the reprinted edition to those who had not received a free copy from the government.

92 HStASt, A 38 Bü. 2, the original German text reads: '[...] Unnd es soll auch gemeltem buchtrucker [Morhart] unnsert halber unbenommen sein, fur sich selbs, vonn gedachter unnser Erklärung merer unnd weitter Exemplaria nach zutruckenn, unnd die seinner gelegennheit nach zuvur kauff. Actum ut in I[u]r[i]s 16 Novembr[is] 1549.'

93 See chapter one.

94 See, for instance, the curious case of the merchant family Van der Meulen in Bremen. They seem to have bought a copy of every ordinance printed in Antwerp to plan their commercial activities, see Lamal (2015), 'Commerce and Good Governance', p. 221.

95 USTC 2212556 (VD16 ZV 31022), USTC 669142 (VD16 ZV 20575), USTC 690039 (VD16 ZV 20415) and USTC 657660 (VD16 ZV 20414).

96 USTC 657653 (VD16 ZV 20574).

The printer could also try to sell them to buyers from outside the duchy, especially officials from other territories. Since the dukes of Württemberg introduced the Reformation quickly and effectively in their territory, the developments in the territory were keenly observed by other rulers. Some of these rulers, such as Count Palatine Otto-Henry, received free copies of the ordinances from Duke Christoph's administration. These rulers could then instruct their own administration to purchase more copies of the books from Morhart. Other rulers who heard of the new legislation and were keen to have a look at the developments in Württemberg could also get copies. To reach such a large audience, Morhart and his heirs sold copies of the books at the Frankfurt Book Fair. Georg Willer already lists several Württemberg publications in his first catalogues of books bought at the Frankfurt book fair.[97] Among them are the *Landesordnung*, the forest ordinance and the construction ordinance, which he bought from Morhart's heirs.[98]

These publications show that Morhart took little financial risk. Almost all of the books he produced during his time in Tübingen were printed for the university and the government. He could, therefore, be sure of selling them either individually or of being paid for an entire edition by the ducal administration. Unlike his predecessors in Tübingen, Morhart did not undertake a printing programme on his own. With this approach he differed decisively from Thomas Anshelm, who wanted to produce humanist works, especially those of his friend and patron Reuchlin. Morhart neither printed any recreational literature nor devotional books. Instead, he produced only books that promised good income and books that would not cause any trouble with the authorities.

Family business. Morhart's legacy

When Ulrich Morhart died, his widow Magdalena took over the print shop, just as Georg Erlinger's widow in Bamberg had done after the death of her husband. In contrast to Magdalena though, Erlinger's widow only ran the shop for two more years, until October 1543, when she sold it to the bishop.[99] This was not a bad deal for her as she received 125 Gulden for her husband's press. The sum certainly made for a good retirement. In Tübingen, Magdalena did not sell her deceased husband's shop; instead, she continued to run it for some 20 years until her sons slowly took over more responsibility.

97 For more information on Willer's catalogues, see Duntze (2013), 'Verlagsbuchhandel und verbreitender Buchhandel von der Erfindung des Buchdrucks bis 1700', pp. 244–247.

98 Fabian (ed.) (1972), *Die Meßkataloge Georg Willers*, pp. 167–170.

99 Reske, p. 61.

What Magdalena did was rather exceptional for a woman until then.[100] In the first 100 years after Gutenberg's invention, many women helped their husbands in their print shops and continued the business once their spouses died. However, very few women ran the business for a long time. Usually they sold the shop within a few years or they remarried so that the new husband could take over the print shop. Magdalena Morhart chose to be independent and thus became one of the first successful woman printers in the Holy Roman Empire.

Her continuation of the only print shop in Württemberg was not unchallenged. She had to fight for this privilege from the very beginning: first a potential rival, and then even opposition from within her own family. In July 1554, only months after the printer Morhart had died, Morhart's son Ulrich the younger opposed his stepmother. He complained to the university senate in Tübingen about the situation among the heirs.[101] However, the senate refused to allow him to keep the print shop all on his own. Ulrich the younger was so upset about the fact that his stepmother continued the shop that even 50 years later Ulrich's son wrote an unusually emotional account about the family dispute in his chronicle.[102]

A few years after the senate's decision, in 1557, Ulrich the younger set up his own press in Tübingen. This was the first time Tübingen had two presses.[103] Yet, Ulrich the younger offered no serious competition to Magdalena's shop, although it would have been possible: his stepmother did not have a privilege for either the government work or the university work. Nevertheless, Ulrich only produced a few books per year. It was Magdalena who continued to attract most of the lucrative orders from the ducal administration. Just like her husband, she printed extensive official works for the government. And, with the important developments under Duke Christoph that manifested themselves in the publication of many official documents, Magdalena ran an even more successful print shop than her husband had. Between 1554–1572 the widow published over 350 editions.[104]

This is impressive enough, but the full evaluation of Magdalena's activity requires a rather different sort of calculation. Historians are increasingly beginning to realise that to calculate output purely in terms of editions, although very convenient, is an insufficient measure of economic activity.[105]

100 For the first in-depth study on Magdalena Morhart's life and her achievements, see Limbach (2019), 'Life and Production of Magdalena Morhart. A Successful Business Woman in Sixteenth-Century Germany', pp. 151–172.

101 UAT, 2/1b, fol. 175.

102 *Haller Haus-Chronik* (1962), pp. 68–69.

103 Widmann (1971b), *Tübingen als Verlagsstadt*, p. 73.

104 Reske, p. 1005.

105 See most recently Kaufmann (2019), *Die Mitte der Reformation*, p. 225.

To assess output in this way, after all, gives equal weight to a one-page broadsheet, which could be printed in a single day, and a long complex folio edition, which might occupy the press for up to two years.

For this reason, bibliographers are increasingly calculating output not just in terms of editions, but also in terms of the number of printed sheets required to make up each edition. This method also helps to estimate how many presses a print shop had, as it draws on the common understanding of workshop practice that a single press could print sufficient copies of one sheet, front and back, each day.[106] So, for instance, a quarto pamphlet of 16 pages represents two printed sheets folded, therefore a putative two-days' work on the press. Larger works obviously take much longer, so if we can account for more than approximately 250 days work in any given year, we can be reasonably confident that this print shop employed more than one press. Although this method disregards print-runs, which could vary considerably, it still allows us to compare and contrast the output of different printers much more accurately. For the purposes of this further analysis, I have recalculated all of Magdalena's output for each year in terms of printed sheets. The results are extremely revealing.

In 1568, Magdalena's output reached 860 sheets.[107] If the three works that appeared without imprint that year can also be attributed to her shop, then production would be even higher with 868 sheets.[108] This was an extraordinarily high number for only one year. As we will see in chapter three, Jaspar von Gennep in Cologne was already very productive when he printed 233 sheets in

106 Gilmont (1998), 'Printing at the dawn of the sixteenth century', p. 17.

107 Here and in the following, I have rounded up to full sheets: USTC 616021 ((VD16 B 7528), 34 sheets), USTC 617002 ((VD16 B 7530), 40 sheets), USTC 617003 ((VD16 B 7529), 35 sheets), USTC 617008 ((VD16 B 7525), 26 sheets), USTC 617012 ((VD16 B 7527), 32 sheets), USTC 617208 ((VD16 B 7526), 26 sheets), USTC 618241 ((VD16 E 1235), 1 sheet), USTC 637963 ((VD16 H 1009), 2 sheets), USTC 638130 ((VD16 A 2585), 2 sheets), USTC 620273 ((VD16 B 7576), 2 sheets), USTC 621954 ((VD16 A 2510), 31 sheets), USTC 611882 ((VD16 S 2463), 12 sheets), USTC 624847 ((VD16 B 5362), 17 sheets), USTC 660554 ((VD 16 A 2632), 4 sheets), USTC 661036 ((VD16 A 2637), 26 sheets), USTC 677218 ((VD16 4501), 3 sheets), USTC 678458 ((VD16 A 2662), 13 sheets), USTC 678459 ((VD16 A 2663), 13 sheets), USTC 678460 ((VD16 A 2664), 13 sheets), USTC 672023 ((VD16 B 5350), 4 sheets), USTC 630640 ((VD16 H 1048), 5 sheets), USTC 641594 ((VD16 A 2610), 136 sheets), USTC 641595 ((VD16 ZV 567), 119 sheets), USTC 641596 ((VD16 A 2609), 120 sheets), USTC 641622 ((VD16 A 2613), 62 sheets), USTC 706029 ((VD16 O 1273), 19 sheets), USTC 706030 ((VD16 O 1272), 19 sheets), USTC 690905 ((VD16 S 2491), 23 sheets), USTC 699736 ((VD16 H 900), 16 sheets), USTC 638120 ((VD16 ZV 7519), 2 sheets), USTC 638143 ((VD16 A 2605), 3 sheets).

108 USTC 638134 ((VD16 S 3286), 2 sheets), USTC 639299 ((VD16 ZV 23071), 1 sheet), USTC 679986 ((VD16 S 3301), 5 sheets).

1546.[109] Magdalena managed to print nearly three times as much as her Cologne colleague. Yet this was not an exceptional year for her. In 1569, the shop was less productive compared to the previous year, but still produced a remarkable 455 sheets.[110]

Soon after Magdalena had inherited the press, her sons from a previous marriage, Georg and Oswald Gruppenbach, joined the business. The payment for the Great Church Order 1559 for the first time includes Georg's name 'the printer in Tübingen, Jörg [sic] Gruppenbach in place of his mother Magdalena Morhart'.[111] From then on, the ducal account books only mention either 'the printer in Tübingen' or his name 'Georg Gruppenbach'. He was now his mother's right hand, responsible for the delivery and the payments of the printed books. Magdalena, on the other hand, was in charge of the print shop. It is her name that appears in the colophon, either as 'Vlrich Morharts Witfraw', 'Vlrich Morharts seligen Witfraw', or 'Vidvae Vlrici Morhardi'.[112] Furthermore, there are numerous receipts and invoices for other printing jobs that reveal more details than the relatively short entries in the ducal account books. These receipts almost exclusively mention that up until 1572 Georg either made a claim 'on behalf of his mother' or received money 'for his mother'.[113]

Magdalena's other son Oswald seems to have remained in the background of the business since his name does not appear in the ducal account books. In the 1560s he worked outside Tübingen, first in Urach and then in Ulm.[114] But from the 1570s onwards, his position must have become more important in the Tübingen shop since he then appeared in some colophons alongside his

109 See page 177.

110 USTC 608153 ((VD16 O 1161), 16 sheets), USTC 629598 ((VD16 H 1033), 3 sheets), USTC 660557 ((VD16 ZV 568), 3 sheets), USTC 617009 ((VD16 B 7532), 21 sheets), USTC 694716 ((VD16 F 2989), 13 sheets), USTC 620435 ((VD16 B 7577), 2 sheets), USTC 553285 ((VD16 ZV 18761), 56 sheets), USTC 553286 ((VD16 ZV 18761), 60 sheets), USTC 553287 ((VD16 ZV 18761), 64 sheets), USTC 632279 ((VD16 ZV 18761), 39 sheets), USTC 628116 ((VD16 B 5373), 24 sheets), USTC 638122 ((VD16 A 2579), 3 sheets), USTC 639277 ((VD16 H 979), 7 sheets), USTC 639317 ((VD16 S 3289), 4 sheets), USTC 641333 ((VD16 B 5367), 12 sheets), USTC 641334 ((VD16 B 5368), 12 sheets), USTC 641623 ((VD16 A 2614), 62 sheets), USTC 660555 ((VD16 A 2633), 3 sheets), USTC 706028 ((VD16 O 1274), 19 sheets), USTC 706789 ((VD16 A 2720), 10 sheets), USTC 706790 ((VD16 A 2719), 10 sheets), USTC 669529 ((VD16 B 5348), 12 sheets).

111 HStASt, A 282 Bd. 1295.

112 USTC 670013 (VD16 W 4493), USTC 669976 (VD16 B 101), USTC 667678 (VD16 B 2029).

113 UAT 8/6,1 no. 15 and nos. 59–67.

114 Reske, pp. 1007, 1017, 1027. For more information on the print shop in Urach, see below.

brother.[115] Presumably his mother was slowly reducing her involvement towards the end of her career, giving Oswald the opportunity to take over more responsibility.

One of the most important publications that Duke Christoph issued during his reign was the *Landrecht* from 1555.[116] In contrast to the *Landesordnung*, the *Landrecht* was issued not only by the duke and his councillors but also with the collaboration of the estates. It was, therefore, an important legal document. Until 1555, every district had its own customary law, which must have often been the cause of confusion and unfair treatment.[117] The *Landrecht* defined, for example, unified civil and procedural law for the whole territory. With the publication of the *Landrecht*, Duke Christoph took an important step into the modern world.

Magdalena Morhart produced this voluminous *Landrecht* as a folio book comprising more than 190 sheets. From the account book of the *Landschreiberei* we know that Magdalena was paid for 1,000 copies of the *Landrecht*, which were brought to Stuttgart upon completion.[118] The amount of copies is striking. As we have seen in the previous chapter, an ordinance that was to be distributed to the officials in every district usually appeared in 250 copies. The many copies of the *Landrecht* were undoubtedly intended for a much larger readership than just the officials in Württemberg.

For the publication and the transport of the 1,000 copies, Magdalena received no less than 300 Gulden. This was an incredible sum of money, being three times as much as a ducal councillor earned in the space of a whole year.[119] Moreover, it was not the only revenue Magdalena received in 1555. On top of the *Landrecht*, Magdalena produced another 15 publications that year. Among the larger works she printed a church ordinance, comprising 13 sheets, a work by Heinrich Bebel with 17 sheets, and Valentin Vannius' treatment of the mass (*De missa*) with 20 sheets.[120] We know that the latter work was also ordered and paid for by Christoph; it was the result of a disputation about the mass between Christoph and the Bishop of Augsburg at the Imperial Diet in 1555.[121] After this dis-

115 Widmann (1971b), *Tübingen als Verlagsstadt*, p. 60.

116 Fuhrmann (1998), 'Amtsbeschwerden, Landtagsgravamina und Supplikationen in Württemberg zwischen 1550 und 1629', p. 90.

117 Schäfer (ed.) (1984), *Reformation in Württemberg*, p. 267.

118 HStASt, A 256 Bd. 40, fol 393r.

119 Kanzleiräte and Oberräte earned 100 Gulden between 1550–1628, on top of natural produce, see Bernhardt (1972), *Die Zentralbehörden des Herzogtums Württemberg und ihre Beamten*, p. 97.

120 USTC 670013 (VD16 W 4493), USTC 657160 (VD16 ZV 1170), USTC 706212 (VD16 W 1197).

121 Schäfer (ed.) (1984), *Reformation in Württemberg*, p. 136.

putation, Christoph arranged the publication of Vannius' work in both Latin and German.[122] Surely Magdalena was also paid by the ducal administration for the church ordinance and the work of Heinrich Bebel. Sadly, no payments for these orders have survived. But we can assume that Magdalena received significant extra revenues from the duke in 1555 on top of the already high payment of 300 Gulden for the *Landrecht*.

In the *Landschreiberei* account book of the years 1556–1557, Magdalena's name appears again.[123] This time, she was paid for the production of the ordinance concerning measurements and calibration. Presumably this is the ordinance *Gemein gleich landtmeß und eych* from 1557.[124] She produced 500 copies and received 45 Gulden in return. The entry also reveals the calculation behind the payment: Magdalena got 1 Gulden for 200 printed sheets.[125] This rate, 1 Gulden for 200 sheets, recurs on numerous other occasions. Over the course of the century, the printers in Tübingen were not only paid by the *Landschreiberei*, but also by the General Church Fund (*Gemeiner Kirchenkasten)*. In contrast to the *Landschreiberei*, the account book of the General Church Fund reveals more information about the payments and the printed books. It usually lists the total amount of sheets printed, the rate for 200 printed sheets, and, in some cases, even the exact date of payment. From the 1550s onwards, the printers in Tübingen were frequently paid for the production of books out of the General Church Fund. Almost all of these payments include the same rate, 1 Gulden for 200 sheets.[126] The details about the payment for the Great Church Order and other books serve as a typical example:

> 700 copies of the Church Ordinance, each comprising 142 sheets, makes 99,400 sheets, then also the new school ordinance and the *Conf[ession] de coena domini*, makes 105,250 sheets in total, for 200 sheets one Gulden, makes 526 Gulden 15 Kreuzer in total.[127]

122 USTC 706212 (VD16 W 1197), USTC 630512 (VD16 W 1200).

123 HStASt, A 256 Bd. 41, fol. 446r.

124 USTC 681505 (VD16 W 4521).

125 The calculation in this particular case does not add up. USTC 681505 (VD16 W 4521) consists of 12 leaves, which translates to only 6 sheets per book. If she was paid for producing 500 copies of this, then she would have only received 15 Gulden. Either the writer of the account book made a mistake, or lucky Magdalena profited from a calculation mistake and received an additional 30 Gulden for her work.

126 On rare occasions the printers are paid for only a few copies of a certain book, such as for Duke Christoph's confession. The authorities bought 41 copies, paying one Batzen each, see HStASt, A 282 Bd 1290.

127 The original German text reads: 'dem Buchdrucker zu Tübingen Jörg Gruppenbach anstatt seiner Mutter für 700 Ex. Kirchenordnungen, jedes zu 142 Bogen, tut 99400 Bogen, und dann Schulordnungen, auch Conf. de coena domini,

Similarly, when he continued his mother's press from 1572, Georg Gruppenbach was frequently paid 1 Gulden for 200 printed sheets. The rate thus remains remarkably stable throughout the entire sixteenth century.

This price stability is quite striking. As we have seen in Erlinger's case, the payments for his letters of passage changed in the 1540s. At the beginning, in 1524, Erlinger received 1 Gulden for 1,000 letters; from 1540 onwards, the price increased by 50 % to 1 ½ Gulden for the same number of letters. So within 15 years the rate had increased significantly. However, in Württemberg the rate did not increase at all for over 50 years. We can only assume that in Württemberg in the second half of the sixteenth century the inflation and prices for paper, ink, and wages did not increase to such a degree that the printers' payment needed to be adjusted.

The rate of 1 Gulden per 200 sheets represents a very high payment. It is nearly twice as much as Magdalena Morhart and Georg Gruppenbach charged on other occasions, as we can see from their invoices to Hans von Ungnad. In the 1560s Magdalena and her sons were involved in the print shop in Urach. It was set up by the Habsburg nobleman Hans von Ungnad, the Captain General of Lower Austria.[128] When he refused anti-Protestant measures, Ungnad quit his career and sought refuge in Protestant Württemberg. There he established the South Slavic Bible Institute in collaboration with Primus Truber, the famous Slovenian reformer, to spread Protestantism among Croats and South Slavs.

The press was heavily funded by Ungnad himself and Duke Christoph.[129] Nevertheless, the costs were tremendous, so Ungnad and Truber tried to obtain more funds from other rulers. To this end, Ungnad sent letters to Protestant princes, including those from Hesse, Saxony, Anhalt, and Brandenburg. In these letters, Ungnad pointed out that his Bible Institute was a charitable organisation, and to underline this argument, Truber and Ungnad presented yearly accounts of their income and expenses to a neutral body: the University of Tübingen. This decision led to extraordinarily detailed accounts of the income and expenses of the press in Urach.

Among these many meticulously written documents one can find several invoices from Georg Gruppenbach for printing books in Tübingen and delivering them to Urach in 1561 and 1562. In contrast to the ducal account books, the printed sheets were not counted in a unit of 200 sheets, but instead in a unit of

5850, tut zusammen 105250 Bogen, je 200 Bogen für 1 fl., tut zusammen: 526 fl. 15 Kr', HStASt, A 282 Bd. 1295.

128 Ehmer (2011), 'Primus Truber, Hans Ungnad von Sonnegg und die Uracher Druckerei 1560–1564', p. 201

129 *Ibid.*, p. 206.

5,000 sheets (one bale of paper).[130] According to the invoices, Gruppenbach charged between 13 and 16 Gulden per bale. So, for example, Gruppenbach delivered 1,000 copies of Luther's *Small Catechism* in Italian, each comprising three sheets of paper.[131] He charged 13 Gulden for the bale and requested a total of 7 Gulden and 13 ½ Batzen for the printed sheets. This payment recurs for other orders from Ungnad. When Gruppenbach delivered the prefaces to five works, including the Croatian Confession, it came to the total amount of 5,750 sheets. For this, he again calculated with 13 Gulden per 5,000 sheets and thus invoiced 14 Gulden, 14 Batzen, and 1 Kreuzer.[132] Later in 1562, Gruppenbach delivered 2,000 prefaces to the New Testament in Croatian, charging 16 Gulden per bale as it was printed on 'good white paper'.[133]

The price difference can certainly partly be explained with the quality of the paper, yet there were probably also more general fluctuations. Ungnad himself bought paper on several occasions for the Bible Institute and the receipts show no indication that the paper was of different quality. The differences in price are striking: they range between 5–7 Gulden for a bale. The papermaker in Urach, Hans Heinzelmann, charged 5 Gulden for a bale, whereas Kaspar Tochtermann in Reutlingen charged 5 on one occasion and 6 on another. At the top of the market was David Getzinger, another paper maker from Reutlingen, who charged 7 Gulden for 5,000 sheets.[134]

This comparison demonstrates just how lucrative it was to print for the government. If Gruppenbach generally received between 12 and 16 Gulden for printing 5,000 sheets of paper, the 25 Gulden he received from the government for the same amount presents a stark difference. With that he could not only meet the different prices for paper, but also have a comfortable surplus that allowed him and his mother to invest in new projects. However, the surplus the printers in Tübingen made must have varied at times according to the changing price for paper. The ducal administration took this into account with their high rate and thus did not need to constantly adjust it.

130 One bale (Ballen) of paper usually comprised 10 *Rieß*, which held 20 *Bücher*, which consisted of 25 sheets of paper ($25 \times 20 \times 10 = 5{,}000$), see Krieg (1953), *Materialien zu einer Entwicklungsgeschichte der Bücher-Preise und des Autoren-Honorars*, p. 17. For more background on the different terminology and paper units in European countries, see Bellingradt (2020), *Vernetzte Papiermärkte. Einblicke in den Amsterdamer Handel mit Papier im 18. Jahrhundert*, p. 51.

131 UAT 8/6a,1, no. 178.

132 UAT 8/6a,1, no. 177.

133 UAT 8/6a,1, no. 181.

134 Unfortunately, the type of paper ordered and whether the difference in prices may have had to do with difference in quality is not specified.

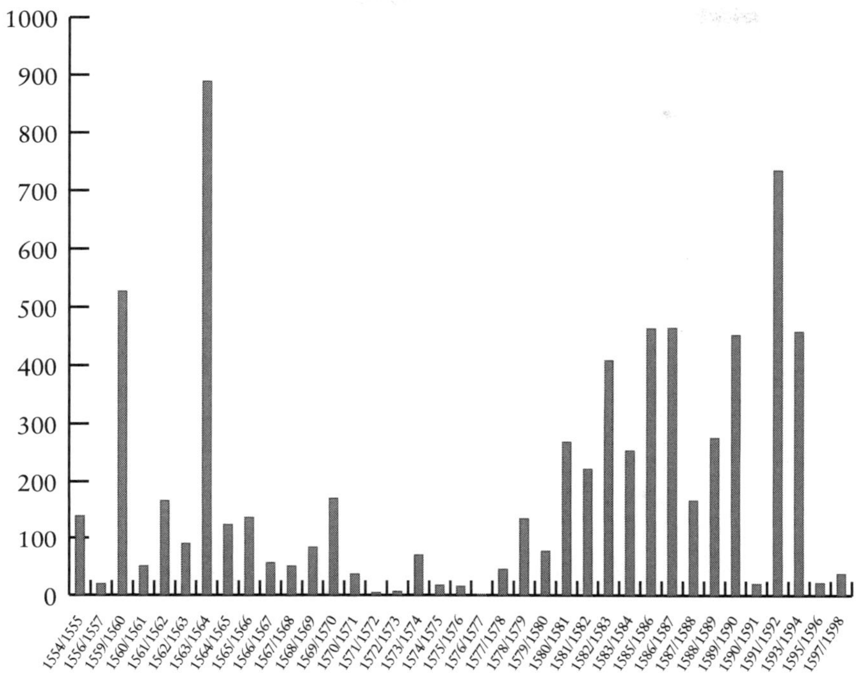

Fig. 2.2. Payments Magdalena Morhart and Georg Gruppenbach received from the General Church Fund (in Gulden). (The account books for the years 1555/1556 and 1557/1558 are missing, and the account books of 1584/1585, 1592/1593, 1594/1595 and 1596/1597 list no payments to printers.)

All in all, the Morhart-Gruppenbach press was paid for nearly 300 editions from the General Church Fund. Some of these payments refer to ordinances. In the financial year of 1552–1553, Ulrich Morhart received 37 Gulden for the *Kastenordnung* and the oath for those in charge of the *Kasten*.[135] One year later he received 25 Gulden for 2,000 copies of the marriage ordinance, and another 42 Gulden for the church ordinance.[136] Furthermore, as we have already seen above, Magdalena received over 500 Gulden for producing the Great Church Order as well as a school ordinance in 1559; USTC 669964 (VD16 W 4492).

The overwhelming majority of the payments in the General Church Fund, however, are not for legal publications, but for theological works. The produc-

135 HStASt, A 282 Bd. 1290; The ordinance is part of USTC 635179 (VD16 W 4509), which contains the *Landesordnung*, the new forest ordinance, and the *Kastenordnung*.

136 HStASt, A 282 Bd. 1291; USTC 681576 (VD16 W 4518); USTC 669964 (VD16 W 4492).

tion of Johannes Brenz' works was frequently sponsored by the ducal administration. All in all, the Morhart-Gruppenbach press published 61 editions by Brenz.[137] Presumably many of those, if not all, were financially supported by the ducal administration. From the account book of the General Church Fund, we can see that, for instance, *De personali unione* in 1561 was financed by the duke; Gruppenbach received 17 Gulden when delivering this work.[138] One of Brenz' publications brought the printer nearly 400 Gulden on its own: his *Catechism*. In his ambition to spread the new faith, Christoph tried to win allies at the French court.[139] Therefore, he sent several Protestant works to France, including Brenz' *Catechism*, translated into French by Heinrich Efferen from Cologne.[140] The translation appeared as an octavo with 472 leaves. So for the production Magdalena needed 59 sheets for every copy. This detail is recorded in the account book of the General Church Fund, according to which Magdalena printed 1,000 copies.[141] The works of Jacob Andreä feature even more prominently in the output of the Morhart-Gruppenbach press.[142] Again, many of those were presumably financed by the ducal government as, for example, Andreä's sermon of 1561, *De Cena Domini*, and his response to Friedrich Staphylus, for which the printers received 22 and 52 Gulden respectively.[143]

Apart from ordinances and theological works, the press in Tübingen also produced larger works for the government. In 1563, Gruppenbach was ordered to publish 1,000 Bibles in Latin to be given to the religious houses. After the Reformation, many religious houses in Württemberg were used to educate the new generation of reformed clerics.[144] Apart from housing, clothing, shoes, and bedding, each student received one Bible from the government.[145] To cater for

137 USTC search: Place - Tübingen, Authorship - Johannes Brenz. Result: 61 editions with Brenz as primary author. Four of these editions were published by Alexander Hock, the rest was produced by either Ulrich Morhart or his successors.

138 HStASt, A 282 Bd. 1296; The payment includes the costs for a missive to the priests about the price increase. This missive consisted probably only of a half or even a quarter sheet, so that the total costs were 1–2 Gulden. The rest of the 17 Gulden remains as payment for Brenz's *De personali unione*.

139 Schäfer (ed.) (1984), *Reformation in Württemberg*, p. 299.

140 Ibid., p. 304.

141 HStASt, A 282 Bd. 1299.

142 USTC search: Place - Tübingen, Authorship - Andreä. Result: 202 editions with Andreä as primary author. 18 of these editions were published by Alexander Hock, the rest were produced by either Ulrich Morhart or his successors; the payment for the following examples: HStASt, A 282 Bd. 1297.

143 HStASt, A 282 Bd. 1297.

144 Schäfer (ed.) (1984), *Reformation in Württemberg*, p. 284.

145 *Ibid.*, p. 231.

this need, Gruppenbach was ordered to produce an edition of the Latin Bible. In the account book of 1563–1564, Gruppenbach received 300 Gulden for the production of the 1,000 Bibles. Yet, this only seems to have been an advance payment. After all, each Bible comprised 209 sheets. To print all copies, the printers in Tübingen thus needed 209,000 sheets (about 42 bales), a considerable investment that was not covered with only 300 Gulden, especially not if the government paid 25 Gulden for a bale. A similarly large work was published in 1569. In this year, Gruppenbach printed the hymnbook by Sigmund Hemmel with notation.[146] Much like the Bibles, it was intended for the cloister schools. In contrast to the Bibles, the printer produced fewer copies, only 100. However, he received quite a good sum for them, namely 158 Gulden.[147] The need for special musical type made the hymnbook more expensive to produce and the ducal administration met the extra costs.

Finally, the printers in Tübingen also printed ecclesiastical books for the government, such as prayers. Some of them are only known to us from the account books. In 1556–1557 Magdalena was paid for 600 prayers against the Black Death.[148] The account book specified that one sheet was needed for each prayer, and Magdalena received 3 Gulden for the production of all of them. This prayer was thus most likely produced as a broadsheet. A few years later, in 1564–1565, she again printed prayers against the Black Death, and this time the account book specifies that Brenz was the author of this particular prayer.[149] Another prayer from 1573, this time against increasing prices, was produced on a half-sheet. Thus to print the 800 prayers, Magdalena only needed 400 sheets and was given 2 Gulden in return. Similar prayers that addressed a recent price increase followed in 1571 and 1586.[150] In addition, the printers also produced prayers against the Turks, especially in 1565, 1566 and 1595.[151]

On top of that, there was another prayer produced that is not evidenced through the account books. Among the documents in the State Archive in Stuttgart regarding issues concerning church and religion, we can find a draft prayer from 1582 entitled 'Common Prayer', which ought 'to be read after the sermon on Sunday'.[152] It is accompanied by a draft order from Duke Ludwig, in which he instructs Georg Gruppenbach to print 700 copies of the prayer in octavo format. After completion, Gruppenbach was to send the prayers to the chancellery upon which he would receive his payment. Unfortunately, we do

146 Bossert (1898), 'Zur Geschichte des Buchhandels in Stuttgart', p. 250.
147 HStASt, A 282 Bd. 1305.
148 HStASt, A 282 Bd. 1293.
149 HStASt, A 282 Bd. 1300.
150 HStASt, A 282 Bd. 1306; HStASt, A 282 Bd. 1322.
151 HStASt, A 282 Bd. 1301; HStASt, A 282 Bd. 1302; HStASt, A 282 Bd. 1331.
152 HStASt, A 63 Bü 59/4.

not know how much Gruppenbach received in the end. But this case suggests that the ducal administration paid for more printed items than only those listed in the account books of the General Church Fund and the *Landschreiberei*.

As we can see, the Morhart-Gruppenbach press served the authorities in Württemberg on many occasions. The printers produced not only ordinances, but also theological works, larger books like Bibles and hymnbooks, and ecclesiastical publications such as prayers. But although the Morhart-Gruppenbach press catered so much for the authorities' needs, the government sometimes relied on other printers. In the years 1561–1562, Duke Christoph ordered several books from Peter Braubach in Frankfurt. He was the former publisher of Johannes Brenz's works before Morhart and Gruppenbach emerged as reliable Protestant printers in Württemberg.[153] In 1561 Duke Christoph ordered one copy of Brenz's *Apologia* and one copy of the Christoph's *Confession against Pedro de Soto*.[154] Several months later, in April 1562, Duke Christoph ordered another 58 copies of those two works, which amounted to a sum of 201 Gulden. The third and last order from Braubach was comparatively small: 50 copies of Brenz's *De maiestate Domini* for only 5 Gulden in total.

In addition, the ducal administration ordered the Lutheran Bible from another printer outside the duchy. In 1564, Duke Christoph ordered 200 copies of the Lutheran Bible from Sigmund Feyerabend in Frankfurt. In the sixteenth century, the Lutheran Bible was principally produced in Saxony and the imperial cities.[155] In Frankfurt, Feyerabend tried to compete with Saxony in the way that he included portraits and dedications to the Protestant princes in the west of the empire. This strategy worked well for Feyerabend. By the time Duke Christoph ordered the copies, the printer-publisher in Frankfurt had produced his fourth edition of the Lutheran Bible within only four years.[156] Considering how voluminous those editions were, this was an exceptional achievement. On 22 April 1564, Sigmund Feyerabend received 600 Gulden, 3 Gulden for each Bible, and 40 Gulden and 40 Kreuzer for the transportation from Frankfurt to Stuttgart and other costs (e.g. taxes).[157]

But for the Morhart-Gruppenbach press, these orders from foreign printers did not present strong competition. Instead, Gruppenbach found a way to be paid even if the books were not produced by his press. Firstly, he acted as buyer for the ducal administration. In 1579, when Gruppenbach returned from the

153 Schäfer (ed.) (1984), *Reformation in Württemberg*, p. 160.

154 HStASt, A 282 Bd. 1297; Bossert (1898), 'Zur Geschichte des Buchhandels in Stuttgart', p. 247.

155 Schäfer (ed.) (1984), *Reformation in Württemberg*, p. 134.

156 USTC 616484 (VD16 B 2747), USTC 616483 (VD16 B 2748), USTC 616482 (VD16 B 2752), USTC 616518 (VD16 B 2756).

157 HStASt, A 282 Bd. 1299.

Frankfurt Fair, he brought with him several books, which he sold to the duke.[158] In the same year, he bought 80 German and five Latin copies of a work against the Council of Trent printed in Strasbourg. For this he received money for transportation from Strasbourg to Tübingen.

Secondly, Gruppenbach extended his business: he became a bookbinder. This way he took his share of the local bookbinding market in Stuttgart and Tübingen. From 1539/1540, Konrad Kuen was a binder and bookseller in Stuttgart.[159] From the mid-1550s onwards, Kuen faced increasing competition, first from Michael Hermann, then also Wilhelm Funk, Jakob Schedel, and David Liesch. In the account book of the General Church Fund, Konrad Kuen and Michael Hermann are frequently mentioned. They regularly earned several Gulden for their work. Then, from 1562 onwards, Gruppenbach joined the bookbinders. On 9 October, he not only produced Brenz's *De Majestati Christ*, but also bound 12 copies for a payment of 3 Gulden;[160] in August 1564, he bound 123 copies of Brenz' *Catechism*, four copies of *De Missa*, and 12 copies of a book on the Council of Trent for a total of 23 Gulden.[161] When he then bought several books at the Frankfurt Fair for the government, he bound them before he gave them to Stuttgart, receiving a total of 52 Gulden for the costs of the books and the binding. Among the most expensive bindings were five copies of the *Concordia*, bringing Gruppenbach 15 Gulden, and a single Bible, which was covered with velvet and silver, for 20 Gulden.[162]

Obstructive cooperation

As fruitful as the relationship between rulers and printers could be, it also suffered from problems and disruptions. To implement the Reformation successfully, Count Palatine Otto-Henry asked one of his officials, Hans Kilian, to open a printing house in the capital Neuburg in 1544.[163] This arrangement, however, lasted only for a couple of years. While Kilian was in the middle of producing a church ordinance for the count, the Schmalkaldic War broke out and imperial troops seized Neuburg, thereby destroying the printing house. It was ten years before Kilian was able to reopen his shop.[164] The printer did his best to catch up on the production, finished the church ordinance, and printed two works by Jean Calvin and Donato Giannotti. In the latter works, Kilian

158 HStASt, A 282 Bd. 1315.
159 Bossert (1898), 'Zur Geschichte des Buchhandels in Stuttgart', p. 248.
160 HStASt, A 282 Bd. 1298.
161 HStASt, A 282 Bd. 1300.
162 HStASt, A 282 Bd. 1316; HStASt, A 282 Bd. 1326.
163 Schottenloher (1927b), *Pfalzgraf Ottheinrich und das Buch*, p. 60.
164 *Ibid.*, pp. 61–62.

inserted dedications to Otto-Henry in which the printer pointed to his misfortune.[165] This, nevertheless, did not persuade Otto-Henry to continue working with the printer. When Otto-Henry became Elector Palatine, he moved to Heidelberg and from 1558 employed another printer to produce official publications.[166]

In Württemberg, the collaboration between rulers and printers was not tested by war but faced problems that were common in the print industry. The ever-increasing orders from the ducal administration as well as the extension of the business meant that Gruppenbach was at times extremely busy. This meant that some orders were not produced as quickly as they could have been. The reprint of the Great Church Order in 1582 illustrates this point very well. In early 1580, Gruppenbach was paid to come to Stuttgart and discuss a new edition of the Great Church Order.[167] After they had come to an agreement, the government issued the new edition at the end of April 1582. This new edition did not greatly differ from the previous one of 1559 and it was given a new preface from the duke that comprised a few leaves[168]

The reprint of the General Church Order should have taken only a few weeks, as Gruppenbach was paid for only 100 copies; a small number compared to the 700 copies his mother had produced in 1559. Back then, Magdalena had received the manuscript of the ordinance in mid-May and had sent the copies by mid-September.[169] The production of the 700 copies had taken her four months, but in the 1580s Gruppenbach needed far longer for a much smaller edition. The ordinance was most likely given to the printer right after it had been issued at the end of April. However, Gruppenbach did not deliver the printed copies until the end of January 1583, a whole nine months after he had received the manuscript.[170]

The government in Stuttgart had to wait that long because Gruppenbach's press was operating at its full capacity in 1582. In that year, the press in Tübingen published no fewer than 33 editions, comprising 560 sheets in total.[171] Some of these publications were quite elaborate, such as Lucas Osiander's *Institutio Christianae religionis*.[172] The octavo book comprised 710 pages. In the same year, Gruppenbach also published the French translation of the *Institutio Christianae*

165 USTC 707876 (VD16 C 306), USTC 690734 (VD16 ZV 21376).
166 Schottenloher (1927b), *Pfalzgraf Ottheinrich und das Buch*, p. 63.
167 HStASt, A 282 Bd. 1315.
168 Reyscher, XII, p. 433.
169 HStASt, A 282 Bd. 1295.
170 HStASt, A 282 Bd. 1318.
171 According to a search in the USTC: Printer - Gruppenbach, Place of Printing - Tübingen, Year - 1582 (result: 33 books), drawing on the same methodology as explained above.
172 USTC 666752 (VD16 O 1212).

religionis with 150 more pages than the original.[173] Most of the publications Gruppenbach produced in 1582 were intended for the ducal administration, so the government probably did not complain about the long waiting time for the church ordinance.

Yet this example shows again that a modern-day historian needs to take into account that the issue date of an ordinance does not necessarily equal the print date. Due to the busy press in Tübingen, the copies of the ordinance did not arrive in Stuttgart before the end of January 1583. There the copies had to be authenticated before they were sent to the officials in the districts. This, in addition to the delivery to the different areas of the duchy, took another few days at least, so that the district officials did not have a copy of the 1582 ordinance in hand before February 1583. Just like we have seen in the previous chapter, the printed copies did not circulate until months after the issue date.

In addition to a busy press, a printer's financial difficulties could also seriously prolong the publication of official work. Although Gruppenbach had inherited his mother's thriving print shop, he faced bankruptcy at the end of his career. From the 1580s onwards, Gruppenbach increasingly faced competition from other printers. In 1586, Philip Apianus, the professor for geometry and astronomy in Tübingen, set up a press in his home.[174] The professor did not publish many works and died shortly after he had started the new venture (1588). Apianus left his equipment to Johann Kircher, who started to produce books in 1593.[175] Kircher was a former assistant of Gruppenbach's and increasingly printed for the university. He was joined by Erhard Cellius, who started printing academic works in 1596.

These developments had serious consequences for Gruppenbach. He lost his grip on one of his most important areas of business: producing books for the university in Tübingen. As a result, Gruppenbach increasingly relied on the production for the ducal administration. At first, this was not a problem since Gruppenbach was ordered to produce many official publications in the 1580s and 1590s. According to the account books of the General Church Fund, Gruppenbach made an average of some 300 Gulden per year in the 1580s. At the beginning of the 1590s, the payments even went as high as 736 Gulden in 1592 and 459 Gulden in 1593.[176]

Towards the end of the century, however, things changed dramatically for Gruppenbach: Duke Friedrich of Württemberg offered the printer Max Fürster

173 USTC 666678 (VD16 O 1215).

174 Widmann, Hans (1971a), 'Professor Philipp Apian als Drucker in Tübingen', p. 224.

175 Reske, p. 1007.

176 HStASt, A 282 Bd. 1327; HStASt, A 282 Bd. 1328; HStASt, A 282 Bd. 1329.

the opportunity to print in Stuttgart.[177] Fürster had previously tried to find employment in Nördlingen, but when he was refused he sent Duke Friedrich a two-coloured broadsheet which showed his printing expertise. The duke appointed Fürster at the end of April 1597. By the end of the year, the printer had received his first payment (2 Gulden), and in the following years he already earned 176 Gulden from the General Church Fund.[178]

With the appointment of Max Fürster, Gruppenbach did not lose all of the orders from the ducal administration. However, the great bulk of books were now produced in Stuttgart. In the account books of the General Church Fund, Gruppenbach's name only appeared on two more occasions after Fürster started printing in Stuttgart. In early 1598, Georg Gruppenbach received 14 Gulden and in January 1600 another 89 Gulden.[179] He never again collected the high payments that he and his mother had earned in previous years. The 736 Gulden Gruppenbach had received in 1592 were now payments of a distant past.

Within a few years, Gruppenbach encountered severe financial problems. In November 1605, he was accused by the University of Tübingen of owing them 1,000 Gulden.[180] When Gruppenbach offered to sell his house, the university refused the offer on the grounds that it was encumbered with mortgages.[181] Towards the end of the month, at least 14 other creditors had accused Gruppenbach of not paying his debts.[182] Things began to look very grim for him. In the following year, Gruppenbach faced enormous debts of 17,000 Gulden and sold all his books to Johann Berner in Frankfurt.[183] However, Gruppenbach remained in the printing business, as we can see from the following interaction with the duke.

Things began to look a bit better in 1606, when Duke Friedrich turned to Gruppenbach once again as Max Fürster had died only a few years after his appointment as *Hofdrucker*. For the publication of the new edition of the *Landrecht*, the duke asked Georg Gruppenbach and his son Philip to estimate the costs for the production of the new publication.[184] To start with the production, however, Gruppenbach and his son needed a considerable investment up front. To this end they asked Melchior Breidner, Philip's stepfather and mayor of Schorndorf, to invest in the business.[185]

177 Reske, p. 990.
178 HStASt, A 282 Bd. 1333; HStASt, A 282 Bd. 1334.
179 HStASt, A 282 Bd. 1333; HStASt, A 282 Bd. 1335.
180 UAT, 2/7, fol. 172.
181 UAT, 2/7, fol. 178.
182 UAT, 2/7, fol. 182.
183 Widmann (1971b), *Tübingen als Verlagsstadt*, p. 72.
184 UAT, 26/3, no. 13.
185 UAT, 26/3, no. 14.

Yet, the production of the *Landrecht* did not bring the desired quick return as it took too long to produce. In June 1606, the duke placed the order of 2,000 copies of the new *Landrecht.*[186] With 145 sheets per copy this meant that the printers had to print 290,000 sheets of paper. This amount of sheets would have taken Magdalena Morhart about a year in 1559.[187] However, things had changed and Georg Gruppenbach did not run a productive print shop anymore. It took more than 18 months to complete the job, and just before the production was finished, missing only the preface, the table of contents, and the final page, Duke Friedrich died.[188] The production immediately came to a standstill as the new duke, Johan Friedrich, first wanted to check if he agreed with the revisions that were made in the *Landrecht*. In March 1608, the duke asked the printer to send four copies as well as the manuscript which was used to set the type.[189] It took more than a whole year until the already printed text was corrected by hand and then send back to the print shop.[190] Finally, in 1610 the book was finished.[191]

The production of the new *Landrecht* had taken the better part of four whole years. This was a long time to wait for the publication of an important legal document. It underlines how the print production of important texts was not always straightforward in the early modern period. The government of Württemberg was not only advanced with the help of printing, but at times was also hindered either by a busy printer whose presses operated at full capacity, or by financially challenged printers who were not able to employ sufficient staff, or invest in the required number of presses.

186 UAT, 26/3, no. 22.

187 The Great Church Order of 1559 was produced in 700 copies with 142 sheets per copy – a total of 99,400 sheets. We know that Magdalena Morhart needed exactly four months to complete the order since the messenger delivered the manuscript on 9 May and the printed copies were delivered on 9 September of the same year, see HStASt, A 282 Bd. 1295. For a translation of the source material, see Limbach (2019), 'Life and Production of Magdalena Morhart', p. 168.

188 Faber (1859), *Die Vorarbeiten zum Württembergischen Land-Recht vom 1. Juni 1610*, p. 19.

189 UAT, 26/3, no. 25.

190 Faber (1859), *Die Vorarbeiten zum Württembergischen Land-Recht vom 1. Juni 1610*, p. 21.

191 It appeared in two editions: USTC 2130511 (VD17 1:016993S) and USTC 2138493 (VD17 7:708509C).

Conclusion

Business interactions between rulers and printers did not always run smoothly. Although the printing press had much to offer early modern governments, it was not always easy to use the new technological innovation. The economic realities of the printing industry made it difficult to keep presses in places such as Württemberg. Even if authorities found printers who dared to take the risk and produce outside the major centres of publication, the financial difficulties the producers experienced could tempt them to disregard official orders, steal from their clients, or produce pamphlets that were not in tune with the government's regulations. On top of that, a busy printing schedule and the lack of sufficient staff could prolong the production of official works significantly.

On the other hand, the relationship between authorities and printers could also be extremely beneficial. For one Württemberg printing house, producing for the authorities became the key to success. Duke Ulrich's and Duke Christoph's aim to elevate the status of their duchy within the Holy Roman Empire led to the production of many publications. The introduction of the Reformation forced the authorities to regulate key issues within the church, such as marriage and blasphemy. The Morhart-Gruppenbach press readily supplied the necessary works and ordinances. This helped the authorities to implement the new faith successfully and establish the duchy as a role model for a Protestant territory.

With the production of these many legal works, Ulrich Morhart and his heirs earned considerable sums of money. Additionally, the printing family was frequently paid for other governmental orders. Reforming a large duchy required more than just books of jurisprudence. Therefore, the authorities frequently paid their printers to produce important reform works such as those of Martin Luther, Johannes Brenz, Lucas Osiander, and Jacob Andreä. These works could reach high print runs and, to the delight of their printers, the government in Stuttgart paid extremely well.

Chapter Three: Governing the German City

As we have seen in the first chapter, print had much to offer to early modern governments. Thanks to Gutenberg's invention, official letters and announcements could be reproduced quickly and easily and sent off to a variety of readers. This enabled territorial rulers to communicate efficiently with their officials in numerous districts. In addition, governors could use printed documents to reach recipients in remote places. By sending out numerous letters, rulers could explain their policies as well as persuade and thus seek support from a large audience. This provided governments with the opportunity to strengthen their position as well as regain power in times of trouble, such as in 1514 when Duke Ulrich faced the uprising of the Poor Conrad.

The city council of Cologne used print similarly to inform a large audience, advertise the city, and assert power in difficult times. However, the council differed decisively from the rulers in Württemberg with regard to the production of printed ordinances. In fact, the magistrates employed the press remarkably little to communicate new regulations. Despite the expansion in government activity in Cologne, which led to some 2,500 police ordinances in the course of the sixteenth century, the council only had 353 ordinances printed before 1601.[1] This was less than 15 % of all ordinances issued.

Given the relationship between the rulers and the ruled in Cologne, this is hardly surprising. Cologne's government, as many other urban governments in

1 Policey K, pp. 284–603, lists a total of 2,571 police ordinances issued by the magistrates in Cologne. On top of that, I found 13 ordinances which were not in Policy K (appendix nos. 28, 29, 31, 36, 48, 54, 76, 111, 143, 239, 240, 284, 371). As for the printed ordinances, the appendix lists 350 ordinances for Cologne (nos. 28–385, excluding nos. 30, 32, 33, 44, 45, 46, 47, 208 which are not police ordinances, but invitations, contracts or explanations). There are three more police ordinances on VD16; as these editions were already known to bibliographers, they do not form part of the appendix which lists only newly found printed editions. The three editions are as follows: one police ordinance which was printed in two separate editions as a pamphlet (Policy K 3377 = USTC 677227 (VD16 K 1808) & USTC 677228 (VD16 ZV 9098)); and an earlier edition of this printed pamphlet (USTC 704779 (VD16 ZV 9097)) which was not integrated into Policy K.

early modern Europe, depended on the consent of their subjects.[2] To gain this consent, the council preferred to communicate new legislation in face-to-face settings where agreement and dissent could be voiced instantly. However, when the city fathers faced several crises in the later decades of the century, such as looming war and a great influx of migrants, they had to give their decisions more permanence. Print was extremely useful for this purpose. By producing broadsheet ordinances to be posted in public, the magistrates in Cologne acted in a similar fashion to their colleagues in Antwerp, where the council also increasingly used print when facing turbulent times during the Dutch Revolt. Yet the magistrates in Cologne only used the press to a limited extent and carefully regulated the information flow in their city. Thus, unlike the dukes in Württemberg, the council had no larger legal works, such as the city's statutes, published in the sixteenth century.[3]

Cologne

In the sixteenth century, Cologne was governed by an elected council. This was a relatively recent development. During the Middle Ages, the city had belonged to the Archbishop of Cologne, who passed laws for everyday life in the city. However, as Cologne became a commercial centre in the twelfth century, merchant families grew increasingly powerful, challenging the archbishop's authority, finally making Cologne a free city.[4] The new freedom was recorded in 1396 when Cologne established its own constitution, the *Verbundbrief*. This unique document prescribed a system of political associations, the *Gaffeln*, which comprised one or more guilds.[5] Every man living in Cologne who had his own household belonged to one of the 22 *Gaffeln* and was thereby able to elect the council.[6] Appointed on a yearly basis, the council consisted of members of all *Gaffeln* and regulated everyday life in the city. Despite its free status, the city was not able to shake off the archbishop's grip completely. Throughout the entire sixteenth century, the archbishop controlled religious life in Cologne and repeatedly tried to regain power over the city, especially in the 1580s.[7]

2 GROTEN (2007), 'Vom Recht der Bürger zum Sorgerecht des Rates', p. 75.

3 The statutes eventually appeared in print in the 1560s, but only on the initiative of an interested party (see below).

4 ISENMANN (1999), 'Die Reichsstadt in der Frühen Neuzeit', p. 45.

5 RB, I, p. XVI.

6 GIEL (1998), *Politische Öffentlichkeit im spätmittelalterlich-frühneuzeitlichen Köln*, p. 159.

7 Policey K, p. 43.

In the early sixteenth century, the council ruled over some 40,000 inhabitants.[8] Confined within only 400 hectares, the city was densely settled.[9] To avoid attacks, the inhabitants had built a large wall that encircled the entire metropolis.[10] This wall, erected in 1180, marked almost the entire jurisdiction of the city council. In contrast to Nuremberg or Augsburg, Cologne had no hinterland attached to it that the council could control. The magistrates ruled only over those people living within the city walls and its immediate surroundings, the *Burgbann*.[11]

Most of the council's subjects made a living from trade. As Cologne was one of the biggest trading centres in the Holy Roman Empire, trade was vital to the economics of the city. Merchants offered a great variety of locally produced cloth, steel, iron, and ironware.[12] In addition, farmers from East Frisia, Oldenburg, and the region around Münster regularly brought their cattle and other livestock to the markets in Cologne.[13] Pigs in particular were of great importance in Cologne, as the metropolis on the Rhine was one of the most important marketplaces for this trade.[14] Thanks to its favourable position on the Rhine, Cologne was well connected to long distance international trade, permitting many salesmen from within the empire and beyond to offer their goods to Cologne citizens. They could do so at several marketplaces like the *Heumarkt* and the *Altermarkt*, the biggest marketplaces in town. These markets were located close to the river and thus easily reachable for merchants who transported their goods by ship.

8 Schilling (2004), *Die Stadt in der frühen Neuzeit*, p. 4.

9 Eiden and Irsigler (2000), 'Environs and Hinterland. Cologne and Nuremberg in the Later Middle Ages', p. 44.

10 Hirschmann (2009), *Die Stadt im Mittelalter*, p. 17.

11 RB, I, p. XV.

12 Mathis (1992), *Die deutsche Wirtschaft im 16. Jahrhundert*, p. 44.

13 Gramulla (1971), 'Kölner Kaufleute im Handel mit dem Ostseeraum am Ende des 15. und 16. Jahrhundert', p. 559.

14 Eiden and Irsigler (2000), 'Environs and Hinterland. Cologne and Nuremberg in the Later Middle Ages', p. 47.

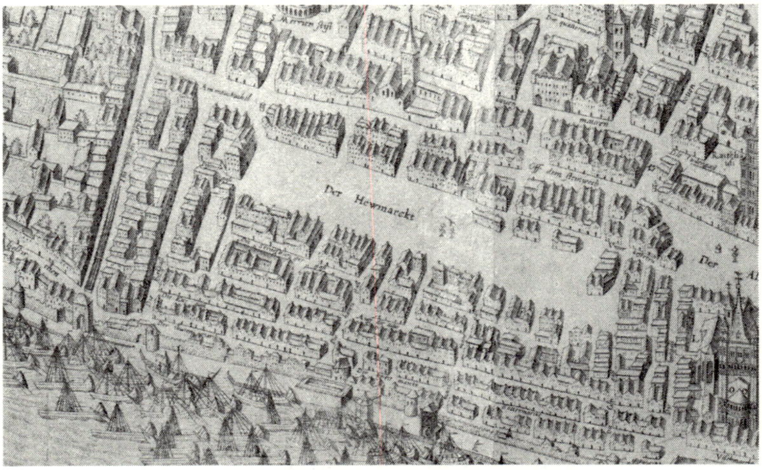

Fig. 3.1. Detail of a map of Cologne produced by Arnold Mercator (1570) showing the *Heumarkt* close to the Rhine.

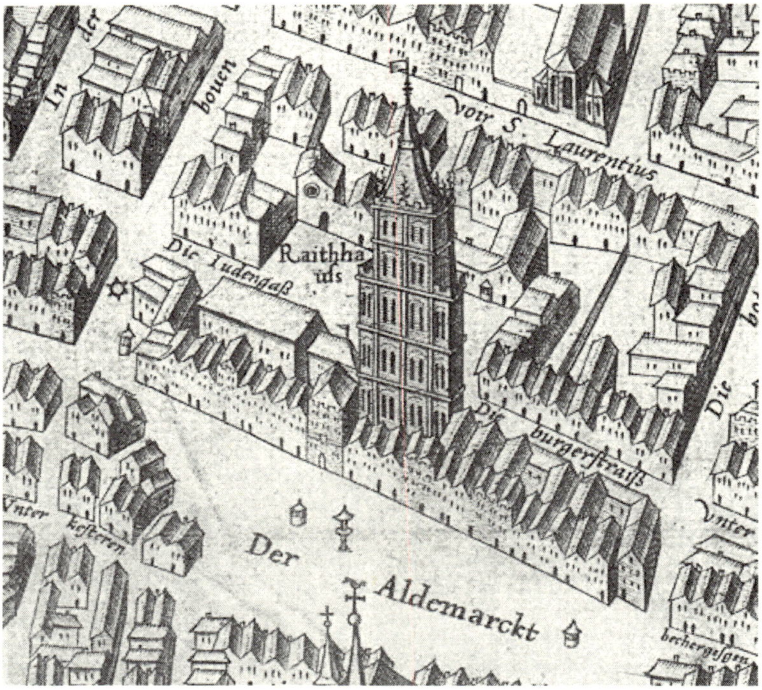

Fig. 3.2. Detail of a map of Cologne produced by Arnold Mercator (1570) showing the *Altermarkt* as well as the town hall east of the Heumarkt.

Proclaiming law and order

Throughout the sixteenth century, especially before 1550, the council communicated most of its decisions orally. With this procedure, the magistrates followed a long-established medieval tradition. Proclaiming law and order in this fashion fulfilled a symbolic function and could be remarkably effective. In the early years, the council commonly employed *Morgensprachen (morning speeches)*, proclamations read out from the balcony of the town hall. Later, to ensure greater efficiency, the magistrates increasingly communicated legislation via the *Gaffeln*. This method ensured that 2,000 inhabitants could be informed about recent legal changes straight away.[15]

In the past, scholars have not attributed much importance to proclamations such as the *morning speeches* in Cologne.[16] They were perceived only as a means to communicate orders, leaving the inhabitants largely in a passive role. Wilhelm Ebel suggests that subjects did not have the opportunity to voice their opinion at such events.[17] However, recent scholarship has contested this assumption and attributed much more importance to civic assemblies.[18] According to this view, the city councils had to ensure that their decision complied with the inhabitants' will.[19] Thus at civic assemblies the magistrates not only read out orders, but also took the temperature of public opinion by testing reactions to the verbal proclamations. This face-to-face interaction was crucial for conducting political affairs in early modern German cities.[20] As the rulers in Cologne were elected on a yearly basis, a custom followed in many German cities at that time, this consensual bond between them and their subjects was particularly important.[21] Unlike the dukes of Württemberg, who inherited power over the territory, the council constantly needed to reinforce its right to rule. Therefore, civic assemblies, such as the *morning speeches* in

15 Giel (1998), *Politische Öffentlichkeit im spätmittelalterlich-frühneuzeitlichen Köln*, p. 152.

16 Hoffmann-Rehnitz (2010), 'Discontinuities: Political Transformation, Media Change, and the City in the Holy Roman Empire from the Fifteenth to Seventeeth Centuries', p. 17.

17 Ebel (1971), *Lübisches Recht*, I, pp. 307–308.

18 Pitz (2001), *Bürgereinigung und Städteeinigung*, pp. 30–33.

19 Hoffmann-Rehnitz (2010), 'Discontinuities: Political Transformation, Media Change, and the City in the Holy Roman Empire from the Fifteenth to Seventeeth Centuries', p. 18.

20 Schlögl, Rudolf (2008), 'Politik beobachten. Öffentlichkeit und Medien in der Frühen Neuzeit', p. 606.

21 Isenmann (2014), *Die Deutsche Stadt im Mittelalter*, p. 352.

Cologne, fulfilled an important function and were a vital tool to legitimise rule and establish consent among the subjects.[22]

In addition to that, the *morning speeches* fulfilled a crucial symbolic function. Every speech was proclaimed from the balcony of the town hall, which faced the *Rathausplatz*.[23] This was not the largest open space in Cologne; both the *Altermarkt* and the *Heumarkt* were much larger. However, in many parts of Europe, including the city of Cologne, the town hall was a powerful visual expression of the council's authority over the city.[24] As it was easily accessible from the major commercial hubs in the city, the town hall was the centre of urban life and used for various purposes.[25] Here, courts announced their decisions, officials proclaimed punishments, and criminals were openly displayed in pillories.[26] By proclaiming recent legislation from the balcony of the town hall, possibly while several convicts were enduring their public shaming, the magistrates displayed their rule clearly.

The practice of proclamations was widespread throughout Europe. We can find ample evidence for this way of communicating new legislation in the Low Countries, Italy, and England.[27] It was also very common in Hanseatic cities. In northern German cities such as Lübeck, Wismar, Greifswald, and Rostock, the respective councils often used such public announcements, commonly called *Bursprake*.[28] These proclamations provided the opportunity for the magistrates to communicate a remarkable array of regulations, including legislation for guard duty, fire protection, road cleaning, trading, and hospitality.[29]

With the practice of stipulating legislation at civic assemblies, the magistracy in Cologne followed a long-established tradition and arguably one that had endured because of its perceived effectiveness. Already in 1328, when the city was still in the hands of the archbishop, the council announced a *morning speech* and instructed every inhabitant to attend.[30] From 1400, especially after Cologne

22 Rituals were also very important in this context, see Krischer (2011), 'Rituale und politische Öffentlichkeit in der Alten Stadt', p. 136.

23 Policey K, p. 8.

24 Friedrichs (2005), 'Das städtische Rathaus als kommunikativer Raum in europäischer Perspektive', p. 159.

25 Schwerhoff and Rau (2004), 'Öffentliche Räume in der Frühen Neuzeit. Überlegungen zu Leitbegriffen und Themen eines Forschungsfeldes', pp. 40–42.

26 Schwerhoff (2004), 'Öffentliche Räume und politische Kultur in der frühneuzeitlichen Stadt', p. 121.

27 Weduwen (2018), *State Communication*, p. 3; Milner (2013), 'Town Criers and the Information Economy of Renaissance Florence', p. 108; Kyle (2015), 'Monarch and Marketplace: Proclamations as News in Early Modern England', p. 774.

28 Isenmann (2014), *Die Deutsche Stadt im Mittelalter*, p. 478.

29 *Ibid.*, p. 478.

30 Policey K, p. 8.

became an imperial city in 1475, the speeches formed an integral part of political life. They took place twice a year, close to the election of the city council: on the feast day of John the Baptist (24 June) and on Christmas Day.[31] During these events, one of the officials read out from the official *morning speech* book, which comprised every official announcement from the mid-fifteenth century onwards.[32] The core of the speech formed a general plea for the inhabitants to remain peaceful, avoid gambling and nightly visits to the streets, and show respect towards the officials as well as the council.

As a response to recent events, the speeches were progressively amended over the years. In 1403, the council extended the speech by adding regulations on fire protection, keeping the streets clean, carrying lanterns at night, as well as the schedule for court sessions.[33] By 1450, the speeches also included prescriptions for the use of coins, exchange rates, as well as general rules for conducting business in Cologne.[34]

If a particular issue required the immediate attention of all inhabitants, the council used separate *Morgensprachen* (*special morning speeches*) to inform their subjects.[35] This procedure was employed in 1523, when the council received the imperial privilege allowing them to confiscate dilapidated houses if the owner refused to pay for repairs or new constructions.[36] To notify their subjects, the two burgomasters as well as their servants went through the entire city and ordered the populace to attend the *special morning speech*. The officials were dressed in their ceremonious garments and held up the burgomasters' symbol of power, their batons.[37] Unfortunately, it is not clear if every speech was announced in such a solemn way or if this was an extraordinary procedure.[38] Nonetheless, it highlights how the magistrates ensured that the bulk of the city's inhabitants took note of the *special morning speech*.

In the first half of the sixteenth century, the council used *special morning speeches* frequently, as they offered the opportunity to disseminate information quickly. The council acted swiftly after it received an imperial mandate in 1536 that had implications for the inhabitants of Cologne. In the 1530s, the imperial city of Münster, north of Cologne, had become the focal point of the Catholic

31 RB, I, p. XVI.
32 Giel (1998), *Politische Öffentlichkeit im spätmittelalterlich-frühneuzeitlichen Köln*, p. 60.
33 RB, I, pp. 60–61, no. 4.
34 Giel (1998), *Politische Öffentlichkeit im spätmittelalterlich-frühneuzeitlichen Köln*, p. 60.
35 Isenmann (2014), *Die Deutsche Stadt im Mittelalter*, p. 478.
36 Policey K, p. 8.
37 *Ibid.*
38 *Ibid.*

forces in the empire when it became the site of the Anabaptist uprising. After the city was recaptured, the emperor tried to crush any attempt of the radicals to regroup. As a result, he urged the city council of Cologne on Friday 24 March 1536 not to accommodate any rebels in the city. The magistracy proclaimed this in a *special morning speech* on Monday 27 March, only shortly after the orders from the emperor were received.[39]

When times got particularly hard, the council even announced speeches closely following each other to reinforce their authority. Shaken by economic hardship in 1482, the magistrates in Cologne faced uproar, which they were only able to control after they had executed several rioters. To explain and thus legitimise its behaviour to its subjects, the council employed several *morning speeches*. The first speech targeted rumours, as the magistrates' severe action was naturally discussed widely in the city. Much to the dismay of the councillors, rumours and accusations spread very quickly, as they did in other European cities.[40] To prevent another uprising, the magistrates forbade invectives with a *special morning speech* on 14 April 1482.[41] Another *special morning speech* followed the next day. This time, the authorities announced that they had banned all rebels who had managed to escape punishment.[42] Offenders who had not left the city were told to do so; even the wives of the rebels had to leave the city. The council declared that every fugitive who came back to Cologne without the permission of the civic authorities would be arrested and immediately executed. This stipulation was enforced several months later, when one fugitive did indeed dare to come back to the city. Undoubtedly, the rebel thought the situation had calmed down by the beginning of September, a whole five months after the riots, but he was mistaken and paid the price. These *morning speeches* announced immediately after the uproar helped the council to communicate its response to the populace in Cologne and thus re-establish order.

Given the size of Cologne's population, however, it is questionable if each and every inhabitant was immediately informed through the oral deliverance of new regulations. As the *morning speeches* were proclaimed from the balcony of the town hall, the listeners had to squeeze into the *Rathausvorplatz* at the end of the *Bürgerstraße* (see fig. 3.2.).[43] Yet, this space was not in any way big enough to accommodate all of Cologne's inhabitants in the early sixteenth century.[44] Even

39 *Ibid.*, no. 1874; RB, IV, p. 379, no. 183.

40 See, for instance, the case of Venice: De Vivo (2007), *Information and Communication in Venice*, p. 90.

41 Ennen (1863–1880), *Geschichte der Stadt Köln*, III, p. 609.

42 This abstract is taken from Ennen (1863–1880), *Geschichte der Stadt Köln*, III, p. 609.

43 Policey K, p. 8.

44 Schilling (2004), *Die Stadt in der frühen Neuzeit*, p. 4.

if only masters and citizens heard the speech with their servants and children staying at home, this would still mean a congregation of several thousand people. Without any technical aids available at that time, it is hard to imagine that people standing far away from the balcony could actually hear every detail of the *morning speech*.

In response, the council progressively relied on other forms of communication. In some cases, the council instructed a town crier to visit several places in the city and read out the latest decisions of the council. This method was already employed as early as 1484, when the magistrates notified their subjects of new coinage regulations.[45] To fulfil his duties, the town crier went to every tavern, bakery, and marketplace, as well as from house to house, to announce the new requirements. The town crier probably used drums to attract people's attention and gather a crowd. This effective practice was often mentioned in later council records from the seventeenth century and may well have been employed regularly far earlier than that.[46]

Attracting attention with music or performances before an imminent proclamation was common practice in medieval and early modern Europe. In Florence, the town criers were usually equipped with trumpets. They were also legally obliged to repeat the proclamation as many as 40 times at the city's most bustling places: in front of churches; on the main squares; on bridges and in front of the city gates.[47] In Dover, when the accession of King James I was made known, the proclamation was preceded by trumpeters, a procession of the town council as well as preachers, a bonfire, the firing of ordnance, and the tolling of bells.[48]

Apart from such proclamations, the city council of Cologne also supplemented *morning speeches* by displaying them on boards attached to the town hall. This practice was also often used by the Court of Holland in the early sixteenth century.[49] Unfortunately, the Cologne council minutes do not allow us to reconstruct the exact procedure; yet we may assume that this was either a manuscript copy of the ordinance pinned to the board or written on a chalkboard. This method was employed as early as 1497, when the council explicitly

45 Policey K, p. 8.

46 *Ibid.*

47 Milner (2013), 'Town Criers and the Information Economy of Renaissance Florence', p. 112.

48 Kyle (2015), 'Monarch and Marketplace: Proclamations as News in Early Modern England', p. 775.

49 Le Bailly (2021), '"Na de publicatie van den niewe ordonnantie." The publication and printing of ordinances for the Court of Holland, 1462–1600'. I would like to express my gratitude to Marie-Charlotte Le Bailly for sharing the manuscript with me before publication.

referred to such a board during their meeting. According to the council minutes, the magistracy tried to limit the circulation of low-grade coins in Cologne and appointed several magistrates to seize these coins. The delegates were instructed to follow the regulations announced in the *morning speech* 'that is displayed on the board attached to the town hall'.[50] Two more ordinances, one banning luxury goods and the other prohibiting usury, were published in the same way.[51]

Such visual display offered great advantages: every inhabitant who did not attend the proclamation or could not understand every detail of it could go to the board to verify the legislation. Exhibiting ordinances this way also helped to settle disputes. If the delegates appointed to collect the coins were challenged by their owners, they could easily reinforce their authority by looking up the details on the board. On top of that, the open display of recent legislation served a symbolic function. Just like a *Roland* statue or a market cross, the exhibited copy of the *morning speech* showed visitors and inhabitants alike that within the city walls one had to obey the rules of the magistrates.[52]

Depending on the topic of the regulations, the council also asked Cologne's priests to inform their congregation about new requirements. In the early sixteenth century, the magistrates employed this method in particular for regulations concerning funerals and prayers.[53] But the magistracy also used the pulpits to disseminate the latest safety measures, such as the ban on storing explosives as well as the testing of a bell to call attention to fires.[54] The latter order in particular reveals the council's care for its subjects: the fire drill needed to be communicated widely so that it would not frighten anyone.[55] Announcing the test via the city's pulpits ensured a smooth procedure without panic.

Lastly, the council increasingly channelled information directly to those who were immediately affected by the ordinances. Throughout the sixteenth century, the council stipulated the prices of meat almost on a weekly basis. These regulations were then always disseminated by word of mouth. When on 10 August 1526 the council determined that beef was to be sold for 7 Heller and mutton for 6 Heller for a period of two weeks, this information was passed on to the market masters.[56] Similarly, when in 1543 the council determined that no printer should produce a book without the approval of the magistrates,

50 RB, I, p. 794, no. 7.
51 Policey K, p. 7.
52 Freitag (2013), 'Städtischer Markt und symbolische Kommunikation', p. 385.
53 Giel (1998), *Politische Öffentlichkeit im spätmittelalterlich-frühneuzeitlichen Köln*, p. 47.
54 *Ibid.*
55 Weinsberg, *Die autobiographischen Aufzeichnungen Hermann Weinsbergs. Digitale Gesamtausgabe*, entry for 1530.
56 RB, III, p. 332, no. 436.

officials informed every printer in Cologne of this new regulation.[57] If the council's decisions affected a larger group of people or even the entire populace, this information was increasingly communicated via the *Gaffeln*. The council already employed this technique in the fifteenth century for *morning speeches* that were of vital importance.[58] This procedure could be remarkably effective as every man with his own household was affiliated to a *Gaffel*, ensuring that some 2,000 inhabitants were informed straight away.[59] The council communicated various new regulations in this way, including the ban on taking up military service outside the city in 1543.[60]

Channelling information via the *Gaffeln* was a very effective way to communicate regulations on law and order quickly. Therefore, the council used fewer *special morning speeches* as the century progressed and increasingly integrated them into one yearly announcement prior to the Corpus Christi Procession (*Große Kölner Gottestracht*). With this procession, Cologne not only honoured Catholic tradition, but also demonstrated civic unity, commemorating the joint effort of erecting a city wall in 1180.[61] In the early days, the magistrates only reminded the populace of certain regulations that ensured the procession could take place as planned: everyone was required to clean the streets in front of their house, to stop dumping dirt in the streets and, if necessary, to remove rummaging pigs from the roads.[62] Since the procession brought together thousands of people, it was a great opportunity to remind a large congregation of certain legislation. Thus, over the years, the magistrates progressively extended the announcement by integrating the topics of *special morning speeches*, such as the use of coins and the imperial privilege to confiscate dilapidated houses.[63] As a result, by the 1590s, the speeches prior to the procession were of considerable length and included a whole array of different regulations.[64] In 1593, the magistrate's speech for the *Gottestracht* stipulated rules not only for blasphemy and hospitality, but also inheritance, firearms, printing, private schools, and even the trade in silk, cloth, and wool. The entire transcript of this particular speech covered nearly 40 pages, a very lengthy speech.[65] By this time the legal

57 RB, V, p. 137, no. 124.

58 See, for instance, the *morning speech* concerning financial difficulties from 18 May 1477, RB, I, p. 581, no. 28.

59 Policey K, p. 13.

60 RB, V, p. 165, no. 349.

61 Giel (1998), *Politische Öffentlichkeit im spätmittelalterlich-frühneuzeitlichen Köln*, p. 78.

62 *Ibid.*, p. 81.

63 *Ibid.*, p. 82.

64 See, for instance, Policey K, no. 3626.

65 HAStK, Best. 30, V 127, fol. 204r–220v.

announcements at the *Gottestracht* served more as a reminder than as a platform to inform and discuss pressing political problems.[66]

Official publications

At first, the emergence of print did little to change the way the authorities in Cologne communicated with their subjects. As the council could inform its subjects about new regulations effectively with oral means of communication, it barely made use of print to address the inhabitants of Cologne. In fact, in the first half of the sixteenth century, the council primarily used print to address a rather different audience, those from outside Cologne. For them, the council produced ordinances in print, as we will see below. Other official publications served three main purposes: to help the city fulfil its administrative obligations, to boost the city's image, and to seek support during turbulent times. These outward-facing functions offer strong echoes of the purposes for which official print was employed in Württemberg.

We see this clearly in the first of these instances, as the city made use of print to fulfil administrative tasks that reached beyond the city walls. One such case was the business of the Hanseatic League. The city was not only a member of the League, but one of its three principal cities.[67] This meant that the city acted as intermediary between the organisers and its members. One of its tasks was to distribute information to a number of cities within Westphalia. When in 1511 the magistrates in Cologne received an invitation to a meeting of the Hansa, the council decided to have 82 copies printed.[68] This way the letter could be sent out to every city and town within Cologne's area of responsibility. In a similar fashion the council distributed another letter to the Westphalian towns in 1526.[69]

Secondly, the printing press offered the opportunity to boost the city's image and to attract visitors. At least three times, in 1483, 1502, and 1581, the council published invitations to shooting contests that took place in the city.[70] Just like Duke Ulrich's widely circulated invitations to horse races, these printed docu-

66 Giel (1998), *Politische Öffentlichkeit im spätmittelalterlich-frühneuzeitlichen Köln*, p. 85.

67 Dollinger (1970), *The German Hansa*, p. 95.

68 Giel (1998), *Politische Öffentlichkeit im spätmittelalterlich-frühneuzeitlichen Köln*, p. 97.

69 *Ibid.*, p. 98.

70 Schnitzler (1992), 'Die Kölner Schützenfeste des 15. und 16. Jahrhunderts – Zum Sportfest in "vormoderner Zeit"', p. 130. I would like to express my gratitude to Jean-Dominique Delle Luche for pointing me in the direction of the 1581 edition. For the two sixteenth-century editions, see appendix nos. 30 and 207.

ments helped to elevate the status of the ruler's territory. In addition, the many guests would spend money on accommodation, food, and drink, providing welcome income for the city. The magistrates in Cologne were not the only ones who employed printed invitations to attract visitors. The councils in Würzburg, Munich, Frankfurt, Augsburg, and Zurich also had such documents produced from the 1480s onwards.[71]

Thirdly, circulating printed documents could help to regain power in turbulent times. Towards the end of the fifteenth century and at the beginning of the sixteenth century, the council repeatedly faced difficult situations. In 1482, 1489, 1503, and 1513, the council's authority was seriously challenged by the inhabitants of Cologne as well as by foreign individuals. On all four occasions the magistrates circulated printed justifications to regain control over the city and assert their power.

As seen above, the year 1482 proved to be particularly challenging for the city council of Cologne. Due to financial difficulties over the previous years, Cologne was facing revolt and uproar.[72] The situation escalated in March when enraged townsmen occupied the town hall and imprisoned several councillors. Alarmed by such an assault on their authority, the rest of the council thought it helpful to spread information about the current developments as quickly as possible to those outside the city walls. The council produced a densely printed broadsheet, comprising over 70 lines, which provided an account of the outrages committed by the 'bad, evil and defiant' men.[73]

This report gives not only the date, but also the exact time of the uproar. The council stated that the people started to gather in front of the city hall on the Monday before Ash Wednesday between 10 and 11 am. Repeatedly, the council emphasised the disrespect of those involved in the uproar, who completely disregarded the oaths they had sworn to the authorities. The magistrates tried their best to neutralise the situation, but the enraged mob would not listen to the 'many good words'. Instead, the 'bad people' imprisoned 31 'friends'. The council was eventually able to restore law and order in the city, but some 'foul' people managed to flee. The long statement specifically named those who managed to leave the city and escape the council's authority: these included Jakob Meyer, called the bad hatter; Peter Mohr, the shoemaker; and Johan von Raitingen, who only had one eye.

With the help of print, the council was able to distribute this account to a large audience. This becomes obvious in the very first line of the wordy report as

71 Eisermann (2000), 'Auflagenhöhen von Einblattdrucken im 15. und frühen 16. Jahrhundert', pp. 161–162.

72 Ennen (1863–1880), *Geschichte der Stadt Köln*, III, p. 586.

73 USTC 744091 (VE15 K-20).

it reads: 'To all princes, dukes and counts as well as their noblemen, knights and servants.' Thanks to a detailed list in the council records, we know that this long broadsheet was sent to at least 78 recipients.[74] This list is truly remarkable as it shows that the city council sought to inform not only direct neighbours, such as the Archbishop of Cologne and the dukes of Jülich and Cleves, but also many southern German cities such as Regensburg, Nuremberg, Ulm, and Strasbourg. Additionally, the archbishops in Mainz and Trier, two of the seven electoral princes, received a copy. This way the council ensured that people close to the emperor and eventually the emperor himself heard an account of the rebellion from the council's perspective.

Much as Duke Ulrich of Württemberg had done, the council of Cologne used print to explain recent disturbances to a large audience and thus seek support. As we have seen in the first chapter, the duke issued a long broadsheet in the aftermath of the Poor Conrad revolt that he sent out to many rulers in the empire. The city council of Cologne employed the same technique. By circulating the account of the event as well as the offenders' names widely, the council drew the attention of a large audience to the events in Cologne. This made it extremely difficult for the banished ringleaders to find a hiding place where people were still unaware of the situation.

Print also proved to be useful when the council faced other problems towards the end of the 1480s.[75] In early 1488, Schweikhard von Sickingen was feuding with the council. The knight felt insulted as the city had punished him when he carried weapons with him (this was against the city's law). To show his outrage, Sickingen robbed several Cologne merchants.[76] As he was backed by both the Elector of Mainz and the Elector Palatine, this presented a serious threat to Cologne's economic life.[77] The council, therefore, published a broadsheet with its own point of view on the feud to appeal to a large audience, which included the emperor.[78] The council's strategy bore fruit. The emperor placed Sickingen under the imperial ban.[79] After this decision, the authorities in Cologne published the ban as well to give wide publicity to the fact that the emperor had, in this instance, sided with the city.[80]

74 Ennen (1863–1880), *Geschichte der Stadt Köln*, III, p. 608.

75 Giel (1998), *Politische Öffentlichkeit im spätmittelalterlich-frühneuzeitlichen Köln*, p. 109.

76 Schmitz (ed.) (1979), *Die Kölner Einblattdrucke*, p. 24.

77 *Ibid.*

78 The broadsheet appeared in two editions: USTC 744093 (VE15 K-24), USTC 744092 (VE15 K-24).

79 Schmitz (ed.) (1979), *Die Kölner Einblattdrucke*, p. 25.

80 USTC 745004 (VE15 F-85).

Print could also serve to influence the council's subjects. With the help of the press, the council was able to make its decision-making processes transparent to its subjects, convincing them that certain acts were necessary.[81] In 1503, the city faced a much more prominent opponent – the Pope. In the previous year the Archbishop of Cologne, who was eager to bring the city back under his control, had convinced Pope Alexander VI to place Cologne under interdict.[82] The council refused to accept this and fought back in print. It published the ban and inserted an appeal to the inhabitants of Cologne to ignore it.[83] On top of that, the council provided each *Gaffel* with a detailed report on the quarrel with the archbishop over the past three years.[84]

From 1512–1513 the city council of Cologne once again faced instances of unrest, which were resolved by the wide circulation of printed documents.[85] On this occasion poor finances, the conflict in Neuss, and corruption within the city council spurred numerous townsmen to arm themselves and express their grievances. In early 1513, several councillors were taken into custody on the grounds that they had breached the law and abused their authority. In just a couple of days all of these prisoners were sentenced to death and executed. During this short time of imprisonment, many citizens wrote to the city council complaining about the accused persons and asking for compensation. Some of these letters were incorporated into accusations against the imprisoned councillors.

The council had these complaints printed. One of these publications contained the complaints about one of the mayors of Cologne in 1512, Johann von Oldendorp. The *Supplicatien und clageschryfften* consist of three claims made by individual burghers who, it was alleged, had suffered severely from their mayor's despotism.[86] One of the complainants was a widow from whom the mayor had unjustly taken money: he had pressed her to pay an alleged outstanding debt of her deceased husband. The widow could not recall any debt owed by her former husband, but Oldendorp insisted and demanded 30 Gulden from her. When the blackmailed woman was not able to pay at once, as she simply did not have the money, Oldendorp physically abused her until she gave him her entire inheritance of 2 Gulden. In her letter to the council the widow asked for repayment of the lost inheritance.

81 Giel (1998), *Politische Öffentlichkeit im spätmittelalterlich-frühneuzeitlichen Köln*, p. 123.
82 *Ibid.*
83 Appendix no. 32.
84 Giel (1998), *Politische Öffentlichkeit im spätmittelalterlich-frühneuzeitlichen Köln*, p. 123.
85 *Ibid.*
86 USTC 710377 (not in VD16).

In addition to this publication, the council had five other complaints printed, each addressing the infamous acts of individual councillors. According to the council's minutes, these printed complaints were intended for the court.[87] The sheets may well have served as evidence against the culprits during the law proceedings. But this does not account for the fact that the complaints were printed instead of just being copied by hand.[88]

The printed complaints fulfilled another function that justified their publication in print. After the events in 1512, the city was in great uproar and the infamous deeds of the council's previous members were widely discussed. In this heated atmosphere, printing the complaints was a calculated strategy. Multiplying the complaints with the help of the press allowed the councillors to hand them to the *Gaffeln* as well as displaying them in public. The council did not stop there. It also sent the confessions of all accused councillors to the *Gaffeln*.[89] This way the inhabitants of Cologne could reconstruct the detailed process of the lawsuit. Being able to read and hear about what the individual councillors had done, made it obvious why they had been imprisoned and sentenced to death. Furthermore, those who had previously made complaints against the imprisoned men, like the widow who was robbed by the mayor, could see that the new city council took their complaints seriously and acted on them. Distributing these printed sheets helped the city council to regain control over the city.

Printing law and order, 1500–1550

It was previously thought that the city council rapidly embraced the use of print for its official business from the beginning of the sixteenth century onwards.[90] The evidence presented here suggests that this perception requires significant refinement. In fact, the council used print only to a very limited extent for its routine business in the first half of the century, just like governments in other European cities did.[91] The situation changed only in the 1560s when Cologne became embroiled in the wider European crisis caused, among other things, by the outbreak of significant religious conflict in northern and western Europe.

87 RB, II, p. 14, no. 99

88 Giel (1998), *Politische Öffentlichkeit im spätmittelalterlich-frühneuzeitlichen Köln*, pp. 128–129.

89 *Ibid.*

90 See, for example, Giel (1998), *Politische Öffentlichkeit im spätmittelalterlich-frühneuzeitlichen Köln*, p. 95.

91 Weduwen (2018), *State Communication*, p. 42, listing evidence for Antwerp, Leiden, Haarlem, Delft and Alkmaar.

For Cologne, this misperception has been facilitated by a lack of precision in the analysis of the bibliographical data.[92] One reason for this is the fact that the inventory of ordinances kept in the city archive was misread. In 1899, the director of the city archive in Cologne, Hermann Keussen, compiled a list of ordinances in a twenty-four-volume collection of early modern edicts.[93] This list served some scholars as proof of the increasing use of the printing press. Yet, Keussen's list contains not only regulations issued by the council, but also those issued by the emperor, the Archbishop of Cologne and neighbouring princes. Among them are, for instance, two imperial coin ordinances from 1524 and one coin ordinance from the Archbishop of Cologne issued three years later.[94] It is true that in some cases the council reprinted imperial ordinances. Yet such publications often include a few lines from the local authotities which marks them as reprints.

In addition to imperial ordinances, Keussen also listed some ordinances that only existed in manuscript form.[95] As a result, out of the 418 editions Keussen lists for the sixteenth century, we can only attribute 268 printed documents to the city council.[96] Most of these printed ordinances were issued after 1550. The remaining 150 ordinances listed by Keussen for the sixteenth century were issued by other authorities or not printed at all.

Unfortunately, the repertory of early modern police ordinances, although very helpful in other respects, introduced further 'ghost' editions.[97] In some cases, the issue date of the ordinance, expressed in Roman numerals, has simply

92 It is unlikely that the low number of ordinances could just be the result of lost evidence. Ordinances were important documents and the council started to collect them from the very beginning. A printer's invoice from 1576 (fig. 4.3.), for instance, reveals that only one of the Cologne ordinances printed between August 1575 and April 1576 did not survive in the city archive, see chapter four. Furthermore, printing items and posting them was only rarely discussed in the council meetings. In most cases the council decided that new regulations were passed on orally, see below.

93 Keussen (1899), 'Inhaltsverzeichniss zu den Sammlungen der Rathsedikte'.

94 *Ibid.*, p. 163, numbers 31, 34 and 39.

95 Most copies in HAStK, Best. 14 (Edikte): 29 are handwritten.

96 See appendix. Additionally, I was able to provide 13 editions from Keussen's list of undated ordinances with more approximate dates, Keussen (1899), 'Inhaltsverzeichniss zu den Sammlungen der Rathsedikte', pp. 316–318, nos. 3892 (appendix no. 41); 3878 (appendix no. 50, 70, 76); 3881 (appendix no. 69); 3889 (appendix no. 72, 86, 212); 3896 (appendix no. 78, 79, 98); 3879 (appendix no. 77, 81, 82); 3880 (appendix no. 83); 3888 (appendix no. 84); 3897 (appendix no. 85); 3891 (appendix no. 91); 3887 (appendix no. 224); 3885 (appendix no. 163, 246); 3886 (appendix no. 285).

97 Ghost editions are publications mentioned in bibliographies or secondary literature for which we have no further proof that an actual copy ever existed.

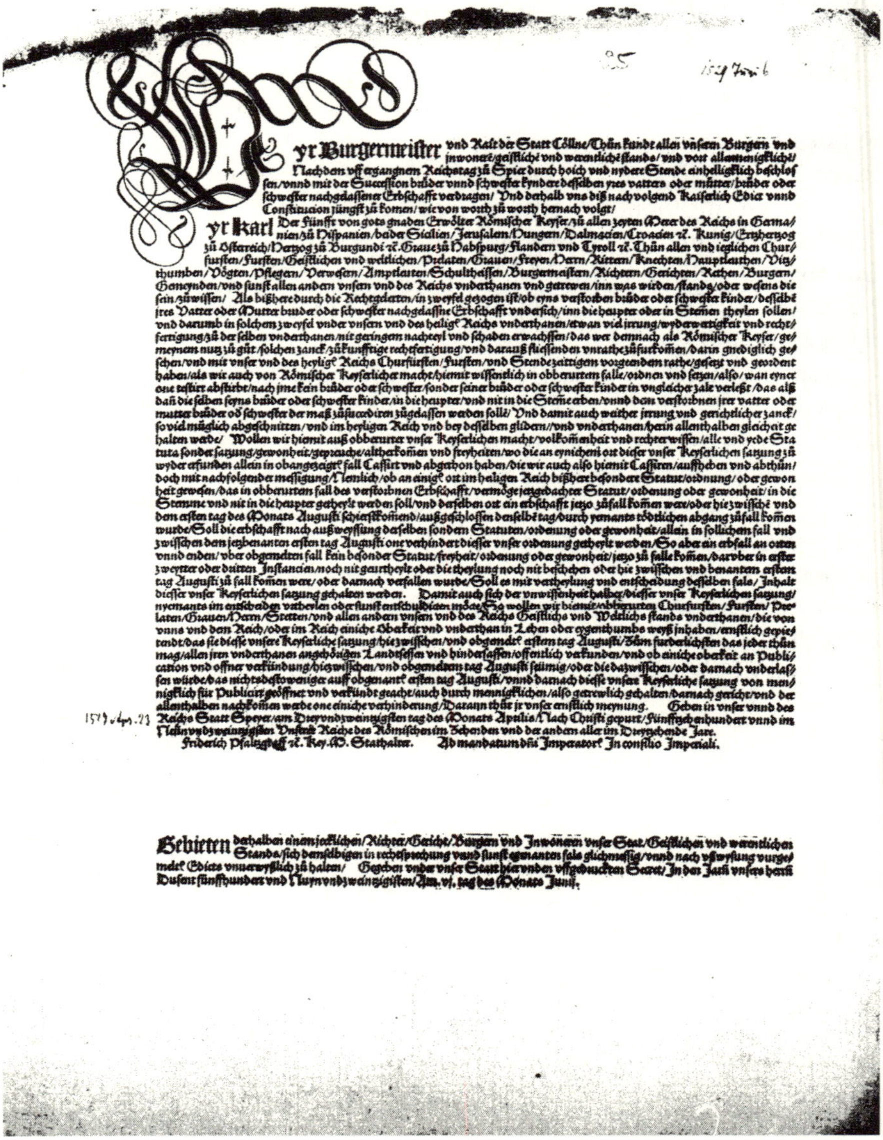

Fig. 3.3. Ordinance regulating inheritance, appendix no. 56. The imperial ordinance from Charles V is framed by an introductory and ending part written by the city council.

been misread. An ordinance regulating the sale of brandy, for instance, bears the date 'xxviij Ianuarij, Anno XCIIII'.[98] Whereas the day had been correctly identified as 28 January, the year has not been listed as [15]94 but instead as [15]44.[99] This introduced a number of ordinances purportedly printed in the 1540s that were actually printed at the very end of the century and were then, in most cases, listed twice in the repertory.[100] Other ordinances could simply not be located and verified.[101] On top of that, some ordinances were recorded as two separate items when in fact the regulations were printed on one and the same document.[102] Lastly, the repertory also inferred printed ordinances just because they were mentioned in later edicts. However, taking into consideration that the council only used the press to a very limited extent, I would suggest that these items were not printed.

After I had tracked down numerous hitherto unknown copies of the ordinances, compiled all their data, including references and links to digital copies, and created a list (see appendix) which was later uploaded to the USTC, I was able to construct the following graph for the first half of the sixteenth century (fig. 3.4.). This graph shows all 38 ordinances printed between 1500 and 1550.[103] Almost all of them contain an issue date at the end of the document that allows us to determine the years of their production, as the documents were generally printed within a few days after the council had agreed on the new regulation.[104] The graph shows that the production of ordinances is evenly spread over the first 50 years, with no distinguishable rise towards the end of the period. In fact, in the 1540s, there were even several years in which the council had no ordinances printed at all. This may partly be explained by the fact that there are 15 undated ordinances that were presumably produced in the mid-sixteenth century.[105] Some of these documents may well have been produced in the 1540s, others were probably produced after 1550. It is unlikely that these

98 Appendix no. 333.

99 Policey K, no. 1942.

100 See, for example, Policey K, no. 1940 (actually 1593); Policey K, no. 1950 (actually 1594); Policey K, no. 1951 (actually 1594); Policey K, no. 1971 (actually 1596); Policey K, no. 1972 (actually 1596); Policey K, no. 2004 (actually 1599); for other ordinances misdated in Policey K, see appendix 164, 200, 246 and 377.

101 See, for example, Policey K 1938.

102 See, for example, Policey K, no. 2712 and 2713, appendix no. 120.

103 See appendix nos. 28–72 (excluding nos. 30, 32, 33, 44, 45, 46, 47 which are not police ordinances, but invitations, contracts or explanations issued by the city council).

104 Limbach (2016), 'Tracing Lost Broadsheet Ordinances Printed in Sixteenth-Century Cologne', p. 498. Appendix nos. 28, 29, 50, 58, 63 were dated approximately.

105 See appendix nos. 73–87.

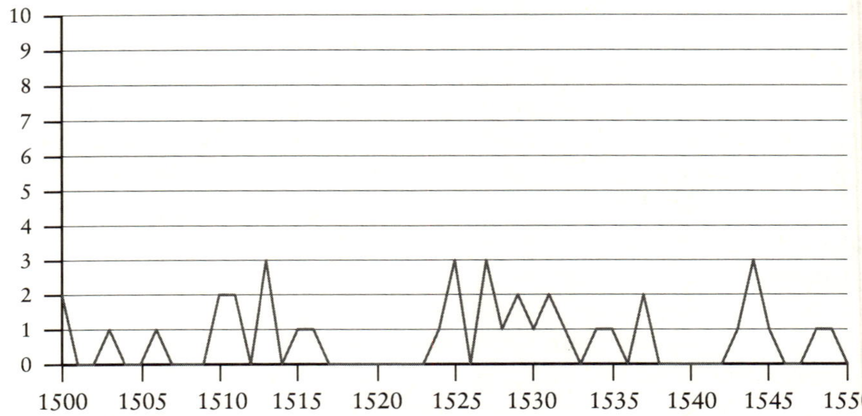

Fig. 3.4. Printed ordinances issued by the city council of Cologne produced in the first 50 years of the sixteenth century.

undated ordinances had an impact on the general trend of the council's use of print. The council only used the press to a limited extent throughout the first half of the sixteenth century.

The 38 dated ordinances produced up to 1550 fulfilled two main purposes: they included complex information, such as exchange rates, or stipulated orders for those who did not belong to a *Gaffel*.[106] As we have seen, the council primarily used oral means, like channelling information via the *Gaffeln*, to communicate new legislation to its subjects. However, such a procedure had one major disadvantage: it excluded foreigners. So, for instance, farmers who brought in their cattle from Neuss or Frisia would not necessarily hear about the new regulations for trading livestock. Similarly, merchants from the Netherlands or the northern part of the empire would not be aware of recent changes in the value of foreign coins in Cologne.

The printing press offered the ideal solution to this problem: the decisions of the council that addressed foreigners were published in print. This way they

106 On two occasions, in 1532 and 1542, this included the clergy living within the city walls. In both cases the council had an ordinance printed in an attempt to collect taxes, see Giel (1998), *Politische Öffentlichkeit im spätmittelalterlich-früh-neuzeitlichen Köln*, pp. 113–122. These two publications are exceptional as they primarily address a small group (the clergy) and not a general audience like the police ordinances or the invitations, contracts or explanations. Therefore, the two publications have not been included in this analysis and the appendix. The later publication (HAStK, A 64 – Convolut 2 – 1540–1552) is now available online: http://historischesarchivkoeln.de:8080/actaproweb/archive.xhtml?id=Vz++++++00102706hupp#Vz______00102706hupp [125/150].

could be affixed to walls, church doors, city gates, marketplaces, the town hall, and other prominent places.[107] On their way to the market, tradesmen from outside Cologne saw the printed edicts, which immediately made them aware of new legislation. Some ordinances even introduced the regulation with headings clearly addressing outsiders. When in 1515 the council published a bread ordinance, the sentence 'This is the ordinance, how, what and when foreign bread can be brought, offered and sold in Cologne' was clearly set apart from the main body of the text (fig. 3.5.).[108] Those foreign bakers who could not read were informed when they passed the city gates and the guards on site read out the ordinance to them. As seen in the first chapter, this was common practice in Tyrol and Württemberg, where ordinances regulating the use of firearms and the behaviour of beggars were read out to foreigners at the borders.

The production of ordinances in print, however, does not render the practice of communicating legislation orally obsolete. Instead, the two ways of communicating regulations coexisted. When in 1524 the council decided to publish legislation on the trade with flour imported from outside Cologne, the magistrates determined that some officials had to proclaim the ordinance at all 12 city gates and then post the printed edicts on the walls.[109] In December 1525, the council accepted a plea from the bakers' guild to prescribe rules for foreign bakers who sold their bread in Cologne. The council had this regulation printed and, again, pinned to the city gates.[110] Eight months later, in August 1526, the council employed the same procedure when the sale of foreign bread was still an issue of major concern.[111]

Although the council used printed ordinances to draw the attention of foreign merchants and tradesmen to recent legislation, it did not print every single ordinance that had implications for foreigners. The magistrates only addressed those issues that posed an immediate threat to their interest and finances. Thus, the council produced three bread ordinances in the years before 1550, when the

107 By the dawn of the sixteenth century, these places were commonly used for displaying ordinances. Already in 1482 two coinage ordinances were posted on the town hall in Munich, see EISERMANN (2003), '"Vil grozer brefe sint angeslagen"', pp. 483–484. See also SCHWERHOFF (2005a), 'Die große Welt im kleinen Raum. Zur Ver-Ortung überlokaler Kommunikationsräume in der Frühen Neuzeit', pp. 370–371.

108 Appendix no. 42. The original German text reads: 'Dyt is die ordenunge, wie, wa und wan[n]e men dat uyßwendige broit herbynnen Coelne brengen, vort veilehaven und v[e]kouffen sall.'

109 RB, III, p. 118 no. 424. Like Jerusalem, Cologne had 12 city gates, see SCHWERHOFF (1991), *Köln im Kreuzverhör*, p. 95.

110 Appendix no. 49 and RB, III, p. 279, no. 914.

111 RB, III, p. 330, no. 408. There is no dated ordinance from August 1526, but it could well be appendix no. 58 (dated c. 1530).

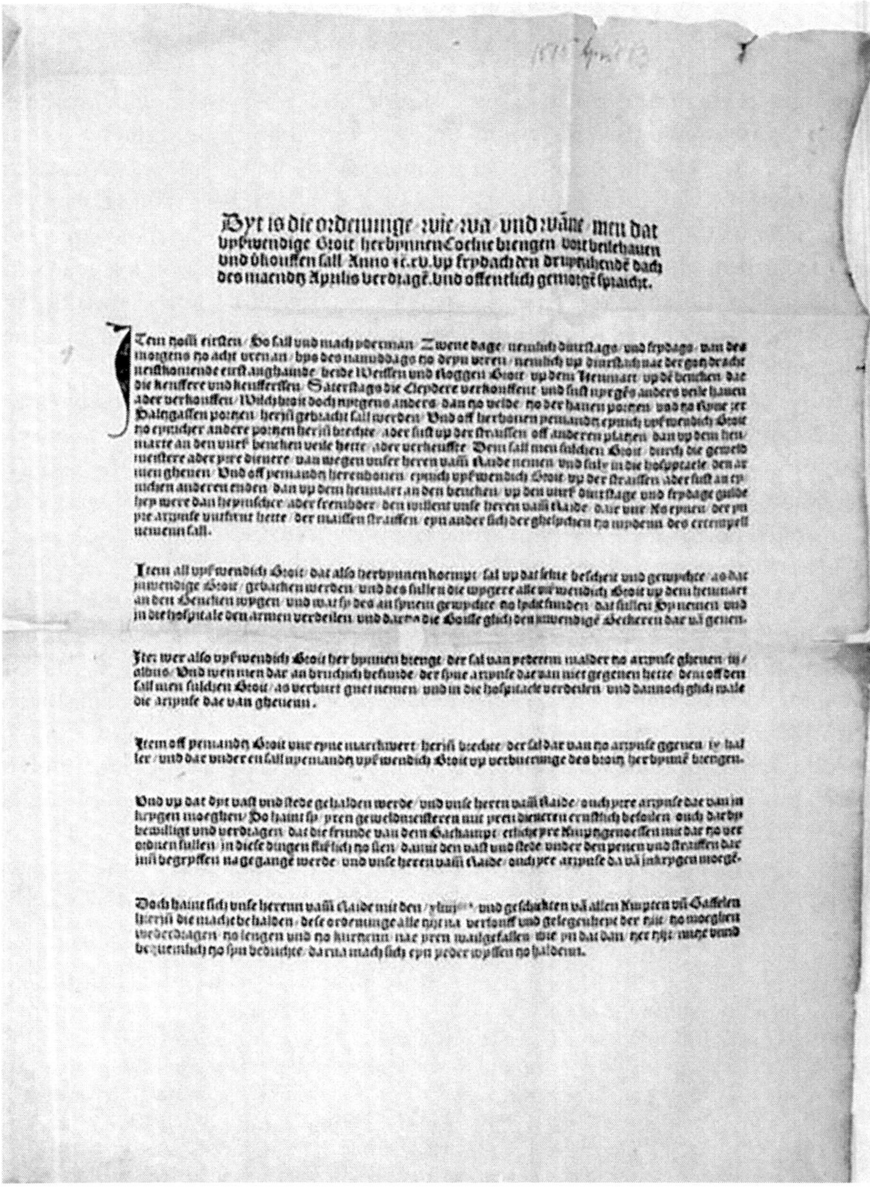

Dyt is die ordenunge / wie / wa / und wanne men dat
upsiwendige Broit herbynnen Coelne brengen vurbeilchauen
und verkouffen sall / Anno xc.xv. up frydach den druytzhende dach
des maendtz Aprilis verdragen. und offentlich gemoigt spraicht.

Fig. 3.5. Bread ordinance with distinct title addressing foreigners, appendix no. 42.

bakers in Cologne were seriously threatened by competition from outside.[112] Bread was one of the most important food products in German cities and offered welcome income not only for those working inside the city walls.[113] In addition, the council had another three ordinances printed that addressed excise, a tax on the sale of goods.[114] Unlike some other cities, the magistracy did not introduce a poll tax but relied solely on excise.[115] In principle, an excise duty had the further advantage that it was easily understood and should have been relatively easy to collect. But that did not prevent repeated attempts at evasion. To ensure that the city's finances remained sound, the magistrates went to considerable pains to make sure that the latest tariffs were made widely known through print.

Other issues that were not an immediate threat to the council's finances, however, did not justify the use of print in the first half of the sixteenth century. This included, among other things, rummaging swine in the street. The animals were not only a concern during processions, but also posed a challenge to the city's hygiene. During the early modern period, various civic governments, including the councils in Nuremberg and Ulm, tried to tackle the problem.[116] In Ulm, owners were only allowed to drive their pigs through the city between 11 am and noon.[117] In Cologne, pigs were a recurring concern for the magistrates. In the early modern period, the metropolis on the Rhine was one of the most important marketplaces for the sale of pigs.[118] Tradesmen from Frisia and the Emsland as well as breeders from more distant places such as Lorraine and Saxony brought their animals to the city on a regular basis. In order to sell them, the traders had to drive their animals through the streets. This not only created noise but also bad smells and dirt as the pigs left behind faeces.

This seems to have been a common problem not only in Cologne, but in many other cities, as we will see when we discuss the parallel case of Antwerp. The presence of pigs in the streets posed problems on multiple occasions. Yet, the council communicated new regulations orally until 1550. In addition to the yearly announcements prior to the Corpus Christi Procession, the council proclaimed regulations for pigs in the streets with a *special morning speech* on 8 April 1510.[119] When the council noticed that the animals were still an issue

112 Giel (1998), *Politische Öffentlichkeit im spätmittelalterlich-frühneuzeitlichen Köln*, p. 338; appendix nos. 42, 49 and 58.

113 Reit (1999), *Lohn und Leistung. Lohnformen im Gewerbe 1450–1900*, p. 263.

114 Appendix nos. 39, 40 and 52.

115 Isenmann (2014), *Die Deutsche Stadt im Mittelalter*, p. 526.

116 *Ibid.*, p. 467.

117 *Ibid.*

118 Eiden and Irsigler (2000), 'Environs and Hinterland. Cologne and Nuremberg in the Later Middle Ages', p. 47.

119 Policey K, no. 1377.

three years later, the magistrates reminded their officials to take better care of the issue.[120] A couple of years later, in early 1517, pigs were again discussed in the council's meeting. This time the magistrates introduced the following punishments: inhabitants of Cologne who infringed the regulations had to pay a fine, and if they transgressed three times, the pigs would be confiscated. Foreigners, however, faced punishments that were much more severe: if a foreigner was caught with his pigs, his animals would be confiscated straight away.[121] The introduction of these fees, however, did not improve the situation for long, and in 1523, 1524, 1549, and 1550 pigs were again troubling the magistrates.[122] Despite this, the magistrates did not have a single ordinance printed until the 1550s that addressed the issue. The council only referred to the many *morning speeches* on this topic when it lamented that pigs in the streets were still a problem in Cologne in the mid-sixteenth century.[123]

Another issue which was frequently discussed in the council meetings but which did not lead to the publication of many printed ordinances (at least at first), was the presence of followers of the new faith in Cologne. Although the council made it very clear that it would not tolerate Lutheranism within its jurisdiction, there were, nevertheless, a number of Protestants in the Catholic city.[124] This is particularly true for the time period between the 1520s to the late 1540s, when Archbishop Hermann von Wied tried to introduce Protestant reform in his territory.[125]

In these two decades, there were many instances when the council discussed the circulation of Luther's books despite the fact that they were banned in Cologne. In October 1523, for instance, the council decided to imprison a man for disregarding the ban on Lutheran books and selling copies.[126] A few months later, in April 1524, Luther's books were sold again in the city. This time the man who sold them also slapped a Dominican monk in the face, presumably during a heated argument about religion.[127] As the situation did not improve, the council decided in August 1524 to instruct every printer and bookseller to neither produce nor sell Lutheran books.[128] Despite the reiteration of the ban,

120 RB, II, p. 136, no. 1120.
121 RB, II, p. 364, no. 27.
122 RB, III, pp. 16–17, no. 146; RB, III, p. 159, no. 833; RB, V, p. 707, no. 413; RB, V, p. 815, no. 394.
123 RB, V, p. 815, no. 394.
124 Schmitz (2017), 'Beten und Lesen im Untergrund', p. 87. See, for instance, RB, III, p. 99, no. 238.
125 Schlüter (2005), *Flug- und Streitschriften zur 'Kölner Reformation'*.
126 RB, III, p. 59, no. 568.
127 RB, III, p. 102, no. 273.
128 RB, III, p. 144, no. 683.

a year later the books were still circulating within the council's jurisdiction and thus the council entrusted officials to confiscate them.[129] Nevertheless, the magistrates could not stop the sale completely, and in 1527, it was brought to the council's attention that Lutheran books were even sold in the cathedral, right under the nose of the Catholic authorities.[130]

For a long time, the magistrates tried to tackle the issue just with more traditional means of communication. When in 1524 the councillors instructed the printers to not publish any books deemed to be heretical, they did so personally.[131] There are no indications in the council minutes around that time that indicate the production of a printed ordinance regulating the sale of heretic books.

Only from the 1540s onwards did the council produce printed ordinances addressing blasphemy, religious dissidence, and the production of books deemed heretical.[132] So, for instance, in 1544 the council decided that blasphemy should be addressed and specifically mentions the production of a printed document.[133] A few years later, on 24 September 1548, the council discussed the appearance of a messenger who had posted the imperial ban of heretic books on a chapel the day before the meeting.[134] The magistrates decided that this ban should be printed and exhibited at all gates and churches. On top of that, copies should be brought to all *Gaffeln*.

With merchants and tradesmen visiting not only from territories within the Holy Roman Empire, but also from countries all over Europe, one issue was crucial to uphold the flourishing trade: the exchange of money. The use of coins was one of the major concerns of the city council during the sixteenth century. In the course of the Middle Ages, the royal privilege of minting coins had been abandoned.[135] From then on many of the princedoms, duchies, bishoprics, and cities had begun to produce their own money. Consequently, a huge variety of different coins circulated within the empire. Merchants paid in Gulden, Mark, Albus, Schilling, Weißpfennig, Raderalbus, Heller, Denare, Pfennig, and many other denominations. By 1500, about 600 local authorities had the privilege to

129 RB, III, p. 242, no. 569.
130 RB, III, p. 394, no. 246.
131 RB, III, p. 144, no. 683.
132 Appendix nos. 68, 70, 71. For appendix no. 50 Policey K states that it was probably produced around 1525 – due to the layout of the document and its content. However, it seems much more likely that the broadsheet was produced in the 1540s, like the other documents addressing this issue.
133 RB, V, p. 226, no. 296. The printed document was issued five days later, see appendix no. 68.
134 RB, V, pp. 624–625, no. 493. The printed document was issued a day later, see appendix no 71.
135 Schmitz (1990), *Die Überlieferung deutscher Texte im Kölner Buchdruck*, p. 271.

mint and – on top of that – forgery was widely practised.[136] On top of that, numerous coins from other European countries found their way into the city. As a result, sixteenth-century Cologne was swamped with a multitude of currencies.

To ensure smooth sales transactions, the council repeatedly addressed the use of coins. Since the 1440s, the magistrates had primarily addressed the issue with oral proclamations.[137] Yet, this did not suffice. If a merchant arrived just one day after the proclamation had taken place, he would not necessarily have heard about the new law. With the help of printed documents, however, the magistrates gave their recent decisions permanence. The new value of specific coins could be openly displayed and consulted long after the oral proclamation.

Printing coin ordinances offered another great advantage. Complex information, such as an overview of the many coins accepted in Cologne as well as their respective value, was now easily accessible. Stipulating such information in public assemblies must have led to disagreement and conflict, as so many details were impossible to communicate in this form. The council probably had to settle many disputes between two disputing parties each claiming they had heard the coin had a different value. The publication of an exchange list was a good way to prevent such disputes and save the councillors' valuable time.

The council used print to produce coin ordinances from an early date. The first edict of this kind had already been printed at the end of the fifteenth century, following the practice of other rulers such as the Elector of Saxony, who had published a similar coin ordinance in 1490 and ordered it to be displayed openly.[138] On 12 March 1493, the magistrates of Cologne agreed with the Archbishop of Cologne as well as the neighbouring Duke of Jülich to introduce new silver coins: Doppelbuschen, Buschen, and Halbe Buschen.[139] The three authorities determined that the old coins could still be used for a couple of months but had to be exchanged by the feast day of St Remigius (1 October).[140]

The printed edict was produced on a half-sheet measuring only 33.0 × 22.4 cm.[141] The text of the ordinance was densely printed and covered more than 70 lines. Much of this text was dedicated to the details of the agreement between the city, the archbishop, and the Duke of Jülich. At the end, the council

136 Whaley (2012), *Germany and the Holy Roman Empire*, I, p. 366. In the early 1480s, local authorities in Northern Germany confiscated 4 tons of forged coins, see Griese (1997) 'Falsche Gulden, gefälschte Ablässe, unerwünschte Bischöfe', p. 50.

137 Giel (1998), *Politische Öffentlichkeit im spätmittelalterlich-frühneuzeitlichen Köln*, pp. 60–61.

138 USTC 745012 (VE15, F-108); the original German text reads: 'durch anschlahu[n]g offentlicher zedeln'.

139 Ennen (1863–1880), *Geschichte der Stadt Köln*, III, pp. 901–902.

140 USTC 744094 (VE15 K-29).

141 See additional information in VE15 (K-29).

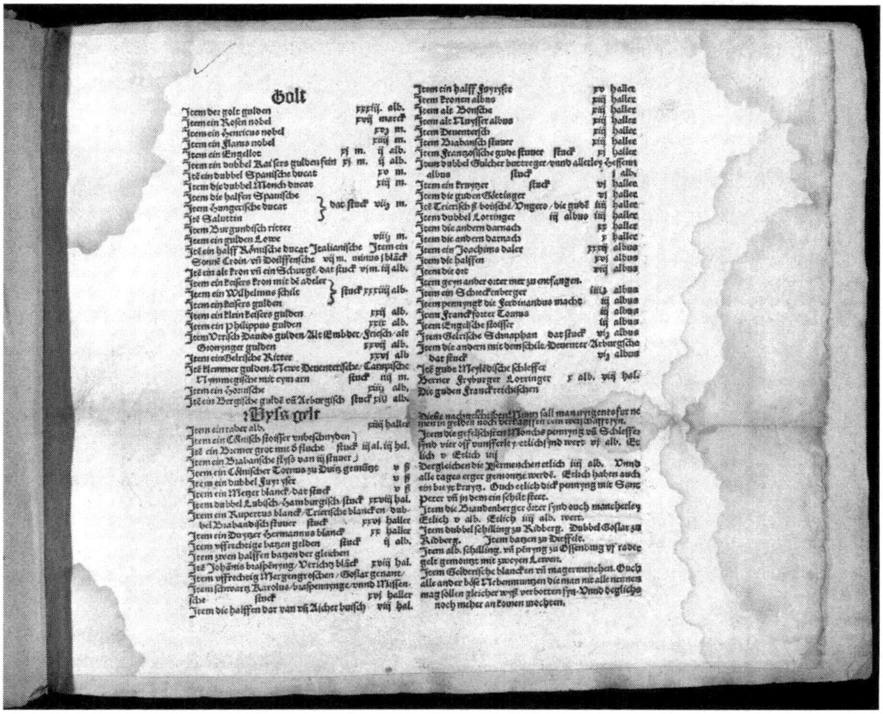

Fig. 3.6. Coin ordinance from around 1500, appendix no. 28.

included additional information about the Gold Gulden and how its value had increased in the last 24 years. The value of a Gold Gulden is given in Weißpfennig for every single year of this period. Whereas in 1468 the Gold Gulden was equivalent to 25 Weißpfennige, its value had increased to 30 Weißpfennige only 11 years later. By the time of the agreement between the city and the two princes, the Gold Gulden was worth 36 Weißpfennige. By including this information, the council facilitated the introduction of the new coins in October. If subjects insisted that they had obtained a Gold Gulden for fewer than 36 Weißpfennig, the council could show precisely how the value had changed over time.

A few weeks later, on 8 May 1493, the council published another ordinance that specified the introduction of new silver coins. In this ordinance the magistrates provided a detailed overview of how exactly the 'light and heavy silver' coins should be exchanged by the feast day of St Remigius.[142] The magistrates

142 USTC 744100 (VE15 K-30); the original German text reads: 'silvere[n] lychte ind swaire muntz'.

appended a list of 21 coins and their respective exchange rates. This list contained coins from neighbouring territories such as Jülich, Cleves, and Neuss, but also from more distant trading centres such as Deventer and Trier. The printed edict also included a sentence at the very end of the text that stated that the regulation was communicated with the help of a *special morning speech*.[143] This illustrates again how the two media, oral proclamation and print, coexisted. With the *morning speech*, the council informed Cologne's inhabitants directly, whereas the printed edict helped to inform the many visitors. This way everyone who traded within the city walls was acquainted with the latest regulations.

The council employed references to *morning speeches* for 20 years after it had started to print ordinances. A coin ordinance from 1506, for example, mentions the *morning speech* at the very end and it is even in capital letters, which demonstrates how important it was for the council to stress the oral proclamation.[144] Traders from outside would know immediately that everyone living in the city was familiar with this new regulation. According to the council's minutes, this particular *morning speech* took place on Monday, 30 March.[145] The printed edict was presumably produced shortly afterwards. The council employed both techniques in 1515 again, when it issued another ordinance on the sale of bread. This ordinance similarly mentions the fact that the new legislation was made known on 13 April with the help of a *morning speech*.[146]

Given the practical benefits of printed coin ordinances, it is hardly surprising that out of the 38 ordinances produced in the first half of the century, 18 addressed the circulation of coins.[147] In the first decade of the century, five out of six printed edicts addressed coinage.[148] The other ordinance specified regulations for the processions of Cardinal Peraudi, the famous indulgence preacher, who visited Cologne in 1503.[149] Undoubtedly, this extraordinary event drew thousands of people to the city. Thus it made sense to produce an ordinance in print to inform every visitor about the procession as well as the regulations surrounding the event. In the following decade, the council had seven ordinances printed, of which three addressed coinage.[150] The other ordinances regulated the sale of foreign bread as well as excise.[151]

143 The original German text reads: 'Dit is uyffgeroissen ind gemorgenspraicht.'
144 Appendix no. 34.
145 RB, I, p. 860, no. 6.
146 Appendix no. 42.
147 Appendix nos. 28, 29, 34, 35, 36, 37, 38, 43, 48, 54, 59, 61, 62, 63, 64, 65, 66, 72.
148 Appendix nos. 28, 29, 34, 35, 36 (nos. 30, 32, 33 are not police ordinances, but an invitation or explanation).
149 Appendix no. 31. On Peraudi's indulgence campaign, see Eisermann (2011), 'Der Ablass als Medienereignis', and Pettegree (2015), *Brand Luther*, pp. 56–58.
150 Appendix nos. 37–43; ordinances addressing coinage: appendix nos. 37, 38, 43.
151 Appendix nos. 39, 40, 41, 42.

The many coinage edicts offer a vivid insight into the variety of currencies circulating in sixteenth-century Cologne, and thus how vital it was to regulate them. From one edict of 1516, it becomes obvious that not only coins from nearby Neuss, but also from other major trading centres like Basel or Frankfurt were commonly used in the Rhineland. Additionally, coins from places even farther away such as Burgundy and Brabant frequently found their way to Cologne.

The coin ordinances printed in Cologne in the first half of the sixteenth century form two different groups, of which one presented recent agreements. The very first printed coin edict from 1493 serves as a prime example. It explained in detail what the city, the archbishop, and the Duke of Jülich had agreed on. This was valid for the next 20 years and was made public not only in Cologne, but also in the archdiocese and the duchy.[152] One year later, in 1494, the three parties decided that the value for silver stipulated in the ordinance was too low, so the ordinance was amended and reissued.[153] The council continued to publish such agreements in the sixteenth century.[154]

The second group of coinage edicts provided conversion tables. These tables give a good overview of foreign currencies and how they related to money used in Cologne. A coin commonly used in the early modern Rhineland was the Albus, which in Cologne equalled 2 Schilling.[155] In an edict of 1516, foreign currencies were converted to this Albus.[156] So, for instance, a Dubbel Gobler was worth as much as 1 Albus at that time. Such information was vital for sixteenth-century traders, and to have it in printed form ensured smooth sales transactions.

'In these dangerous times' – printed ordinances in Cologne 1550–1600

From the mid-sixteenth century onwards, the council made increasing use of print to communicate regulations, as fig. 3.7. shows. The total of 300 dated ordinances printed between 1550 and 1600 represents a 600 % increase over the number of ordinances produced in the previous 50 years (38 items).[157] This

152 Schmitz (ed.) (1979), *Die Kölner Einblattdrucke*, p. 27. In his catalogue, the two broadsheets can be found as numbers 20 and 82.

153 USTC 744103 (VE 15 K-28); Schmitz (ed.) (1979), *Die Kölner Einblattdrucke*, p. 27.

154 See, for instance, appendix nos. 37 and 38.

155 Giel (1998), *Politische Öffentlichkeit im spätmittelalterlich-frühneuzeitlichen Köln*, p. 358.

156 Appendix no. 43.

157 Appendix nos. 88–385 (excluding no. 208, which is an invitation and not a police ordinance) and the three guard ordinances in pamphlet form: USTC

means that the average number of ordinances produced per year rose significantly, from one to six. In the first 50 years, the number of ordinances had been more or less evenly spread. While some of this increase may be explained with a general rise in documentation, we see that the numbers fluctuated and peaked in particularly troublesome years, especially in the time between 1560 and 1590, when Cologne experienced much turbulence. In 1581, the council was exceptionally active, producing a total of 17 ordinances in print.[158] As can be seen below, this was an extraordinarily difficult year to which the magistrates reacted with a number of regulations that were not only communicated orally but also printed and exhibited. After this peak, however, the number of ordinances per year declined again until in the 1590s only an average of seven ordinances were produced per year.

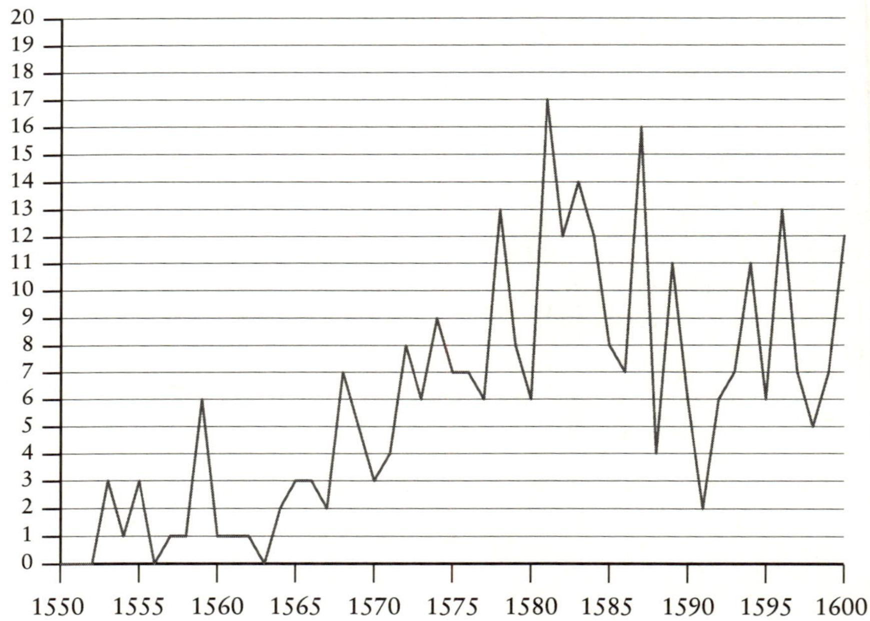

Fig. 3.7. Printed ordinances issued by the city council of Cologne produced in the last 50 years of the sixteenth century.

677227 (VD16 K 1808), USTC 704779 (VD16 ZV 9097) and USTC 677228 (VD16 ZV 9098).

158 Appendix nos. 205–222 (excluding no. 208, which is an invitation and not a police ordinance).

The rise in printed ordinances reflects the overall inflation of ordinances issued in the second half of the sixteenth century.[159] Fig. 3.8. shows the total amount of ordinances issued per year with the printed ones displayed in a darker colour. We can see this particularly clearly between 1560–1600, when the council issued an average of 34 ordinances per year. Again, we see that the number of ordinances is particularly high in the 1580s, especially in the early years; in 1581, 1582, and 1583, the council issued 42, 41, and 48 ordinances, of which 17, 12, and 14 were printed.[160] Then, just like the number of printed ordinances, the total number of ordinances dropped in 1591.

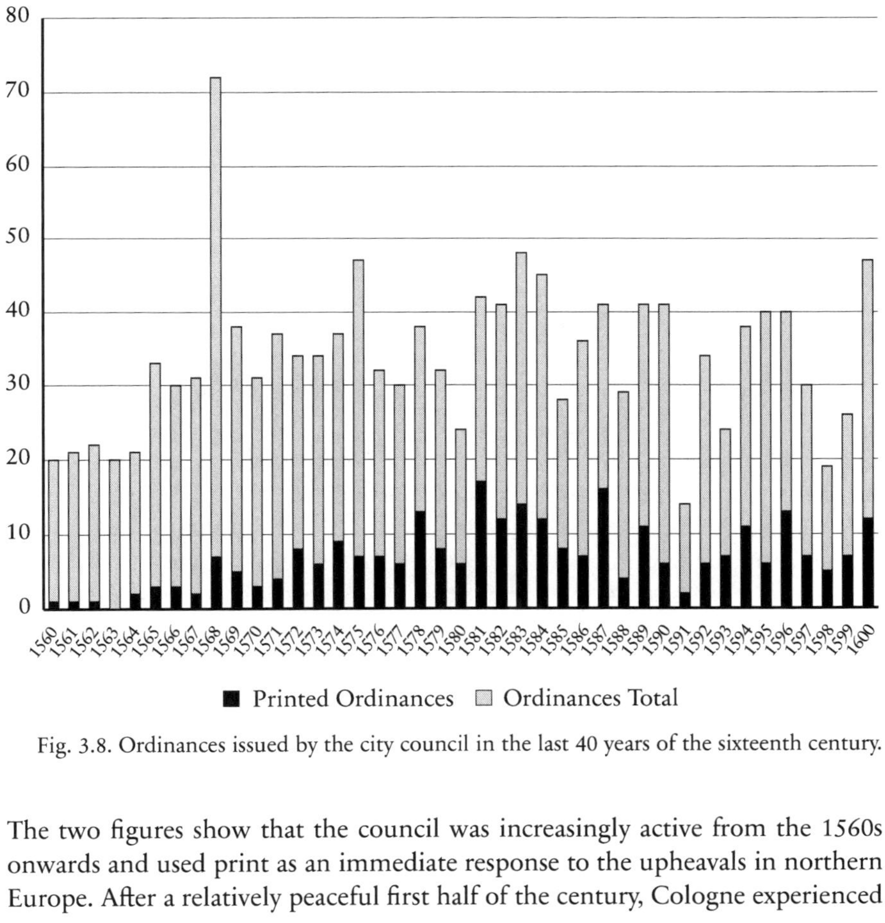

Fig. 3.8. Ordinances issued by the city council in the last 40 years of the sixteenth century.

The two figures show that the council was increasingly active from the 1560s onwards and used print as an immediate response to the upheavals in northern Europe. After a relatively peaceful first half of the century, Cologne experienced

159 This data visualises the ordinances listed in Policey K, nos. 2472–3890.

160 Policey K nos. 3170–3300; appendix nos. 205–248 (excluding no. 208, which is an invitation and not a police ordinance).

considerable turbulence in the years after 1550. Economically, the Little Ice Age caused significant harvest failures and widespread food shortages; politically, the city had to defend its freedom, which culminated in the 1580s when the Archbishop of Cologne on several occasions threatened to take over the city.[161] The Counter-Reformation as well as continuous warfare all over the continent brought further disturbance and triggered a wave of refugees from northern and western Europe seeking shelter in the northern part of the empire.[162] From the start of the Dutch Revolt in 1566, thousands of people left their homes to find peace in other countries. These refugees were joined by people fleeing from the Wars of Religion in France, especially after the St Bartholomew Massacre in 1572.[163] As a result, Europe witnessed a mass exodus of approximately 250,000 people.[164]

Many crossed the borders to the Holy Roman Empire and settled in large trading centres, such as Basel and Strasbourg. Cologne in particular attracted many different groups of foreigners.[165] As the city had long-established trading relations with the Netherlands, numerous merchants took the opportunity to find refuge and continue their businesses in the metropolis on the Rhine.[166] On top of that, the rich religious infrastructure appealed to numerous Catholic clerics, including expelled bishops from Roermond, Middelburg, 's-Hertogenbosch and Leeuwarden.[167] For them, Cologne became a safe haven in times of religious unrest.

It is difficult to estimate how much of an impact the many migrants had on the total number of inhabitants in sixteenth-century Cologne. It has been estimated that about 2,000 refugees from the Netherlands settled in the city in the first decade after the Dutch Revolt (1568–1578).[168] The fall of Antwerp in 1585 brought a similar number of migrants.[169] Yet, the total number of inhabitants fluctuated in this time, especially since many foreigners only stayed for a short period of time. The efforts of the council to limit the rights of Protestants, especially from the 1570s onwards, caused thousands to leave the city.[170]

161 Schwerhoff (1991), *Köln im Kreuzverhör*, p. 40.

162 Schilling (1972), *Niederländische Exulanten im 16. Jahrhundert*, p. 13.

163 Grell (1994), 'Merchants and ministers: the foundation of international Calvinism', p. 256.

164 Grell (2011), *Brethren in Christ. A Calvinist Network in Reformation Europe*, p. 4.

165 Janssen (2014), *The Dutch Revolt and Catholic Exile in Reformation Europe*, p. 62.

166 Janssen (2012), 'The Counter-Reformation of the Refugee: Exile and the Shaping of Catholic Militancy in the Dutch Revolt', p. 678.

167 Janssen (2014), *The Dutch Revolt and Catholic Exile in Reformation Europe*, p. 65.

168 Schilling (1972), *Niederländische Exulanten im 16. Jahrhundert*, p. 59.

169 *Ibid.*

170 Mallinckrodt (2005), *Struktur und kollektiver Eigensinn. Kölner Laienbruderschaften im Zeitalter der Konfessionalisierung*, p. 88.

As modern-day scholars have no reliable accounts on the total number of inhabitants in Cologne at that particular time, it is difficult to assess to what extent the number of inhabitants grew from the 1560s onwards. There are unfortunately no tax lists that would provide us with a clearer picture, not least because, as we have seen, Cologne did not introduce poll taxes but instead relied on excise.[171]

Yet, personal accounts of contemporaries show that the many foreigners were clearly visible to the inhabitants of Cologne. Economically the city benefitted from the many, mostly wealthy, refugees.[172] However, the sudden presence of thousands of foreigners also caused severe problems. The diary of Hermann Weinsberg, a councillor who noted meticulously any event worth remembering, offers us unique insights into the reactions of the townspeople towards the many refugees.[173] On 2 January 1570, Weinsberg noted a discussion between several council members and various clerics. Whereas the councillors pointed out that the high number of foreigners drove up prices of every day necessities, such as charcoal, meat, fish, and butter, some of the clerics insisted that Cologne had to have pity for the misery of the refugees and thus needed to welcome them with compassion.[174]

This discussion probably reflected the mixed feelings of most inhabitants, torn between their Christian ideals and economic realities. In addition to the shortage of food supplies, the sheer number of migrants put pressure on the housing market. Weinsberg's diary, again, offers us great insights into the changed circumstances in the second half of the sixteenth century. On 16 March 1580, Weinsberg observed that 'the city was full with people so that no house [in Cologne] was unoccupied because of the war in the Netherlands'.[175] For Weinsberg, who earned an extra income as a landlord, this was not a particular problem: quite the contrary, in fact, as he could easily rent his properties during this time. Yet, for the civic authorities, the overcrowding posed particular problems, not least issues of hygiene and security.

171 Gibbs (2009), 'Immigration and Civic Identity in Sixteenth-Century Cologne', p. 55.

172 Janssen (2014), *The Dutch Revolt and Catholic Exile in Reformation Europe*, p. 71.

173 Hermann Weinsberg's fascinating account on sixteenth-century Cologne has recently gained more attention in the Anglophone world, see Lundin (2012), *Paper Memory.*

174 Weinsberg, *Die autobiographischen Aufzeichnungen des Hermann Weinsberg. Digitale Gesamtausgabe*. Available at www.weinsberg.uni-bonn.de. The original text reads: 'weren sei uis barmherzicheit in irem ellende zu herbergen'.

175 *Ibid.* The original German text reads: 'Die stat war eitz durch und durch mit folk besatz, das kein heuser ledich stunden, das macht der kreich in den Nederlanden.'

In order to implement new legislation effectively, which upheld certain hygienic standards as well as guaranteeing security, the council could no longer communicate regulations solely via the *Gaffeln*. Numerous foreigners were not affiliated to a *Gaffel*, as membership was restricted and could only be obtained in two ways.[176] First and foremost, foreigners could purchase citizenship.[177] Yet, this involved a considerable sum of money, which not all foreigners had at their disposal, especially after a long and difficult journey to safety. Secondly, foreigners could join a *Gaffel* by becoming lawful residents, swearing an oath to support the city. This option, however, was only available for Catholics. After the influx of migrants, the council increasingly, and successfully, tried to limit the rights of Protestants in Cologne. Finally, many foreigners only stayed in Cologne for a short period of time. Once the conflict in their hometowns had calmed down, as for example after the surrender of Antwerp, numerous migrants returned to their home soil, a movement very much encouraged by the Habsburgs.[178] Undoubtedly, those who just waited in Cologne until the worst was over did not trouble themselves with becoming active in the political life of the city by, for instance, seeking affiliations to a *Gaffel*.

Therefore, to inform everyone living inside the city walls, including those who did not belong to a *Gaffel*, the council increasingly relied on other methods to communicate new regulations. The dual practice of displaying the ordinances publicly as well as proclaiming them orally, promised more success. The posted announcements then served as a visual reminder of what had been proclaimed. Although the many printed ordinances in the second half of the sixteenth century do not, unfortunately, contain instructions for their publication, we may well assume that many were published in exactly the same fashion as the bread ordinance in 1524 or the coin ordinance in 1484.[179]

Posting ordinances within the city also promised other benefits for the councillors. Firstly, the placards showed that the city fathers were trying to solve current problems. By displaying numerous orders on walls, doors, and buildings, the magistrates emphasised their activity: a good response to crisis. Secondly, the ordinances conveyed the perspective of the city council on recent events. Such an official view was especially important during the Cologne War, which was accompanied by dozens of news sheets, pamphlets, and printed reports.[180] Among these many publications, the broadsheets clearly stood out.

176 Janssen (2011), 'Quo Vadis? Catholic Perceptions of Flight and the Revolt of the Low Countries, 1566–1609', p. 482.

177 Deeters (1987), 'Das Bürgerrecht der Reichsstadt Köln seit 1396', pp. 5–9.

178 Janssen (2014), *The Dutch Revolt and Catholic Exile in Reformation Europe*, p. 135.

179 See above.

180 Schnurr (2009a), *Religionskonflikt und Öffentlichkeit. Eine Mediengeschichte des Kölner Krieges (1582 bis 1590)*.

Thirdly, the placards served as symbols of power. On the way to conduct their daily business, the inhabitants of Cologne were constantly reminded that the magistrates were in charge of implementing new legislation and ruled over the city. In an age where symbols were of vital importance to rulership, manifesting authority in such a visual way was an important means to communicate power.[181]

Lastly, the magistrates also increased their use of the city's pulpits, especially when bad weather conditions threatened the city. In contrast to other ordinances, the text of the regulations intended to be read out by priests did not start with 'We mayors and council of Cologne', but instead with 'Following the wishes of the city council of Cologne the pastors and preachers should announce the following from the pulpit to the people next Sunday.'[182] By late 1580, the city had endured a long drought during both the summer and autumn months, which affected its water supply. Therefore, in November, the council distributed a printed ordinance among the priests so that they could instruct their congregations that every household had to have a cask of water ready in case of fires.[183] Later that month, the council used the pulpits again to order everyone to send a strong man to help with the reinforcement of the river banks.[184] The annual celebration of the 'Peter-Winkel-Feuer' posed a particular threat at that time. The ritual, also known as *Petri-Kettenfeier*, took place every year on 1 August to commemorate St Peter's liberation from his chains in Jerusalem where King Herod had imprisoned him. For the celebration, people gathered in front of bonfires built on the streets with the bravest men jumping over the flames.[185] As Cologne suffered from drought, the council wanted to prevent any fire from spreading. Whereas in 1568 and in July 1580, the council only instructed the priests orally to communicate that every inhabitant of Cologne should abstain from the annual celebrations, it used a printed document in 1581.[186]

181 Stollberg-Rilinger and Neu (2013), 'Einleitung', pp. 24–25.

182 See, for example, appendix no. 312. The original German text reads: 'Auff begeren eines Erbaren Rahts der Statt Cölln sollen die Herrn Pastoren und Predicanten negst Sontag [...] dem Volck auff der Cantzel verkündigen.'

183 Appendix no. 200.

184 Appendix no. 203.

185 Bächtold-Stäubli (ed.) (1927–1942), *Handwörterbuch des deutschen Aberglaubens*, VI, col. 1526.

186 Giel refers to the council minutes as well as a handwritten copy, see Giel (1998), *Politische Öffentlichkeit im spätmittelalterlich-frühneuzeitlichen Köln*, p. 47, fn. 27; appendix no. 213. In this context it is very interesting that no printed ordinance addressed the consequences of bad weather when, for instance, in 1570/1571 Cologne experienced heavy snow or, on another occasion, the river iced up all

In these troubled and difficult times, the magistrates also took steps to limit the spread of diseases. Already in 1558, the council published its first regulation on this matter, banning the discharge of dirt in the streets as well as limiting the presence of sick people in certain areas.[187] The ordinance also banned everyone from keeping their pigs in the streets. As mentioned above, in the first half of the sixteenth century, the council addressed problems with pigs solely by word of mouth. Now in 1558, the council included regulations concerning pigs in their printed ordinance. To encourage obedience, the council appointed several officials to keep the streets clean. The magistrates also stipulated that beggars and sick people who had open wounds or suffered from other diseases should dress their wounds appropriately and avoid sitting on the road or in front of churches. Separating the healthy from the sick in this manner certainly helped to combat the spread of diseases.

Over the next decades, when Cologne hosted an ever-increasing number of refugees, the council repeatedly issued regulations for dirt and excrement. In November 1568, the magistrates again banned pigs from the streets.[188] A few months later, in July 1569, the council issued another edict that addressed the pollution of watering holes in the city.[189] The city's hygiene and its supply of clean drinking water was now a top priority for the council. Up to the end of the sixteenth century, the council would produce five more ordinances to uphold standards of hygiene in the city.[190]

Another pressing concern was the issue of the city's safety. This holds especially true during the turbulent time of the Cologne War (1582–1590). During the entire sixteenth century, the council lived in constant fear that the archbishop, as former overlord, might bring the city back under his control. When Archbishop Gebhard Truchsess von Waldburg converted to Protestantism in 1582, this precipitated an armed conflict that not only affected the archbishopric but also the imperial city.

After 1550, the council issued no fewer than 57 ordinances addressing various security matters.[191] This was an impressive amount: it meant that one in six

the way down to its bed in the 1560s. For more information on these weather phenomena, see Behringer (2010), *A Cultural History of Climate*, pp. 136 and 91.

187 Appendix no. 96.

188 Appendix no. 122.

189 Appendix no. 124.

190 Appendix nos. 158, 229, 293, 313, 356.

191 Appendix nos. 100, 101, 115, 119, 120, 125, 132, 140, 145, 150, 163, 164, 166, 169, 192, 200, 213, 216, 219, 220, 223, 230, 232, 233, 235, 236, 237, 239, 240, 241, 243, 244, 245, 246, 247, 248, 254, 260, 262, 263, 264, 267, 270, 271, 272, 285, 292, 300, 303, 310, 325, 336, 365, 372 and USTC 677227 (VD16 K 1808), USTC 677228 (VD16 ZV 9098), USTC 704779 (VD16 ZV 9097).

ordinances addressed security at that time. Several of these ordinances included the council's guarantee of safe conduct for those who brought victuals to the city. Already in 1528, 1529, and 1531, the city had issued such printed ordinances.[192] After the outbreak of the Dutch Revolt, the magistrates had such safe conduct ordinances printed again.[193] In one of the ordinances, dated 1576, the councillors even explicitly mentioned the protection of Dutch traders.[194] In this way the councillors tried to limit disputes between the refugees and the Dutch merchants who might have contrasting ideas about recent developments in their home country.

The city's security was also threatened by criminals, who infiltrated the city alongside the many migrants. The council was determined to keep track of everyone who settled in Cologne. In April 1569, the councillors published an edict that ordered every foreigner who had not announced his presence to the authorities to leave Cologne within three days.[195] Several years later, in February 1574, the council had an ordinance published that instructed everyone who hosted beggars and foreigners to keep a close eye on them and report any suspicious activities.[196] The sixteenth century saw an increase in beggars, who were particularly drawn to Cologne with its rich religious culture that cared for those in need.[197] With the ordinance the council also informed its subjects that several officials were in charge of searching houses and entitled to arrest everyone who appeared to act against the city's law. Only two years later, foreigners and beggars were again a major concern for the authorities. This time the council published an ordinance to be read out from all pulpits in Cologne. The preachers were to instruct their congregation that every beggar who had come to the city in the past seven years had to leave.[198]

It is not surprising that the defence of the city was of utmost importance and had to be improved significantly to meet the challenges posed by the developments post-1550. Since 1396, when Cologne had established its own constitution, the *Gaffeln* were in charge of guarding the city, and their duties were specified in two ordinances, a *Wachtmeisterrolle* and a guard ordinance from

192 Appendix nos. 55, 57, 60.
193 Appendix nos. 115, 132, 145, 169.
194 Appendix no. 169.
195 Appendix no. 125.
196 Appendix no. 150.
197 Irsigler (1980), 'Bettler, Dirnen und Henker im spätmittelalterlichen und frühneuzeitlichen Köln. Zur Analyse sozialer Randgruppen', pp. 37–38.
198 Appendix no. 165. In Antwerp, the authorities even handed out printed chits on which they wrote the beggar's name, telling them to leave the city within 24 hours, see Pettegree (2017b), 'Broadsheets: Single-Sheet Publishing in the First Age of Print. Typology and Typography', p. 21.

1462.[199] According to these two handwritten documents, every *Gaffel* elected a number of members who were on duty during the night.[200] During peaceful times, the selection of two *Gaffeln* sufficed, so that the 22 *Gaffeln* were able to take turns. Yet, when Cologne was facing troubles, the councillors needed to increase patrols and thus summoned the representatives of all *Gaffeln*.

During the first half of the sixteenth century, this system worked well. As a result, the council did not need to introduce any larger changes and manuscript copies of the guard ordinances sufficed.[201] If necessary, the magistrates created another handwritten copy and gave it to the officials in charge. In case people disregarded parts of the regulation, the council ordered the officials to remind the offenders of the details of the guard ordinance. On other occasions, the magistrates read out relevant parts of the ordinance, as for instance in 1525, when the council reminded the captains and tower master of the part of the ordinance concerning public gatherings.[202] When in 1550 it was brought to the attention of the council that the guard was mismanaged, the council solved the problem by instructing the patrolmen to be more vigilant.[203]

Yet, severe threats in the 1580s revealed that the city's defence was anything but effective when it came to war. During that time, rumour and misinformation spread particularly quickly, and in 1581, 1582, and 1583, several rumours about the archbishop's alleged plan to invade the city led to chaos.[204] This clearly revealed the flaws of the organisation of the guard.[205] Following these incidents, the magistrates swiftly composed a new guard ordinance that divided the city into eight districts with further subdivisions, the so-called flags.[206] From then on, these districts were in charge of guaranteeing safety. This new organisation promised a much larger group of some 7,000 guardsmen since the council determined that every man between 18–70 years had to fulfil his duty, with the exception of those who were sick, foreigners, and students.[207]

199 Policey K, no. 773; Heinzen (1939), *Zunftkämpfe, Zunftherrschaft und Wehrverfassung in Köln*, p. 47.

200 *Ibid.*

201 RB, III, p. 4, no. 32.

202 RB, III, p. 281, no. 933.

203 RB, V, p. 765, no. 80.

204 Schnurr (2009), '"Jedem anbringer gleub ich so balt nit." Informationsbeschaffung und Mediennutzung des Kölner Bürgers Hermann Weinsberg während des Kölner Kriegs (1582 bis 1590)', p. 179. A soldier was held accountable for spreading such rumours and was quartered, see Schwerhoff (1994), 'Die goldene Freiheit der Bürger', p. 103.

205 Heinzen (1939), *Zunftkämpfe, Zunftherrschaft und Wehrverfassung in Köln*, p. 96.

206 Jilka (1990), 'Aspekte des bürgerlichen Wachdienstes in Köln im 18. und 19. Jahrhundert', p. 80.

207 Holt (1927), 'Die militärische Einteilung der Reichsstadt Köln von 1583–1794', p. 137.

The council recorded these new regulations in a guard ordinance that was published in print in 1583. Unlike the other regulations that the council had printed from 1450 onwards, this new guard ordinance was not published as a single sheet, but as a pamphlet. The ordinance was very detailed, containing no fewer than 106 paragraphs and covering more than 25 pages.[208] Because of its length, it might well have been more convenient to publish it as a pamphlet rather than a broadsheet. However, if an ordinance was intended to be hung up, the council would issue it as a broadsheet, even if that meant that several sheets needed to be pasted together. The coin ordinance from 1564 illustrates this point very well. With its 150 illustrations in various sizes, the broadsheet was of extraordinary length: it measured over one metre in height.[209] We will also see below that the council published other lengthy ordinances as broadsheets in the seventeenth century.

In 1583, the council had the guard ordinance produced as a pamphlet so that the officials and guardsmen could obtain their own copy and carry it with them at all times.[210] As mentioned in the first chapter, this was a strategy often employed by the authorities in Württemberg and Saxony, who ordered their officials to keep certain ordinances on them.[211] For the authorities in Cologne, this was also a rewarding strategy. During the entire sixteenth century, Cologne suffered from conflicts among the guards who disputed and contested the regulations. On numerous occasions, the council had to combat these difficulties by reminding the officials how they were meant to do their duty. The new organisation of the guard in 1583 brought new complexities with it and would have undoubtedly caused new waves of dissent if it had solely been communicated orally. By publishing the ordinance in pamphlet form, the council pre-empted some of these problems.

For the officials and the guardsmen, the purchase of the guard ordinance was mandatory. Although the guard ordinance from 1583 and its amended versions in 1585 and 1586 do not contain the explicit order to buy the pamphlets, later ordinances as well as the imprints on the pamphlets themselves support this claim.[212] In the decades after the publication of the guard ordinances, the

208 Appendix no. 241.

209 Appendix no. 106.

210 In other cities, health and safety regulations were also published as pamphlets, for instance, the fire ordinance in Dresden, first published in print in 1558, see Lasch (2010), '"Es sey das Fewer in der Stadt." Textpragmatische und -grammatische Überlegungen zu vormodernen Feuerordnungen', II, p. 764.

211 See chapter one.

212 Appendix no. 241 (1583) and USTC 704779 (VD16 ZV 9097) (1585). The 1586 ordinance appeared in two editions: USTC 677227 (VD16 K 1808), USTC 677228 (VD16 ZV 9098).

council had three fire ordinances printed, each containing the council's instruction to obtain a copy of the printed item. At the end of the first ordinance of this kind, published in 1604, the council included the sentence: 'It is our [...] order that every [...] citizen should buy a copy from the printer, who is mentioned at the end of this document, for a small sum so that everyone can post it in their houses to have it always before the eyes.'[213] The same sentence appeared on later editions of this ordinance printed in 1633 and 1642 respectively.[214] On top of that, the guard ordinances from 1583, 1585, and 1586 all included an imprint clearly visible on the title page. With this display of the printer's name, the ordinances deviated significantly from the other ordinances produced in the sixteenth century, which do not contain any information about the print house.[215] In contrast to the majority of the ordinances, these were not only produced to be exhibited in key places; they were produced in much larger print runs so that the inhabitants of Cologne could buy their own copy.

Coin ordinances continued to be the most frequently produced regulations in print. The many Dutch and French immigrants made the regulation of coins an even bigger issue in the second half of the sixteenth century than it had been in the first 50 years. Whereas in the 1560s the council had only eight coin ordinances printed, this number increased in the next two decades.[216] As the migration continued in the 1570s and 1580s, the council had no fewer than 34 coin ordinances printed.[217] Some of these ordinances primarily regulated the use of Dutch coins listing specifically the 'forbidden gold and silver coins produced in the Netherlands'.[218]

In addition to presenting complex information, printing coinage ordinances offered a great advantage in contrast to oral proclamations; it was now possible to include illustrations of the coins. Early modern coins often showed coats of

213 This fire ordinance from 1604 was produced as a very long broadsheet. The original German text reads: 'Ist unser [...] befelch, dß alle [...] Bürger, wie die geschaffen, dise Ordnung bey dem Drucker hier hierunden benant, für ein geringes sollen gelden, in ihren Häusern stehts fu[e]r Augen zu haben, anzuschlagen', HAStK, Best. 30/N (Nachträge), A N/20, fol. 20, available online: http://historischesarchivkoeln.de:8080/actaproweb/archive.xhtml?id=Vz++++++00176565Paprless#Vz______00176565Paprless [28/79] & [29/79].

214 Policey K, p. 8; The later ordinance actually appeared in two editions: one dating from 30 January 1642, the other from 31 January 1642, both are in KSM.

215 There are only three coin ordinances with an imprint: appendix nos. 88, 106, 109. The many illustrations and the fine craft of these ordinances should serve to advertise the printer's expertise.

216 Appendix nos. 105, 106, 108, 109, 111, 112, 114, 117.

217 Appendix nos. 136, 138, 141, 172, 173, 174, 175, 176, 178, 179, 180, 181, 182, 183, 185, 193, 201, 210, 211, 212, 214, 224, 225, 227, 238, 250, 251, 275, 283, 284, 294, 295, 296, 302,

218 See, for example, appendix no. 175.

arms or reproductions of either local bridges or buildings. For someone who had never seen such images before, it was hard to identify the coin solely from a description. With the help of a woodcut illustration on printed ordinances, the coins could now easily be identified visually.[219]

Illustrations were often used to complement edicts concerning forbidden coins. An average ordinance of this kind would focus primarily on the description of the coinage, accompanied by the reason why it was prohibited to use it. This way, in 1597, the city council stated that Nobles (Rosennobel) were forbidden in Cologne. The magistrates explained this ban by stating that these coins had often been forged in the past: 'many forged Rosennobel have been spent'.[220] For guidance, the council had included two illustrations of the front and back of the coin on the printed sheet.

Despite the advantages that print offered with regard to producing coin ordinances, however, the city council had initially been quite reluctant to exploit this technical opportunity. Although embracing printing, the magistrates were at first not in favour of woodcut illustrations. It was probably the additional costs of woodcuts or the technical challenges that caused the council to hesitate. For whatever reason, very few printed edicts produced in the early sixteenth century contained illustrations. Yet, with the influx of foreigners and their coins, it was imperative for the council to make the coins easily identifiable. Just as the number of printed coin edicts increased, they included more and more illustrations. So, for instance, an edict of 12 July 1553 contains a conversion table and both front and back illustrations of a coin from Liège.[221] One edict from 1564 comprised over 150 illustrations in various sizes.[222]

One senses that this shift from traditional practice to print was somewhat reluctant. In the major political issues that faced German cities during the sixteenth century, Cologne had generally made conservative choices. Therefore, one may assume that the city fathers would have also preferred to continue using more traditional means of communication to school their subjects.

So it is worth concluding this chapter with a brief comparison of Cologne's responses to political crises and the increasing demands placed on civic govern-

219 Interestingly, almost all illustrated coin ordinances listed in the appendix show woodcut illustrations. There is only one exception where the front and the back of a coin is depicted with the help of an engraving (appendix no. 357). The typical flattened square area around the illustration clearly shows how much more pressure was applied when the engraving was printed. It was probably the higher costs associated with this technique that dissuaded the council from using engravings more frequently.

220 Appendix no. 357.

221 Appendix no. 88.

222 Appendix no. 106.

ments with that of other cities. A classic opportunity is provided by the extraordinary archival riches in Antwerp. Antwerp was, like Cologne, a major trading city and information hub. Indeed, in the sixteenth and seventeenth centuries, the Low Countries relied on Cologne as a major trading partner and as a source for many of the news reports that flowed to the Netherlands from Germany and beyond. So it is worth asking how Antwerp, the most expansive trading metropolis of north-west Europe, experiencing similar significant population flows as a result of economic and religious disruption, coped with the same challenges as the magistrates in Cologne.

Printing ordinances to overcome times of trouble in Antwerp

The civic government in Antwerp used print as an immediate response to the turmoil of the later sixteenth century. We are in the fortunate position of having a wonderful body of material for this major trading centre that allows us to trace the ambitions of the magistrates in sixteenth-century Antwerp. From 1555 onwards, the printer Christopher Plantin produced hundreds of broadsheet ordinances for the civic authorities. As a man who conducted his business very carefully, Plantin kept a copy of almost every ordinance he produced for the city council.[223] This marvellous collection, now housed in the Plantin-Moretus Museum, gives us unique insights into the accelerated process of state communication in Antwerp.

Plantin's collection reveals that just like the magistrates in Cologne, Antwerp's city fathers were slow to adopt print at first. Until the mid-sixteenth century, the Flemish magistrates relied primarily on oral communication to stipulate new regulations and thus had only a handful of ordinances appear in print.[224] This was despite the fact that Antwerp attracted many immigrants and as a result grew significantly before 1550: whereas Antwerp counted some 33,000 inhabitants in 1480, this number had nearly tripled to 84,000 in 1542.[225] Yet, unlike the many migrants who came to Cologne, the foreigners in Antwerp meant to stay and were integrated into political life.

Only when Antwerp faced major turmoil and outbursts of violence spurred by the Dutch Revolt did the council try to combat the crisis by changing its manner of communication. From the late 1570s onwards, the authorities in Antwerp increasingly used print to communicate new legislation as quickly and efficiently as possible. Many of the new regulations were published in broadsheet

223 Voet (ed.) (1980–1983), *The Plantin Press (1555–1589)*, I, pp. 107–154.
224 USTC search: Authorship - Antwerpen, see, for instance, USTC 408276.
225 Meester (2016), 'To Kill Two Birds with One Stone: Keeping Immigrants in by Granting Free Burghership in Early Modern Antwerp', p. 96.

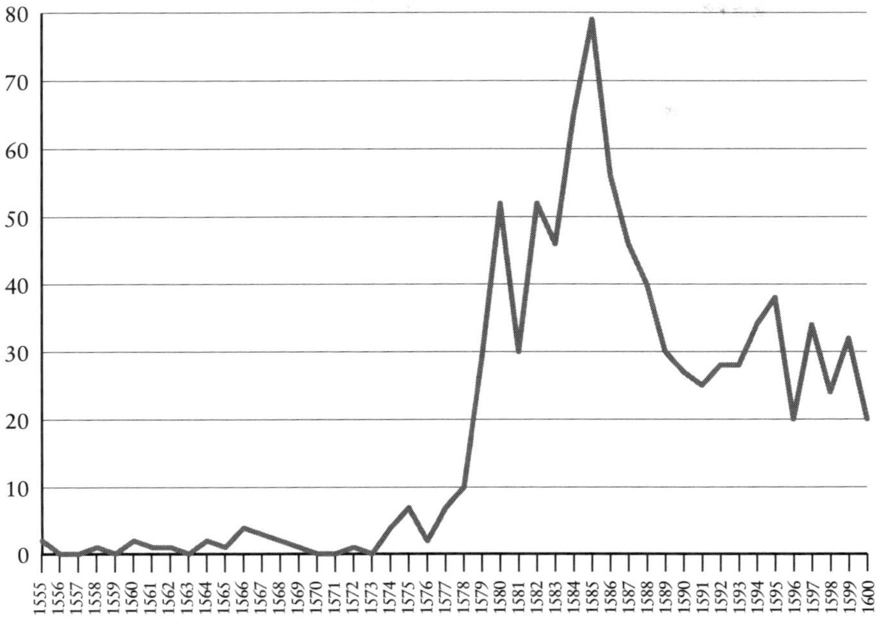

Fig. 3.9. Ordinances issued by the city council in Antwerp produced as broadsheets, 1555–1600 (based on Voet (ed.) (1980–1983), The Plantin Press (1555–1589), I, pp. 107–154.)

form to allow for public display. Fig. 3.9. shows just how closely connected the production of print ordinances was with political and economic crises. The production of ordinances rose rapidly in the early 1580s, when Antwerp faced severe problems eventually leading to the devastating siege of the city in 1584–1585 and the mass emigration that followed its fall. As a result, the city lost much of its economic importance.

Much like their colleagues in Cologne, the councillors in Antwerp were anxious to keep track of every foreigner who came to the city, especially during the testing years in the early 1580s. On 8 March 1580, the magistrates ordered all people who had recently settled in the city to register their names.[226] On the same day, the magistrates also stipulated that every peasant who had fled to the city in recent times had to leave Antwerp within eight days.[227] A few months later, the magistrates were still troubled by foreigners. On 28 July 1580, the council prescribed detailed regulations about the persons who were to be tolerated in the city and those who were not.[228] This placard was most likely

226 USTC 412101.
227 USTC 412102.
228 USTC 412118.

then put up near the city gates so that the officials on site could read it out to any newcomer. Over the following years, the council repeatedly targeted beggars and eventually declared that those who were not authorised had to be driven out of the city.[229]

The Antwerp ordinances also reveal that the Calvinist council was not only troubled by enemies from outside, but also faced opposition within its jurisdiction. Adolescents repeatedly stirred up unrest within the city. The magistrates tried to control this wanton youth and their mischief by issuing ordinances.[230] The winter of 1584 was particularly hard to endure for the inhabitants of Antwerp. By that point, the city had been under siege for several months already. The harsh weather brought with it hunger and starvation, which led some citizens to trade with the Spanish. The council addressed this problem with two ordinances, both published in December 1584, which banned the inhabitants of Antwerp from communicating and doing any business with the enemy.[231]

Just as had been the case with the Cologne authorities, the city fathers of Antwerp tried to regulate the city's hygiene on numerous occasions. In late February 1582, the council had a detailed ordinance printed that included a number of regulations, addressing the cleaning of streets as well as precautions against fire.[232] Just like in Cologne, rummaging pigs presented a matter of concern for the magistrates, who banned the animals from the streets in October 1583 and May 1584.[233]

In contrast to the magistrates in Cologne, who never printed more than 18 ordinances in a single year, the councillors in Antwerp issued 79 printed ordinances in the peak year 1585.[234] This may reflect the relative severity of the crisis, but it is clear, too, that the Antwerp authorities embraced the potential of print rather more readily. The majority of the Antwerp ordinances addressed taxes and supplies, most notably of food, which was obviously crucial for a besieged city. In contrast to the Cologne ordinances, the Antwerp regulations were also stricter. Whereas in Cologne lepers were ordered to avoid certain places, the Dutch magistrates declared that lepers were no longer tolerated within the city walls.[235] In times of growing unease there was little room for compassion.

In the 1580s, the magistracy progressively prepared the city for defence. During this time, the magistrates issued several ordinances per year that aimed at the erection and maintenance of the city's fortification. The ordinances printed

229 USTC 412187, USTC 412308.
230 USTC 412095, USTC 412199, USTC 412238, USTC 412253.
231 USTC 412293, USTC 412298.
232 USTC 412155.
233 USTC 412235, USTC 412264.
234 Voet (ed.) (1980–1983), *The Plantin Press (1555–1589)*, I, pp. 131–139.
235 USTC 412153.

in 1582 allow us to trace exactly how the city equipped itself for the ensuing siege. In June, the magistrates regulated how stone and other material that could be used for the fortifications should be transported to the city.[236] Two months later the council declared that all houses, buildings, and even hedges within 500 paces of the outer side of the city's fortifications should be pulled down.[237] This way the officials and townsmen could see their attackers long before they reached the walls. Finally, in September, the council ordered every wagoner to unload earth and gravel for the fortification of the dikes.[238] During the siege, the magistrates continued their efforts to maintain their fortification, although their efforts were ultimately in vain.

In addition to the many broadsheet editions, the civic government in Antwerp had several larger legal works printed, among them, most notably, the *Rechten ende Costumen van Antwerpen* in 1582.[239] This included various privileges of the city as well as other vital documents that recorded the city's rights.[240] For many years, the Habsburg central authorities had urged the magistrates to produce a homologised compendium of the customary law of Antwerp in print.[241] Yet, only when the council's rule was threatened was this plan put into action. After several years of compiling and editing the draft, the book was finally produced in print in late 1582.[242]

In contrast to the Duke of Württemberg, however, who circulated his legal works widely to legitimise his authority, the edition of the customary law in Antwerp was intended just for internal use.[243] Only the council could use the book, and if a lawyer or notable of the city wanted to consult it, he could only do so under the direct supervision of the city authorities. Therefore, the council ordered the printer, Christopher Plantin, to print only 400 copies and have them delivered directly to the authorities. Plantin was strictly forbidden to print, sell, or distribute any other copy beyond this official order.[244]

The council's limited use of print

As we have seen, the council in Cologne progressively produced more broadsheet ordinances in the years after 1550. Despite this increase in printed

236 USTC 412171.
237 USTC 412180.
238 USTC 412186.
239 USTC 401932.
240 Holthöfer (ed.) (1986), *Gesetzgebung in Europa im Spiegel alter Drucke*, p. 19.
241 Voet (ed.) (1980–1983), *The Plantin Press (1555–1589)*, I, p. 155.
242 USTC 401932.
243 Voet (ed.) (1980–1983), *The Plantin Press (1555–1589)*, I, p. 156.
244 *Ibid.*

ordinances, however, the overall production of official publications in Cologne was still low compared to the Duchy of Württemberg. The dukes, as seen in the first chapter, issued a *Landesordnung* at the end of the fifteenth century and it was progressively amended throughout the sixteenth century. When these amendments came to a provisional conclusion in 1567, the *Landesordnung* comprised a great variety of different legislation, including regulations of religious issues, foreign military service, schools, vineyards, and the sale of crops, meat, wool, and wood. Duke Christoph used these law codes strategically to establish Württemberg as the prototype of a Protestant territory. This way he could boost the duchy's profile after the turbulent rule of Duke Ulrich and strengthen the duchy's position within the empire.

The magistrates in Cologne did not need to boost the city's profile to such a degree. In contrast to many other cities and territories, Cologne did not undergo significant change in the sixteenth century. It was the only major city in the empire that remained Catholic.[245] Many other cities that embraced the new faith employed printed city statutes that regulated primarily religious issues such as blasphemy, marriage, and adultery, but also treated economic matters. One of the first city statutes was issued in Erfurt in 1551.[246] The short quarto pamphlet comprised only 11 leaves, but addressed key matters such as blasphemy, drinking, clothing, and baptism. Only a few years later, similar statutes appeared in print in Augsburg.[247] These statutes were produced as a folio pamphlet comprising 14 leaves. Similarly, the city council of Rostock issued a comprehensive police ordinance in 1576 in quarto with 56 leaves.[248] With these printed ordinances, the cities could assert their rights in the aftermath of the Reformation. This, however, was not an issue for Cologne.

The suggestion that the council in Cologne did not need printed statutes to assert its position within the empire is given further credence by the fact that other essential legal documents were not produced in print either. The *Verbundbrief* of 1396, Cologne's constitution, only existed in handwritten form throughout the entire sixteenth century. The council kept one copy in its possession tucked away safely in a chest with a golden crown.[249] In addition, each *Gaffel* had its own handwritten copy. In case the *Verbundbrief* was required in a lawsuit

245 For more information on why Cologne never embraced the new faith, see Scribner (1976), 'Why was there no Reformation in Cologne' and Groten (1999), 'Die nächste Generation: Scribner's Thesen aus heutiger Sicht', pp. 110–113.

246 USTC 648850 (VD16 E 3744).

247 USTC 610528 (VD16 A 4126).

248 USTC 684628 (VD16 R 3184).

249 Militzer (ed.) (1996), *Stadtrat, Stadtrecht, Bürgerfreiheit*, pp. 37–38.

outside Cologne, the magistrates had a scribe copy the text and send it to the recipient.[250] After they had used the text for their purposes, the recipient had to deliver the copy back to Cologne. Similarly, the *Transfixbrief* of 1513, an important addition to the *Verbundbrief*, was not printed in the sixteenth century. Here, again, handwritten copies sufficed.

Even the publications of the imperial police ordinances issued in 1530, 1548, and 1570 did not stimulate any publications from the city council. The magistrates simply passed on new legislation orally, as we can see from the council minutes. In mid-November 1548, the magistrates determined that several members should go through the imperial police ordinance to decide which rules applied to Cologne. After the magistrates had looked through the ordinance, they decided that one of the few things Cologne traders needed to know was the fact that no stretched cloths should be sold over the next six months.[251] The council determined that this information should be passed on to the merchants in Cologne. In addition, one council member had to tell those travelling to England about the new cloth regulation. Later, in June 1549, the councillors determined that the goldsmiths as well as the tailors needed to be informed about new regulations in the imperial police ordinance.[252] According to the ordinance, the goldsmiths needed to use a specific sign, which they presented to the council at the end of August.[253] To communicate this information the council did not need print.

Yet, there were a number of citizens within Cologne who thought it important to have fundamental legal texts in printed form. Some of these texts appeared in print over the sixteenth century. However, these publications were presumably not ordered by the magistrates: they were paid for by interested parties within Cologne. The citizens' rights and freedoms here serve as an example. Already in the mid-fifteenth century, the council had composed a document intended to protect citizens from assault, violence, and constraint.[254] The text asserted the privacy of people's homes and laid down legislation for arrests as well as rights before the court.[255] After the uproar in 1513, the magistrates determined to have this document printed and have one copy brought to each *Gaffel*.[256] Yet, the production in print was not put into action

250 RB, III, p. 277, no. 901; RB, III, p. 281, no. 932.
251 RB, V, p. 647, no. 642.
252 RB, V, p. 691, no. 289.
253 RB, V, p. 711, no. 438.
254 Schwerhoff (1994), 'Die goldene Freiheit der Bürger', p. 106.
255 Giel (1998), *Politische Öffentlichkeit im spätmittelalterlich-frühneuzeitlichen Köln*, p. 132.
256 RB, II, p. 17, no. 127.

and only manuscript copies were used.[257] Only in 1529 was a small pamphlet printed, but in all probability this was an edition published either on an interested party's or even the printer's initiative.[258]

The collection of statutes in 1562 was another publication produced on the initiative of a printer rather than by the civic government.[259] In the preface, the author identified himself as the printer who wanted to serve the inhabitants of Cologne and the commonweal with this publication. He argues that the inhabitants needed to know what they could or could not do to help the city thrive. One can easily follow his argumentation because at that point in time only the *Gaffeln* and the council possessed important regulations in handwritten form. If a merchant wanted to look up particular legislation, he could not easily do so without consulting a *Gaffel* or the council first. The publication in print, therefore, met a need, even if the compilation did not include every regulation.[260]

To avoid any problems with the authorities, the book was produced clandestinely. Since it was not a publication commissioned by the city council and the copies were sold freely, we would expect to see the printer's name on the title page or in the colophon. Nevertheless, the book does not include this vital information.[261] Furthermore, the printer emphasises his good intentions in the preface, stating repeatedly how useful the publication is for everyone and that he compiled the book solely in 'good faith'. Surely this was a way to get into the council's good books in case the magistrates thought of prosecuting the printer.

Conclusion

On 25 December 1542, when the newly elected council in Cologne took office, the magistrates were presented with an immediate problem: close to the church of St Mariengraden, located near the cathedral, several placards informed Cologne's inhabitants about the latest regulations on religious issues.[262] In addition to the text, the placards included three crowns, a part of the city's coat of arms. For passers-by the placards appeared to be official publications, printed and posted up by the council of Cologne.

257 Giel refers to a statement made by Joachim Deeters, who has worked extensively with the archivalia preserved in the city archive of Cologne, GIEL (1998), *Politische Öffentlichkeit im spätmittelalterlich-frühneuzeitlichen Köln*, p. 132.

258 USTC 640296 (VD16 K 1806).

259 USTC 608010 (VD16 ZV 9096).

260 GIEL (1998), *Politische Öffentlichkeit im spätmittelalterlich-frühneuzeitlichen Köln*, p. 133.

261 The book appeared in two editions: USTC 608010 (VD16 ZV 9096) and USTC 2213379 (VD16 ZV 30617).

262 RB, V, p. 122, no. 1.

Yet, this was not the case. The placards had not been produced by the council, and their exhibition caused the new magistrates a feeling of unease. Therefore, the new magistracy determined to act quickly. It appointed several officials to find the offender who had ordered these seemingly official publications as well as the printer who had facilitated the manufacture.[263] It did not take long for the officials to trace down the offender, and already on 1 January 1543, the printer was put in prison.[264]

This case shows how seriously the council of Cologne took the circulation of unofficial information in print and how severe the punishments could be. From the council's perspective, the printer responsible had facilitated a severe crime; the circulation of official information in print within Cologne was the privilege of the council. Only if the magistrates agreed on the publication of certain regulations were they produced and displayed publicly. Everyone who disregarded this undermined the authority of the council.

Despite the demand for legal works and announcements in print, the council only used the press to a limited degree. For urban governments, like the magistracy in Cologne, print was not an innovation that changed the mode of communication immediately. In fact, in the first half of the sixteenth century, the council continued to employ oral means such as public assemblies and channeling information via the *Gaffeln*. This was an effective way of informing a great number of people about recent legal changes and helped the council to create consensus among the ruled – a vital task for the elected council. When the council used print, it did so primarily to communicate with outsiders. The press helped to distribute information on Hanseatic issues, to explain recent turbulence, and thus encouraged support from other cities as well as the emperor. In addition, printed placards displayed on the way to the marketplaces made foreign tradesmen aware of new regulations concerning coinage.

However, throughout the turbulent second half of the sixteenth century, when Cologne hosted an increasing number of religious refugees and faced conflicts with the archbishop, the council increasingly employed print to communicate law and order. This included mostly health and safety regulations, which were of vital importance for a densely populated city at war. On top of that, the production of the new guard ordinance in pamphlet form was extremely useful, especially after the guard had undergone significant change in the 1580s. By making the pamphlet widely available, the council allowed everyone who had to fulfil guard duty to have the relevant regulations at hand.

263 RB, V, p. 122, no. 2.
264 RB, V, p. 123, no. 8.

Chapter Four: The Council's Printers

Commissions from the council of Cologne were sought after in the local publishing fraternity, but not only because of their economic benefit. Unlike their colleagues in Württemberg, who often made a good living by producing for their local government, the printers in Cologne did not receive hefty returns for their official publications. Instead of money, the printers were keen to obtain the prestige that the involvement with the civic government brought with it. The printers who enjoyed a good reputation among the political elite in Cologne were frequently entrusted with producing for other official bodies, especially for those authorities close to the city, such as the Archbishop of Cologne and the dukes of Jülich-Cleves-Berg. For these rulers, Cologne was the closest print centre and they frequently had their publications produced there. In some cases, the involvement with other governments was so fruitful that the printers left Cologne to set up a press in their territory.

This chapter will argue that the increase in printed ordinances in the second half of the sixteenth century led to an interesting development in the market for official print. From the very beginning of print, Cologne was one of the most important print centres in the empire. Over 100 printers were active in the metropolis on the Rhine in the 140 years before 1601. Despite this abundance of shops, however, the council only entrusted a handful of printers with the production of official announcements and ordinances. In fact, there was often only one printer at a time producing the majority of official work. However, just like in Württemberg, printers worked for the council on the basis of individual orders and did not receive an annual salary, as they did, for instance, in many cities in the Low Countries.[1]

Although the overwhelming majority of the council's publications lack imprints, I was, nevertheless, able to deduce which printing houses presumably produced most of the ordinances by analysing their woodcuts.[2] The identified

1 From 1577 onwards, official state printers received an annual salary in Leiden, Antwerp, Arnhem, Middelburg, Franeker, Utrecht, Kampen, Deventer, Zwolle, and Groningen, see Weduwen (2018), *State Communication*, pp. 84–85.

2 Interestingly, Cologne ordinances are only adorned with woodcuts and not with engravings. There is only one exception: a coin ordinance from 1597 with a depiction of a Rosennobel (appendix no. 357).

publications reveal that the council preferred to employ printers who had been in Cologne for several years and thus proven their skills and reliability. They were not always among the most successful businesses, but they managed to keep their shops open for several years or even decades. Up until 1550, the owners of small print shops close to the town hall supplied the majority of ordinances. When the civic authorities, however, made use of the press to a larger extent in the second half of the sixteenth century, the market changed significantly. During this latter period, almost all civic ordinances were produced by printers who were part of the political elite in Cologne. Both Jaspar von Gennep and Maternus Cholinus were prolific figures in Cologne's print industry and increasingly interested in working for the council as well as other authorities.

This shift to the larger print houses was ideal for the authorities. As the council progressively included images in its announcements, it needed printers who were willing to invest in the required woodcuts. Although the printers would receive additional reimbursement when they printed with woodcuts, they had to aquired the woodblocks on their own.[3]

Cologne as a print centre

Cologne was among the first German cities to embrace printing. Already in 1464, only a few years after Gutenberg first experimented with moveable type, Ulrich Zell brought the new technology to the city on the Rhine. Born in Hanau, close to Gutenberg's home town, Zell first moved to Mainz to work in Peter Schöffer's print shop before he turned his attention to the large trading centre in the north with its distinguished university.[4] The printer was right to assume that the academic institution would welcome the innovation of producing texts quickly and cheaply, and from the very beginning Zell ran a successful business.[5] He was swiftly joined by other entrepreneurs who found fertile ground for printing, and within a short space of time, Cologne became one of the most important print centres in the Holy Roman Empire. The city's presses produced no fewer than 1,500 imprints before 1501.[6] This placed Cologne among the most important print centres in Europe, behind only Venice, Paris, and Rome.

3 The printer Maternus Cholinus lists additional costs for 'etliche Münzstock gedruckt' in his invoice for the two occassions he produced a coin ordinance (both dated mid-April 1576), see fig. 4.3.

4 SCHMITZ (1990), *Die Überlieferung deutscher Texte im Kölner Buchdruck*, p. 8.

5 CORSTEN (1965), 'Ulrich Zells deutschsprachige Drucke', p. 110.

6 USTC search: Place - Köln, Date - 1450–1500.

In the course of the sixteenth century, Cologne continued to occupy a significant position within the print world. As it was the most prominent German city cleaving to the old faith, Cologne became the centre for Catholic publishing in the empire. During the course of the sixteenth century, Cologne's printing houses produced no fewer than 3,000 religious works, more than one third of the overall output of the 8,000 imprints published in sixteenth-century Cologne.[7] Many of the books were directed against the new faith, especially during the reform attempts of Cologne's Archbishop Hermann von Wied.[8]

Throughout the century, the print industry attracted many workers and entrepreneurs from all over Europe. Some, such as Johann von Solingen in 1517, did not prosper and left the city after a few unproductive months.[9] Similarly, Renerus Tremoniensis, who came from close-by Dortmund, seems to have produced very little before he closed his shop in 1567, the same year he had opened it.[10] Others were more fortunate and stayed in Cologne for years or even decades, in some cases establishing long-lasting family businesses. Among the most successful ones were those print shops of the families of Quentel, Birckmann, Gymnich, and Cholinus and their respective heirs and successors.[11]

Dozens of different printing houses were active in the city on the Rhine before 1601, as fig. 4.1. shows.[12] These provided the authorities with ample choice when they wanted to produce official documents. Unlike the dukes in Württemberg, the magistrates had many print shops right on their doorstep at any given time. Already in 1500, the council could select from eight printing houses for the production of their coin ordinances. This number grew steadily, especially from the 1530s onwards, as many printers settled in Cologne. In 1560, no fewer than 11 printers operated a print shop at the same time and in 1580 there were 12.

7 USTC search: Date - 1500–1600, Subject - Religious.

8 Schlüter (2005), *Flug- und Streitschriften zur 'Kölner Reformation'*, p. 3.

9 Reske, p. 446.

10 Reske, p. 487; USTC 623770 (VD16 ZV 784).

11 Enderle (1999), 'Die Buchdrucker der Reichsstadt Köln und die katholische Publizistik zwischen 1555 und 1648', pp. 171–172.

12 The data is taken from Reske, pp. 458–499; the graph shows every printer working in Cologne for three consecutive years or longer.

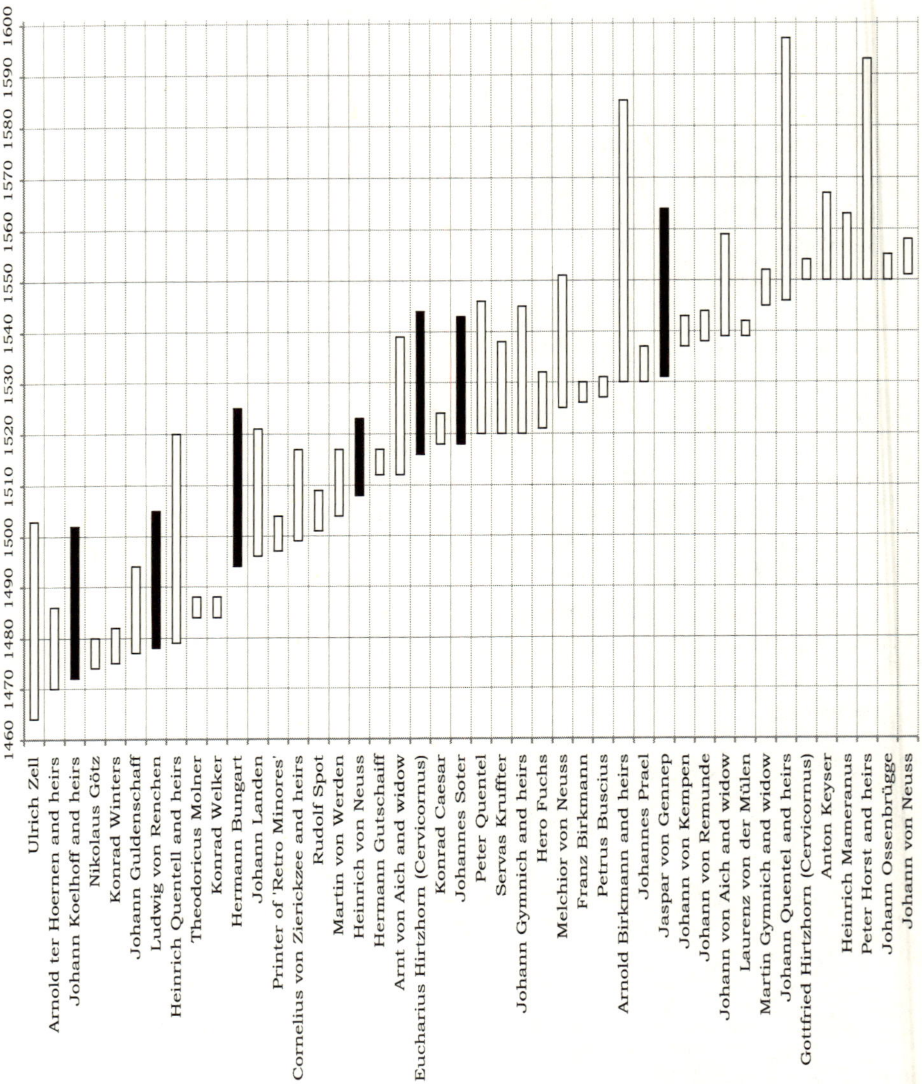
1460
1470
1480
1490
1500
1510
1520
1530
1540
1550
1560
1570
1580
1590
1600
Ulrich Zell
Arnold ter Hoernen and heirs
Johann Koelhoff and heirs
Nikolaus Götz
Konrad Winters
Johann Guldenschaff
Ludwig von Renchen
Heinrich Quentell and heirs
Theodoricus Molner
Konrad Welker
Hermann Bungart
Johann Landen
Printer of 'Retro Minores'
Cornelius von Zierickzee and heirs
Rudolf Spot
Martin von Werden
Heinrich von Neuss
Hermann Gutschaiff
Arnt von Aich and widow
Eucharius Hirtzhorn (Cervicornus)
Konrad Caesar
Johannes Soter
Peter Quentel
Servas Kruffter
Johann Gymnich and heirs
Hero Fuchs
Melchior von Neuss
Franz Birkmann
Petrus Buscius
Arnold Birkmann and heirs
Johannes Prael
Jaspar von Gennep
Johann von Kempen
Johann von Remunde
Johann von Aich and widow
Laurenz von der Mülen
Martin Gymnich and widow
Johann Quentel and heirs
Gottfried Hirtzhorn (Cervicornus)
Anton Keyser
Heinrich Mameranus
Peter Horst and heirs
Johann Ossenbrügge
Johann von Neuss

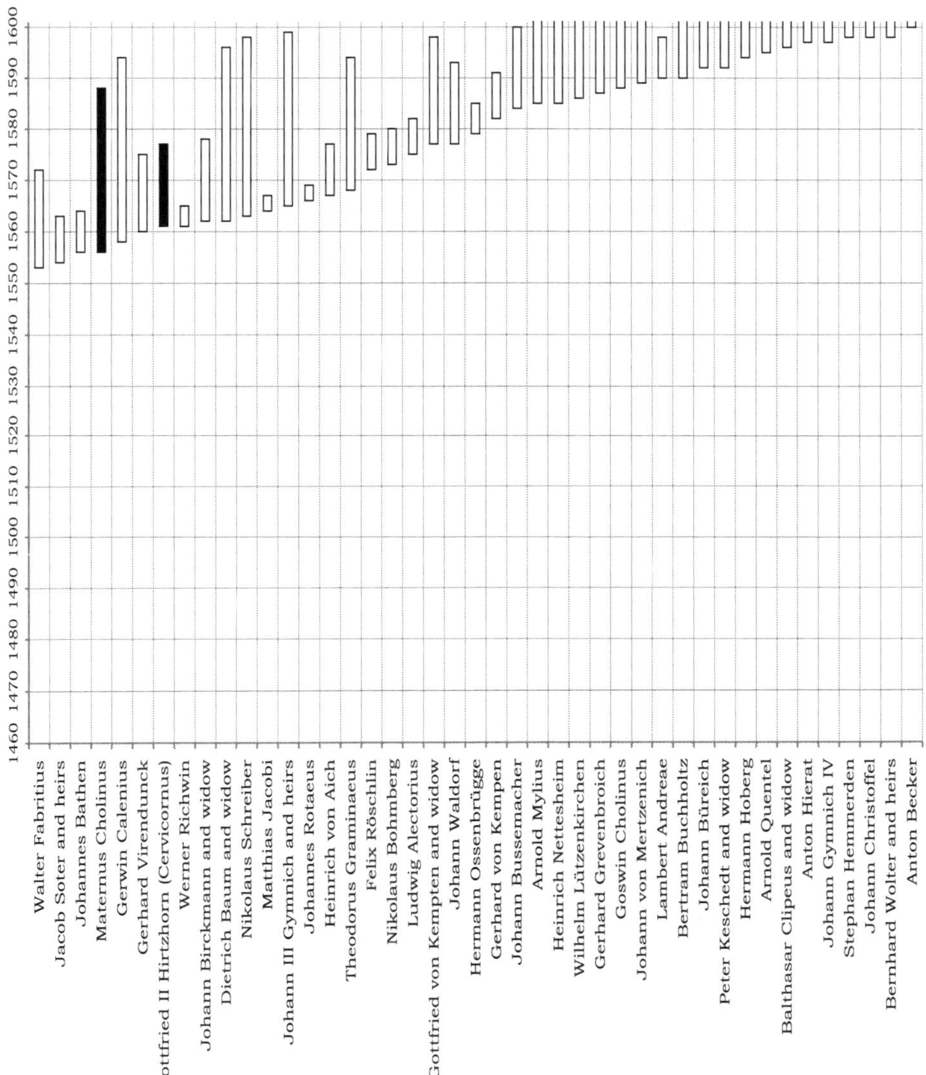

Fig. 4.1. Printers working in Cologne between 1464 and 1600 with those producing for the council in black (based on GW, TW and Reske).

Printing for municipal governments

Producing official documents for the city council in Cologne was far less financially rewarding than printing for the authorities in Württemberg. Whereas Ulrich Morhart and his family made a comfortable living by publishing books for the dukes in southern Germany, the printers in Cologne made comparatively little from the council's orders. In contrast to the dukes, the magistrates did not order the production of any complex legal works, such as city statutes or collections of ordinances. A large sum, such as the 300 Gulden Magdalena Morhart received for the *Landrecht* in Württemberg, the equivalent of the annual salary of three ducal councillors, was never paid to a local printer by the council of Cologne.[13] Similarly, the council did not order the production and the distribution of theological works. As we will see below, such books were financed by the archbishop, the cathedral capital, and the many religious orders in the city. Therefore, no printer received a council payment as high as the 400 Gulden Magdalena Morhart earned when she produced Johannes Brenz' *Catechism*.[14]

That is not to say, however, that working for municipal governments generally brought little return. Producing for Protestant magistracies was much more financially rewarding than working for the Cologne magistrates. Although city rulers tended to employ more traditional means to communicate, both the urban governments in the Reformed cities Nuremberg and Augsburg employed the press from an early stage to help advance religious change in their jurisdiction. Just like the authorities in Württemberg, the two councils paid their printers for every individual order, as can be demonstrated from several surviving invoices. The documents show that the city council of Augsburg paid both Melchior Ramminger and Silvan Otmar for publishing the *Edict of Worms* in the 1520s.[15] In the following years, the magistrates continued to employ Silvan Otmar and reimburse him for every official publication he had printed in the years 1522–1537.[16]

Silvan Otmar was a well-known printer in Augsburg, not least because of his extremely successful career. He learned to print in his father's shop, which had been in business since 1502.[17] From 1513, Otmar published books under his own name and eventually took over his father's printing house a few years later. Within the first ten years, Otmar doubled his assets from 270 Gulden to 600 Gulden.[18] This extraordinary success, undoubtedly a result of his close con-

13 See chapter two.
14 See page 97.
15 Künast (1997), *'Getruckt zu Augspurg'*, p. 202.
16 Schottenloher (1940), 'Silvan Otmar in Augsburg, der Drucker des Schwäbischen Bundes 1519–1535', p. 284.
17 Reske, p. 33.
18 Künast (1997), *'Getruckt zu Augspurg'*, p. 56.

nection to the city council, placed Otmar firmly among the publishing elite in Augsburg.

At the same time in Nuremberg, Jobst Gutknecht also began to print for the authorities. Like Otmar, Gutknecht started his business in the decade between 1510–1520, and from the very beginning, he concentrated on official work for local rulers. In 1516, he published the procedure for the judgment of capital crimes issued by the Margrave of Brandenburg-Ansbach and Kulmbach.[19] A few years later, the printer started to supply ordinances for the municipal government in Nuremberg, such as the alms ordinance of 1522.[20] The printers' invoices that have survived provide us with invaluable insights into the immense scope of the government publications of Protestant city councils.[21]

Otmar's and Gutknecht's invoices testify to how financially lucrative it could be to work for a city council that made active use of print. The magistrates in the southern imperial cities employed this technical innovation far more than their colleagues in Cologne, issuing for instance a church ordinance as well as a police ordinance, both comprising a variety of laws. In 1533, Gutknecht received a total of 66 Gulden from the council in Nuremberg for producing a church ordinance in 400 copies.[22] His colleague Silvan Otmar earned a similar amount when he produced the Augsburg police ordinance in 1537. Unfortunately, Otmar does not specify in his invoice how many copies he delivered to the council. Nevertheless, the payment of 77 Gulden undeniably included several hundred copies of the *Policeyordnung*.[23]

In addition to these larger legal works, the urban governments in Nuremberg and Augsburg often published new regulations not as a single-sheet but as a pamphlet. The legal complexities of the new faith rendered pamphlets much more practical than broadsheets.[24] When the council in Augsburg issued an ordinance in 1522 regulating weddings, the magistrates had it produced as a pamphlet consisting of five leaves.[25] In the same year, the council agreed on an ordinance addressing the distribution of alms, which was printed in the same format and size.[26]

19 It appeared in two editions: USTC 616917 (VD16 B 6936), USTC 616918 (VD16 B 6937).

20 USTC 648630 (VD16 N 2019).

21 Keunecke (1987), 'Jobst Gutknecht – Der Drucker des Nürnberger Rates', pp. 151–153.

22 *Ibid.*

23 USTC 610523 (VD16 ZV 24719).

24 For the difference between broadsheet and pamphlet ordinances, see chapter one.

25 USTC 610519 (VD16 ZV 16139).

26 USTC 610520 (VD16 A 4106). For an English translation of the ordinance text, see: Tlusty (ed.) (2012), *Augsburg during the Reformation Era*, pp. 82–83.

Naturally, these slightly longer ordinances brought the printers more income than single sheets. Whereas Otmar usually received 1 Pfund (approximately 1/3 Gulden) for 100 single-sheet ordinances, he received about three times as much, namely 1 Gulden, when he produced the wedding ordinance and the alms ordinance.[27] In Nuremberg, the council also asked for many ordinances in pamphlet form, which Jobst Gutknecht readily supplied. When on 27 March 1537 the council regulated blasphemy and the custom of pledging health, Gutknecht printed the ordinance as a quarto pamphlet with eight leaves.[28] For its production, the printer required two sheets of paper, as he specified in his invoice.[29] In the same year, the printer also delivered an ordinance for the sale of meat, which comprised four sheets of paper, and a forest ordinance with six and a half sheets per copy. For these editions Gutknecht received 4 and 6 Gulden respectively.

All of these official publications and ordinances provided Gutknecht and Otmar with generous revenues. In Nuremberg, Gutknecht received more than 89 Gulden in 1533 and a total of 23 Gulden for the years 1534–1537. His colleague Silvan Otmar obtained on average about 2 1/2 Gulden per year (1522–1535) from the local authorities. In the latter half of the 1530s, his payments increased significantly, with the printer earning no less than 29 Gulden in one single year, 1536. In the next year, the production of the *Policeyordnung* pushed Otmar's income to a total of 77 Gulden.

On top of these already very lucrative payments from their respective councils, the printers in Nuremberg and Augsburg could also make money by selling ordinances to other authorities or on a commercial market. Being entrusted with the publication of the Nuremberg church ordinance was a great success for Gutknecht. He not only sold 400 copies to the city council but also 1,000 copies to the Margrave of Brandenburg-Ansbach, who had formulated the ordinance in collaboration with the magistracy.[30] As the publication was highly sought after, the printer produced a third edition of the ordinance to be sold in his print shop. The three editions appeared in folio, quarto, and octavo format. We may well assume that the two large formats were intended for the local governments, whereas the small edition was sold to interested individuals. In Augsburg, Otmar could also hope for good revenues when he printed the police ordinance in 1537. It appeared in two editions: one in folio and one in quarto

27 He received 2 Gulden, 1 Pfund, and 15 Schilling for each ordinance which appeared in 300 copies. This equals approximately 1 Gulden for 100 copies.

28 USTC 674770 (VD16 N 1988).

29 Keunecke (1987), 'Jobst Gutknecht – Der Drucker des Nürnberger Rates', p. 153.

30 *Ibid.*, p. 152.

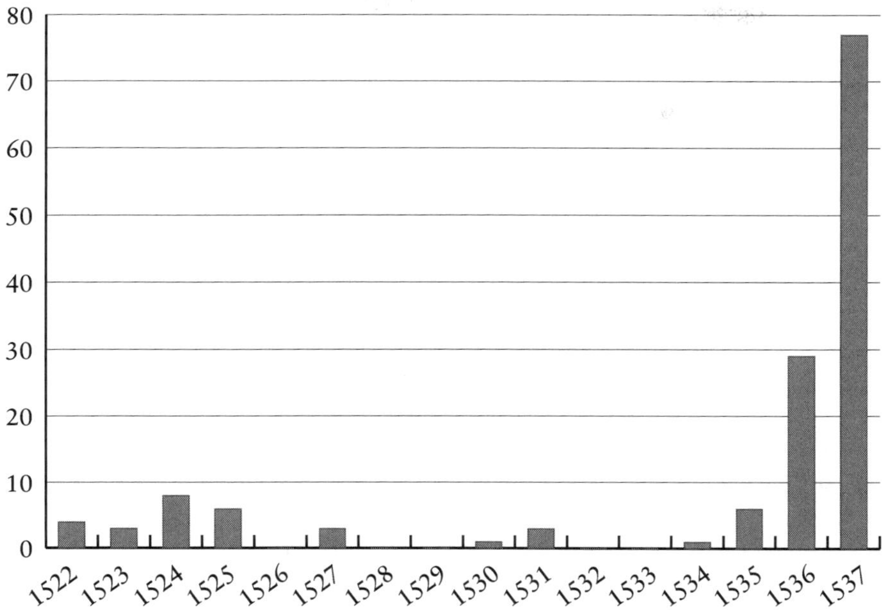

Fig. 4.2. Payments Otmar Silvan received from the city council of Augsburg to produce official publications (in Gulden).

format.[31] Whereas the folio edition undoubtedly went to the council and its officials, Otmar sold the smaller edition commercially.

Printing these many official publications was a very attractive side business for both Otmar and Gutknecht, allowing the printers to embark on more cost-intensive projects. After Otmar started to work in Augsburg, catering increasingly for official needs, he moved from smaller publications to larger theological books such as Anton Corvinus' *Interpretation of the Epistles*, consisting of some 270 leaves.[32] Similarly, Jobst Gutknecht ran a successful business, publishing over 500 books throughout the 28 years he worked in Nuremberg.[33] Among these many imprints was one edition of Luther's New Testament, comprising over 400 leaves.[34]

31 Folio: USTC 610523 (VD16 ZV 24719), quarto: USTC 610524 (VD16 A 4125).
32 USTC 670379 (VD16 C 5367).
33 USTC search: Printer - Gutknecht, Date - 1514–1541.
34 USTC 627817 (VD16 B 4376).

In contrast to this, Cologne printers could not secure such income from producing the council's publications. The ordinances were not intended for a commercial market, and, as we have seen in the third chapter, printers who were caught producing unauthorised official publications faced immediate imprisonment. The only exception to this was the printed guard ordinance, which every household in Cologne was required to possess. In this case, the printer must have produced a very substantial number of copies. Similar publications in Nuremberg, which were also distributed to every household, were produced in some 5,000 – 7,000 copies.[35] It seems very likely that the council in Cologne had at least 6,500 copies of the ordinance produced, as there were some 6,200 households in Cologne at the time the guard ordinance was issued.[36] This excluded the 1,600 clerics with their servants, as well as the 1,200 students in town.

The day-to-day production of ordinances did not provide the producer with substantial returns. As the broadsheet ordinances were intended to be hung up in specific places, such as the markets, they were usually only produced in 100–200 copies. On 11 December 1510, the printer Hermann Bungart received 32 Marks for 'letters concerning coins'.[37] It is not unusual that the council referred to ordinances as letters; in this instance, the word was also often used as a synonym for broadsheets. The amount of 32 Marks suggests that some 200 copies were printed, twice as many as the Hansa invitations for which Heinrich von Neuss would receive 14 Mark one year later (see below). Similarly, when the magistrates agreed on a new coinage ordinance in August 1527, they decided to have the document produced in 100 copies.[38] Five years later, the magistrates ordered the production of another coin ordinance, which would probably have been printed in the same number of copies.[39] As the amount did not seem to have sufficed, the council ordered another 100 copies a few days later.[40]

These small edition sizes were not unusual. The major trading centres in the southern part of the empire also produced their broadsheet ordinances in 100–200 copies. According to the invoices Otmar presented to the Augsburg magistrates in the 1520s, he printed five broadsheets in 100 copies, such as the

35 Keunecke (1987), 'Jobst Gutknecht – Der Drucker des Nürnberger Rates', p. 154.

36 Kellenbenz (1975), 'Wirtschaftsgeschichte Kölns im 16. und beginnenden 17. Jahrhundert', I, p. 327.

37 HAStK, Best. 70 A 98, fol. 395v. The German original reads: 'H[er]mano van ketwich [Bungart] boichdrucker van gedruckten breven die muntze beruend – xxxii mr.'

38 RB, III, p. 438, no. 662. The ordinance itself was most likely printed without an issue date, and this is why it does not appear in the graph in chapter three.

39 Appendix no. 61; Giel (1998), *Politische Öffentlichkeit im spätmittelalterlich-frühneuzeitlichen Köln*, p. 93.

40 RB, IV, p. 93, no. 111.

cloth ordinance and the trade ordinance, both issued in 1524.[41] In addition to that, the printer supplied a coin ordinance in 150 copies and a regulation concerning Lutheranism in 200 copies. Only on rare occasions did the numbers exceed this. In 1524, Otmar delivered 650 copies of a tax ordinance; the previous year, he had printed as many as 800 copies of a broadsheet edition. In Nuremberg, the average broadsheet ordinance was produced in a slightly higher print run. This is not surprising as the council governed the biggest territory of all imperial cities, covering some 6,200 square km.[42] Unlike in Cologne, the council's jurisdiction stretched far beyond the city walls, comprising over 70 villages.[43] Therefore, it did not suffice to exhibit printed ordinances only within the city walls. To communicate new regulations effectively, the council had to send out a number of copies to the villages and, therefore, usually had their broadsheets produced in 200–400 copies.[44]

As the council in Cologne increasingly channelled information via the *Gaffeln*, the average number of copies per ordinance decreased. The magistracy only needed 22 copies of each ordinance to inform the political associations, some copies to be hung up in prominent places, and finally some copies for filing. A very detailed contemporary invoice from the 1570s shows that the city council of Cologne had its broadsheet ordinances produced in 50–60 copies (fig. 4.3.). The invoice is a truly fascinating document. It gives us insights into the remarkably efficient production of ordinances, usually ready for publication at the latest within three days after the council's meeting.[45] In his invoice from 1576, the printer Maternus Cholinus also gives us a clear indication of how many copies he produced of each ordinance.[46] On 13 April, Cholinus printed a

41 For this and the following information on print runs, see Schottenloher (1940), 'Silvan Otmar in Augsburg, der Drucker des Schwäbischen Bundes 1519–1535', p. 284. The printer uses the word *Zettel*, which indicates that these ordinances were produced as a broadsheet.

42 Eiden and Irsigler (2000), 'Environs and Hinterland. Cologne and Nuremberg in the Later Middle Ages', p. 53.

43 Endres (1988), 'Nürnberg in der Frühneuzeit', p. 142.

44 Keunecke (1987), 'Jobst Gutknecht – Der Drucker des Nürnberger Rates', pp. 151–154.

45 Limbach (2016), 'Tracing Lost Broadsheet Ordinances Printed in Sixteenth-Century Cologne', p. 498. There could, however, be a slight delay between the time of the council's meeting, in which the ordinance was agreed on, and the issue date displayed on the printed ordinance. The two blasphemy ordinances from the 1540s serve to illustrate this point (see chapter three): In 1544, there were five days between the council's decision and the issue date of the ordinance. In the case of the imperial ordinance, an entire month passed, probably because it took more time to prepare imperial ordinances.

46 HAStK, Best. 90 A 225 fol. 12.

coin ordinance in three editions: one issued by the city council in Aachen and the other two issued by the councils in Dortmund and Cologne respectively. The printer produced 100 copies of the Aachen edition asking for 2 Taler reimbursement.[47] The other two editions appeared in 50 and 60 copies respectively, for which Cholinus charged 1 Taler each. As he charged the same price for the other listed ordinances, we may infer that the printer also produced these in 50–60 copies.

The print runs of official publications produced in sixteenth-century Cologne were generally quite low. As we have seen in the previous chapter, the explanation of the uproar in 1482 was sent to 78 recipients, including neighbouring rulers and other urban governments. Although the council probably kept some copies for administrative purposes, it is unlikely that the print run exceeded 100 copies. The invitation to the meeting of the Hansa in 1511 was produced in a similar number: when the council received the letter from Lübeck, the magistrates had it produced in 82 copies, which were then distributed to Westphalian towns.[48]

Such small print jobs did not bring substantial financial rewards. The production of the 82 Hansa invitations brought the printer only 14 Marks.[49] In the early sixteenth century, this was not very much, equalling about 3 ½ Gulden.[50] This was a relatively small reward, as the comparison to the annual salary of a town clerk in Cologne reveals. In 1513, only two years after Heinrich von Neuss received his payment for the printed invitations, the magistrates stipulated that the town clerk Albertus Potgieter should be paid 110 Gulden on top of 10 ell of English cloth every year.[51]

The only official publications produced in many more copies were the invitations to the shooting competitions, as they were intended to appeal to a transregional audience. Although we lack exact print runs of the invitations sent out in 1483 and 1501, we may imagine that the documents existed in hundreds of copies, as they did in other cities. Whereas the city council in Mainz produced its invitation in 350 copies, both the city councils of Munich and Zurich had

47 In the invoice, Taler is shortened to 'dal' and Albus to 'alb'. A copy of the Aachen edition is online at USBK (SB1051) http://www.ub.uni-koeln.de/cdm/ref/collection/rheinmono/id/699436; see fig. 4.30.

48 See chapter three, subchapter 'Official publications'.

49 HAStK, Best. 70 A 98, fol. 414, see Giel (1998), *Politische Öffentlichkeit im spätmittelalterlich-frühneuzeitlichen Köln*, p. 97.

50 Two years after Heinrich von Neuss received 14 Marks, on 20 May 1513, the council decided to pay 42 Gulden to four guardsmen, stating that 1 Gulden was worth 4 Marks, see RB, II, p. 52, no. 431.

51 RB, II, p. 17, no. 130. For more information on the town clerk Albert Potgieter, see RB, p. XXVIII.

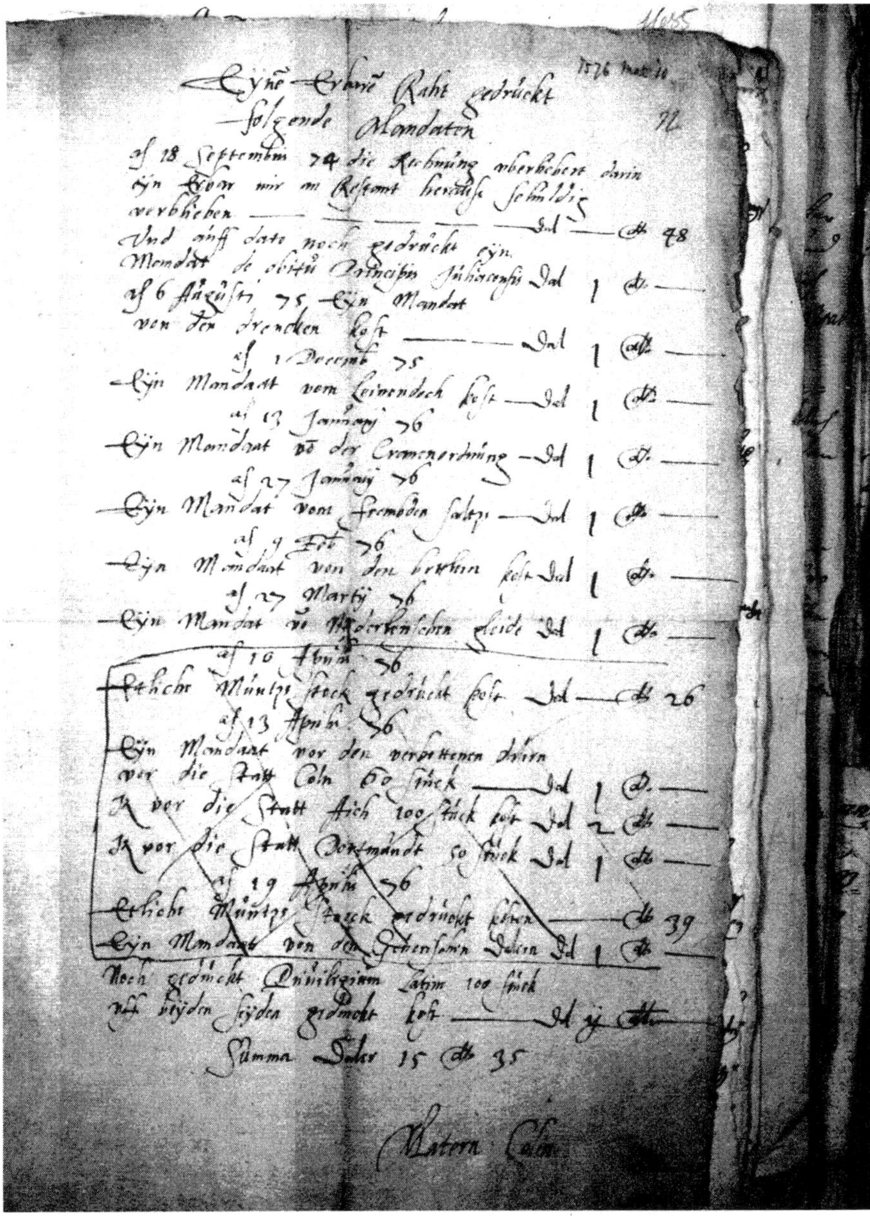
Eynē Erbarē Raht gedrückt
folgende Mandaten
af 18 Septembris 74 die Rechnung uberhebert darin
eyn [illegible] mir an Restant [illegible] schuldig
verblieben — Dal — alb 48
Und auff date noch gedrückt eyn
Mandat de obitu Principis Juliacensis Dal 1 alb —
af 6 Augusti 75 Eyn Mandat
von der drencken kost — Dal 1 alb —
af 1 Decemb 75
Eyn Mandat vom Leinendoch kost — Dal 1 alb —
af 13 Januarij 76
Eyn Mandat vō der Cramerordnung — Dal 1 alb —
af 27 Januarij 76
Eyn Mandat vom fremden saltz — Dal 1 alb —
af 9 Feb 76
Eyn Mandat von den [illegible] kost Dal 1 alb —
af 27 Martij 76
Eyn Mandat vā Niderlendischen kleidr Dal 1 alb —
af 10 Aprilis 76
Etliche Müntz stuck gedrückt kost Dal — alb 26
af 13 Aprilis 76
Eyn Mandat vor den verbottenen [illegible]
vor die statt Coln 60 stuck — Dal 1 alb —
It vor die statt Aich 100 stuck kost Dal 2 alb —
It vor die statt Dortmundt 50 stuck Dal 1 alb —
af 19 Aprilis 76
Etliche Müntz stuck gedrückt kosten — alb 39
Eyn Mandat von den [illegible] Dal 1 alb —
Noch gedrückt Privilegium Latin 100 stück
uff beyden syden gedrückt kost — Dal ij alb
Summa Daler 15 alb 35
Matern Colin

Fig. 4.3. Cholinus' invoice presented to the city council in 1576.

their documents printed in 600 copies.[52] We may infer that the Cologne edition, inviting participants to a contest in 1483, existed in a similarly high number of copies, especially since it was produced in two editions.[53] The edition produced about two decades later may even have topped these numbers, as the competition was intended to be a major event, including even a lottery; the participants were promised big prizes and the documents were sent out over nine months in advance to allow participants from more distant territories to travel to Cologne.[54]

Some of these documents could involve complex designs, including various images, as for instance the coat of arms of the host city. In many cases, the broadsheets also show depictions of the targets to help contestants practise for the event. In a time before standardised measurement, this was of great importance for foreign contestants.[55] Naturally, these illustrations drove up the prices for their production, yet they also brought higher compensations.

The Cologne edition of 1501 (fig. 4.4.) is an extraordinary example showing just how elaborate these invitations could be. For the edition, the printer employed various detailed woodcuts, such as a large coat of arms in the top centre of the broadsheet, and a representation of the size as well as the distance to the target. On top of that, the broadsheet was adorned with illustrations of the permitted weapons: crossbows and firearms. Lastly, the broadsheet also included a depiction of the lottery drawing, in which the official drew the winning tickets out of two cask-sized pots adorned with the city's coat of arms.

For the production of this beautiful broadsheet edition, the printer Johannes Koelhoff received the impressive amount of 17 Gulden.[56] This relatively high investment paid off: the event brought the city a huge surplus. Although only some 350 shooters competed for the prizes, a relatively low number of participants for such a big event, the lottery was a real success.[57] The city was able to sell some 60,000 lottery tickets, raising a total of 4,300 Gulden.[58] The printer commissioned to print the lottery tickets would also have earned a decent fee, though

52 Eisermann (2000), 'Auflagenhöhen von Einblattdrucken im 15. und frühen 16. Jahrhundert', pp. 161–162.

53 USTC 744098 (VE15 K-21); USTC 744099 (VE15 K-22).

54 Appendix no. 30. The event took place on 1 August 1502, and the document was issued on 16 November 1501, presumably printed and sent out quickly afterwards, see BC, no. 353.

55 Ostermann (2000), 'Zu den gedruckten Schützenbriefen des 15. Jahrhunderts', p. 430.

56 HAStK, Best. 70 A 99A, fol. 4. The German original reads: 'Item Johan Kolhoff vm die vysgesante gedruckte brieve gegeven – xvij guld.'

57 Giel (1998), *Politische Öffentlichkeit im spätmittelalterlich-frühneuzeitlichen Köln*, p. 104.

58 Ewald (1933), 'Die Rheinischen Schützengesellschaften', p. 60.

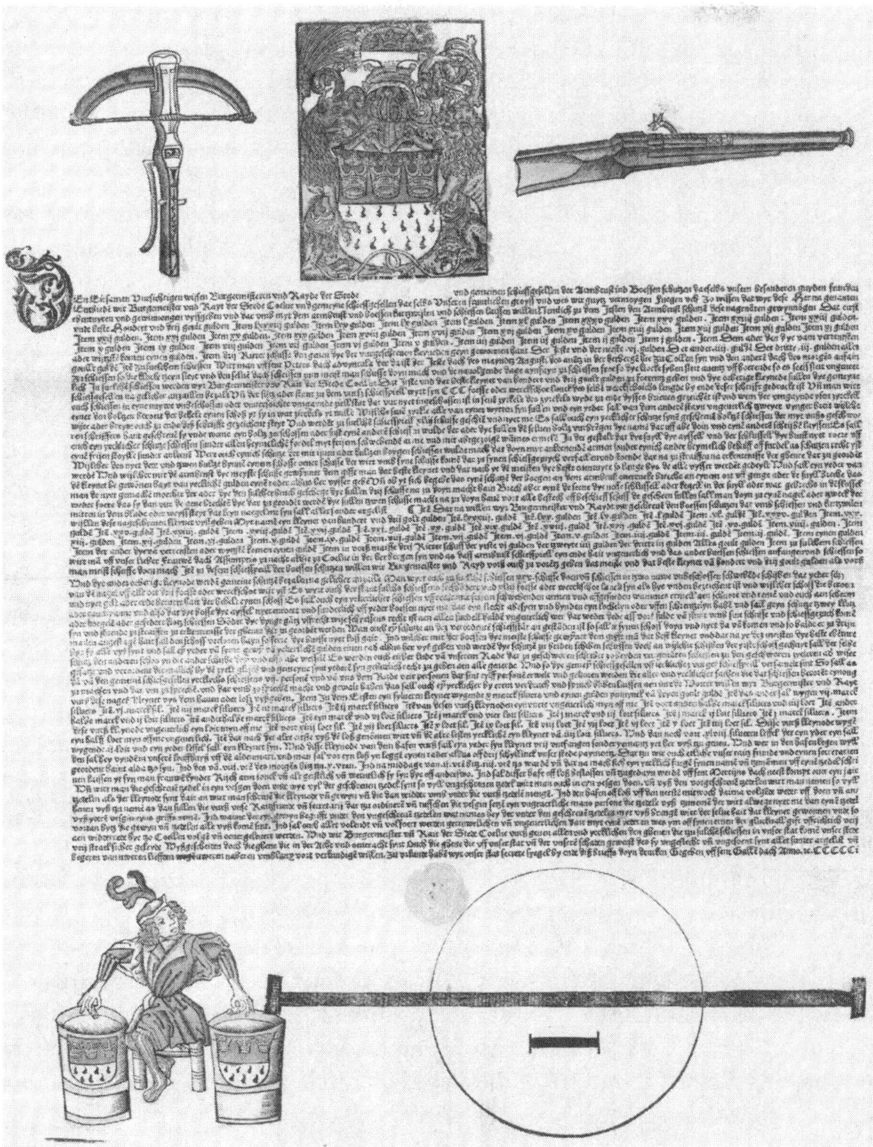

Fig. 4.4. Invitation to a shooting contest in Cologne, printed 1501, appendix no. 30.

sadly no copies survive. The council of Zurich was not nearly as successful when it only managed to sell 24,000 tickets at a local lottery a few years later.[59] Despite the expenditure of some 2,500 Gulden for the organisation of the big event in Cologne, the city made 1,800 Gulden profit.[60] This was a handsome sum. The council in Munich was not as fortunate when it organised a shooting contest and a lottery in 1486 and only had a surplus of some 43 Gulden.[61]

Yet, the payment of 17 Gulden for the production of printed invitations was exceptional. Most shooting competitions that took place in Cologne were much smaller in scale than the one in 1502. When in the mid-sixteenth century the council decided to host another match, it specified that only marksmen from neighbouring cities and villages could be invited.[62] As those from areas near Cologne were familiar with local rules and traditions, probably following them as well, there was no need to include an indication of the competition rules on the printed invitations. The council did not organise a lottery for every match either.

'Our well-known and trusted printer' – prestigious print orders

It is worthy of note that despite the relatively small returns offered by official publications, printing for the council in Cologne was still a job keenly sought after. Although the magistrates usually only placed small orders, the owners of big print firms were increasingly interested in these jobs, especially from the mid-1550s onwards. In the latter half of the sixteenth century, Cologne ordinances were almost exclusively produced by two of the most prolific publishers, Jaspar von Gennep and Maternus Cholinus (cf. fig. 4.1).

The two printers knew that being the trusted producers for the political elite in the city brought their printing houses much prestige. In Augsburg, Silvan Otmar enjoyed a particularly good reputation among the authorities, as was demonstrated by a letter from the local council. In its letter to the magistrates in Heilbronn, the council referred to Otmar as their 'well-known and trusted' printer, who was responsible for the document enclosed.[63] Such positive evaluation travelled far beyond the city's jurisdiction. At a time when many authors complained about stingy, illiterate, and careless printers, it was of utmost

59 OSTERMANN (2000), 'Zu den gedruckten Schützenbriefen des 15. Jahrhunderts', p. 406.
60 EWALD (1933), 'Die Rheinischen Schützengesellschaften', p. 60.
61 OSTERMANN (2000), 'Zu den gedruckten Schützenbriefen des 15. Jahrhunderts', p. 405.
62 RB, V, p. 821, no. 433.
63 SCHOTTENLOHER (1940), 'Silvan Otmar in Augsburg, der Drucker des Schwäbischen Bundes 1519–1535', p. 285.

importance to find scrupulous businessmen who took great care in handling official orders.

This was especially true for legal publications commissioned by the authorities. It was of importance that the government knew its secrets were safe with the printer, particularly during the difficult times of the Reformation. A simple mistake could easily lead to uproar, just as it happened in Edinburgh when the king tried to introduce a new reform.[64] Although the king kept this quiet for a long time, the corrected proof sheets of his reform were reused thoughtlessly, thereby making the king's plans involuntarily public much sooner than he had hoped. What followed was a number of violent protests against the reform. It was, therefore, crucial for authorities to know how trustworthy a printer was. The frequent employment and generous remarks of the local authorities signalled to many other governing bodies that Otmar was a suitable supplier who delivered on time, printed documents without errors and, most importantly, could be trusted with sensitive orders.

As the printer enjoyed the Augsburg council's trust, other authorities in the southern part of the empire frequently placed their orders at Otmar's printing shop. From 1523, shortly after he started producing for the city council, Otmar printed several legal works issued by rulers in the Habsburg heredity lands, including the Duke of Styria and the Duke of Carinthia.[65] The printer also published ordinances from other city councils, such as those of Zurich and Bern.[66] One of Otmar's best clients was the Swabian League. Founded in 1488, the League comprised many towns, abbeys, and knights who, among other things, hoped to counterbalance Wittelsbach power in the southern empire.[67] It has been estimated that Otmar's involvement with the Swabian League started in 1522, yet the first payment may have even preceded this date, as the printer produced an announcement from the League as early as 1519.[68] Until the dissolution of the League in 1534, the association frequently entrusted Otmar with its work. Most of the publications were small pamphlets comprising only a few leaves, but on several occasions the printer also delivered larger works with some 20–30 leaves, bringing him welcome profit.[69]

64 Parker (2013), *Global Crisis*, pp. 333–334. In Antwerp, the printer was told to destroy all manuscript and proof copies after printing a sensitive document. Voet (ed.) (1980–1983), *The Plantin Press (1555–1589)*, I, p. 156.

65 USTC 635318 (VD16 S 8760), USTC 657411 (VD16 ZV 8829).

66 See, for instance, USTC 608206 (VD16 Z 572), USTC 608575 (VD16 B 1880), USTC 689888 (VD16 B 1896).

67 Whaley (2012), *Germany and the Holy Roman Empire*, I, p. 77.

68 Schottenloher (1940), 'Silvan Otmar in Augsburg, der Drucker des Schwäbischen Bundes 1519–1535', p. 285; USTC 608219 (VD16 S 4564).

69 USTC 608217 (VD16 S 4569).

Undoubtedly, Otmar was paid for most of his editions by the authorities who issued them, such as the Swabian League or the dukes in Austria. Yet, some of the above-mentioned publications were also commissioned by the city council of Augsburg. This holds especially true for imperial publications. As an imperial city, Augsburg was obliged to communicate the emperor's orders to its subjects, and in several cases, the magistrates did so by printing the documents and having them exhibited. Thus when Charles V issued a mandate regulating Anabaptism on 28 January 1528, the council instructed Otmar to print 100 copies.[70]

Similarly, in Cologne the city council paid for the production of several imperial announcements. On some ordinances it included extra words above and below the imperial text. As already seen above, fig. 3.3. shows an imperial mandate issued on 6 June 1529.[71] It contains both an introductory and ending part to Charles V's order which clearly marks it as a local re-production of an imperial ordinance. Another example from the council's minutes even reveals the print run for such publications. When in June 1544 the council received Charles V's mandate banning anyone from taking up French military service, the magistrates determined that the ordinance should be published in 100 copies.[72]

A good reputation among the political elite, like that enjoyed by Silvan Otmar, was extremely valuable for printers in Cologne. The city was surrounded by rulers who did not have a print shop at their disposal and frequently employed Cologne printers for their work. This included not only immediate neighbours such as the Archbishop of Cologne, the dukes of Jülich-Cleves-Berg, and the Count of Moers, but also rulers from more distant territories such as the Archbishop of Liège and the Bishop of Würzburg. These rulers tended to employ the same printers who worked for the city council. Therefore, the printers who were favoured by the magistrates would attract many more orders from other rulers, especially as the century progressed and the printing press became a vital tool for early modern governments.

The first printer the council continuously entrusted with official work was Ludwig von Renchen.[73] He was a cautious businessman and tried to minimise the risks of the early modern print industry throughout his entire life. When he set up shop in 1475, he worked exclusively as a printer for other publishers,

70 Schottenloher (1940), 'Silvan Otmar in Augsburg, der Drucker des Schwäbischen Bundes 1519–1535', p. 284. As the printer refers to the publication as printed on *Zettel*, this was most likely a broadsheet publication intended for public display.

71 Appendix no. 56.

72 Appendix no. 69; RB, V, p. 212, no. 180.

73 Schmitz (1990), *Die Überlieferung deutscher Texte im Kölner Buchdruck*, p. 339.

focussing on theological books as well as humanist works.[74] This was a safe strategy for a printer in the incunabula age. After seven years, when he had accumulated enough capital, Renchen opened his own independent print shop in late 1482. As a printer, Renchen still aimed to reduce the risks of the print business and, therefore, continued to produce books for two successful publishers in Cologne, Johann Koelhoff the elder and Heinrich Quentel.[75] In the following years, Renchen concentrated on the production of liturgical books, devotional works, and schoolbooks, publications that promised good sales.[76]

From the very beginning, Renchen knew how valuable official orders were. He, therefore, chose the position of his printing house with great care, establishing business premises close to the town hall. The shops of Renchen's colleagues were at least several minutes away from the municipal building. Ulrich Zell worked near St Mary's church, ten minutes south of the *Altermarkt*, the market square in front of the town hall.[77] His competitor Heinrich Quentel operated in a shop near the cathedral and, in this way, was ideally placed to cater for the needs of the many visitors and pilgrims who came to visit the site.[78] Renchen, in contrast, was well situated to attract the attention of the authorities.

Renchen's careful consideration of his place of business bore fruit, and in the following years, he was entrusted with a number of official publications. During the fifteenth century, the council employed him for the production of the majority of its ordinances. His involvement with the political elite in the city brought further orders from other authorities. When in 1494, the magistrates in Cologne came to an agreement with the archbishop on the use of specific coins, Renchen produced the edition for the council as well as the edition for the Archbishop.[79] This was easily done, as Renchen only needed to set up the type once and adapt it to the wishes of the respective authorities. In this way, he could supply both editions in a very short space of time. In addition to the archbishop of Cologne, Renchen also produced a broadsheet for the Bishop of Liège, Johann II.[80] From the mid-1490s, Renchen increasingly printed documents for neighbouring princes. In these years, the printer supplied four editions for the Count of Moers, the ruler of a small territory north of Cologne.[81] The territory was eventually taken over by the Count of Wied, for whom Renchen

74 Schmitz (ed.) (1979), *Die Kölner Einblattdrucke*, p. 51.

75 *Ibid.*

76 Reske, p. 459.

77 Schmitz (1990), *Die Überlieferung deutscher Texte im Kölner Buchdruck*, p. 312.

78 Ennen (ed.) (1865), *Katalog der Inkunabeln in der Stadt-Bibliothek zu Köln*, p. xv.

79 USTC 745656 (VE15 H-22, archbishop's edition), USTC 744103 (VE15 K-28, council's edition).

80 USTC 746211.

81 VE15 V-22 – V-25.

also published four editions; all of them in broadsheet form.[82] The printer even seems to have obtained a privilege for producing official documents for the Duke of Jülich.[83] From 1494 onwards, Renchen was the only printer who produced ordinances and privileges for the duke. Before this, Johann Koelhoff the younger had printed two ordinances for Jülich.[84]

Renchen was the printer who produced nearly half of the council's ordinances in the incunabula age (5 out of 12), but he was not the exclusive supplier.[85] The very first printed announcement from the city council, the explanation of the uproar in 1482, appeared a few months before Renchen opened his printing house. Here, it was Johann Koelhoff the elder who supplied the printed copies.[86] In addition to this publication, Koelhoff also produced the two editions of the invitation to the shooting competition in 1483 as well as the magnificent invitation in the early sixteenth century.[87] However, after these initial publications, Renchen took over the work. Over the next six years, he supplied almost all the other publications for the city council. These included the justifications concerning the feud with Swicker von Sickingen and various coin ordinances.[88]

After Renchen started printing for the civic government, Johann Koelhoff only produced for the council on one more occasion; perhaps Renchen was too busy with other work in that particular year.[89] In 1490, the council complained to King Maximilian about various princes who had deliberately sabotaged Cologne's privileges on the Rhine. In the same year, Renchen produced a dictionary of German and Low German.[90] The printer produced the dictionary as a quarto that comprised no fewer than 180 leaves, a total of 45 sheets. As Renchen only operated a small print shop, he was probably too occupied with the production of the dictionary to focus his attention on other publications, including those ordered by the council. Consequently, Koelhoff supplied the announcement.

82 USTC 749825 (VE15 W-41), USTC 749826 (VE15 W-42), USTC 749827 (VE15 W-43), USTC 749828 (VE15 W-44).
83 Schmitz (ed.) (1979), *Die Kölner Einblattdrucke*, p. 52.
84 USTC 749832 (VE15 W-36), 749833 (VE15 W-37).
85 VE15 K-20 – K-32; Renchen supplied VE15 K-23, 24, 28, 29, 30.
86 USTC 744091 (VE15 K-20).
87 See chapter three, USTC 744098 (VE15 K-21), USTC 744099 (VE15 K-22).
88 USTC 744092 (VE15 K-23), USTC 744093 (VE15 K-24), USTC 744094 (VE15 K-29), USTC 744100 (VE15 K-30), USTC 744101 (VE15 K-31), USTC 744103 (VE15 K-28).
89 The ordinance appeared in two very similar editons, see: USTC 744095 (VE15 K-26) and USTC 744096 (K-27). For a reproduction of the latter, see Schmitz (ed.) (1979), *Die Kölner Einblattdrucke*, Tafel no. 35.
90 USTC 742199.

Despite the fact that Renchen produced many official broadsheets for the council, he was not able to secure the market for imperial ordinances. Although the printer published two of Maximilian I's mandates, there were other printers who shared this market.[91] Heinrich Quentel printed a royal announcement concerning the Count of Nassau in 1494.[92] From then on, Johann Landen, Hermann Bungart, and others produced royal and imperial documents.[93] This indicates that in the fifteenth century, the Cologne magistrates and the imperial chancellery did not appoint one and the same printer.

Renchen was also unable to secure the market for official religious publications, most importantly indulgences. From the very beginning of moveable type in Cologne, printers produced various editions of these rewarding publications. They were extremely lucrative orders: the authorities would request thousands of copies and the whole edition was paid for by a single client.[94] Ulrich Zell started producing indulgences in 1467, only a few years after he had begun printing.[95] Before the end of the century, Zell would publish a total of 20 different broadsheet indulgence certificates.[96] Although Zell produced many broadsheet editions for the papal legate Peraudi, he did not have a monopoly on this kind of print.[97] Only a decade after Zell had begun to publish indulgences, the printer faced competition from one of his former students, Arnold ter Hoernen. It was ter Hoernen who in 1479 and 1480 catered almost exclusively for this promising market.[98] Ter Hoernen's supremacy would not last very long, however, since he died in 1482.[99] From then on, Ulrich Zell once again supplied official religious broadsheets. As the number of orders increased constantly, Ulrich Zell later shared the market with Johann Koelhoff the elder, who started printing indulgences from 1485.[100] Only towards the very end of the century, after he had been printing for over a decade, did Renchen produce an indulgence.[101] This seems to be the only religious broadsheet the printer produced during his lifetime.

91 The two editions produced by Renchen: USTC 747071 (VE15 M-48), USTC 747114 (VE15 M-44).
92 USTC 747077 (VE15 M-29).
93 USTC 747123, USTC 747074 (VE15 M-105); for Bungart see below.
94 Indulgences could be produced in 10,000 copies, see Eisermann (2017b), 'Fifty Thousand Veronicas. Print Runs of Broadsheets in the Fifteenth and Early Sixteenth Centuries', pp. 80–92.
95 USTC 748372 (VE15 R-3), USTC 748373 (VE15 R-4).
96 USTC search: Printer - Zel*, Format - Broadsheet.
97 Schmitz (ed.) (1979), *Die Kölner Einblattdrucke*, p. 42.
98 *Ibid.*, pp. 45–46.
99 Schmitz (1990), *Die Überlieferung deutscher Texte im Kölner Buchdruck*, p. 317.
100 Schmitz (ed.) (1979), *Die Kölner Einblattdrucke*, p. 42.
101 USTC 745047 (VE15 G-7).

Although Renchen worked in Cologne until 1505, he lost the business of the council in 1494 to one of his competitors, Hermann Bungart. Bungart had entered the print world of Cologne only one year previously, yet he focussed on official publications from the very beginning. As already seen, Bungart was one of the printers who produced royal and imperial mandates while Ludwig von Renchen was still active. Bungart's first book appeared in mid-December 1494, and by the following year, he had already printed two official broadsheet publications.[102] One of them was a mandate from Maximilian I regulating blasphemy. The other edition was an order from the Cologne magistrates: an undated coin ordinance. Although the document bears neither a dated imprint nor an issue date, the conversion table included on the broadsheet allows us to date the edition to 1495. This was the only year in which 1 Gold Gulden equalled 39 Albus, exactly as described in the table on the broadsheet.[103]

From 1495 onwards, Bungart frequently worked for the council. In the first quarter of the sixteenth century, the council commissioned 24 broadsheets.[104] Many of these publications regulated the use of coins, with others addressing the import of bread from rural areas surrounding Cologne as well as tax issues. It appears that 14 of these publications were supplied by Bungart, as the type used for these publications clearly points in his direction.[105] The printer might even have generated another eight editions until his death in 1527, however, the type on these broadsheets does not provide any clear indication.[106] In addition to these ordinances, Bungart printed the sheets complaining against the councillors during the uproar in 1513, which the new council used to justify its policy to the inhabitants of Cologne.[107]

Just like Renchen, Bungart was soon entrusted with the production of official work for other authorities. In 1501, the printer supplied an announcement made by the Archbishop of Cologne.[108] A couple of years later, in 1503, the printer produced indulgences, pamphlets, and probably even legends of saints for the papal legate Peraudi.[109] Since Zell and Koelhoff the younger had

102 Reske, p. 460; Schmitz (ed.) (1979), *Die Kölner Einblattdrucke*, p. 58; note: another broadsheet attributed to Bungart was most likely produced by Jakob Köbel in Oppenheim, see Schanze (2000), 'Inkunabel oder Postinkunabel?', p. 91.

103 Schmitz (ed.) (1979), *Die Kölner Einblattdrucke*, p. 58.

104 Appendix nos. 28–51.

105 The type was analysed by Borchling and Claussen, see BC, I, pp. 163–362. Appendix nos. 31, 32, 33, 34, 35, 36, 40, 41, 43, 44, 45, 46, 47, 49.

106 Reske, p. 460. Appendix nos. 28, 29, 42, 48, 50, 51, 52, 53.

107 See chapter three, e. g. USTC 710377 (VD16 S 10213); Schmitz (1990), *Die Überlieferung deutscher Texte im Kölner Buchdruck*, p. 348.

108 USTC 656933 (VD16 K 1727).

109 Rautenberg (1996), *Überlieferung und Druck. Heiligenlegenden aus frühen Kölner Offizinen*, p. 182.

died in 1502 and 1503 respectively, Bungart was able to dominate the market.[110] However, this was only for a short period, since Peraudi only stayed in Cologne for a few weeks.[111] Then, in 1506, Bungart collaborated with another printer to produce an *Ordinarius* for the Diocese of Trier, and in 1516, he again produced indulgences, this time for the papal legat Johannes Angelus Arcimboldus.[112]

Although Bungart produced most of the ordinances for the city council until his death in 1527, he was, like Renchen, not the only printer appointed by the government at that time. His competitor Heinrich von Neuss produced at least three editions for the magistrates while Bungart was active.[113] In all three cases, the documents consisted of an agreement between the city council and the Duke of Jülich, which may indicate that Heinrich von Neuss was producing for the neighbouring duke as well. Thus it was probably easier for the city council to ask him, instead of Bungart, to print the respective ordinance for the council. Like Renchen in 1494, when he supplied ordinances for both archbishop and council, Heinrich von Neuss could just keep the frame in standing type, make minimal changes, and print it again for the council and the Duke of Jülich.

Heinrich von Neuss must have received the order from the council as welcome news. He was facing financial difficulties in both years in which he produced ordinances for the municipal government. Two of the ordinances appeared in 1511, the very year in which Heinrich von Neuss suffered from a severe decline in his production. This was rather unexpected, as after a promising start in 1508, Heinrich von Neuss' production rose steadily.[114] When he experienced difficulties securing work in 1511, he was able to receive at least some income by publishing the only two official broadsheets the city council issued that year. The second time Heinrich von Neuss produced for the council was in 1517. Again, his production had suffered a decline and the council's order helped him through this difficult time.[115]

Although Heinrich von Neuss was active in Cologne until 1523, the council entrusted Herrmann Bungart with the production of most ordinances, probably

110 *Ibid.* For reproductions of some of Koelhoff's indulgences, see https://www.monasterium.net//mom/IlluminierteUrkunden/1502–99–99_Nuernberg/charter

111 Rautenberg (1990), 'Der päpstliche Gesandte und Ablaßkommissar Raymundus Peraudi als Auftraggeber des Druckers Hermann Bungart', p. 188.

112 Reske, p. 460; Duntze and Eisermann (2017), 'Beichtbriefe und Formulardrucke für die Livlandkampagnen und für den Vertrieb des Petersablasses durch Arcimboldi', p. 258. For reproductions of the indulgences, see https://www.monasterium.net/mom/IlluminierteUrkunden/1515-99-99_Muenchen/charter and https://www.monasterium.net/mom/IlluminierteUrkunden/1516-99-99_Stralsund/charter

113 Appendix nos. 37, 38, 39.

114 Schmitz (1990), *Die Überlieferung deutscher Texte im Kölner Buchdruck*, p. 352.

115 *Ibid.*, p. 353.

because Heinrich von Neuss' shop was situated farther away from the centre of political life in Cologne. His printing house was in an old mansion called 'Leopard' on the 'Eigelstein', north of the cathedral and thus some distance from the town hall.[116] A messenger would have to walk at least 15 minutes to bring a manuscript to Heinrich von Neuss' shop. It was much more convenient to take the manuscript across the market square to Hermann Bungart's printing house.

Another printer who probably printed for the municipal government in Cologne during Hermann Bungart's time was Johannes Soter. This printer seems to have supplied at least one ordinance in 1527, which has, unfortunately, not survived to the present day.[117] In this year, the Archbishop of Cologne issued an ordinance that contained the details of an agreement on coins between him and the Elector Palatine. As the agreement also had implications for the many tradesmen conducting business in the imperial city, it seems very likely that the council had a similar ordinance printed to be exhibited to visitors. This assumption is given credence by the survival of a copy of the archbishop's coin ordinance annotated by a council scribe.[118] The annotations suggest that the scribe was making the necessary adjustment for the printing of an edition for the council. The archbishop's edition opens with the title of the ruler, and the city scribe wrote the respective title of the council in the free space above the first line: 'Wir Bürgermeister und Rat der löblichen unser kayserlichen und des heiligen Reiches freyer Stat Köln tuen kundt.' The scribe also changed minor parts within the text such as crossing out the word 'territory' (*land*) and replaced it with 'city' (*stadt*). In this way, the printer could easily make the small amendments necessary to produce a similar ordinance for the magistrates. Undoubtedly, this would have been done by Soter, who had already produced the archbishop's edition. Depending on how quickly the city scribe worked, the printer may have even kept the existing type set up, then amended the respective parts, and produced the broadsheet for the city council as soon as he received the changes. This also happened in 1573, when the council kept only an annotated copy instead of preserving a copy of the amended printed version.[119] This sufficed as a future reference tool for the council.

Apart from this coin ordinance for the city council that has sadly not survived, Soter may have produced other regulations for the city council. He operated his printing house from 1518 to 1543, and during this time, the council had a total of 21 documents printed that cannot be assigned with certainty to one printer.

116 Reske, p. 463; Ennen (1863–1880), *Geschichte der Stadt Köln*, I, p. 678.

117 Appendix no. 54.

118 HAStK, Best. 14 (Edikte): 14, Nr. 16.

119 Limbach (2016), 'Tracing Lost Broadsheet Ordinances Printed in Sixteenth-Century Cologne', p. 502; appendix no. 143.

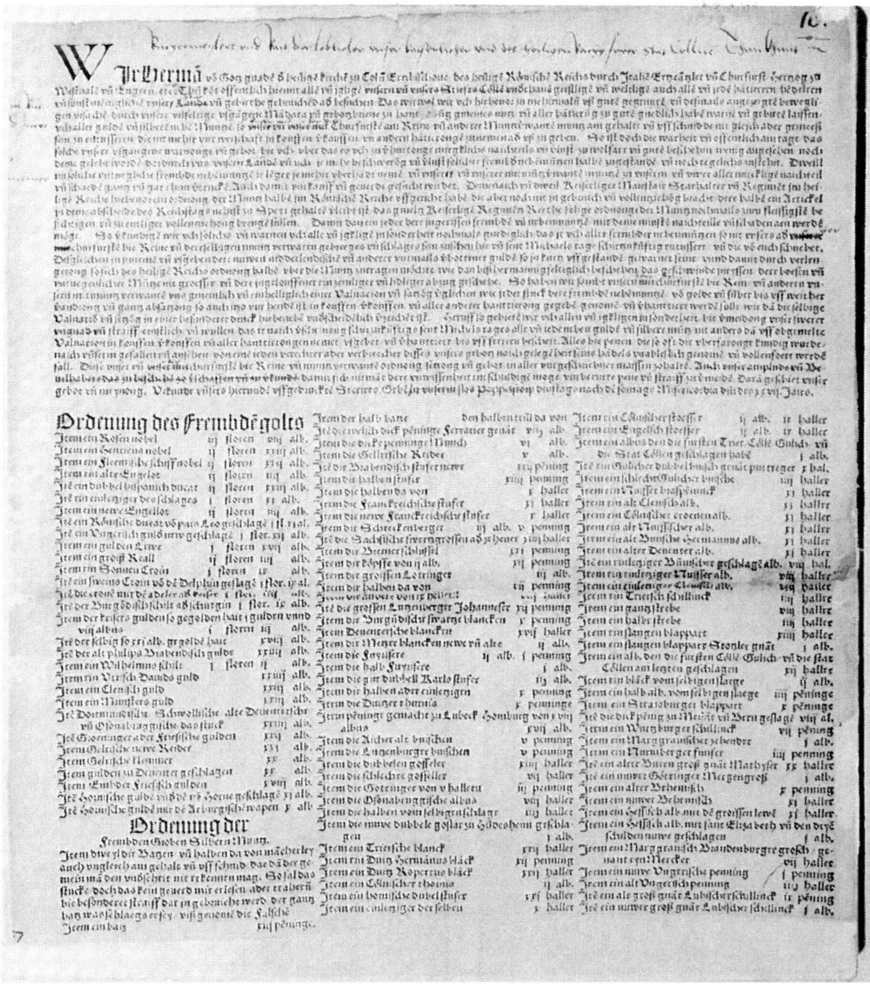

Fig. 4.5. Annotated copy of a coin ordinance from 1527, issued by the Archbishop of Cologne.

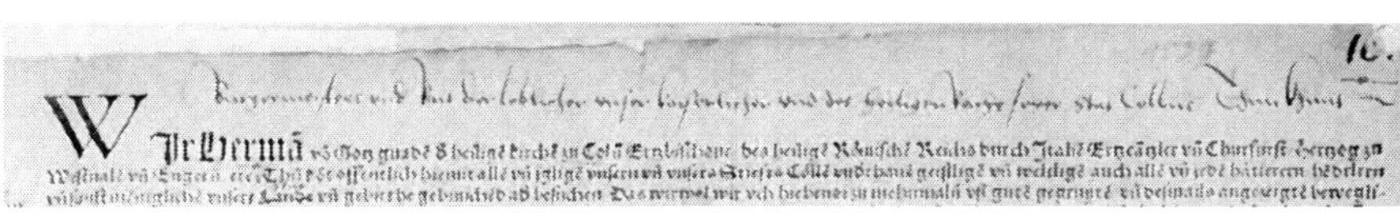

Fig. 4.6. Detail of the annotations.

This includes 18 dated ordinances as well as three undated ones that seem to have been produced in the mid-sixteenth century. Soter may well have been the producer of some of them, yet unfortunately we cannot assign any documents to his shop with certainty. It is, however, unlikely that Johannes Soter produced many official broadsheets for the magistrates in Cologne since in the early 1530s Eucharius Hirtzhorn was entrusted with the magistrates' official work and produced at least three broadsheets for the city council.[120]

Soter produced for various other rulers in the Rhineland as well as the city council. As the printer supplied the coin ordinance for the Archbishop of Cologne, he probably also provided other official documents commissioned by religious authorities in Cologne. This may include two pamphlets with official statements from the Duke of Saxony and the Landgrave of Hesse.[121] To pen a Catholic response to these statements, it was certainly handy to have them in printed form produced by a trusted printer.

In contrast to his predecessors, Soter took his involvement with the Duke of Jülich-Cleves-Berg a step further and left Cologne to move to the Duke's territory. Already in his Cologne time, in the early 1530s, Soter had printed a church ordinance issued by the duke, probably commissioned by the ruler.[122] A few years later, in 1537, Soter bought a paper mill in the territory and opened a printing house next to it.[123] Here, the printer produced various religious books, including the works of Philip Melanchthon and Johannes Eck, which certainly were of use to a prince who hoped to introduce the Reformation in his territory. While he was in the duchy, the printer probably supplied the five broadsheet ordinances that the dukes issued between 1537 and 1543.[124] Soter's press was of particular importance for William in the last two years, as the Duke was facing war with the emperor after he had invaded parts of the Habsburg Netherlands.[125] The duke justified his claims in several official publications, both in German and in Latin, which Soter readily supplied.[126] The relationship between

120 Appendix nos. 59, 61, 62.

121 USTC 707826 (VD16 S 775), USTC 671536 (VD16 ZV 23340); in Württemberg, the Catholic government also had Morhart print Luther pamphlets so that they could respond to them, see chapter two, subchapter 'Ulrich Morhart – the loyal servant'.

122 USTC 700399 (VD16 K 1284).

123 Reske, p. 917.

124 Landesarchiv Nordrhein-Westfalen, Handschriften L II 7, Band 1 & Handschriften L II 8, see entries in bibliography for 'Jülich – Cleves – Berg'.

125 Esser (2012), *The Politics of Memory. The Writing of Partition in the Seventeenth-Century Low Countries*, p. 248.

126 USTC 705919 (VD16 K 1287), USTC 615895 (VD16 B 1829), USTC 665839 (VD16 A 3912).

the printer and the duke came to a sudden end when both William and Soter died in 1543.

Soter's successor in producing Cologne ordinances, Eucharius Hirtzhorn, followed Soter's example and also moved to another jurisdiction to cater for the needs of the local ruler. Hirtzhorn was working in Cologne as early as 1516 and was thus well known in the city when he started producing for the authorities.[127] In the early 1530s, Hirtzhorn secured at least three orders from the magistracy, delivering coin ordinances with detailed exchange rates.[128] These publications probably sparked the interest of Philip, Landgrave of Hesse, one of the leading figures in the Reformation and confidant of Duke Ulrich of Württemberg. In 1536, the landgrave tempted Hirtzhorn to move to the capital of his territory, Marburg, about 150 kilometres east of Cologne.[129] The small town had enjoyed much recent attention after Philip founded the first Protestant university in the German lands.[130] As the previous university printer had left in 1535, Marburg was without a printer and desperately needed one. Hirtzhorn moved to Marburg to produce for both the new academic institution and the government.

The new office was quite lucrative and there was plenty for Hirtzhorn to do from the very start. After the previous printer had left, numerous academic manuscripts were still waiting to be put to press. Hirtzhorn received an annual salary of 50 Gulden for his work, which, as we have seen in the second chapter, was both unusual at the time as well as a good sum of money. In addition to this already generous payment, the printer received an extra 200 Gulden to help him move to Marburg and buy the necessary equipment.[131]

However, Hirtzhorn's endeavour in Marburg did not go well. He spent most of his time in his shop in Cologne and delegated his son Gottfried to oversee the shop in Marburg. Following the establishment of his father's business relationship with the university, young Gottfried matriculated in Marburg and began to pursue a degree.[132] Supervised only by a student, the production of Hirtzhorn's shop in Marburg seems to have been neglected, and output was very low. In the first year, the shop produced 11 books: a total of 86 sheets.[133] This was not much,

127 Reske, p. 465.
128 Appendix nos. 59, 61, 62.
129 Reske, p. 653.
130 Rudersdorf (1992), 'Hessen', p. 264.
131 Reske, pp. 653–654.
132 *Ibid.*, p. 476.
133 This again draws on the same methodology explained in chapter two. USTC 608552 ((VD16 M 5661), 4 sheets), USTC 648945 ((VD16 C 3294), 4 sheets), USTC 668023 ((VD16 E 873), 44 sheets), USTC 688140 ((VD16 B 3160), 4 sheets), USTC 611367 ((VD16 E 651), 4 sheets), USTC 678578 ((VD16 E 673), 6 sheets), USTC 683709 ((VD16 ZV 26883), 4 sheets), USTC 673464

especially since the Marburg scholars were kept waiting for various publications. In contrast, in 1534, Hirtzhorn had published ten editions with a total of 352 sheets in his Cologne shop.[134] The second year in Marburg was even less productive than the first.

Not surprisingly, Marburg's academic community was far from satisfied. The scholars complained to the landgrave's chancellery that paid Hirtzhorn's salary.[135] In their complaint, the scholars voiced their concerns that Hirtzhorn spent much more time in Cologne than in Marburg. The professors also objected to Hirtzhorn's character, as he was a naïve and unmannerly man, and demanded that Hirtzhorn be dismissed. They proposed that instead of the Cologne printer, the Landgrave of Hesse should encourage a printer from Frankfurt, Christian Egenolff.[136]

This complaint was grist to the chancellery's mill. Despite a regular payment and a considerable investment for the shop, Hirtzhorn had managed to accumulate a debt of 100 Gulden to the landgrave. The professors' complaint was, therefore, the confirmation that the printer was not as reliable as previously thought. In 1538, only two years after he had tempted the printer to come to Marburg, Philip of Hesse dismissed Hirtzhorn and, following the professors' advice, appointed Christian Egenolff from Frankfurt as the new university printer in Marburg. This would turn out to be a much more fruitful endeavour, with Egenolff producing over 80 imprints in the following years.[137]

After his short interlude in Marburg, Hirtzhorn focussed on his production in Cologne once again. He may have continued to print for the council, yet if he did do so, he did not employ any of the initials he had previously used for the magistrates' publications. It seems, however, very unlikely that Hirtzhorn worked for the magistrates again, partly because of his previous work for a Protestant government. Although he had good ties to theologians in Cologne and seems to have been a Catholic himself, he still ended up on Pope Paul IV's Index from 1559.[138] Furthermore, a printer who had been dismissed by one

((VD16 C 5407), 10 sheets), USTC 701873 ((VD16 H 2894), 2 sheets), USTC 630144 ((VD16 ZV 26493), 2 sheets), USTC 630500 ((VD16 C 5411), 2 sheets).

134 USTC 683402 ((VD16 ZV 12308), 9 sheets), USTC 663926 ((VD16 H 4705), 31 sheets), USTC 657567 ((VD16 J 959), 178 sheets), USTC 652911 ((VD16 A 1112), 8 sheets), USTC 626441 ((VD16 H 215), 86 sheets), USTC 626053 ((VD16 E 3482), 4 sheets), USTC 626026 ((VD16 E 3406), 5 sheets), USTC 626001 ((VD16 E 2516), 25 sheets), USTC 617539 ((VD16 P 3519), 5 sheets), appendix no. 61 (1 sheet).

135 Reske, p. 654.

136 Schmitz (1990), *Die Überlieferung deutscher Texte im Kölner Buchdruck*, p. 373.

137 USTC search: Printer - Christian Egenolff, Place - Marburg, Date - 1538–1545.

138 Schmitz (2017), 'Beten und Lesen im Untergrund', pp. 99–100. Note that Hirtzhorn is listed as a printer in Marburg, although this shop had been closed

ruler for being slow and unreliable was not the best candidate for employment with another government. In sixteenth-century Cologne, the officials would undoubtedly have heard about Hirtzhorn's failure in Marburg – either from an envious colleague or travellers from Hesse – and would, therefore, have been reluctant to take him back.

Small print produced in big print shops

In the second half of the sixteenth century, when the council printed to a greater extent, the magistracy in Cologne turned to the most prolific and financially robust print shops: those of Jaspar von Gennep and Maternus Cholinus. The latter is known to have produced for the council, yet little was previously known about the nature of his official work.[139] The following will present a more complete picture of Cholinus' activities for the council as well as his involvement with other religious and secular authorities. In addition, it will be demonstrated that the local authorities in Cologne also employed Jaspar von Gennep, a fact which, until now, has escaped scholarly attention. Although almost all official publications in Cologne lack imprints, I can identify Gennep as the most likely candidate to have produced many ordinances issued in the second half of the sixteenth century. Here, I will base my investigation on woodcut images, especially those of coins. This investigation will be supplemented by a survey of initial woodcut decorations. Based on my findings, I can demonstrate that Gennep very likely supplied at least 20 ordinances for the city council.[140]

With this high number, Jaspar von Gennep supplied the majority of official broadsheets for the council from the 1550s until his death in 1564. Although Gennep produced most of these ordinances without imprints, there are three that include the printer's name. With the help of the woodcuts on these documents, as well as images used in his other publications, numerous other ordinances can be assigned with much certainty to Gennep's press. The first edition Gennep produced for the city council was issued in 1545. Over the next 19 years, Gennep produced another 12 dated editions and seven undated edicts. As the council had 23 dated as well as 15 undated editions printed in this period, we can assume that Gennep printed more than 50 % of all ordinances.

For the council, Gennep was the ideal candidate to provide civic announcements. As we have seen in the third chapter, the magistrates in Cologne banned

for over 20 years by the time the Index was published, *Die Indices librorum prohibitorum des sechzehnten Jahrhunderts*, ed. Reusch (1886), p. 207.

139 Schmitz (1990), *Die Überlieferung deutscher Texte im Kölner Buchdruck*, p. 403.

140 Appendix nos. 70, 72, 79, 80, 82, 86, 87, 88, 89, 90, 91, 92, 93, 94, 96, 98, 102, 104, 105, 106.

an increasing number of Dutch coins in the second half of the sixteenth century. To ensure that these ordinances were observed, it was crucial to include images of the coins in the broadsheets, allowing the inhabitants of Cologne to identify the coins at first sight. This was Gennep's great advantage: he had distinguished himself from his colleagues by his willingness to invest in a variety of woodcut images of coins. The council paid extra money when ordinances contained woodcuts, but this could have taken months, maybe even years.[141] In the meantime, Gennep had to balance his investment. For the small print shops, such as those of Renchen and Bungart, this might have been impossible; yet Gennep, as a more financially-secure printer, was able to do so.

Obtaining a variety of coin woodcuts made Gennep also the ideal supplier for coinage ordinances issued by other authorities. The Cologne magistrates were not the only rulers who increasingly banned Dutch coins from their jurisdiction. When the Duke of Jülich-Cleves-Berg issued regulations for the use of these coins in 1560, Gennep supplied the publication for which he employed several images used previously on Cologne publications.[142] The printer also used his woodcuts to produce ordinances for authorities in more distant territories such as the Archbishopric of Trier in 1564.[143] This broadsheet shows over 60 images as well as a large woodcut decoration at the bottom of the sheet, bearing a striking resemblance to the ordinance Gennep produced for the Cologne council in the same year.

Gennep had a very successful career right from the start. When he began to print in 1531, he ran his business in the house 'Zum Wilden Mann', the workshop previously used by Hermann Bungart.[144] Gennep was thus well situated in the market place in front of the town hall, the centre of political life in Cologne. Unlike Bungart, however, Gennep joined the urban elite, as only a few years after he had set up shop in Cologne, in 1539 at the latest, he was elected *Burggraf*, an office which oversaw the city court.[145]

His affiliation with the civic elite soon secured him valuable orders from other authorities as well as privileges. As the printer knew both Latin and the Bible, skills not every printer possessed, he was well equipped to produce religious

141 Cholinus' invoice shows that he received additional money for the two coin ordinances which included woodcuts. The additional costs are listed as 'etliche Müntzstock gedruckt', see fig. 4.3. He also had to wait up to 14 months for his payment, see below.

142 HAStK, Best. 14 (Edikte): 14, Nr. 37.

143 HAStK, Best. 14 (Edikte): 14, Nr. 38/39. The ordinance shows Gennep's imprint; however, it does not include a date. Nevertheless, the year has been added by a contemporary hand on the back of the broadsheet 'Ao 64'.

144 Reske, p. 473.

145 Isenmann (2014), *Die Deutsche Stadt im Mittelalter*, p. 482; Reske, p. 473.

works. In the following years, Gennep worked repeatedly for the Carthusians, a Catholic order based in Cologne.[146] By 1543, he had produced no fewer than 33 books for the Carthusians; this was nearly every second book he printed at that time.[147] On top of that, only five years after his election as *Burggraf*, Gennep obtained an imperial privilege to produce Catholic books.[148] Soon after that, he also became the official printer of the cathedral chapter.[149] Among his most notable publications were the books directed against Hermann von Wied, the archbishop who tried to convert Cologne to Protestantism.[150] During the Counter-Reformation, Jaspar von Gennep's press became an indispensable tool for the Catholic response to the archbishop's publications.[151]

Work for the Catholic authorities fuelled the printer's presses, and in the 1540s, Gennep's output rose significantly. In the 1530s, Gennep's output was relatively modest. In 1532, he produced only two editions with a total of 13 sheets.[152] While his output had risen by the end of the following year (1533), it was still relatively low – a total of five editions, which amounted to 96 sheets.[153] During the religious upheaval, however, Gennep's production rose significantly. The Catholic response to Hermann's attempted reform was energetic. In 1546 alone, Gennep produced a total of 19 editions, among them five pamphlets issued by the cathedral chapter and three books written by Johann Gropper, one of the archbishop's antagonists.[154] This busy year pushed

146 Duntze (2012), 'Gennep, Jaspar von', col. 551.

147 Duntze (1999), *Die Kölner Offizin des Jaspar von Gennep*, p. 28.

148 Gennep obtained the privilege on 15 January 1544, see Keussen, (1918), 'Regesten und Auszüge zur Geschichte der Universität Köln' p. 433. Obtaining such privileges was common practice in Italy, France, England, and the Holy Roman Empire from the end of the fifteenth century onwards, see Machill (ed.) (1974), *Handbuch des Buchhandels*, p. 37.

149 Reske, p. 473.

150 Schlüter (2005), *Flug- und Streitschriften zur 'Kölner Reformation'*, p. 13; Schlüter (1993), 'Der Streitschriftenkrieg um den Reformationsversuch in den Jahren 1543–1547', pp. 83–88.

151 Schlüter (2005), *Flug- und Streitschriften zur 'Kölner Reformation'*, p. 13.

152 USTC 628543 ((VD16 L 2298), 7 sheets), USTC 610577 ((VD16 ZV 8709), 6 sheets).

153 USTC 683753 ((VD16 J 1197), 30 sheets), USTC 636511 ((VD16 ZV 6104), 1 sheet), USTC 626442 ((VD16 H 229), 51 sheets), USTC 665004 ((VD16 J 1184), 13 sheets), USTC 666599 ((VD16 B 5749), 1 sheet). Schmitz (1990), *Die Überlieferung deutscher Texte im Kölner Buchdruck*, p. 121, mentions one further edition that Gennep had printed by Eucharius Hirtzhorn 1533. Unfortunately, Schmitz provides neither book format nor foliation.

154 USTC 647333 ((VD16 K 1799), 2 sheets), USTC 607902 ((VD16 E 1212), 9 sheets), USTC 613258 ((VD16 K 1772), 4 sheets), USTC 617970 ((VD16 G 3390), 8 sheets), USTC 617973 ((VD16 ZV 24633), 8 sheets), USTC 657515 ((VD16 M 6179), 8 sheets), USTC 629035 ((VD16 F 285), 4 sheets), USTC 611956

Gennep's output to a total of 229 sheets; it had thus multiplied significantly since his modest beginning in the 1530s.

From 1545 at the latest, Jaspar von Gennep started producing official publications for the city council of Cologne. In the following years, before he died in 1564, Gennep most likely produced at least 21 broadsheet editions for the civic government. Fortunately, in contrast to all his predecessors, he supplied three broadsheet editions with imprints. Two of these broadsheets were produced for the city council, whereas the third was a publication issued by the Duke of Jülich-Cleves-Berg.[155] The woodcut illustrations used on these editions suggest that another 19 editions for the city council were produced in his print shop.

We may well assume that Gennep produced more editions, maybe even every edition between 1545 and his death in 1564, but there is a lack of sources to support this claim. Unfortunately, not every official broadsheet in the possession of the city archive in Cologne was microfilmed. Following the collapse of the building which housed the archive in 2009, we often have to make do with broadsheets that have survived in only digital form. For the period during which Gennep worked for the government, 17 editions cannot be assigned with certainty. The low quality of a microfilm does not allow type analysis, and the woodcuts on the broadsheets do not point clearly in Gennep's direction either. Therefore, we cannot verify the assumption that Gennep was the only printer producing for the council in the years 1545–1564. However, we can assume that he produced at least 50 % of the broadsheets the council issued during these years.

Gennep's imprint appeared in July 1553 for the first time on an ordinance that stipulated the value of various foreign coins.[156] To aid the reader, the different values were accumulated in a table in the centre of the broadsheet. According to this table, for instance, the Gold Gulden is fixed at 52 Albus. In addition to the table, the broadsheet ordinance included two images of a coin produced in Liège, both front and back, on the right hand side next to the table. To structure the text, Gennep used three initials: one large initial at the

((VD16 F 1118), 10 sheets), USTC 632233 ((VD16 K 1775), 7 sheets), USTC 707289 ((VD16 ZV 9076), 1 sheet), USTC 669151 ((VD16 K 1812), 6 sheets), USTC 676669 ((VD16 ZV 9073), 1 sheet), USTC 684665 ((VD16 N 69), 152 sheets), USTC 691900 ((VD16 D 904), 3 sheets), USTC 693369 ((VD16 V 578), 2 sheets), USTC 629756 ((VD16 ZV 9356), 2 sheets), appendix nos. 85, 102 (1 sheet each); Gennep also produced USTC 654605 (VD16 B 4890), however, the amount of sheets remains unknown.

155 Appendix nos. 88, 106 and HAStK, Best. 14 (Edikte): 14, Nr. 37,1–2. The broadsheet has been separated into two pieces.

156 Appendix no. 88.

WJr Bürgermeistere vnd Rath der Stadt Cöllen/ Thün allen vnd jedern vnsern Bürgern/ Inwo-

Fig. 4.7. Coin ordinance from 1553 with Gennep's imprint at the bottom right, appendix no. 88.

beginning of the text (the letter 'W'), and two smaller initials (the letters 'N' and 'D') at the bottom of the text (fig. 4.7.). At the very bottom of the text, we see the printer's imprint on the right hand side.

The second ordinance which Gennep provided with an imprint appeared in July 1564. The document was one of the last ordinances the printer supplied before he died later that year.[157] This ordinance is in many ways a masterpiece. Again, it is a coin ordinance listing coins that were not permitted in Cologne. For guidance, it includes no fewer than 154 images of the coins mentioned, with a large 'W' woodcut initial placed at the beginning of the text. With its many images, the document was so long that four sheets had to be glued together; the whole document is over one metre long. This elaborate reference tool is of very fine quality. Its remarkable illustrations demonstrate very effectively what a vital tool printing was for this particular area of government regulation. It is impossible to conceive how an ordinance of this type could have been disseminated effectively purely by oral proclamations.

157 Appendix no. 106.

Fig. 4.8. Upper part of the coin ordinance issued in 1564 with the large 'W' initial, appendix no. 106 (with links to all parts of the ordinance).

Gennep's third coin ordinance dates from 1560.[158] Again, it provides an overview of forbidden coins with no fewer than ninety woodcuts. In contrast to the other ordinances, Gennep did not produce it for the city council but for the Duke of Jülich-Cleves-Berg. Although the duke's name is not given at the beginning of the ordinance, the text at the bottom of the broadsheet reveals that the ordinance was issued in Cleves. Thus we may well assume that Gennep worked for the duke, just like other council printers did before him.

Comparison of the coin woodcuts used in these broadsheets with other Cologne publications provides the key to demonstrating whether these anonymous editions were produced in Gennep's printing house. Coin woodcuts used

158 HAStK, Best. 14 (Edikte): 14, Nr. 37,1–2. The broadsheet has been separated into two pieces.

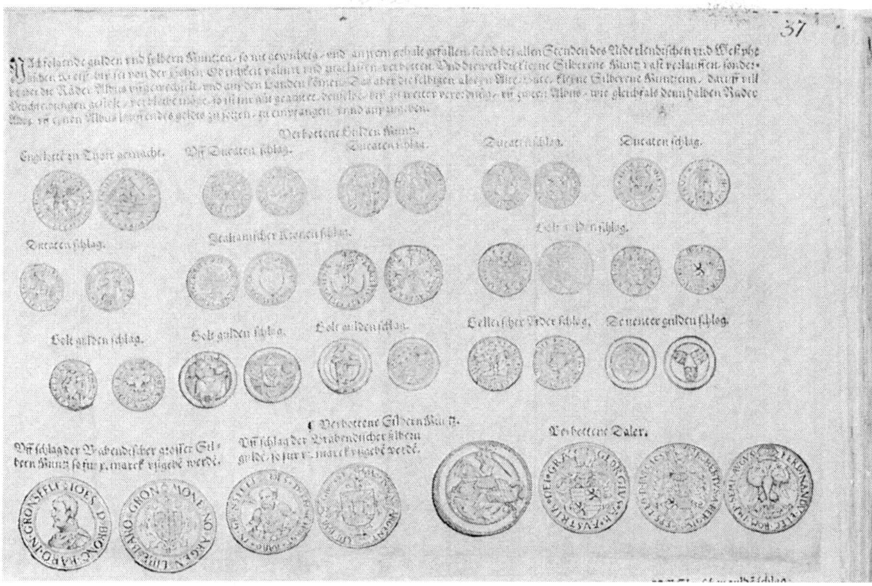

Fig. 4.9. Detail of the ordinance issued by the Duke of Jülich-Cleves-Berg in 1560.

in different shops reveal subtle but noticeable differences.[159] This can be illustrated by an example taken from a slightly later period than the one in which Gennep worked. In 1577, the emperor issued an overview of newly minted coins that were prohibited within the entire empire. The broadsheet included 40 coins and was printed in Frankfurt by a printer who held an imperial privilege.[160] Drafted after the Frankfurt model, the city council of Cologne issued a similar ordinance and had it printed in the same year. For this ordinance, the Cologne printer Maternus Cholinus used his own woodcuts, which were very similar to those of his Frankfurt colleague. However, the keen observer can notice subtle but distinct differences between the Frankfurt images and their Cologne imitations. This holds especially true for the depiction of the Taler from Holland:

159 Gennep may have passed on the woodblocks to another printer, as it happened before in Cologne, see SCHMITZ (1990), *Die Überlieferung deutscher Texte im Kölner Buchdruck*, p. 80. This, however, seems unlikely as all known cases of exchanged woodcuts were for publications sold on the commercial market. In contrast, almost all Cologne ordinances, were produced for the council's use in a small amount of copies.

160 HAStK, Best. 14 (Edikte): 14, Nr. 64 b.

Fig. 4.10. Frankfurt edition from 1577.

Fig. 4.11. Cologne edition from 1577, appendix no. 172.

At first sight, the two images of the coin look very similar. On one of the Frankfurt images, we see a lion encircled by an inscription reading 'CONFIDENS DNO NON MOVETVR'. The other image shows a man dressed in armour with a cape and a coat of arms in front of him. The man is also encircled by an inscription that includes the date 1576 (at the bottom), the date the coin was produced. In the woodcut Cholinus employed for the Cologne edition, the lion has a fuller mane as well as better defined legs and tail. As the letters in the inscription are smaller than in the Frankfurt image, the text includes a round sign as a space holder just above the lion's head. There is no such sign in the Frankfurt woodcut. The image of the man differs also from the Frankfurt model. The coat of arms in front of him is adorned and the man rests his right hand on a long stick. Apart from that, the man's cape is flowing freely with some space left in the frame of the image.

Images of the same woodcuts, however, do not show such distinct differences. This becomes obvious in the depiction of the Lüttich (Liège) Taler on two Cologne editions printed in 1553 and 1555 respectively:

Fig. 4.12. Coin ordinance from 1553, appendix no. 88.

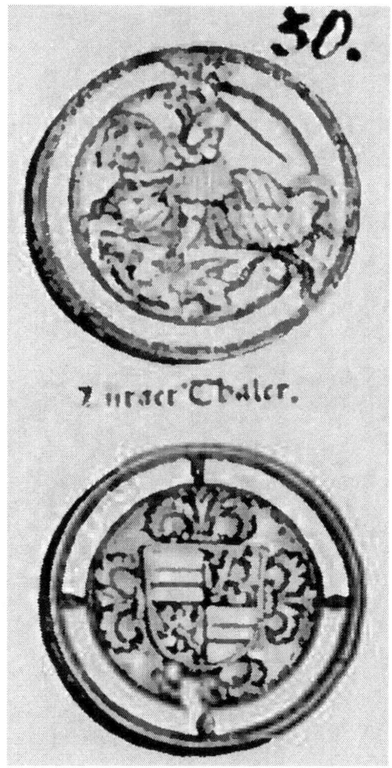

Fig. 4.13. Coin ordinance from 1555, appendix no. 92.

Although one image is slightly tilted and one copy slightly sharper, there are no differences between the illustrations. They have the same proportions, details, and design. Therefore, we can assume that the printer who produced the coin ordinance from 1553, Jaspar von Gennep as the imprint shows (see fig. 4.7.), also produced the ordinance two years later.

Gennep presumably used the two woodcut images of the Lüttich Taler for four editions; this includes the long coin ordinance from 1564.[161] The fact that the long coin ordinance contains Gennep's imprint helps confirm the validity of

161 Appendix nos. 72, 92, 105, 106.

this methodology. This suggests that Gennep had possessed the two woodcuts of the Lüttich Taler since at least the 1550s and used them for every suitable coin ordinance he produced between 1550 and 1564. During this time, the printer also employed the Lüttich Taler woodcut for other rulers' publications, such as the ones he supplied for the Archbishop of Trier as well as the Duke of Jülich-Cleves-Berg.

The ordinance issued by the Duke of Jülich-Cleves-Berg (fig. 4.9.) helps us to identify two further broadsheets produced most likely in Gennep's shop. The first is an undated coin ordinance for Cologne, which shows 20 images including numerous woodcuts included on the duke's ordinance.[162] Among them are two Brabant coins (four images) and two corunas (four images), which exhibit striking similarities to the 1560 edition (fig. 4.14. and 4.15.). Thus the conclusion that can be drawn is that Gennep most likely printed the ordinance.

Fig. 4.14. Images of a Brabant coin on the 1560 edition for the Duke of Jülich-Cleves-Berg.

Fig. 4.15. Images of a Brabant coin on an undated coin ordinance for the city council, appendix no 86.

162 Appendix no. 86.

The second edition we can assign to Gennep is another undated coin regulation, showing 34 coins in total. At the very bottom of the ordinance, the printer inserted six images of forbidden Heller.[163] The resemblance of the images in this example is even more striking than in the previous examples: the woodcuts reveal the same usage marks. On both editions, two of the woodcuts are missing parts of their frame at exactly the same position (fig. 4.16. and 4.17.). Therefore, it is very plausible to assume that Gennep also created this undated edition in his printing house.

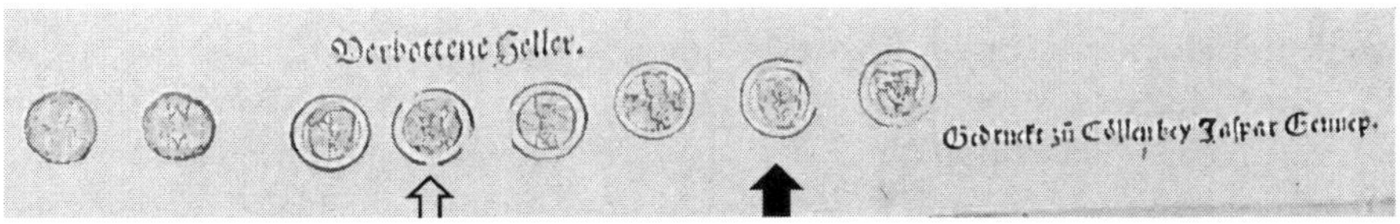

Fig. 4.16. Edition issued by the Duke of Jülich-Cleves-Berg, with Gennep's imprint (1560).

Fig. 4.17. Undated edition with the same woodcuts (missing parts of their frame), appendix no 87.

In addition to the many coin woodcuts, Gennep employed various initials that suggest further official broadsheets were produced in his shop. The biggest and most noticeable decoration is the large and very fine 'W' initial (fig. 4.18.). By using this large and eye-catching woodcut, the printer emphasised the importance of the broadsheet. For every passer-by who saw such a broadsheet pinned to a wall, it was perfectly clear that the text on the publication was imperative. The printer used this particular decorated initial on the 1564 coin ordinance, his masterpiece, and most likely on a further four editions.[164]

Fig. 4.18. Excerpt from the coin ordinance of 1564 with the large 'W' initial, appendix no 106.

163 Appendix no. 87.
164 Appendix nos. 79, 80, 94, 102.

The earliest dated broadsheet that shows this initial appeared in 1555 on an ordinance regulating blasphemy and the production of lampoons.[165] This early use of the initial shows that the printer employed the woodcut at least for the last nine years of his life (1555–1564). Gennep included the large 'W' initial in two undated broadsheets he supplied for the city council in Cologne. One of them is an ordinance regulating the import of foreign bread, mentioned in the third chapter, a pressing concern for Cologne from the early days onwards. The other defined regulations for shipping.[166]

In addition to the large 'W' initial, Gennep used a variety of less elaborate small initials that were adorned to a limited extent. The coin ordinance from 1553 includes a selection of three initials (fig. 4.19.). The small 'W' initial at the top is decorated with floral illustrations and includes a little pedestal beneath the letter. Gennep used this initial for three editions, one of which also includes the same images of the Lüttich Taler.[167]

Wir Bürgermeistere vnd Rath der Stadt Cöllen/ Thün allen vnd jedern vnsern Bürgern/ Inwoneren vnd sunst jedermenigklich hiemit zu wyssen.

Gedruckt bey Jaspar von Gennep.

Fig. 4.19. Coin ordinance from 1553 with Gennep's imprint at the bottom right, appendix no. 88.

165 Appendix no. 94.
166 Appendix nos. 79, 80.
167 Appendix no. 72 (which also includes the Lüttich Taler), appendix no. 76, 90.

Gennep presumably reused the other small woodcut initials as well. We can find the small 'N' initial on an undated broadsheet from the mid-sixteenth century.[168] Moreover, the small 'D' appears on an ordinance issued in July 1553, as well as on the broadsheet from 1558 that regulated pigs in the streets (fig. 4.20.).[169] The pig ordinance shows that Gennep had an entire set of the smaller initials, including not only the letters 'N' and 'D', but also 'A', 'W', and 'J'.

den sollen.
A Nfengkli
knecht dat
Item solle
ten/erde/schre
fuert werden/
fledicheit her k
wurde/sollen
men sich der be
wurde/Und s
Dergleiche
platzen bestre
gebott der vur
Werckhuisern
W Eiters
vnd zuf
vnnd m
betretten wur
vnd widder v
Item es so
den vnd helpli
Dergleich
verstoerenn.
J Tem di
befunde
len gesej
betretten wer
D Weil a
warnd
stattet

Fig. 4.20. Ordinance from 1558 with regulations for pigs in the streets, appendix no. 96.

168 Appendix no. 81.
169 Appendix nos. 89, 96.

These small initials were not only employed for official broadsheets; Gennep used them for other publications as well, such as his account of the Council of Trent.[170] The first German edition of this celebrated work was produced in 1564.[171] After translating the Latin document himself, the printer published a book with 96 leaves. On folio xxj Gennep inserted the small 'D' initial as well as the 'I' initial (fig. 4.21.).

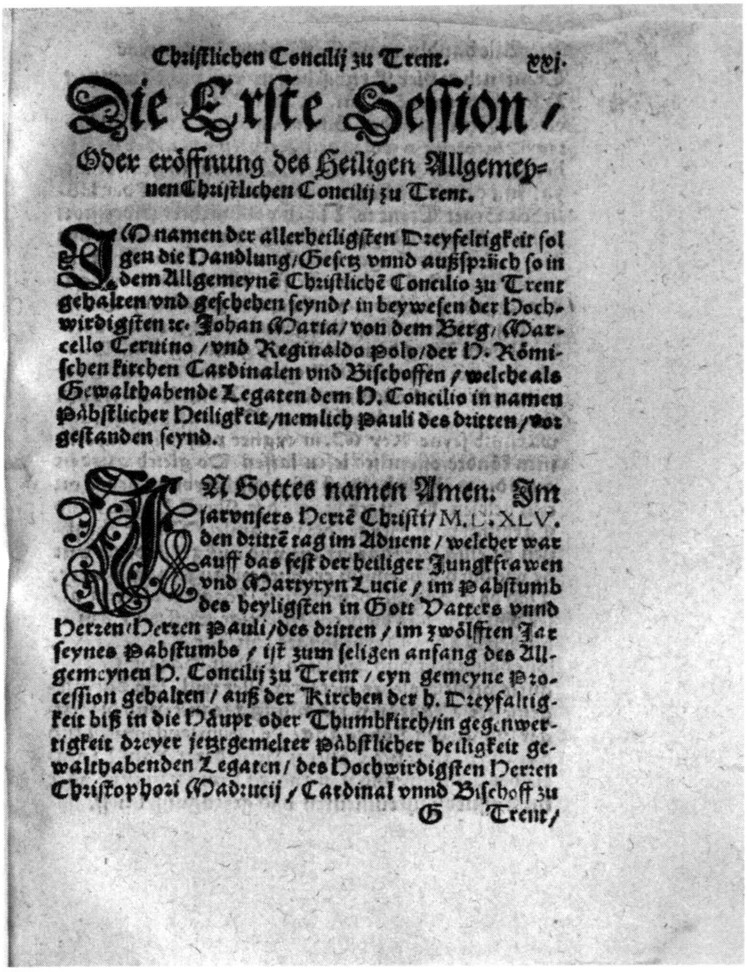

Christlichen Concilij zu Trent. xxj.

Die Erste Session/

Oder eröffnung des Heiligen Allgemeynen Christlichen Concilij zu Trent.

IN namen der allerheiligisten Dreyfeltigkeit folgen die Handlung/Gesetz vnnd außsprüch so in dem Allgemeynē Christlichē Concilio zu Trent gehalten vnd geschehen seynd/ in beywesen der Hochwirdigisten ꝛc. Johan Maria/ von dem Berg/ Marcello Ceruino/vnd Reginaldo Polo/der H. Römischen kirchen Cardinalen vnd Bischoffen/ welche als Gewalthabende Legaten dem H. Concilio in namen Päbstlicher Heiligkeit/nemlich Pauli des dritten/vorgestanden seynd.

IN Gottes namen Amen. Im jar vnsers Herrē Christi/ M.D.XLV. den drittē tag im Aduent/ welcher war auff das fest der heiliger Jungkfrawen vnd Martyryn Lucie/ im Pabstumb des heyligsten in Gott Vatters vnnd Herren/Herren Pauli/des dritten/ im zwölfften Jar seynes Pabstumbs/ ist zum seligen anfang des Allgemeynen H. Concilij zu Trent/ eyn gemeyne Procession gehalten/ auß der Kirchen der h. Dreyfaltigkeit biß in die Häupt oder Thumbkirch/in gegenwertigkeit dreyer jetztgemelter Päbstlicher heiligkeit gewalthabenden Legaten/ des Hochwirdigsten Herren Christophori Madrucij/ Cardinal vnnd Bischoff zu

G Trent/

Fig. 4.21. Folio xxj from Gennep's 1564 translation of the proceedings of the council of Trent, USTC 610813 (VD16 K 2064).

170 USTC 610813 (VD16 K 2064).

171 Corsten (1988), 'Drucken oder drücken', p. 97.

The set of small initials Gennep used on the 1558 broadsheet (fig. 4.20) allows us to identify two more broadsheet editions that he produced for the city council.[172] One of them is a coin ordinance reinforcing an earlier regulation passed by both the Archbishop of Cologne and the Duke of Jülich-Cleves-Berg (fig. 4.22.). The document reveals that Gennep even had a third small 'W' woodcut initial. It is very similar to the small 'W' initial with the floral illustrations on the 1553 coin ordinance that includes the Lüttich Taler (fig. 4.7.). Yet, it differs slightly from it. The floral arrangements are somewhat different and, most notably, the letter does not stand on a small pedestal.

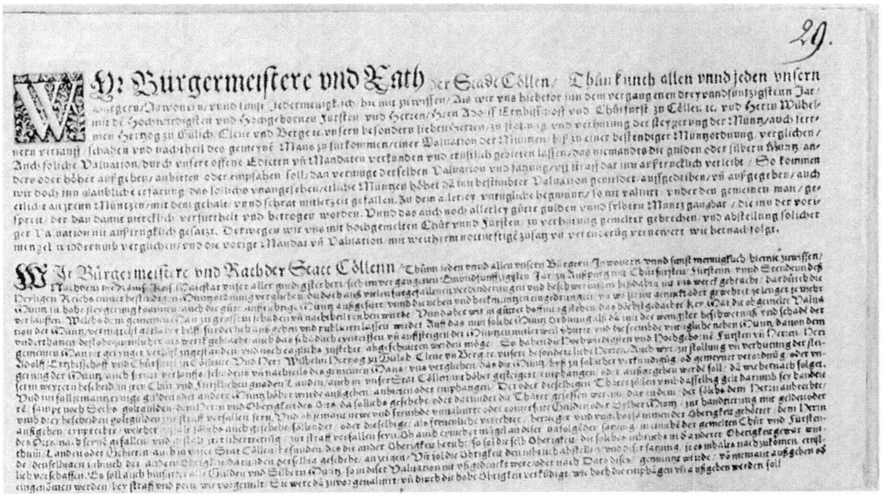
29.

WIr Bürgermeistere vnd Rath der Stadt Cöllen/ Thun kunth allen vnnd jeden vnsern

WIr Bürgermeistere vnd Rath der Statt Cöllenn

Fig. 4.22. Undated coin ordinance with small 'W' initial in the middle of the text and another 'W' initial at the top, appendix no. 91.

This 'W' initial without pedestal means that we can assume Gennep produced another broadsheet as well.[173] The ordinance was issued on 10 July 1555 and regulated matters concerning Anabaptists, blasphemy, and the censorship of printed publications.

We can identify more of Gennep's official broadsheets by comparing their initials to those of other publications produced in his shop. In 1545, Gennep printed Johann Gropper's response to Martin Bucer as a folio consisting of some 80 leaves.[174] On folio xx verso, the printer used a 'W' initial that is rather special.

172 Appendix nos. 91, 98.
173 Appendix no. 93.
174 USTC 637052 (VD16 G 3389).

The letter appears to be made out of wood with numerous elaborate flourishes on the ornated letter. Gennep reused this extraordinary initial on the council ordinance that bans lampoons.[175] It even has the same damaged spot on the bottom left-hand side. Unfortunately, the ordinance does not include an issue date, though it has been assumed that the council agreed on the regulation on 2 October 1545.[176]

Fig. 4.23. Fol. xx verso from Gennep's 1545 Gropper edition, USTC 637052.

Fig. 4.24. Broadsheet edition from 1545 with the same initial, appendix no. 70.

The Gropper edition also contains a large 'A' initial that looks as if it were from the same set of woodcuts that also contains the large 'W' initial on Gennep's coin ordinance of 1564. The printer employed the 'A' initial both on the title page of the Gropper edition and on fol. ii (fig. 4.25.). Three years before the printer produced this book, in 1561, he utilised the woodcut initial for an ordinance regulating wages for day labourers (fig. 4.26.).[177]

The above examples show that Gennep most likely produced at least 21 ordinances for the city council, including two editions in which the printer inserted his name in the imprint. With the help of a coin ordinance issued by the Duke of Jülich-Cleves-Berg, we can recreate Gennep's great repertoire of coin woodcuts. These coin images allow us to attribute five official broadsheets to Gennep's shop. This can be extended by an analysis of the printer's woodcut initials: the large 'W' initial appears on another four broadsheet editions. The smaller 'W' initial with the letter standing on a small pedestal helps us to identify two further editions. In addition, the small 'N' and 'D' initials as well as the small 'W' initial

175 Appendix no. 70.
176 Policey K, no. 1963.
177 Appendix no. 104.

allow us to attribute a further six broadsheets to Gennep's printing house. Finally, we can identify two more editions with the help of initials the printer employed for other publications.

Fig. 4.25. Large 'A' initial on title page of Gennep's Gropper edition from 1545, USTC 637052.

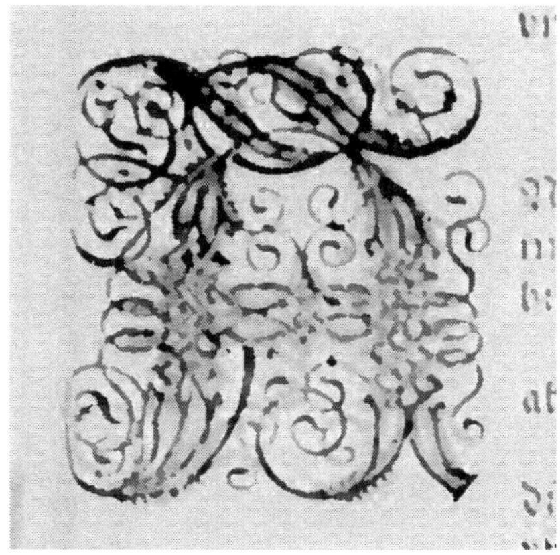

Fig. 4.26. Large 'A' initial on a broadsheet ordinance from 1561, appendix no. 104.

The printing councillor

Jaspar von Gennep died only months after he had produced the coin ordinance with 154 illustrations. The council then commissioned publications from Gottfried Hirtzhorn the younger, who was active in Cologne between 1561 and 1577.[178] Gottfried was the grandson of Eucharius Hirtzhorn, who, as we have seen previously, had also undertaken commissions for the council in the 1530s. Gottfried's father, Gottfried the elder, was the student in Marburg who oversaw the print shop of his father, Eucharius. After the Marburg venture failed, Gottfried the elder briefly tried his luck as a printer in Cologne. Unfortunately, shortly after he had set up his shop in 1550, he was imprisoned for producing heretic books.[179] This finally led him to move to Antwerp, where he hoped to make a fresh start.

Cautioned by his father's failure, Gottfried the younger tried to minimise the risks of the print industry from the very beginning. In 1561, Gottfried moved back to his father's and grandfather's earlier place of business and started off by printing for big publishers in Cologne, such as Maternus Cholinus and the heirs

178 Reske, p. 483.
179 Schmitz (1990), *Die Überlieferung deutscher Texte im Kölner Buchdruck*, p. 136.

of Arnold Birckmann.[180] In fact, in the first two years, Hirtzhorn worked almost exclusively for Maternus Cholinus.[181] This allowed him to save some capital and wait for a good opportunity to extend his business.

This opportunity came in 1564, three years after Gottfried had set up shop. In this year, the printer started to produce books on his own, thus escaping from his safe but low-income existence as a printer paid by a publisher (*Lohndrucker*). We can be reasonably confident in saying that Jaspar von Gennep's death in 1564 encouraged Gottfried to face the competitive world of printing as an independent producer. After Gennep died, his shop was not taken over by an heir or successor and his type and woodcuts were sold. Gottfried seized this opportunity and bought some of Gennep's material. With this material Gottfried produced a large coin ordinance in May 1565, which he provided with an imprint.[182]

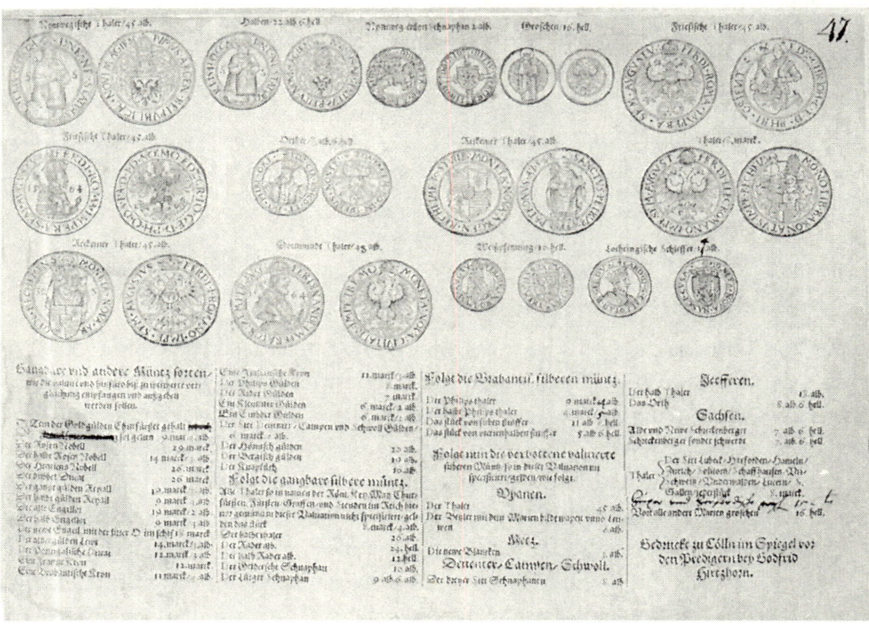

Fig. 4.27. Hirtzhorn's coin ordinance from 1565 including a variety of Gennep's woodcuts. His imprint is at the bottom right, appendix no. 109.

180 Reske, p. 483.
181 In 1562, Hirtzhorn produced only one book without Cholinus mentioned as a publisher (USTC 686163, (VD16 ZV 14675)).
182 Appendix no. 109. The different parts of the broadsheets have been separated in HAStK, Best. 14 (Edikte). Thus the ordinance stretches over five folios (fol. 42, 44, 45, 46, 47). The parts definitely belong together, as Gottfried added the value

This ordinance includes a variety of images that we have already encountered in Gennep's editions. Among them are, for instance, six images of coins produced in Nijmegen: two images of a Taler, two images of a Groschen, and two images of the local Snaphaß. In addition, the two images of the Reckener Taler are identical to Gennep's woodcuts, as becomes clear from crucial details, such as the number 30 next to St Peter (fig. 4.28. and fig. 4.29., most coins up until then do not show any numerals). The same number is included in the shield of the double-headed eagle in the other image.

Fig. 4.28. Reckener Taler on Gennep's coin ordinance from 1564, appendix no. 106.

Fig. 4.29. Same Reckener Taler on Hirtzhorn's coin ordinance from 1565, appendix no. 109.

Right from the start of his career as an individual printer, Hirtzhorn did what every printer producing for the council had done before him: he published for other authorities. In 1564, he published legislation issued by Philip II, King of Spain, as a medium-sized quarto pamphlet.[183] In the following years Hirtzhorn continued to print for Philip and also produced announcements from William of Orange.[184]

Hirtzhorn produced civic ordinances only for a short period of time, maybe just for a year. His family had a susceptibility to Protestantism that was not well received by the Catholic council.[185] Eventually, he succumbed to the same temptation as his father: Gottfried printed Protestant works that promised quick returns, especially when Cologne hosted many Dutch refugees. To avoid trouble with the authorities, he produced the Luther Bible in Low German with a fake imprint stating that the book was printed in Frankfurt.[186] Nevertheless, the

of each coin over their images. This is a rather unusual practice and cannot be found on many other coin ordinances.

183 USTC 636509 (VD16 B 6879).

184 For publications issued by William of Orange, see, for example, USTC 421573 (not in VD16), USTC 411058 (not in VD16) and USTC 410000 (not in VD16). For publications issued by Philip II, see, for example, USTC 415164 (not in VD16).

185 Schmitz (1990), *Die Überlieferung deutscher Texte im Kölner Buchdruck*, p. 242.

186 *Ibid.*, p. 206

council was able to trace the Bible back to Hirtzhorn's shop.[187] As the magistrates were not keen to employ a printer who broke their rules, this offence cost him future employment by the council. Therefore, Hirtzhorn's imprint does not appear on any later broadsheet ordinances. The offence might have had an even stronger impact than previously assumed, as after this incident his overall production declined steadily. Although he was active until 1577, in the last seven years he produced only five books.[188]

After this short interlude, another big Catholic publisher took over the work for the council: Maternus Cholinus. In the second half of the sixteenth century, Cholinus had an impressive career in Cologne and became one of the most influential printers. For the council, employing Cholinus had obvious benefits. As the printer had deep pockets – it has been suggested that he made up to 70 % gross profit from his editions – he could step in if the council experienced financial difficulties.[189] Cholinus did not depend on timely payments for the produced ordinances either. Instead, the magistrates were able to delay months or even years before meeting their obligations. The printer's invoice from 1576 suggests that the council used this opportunity of late payments, and when it actually did pay, it did not even settle the whole sum. On 10 May 1576 Cholinus presented an invoice in which he listed the mandates he had produced for the council since his last payment (fig. 4.3.). According to this invoice, the council last paid Cholinus in September 1574, but not in full, as the sum of 48 Albus remained outstanding. Below this statement, the printer listed eight ordinances that he had produced from August 1575 to April 1576.[190]

Cholinus seems to have been the only supplier of ordinances for the council from 1574 at the latest until his death in 1588.[191] During this time, he

187 *Ibid.*, p. 24.

188 Reske, p. 483. The books are: USTC 678301 ((VD16 N 1831), 1570), USTC 415164 ((not in VD16), 1570), USTC 415393 ((not in VD16), 1572), USTC 615704 ((VD16 ZV 6480), 1574), USTC 671478 (equals USTC 412650 and USTC 406372, (VD16 ZV 2372), 1577).

189 For Cholinus' income, see Reuter (1958), 'Zur Wirtschafts- und Sozialgeschichte des Buchdruckgewerbes im Rheinland bis 1800', p. 682; in Nuremberg, the council asked a printer twice for a credit of several thousand Gulden, see Kempkens (2014), 'Der Erfolg der Prognostica auf dem Buchmarkt in der Frühen Neuzeit', p. 12.

190 The coin ordinance from 13 April 1576 appeared in three editions, one for Cologne, one for Dortmund, and one for Aachen, interestingly all paid for by the city council of Cologne, see Limbach (2016), 'Tracing Lost Broadsheet Ordinances Printed in Sixteenth-Century Cologne', p. 496.

191 Schmitz (1990), *Die Überlieferung deutscher Texte im Kölner Buchdruck*, p. 182; Zaretzky (1912), 'Ein Quentelsches Rechnungsbuch aus der zweiten Hälfte des 16. Jahrhunderts', pp. 87–88.

produced 132 ordinances for the Cologne government.[192] From his invoice we know that he printed official announcements from at least 1574 onwards. Yet, as Cholinus also used the woodcuts that had previously belonged to Gennep, it is hard to say when exactly Cholinus produced his first broadsheet for the magistrates. It seems, however, likely that Cholinus took over the woodcuts from Hirtzhorn when he stopped working for the council.

Almost all of Cholinus' ordinances lack imprints. Nevertheless, we can assign seven Cologne ordinances to his print shop with the help of his invoice.[193] One of the ordinances the printer produced was issued in April 1576. Here, we see that Cholinus used Gennep's earlier woodcut, the large 'W' initial. The ordinance, issued in the name of the city council of Aachen but interestingly

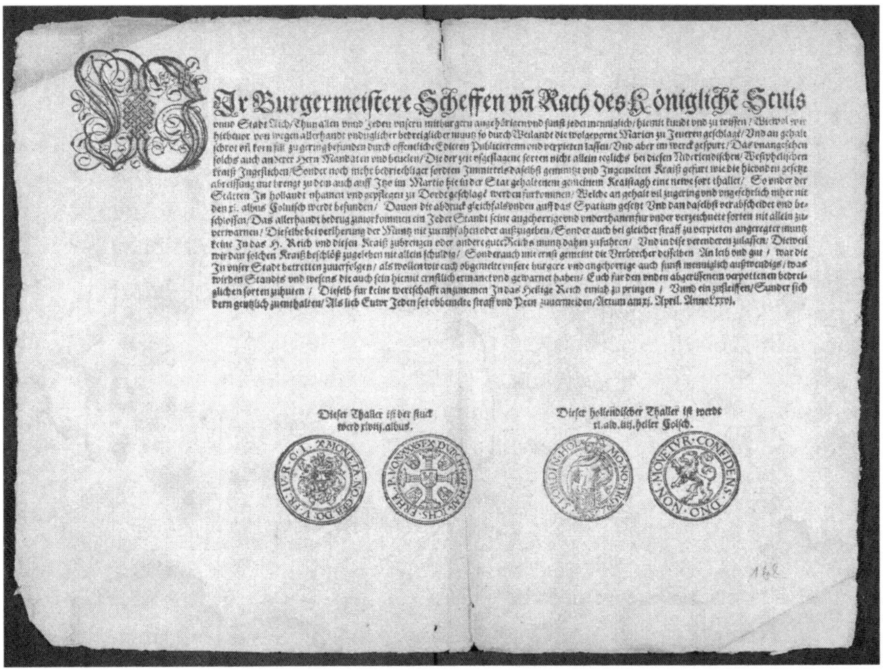

Fig. 4.30. Coin ordinance issued by the city council of Aachen in April 1576, printed by Maternus Cholinus using Gennep's initial.

192 Appendix nos. 158, 160, 165–290, 292; Cholinus also produced the three guard ordinances in pamphlet form, which all reveal his imprint: USTC 704779 (VD16 ZV 9097), USTC 677227 (VD16 K 1808), USTC 677228 (VD16 ZV 9098).

193 Appendix nos. 158, 160, 165, 167, 168, 170, 171. Only the Cologne edition of the coin ordinance from April 1576 could not be located; see fig. 4.3.

paid for by the Cologne council, appears in the invoice as: 'on 13 April 1576 a mandate addressing forbidden Taler'.[194]

By the time Cholinus started to produce for the council, he had been in Cologne for a long time and looked back on a great career. The printer was probably born in 1525 in Arlon, a city in the Duchy of Luxemburg.[195] Cholinus came to Cologne in his early twenties and began to work as a bookseller.[196] He became a publisher in 1552 and his first book was an extensive work of Pope Innocent III, a large folio with no fewer than 364 leaves.[197] At first his business did not go well, and in the 1560s, Cholinus complained repeatedly about his modest means.[198] When in 1562 he wanted to buy the building housing his print shop, he could only afford half of it. Yet, the printer only had to endure this financial squeeze for a few years, as towards the end of the century, Cholinus' shop was one of the four most prominent publishing houses in Cologne.[199]

The secret of his success consisted of several ingredients. Firstly, Cholinus was aware of the pitfalls in the print industry. Like some of his predecessors, he started off as a bookseller.[200] This gave him a feel for the market and allowed him to identify the items promising the highest returns. Only after he had had the chance to observe the market thoroughly for a good number of years did Cholinus dip his toe into the waters and issue his own publications.[201] He continued to do this for another couple of years until he finally began to print in 1559.[202] In this way, Cholinus edged forward, step-by-step, into the world of the printed book.

Secondly, Cholinus focussed on Catholic books and made sure that he would have little competition. Just like Gennep, Cholinus printed many works by Catholic authors directed against the Reformation.[203] This included most prominently the Jesuits, who had established a community in Cologne in 1544.[204]

194 The original German text reads: 'a[u]f 13 Aprili [15]76 Eyn Mandaat von den verbottenen dalern'. As the issue date in the ordinance is 'xi. April' (fig. 4.30.), it shows that Cholinus supplied the broadsheets two days after the council issued the ordinance.

195 Peuckert (2011), 'Materne Cholinus, un imprimeur arlonais à Cologne (1525–1588)', p. 30.

196 Schmitz (1990), *Die Überlieferung deutscher Texte im Kölner Buchdruck*, p. 402.

197 USTC 679617 (VD16 ZV 8581).

198 Schmitz (1990), *Die Überlieferung deutscher Texte im Kölner Buchdruck*, p. 402.

199 Enderle (1999), 'Die Buchdrucker der Reichsstadt Köln und die katholische Publizistik zwischen 1555 und 1648', p. 171.

200 Schmitz (1990), *Die Überlieferung deutscher Texte im Kölner Buchdruck*, p. 402.

201 Reske, p. 481.

202 *Ibid.*

203 Janssen (2014), *The Dutch Revolt and Catholic Exile in Reformation Europe*, p. 112.

204 Heal (2007), *The Cult of the Virgin Mary in Early Modern Germany*, p. 207.

To secure this promising market for himself, Cholinus obtained imperial privileges for some of his books in 1560 that stipulated that no one could reprint his books for a period of ten years.[205] One year later he obtained another privilege that enabled Cholinus to be the only printer who could publish Petrus Canisius' *Catechism*.[206]

Thirdly, like his predecessors, Cholinus focussed on publications for other authorities. As we have seen with Johann Otmar, who was recommended as a trusted printer to authorities outside Augsburg, the work for the municipal government in Cologne most likely helped Cholinus to secure orders from other governments, too. In his case, these authorities included the Archbishop of Cologne as well as the Prince-Bishop of Würzburg.[207] Their orders were especially lucrative because the clients paid for the entire production, which meant that the printer was not left with unsold stock (the nail in the coffin for many printers in the sixteenth century). These commissions could include large works that would bring Cholinus hundreds of Gulden.

This is very well illustrated by the Prince-Bishop of Würzburg's order from 1585. In that year, Cholinus printed 1,600 breviaries consisting of one complete edition as well as one edition in two parts.[208] The payment for the breviaries was extraordinary: Cholinus received no less than 1,882 Gulden for the order – a sum not even Magdalena Morhart or her son came close to earning with one commission. In his invoice, Cholinus charged 1 Gulden for 75 sheets. As we have seen in the second chapter, Magdalena Morhart and her son Georg Gruppenbach received on average one Gulden for 200 sheets, and that was already a comparatively good payment. Although Cholinus probably had more costs than his colleagues in Württemberg – the breviaries included many rubricated pages requiring extra work – the printer was still paid extraordinarily well for this order.

The fourth and arguably most important key to Cholinus' success was the fact that he participated actively in political life. As soon as he came to Cologne, Cholinus became a member of the shoemakers' *Gaffel*.[209] Although the book-

205 Juchhoff (1957), 'Cholinus, Maternus', p. 213.

206 Schmitz (1990), *Die Überlieferung deutscher Texte im Kölner Buchdruck*, p. 451.

207 USTC 617085 (VD16 ZV 22256), USTC 617121 (VD16 ZV 22255), USTC 617122 (VD16 ZV 20019).

208 Ruland (1863), 'Zur Druckgeschichte des vom Fürstbischof Julius zu Würzburg herausgegebenen Breviarium secundum usum ecclesiae Herbipolensis von 1575', pp. 222–223.

209 Heitjan (1970), 'Die Stellung der Buchgewerbetreibenden in der Stadt Köln und zu ihrer Universität (15. bis 18. Jahrhundert)', col. 1142. Heitjan argues that Cholinus was a member of the *Gaffel* from before 1550. As Cholinus came to Cologne in 1547, it seems likely that he joined the *Gaffel* as soon as he arrived.

seller had little to do with shoes, it is not surprising that he joined this particular *Gaffel*. Despite the fact that the book business thrived in Cologne, there was no designated *Gaffel* for book sellers, publishers, and printers. Just as in other cities, such as Mainz, Strasbourg, Basel, and Zurich, those involved in the book world could choose a guild to which they wanted to be affiliated.[210] Cholinus' political involvement did not stop there. In the following years he held several offices.[211] Moreover, from 1565, only a few years after he had started printing in Cologne, Cholinus was elected to the council on a regular basis.[212] This frequent interaction with the political elite brought him many orders including ordinances.

Conclusion

Cholinus' extremely successful career shows that printing for the civic government was a job worth taking, despite the relatively small payments involved. Producing for the authorities in Cologne was nowhere near as financially rewarding as catering for the needs of the Württemberg dukes, or the city councils in Nuremberg and Augsburg. With an average print-run of some 50–60 copies, Cologne broadsheets brought fewer rewards for printers. Nevertheless, printing broadsheets for the magistrates in Cologne conferred prestige. A positive evaluation from the local civic government signalled to many rulers outside Cologne that the printer entrusted with their work was both capable and reliable. Printers who worked for the magistrates in Cologne frequently produced for other authorities, including the dukes of Jülich-Cleves-Berg and the Archbishop of Cologne. Such official orders could be extremely lucrative, as Cholinus' invoice for the production of breviaries shows.

Printing for the council in Cologne became more competitive, as the demand for official publications grew in the sixteenth century. At the beginning, the small printing houses close to the town hall catered for the market of official publications. This changed, however, around the 1540s when the prolific figures of Cologne's print industry took over production. As a thorough woodcut analysis of the broadsheets shows, both Jaspar von Gennep and Maternus Cholinus were increasingly interested in securing official orders.

For the council this shift from small to large print houses was a positive development. The magistrates needed a financially strong printer who was willing to invest in woodcuts necessary for the publication of coin ordinances.

210 Gramlich (1994), *Rechtsordnungen des Buchgewerbes im Alten Reich*, p. 24.
211 Reske, pp. 481–482.
212 Deeters (ed.) (2013), *Rat und Bürgermeister in Köln 1396–1797*, p. 180.

Jaspar von Gennep supplied multiple broadsheets with various coin images, which helped to control the circulation of coins after the outbreak of the Dutch Revolt. The financially robust print shops also allowed the council leeway with its payment. As a successful businessman, Maternus Cholinus could easily afford to wait months, even years, before he received his payment from the council.

Conclusion

In March 1606, after the death of *Hofdrucker* Max Fürster, Duke Friedrich of Württemberg encountered a publishing problem: he intended to put to press a new edition of the *Landrecht*, but he was unable to find a printer. In this time of need, the duke turned to Georg Gruppenbach, the printer who had served the authorities in Württemberg for decades but had crumbled financially after he had lost most of the official orders to the *Hofdrucker*. In his letter to the university senate, who oversaw the Württemberg book trade legally, the duke expressed his sympathy to his former loyal servant and his hope that the latter would be able to help:[1]

> We are very sorry to hear that Gruppenbach is currently in such an unpleasant and miserable state caused by his great debts (although he cannot be accused of living extravagantly). Despite his situation, however, we have no qualms about graciously supporting him and we hope that through this work he will be able to obtain food in an honest way because we and our estates consider it as important to do such a charitable deed. So we would like you to ask Gruppenbach and his son if they are in the position to produce our new *Landrecht*.[2]

Although claiming to act out of compassion, Duke Friedrich had little choice but to employ Gruppenbach once again if he wanted to keep the production costs at bay. The *Landrecht* comprised some 300 sheets of paper per copy, and it was intended to be printed in an edition of 1,800 copies with an estimated cost of no less than 1,800 Gulden.[3] The expense would undoubtedly have risen

1 Brinkhus (1998), 'Zwischen Privilegien und Zensur. Das Verhältnis von Buchgewerbe und Universität', p. 13.

2 UAT, 26/3 no. 13, the original German text reads: 'Wann wir nun In gnaden zu hertzen füoren, In was Laidigen erbärmlichen Zustand er Gruppenbach (der sonsten für sein Persohn üppigen, übermaßigen Haußhaltens nit zubeschuldigen) mit überhäuffen großen schuldenlast gerhaten, allß setzen wir In kein bedencken, Ime, da er sich hierdurch an etwas außwückhlen und widerumb zu einer ehrlichen nahrung gelangen möchte, In gnaden zuwillfahren allein, will uns und unßere gehorsamen Landschafft an solchen hochwüchtigen gemainnützigen Werck mercklich will gelegen. Demnach wolt ir Ime Gruppenbach zusambt seinem Sohne für Euch erfordern, und von Inen erkundig[en], ob und welcher gestalltt Sie solch Werckh verlegen und vorttreiben wollten.'

3 UAT, 26/3 no. 19: On 23 April 1606, Georg Gruppenbach and his son wrote a letter to the duke informing him that the production of the new *Landrecht* will

significantly if the vast number of sheets had to be transported from Strasbourg or Basel. But reducing transportation costs by relying on the only printer left in Württemberg came with another price: a massive delay of four years.[4]

The dilemma both Duke Friedrich and Georg Gruppenbach experienced in 1606 offers an intriguing example of the complexities of publishing official work. For rulers, the invention of print was a gift, but one that was not always easy to use, especially when it was difficult to find a suitable printer. The publication of official work was thus shaped by the economic realities of the new business. For printers, working for the state could be lucrative but also came with major disadvantages: Gruppenbach, whose parents had made easy profits from producing for the authorities in Württemberg, lost everything as soon as another printer started to work for the duke.

The preceding pages have attempted to shed light on the complex production process of official publications in sixteenth-century Germany. The two case studies analysed in this book powerfully illustrate that the adoption of print by governments was not an inevitable result of technical progress. Although the press was eagerly embraced by some rulers, others were more reluctant to employ it. By comparing and contrasting government use of print in Württemberg and Cologne, this study suggests that the creation of official publications in print was determined by five factors, enumerated below.

Intention

Above all, the purpose of the document determined whether or not it was printed. Rulers who intended to inform only an individual or a small group of people did so with the help of more traditional means, such as oral communication and letters, and this continued throughout the entire sixteenth century. In this manner, the city council of Cologne passed on most of its decisions to the officials in charge or to the *Gaffeln*. In Württemberg, the rulers also relied on traditional means to interact with their representatives or other authorities outside the duchy.

It was extremely handy, however, to print documents that were intended to be used as a reference tool, such as coin ordinances containing illustrations or exchange rates, or announcements intended to inform those who were not part of the political life of the jurisdictions, such as foreigners or refugees. This holds

cost 900 Gulden; UAT, 26/3 no. 22: In his letter from 10 June 1606, Duke Friedrich stated that the production will cost at least twice as much as Gruppenbach's estimation since the *Landrecht* is much larger than the one published in 1585.

4 The reasons for this delay are explained at the end of chapter two.

especially true for documents intended to reach a large audience, including the entire territory or a group of people beyond its boundaries. Thanks to moveable type, the authorities could produce invitations to shooting competitions or horse races in hundreds of copies to be distributed widely. Through ostentatious hospitality, they could advertise the government's reputation and even improve their finances by hosting a lucrative event.

The swift distribution of documents proved particularly useful during times of political upheaval. Rulers who had experienced a decisive blow against their authority were able to employ the press to seek support. By spreading the official point of view on a revolt, the authorities could help bolster their power. When confronted with popular unrest, governments in both Cologne and Württemberg disseminated their versions of the events widely, in this way discrediting the rebels and seeking support in tracking down fugitives. Similarly, the printing press helped tremendously to implement the new faith in Württemberg. With Ulrich Morhart and his heirs' help, the dukes made available numerous theological works including, catechisms, prayers, and the Bible.

Size of jurisdiction

The second decisive factor in determining the extent of government use of print was the size of the ruler's jurisdiction. Württemberg was one of the largest territories in the empire, with some 60 districts. To inform each and every district official, the dukes sent out copies of all of their regulations to the district officials, who proclaimed the new regulations in public. The invention of print facilitated this procedure considerably. From the very beginning the rulers of Württemberg adopted the new medium to help disseminate their ordinances in the duchy.

The council in Cologne, on the other hand, oversaw a much smaller jurisdiction. This allowed for more frequent face-to-face interactions between rulers, officials, and subjects than in the duchy. The close proximity of rulers and ruled in Cologne, therefore, rendered sending out multiple letters on the council's decisions unnecessary. Instead, the government could easily pass on new legislation to the city's population in a variety of ways, including oral proclamations. This method of communication worked well and was not changed by the appearance of print.

Type of government

Closely connected to the size of the jurisdiction is the third factor that determined the adoption of print: the type of government. In Württemberg, rule was hereditary and, therefore, accepted to a certain degree. This is not to say that the duke's rule was uncontested; the expulsion of Duke Ulrich in 1519 is testament to this. Yet, it was taken for granted that the duke and his councillors would issue new legislation in the capital that would then be printed and made known in the duchy.

By contrast, rule in Cologne was exercised by a council elected biannually. This system implied that the magistrates needed to negotiate their power on a frequent basis. For this, they relied much more on empowering interactions with their subjects than the dukes in Württemberg. These interactions were conducted in several ways including processions, rituals, and proclamation of legislation that allowed for face-to-face encounters. As the inhabitants were informed about new regulations at these events, it was unnecessary to produce them in print as well.

Special circumstances

This tradition, however, changed significantly when special circumstances presented themselves. The influx of migrants, looming war, and ensuing sieges brought major disruptions to urban life, posing serious challenges to the city fathers. To combat the spread of disease and prevent any upheaval, the council in Cologne increasingly had their ordinances printed and exhibited in public places. The many broadsheets on the walls of Cologne testified to the government's activities to restore peace and order in the city. Just like in Antwerp, the ordinances showed the inhabitants that the rulers were anything but passive in these times of trouble.

The introduction of the Reformation also presented a disruption of tradition and brought with it a variety of issues that needed to be addressed by legislation. Therefore, the Reformed movement evoked similarly increased activity by the cities' rulers in both Nuremberg and in Augsburg and the dukes of Württemberg. Here the new faith was quickly introduced and inspired the authorities to publish extensive legislation on the Protestant movement, not least church ordinances that defined religious complexities in great detail.

Local print industry

Lastly, even if governments embraced the new technical innovation, their use of the press was determined by the economics of the print industry. This posed particular problems for governments in more remote areas of the empire, as, unless the authorities were willing to pay the printer a high salary or entrust him with frequent orders, they had problems keeping a reliable printer in their territory. The printer would soon encounter financial problems, which could lead to sloppy work. Worse, they could disregard the agreements between them and their employers. This defiance could include theft, such as committed by Saltzer in Lauingen, who took 200 kilograms of printing material with him when he left. It could also include using the ruler's equipment, which would then need replacement, as was the case with Höller in Tyrol. Poor printers who were in desperate need of additional income were also tempted to produce books that the authorities disapproved of, such as Wehrlich who printed Lutheran pamphlets under the watchful eyes of the Habsburgs in Stuttgart.

Rulers close to a print centre, or civic governments who ruled over a large print industry, were much more fortunate in this respect. They could choose from a number of printers who were keen to attract official business, as this secured them orders from other authorities. Throughout the sixteenth century, many rulers seem to have preferred the most prolific and financially robust printers in the print centres as they could allow the governments some leeway with payments. This was a great advantage for state coffers frequently burdened with expenses for wars.

With these results, the previous pages make a substantial contribution to existing scholarship on book history. By focussing on the producers of official print, this analysis shows that printers sought the patronage of the state from the very beginning. We can see that Jane McLeod's important point – rulers and printers had common interests – not only holds true for eighteenth-century France but also for Germany two centuries earlier.[5] The most successful printers who worked for German authorities, Jaspar von Gennep, Maternus Cholinus, and the Morharts, were loyal subjects who entertained good relations with the ruling elite. And their involvement with rulers did not stop there: the businessmen were often not only working for local governments but were also part of them. Their close relationship to the governments secured many attractive orders from Stuttgart or Cologne and earned them a good reputation far beyond their workplaces.

5 McLeod (2011), *Licensing Loyalty. Printers, Patrons, and the State in Early Modern France.*

This is a crucial point and one that has not been stressed enough in previous studies. Producing for local rulers, and thus attracting more orders from other official bodies, was the key to success for many; it was precisely these official orders that made the difference between solvency and bankruptcy. In this study, we can see in detail how attractive it was to publish for local rulers: in some years, the Morharts received as much money as a ducal councillor did.

This research also provides a much more complete picture of the individuals who worked for the authorities in Württemberg and Cologne and contextualises official publications within their overall production. For the first time, we can see how many different editions the various printers supplied for the dukes of Württemberg, the city council of Cologne, as well as other official bodies. On top of that, we now know the exact production figures for hundreds of publications that were printed for the court in Stuttgart. Thus the results of this thesis deepen considerably our knowledge of a publishing trade where profit and prestige were more easily found in smaller jobs, swiftly accomplished, than in the large projects that have thus far attracted most interest from scholars.

Despite these advantages for printers, however, the previous pages also present the downside of publishing for the state in the sixteenth century. We learn that the office of the *Hofdrucker* was not institutionalised at that point for various reasons. This finding adds significantly to the pioneering work of Karl Schottenloher, who provided the first general, albeit very brief, overview of the interaction between rulers and printers.[6] His case of the unfortunate Höller in Tyrol proves to be no exception, as the fates of Hans von Wehrlich and Emanuel Saltzer demonstrate.

The preceding chapters also provide important findings for legal historians, especially those analysing early modern ordinances. As I worked extensively with the volumes of the repertory of police ordinances, I was able to complement them in various ways. This includes the recording of new material, which can be found in a number of archives, libraries, and museums that were not previously systematically checked for official documents from the sixteenth century. In addition, we now know who exactly produced the many ordinances mentioned in the repertory.

By tracing the process from the creation of a draft announcement, its production in print, and finally its distribution, this study reveals precisely how new regulations were communicated. With the help of printed documents, officials could read out the latest regulations at key sites in the territory, stick the documents up on walls for everyone to consult, and use them as a reference tool

6 Schottenloher (1944/1949), 'Der Frühdruck im Dienste der öffentlichen Verwaltung', pp. 138–148.

like the fish ordinance with its measurements. This way, the printing press proved to be a vital tool for regulating German society in the sixteenth century.

Yet, printed legislation was not only used to communicate new rules. This study reveals that printed ordinances could also help to build the ruler's reputation and create consent among others outside their territory. As we have seen in chapter one, the rulers of Württemberg used printed regulations to legitimise their rule over the duchy and secure their position both within and outside the territory. By circulating widely the marriage ordinance, the Great Church Order, and the *Landesordnungen*, the dukes tried to establish the duchy as a role model for a Protestant state. When one considers the various ordinances that were heavily influenced by the Württemberg model, it seems that the dukes had at least some success with their strategy.

As helpful as print could be, the press was not always as straightforward to use as previous studies suggest. Instead, the production of legal texts in print could be quite complex and time-consuming. In some cases, the new legislation did not reach the officials until months later. Only then could the legislation be made known in every part of the territory, a vital point to keep in mind when studying the communication and implementation of new legislation in the sixteenth century.

Sources and bibliography

Archival sources

DHM: Deutsches Historisches Museum Berlin

Dokumente I
Do 94/56, Do 94/57, Do 94/58, Do 94/59, Do 94/60, Do 94/61, Do 94/63, Do 94/64, Do 94/65, Do 94/68, 1989/1041, 1989/1043, 1989/1045.1, 1989/1046, 1989/1047, 1989/1049, 1989/1050, 1989/1051, 1989/1052, 1989/1053, 1989/1054, 1989/1055, 1989/1056, 1989/1107, Do 2009/303

HAStK: Historisches Archiv der Stadt Köln (Microfilm)

Best. 14
Edikte: Band 1, 2, 3, 4, 5, 6, 7, 8, 9, 10, 11, 12, 13, 14, 15, 16, 17, 18, 19, 20, 21, 22, 23, 24, 25, 26, 27, 28

Best. 30
Verfassung und Verwaltung: N 20, N 47, N 256, N 342, N 404, N 751, N 862, V 107, V 127

Best. 33
Militaria: A 45, A 53, A 64

Best. 70
Rechnungen: A 98, A 99A

Best. 90
Handel: A 1, A 74, A 79, A 155, A 197, A 206, A 225, A 323, A 321, A 323, A 349, A 335, A 336, A 339, A 342, A 349, A 372, A 382, A 390, A 393, A 398, A 424, A 429, A 437, A 439, A 446, A 510, A 520, A 539, A 549, A 550, A 560, A 921, A 927

Best. 95
Zunft: A 29, A 182, A 428, A 459, A 462

HStASt: Hauptstaatsarchiv Stuttgart

A 17
Kanzleisachen: Büschel 1, 2, 71, 72, 87, 88, 89

A 38
'Landesordnung - Policey' - Landesweite Regelungen zur inneren Ordnung: Büschel 1, 1/1, 1/2, 1/3, 2, 2/1, 2/2, 2/3, 3, 3/1, 3/2, 3/3, 4, 5, 6, 6/1, 6/2, 7, 8, 9, 10, 12, 13, 14, 15, 16, 17, 19, 20, 21

A 39
Generalreskripte: Büschel 1, 2, 3

A 45
Aufstand 'Armer Konrad': Büschel 10

A 56
Juden: Büschel 1

A 58
Landwirtschaft, Gewerbe, Handel: Büschel 1b, 26

A 63
Religions- und Kirchensachen: Büschel 2/6, 2/7, 3/5, 7/22, 16/10, 22/4, 23/2, 24/1, 59/4, 70/8

A 84
Vertreibung Herzog Ulrichs: Büschel 29

A 238
Oberrat, Generalreskripte und Druckschriften: Büschel 1, 2, 3, 4, 5, 6, 7, 8, 9, 10

A 251
Rentkammer, Bändereihen: Band 107, 108, 109

A 252
Rentkammer, Diener- und Besoldungsbücher: Band 1, 2, 3

A 256
Landschreiberei: Band 4, 5, 6, 7, 8, 9, 10, 11, 12, 13, 14, 15, 16, 17, 18, 19, 20, 21, 22, 23, 24, 25, 26, 27, 28, 29, 30, 31, 32, 33, 34, 35, 36, 37, 38, 39, 40, 41, 42, 43, 44, 45, 46, 47, 48, 49, 50, 51, 52, 53, 54, 55, 56, 57, 58, 59, 60, 61, 62, 63, 64, 65, 66, 67, 68, 69, 70, 71, 72, 73, 74, 75, 76, 77, 78, 79, 80, 81, 82, 83, 84, 85, 86, 87

A 282
Kirchenkastenverwaltungsrechnungen: Band 1288, 1289, 1290, 1291, 1292, 1293, 1294, 1295, 1296, 1297, 1298, 1299, 1300, 1301, 1302, 1303, 1304, 1305. 1306, 1307, 1308, 1309, 1310, 1311, 1312, 1313, 1314, 1315, 1316, 1317, 1318, 1319, 1320, 1321, 1322, 1323, 1324, 1325, 1326, 1327, 1328, 1329, 1330, 1331, 1332, 1333, 1334, 1335, 1336

G 41
Herzog Ulrich (1487–1550): Büschel 11

H 54
Bauernkrieg: Büschel 50

H 57
Münzsachen: Büschel 6

J 17
Sammlung Pfaff: Büschel 12, 13, 14, 15

KSM: Kölnisches Stadtmuseum

Verordnungen

UAT: Universitätsarchiv Tübingen

2
Regesten zu den Protokollen des Akademischen Senats 1524–1776

8/1,1
Buchhändler und Buchdrucker (1522–1623)

8/6a,1
Slavischer Buchdruck (1559–1564); Teil 1 Rechnungen

26/3
Landrecht und Landesordnung

USBK: Universtitäts- und Stadtbibliothek Köln

Einblattsammlung
RH Kasten 1549
RH Kasten 1567
RH Kasten 1570
SB1051 (frühere Signatur: RHV2240)

WLB: Württembergische Landesbibliothek Stuttgart

Cod. iur. 2° 308
Band 3

HBF
206, 2751, 2774

HBFa
206, 282, 882

HBFC
1, 2, 4, 6, 8, 9, 10, 13, 15, 18, 20, 21, 25, 26, 27, 28, 31, 33, 34, 37, 43, 45, 48, 54, 57, 58, 59, 60, 61, 61a, 62, 62a, 63, 63a, 64, 65, 66, 67, 68, 69, 70, 71, 73, 75, 77, 78, 83, 105

Early modern printed books not listed in the appendix

Andreae, Jakob, *Christliche notwendige und ernstliche erinnerung nach dem lauff der irrdischen Planetengestelt darauß ein jeder einfaeltiger Christ zusehen was für glück oder unglück Teutschlandt diser zeit zugewarten* (Tübingen: haer. Ulrich I Morhart, 1568), USTC 621954 (VD16 A 2510)

Andreae, Jakob, *Christliche trostschrifft an die armen betruebten Christen* (Tübingen: haer. Ulrich I Morhart, 1564), USTC 621820 (VD16 A 2552)

Andreae, Jakob, *Disputatio de duabus naturis in Christo.atque earundem idiomatum, sive proprietatum communicatione* (Tübingen: haer. Ulrich I Morhart, 1569), USTC 638122 (VD16 A 2579)

Andreae, Jakob, *Disputatio de judice in controversiis de fide et religions Christiana. Deo juuante prasside Jacobo Andreae, sacrosanctae theologiae doctore ac professore scholae et ecclesiae Tubingensia praeposito et cancellario praeceptore suo M. Michael gammelius vayhingensis, die 9. Julii exercitii causa publicè respondebit* (Tübingen: haer. Ulrich I Morhart, 1568), USTC 638130 (VD16 A 2585)

Andreae, Jakob, *Disputatio de trinitate* (Tübingen: haer. Ulrich I Morhart, 1568), USTC 638143 (VD16 A 2605)

Andreae, Jakob, *Drey und dreissig predigen von den fuernemmsten spaltungen in der Christlichen religion so sich zwischen den Baepstischen, Lutherischen, Zwinglischen, Schwenckfeldern und widerteuffern halten* (Tübingen: haer. Ulrich I Morhart, 1568), USTC 641594 (VD16 A 2610)

Andreae, Jakob, *Drey und dreissig predigen von den fuernemmsten spaltungen in der Christlichen religion so sich zwischen den Baepstischen, Lutherischen, Zwinglischen, Schwenckfeldern und widerteuffern halten* (Tübingen: haer. Ulrich I Morhart, 1568), USTC 641595 (VD16 ZV 567)

Andreae, Jakob, *Drey und dreissig predigen von den fuernemmsten spaltungen in der Christlichen religion so sich zwischen den Baepstischen, Lutherischen, Zwinglischen, Schwenckfeldern und widerteuffern halten* (Tübingen: haer. Ulrich I Morhart, 1568), USTC 641596 (VD16 A 2609)

Andreae, Jakob, *Dreyzehen predigen vom Türcken. In woelchen gehandelt vürdt von seines Regiments, ursprung, glauben und religion vom Türckischen Alcoran unnd desselben grundtlicher widerlegung* (Tübingen: haer. Ulrich I Morhart, 1568), USTC 641622 (VD16 A 2613)

Andreae, Jakob, *Dreyzehen predigen vom Türcken. In woelchen gehandelt würdt von seines Regiments, ursprung, glauben unnd religion* (Tübingen: haer. Ulrich I Morhart, 1569), USTC 641623 (VD16 A 2614)

Andreae, Jakob, *Gratulation das die prediger und lehrer im Hertzogthumb Bayern Lutherisch worden* (Tübingen: haer. Ulrich I Morhart, 1568), USTC 660554 (VD 16 A 2632)

Andreae, Jakob, *Gratulation das die prediger und lehrer im Hertzogthumb Bayern Lutherisch worden* (Tübingen: haer. Ulrich I Morhart, 1569), USTC 660557 (VD16 ZV 568)

Andreae, Jakob, *Gratulation das die prediger und lehrer im Hertzogthumb Bayern Lutherisch worden* (Tübingen: haer. Ulrich I Morhart, 1569), USTC 660555 (VD16 A 2633)

Andreae, Jakob, *Grundtliche widerlegung der vermeindten ursachen, darumb ettlich von der Christlichen und in Gottes wort gegründter Augspurgischen Confeßion zum verdampten Bapst umb abgefallen* (Tübingen: haer. Ulrich I Morhart, 1568), USTC 661036 (VD16 A 2637)

Andreae, Jakob, *Notwendige erinnerung von der Teutschen Bibel dolmetschung sampt widerlegung aller der ursachen darumb die Baepstischen den layen die Bibel zulesen verbietten* (Tübingen: haer. Ulrich I Morhart, 1568), USTC 678458 (VD16 A 2662)

Andreae, Jakob, *Notwendige erinnerung von der Teutschen Bibel dolmetschung sampt widerlegung aller der ursachen darumb die Baepstischen den layen die Bibel zulesen verbietten* (Tübingen: haer. Ulrich I Morhart, 1568), USTC 678459 (VD16 A 2663)

Andreae, Jakob, *Notwendige erinnerung von der Teutschen Bibel dolmetschung sampt widerlegung aller der ursachen darumb die Baepstischen den layen die Bibel zulesen verbietten* (Tübingen: haer. Ulrich I Morhart, 1568), USTC 678460 (VD16 A 2664)

Andreae, Jakob, *Widerruff daß die münch und pfaffen im Hertzogthumb Bayern wider das zeugnuß ires gewissens und die geoffenbarte warheit Baepstisch sein und bleiben woellen* (Tübingen: haer. Ulrich I Morhart, 1569), USTC 706789 (VD16 A 2720)

Andreae, Jakob, *Widerruff daß die münch und pfaffen im Hertzogthumb Bayern wider das zeugnuß ires gewissens und die geoffenbarte warheit Baepstisch sein und bleiben woellen* (Tübingen: haer. Ulrich I Morhart, 1569), USTC 706790 (VD16 A 2719)

Antwerpen, *Gheboden ende uuytgheroepen, 01.09.1582. Alsoo de dijcken inde Nieuwstadt alhier seer swack ende onsterck zijn* (Antwerpen: Christophe Plantin, 1582), USTC 412186

Antwerpen, *Gheboden ende uuytgheroepen, 03.09.1582. Men gebiet alle arme menschen van deser stadt niet gheboren te vertrecken binnen acht dagen* (Antwerpen: Christophe Plantin, 1580), USTC 412187

Antwerpen, *Gheboden ende uuytgheroepen, 03.10.1583. Alsoo de straten deser stadt seer met vuylnisse hoopen zijn vervult ende diversche verckenen inder stadt opghehouden worden. Soo dat niemandt en sal mueghen ergens houden oft opvoeden eenighe verckens* (Antwerpen: Christophe Plantin, 1583), USTC 412235

Antwerpen, *Gheboden ende uuytgheroepen, 04.04.1584. Alsoo eenighe kinderen ende onder hen groote jongers ghemenghelt tieren ende regimenten d'een tegens den anderen, dat niemandy jonck oft oudt eenighe veresamelinghe te maken* (Antwerpen: Christophe Plantin, 1584), USTC 412253

Antwerpen, *Gheboden ende uuytgheroepen, 04.08.1582. Alsoo tot versekeringhe van deser stadt alle huysen, edificien staende rontsomme deser stadt, casteele ende de nieuwe gordijne souden worden afgebroken* (Antwerpen: Christophe Plantin, 1582), USTC 412180

Antwerpen, *Gheboden ende uuytgheroepen, 07.02.1582. Alsoo eenighe lazarussen binnen deser stadt te comen, ende aldaer te bedelen* (Antwerpen: Christophe Plantin, 1582), USTC 412153

Antwerpen, *Gheboden ende uuytgheroepen, 08.01.1583. Alsoo groote vergaderinghe van jongers bedrijvende groote ongheregeltheden ende foulen. Soo men gebiedt den ouders ende meesters datse heure kinders ende jongers thuys ende vander straten oft vesten houden* (Antwerpen: Christophe Plantin, 1583), USTC 412199

Antwerpen, *Gheboden ende uuytgheroepen, 08.03.1580. Dat alle de huyslieden die binnen dese stadt zijn gheweken binnen acht dagen vertrecken* (Antwerpen: Christophe Plantin, 1580), USTC 412102

Antwerpen, *Gheboden ende uuytgheroepen, 08.03.1580. Men beveelt dat alle de persoonen die binnen twee jaren van buyten alhier zijn commen woonen selen schuldich wesen te kennen te gheven sijnen naem* (Antwerpen: Christophe Plantin, 1580), USTC 412101

Antwerpen, *Gheboden ende uuytgheroepen, 09.05.1584. Alsoo door twroeten vanden verckenen (die langs den straten ende weghen loopen) in vuylnissen, mishoopen, dat nyemandt eenighe verckenen op oft langs der straten en sal moghen laten gaen* (Antwerpen: Christophe Plantin, 1584), USTC 412264

Antwerpen, *Gheboden ende uuytgheroepen, 13.06.1582. Dat alle karrelieden die eenighen savel sullen vueren van elcke karre nier meer moghen nemen dan drye stuyvers een oort* (Antwerpen: Christophe Plantin, 1582), USTC 412171

Antwerpen, *Gheboden ende uuytgheroepen, 14.11.1583. Alsoo groote jonghers opde straten, mercten, kerchoven ende alomme elders vergaderinghe te maken vechten. Soo dat niemandt versamelinghe te maken, te vechten* (Antwerpen: Christophe Plantin, 1583), USTC 412238

Antwerpen, *Gheboden ende uuytgheroepen, 14.12.1584. Alsoomen bevindt dat sommighe met den ghemeynen landts-vyant te handelen, dat niemandt hem en vervoordere den vyant hulpe oft bystant te doen* (Antwerpen: Christophe Plantin, 1584), USTC 412293

Antwerpen, *Gheboden ende uuytgheroepen, 18.02.1582. Men ghebiedt alle herbergiers ende ingesetenen opten stadthuyse over te brenghen de persoonen met naem ende toenaem binnen hunnen huyse gheforiert oft gelogeert wesende* (Antwerpen: Christophe Plantin, 1582), USTC 412155

Antwerpen, *Gheboden ende uuytgheroepen, 27.02.1585. Alsoomen bevindt dat diversche ledich-gangers ende vagabonden hen binnen deser stadt begheven ende blyven houdende* (Antwerpen: Christophe Plantin, 1585), USTC 412308

Antwerpen, *Gheboden ende uuytgheroepen, 28.07.1580. Alsoo is geordineert dat die persoonen uuyt deser stadt geseght sijnde niet en souden wederom keeren ende dat nochtans sommige alhier weder te keeren* (Antwerpen: Christophe Plantin, 1580), USTC 412118

Antwerpen, *Gheboden ende uuytgheroepen, 30.01.1580. Alzoemen dagelijcx siet op sondaghen ende vierdaghen grooote vergaderinghe van jongers ende kinderen achter straten, bedryvende groote ongeregeltheyt ende foulen* (Antwerpen: Christophe Plantin, 1580), USTC 412095

Antwerpen, *Gheboden ende uuytgheroepen, 31.12.1584. Alsoomen bevindt dat sommighe met den ghemeynen lants vyant te handelen, dat niemandt hem en vervoordere den vyant hulpe oft bystant te doen* (Antwerpen: Christophe Plantin, 1584), USTC 412298

Antwerpen, *Ordinancie, 21.07.1542, aengaende der stadt ende burgers bewaerenisse* (Antwerpen: Martinus I Nutius, 1542), USTC 408276

Antwerpen, *Rechten, ende costumen van Antwerpen* (Antwerpen: Christophe Plantin, 1582), USTC 401932

Arntss, Hendrik, *Compendium chronici geldrici scriptum ab Henrico aquilio arnemiense* (Cologne: excudebat Renerus Tremoniensis Renerus Tremoniensis, 1567), USTC 623770 (VD16 ZV 784)

Asclepius, Nikolaus, *Petrus lavans. Item psalmus nonus; carmine lyrico* (Marburg: Eucharius Cervicornus, 1536), USTC 683709 (VD16 ZV 26883)

Augsburg – Rat, *Ains erbern rats der stat Augspurg ordnung die allmusenherrn und verwalter der armen dürfftigen daselbs belangend* (Augsburg: Silvan Otmar, 1522), USTC 610520 (VD16 A 4106)

Augsburg – Rat, *Ains erbern rats der stat Augspurg ordnung die hochzeit betreffend* (Augsburg: Silvan Otmar, 1522), USTC 610519 (VD16 ZV 16139)

Augsburg – Rat, *Ains erbern rats der stat Augspurg zucht und pollicey ordnung* (Augsburg: Silvan Otmar, 1537), USTC 610523 (VD16 ZV 24719)

Augsburg – Rat, *Ains erbern rats der stat Augspurg zucht und pollicey ordnung* (Augsburg: Silvan Otmar, 1537), USTC 610524 (VD16 A 4125)

Augsburg – Rat, *Ains ersamen Raths der stat Augspurg zucht unnd policey ordnung* (Augsburg: Melchior Kriegstein, 1553), USTC 610528 (VD16 A 4126)

Baden-Durlach, Karl II, Markgraf von, *Kirchenordnung. Wie die inn der Marggraveschafft Baden, Pfortzheimer theils auch andern Marggraff Carlins zu Baden und hochberg Marggraveschafft Landtschafften und Herrschafften soll angericht und gehalten werden* (Tübingen: haer. Ulrich I Morhart, 1556), USTC 669976 (VD16 B 101)

Bebel, Heinrich, *Facetiarum Heinrici bebelii, poetae a. D.Maximiliano laureati, libri tres* (Tübingen: haer. Ulrich I Morhart, 1555), USTC 657160 (VD16 ZV 1170)

Bern – Rat, *Antwurt schulthaissen klainen und grossen rats der statt Bern auff die außgangne missive der acht orten botschafften zu Lucern versampt an sy schrifftlich gelanget und*

demnach in viltruckten buechlien außgespraittet (Augsburg: Silvan Otmar, 1528), USTC 608575 (VD16 B 1880)
Bern – Rat, *Ratschlag halltender disputation zu Bernn* (Augsburg: Silvan Otmar, 1528), USTC 689888 (VD16 B 1896)
Biblia – VT – Psalmi, *Psalmi ex Hebraica veritate in Latinam conversi* (Marburg: Eucharius Cervicornus, 1536), USTC 688140 (VD16 B 3160)
Biblia – NT – Evangelia, *Evangelium secundum Matthaeum, per Erasmum Roterodamum ad Graecam veritatem fidelissime versum, ac postremo ab ipso recognitum* (Cologne: excudebat Jaspar von Gennep, 1546), USTC 654605 (VD16 B 4890)
Biblia – NT, *Das New Testament* (Nuremberg: Jobst Gutknecht, 1527), USTC 627817 (VD16 B 4376)
Biblia – NT, *Novi Testamenti totius aeditio longe optima et accuratissima. Nam praeter canones illos Eusebii et paraclesin ad evangelicae philosophiae studiu accesserunt etiam nonnulla paraclesis ad evangelicae philosophiae studium paraclesis, id est adhortatio ad sanctissimum ac saluberrimum Christianae philosophiae stadium* (Tübingen: Ulrich I Morhart, 1523), USTC 676054 (VD16 B 4241)
Biblia, *Biblia das ist die gantze heylige schrifft Teutsch* (Frankfurt am Main: Johann Zöpfel, Johann Rasch & Sigmund Feyerabend, 1560), USTC 616482 (VD16 B 2752)
Biblia, *Biblia das ist die gantze heylige schrifft Teutsch. Sampt einem register und schoenen figuren* (Frankfurt am Main: Johann Zöpfel & Sigmund Feyerabend, 1560), USTC 616484 (VD16 B 2747)
Biblia, *Biblia das ist die gantze heylige schrifft Teutsch. Sampt einem register und schoenen figuren* (Frankfurt am Main: Johann Zöpfel & Sigmund Feyerabend, 1560), USTC 616483 (VD16 B 2748)
Biblia, *Biblia das ist die gantze heilige schrifft Teutsch. Sampt einem vollkommenen register und argumenten darueber* (Frankfurt am Main: Georg I Rab, haer. Weigand Han & Sigmund Feyerabend, 1562), USTC 616518 (VD16 B 2756)
Bidenbach, Wilhelm, *Consensus Jesuitarum et Christianorum in doctrina religionis. Ubi examinantur propositiones confeßionis Augustinianae: quibus ceu catholicis pronunciatis, D. Hieronymus torrensis Jesu ita, summam totius Jesu iticae theologiae complecti voluit* (Tübingen: apud haer. Ulrich I Morhart, 1568), USTC 624847 (VD16 B 5362)
Bidenbach, Wilhelm, *Das verleugnete Bapstumb. Beweisung, daß noch bey menschen gedechtnuß erst vor sechtzig jaren in Teutschland von des menschen eignen krefften die sünd zubuessen unnd ewigs leben zuerwerben falsch* (Tübingen: haer. Ulrich I Morhart, 1569), USTC 628116 (VD16 B 5373)
Bidenbach, Wilhelm, *Drey Christliche troestliche predigen uber der leich weilund des durchleuchtigen Herrn Christoffen Hertzogen zu Württemberg und Teck Graven zu Mümpelgart* (Tübingen: haer. Ulrich I Morhart, 1569), USTC 641333 (VD16 B 5367)
Bidenbach, Wilhelm, *Drey Christliche troestliche predigen uber der leich weilund des durchleuchtigen Herrn Christoffen Hertzogen zu Württemberg und Teck Graven zu Mümpelgart* (Tübingen: haer. Ulrich I Morhart, 1569), USTC 641334 (VD16 B 5368)
Bidenbach, Balthasar, *Kurtzer unnd warhafftiger bericht von dem hochloeblichen und Christlichen leben auch seligem Absterben weilundt des durchleuchtigen hochgebornen Fürsten unnd Herrn, Herrn Christoffen Hertzogen zu Wirtemberg* (Tübingen: haer. Ulrich I Morhart, 1569), USTC 669529 (VD16 B 5348)
Bidenbach, Balthasar, *Leichpredig bey der Begrebnuß weilund deß durchleuchtigen hochgebornen Fürsten unnd Herrn, Herrn Eberhardten Hertzogen zu Würtemberg und Theck, Graven zu Mümpelgart etc. Gethon zu Tübingen den 8. Maii anno 1568* (Tübingen: haer. Ulrich I Morhart, 1568), USTC 672023 (VD16 B 5350)

Blomevenna, Petrus, *Informatio succincta, de vario modo adorandi deum, sanctos et homines. Per venerabilem patrem D. Petrum leydeñ. Priorem carthusiensium in Colonia, et visitatorem provincie Rheni. Reuisum et approbatum per eximium magistrum nostrum Arnoldum de tongari, sacre theologiae doctorem* (Cologne: Jaspar von Gennep, 1533), USTC 666599 (VD16 B 5749)

Brabant, *Die blyde incomste den Hertochdom van Brabant in voortiiden by hueren landsheeren verleent* (Cologne: Gottfried II Cervicornus, 1564), USTC 636509 (VD16 B 6879)

Brabant, *Die blyde incomste den Hertochdom van Brabant verleent* (Cologne: Gottfried II Cervicornus, 1577), USTC 412650 (equals USTC 671478 and USTC 406372) (VD16 ZV 2372)

Brandenburg-Ansbach und Kulmbach, Kasimir, Markgraf von, *Brandenburgische halszgerichtsordnung* (Nuremberg: Jobst Gutknecht, 1516), USTC 616917 (VD16 B 6936)

Brandenburg-Ansbach und Kulmbach, Kasimir, Markgraf von, *Brandenburgische halszgerichtsordnung* (Nuremberg: Jobst Gutknecht, 1516), USTC 616918 (VD16 B 6937)

Brassicanus, Johann Alexander, *In florentissimum principem Ferdinandum Austrium, stutgardiam nuper ingressum io. Alexandri Brassicani elegeia gratulatoria. Eiusdem in caldum psychrologum disticha, nobiliss.iuueni dñ Christophoro truchses baroni ex vualdpurg nuncupata. In caldum psychrologum disticha* (Stuttgart: excudebat Hans von Erfurt, 1522), USTC 665745 (VD16 B 7150)

Brenz, Johannes, *Bervis et perspicua psalmorum Davidis explicatio. Decas quinta* (Tübingen: haer. Ulrich I Morhart, 1568), USTC 616021 (VD16 B 7528)

Brenz, Johannes, *Brevis et perspicua explicatio psalmorum Davidis. Decas nona* (Tübingen: haer. Ulrich I Morhart, 1568), USTC 617002 (VD16 B 7530)

Brenz, Johannes, *Brevis et perspicua explicatio psalmorum Davidis. Decas octava* (Tübingen: haer. Ulrich I Morhart, 1568), USTC 617003 (VD16 B 7529)

Brenz, Johannes, *Brevis et perspicua explicatio psalmorum Davidis. Decas tertia* (Tübingen: haer. Ulrich I Morhart, 1568), USTC 617008 (VD16 B 7525)

Brenz, Johannes, *Brevis et perspicua explicatio psalmorum Davidis. Decas quinta* (Tübingen: haer. Ulrich I Morhart, 1568), USTC 617012 (VD16 B 7527)

Brenz, Johannes, *Brevis et perspicua explicatio psalmorum Davidis. Decas decima* (Tübingen: apud haer. Ulrich I Morhart, 1569), USTC 617009 (VD16 B 7532)

Brenz, Johannes, *Brevis et perspicua psalmorum Davidis explicatio. Decas tertia* (Tübingen: haer. Ulrich I Morhart, 1568), USTC 617208 (VD16 B 7526)

Brenz, Johannes, *Catechismus praecipva et necessaria capita Christianae et syncerae religionis complectens. Joan. Brent. Pro scholis in ducatu Wirtemberg* (Tübingen: haer. Ulrich I Morhart, 1568), USTC 620273 (VD16 B 7576)

Brenz, Johannes, *Catechismus, praecipva et necessaria capita Christianae et syncerae religionis complectens. Joan. Brent. Pro scholis in ducatu Wirtembergico* (Tübingen: apud haer. Ulrich I Morhart, 1569), USTC 620435 (VD16 B 7577)

Brenz, Johannes, *Le catechism* (Tübingen: haer. Ulrich I Morhart, 1563), USTC 16488 (VD16 B 7575)

Bruderschaft, *Die broderschaff van unser lieuer frauwen Bedroiffniß, mit innigen gebeden und oiffungen* (Cologne: Jaspar von Gennep, 1533), USTC 636511 (VD16 ZV 6104)

Calvin, Jean, *Zween sendbrief Johannis Calvini* (Neuburg an der Donau: Hans Kilian, 1557), USTC 707876 (VD16 C 306)

Charles V, Emperor, *Der Roemischen Keiserlichen Majestat ordnung und Reformation guter pollicey zu befuerderung des gemeinen nutz auff dem Reichstag zu Augspurg*, (s.l.: s.n., 1548), USTC 634336 (VD16 D 1058)

Charles V, Emperor, *Laetus introitus: die blyde incomst den hertochdomme van Brabandt, in voirtyden by hueren landsheeren verleent, ende van Keyser Carolo den V. geconfirmeert, ende by Philips sijnen sone ghesworen. Anno M.D.XLIX. Met summarien (06.05.1577)* (Cologne: Gottfried II Cervicornus, 1577), USTC 406372 (equals USTC 671478 and USTC 412650), (VD16 ZV 2372)

Charles V, Emperor, *Sacratissimae imperatoriae Maiestatis domini nostri clementissimi declaratoria sententia et decretum cum insertione mandati executorii poenalis, in quibus imperatoria Maiestas ad plenum exnunc ut extunc revocat, cassat, annullat* (Cologne: Jaspar von Gennep, 1546), USTC 691900 (VD16 D 904)

Cicero, Marcus Tullius, *Elegantissima M. T. Ciceronis oratio pro lege manilia sive de imperatore deligendo, separatim hac forma, ut in scholis praelegi possit, accuratius excus* (Marburg: Eucharius Cervicornus, 1536), USTC 648945 (VD16 C 3294)

Cochlæus, Johannes, *Responsio Johannis cochlei in epistolam cuiusdam Lutherani* (Stuttgart: Hans von Erfurt, 1524), USTC 690857 (VD16 C 4376)

Corvinus, Antonius, *De miserabili monasteriensium anabaptistarum obsidione, excidio, memorabilibus rebus tempore obsidionis in urbe gestis, regis, knipperdollingi, ac krechtingi, confessione et exitu libellus Antonii corvini ad Georgium spalatinum scriptus* (Marburg: apud Eucharius Cervicornus, 1536), USTC 630500 (VD16 C 5411)

Corvinus, Antonius, *Kurrtze Außlegung der Episteln so auf die Sontag durch das gantz jar in der Kirchen gelesen werden. Für arme Pfarrherren und haußuätter gestellt* (Augsburg: Silvan Otmar, 1539), USTC 670379 (VD16 C 5367)

Corvinus, Antonius, *Loci in evangelia cum dominicalia tum de sanctis, ut vocant, ita adnotati, ut vel commentarii vice esse possint* (Marburg: apud Eucharius Cervicornus, 1536), USTC 673464 (VD16 C 5407)

Dominicus (Nanus Mirabellius), *Polyanthea opus suavissimis floribus exornatum, authore dominico nano mirabellio, ciue albense, artiumque doctore, ad communem reipublicae literariae utilitatem, longe qua antea auctius factum, et ab innumeris erroribus vindicatum* (Cologne: Jaspar von Gennep, 1546), USTC 684665 (VD16 N 69)

Dryander, Johann, *Anatomia capitis humani, in Marpurgensi academia superiori anno, publice exhibita, per Johannem dryandrum medicum* (Marburg: Eucharius Cervicornus, 1536), USTC 611367 (VD16 E 651)

Dryander, Johann, *Novi annuli astronomici, per Johannem dryandrum medicum atque mathematicum, nuper anno vicesimonono, excogitati, atque hactenus, ex crebra eiusdem instrumenti, in diversis scholis professione, mirum in modum, aucti, canones, atque explicatio succincta. Praefatio eiusdem autoris, ad illustriss. Principem atque D. Johannem comitem et Palatinu Rheni etc. Qua annulum, ex suo solius invento prodiisse, contra quosdam, qui falso sese annuli autores, mentiti sunt, inconuincibilibus argumentis conuincit* (Marburg: Eucharius Cervicornus, 1536), USTC 678578 (VD16 E 673)

Eberlin von Günzburg, Johann, *Der clocker thurn bin ich genant und meld hie d' von Güntzburg schand wie vol ich nur ein steinhauff bin, zwingt mich doch des Evangelisten sin, dann sie mich habend mißgebraucht mit mir gestrafft den armen hauff dem Christus selb sein wort verheißt* (Tübingen: Ulrich I Morhart, 1523), USTC 632970 (VD16 E 129)

Ecclesia catholica - Breviarium - Wurzburg, *Breviarii secundum usum ecclesiae Herbipolensis emendati, in melioremque nunc ordinem digesti, jussu et authoritate D. Julii, episcopi Herbipolensis, et Franciae orientalis ducis, pars hyemalis* (Cologne: apud Maternus Cholinus, 1575), USTC 617085 (VD16 ZV 22256)

Ecclesia catholica - Breviarium - Wurzburg, *Breviarium secundum usum ecclesiae Herbipolensis emendatum, in melioremque nunc ordinem digestum. Jussu et authoritate*

D. Julii, episcopi Herbipolensis, et Franciae orientalis ducis (Cologne: apud Maternus Cholinus, 1575), USTC 617121 (VD16 ZV 22255)

Ecclesia catholica - Breviarium - Wurzburg, *Breviarium secundum usum ecclesiae Herbipolensis emendatum, in melioremque nunc ordinem digestum. Jussu et authoritate d Julii, episcopi Herbipolensis, et Franciae orientalis ducis* (Cologne: apud Maternus Cholinus, 1575), USTC 617122 (VD16 ZV 20019)

Engelbrecht, Anton, *Abconterfeytung und ware gründtliche beschreibung Martin Butzers list geschwindigkeit falsch betrueg wanckelmütigkeit* (Cologne: Jaspar von Gennep, 1546), USTC 607902 (VD16 E 1212)

Engelhart, Leonhard, *Carmen ex esslinga sacri imperIII urbe disce dentis, M. Leonhardi engelhart Halensis* (Tübingen: haer. Ulrich I Morhart, 1568), USTC 618241 (VD16 E 1235)

Erasmus, Desiderius, *De praeparatione ad mortem liber cum primis pius, nunc primum et conscriptus et editus* (Cologne: Eucharius Cervicornus, 1534), USTC 626026 (VD16 E 3406)

Erasmus, Desiderius, *Opus de conscribendis epistolis, ex postrema autoris recognitione emendatius editum. Cum annotationibus marginalibus, que partim artificium, partim autorum locos explicant. Additus est index rerum copiosus* (Cologne: Eucharius Cervicornus, 1534), USTC 626001 (VD16 E 2516)

Erasmus, Desiderius, *Purgatio adversus epistolam non sobriam Martini luteri* (Cologne: Eucharius Cervicornus, 1534), USTC 626053 (VD16 E 3482)

Erfurt – Rat, *Eins erbarn rathes der Stadt Erffurdt ordenunge zu guter pollicey dienlich* (Erfurt: Barbara Sachse, 1551), USTC 648850 (VD16 E 3744)

Fabricius, Franz, *De balneorum naturalium praecipve eorum, quae sunt aquisgrani et porceti, natura et facultatibus, et qua ratione illis utendum sit, libellus perutilis* (Cologne: excudebat Jaspar von Gennep, 1546), USTC 629035 (VD16 F 285)

Ferdinand I, Herzog von Kärnten, *Ferdinannd von Gottes gnaden Printz und infannt in Hispanien, Ertzhertzog zu Osterreich, Hertzog zu Burgundien. Wiewol unnser fründt der Bischove von Bamberg sich in kain disputation lassen will, wie dann unnser gemüet auch nit ist, ob seiner lieb gueter in unnserm Fürstenthumb Kerndten (on mittel gelegen) im pundt seyen oder nit* (Augsburg: Silvan Otmar, 1526), USTC 657411 (VD16 ZV 8829)

Ferrarius, Johannes, *Ad titulum pandectarum, de regulis juris, integer commentaries* (Marburg: apud Eucharius Cervicornus, 1536), USTC 668023 (VD16 E 873)

Fiordibello, Antonio, *De auctoritate ecclesiae, ad amplißvirum Jacobum sadoletum, episcopum carpentoractensem, sanctae Romanae ecclesiae presbyterum cardinalem* (Cologne: excudebat Jaspar von Gennep, 1546), USTC 611956 (VD16 F 1118)

Fontanus, Jacobus, *Ad Adrianum pont.m. Jacobi Fontani judicis appellationum rhodiorum epistola elegantiß. Mißa e rhodo, post deuictam a crudelißimo Christianorum hoste turcha insulam* (Tübingen: Ulrich I Morhart, 1523), USTC 608786 (VD16 F 1839)

Fridericus III, Imperator, *Ausschreiben an alle Stände des Reiches mit der Wiederholung der Weisung, gegen Swicker von Sickingen und seine Anhänger und Helfer vorzugehen, über die wegen Gewalttätigkeit und Raub, verübt an den Bürgern der Stadt Köln die Reichsacht verhängt worden ist. Linz, 15 Nov. 1489* (Cologne: Ludwig von Renchen, 1489), USTC 745004

Frischlin, Nicodemus, *Stipendium Tubingense, illustrissimi principis ac domini, domini Ludovici, ducis Wirtembergici unà cum superattendentibus et magistris domus omnibus: itemque gymnasia monastica, cum eorum abbatibus, descripta carmine* (Tübingen: apud haer. Ulrich I Morhart, 1569), USTC 694716 (VD16 F 2989)

Gaguin, Robert, *Litterae indulgentiarum pro ordine S. Trinitatis, 1498* (Cologne: Ludwig von Renchen, 1498), USTC 745047

Geldorpius, Henricus Castritius, *Belgicae liberandae ab Hispanis hypodeixis, ad p. P. D. Gvilielmum Nassavium, principem aurantium. Anno M. D. LXXi. April. XVII. Exhibita. Ac nunc demum in lucem edita* (Cologne: Gottfried II Cervicornus, 1574), USTC 615704 (VD16 ZV 6480)

Gesetze Steiermark, *Des loblichen Fürstentums erbhuldigung in dem fünfzehnhundertund-zwanzigsten auch nachfolgend des einundzwanzigsten jars bescheen, samt handlung der Landtage* (Augsburg: Jobst de Negker, Silvan Otmar, 1523), USTC 635318 (VD16 S 8760)

Giannotti, Donato, *Res publica venetum. Der grossen commun der statt Venedig ursprung erbawung und aufnemung* (Neuburg an der Donau: Hans Kilian, 1557), USTC 690734 (VD16 ZV 21376)

Gropper, Johann, *An die Roemsche Keyserliche Majestat unsern allergnedigsten Herren warhafftige antwort und gegenberichtug uff Martini Buceri freuenliche clage und angeben* (Cologne: Jaspar von Gennep, 1545), USTC 637052 (VD16 G 3389)

Gropper, Johann, *Capita institutionis ad pietatem, ex sacris scripturis et orthodoxa catholicae ecclesiae doctrina et traditione excerpta, in usum pueritiae apud divum gereonem, Coloniae agrippinae* (Cologne: excudebat Jaspar von Gennep, 1546), USTC 617970 (VD16 G 3390)

Gropper, Johann, *Capita institutionis ad pietatem, ex sacris scripturis et orthodoxa catholicae ecclesiae doctrina et traditione excerpta, in usum pueritiae apud divum gereonem, Coloniae agrippinae* (Cologne: Jaspar von Gennep, 1546), USTC 617973 (VD16 ZV 24633)

Hadrianus VI, *Breve ad Fridericum Saxoniae ducem adversus Lutherum* (Tübingen: Ulrich I Morhart, 1523), USTC 617061 (VD16 ZV 8861)

Haimo Halberstadensis, *Homiliarum, nunc tertio diligentissimè excusarum pars hyemalis, (aestivalis.) additi sunt sermones aliquot pulcherrimi eiusdem haymonis in epistolas canonicas* (Cologne: Eucharius Cervicornus, 1534), USTC 626441 (VD16 H 215)

Haimo Halberstadensis, *In omnes psalmos pia, brevis ac dilucida explanatio, quam ille veluti spiritualis apicula, ex omnium veterum hortis ac pratis florentissimis decerpsit, quo simplicibus et occupatis esset parata saluberrimi mellis copia. Aeditio secunda* (Cologne: Jaspar von Gennep, 1533), USTC 626442 (VD16 H 229)

Hebsacker, Matthias, *Trunckenheit. Das schandtlich und schaedlich laster mit allen seinen verderblichen eigenschafften* (Tübingen: haer. Ulrich I Morhart, 1568), USTC 699736 (VD16 H 900)

Heerbrand, Jakob, *De electione et praedestinatione divina disputatio* (Tübingen: haer. Ulrich I Morhart, 1569), USTC 629598 (VD16 H 1033)

Heerbrand, Jakob, *De nova religione seu fide disputatio* (Tübingen: haer. Ulrich I Morhart, 1568), USTC 630640 (VD16 H 1048)

Heerbrand, Jakob, *Disputatio contra purgatorium* (Tübingen: haer. Ulrich I Morhart, 1569), USTC 639277 (VD16 H 979)

Heerbrand, Jakob, *Disputatio de coniugio* (Tübingen: haer. Ulrich I Morhart, 1568), USTC 638120 (VD16 ZV 7519)

Heerbrand, Jakob, *Disputatio de omnium prima et antiquissima religione, ex genes. Capite tertio. Praeside Jacobo heerbrando Tubingensis academiae rectore sacrosanctae theologiae doctore et eiusdem scholae professore ordinario, domino et praeceptore suo omni reverentia colendo, M. Martinus rieger cantharopolitanus, ad subiecta cum quaestione themata, 7. Calendas julias, loco et hora consuetis pro ingenii sui viribus respondebit* (Tübingen: haer. Ulrich I Morhart, 1568), USTC 637963 (VD16 H 1009)

Hemmeln, Sigmund, *Der gantz psalter Davids wie derselbig in teutsche gesang verfasset mit vier stimmen kunstlich und lieblich von newem gesetzt (Discantus)* (Tübingen: apud haer. Ulrich I Morhart, 1569), USTC 553285 (VD16 ZV 18761)

Hemmeln, Sigmund, *Der gantz psalter Davids wie derselbig in teutsche gesang verfasset mit vier stimmen kunstlich und lieblich von newem gesetzt (Altus)* (Tübingen: apud haer. Ulrich I Morhart, 1569), USTC 553286 (VD16 ZV 18761)

Hemmeln, Sigmund, *Der gantz psalter Davids wie derselbig in teutsche gesang verfasset mit vier stimmen kunstlich und lieblich von newem gesetzt (Bassus)* (Tübingen: apud haer. Ulrich I Morhart, 1569), USTC 553287 (VD16 ZV 18761)

Hemmeln, Sigmund, *Der gantz psalter Davids wie derselbig in teutsche gesang verfasset mit vier stimmen kunstlich und lieblich von newem gesetzt (Tenor)* (Tübingen: apud haer. Ulrich I Morhart, 1569), USTC 632279 (VD16 ZV 18761)

Henrichmann, Jacob, *Grammaticae institutiones. Exhortatio eiusdem ad pueros ut eloquentiae studeant ars condendorum carminu Henrici bebelii justingensis poetae laureati cum additionibus per autorem ipsum emendata racemationes eiusdem centimetru mauri seruli honorati grammatici* (Tübingen: in aedibus Thomas Anshelm, 1516), USTC 668695 (VD16 H 2025)

Hessen, Philip I., Landgraf von, *Landtgravisch Ausschreyben der furhabenden gewerb und rustung. Copei eyner angetzogen Bundtnus so durch Koenigliche Majestat zu Hungern unnd Boehemen unnd etlich Chuerfurstenn unnd Furstenn auffgericht sein soll* (Cologne: Johann Soter, 1528), USTC 671536 (VD16 ZV 23340)

Hessen, Philip I., Landgraf von, *Unser Philipsen von Gottes gnaden Lantgraven zu Hessen underthanen und lieben getreuwen von der Ritterschafft Stetten und Landschafft so wyr Freitags nach Kiliani an. M.D. XXXII. ghein Homburg in Hessen dero hülffe halb so Roem.Key. Mt widder den Turcken bewilligt zu uns erfordert haben einer gemeiner stewer unndertheniglich bewilligten anlage und ordnung* (Marburg: Eucharius Cervicornus, 1536), USTC 701873 (VD16 H 2894)

Hollande, Willem I, stathouder de, *Allen ende elckerlycken capiteynen crijchsluyden van Nederlant wenschet de prince van Oraengien gheluck ende salicheyt (in onsen vertlegher by Arweyler, 14.09.1568)* (Cologne: Gottfried II Cervicornus, 1568), USTC 410000 (not in VD16)

Hollande, Willem I, stathouder de, *Verklaers ende uutschrift des vorsten ende heeren, heer Willem, prince van Orangien etc ende zijner excellentien nootsakelicke defensie teghen den duca de Alba ende zijne grouwelijcke tyrannys* (Cologne: Gottfried II Cervicornus, 1568), USTC 411058 (not in VD16)

Hollande, Willem I, stathouder de, *Willem byder gratien Gods prince toe Orangien. Allen ghetrouwen ondersaten des con. maj. in den Nederlanden, saluyt* (Cologne: Gottfried II Cervicornus, 1568), USTC 421573 (not in VD16)

Homer, *Batrachomyomachia homeri poetarum omnium principis, odysseae libri XXIIII. Raphaële regio volaterrano interprete. Eiusdem batrachomyomachia, id est, ranarum et muriu pugna, aldo manutio Romano interprete eiusdem hymni deorum trigintaduo, iodoco velareo verbrokano interprete herodoti halicarnassei libellus, homeri vitam continens, Conrado heresbachio interprete. Cum indice homeru bios hymni deorum trigintaduo hymnoi libellus homeri vitam continens* (Cologne: Eucharius Cervicornus, 1534), USTC 663926 (VD16 H 4705)

Innocentius III, *Opera d.innocentii pontificis maximi, eius nominis III. Viri eruditissimi simul atque gravissimi, quae quidem hactenus obtineri potuerunt omnia, ad diversa, antiqua fideque digna exemplaria, sedulò, studioseque castigata, et partìm iam primum in lucem edita, et in unum volumen congesta. Cum indice* (Cologne: Johann von Neuß, Maternus Cholinus, 1552), USTC 679617 (VD16 ZV 8581)

Josephus, Flavius, *Antiquitatum libelli quinque babyloniaka de judicio temporum flavii Josephi Hebraei antiquitatum judaicarum libri XX* (Cologne: Gottfried Hittorp, Eucharius Cervicornus, 1534), USTC 657567 (VD16 J 959)

Jülich – Cleves – Berg, Johann III, Herzog von, *Van Gots genadenn. Wir Johan Hertzog zu Cleef Gulich unnd Berg Graff zu der Marck unnd Ravenßberg Doin kunt* (Cologne: Johannes Soter, 1533), USTC 700399 (VD16 K 1284)

Jülich – Cleves – Berg, Johann III, Herzog von, *Von Gotz gnaden wir Johan - Münzordnung, Kleve 21.01.1537* (Solingen: Johannes Soter, 1537), USTC 2507379 (not in VD16, broadsheet, copy in Landesarchiv Nordrhein-Westfalen, Handschriften L II 7, Band 1)

Jülich – Cleves – Berg, Johann III, Herzog von, *Van Gotz gnaden wir Johan – Das Einschleichen, Durchziehen und Aufhalten fremder herrenloser Kriegsknechte und anderer Vagabunden wird streng verboten, Kleve 03.07.1538* (Solingen: Johannes Soter, 1538), USTC 2507380 (not in VD16, broadsheet, copy in Landesarchiv Nordrhein-Westfalen, Handschriften L II 7, Band 1)

Jülich – Cleves – Berg, Wilhelm V, Herzog von, *Warhafftiger und gruntlicher bericht der gerechtigkeitt unnd rechtmessiger possession des durchleuchtigen hochgebornen Fursten und Herrn, Herrn Wilhelms Hertzogen zu Gulch Geldren Cleef und Berg Graven zu der Marck Zutphen und Ravenszberg Hern zu Ravenstein etc. Zu dem Hertzogthumb Geldren und Graffschafft Zutphen auff dem Reichstag zu Speir im jair M.D.XLII. ubergeben* (Solingen: Johann Soter, 1542), USTC 705919 (VD16 K 1287)

Jülich – Cleves – Berg, Wilhelm V, Hertzog zu Gulich - *Aufgebot der bewaffneten Landmacht zur Beschützung des bedrohten Fürstentums Jülich, 00.10.1542* (Solingen: Johannes Soter, 1538), USTC 2507381 (not in VD16, broadsheet, copy in Landesarchiv Nordrhein-Westfalen, Handschriften L II 7, Band 1)

Jülich – Cleves – Berg, Wilhelm V, Herzog von, *Bericht uff den vermeinten fuergestalten andstandt zu Nuerenberg* (Solingen: Johann Soter, 1543), USTC 615895 (VD16 B 1829)

Jülich – Cleves – Berg, Wilhelm V, Herzog von, *Wilhelm Hertzog zu Guylich, so ist unser bevelh, das ir dry fridage nacheynander gemeynen gebeth halden - Anordnung eines Landesgebetes zur Abwendung des Krieges, der Pest und der Teuerung, Gladbach 17.03.1543* (Solingen: Johannes Soter, 1543), USTC 2507052 (not in VD16, broadsheet, copies in Landesarchiv Nordrhein-Westfalen, Handschriften L II 7, Band 1 &Handschriften L II 8)

Jülich – Cleves – Berg, Wilhelm V, Herzog von, *Wilhelm Hertzoch zu Gulich - Wilhelm von der Leyen wird zum Befehlshaber der Landmacht ernannt, die Beamten werden angewiesen die Untertanen in guter Kriegsrüstung bereit zu halten, Gladbach 20.07.1543* (Solingen: Johannes Soter, 1543), USTC 2507053 (not in VD16, broadsheet, copies in Landesarchiv Nordrhein-Westfalen, Handschriften L II 7, Band 1 & Handschriften L II 8)

Kastl, Johannes von, *De adherendo deo nudato intellectu et affectu, et ultima hominis perfectione, libellus plane piissimus. Farrago item piarum precum* (Cologne: Jaspar von Gennep, 1532), USTC 610577 (VD16 ZV 8709)

Köln – Domkapitel, *Artickell eins ehrwirdigen dhomcapittels so den weltlichen stenden nemlich Gravenn Ritterschafft Stetten unnd gemeiner Landtschafft des Ertzstiffts Coellen, wan dieselben uff das beschehen beschreiben ankomen weren, solten sein vorgelesen worden uff den neunten tag des monats Septembris anno 1546* (Cologne: Jaspar von Gennep, 1546), USTC 613258 (VD16 K 1772)

Köln – Domkapitel, *Delectorum per capitulum metropolitanum, universitatem et clerum urbis metropolitanae Coloniensis, censura de mediis concordiae conceptis à delectis status secularis eiusdem dioscesis in causa religionis. E Germanico in Latinum sermonem per quendam religiosum fratrem conversa* (Cologne: Jaspar von Gennep, 1546), USTC 632233 (VD16 K 1775)

Köln – Domkapitel, *Ein underthenig bitlich und flehelich schreiben so ein erwirdig thumbcapittel dem hochwirdigsten Ertzbischoffen und Chuerfuersten zu Coelln in zeit der insinuation des Keyserlichen decrets unnd mandats undertheniglich uberantwortenn haben lassen* (Cologne: Jaspar von Gennep, 1546), USTC 647333 (VD16 K 1799)

Köln – Domkapitel, *Nachdem wir jüngst uß etlichen notwendigen und unvermeidtlichen ursachen daran disem Ertzstifft und allen ingesessen desselben am hoechsten gelegen die drey weltliche Stende vermoege der Erblandtvereinung (die uns des zu thun macht und gewalt gibt) zu uns hieher gen Coelnn thun beschreiben* (Cologne: Jaspar von Gennep, 1546), USTC 676669 (VD16 ZV 9073)

Köln – Domkapitel, *Wolgebornen vettern ernfesten frommen vorsichtigen und ersamen lieben besondern gustige und gute freunde e.l. Und ir andern wissen onzweiffel euch wol zu erinnern wie offt wir euch als unsere liebe erbeinigungsverwandten unnd mitglidder dißes alten unnd loeblichen Ertzstiffts schrifftlich und müntlich ermant und gebetten haben bei unser alten Catholischen religion bestendig zu pleiben* (Cologne: Jaspar von Gennep, 1546), USTC 707289 (VD16 ZV 9076)

Köln – Erzbischof, Hermann von Hessen, Eynnunge vnd fruntlich verstant van hundert Jaren (Cologne: Heinrich Bungart, 1501), USTC 656933 (VD16 K 1727)

Köln – Rat, *Abdruck und gemeiner begriff der pollicey ordnungen plebisciten unnd statuten der alten loeblichen Freyen Reichsstadt Coellen* (s.l.: s.n., 1562), USTC 608010 (VD16 ZV 9096)

Köln – Rat, *Abdruck vnd gemeiner begriff der Pollicey Ordenungen Plebisciten, vnd Statuten der alten loblichen freyen Reichs Stadt Coellen* (s.l.: s.n., 1562), USTC 2213379 (VD16 ZV 30617)

Köln – Rat, *Ausschreiben betreffend einen Aufruhr in der Stadt am 18 Feb. 1482 und Bestrafung der Rädelsführer* (Cologne: Johann Koelhoff, 1482), USTC 744091

Köln – Rat, *Ausschreiben von Bürgermeister und Rat von Köln über ihren Handel mit Swicker von Sickingen. 31 Jan. 1489* (Cologne: Ludwig von Renchen, 1489), USTC 744093

Köln – Rat, *Ausschreiben von Bürgermeister und Rat von Köln über ihren Handel mit Swicker von Sickingen. 31 Jan. 1489* (Cologne: Ludwig von Renchen, 1489), USTC 744092

Köln – Rat, *Bekanntmachung über Münzeinigung mit dem Erzbischof von Köln und dem Herzog Wilhelm von Jülich* (Cologne: Ludwig von Renchen, 1493), USTC 744094

Köln – Rat, *Bürgermeister und Rat der Stadt Köln: Beschwerdeschrift wegen Beeinträchtigung der Zollprivilegien* (Cologne: Johann Koelhoff, 1490), USTC 744095

Köln – Rat, *Bürgermeister und Rat der Stadt Köln: Beschwerdeschrift wegen Beeinträchtigung der Zollprivilegien* (Cologne: Johann Koelhoff, 1490), USTC 744096

Köln – Rat, *Dit is der Stadt Coelne recht und burger freyheyt* (Cologne: s.n., 1529), USTC 640296 (VD16 K 1806)

Köln – Rat, *Einladung des Rats und der Schiessgesellen der Stadt Köln zum Armbrustschiessen* (Cologne: Johann Koelhoff, 1483), USTC 744098

Köln – Rat, *Einladung des Rats und der Schiessgesellen der Stadt Köln zum Armbrust-Schiessen, verbunden mit einem Glückshafen. (Invitation issued on 9 Apr. 1483 to a shooting match on 16 June 1483)* (Cologne: Johann Koelhoff, 1483), USTC 744099

Köln – Rat, *Erklärung wie men die Silveren Lychte ind Swaire* (Cologne: Ludwig von Renchen, 1493), USTC 744100

Köln – Rat, *Münzordnung: Valvatio oder Ordnung des Rates der Stadt Köln über die goldenen und silbernen Münzen* (Cologne: Ludwig von Renchen, 1493), USTC 744101

Köln – Rat, *Münzvertrag zwischen Erzbischof Hermann IV von Köln, Herzog Wilhelm IV von Jülich und dem Rat der Stadt Köln* (Cologne: Ludwig von Renchen, 1494), USTC 744103

Köln – Rat, *Wacht Ordnung* (Cologne: Maternus Cholinus, 1585), USTC 704779 (VD16 ZV 9097)

Köln – Rat, *Newe Gemeine Wachtordnung* (Cologne: Maternus Cholinus, 1586), USTC 677228 (VD16 ZV 9098)

Köln – Rat, *Newe Gemeine Wachtordnung* (Cologne: Maternus Cholinus, 1586), USTC 677227 (VD16 K 1808)

Köln – Rat, *Supplication und clageschryften die gegen Heren Johan van Oldendorpinge-schreven und overgegeven synt worden* (Cologne: Hermann Bungart, 1513), USTC 710377 not in VD16

Köln – Stände, *Instruction in namen der dreier wertlicher stendt des Ertzstiffts Coellen an die erwirdigen wolgebornen und hochgelerten Hern Thumbkepler unnd Cantzler etc. ferrer an eyn erwirdig Thumcapitel unnd andere darzu gehoerige* (Cologne: Jaspar von Gennep, 1546), USTC 669151 (VD16 K 1812)

Köln, Erzbischof von, *Münzordnung: Ordnung der goldenen und silbernen Münzen. Brühl, 1 Dec. 1494* (Cologne: Ludwig von Renchen, 1494), USTC 745656

Laguna, Andrés de, *De victus et exercitiorum ratione, maxime in senectute observanda, ad reverendum, illustrem, atque magnificum virum, D. D. Ioannem, diminum ab epstein, et mintzburg, comitem in Dietz, gymnasiarcham metropolitanae Coloniensis ecclesiae longe digniß. Et C. Andreae a lacuna, secobiensis, philiatri, perioche* (Cologne: excudebat Jaspar von Gennep, 1546), USTC 629756 (VD16 ZV 9356)

Landsberg, Johannes Justus, *Jesu Christi ad animam peccatricem nondum conversam, interna exhortatio. Jesu Christi ad animam fidelem epistola sive alloquia. Regulae duae discipulorum Christi. Hymni aliquot pii. Exercitium amoris ad sanctissimam trinitatem* (Cologne: Jaspar von Gennep, Kartause St. Barbara, 1533), USTC 665004 (VD16 J 1184)

Landsberg, Johannes Justus, *Pharetra divini amoris, variis ignitisque aspirationibus, orationibus atque exercitiis referta* (Cologne: Jaspar von Gennep, Kartause St. Barbara, 1533), USTC 683753 (VD16 J 1197)

Latomus, Bartholomaeus, *Epitome commentariorum dialecticae inventionis, Rodolphi Agricolae* (Cologne: Eucharius Cervicornus, 1534), USTC 652911 (VD16 A 1112)

Liège Johann II, bishop of, *Klage gegen Eberhard Rupprecht von Arenberg und Genossen, 5 Jan. 1486* (Cologne: Ludwig von Renchen, 1486), USTC 746211

Loer, Dierick, *Catalogus d'dionysii carthusiani, doctoris extatici vita, simul et operum eius fidissimus catalogus. Fidissimus catalogus* (Cologne: excudebat Jaspar von Gennep, 1532), USTC 628543 (VD16 VD16 L 2298)

Luther, Martin, *Ermanunge zum frid auff die zwoelff artickel der bawrschafft in Schwaben* (Tübingen: Ulrich I Morhart, 1525), USTC 653520 (VD16 L 4689)

Luther, Martin, *Warnunge an seine lieben Deudschen vor etlichen jaren geschrieben auff diesen fall so die feinde Christlicher warheit diese Kirchen und land darinne reine lere des Evangelii geprediget wird mit krieg überziehen und zerstoeren wolten* (Tübingen: Ulrich I Morhart, 1546), USTC 706039 (VD16 L 7349)

Luther, Martin, *Wider die mordischen unnd reübischen rotten der bawren* (Tübingen: Ulrich I Morhart, 1525), USTC 706700 (VD16 L 7498)

Maximilian I, Emperor, *Ausschreiben betreffend den abgesetzten Herzog Eberhard II von Württemberg. Innsbruck, 19 Nov. 1499* (Tübingen: Johann Otmar, 1499), USTC 746967

Maximilian I, Emperor, *Ausschreiben betreffend die Unterstützung seiner politischen Absichten gegen Franzosen und Türken durch die Niederländer. Grave, 26 Jan. 1498* (Cologne: Retro Minores (Martin von Werden), 1498), USTC 747074

Maximilian I, Emperor, *Ausschreiben gegen Karl von Egmont wegen Anmassung des Herzogtums Jülich. Worms, 31 Aug. 1495* (Cologne: Ludwig von Renchen, 1495), USTC 747071

Maximilian I, Emperor, *Ausschreiben zugunsten des Grafen Johann von Nassau betreffend die Befreiung vom Reichshofgericht zu Rottweil und von den westfälischen Femegerichten. Speyer, 8 June 1494* (Cologne: Heinrich Quentell, 1494), USTC 747077

Maximilian I, Emperor, *Landfrieden, Ordnung des Kammergerichts. Worms, 7 et 17 Aug. 1495* (Cologne: Johann Landen, 1496), USTC 747123

Maximilian I, Emperor, *Landfrieden. Worms, 7 Aug. 1495* (Cologne: Ludwig von Renchen, 1495), USTC 747114

Melanchthon, Philipp, *Annotationes, omnium eruditiss. In evangelium Matthaei, pro communi Christianismi commodo* (Tübingen: Ulrich I Morhart, 1523), USTC 611675 (VD16 M 2494)

Melanchthon, Philipp, *In evangelium Joannis, annotationes Philippi Melanchthonis* (Tübingen: Ulrich I Morhart, 1523), USTC 665690 (VD16 M 2480)

Melanchthon, Philipp, *In obscuriora aliquot capita geneseos Philip. Melanch. Annotationes* (Tübingen: Ulrich I Morhart, 1523), USTC 662638 (VD16 M 3461)

Mithoff, Burkhard, *Annuli cum sphaerici tum mathematici usus et structura, opera D. Burchardi mithobii neapolitani, celeberrimae academiae Marpurgeñ mathematic* (Marburg: apud Eucharius Cervicornus, 1536), USTC 608552 (VD16 M 5661)

Monsenus, Johannes, *Finitiva scriptis e canonicis decisio, ab apostolorum prouenire consuetudine, populo sub panis tantum specimine sacram synaxim esse tribuendam* (Cologne: excudebat Jaspar von Gennep, 1546), USTC 657515 (VD16 M 6179)

Neue Zeitung, *Newe Zeytung auß Niderland. Warhafftige beschreibung und summarische erzelung der fuernembsten handlungen so mit schlagen stoett und schiff eroberung vom ersten tag Aprilis biß auff den 28. May zwischen dem Herrn von lumy Graff Ludwig von Nassaw und irer widerpart nemlich dem Cardinalischen diener Duc de Alba und seinem anhang ergangen ist inn diesem 1572. jar. Alles auß Niderlendischer sprach fleissig in hoch Teutsch verfertiget* (Lauingen: Emanuel Saltzer, 1572), USTC 677756 (VD16 N 688)

Nonnus Panopolitanus, *Nonnoy nonnu poietu panopolitu metabole tu kata Joannen hagiu evangeliu, dia stichon heroikon. Nonni panopolitani poëtae, conversio evangelii secundum iounnem, Graecis versibus conscripta* (Cologne: Maternus Cholinus, Gottfried II Cervicornus, 1570), USTC 678301 (VD16 N 1831)

Noot, Jan van der, *Verscheiden poetixe wercken* (Cologne: Gottfried II Cervicornus, 1572), USTC 415393 (not in VD16)

Nürnberg – Rat, *Eins rats der stat Nürmberg ordnung des grossen allmusens haußarmer leut* (Nuremberg: Jobst Gutknecht, 1522), USTC 648630 (VD16 N 2019)

Nürnberg – Rat, *Mandat eins erbern Raths der stat Nuermberg das gotslestern und zutrinckens belangent* (Nuremberg: Jobst Gutknecht, 1537), USTC 674770 (VD16 N 1988)

Osiander, Lucas, *Ableinung der lugen verkerungen unnd loesterungen mit denen bruder Johann naß in seinen centuriis der Evangelischen warheiten (wie ers nennet) die Christlich lehr der Augspurgischen Confeßion unwarhafftig und schmaelich antastet* (Tübingen: haer. Ulrich I Morhart, 1569), USTC 608153 (VD16 N 1988)

Osiander, Lucas, *Institutio Christianae religionis* (Tübingen: excudebat Georg Gruppenbach, 1582), USTC 666752 (VD16 O 1212)

Osiander, Lucas, *Institution de la religion chrestienne. Mise en lumiere. Par lucas osiander D. Escrite principalement pour lusage des eglises de france, et du pays bas* (Tübingen: Georg Gruppenbach, 1582), USTC 666678 (VD16 O 1215)

Osiander, Lucas, *Warnung vor der falschen lehr und phariseischen gleißnerey der Jesuiter* (Tübingen: haer. Ulrich I Morhart, 1568), USTC 706029 (VD16 O 1273)

Osiander, Lucas, *Warnung vor der falschen lehr und phariseischen gleißnerey der Jesuiter* (Tübingen: haer. Ulrich I Morhart, 1568), USTC 706030 (VD16 O 1272)

Osiander, Lucas, *Warnung vor der falschen lehr und phariseischen gleißnerey der Jesuiter* (Tübingen: haer. Ulrich I Morhart, 1569), USTC 706028 (VD16 O 1274)

Persius Flaccus, Aulus, *Satyrae, obscurißimae alioqui, luculentißima eophrasi simul et scholiis doctißimi viri iohannis Murmellii illustratae. Adiecta est epistola hermanni buschii, ad intelligentiam persii multum conducens* (Cologne: Eucharius Cervicornus, 1534), USTC 683402 (VD16 ZV 12308)

Philip II, King of Spain, *Translaet vande brieven van gratie ende pardoen generael gegeven ter saken vande voorledene troublen (Madrid, 16.11.1569)* (Cologne: Gottfried II Cervicornus, 1570), USTC 415164 (not in VD16)

Plinius Minor, *Illustrium virorum ab urbe condita liber unus* (Cologne: Eucharius Cervicornus, 1534), USTC 617539 (VD16 P 3519)

Radulphus, Frater, *Indulgentia (to benefactors of the Order of the Holy Trinity) 1467* (Cologne: Ulrich Zell, 1467), USTC 748372

Reninger, Johannes, *Zu trost allen menschen die von wegen sindtfluß manigfaltig betriepte hertzer habent und zu nutz allen secten unnd staenden zu vor an den so in den oebern secten seind* (Tübingen: Ulrich I Morhart, 1523), USTC 707773 (VD16 ZV 4300)

Rostock – Rat, *Policey ordnung eines erbarn rhats der Stadt Rostock. publiciret anno M. D. LXXVI. Den 14. Aprilis* (Rostock: Augustin I Ferber, 1576), USTC 684628 (VD16 R 3184)

Sachsen, Georg, Herzog von, *Zuvermercken mit was truglicher unwarheyt die kinder dieser boshafftigen welt bei unsern zeiten sich bearbeiten zwuschen Koenigen Georg von Gots gnaden Hertzog zu Sachsen etc. Philipsen Landtgraven zu Hessen schrifft an Hertzog Georgen von Sachsen* (Cologne: Johann Soter, 1528), USTC 707826 (VD16 S 775)

Sachsen, Johann Friedrich I., Kurfürst von, Hessen, Philipp, Landgraf von, *Bestendige vnde warhafftige verantwortung auch im Rechten gegruendete widerlegung* (Magdeburg: Michael Lotter, 1546), USTC 633083 (VD16 S 995)

Sachsen, Johann Friedrich I., Kurfürst von, Hessen, Philipp, Landgraf von, *Warhafftiger bericht vn Summari außfuerung, Warumb jnen zu vnschulden auffgelegt wirdet* (s.l.: s.n., 1546), USTC 2212481 (VD16 ZV 30277)

Sachsen, Johann Friedrich I., Kurfürst von, Hessen, Philipp, Landgraf von, *Bestendige vnd warhafftige, verantwortung auch im Rechten gegruendete widerlegung* (Ulm: Hans Varnier, 1546), USTC 633132 (VD16 S 997)

Sachsen, Johann Friedrich I., Kurfürst von, Hessen, Philipp, Landgraf von, *Warhafftiger bericht und summari außfuerung warumb inen zu unschulden auffgelegt wirdt* (Nuremberg: s.n., 1546), USTC 633112 (VD16 S 1071)

Sachsen, Johann Friedrich I., Kurfürst von, Hessen, Philipp, Landgraf von, *Warhafftiger bericht und summari außfuerung warumb inen zu unschulden auffgelegt wirdet* (Augsburg: s.n., 1546), USTC 633136 (VD16 S 1075)

Sachsen, Johann Friedrich I., Kurfürst von, Hessen, Philipp, Landgraf von, *Warhafftiger bericht und summari außfuehrung warumb inen zu unschulden auffgelegt wirdet* (Nuremberg: Johann Vom Berg & Ulrich Neuber, 1546), USTC 633113 (VD16 S 1072)

Sachsen, Johann Friedrich I., Kurfürst von, Hessen, Philipp, Landgraf von, *Warhafftiger bericht vn Summari außführung Warumb jnen zu vnschulden auffgelegt wirdet* (s.l.: s.n., 1546), USTC 2214459 (VD16 ZV 29142)

Sachsen, Johann Friedrich I., Kurfürst von, Hessen, Philipp, Landgraf von, *Warhafftiger bericht und summari außfürung warumb inen zu unschulden auffgelegt wirdet* (Marburg: Andreas Kolbe, 1546), USTC 633114 (VD16 S 1079)

Sachsen, Johann Friedrich I., Kurfürst von, Hessen, Philipp, Landgraf von, *Warhafftiger bericht und summari außfuehrung warumb inen zu unschulden auffgelegt wirdet* (Erfurt: Melchior I Sachse, 1546), USTC 633078 (VD16 S 1076)

Sachsen, Johann Friedrich I., Kurfürst von, Hessen, Philipp, Landgraf von, *Warhafftiger bericht unnd summari außfuerung warumb inen zu unschulden auffgelegt würt* (s.l.: s.n., 1546), USTC 633133 (VD16 ZV 13618)

Sarcerius, Erasmus, *De institutione scholae sigensis, M. Erasmi sarcerii annaemontani* (Marburg: apud Eucharius Cervicornus, 1536), USTC 630144 (VD16 ZV 26493)

Schegkius, Jacobus, *Antilogia Jacobi schegkii schorndorffensis, qua refellit XXVII. Propositiones serutianae haereseos, quibus impiè statuitur solius patris essentia et persona Deus esse verus exclusiuè, filius autem, et spiritus s. Impiè negantur personaliter subsistere in essentia divina* (Tübingen: haer. Ulrich I Morhart, 1568), USTC 611882 (VD16 S 2463)

Schegkius, Jacobus, *Disputatio de febribus. Praeside excellentissimo viro, D. Jacobo scekgio, philosophiae et medicinae doctore eximio, praeceptore et patrono suo, M. Tilemannus hamelius, Brunsvicensis, ad subscriptas cum quaestione positiones, pro virili, deo adiuuante, publicè respondebit. In aula nova, die decima septima septembris, hora septima* (Tübingen: haer. Ulrich I Morhart, 1568), USTC 639299 (VD16 ZV 23071)

Schegkius, Jacobus, *Responsum Jacobi schegkii schorndorffensis, ad Simonis Simonii libellum vanissimum* (Tübingen: haer. Ulrich I Morhart, 1568), USTC 690905 (VD16 S 2491)

Schnepff, Dietrich, *Disputatio de poenitentia* (Tübingen: s.n., 1568), USTC 638134 (VD16 S 3286)

Schnepff, Dietrich, *Disputatio de propositione Paulina* (Tübingen: haer. Ulrich I Morhart, 1569), USTC 639317 (VD16 S 3289)

Schnepff, Dietrich, *Oratio cum funus duceretur illustrißimo principi et domino d.eberharto duci Wirtenbergensi anno M. D. LX VIII* (Tübingen: s.n., 1568), USTC 679986 (VD16 S 3301)

Schwäbischer Bund, *Abschid des gemainen bundtsversamlungstags so auf der Hailigen drey Künig tag anno etc. XXXII. gen Augspurg fürgenommen worden ist* (Augsburg: Silvan Otmar, 1532), USTC 608217 (VD16 S 4569)

Schwäbischer Bund, *Abschid des gemainen punds versamlung tags so auff Sant Andreas des Hailigen zwoelffpotten tag anno etc. XVIIII. gen Augspurg fürgenommen worden ist* (Augsburg: Silvan Otmar, 1519), USTC 608219

Schwäbischer Bund, *Wie man für die Bundesverwandten Gott den Allmächtigen bitten soll, beschlossen auf dem Tag zu Esslingen* (Tübingen: Johann Otmar, 1500), USTC 748837

St Trinitatis, *Indulgentia (to benefactors of the Order of the Holy Trinity) 1467* (Cologne: Ulrich Zell, 1467), USTC 748373

Steenhouwer, Johan, *Praeclarissimae quaeque sententiae, ex C. Plinii secundi naturalis historiae libris, compendio selectae, a Joanne lithocomo. In usum studiosorum, qui sibi totum illud opus commode prae pecuniae inopia comparare nequeunt* (Cologne: excudebat Gottfried II Cervicornus, 1562), USTC 686163 (VD16 ZV 14675)

Stöffler, Johannes, *Expurgatio adversus divinationum XXIIII anni suspitiones, à quibuscuque idigne sibi offusas, nominatim aut à Georgio tanastetter collimitio lycoripensi, medico et mathematico, in eo libello quem ipse consolatorium inscripsit* (Tübingen: Ulrich I Morhart, 1523), USTC 667966

Trient – Konzil, *Alle handlung und session des allgemeynen und Christlichen Concilii zu Trent under Pabst Paulo dem Dritten angefangen und nach Absterben Julii des dritten under pio dem Vierdten im jar M.D.LXIII. Gottseligklich beschlossen* (Cologne: Jaspar von Gennep, 1564), USTC 610813 (VD16 K 2064)

Ungarn, Niederlande Statthalterin Maria von, *Confutatio defensionis ducis clivensis super jure ducatus Geldriae ac comitatus zutphaniae* (Solingen: Johann Soter, 1543), USTC 665839 (VD16 A 3912)

Veltkirch, Johann Toltz von, *Commentarii in universam physicam Aristotelis, distincti libris IIII. Iam recens accuratissime recogniti* (Tübingen: haer. Ulrich I Morhart, 1557), USTC 667678 (VD16 B 2029)
Verallo, Girolamo, *Sententia diffinitiva per reverendissimum in Christo patrem et amplissimum dominum D. Hieronymum archiepiscopum rossanensem, apostolicae sedis nuncium cum potestate legati de latere ad imperatoriam maiest. Etc. Pro reverendis, illustribus et venerabilibus dominis, subdecano et capitulo ecclesiae Coloniensis, contra eiusdem ecclesiae decanum et suos complices adversarios lata et promulgat* (Cologne: Jaspar von Gennep, 1546), USTC 693369 (VD16 V 578)
Vocabularius, *Vocabularius ex quo* (Cologne: Ludwig von Renchen, 1490), USTC 742199

Wanner, Valentin, *De missa judicium valentini vannii pastoris ecclesiae quae est in candtstatt* (Tübingen: haer. Ulrich I Morhart, 1555), USTC 630512 (VD16 W 1200)
Wanner, Valentin, *De missa* (Tübingen: haer. Ulrich I Morhart, 1555), USTC 630510 (VD16 W 1195)
Wanner, Valentin, *Was von der Meß zuhalten sey bedencken auß der hayligen geschrifft und den allten lehrern der Kirchen gezogen* (Tübingen: haer. Ulrich I Morhart, 1555), USTC 706212 (VD16 W 1197)
Wied, Wilhelm, Graf von, *Urkunde, durch die dem Herzog Wilhelm IV von Jülich, die Verpfändungssumme für die Ortschaften Brüggen, Dülken, Dahlen, Venrath und Süchteln um 25000 Gulden gekürzt wird. 24 Jan. 1493* (Cologne: Ludwig van Renchen, 1493), USTC 749825
Wied, Wilhelm, Graf von, *Urkunde, durch die er Born, Sittart und Süstren an Herzog Wilhelm* (Cologne: Ludwig von Renchen, 1494), USTC 749826
Wied, Wilhelm, Graf von, *Urkunde, durch die er Brüggen, Dülken, Dahlen, Venrath und Süchteln an Herzog Wilhelm IV von Jülich abtritt. 21 June 1494* (Cologne: Ludwig von Renchen, 1494), USTC 749827
Wied, Wilhelm, Graf von, *Urkunde, durch die er Wassenberg an Herzog Wilhelm IV von Jülich abtritt. 21 June 1494* (Cologne: Ludwig von Renchen, 1494), USTC 749828
Worms, *Ain anzaygunng der Fürsten unnd Herren so auff dem yetzt gehalten Reichstag zu Wurmbs in eygner person erschinen seindt. Im jar. M.D.und.XXI.* (Worms: Hans von Erfurt, 1521), USTC 609665 (VD16 A 3019)
Württemberg, *Ausschreiben betreffend die Irrungen mit Eberhard, Herzog von Württemberg. Vertrag zwischen den Herzögen Ulrich und Eberhard und Verzichtserklärung Eberhards. Horb, 15 June 1498* (Pforzheim: Thomas Anshelm, 1498), USTC 749566
Württemberg, Christoph, Herzog von, *Des Fürstenthumbs Wirtemberg newe landtsordnung* (Tübingen: Ulrich I Morhart, 1552), USTC 635179 (VD16 W 4509)
Württemberg, Christoph, Herzog von, *Kirchen ordnung wie es mit der leere und Ceremonien im Fürstenthumb Wirtemberg angericht und gehalten werden soll* (Tübingen: Ulrich I Morhart, 1553), USTC 669885 (VD16 W 4491)
Württemberg, Christoph, Herzog von, *Kirchenordnung. Wie es mit der leere und Ceremonien im Fürstenthumb Wirtemberg angericht und gehalten werden soll* (Tübingen: Ulrich I Morhart, 1553), USTC 669964 (VD16 W 4492)
Württemberg, Christoph, Herzog von, *Kirchenordnung. Wie es mit der lehre und Ceremonien im Fürstenthumb Würtemberg angericht und gehalten werden soll* (Tübingen: haer. Ulrich I Morhart, 1555), USTC 670013 (VD16 W 4493)
Württemberg, Christoph, Herzog von, *Newe bawordnung des Fürstenthumbs Würtemberg* (Tübingen: haer. Ulrich I Morhart, 1568), USTC 677218
Württemberg, Christoph, Herzog von, *Ordnung in eesachen* (Tübingen: Ulrich I Morhart, 1553), USTC 681576 (VD16 W 4518)
Württemberg, Christoph, Herzog von, *Ordnung wie im Fürstenthumb Würtemberg ein gemein gleich landtmeß und eych angericht werden und auff Jacobi angeen soll* (Tübingen: haer. Ulrich I Morhart, 1557), USTC 681505 (VD16 W 4521)

Württemberg, Christoph, Herzog von, *Von Gottes gnaden unser Christoffs Hertzogen zu württemberg und zu teckh Graven zu Mümpelgart etc. Summarischer und einfaeltiger begriff wie es mit der lehre und Ceremonien in den Kirchen unsers Fürstenthumbs auch derselben Kirchen anhangenden sachen und verrichtungen bißher geuebt unnd gebraucht auch fürohin mit verleihung Goettlicher gnaden gehalten und volzogen werden solle* (Tübingen: haer. Ulrich I Morhart, 1559), USTC 703883 (VD16 W 4527)

Württemberg, Eberhard der Ältere Graf von, *Antwort auf das Schreiben des Grafen Eberhard des Jüngeren vom 9 Mar. 1488 (24 Apr. 1488)* (Ulm: Johann Zainer, 1488), USTC 744542

Württemberg, Eberhard der Ältere Graf von, *Bekanntmachung betreffend die Eröffnung der Universität Tübingen. Issued at Urach, 3 July 1477* (Blaubeuren: Conrad Mancz, 1477), USTC 744537

Württemberg, Eberhard der Ältere Graf von, *Schreiben an die Schweizer Eidgenossenschaft betreffend Hermann von Eptingen. Issued at Urach, 15 Feb. 1478* (Blaubeuren: Conrad Mancz, 1478), USTC 744538

Württemberg, Eberhard der Ältere Graf von, *Schreiben an Herzog Sigismund von Oesterreich betreffend die Herrschaft Hohenberg. Issued at Urach, 18 Oct. 1476* (Reutlingen: Michael Greyff, 1476), USTC 744536

Württemberg, Eberhard der Ältere, Graf von, *Stiftungsbriefe für das Stift S. Peter zum Einsiedel im Schönbuch* (Ulm: Johann Reger, 1493), USTC 744543

Württemberg, Eberhard der Jüngere, Herzog von, *Ausschreiben betreffend Einziehung des gemeinen Pfennigs gegen die Türken und Reichsfeinde (5 Oct. 1496)* (Reutlingen: Michael Greyff, 1496), USTC 744544

Württemberg, Ferdinand, Statthalter in, *Der lanndschafft zu Wirttemperg freyhait* (Stuttgart: Hans von Erfurt, 1522), USTC 633889 (VD16 ZV 15615)

Württemberg, Ferdinand, Statthalter in, *Ordnung wie es obligender clemi und theürung halb in allen aembtern mit den bettlern gehalten werden soll* (Tübingen: Ulrich I Morhart, 1531), USTC 681631 (VD16 W 4463)

Württemberg, Ferdinand, Statthalter in, *Triumph und Victoria: wie der durchleüchtigest Christenlich und hochgeborn Fürst und Herr, Herr Ferdinandus: Printz und infant in Hispanien Ertzhertzog zu Osterreich Hertzog zu Burgudi etc. Auff den XXV. Tag des monats May. Anno etc. Im zwayundzwaintzigisten zu Stutgarten ingeritten unnd loblich empfangen ist* (Stuttgart: Hans von Erfurt, 1522), USTC 699455 (VD16 T 2013)

Württemberg, Johann Friedrich, *Des Hertzogthumbs Württemberg Ernewert Gemein Landtrecht* (Tübingen: Georg Gruppenbach und Melchior Breidner, 1609 ie 1610), USTC 2138493 (VD17 7:708509C)

Württemberg, Johann Friedrich, *Des Hertzogthumbs Württemberg Ernewert Gemein Landtrecht* (Tübingen: Georg Gruppenbach und Melchior Breidner, 1609 ie 1610), USTC 2130511 (VD17 1:016993S)

Württemberg, *Ordnung und Regiment des Fürstentums Württemberg* (Strasbourg: Thomas Anshelm, 1498), USTC 749932

Württemberg, Ulrich, Herzog von, *Ansuchen Hertzog Ulrichs zu Wirtemberg und Landgrave Philipsen zu Hessen bey Kei. Majest. und Koeniglicher wirde zu Ungern etc. des Hertzogthums Wirtemberg halben* (s.l.: s.n., 1534), USTC 611790 (VD16 W 4439)

Württemberg, Ulrich, Herzog von, *Ansuchen Hertzog Ulrichs zu Wirtemberg und Landgrave Philipsen zu Hessen bey Kei. Ma. und Koewir. zu Ungern etc. des Hertzogthumbs Wirtemberg halber* (Wittenberg: Nickel Schirlentz, 1534), USTC 611789 (VD16 W 4442)

Württemberg, Ulrich, Herzog von, *Ansuchüng Hertzog Ulrichs zu Wirtemberg und Landgrave Philipsen zu Hessen bey K.W. zu Hungern etc. Des Hertzogthumbs Wirtemberg halber* (Marburg: Franz Rhode, 1534), USTC 611791 (VD16 W 4441)

Württemberg, Ulrich, Herzog von, *Ansuchung unser Hertzog Ulrichs zu Wirtemberg und Landtgrave Philipsen zu Hessen etc. Bey Roe. Key. Ma. des Furstenthnmb. Wirtembergs halber* (Marburg: Franz Rhode, 1534), USTC 611795 (VD16 W 4437)

Württemberg, Ulrich, Herzog von, *Aus schribung und enschüldigung Hertzog Ulrich von Gots gnaden Hertzog zu Wirtenberg und zu tegk Grave zu Mimpelgart: Ludwig von Hutten anß schrybens mit sampt seyn fründen* (Heidelberg: Jakob Stadelberger, 1516), USTC 614124 (VD16 W 4441)

Württemberg, Ulrich, Herzog von, *Der durchleüchtigen hochgebornen Fursten unnd Hernn Hern Ulrichs Hertzogen zu Wirtemberg etc. Unnd Hern Philipsen Landtgraven zu Hessen Graven zu Catzenelnpogen etc. ansuchung bey Key. M. Und Koenig. W. sampt andern schrifften des Hertzogthumb Wirtembergs halber* (Marburg: Franz Rhode, 1534), USTC 633121 (VD16 W 4440)

Württemberg, Ulrich, Herzog von, *Der durchlüchtigen hochgebornen Fürsten und Herren, Herren Ulrichen Hertzogen zu Wirtemperg und teckh etc. und Philipsen Landgraven in Hessen Graven zu Catzenelnbogen etc. auschriben die fürgenomen recuperation und eroberung des Fürstenthumbs Wirtemperg belangende* (Basel: Thomas Wolff, 1534), USTC 633140 (VD16 ZV 15612)

Württemberg, Ulrich, Herzog von, *Des Fürstenthumbs Wirtemberg newe Landsordnung* (Tübingen: Ulrich I Morhart, 1536), USTC 635178 (VD16 W 4453)

Württemberg, Ulrich, Herzog von, *Gegenantwort der Durchleüchtige Hochgeborne Fürsten vnd Herrn/ Herr Vlrichs Hertzog zů Wirttemberg Vnd Herr Philips Landtgraff zů Hessen. Auff Künig Ferdinandi Antwort* (Strasbourg: Jakob Frölich, 1534), USTC 2214008 (VD16 ZV 29013)

Württemberg, Ulrich, Herzog von, *Newe Zeytung. Wirttembergische unnd Landtgraevische gemeyne auszschreybung yetzundt fürhabens* (Strasbourg: Jakob Frölich, 1534), USTC 677827 (VD16 ZV 15613)

Württemberg, Ulrich, Herzog von, *Gemein Kirchen Ordnung wie die diser zeit allenthalb im Fürstenthumb Wirtemberg gehalten soll werden* (Tübingen: Ulrich I Morhart, 1536), USTC 659058 (VD16 W 4451)

Württemberg, Ulrich, Herzog von, *Grund und ursach des fürgenommen zugs inn das land Wirttemberg durch die durchleüchtigen hochgebornen Fürsten und Herren, Herrn Ulrichen Hertzogen zu Wirttemberg und Philipsen Landtgraven zu Hessen. Auch weitter Hertzog Ulrichs verantwurttung die acht betreffendt so in seine mißgoenner faelschlich geschuldigt haben* (Tübingen: Ulrich I Morhart, 1534), USTC 660971 (VD16 W 4452)

Württemberg, Ulrich, Herzog von, *Grund vnd vrsach des fürgenommen Zugs inn das Land Wirttemperg Durch die Durchleüchtigen Hochgebornen Fürsten vnnd Herren/ Herrn Vlrichen Hertzogen zů Wirttemperg Vnd Philipsen Landtgrauen zů Hesszen* (Strasbourg: Jakob Frölich, 1534), USTC 2214137 (VD16 ZV 29014)

Württemberg, Ulrich, Herzog von, *Illustriss. Principum, Ulrichi ducis vvirtempergensis, et Philippi Lantgravii Hessiae, pro ducatu vvirtempergensi, ad Carolum V. Imp. et Ferdinandum regem, supplices libelli. Aliaque in eandem caussam scripta* (Marburg: Franz Rhode, 1534), USTC 668887 (VD16 W 4443)

Württemberg, Ulrich, Herzog von, *Ordnung eins gemeinen kasten für die armen wie der allenthalb im Fürstenthumb Wirtemberg angericht soll werden* (Tübingen: Ulrich I Morhart, 1536), USTC 681571 (VD16 W 4454)

Württemberg, Ulrich, Herzog von, *Ordnung in eesachen* (Tübingen: Ulrich I Morhart, 1535), USTC 681575 (VD16 ZV 27244)

Württemberg, Ulrich, Herzog von, *Ulrich (von Gotes gnaden) Hertzog zu Wirtemperg und zu tegke Grave zu Mümppelgart etc. Unsern grus zu vor lieben getreuen* (Tübingen: Thomas Anshelm, 1515), USTC 701569 (VD16 W 4455)

Württemberg, Ulrich, Herzog von, *Warhafftig underrichtung der uffruern unnd handlungen sich im Fürstenthumb Wirtemperg begeben* (Tübingen: Thomas Anshelm, 1514), USTC 705112 (VD16 W 4458)

Württemberg, Ulrich, Herzog von, *Warhafftig underrichtung der uffruern unnd handlungen sich im Fürstenthumb Wirtemperg begeben* (Tübingen: Thomas Anshelm, 1514), USTC 705111 (VD16 W 4457)

Württemberg, Ulrich, Herzog von, *ERklaerung etlicher Artickel da in Roe. Kei. Maie. vnsers allergnaedigsten herrn außgekündten Pollicei Ordnung jedem Churfürsten ... auferlegt würdt nach eines jeden Landts art erleutterung zuthun vnd darüber ordnung zugeben wie die sambt der Keiserlichen Pollicei ordnung fürterhin in dem Fürstenthumb Wirtemberg gehalten werden sollen* (Tübingen: Ulrich Morhart, 1549), USTC 2214584 (VD16 ZV 30767)

Württemberg, Ulrich, Herzog von, *Wirtembergische unnd Lanndtgraevisch auszschreiben fürhabender rüstung* (Frankfurt am Main: Christian I Egenolff, 1534), USTC 707151 (VD16 W 4438)

Zürich – Rat, *Abschid der Stette Zürich Bern unnd Sant Gallen von wegen der widerteüffer auszgangen (anno etc. XXVII.)* (Augsburg: Silvan Otmar, 1527), USTC 608206 (VD16 Z 572)

Edited primary sources

Briefwechsel des Herzogs Christoph von Wirtemberg, ed. Victor Ernst, 4 vols, Stuttgart: Kohlhammer, 1899–1907

Die Amerbachkorrespondenz, ed. Alfred Hartmann and Beat Rudolf Jenny, 11 vols, Basel: Verlag der Universitätsbibliothek, 1942–2010

Die Indices librorum prohibitorum des sechzehnten Jahrhunderts, ed. Fr. Heinrich Reusch, Tübingen: Laupp, 1886

Haller Haus-Chronik, ed. Historischer Verein für Württembergisch Franken, Schwäbisch Hall: Eppinger, 1962

The 'Musica instrumentalis deudsch' of Martin Agricola. A treatise on musical instruments, 1529 and 1545, ed. and trans. William Hettrick, Cambridge: Cambridge University Press, 1994

Internet sources

15c Book Trade, http://15cbooktrade.ox.ac.uk

Deutsches Rechtswörterbuch, https://drw-www.adw.uni-heidelberg.de

EMo Book Trade, http://emobooktrade.unimi.it

GW, Gesamtkatalog der Wiegendrucke, http://www.gesamtkatalogderwiegendrucke.de

USTC, Universal Short Title Catalogue, http://www.ustc.ac.uk

VD16, Verzeichnis der im deutschen Sprachbereich erschienenen Drucke des 16. Jahrhunderts, http://www.vd16.de

VD17, Verzeichnis der im deutschen Sprachbereich erschienenen Drucke des 17. Jahrhunderts, http://www.vd17.de

Weinsberg, Hermann, *Die autobiographischen Aufzeichnungen Hermann Weinsbergs. Digitale Gesamtausgabe*, www.weinsberg.uni-bonn.de

Works of reference

Borchling, Conrad, Claussen, Bruno (eds.) (1976), *Niederdeutsche Bibliographie. Gesamtverzeichnis der niederdeutschen Drucke bis zum Jahre 1800*, 3 vols, Utrecht: Hes Publishers

Cockx-Indestege, E., Glorieux, G., Beeck, B. op de (eds.) (1968–1994), *Belgica typographica 1541–1600. Catalogus librorum impressorum ab anno MDXLI ad annum MDC in regionibus quae nunc Regni Belgarum partes sunt*, 4 vols, Nieuwkoop: De Graaf

Eisermann, Falk (ed.) (2004), *Verzeichnis der typographischen Einblattdrucke des 15. Jahrhunderts im Heiligen Römischen Reich Deutscher Nation*, Wiesbaden: Reichert

Ennen, Leonard (ed.) (1865), *Katalog der Inkunabeln in der Stadt-Bibliothek zu Köln*, Cologne: Greven

Faust, Ingrid, Barthelmess, Klaus, Stopp, Klaus (eds.) (1998–2010), *Zoologische Einblattdrucke und Flugschriften vor 1800*, 6 vols, Stuttgart: Hiersemann

Geisberg, Max (ed.) (1984), *The German Single-Leaf Woodcut 1500–1550*, revised and edited by Walter L. Strauss, 4 vols, New York: Hacker

Harms, Wolfgang, Schilling, Michael (eds.) (1985–1997), *Deutsche Illustrierte Flugblätter des 16. und 17. Jahrhunderts*, 7 vols, Tübingen: Niemeyer

Hughes, P. L., Larkin, J.F. (eds.) (1964–1969), *Tudor Royal Proclamations*, 3 vols, New Haven (CT): Yale University Press

Kelly, James, Lyons, Mary Ann (eds.) (2014), *The Proclamations of Ireland 1660–1820*, 5 vols, Dublin: Irish Manuscripts Commission

Keussen, Hermann (1899), 'Inhaltsverzeichniss zu den Sammlungen der Rathsedikte 1493–1819', in: *Mittheilungen aus dem Stadtarchiv von Köln* 29, pp. 159–336

Nijhoff, W., Kronenberg, M.E. (eds.) (1923–1971), *Nederlandsche bibliographie van 1500 tot 1540*, 3 vols, 's-Gravenhage: Nijhoff

Paas, John Roger (ed.) (1985–2017), *The German Political Broadsheet, 1600–1700*, 14 vols, Wiesbaden: Harrassowitz

Pettegree, Andrew, Walsby, Malcolm (eds.) (2010), *Netherlandish Books. Books published in the Low Countries and Dutch books published abroad before 1601*, 2 vols, Leiden: Brill

Pollard, A.W., Redgrave, G.R. (eds.) (1976–1991), *A Short-title Catalogue of Books Printed in England, Scotland & Ireland and of English Books Printed Abroad 1475–1640*, 2nd ed, 3 vols, London: Bibliographical Society

Reske, Christoph (2015), *Die Buchdrucker des 16. und 17. Jahrhunderts im deutschen Sprachgebiet*, 2nd ed, Wiesbaden: Harrassowitz

Schmitz, Wolfgang (ed.) (1979), *Die Kölner Einblattdrucke des 15. Jahrhunderts*, Cologne: Wamper

Sybel, Heinrich von, Sickel, Theodor von (eds.) (1880/1891), *Kaiserurkunden in Abbildungen*, 2 vols, Berlin: Weidmannsche Buchhandlung

Tlusty, Ann (ed.) (2012), *Augsburg during the Reformation Era. An Anthology of Sources*, Indianapolis: Hackett Publishing Company

Valkema Blouw, Paul (ed.) (1998), *Typographia Batava 1541–1600. Repertorium van boeken gedrukt in Nederlanden tussen 1541 en 1600*, 2 vols, Nieuwkoop: De Graaf

Voet, Léon (ed.) (1980–1983), *The Plantin Press (1555–1589). A Bibliography of the Works Printed and Published by Christopher Plantin at Antwerp and Leiden*, 6 vols, Amsterdam: Van Hoeve

Secondary sources

AREND, SABINE, HAAG, NORBERT, HOLTZ, SABINE (eds.) (2013), *Die württembergische Kirchenordnung von 1559 im Spannungsfeld von Religion, Politik und Gesellschaft*, Epfendorf/Neckar: Bibliotheca-Academica-Verlag

AREND, SABINE (2014), '"Lasset alles züchtiglich vnd ordentlich zugehen." Vorstellungen von "guter Ordnung" in den evangelischen Kirchenordnungen des 16. Jahrhunderts', in: DINGEL, IRENE, KOHNLE, ARMIN (eds.), *Gute Ordnung. Ordnungsmodelle und Ordnungsvorstellungen in der Reformationszeit*, Leipzig: Evangelische Verlagsanstalt, pp. 31–47

AREND, SABINE, DÖRNER, GERALD (eds.) (2015), *Ordnung für die Kirche – Wirkungen auf die Welt. Evangelische Kirchenordnungen des 16. Jahrhunderts*, Tübingen: Mohr Siebeck

AURICH, FRANK (2000), *Die Anfänge des Buchdrucks in Dresden. Die Emserpresse 1524–1526*, Dresden: Sächsische Landesbibliothek – Staats- und Universitätsbibliothek

BÄCHTOLD-STÄUBLI, HANNS (ed.) (1927–1942), *Handwörterbuch des deutschen Aberglaubens*, 14 vols, Berlin: De Gruyter

BANGERT, JULIA (2019), *Buchhandelssystem und Wissensraum in der Frühen Neuzeit*, Berlin: De Gruyter

BECK VARELA, LAURA (2016), 'The Diffusion of Law Books in Early Modern Europe. A Methodological Approach', in: MECCARELLI, MASSIMO, SOLLA SASTRE, MARÍA JULIA (eds.), *Spatial and Temporal Dimensions for Legal History. Research Experiences and Itineraries*, Frankfurt: MPI for European Legal History, pp. 195–240

BEHRINGER, WOLFGANG (2010), *A Cultural History of Climate*, trans. PATRICK CAMILLER, Cambridge: Polity

BEIK, WILLIAM (1997), *Urban Protest in Seventeenth-Century France. The Culture of Retribution*, Cambridge: Cambridge University Press

BELLINGRADT, DANIEL (2011), *Flugpublizistik und Öffentlichkeit um 1700. Dynamiken, Akteure und Strukturen im urbanen Raum des Alten Reiches*, Stuttgart: Steiner

BELLINGRADT, DANIEL (2012), 'The Early Modern City as a Resonating Box. Media, Public Opinion, and the Urban Space of the Holy Roman Empire, Cologne, and Hamburg ca. 1700', in: *Journal of Early Modern History* 16, pp. 201–240

BELLINGRADT, DANIEL (2020), *Vernetzte Papiermärkte. Einblicke in den Amsterdamer Handel mit Papier im 18. Jahrhundert*, Cologne: Halem

BERNHARDT, WALTER (1972), *Die Zentralbehörden des Herzogtums Württemberg und ihre Beamten 1520–1629*, Stuttgart: Kohlhammer

BLICKLE, PETER (1973), *Landschaften im Alten Reich. Die staatliche Funktion des gemeinen Mannes in Oberdeutschland*, Munich: Beck

BLICKLE, PETER (2003), 'Beschwerde und Polizeien. Die Legitimation des modernen Staates durch Verfahren und Normen', in: BLICKLE, PETER, KISSLING, PETER, SCHMIDT, HEINRICH RICHARD (eds.), *Gute Policey als Politik im 16. Jahrhundert. Die Entstehung des öffentlichen Raumes in Oberdeutschland*, Frankfurt am Main: Klostermann, pp. 549–568

BLICKLE, PETER (2004), *Die Revolution von 1525*, 4th ed, Munich: Oldenbourg

BLOCKMANS, WIM, HOLENSTEIN, ANDRÉ, MATHIEU, JON (eds.) (2009), *Empowering Interactions. Political Cultures and the Emergence of the State in Europe 1300–1900*, Aldershot: Ashgate

BOELCKE, WILLI A. (1987), *Wirtschaftsgeschichte Baden-Württembergs von den Römern bis heute*, Stuttgart: Konrad Theiss

BOSSERT, GUSTAV, (1898), 'Zur Geschichte des Buchhandels in Stuttgart unter Herzog Christoph und in den ersten Jahren des Herzogs Ludwig. Nach Rechnungen des Kirchenkastens', in: *Württembergische Vierteljahrshefte für Landesgeschichte* 7, pp. 246–252

Bowen, Karen L., Imhof, Dirk (2008), *Christopher Plantin and Engraved Book Illustrations in Sixteenth-Century Europe*, Cambridge: Cambridge University Press

Brecht, Martin, Ehmer, Hermann (eds.) (1984), *Südwestdeutsche Reformationsgeschichte. Zur Einführung der Reformation im Herzogtum Württemberg 1534*, Stuttgart: Calwer Verlag

Brinkhus, Gerd (1998), 'Zwischen Privilegien und Zensur. Das Verhältnis von Buchgewerbe und Universität', in: Brinkhus, Gerd, Lagler, Wilfried, Pachnicke, Claudine (eds.), *Eine Stadt des Buches. Tübingen 1498–1998*, Tübingen: Kulturamt, pp. 11–20

Bruni, Flavia (2017a), 'Early Modern Broadsheets between Archives and Libraries: Toward a Possible Integration', in: Pettegree, Andrew (ed.), *Broadsheets. Single-Sheet Publishing in the First Age of Print*, Leiden: Brill, pp. 33–54

Bruni, Flavia (2017b), 'In the Name of God: Governance, Public Order and Theocracy in the Broadsheets of the Stamperia Camerale of Rome', in: Pettegree, Andrew (ed.), *Broadsheets. Single-Sheet Publishing in the First Age of Print*, Leiden: Brill, pp. 143–161

Buchwald, Georg (1934), 'Kleine Notizen aus Rechnungsbüchern des Thüringischen Staatsarchivs (Weimar)', in: *Archiv für Reformationsgeschichte* 31, pp. 206–218

Burkart, Lucas (2019), 'Early Book Printing and Venture Capital in the Age of Debt. The Case of Michel Wenssler's Basel Printing Shop (1472–1491)', in: Graheli, Shanti (ed.), *Buying and Selling. The Business of Books in Early Modern Europe*, Leiden: Brill, pp. 23–54

Chittolini, Giorgio, Willoweit, Dietmar (eds.) (1992), *Statuten, Städte und Territorien zwischen Mittelalter und Neuzeit in Italien und Deutschland*, Berlin: Duncker & Humblot

Claus, Helmut (ed.) (1987), *Das Leipziger Druckschaffen der Jahre 1518–1539*, Gotha: Veröffentlichungen der Forschungsbibliothek Gotha

Cohn, Henry J. (1987), 'Church Property in the German Protestant Principalities', in: Scott, Tom, Kouri, E. I. (eds.), *Politics and Society in Reformation Europe*, Basingstoke: Palgrave Macmillan, pp. 158–187

Corsten, Severin (1965), 'Ulrich Zells deutschsprachige Drucke', in: *Gutenberg-Jahrbuch* 40, pp. 110–117

Corsten, Severin (1988), 'Drucken oder drücken. Die Erfindung Gutenbergs im Munde der Zeitgenossen', in: Corsten, Severin (ed.), *Untersuchungen zum Buch- und Bibliothekswesen*, Frankfurt am Main: Lang, pp. 84–104

Creasman, Allyson (2012), *Censorship and Civic Order in Reformation Germany, 1517–1648. 'Printed Poison & Evil Talk'*, Farnham: Ashgate

Daybell, James (2012), *The Material Letter in Early Modern England. Manuscript Letters and the Culture and Practice of Letter-Writing, 1512–1635*, Basingstoke: Palgrave Macmillan

De Vivo, Filippo (2007), *Information and Communication in Venice. Rethinking Early Modern Politics*, Oxford: Oxford University Press

Decker-Hauff, Hansmartin (ed.) (1966), *Geschichte der Stadt Stuttgart. Von der Frühzeit bis zur Reformation*, Stuttgart: Städt. Sparkasse Stuttgart

Deen, Femke (2015), *Publiek debat en propaganda in Amsterdam tijdens de Nederlandse Opstand: Amsterdam 'Moorddam' (1566–1578)*, Amsterdam: Amsterdam University Press

Deeters, Joachim (1987), 'Das Bürgerrecht der Reichsstadt Köln seit 1396', in: *Zeitschrift der Savigny-Stiftung für Rechtsgeschichte, Germanistische Abteilung* 104,1, pp. 1–83

Deeters, Joachim (ed.) (2013), *Rat und Bürgermeister in Köln 1396–1797. Ein Verzeichnis*, Cologne: Historisches Archiv der Stadt Köln

Delle Luche, Jean-Dominique (2014), 'Schützenfeste und Schützengesellschaften in den Residenzstädten. Konfigurationen zwischen Stadt und Fürsten im 15. und 16. Jahrhundert (Pforzheim, Würzburg, Ansbach, Stuttgart), in: Hirschbiegel, Jan, Paravicini, Werner in Zusammenarbeit mit Kurt Andermann (eds.), *In der Residenzstadt. Funktionen, Medien, Formen bürgerlicher und höfischer Repräsentation*, Ostfildern: Jan Thorbecke Verlag, pp. 157–174

Dixon, C. Scott (2002), *The Reformation in Germany*, Oxford: Blackwell Publishers

Doig, James (1998), 'Political Propaganda and Royal Proclamations in Late Medieval England', in: *Historical Research* 71, pp. 253–280

Dollinger, Philippe (1970), *The German Hansa*, Stanford (CA): Stanford University Press

Dondi, Christina, Harris, Neil (2014), 'Exporting Books from Milan to Venice in the Fifteenth Century: Evidence from the Zornale of Francesco de' Madiis', in: *La Bibliofilía* 116, pp. 121–148

Dooley, Brendan, Baron, Sabrina A. (eds.) (2001), *The Politics of Information in Early Modern Europe*, London: Routledge

Dumolyn, Jan et al. (eds.) (2014), *The Voices of the People in Late Medieval Europe. Communication and Popular Politics*, Turnhout: Brepols

Duntze, Oliver (2010), 'Verlagsbuchhandel und verbreitender Buchhandel von der Erfindung des Buchdrucks bis 1700', in: Rautenberg, Ursula (ed.) *Buchwissenschaft in Deutschland. Ein Handbuch*, Berlin: De Gruyter, pp. 201–256

Duntze, Oliver (2012), 'Gennep, Jaspar von', in: Kühlmann, Wilhelm, Müller, Jan-Dirk, Schilling, Michael, Steiger, Johann Anselm, Vollhardt, Friedrich (eds.), *Frühe Neuzeit in Deutschland 1520–1620. Literaturwissenschaftliches Verfasserlexikon*. Vol. 2, Berlin: De Gruyter, cols. 550–557

Duntze, Oliver, Eisermann, Falk (2017), 'Beichtbriefe und Formulardrucke für die Livlandkampagnen und für den Vertrieb des Petersablasses durch Arcimboldi', in: Bünz, Enno, Kühne, Hartmut, Wiegand, Peter (ed.) *Johann Tetzel und der Ablass. Begleitband zur Ausstellung 'Tetzel – Ablass – Fegefeuer'. Mönchenkloster und Nikolaikirche Jüterbog vom 8. September bis 26. November 2017*, Berlin: Lukas Verlag, pp. 243–266

Ebel, Wilhelm (1971), *Lübisches Recht*, Lübeck: M. Schmidt-Römhild

Ehmer, Hermann (2011), 'Primus Truber, Hans Ungnad von Sonnegg und die Uracher Druckerei 1560–1564', in: Lorenz, Sönke, Schindling, Anton, Setzler, Wilfried (eds.), *Primus Truber 1508–1586. Der slowenische Reformator und Württemberg*, Stuttgart: Kohlhammer, pp. 201–216

Eiden, Herbert, Irsigler, Franz (2000), 'Environs and Hinterland. Cologne and Nuremberg in the Later Middle Ages', in: Galloway, James A. (ed.), *Trade, Urban Hinterlands and Market Integration c. 1300–1600*, London: Working Papers Series. Center for Metropolitan History, pp. 43–57

Eisenstein, Elizabeth L. (1979), *The Printing Press as an Agent of Change. Communications and Cultural Transformations in Early-Modern Europe*, Cambridge: Cambridge University Press

Eisermann, Falk (1998), '"Darnach wisset euch zu richten." Maximilians Einblattdrucke vom Freiburger Reichstag', in: Schadek, Hans (ed.), *Der Kaiser in seiner Stadt. Maximilian I. und der Reichstag zu Freiburg 1498*, Freiburg im Breisgau: Kore, pp. 198–215

Eisermann, Falk (2000), 'Auflagenhöhen von Einblattdrucken im 15. und frühen 16. Jahrhundert', in: Honemann, Volker, Griese, Sabine, Eisermann, Falk,

Ostermann, Marcus (eds.), *Einblattdrucke des 15. und frühen 16. Jahrhunderts*, Tübingen: Niemeyer, pp. 143–177

Eisermann, Falk (2002), 'Buchdruck und politische Kommunikation. Ein neuer Fund zur frühen Publizistik Maximilians I.', in: *Gutenberg-Jahrbuch* 77, pp. 76–83

Eisermann, Falk (2003), '"Vil grozer brefe sint angeslagen". Typographie und öffentliche Kommunikation im 15. Jahrhundert', in: Miedema, Nine, Suntrup, Rudolf (eds.), *Literatur – Geschichte – Literaturgeschichte. Festschrift für Volker Honemann zum 60. Geburtstag*, Frankfurt am Main: Peter Lang, pp. 481–502

Eisermann, Falk (2006), 'Archivgut und chronikalische Überlieferung als vernachlässigte Quelle der Frühdruckforschung', in: *Gutenberg-Jahrbuch* 81, pp. 50–61

Eisermann, Falk (2011), 'Der Ablass als Medienereignis. Kommunikationswandel durch Einblattdrucke im 15. Jahrhundert', in: Hamm, Berndt, Leppin, Volker, Schneider-Ludorff, Gury (eds.), *Media Salutis. Gnaden- und Heilsmedien in der abendländischen Religiosität des Mittelalters und der Frühen Neuzeit*, Tübingen: Mohr Siebeck, pp. 121–144

Eisermann, Falk (2017a), 'Die Einblattdrucke Peter Schöffers', in: *Wolfenbütteler Notizen zur Buchgeschichte* 42, pp. 9–20

Eisermann, Falk (2017b), 'Fifty Thousand Veronicas. Print Runs of Broadsheets in the Fifteenth and Early Sixteenth Centuries', in: Pettegree, Andrew (ed.), Broadsheets. Single-Sheet Publishing in the First Age of Print, Leiden: Brill, pp. 76–113

Enderle, Wilfried (1999), 'Die Buchdrucker der Reichsstadt Köln und die katholische Publizistik zwischen 1555 und 1648', in: Mölich, Georg, Schwerhoff, Gerd (eds.), *Köln als Kommunikationszentrum. Studien zur frühneuzeitlichen Stadtgeschichte*, Cologne: DuMont, pp. 167–182

Endres, Rudolf (1988), 'Nürnberg in der Frühneuzeit', in: Krüger, Kersten (ed.), *Europäische Städte im Zeitalter des Barock. Gestalt – Kultur – Sozialgefüge*, Cologne: Böhlau, pp. 141–167

Ennen, Leonard (1863–1880), *Geschichte der Stadt Köln*, 5 vols, Cologne: Schwann

Esser, Raingard (2012), *The Politics of Memory. The Writing of Partition in the Seventeenth-Century Low Countries*, Leiden: Brill

Ewald, Wilhelm (1933), 'Die Rheinischen Schützengesellschaften', in: *Zeitschrift des Rheinischen Vereins für Denkmalpflege und Heimatschutz* 26, pp. 69–96

Faber, Eduard von (1859), *Die Vorarbeiten zum Württembergischen Land-Recht vom 1. Juni 1610*, Stuttgart: Julius Weise

Fabian, Bernhard (ed.) (1972), *Die Meßkataloge Georg Willers. Herbstmesse 1564 bis Herbstmesse 1573*, Hildesheim: Olms

Febvre, Lucien, Martin, Henri-Jean (1958), *L'apparition du livre*, Paris: Albin Michel

Franz, Monika (2003), *Die Landesordnung von 1516/1520. Landesherrliche Gesetzgebung im Herzogtum Bayern in der ersten Hälfte des 16. Jahrhunderts*, Munich: Beck

Freist, Dagmar (1997), *Governed by Opinion. Politics, Religion, and the Dynamics of Communication in Stuart London, 1637–1645*, London / New York: Tauris

Freitag, Werner (2013), 'Städtischer Markt und symbolische Kommunikation', in: Stollberg-Rilinger, Neu, Tim, Brauner, Christina (eds.), *Alles nur symbolisch? Bilanz und Perspektiven der Erforschung symbolischer Kommunikation*, Cologne: Böhlau, pp. 379–400

Friedrichs, Christopher R. (2005), 'Das städtische Rathaus als kommunikativer Raum in europäischer Perspektive', in: Burkhardt, Johannes, Werkstetter, Christine (eds.), *Kommunikation und Medien in der Frühen Neuzeit*, Munich: Oldenbourg, pp. 159–174

Fuhrmann, Rosi (1998), 'Amtsbeschwerden, Landtagsgravamina und Supplikationen in Württemberg zwischen 1550 und 1629', in: Blickle, Peter (ed.), *Gemeinde und Staat im Alten Europa*, Munich: Oldenbourg, pp. 69–148

Fuhrmann, Bernd (2013), 'Holzversorgung, Waldentwicklung, Umweltveränderungen und wirtschaftliche Tendenzen in Spätmittelalter und beginnender Neuzeit', in: *Vierteljahrschrift für Sozial- und Wirtschaftsgeschichte* 100,3, pp. 311–327

Füssel, Stephan (2005), *Gutenberg and the Impact of Printing*, translated by Douglas Martin, Aldershot: Ashgate

Geldner, Ferdinand (1964), 'Das Rechnungsbuch des Speyrer Druckherrn, Verlegers und Großbuchhändlers Peter Drach. Mit Einleitung, Erläuterung und Identifizierungslisten', in: *Archiv für Geschichte des Buchwesens* 5, col. 1–196

Gestrich, Andreas (2006), 'The Public Sphere and the Habermas Debate', in: *German History* 24, pp. 413–430

Gibbs, Janis M. (2009), 'Immigration and Civic Identity in Sixteenth-Century Cologne', in: Plummer, Elizabeth, Barnes, Robin (eds.), *Ideas and Cultural Margins in Early Modern Germany. Essays in Honor of H. C. Erik Midelfort*, Farnham: Ashgate, pp. 49–62

Giel, Robert (1998), *Politische Öffentlichkeit im spätmittelalterlich-frühneuzeitlichen Köln (1450–1550)*, Berlin: Duncker & Humblot

Gilmont, Jean-Francois (1998), 'Printing at the dawn of the sixteenth century', in: Gilmont, Jean-Francois (ed.), *The Reformation and the Book*, translated by Karin Maag, Aldershot: Ashgate, pp. 10–20

Grafton, Anthony (1980), 'The Importance of Being Printed', in: *The Journal of Interdisciplinary History* 11, pp. 265–286

Graheli, Shanti (ed.) (2019), *Buying and Selling. The Business of Books in Early Modern Europe*, Leiden: Brill

Gramlich, Jürgen (1994), *Rechtsordnungen des Buchgewerbes im Alten Reich. Genossenschaftliche Strukturen, Arbeits- und Wettbewerbsrecht im deutschen Druckerhandwerk*, Frankfurt am Main: Buchhändler-Vereinigung

Gramulla, Susanna (1971), 'Kölner Kaufleute im Handel mit dem Ostseeraum am Ende des 15. und im 16. Jahrhundert', in: *Mitteilungen aus dem Stadtarchiv von Köln* 60, pp. 553–598

Grell, Ole Peter (1994), 'Merchants and ministers: the foundation of international Calvinism', in: Pettegree, Andrew, Duke, Alastair, Lewis, Gillian (eds.), *Calvinism in Europe, 1540–1620*, Cambridge: Cambridge University Press, pp. 254–273

Grell, Ole Peter (2011), *Brethren in Christ. A Calvinist Network in Reformation Europe*, Cambridge: Cambridge University Press

Grendler, Paul (1981), *Culture and Censorship in Late Renaissance Italy and France*, London: Variorum Reprints

Griese, Sabine (1997), 'Falsche Gulden, gefälschte Ablässe, unerwünschte Bischöfe. Einblattdrucke als publizistische Gattung im Spätmittelalter', in: *Verhandlungen des Historischen Vereins für Oberpfalz und Regensburg* 137, pp. 49–67. Available online: https://www.heimatforschung-regensburg.de/2421/1/1381096_DTL1501.pdf

Grillo, Manuela (2014), *Leggi e bandi di antico regime*, Cargeghe: Editoriale documenta

Groten, Manfred (1999), 'Die nächste Generation: Scribner's Thesen aus heutiger Sicht', in: Schwerhoff, Gerd, Mölich, Georg (eds.), *Köln als Kommunikationszentrum. Studien zur frühneuzeitlichen Stadtgeschichte*, Cologne: Dumont, pp. 110–113

Groten, Manfred (2007), 'Vom Recht der Bürger zum Sorgerecht des Rates. Zur Veränderung der Sprache des innerstädtischen Diskurses in Köln im späten 16. Jahrhunderts', in: *Jahrbuch des Kölnischen Geschichtsvereins* 78, pp. 71–88

Groten, Manfred, Huiskes, Manfred (eds.) (1988–2003), *Beschlüsse des Rates der Stadt Köln, 1320–1550. Die Ratsmemoriale und ergänzende Überlieferung, 1320–1543*, 6 vols, Düsseldorf: Droste

Habermas, Jürgen (1962), *Strukturwandel der Öffentlichkeit. Untersuchungen zu einer Kategorie der bürgerlichen Gesellschaft*, Neuwied: Luchterhand

Habermas, Jürgen (1989), *The Structural Transformation of the Public Sphere. An Inquiry into a Category of Burgeois Society*, translated by Thomas Burger, Cambridge (MA): MIT Press

Hardy, Duncan (2018), *Associative Political Culture in the Holy Roman Empire. Upper Germany, 1346–1521*, Oxford: Oxford University Press

Harris, Tim (ed.) (2001), *The Politics of the Excluded, c. 1500–1850*, Basingstoke: Palgrave

Härter, Karl (2002), 'Gesetzgebungsprozess und gute Policey. Entstehungskontexte, Publikation und Geltungskraft frühneuzeitlicher Policeygesetze', in: *PoliceyWorkingPapers* 3, pp. 1–32. Available online: http://www.univie.ac.at/policey-ak/pwp/pwp_03.pdf

Härter, Karl (2010a), 'Security and 'Gute Policey' in Early Modern Europe. Concepts, Law, and Instruments', in: *Historical Social Research* 35, pp. 41–65

Härter, Karl (2010b), 'Statut und Policeyordnung. Entwicklung und Verhältnis des Statutarrechts zur Policeygesetzgebung zwischen spätem Mittelalter und Früher Neuzeit in mitteleuropäischen Reichs- und Landstädten', in: Drossbach, Gisela (ed.), *Von der Ordnung zur Norm. Statuten in Mittelalter und Früher Neuzeit*, Paderborn: Ferdinand Schöningh, pp. 127–152

Härter, Karl (2018), *Strafrechts- und Kriminalitätsgeschichte der Frühen Neuzeit*, Berlin: De Gruyter Oldenbourg

Härter, Karl, Stolleis, Michael (eds.) (1996), *Repertorium der Policeyordnungen der Frühen Neuzeit.* Vol. 1: *Deutsches Reich und geistliche Kurfürstentümer*, Frankfurt am Main: Klostermann

Heal, Bridget (2007), *The Cult of the Virgin Mary in Early Modern Germany*, Cambridge: Cambridge University Press

Heinzen, Toni (1939), *Zunftkämpfe, Zunftherrschaft und Wehrverfassung in Köln*, Cologne: Verlag des Kölnischen Geschichtsvereins

Heitjan, Isabel (1970), 'Die Stellung der Buchgewerbetreibenden in der Stadt Köln und zu ihrer Universität (15. bis 18. Jahrhundert)', in: *Archiv für Geschichte des Buchwesens* 11, cols. 1129–1358

Helmers, Helmer J. (2015), *The Royalist Republic. Literature, Politics, and Religion in the Anglo-Dutch Public Sphere, 1639–1660*, Cambridge: Cambridge University Press

Hespanha, António Manuel (2008), 'Form and Content in Early Modern Legal Books. Bridging the Gap between Material Bibliography and the History of Legal Thought', in: *Rechtsgeschichte Rg* 12, pp. 12–50

Hirsch, Rudolf (1953), 'The first printed Protestant 'Eheordnung'', in: *Gutenberg-Jahrbuch* 28, pp. 96–97

Hirsch, Rudolf (1974), *Printing, Selling and Reading, 1450–1550*, Wiesbaden: Harrassowitz

Hirschmann, Frank G. (2009), *Die Stadt im Mittelalter*, Munich: Oldenbourg

Hoffmann-Rehnitz, Philip R. (2010), 'Discontinuities: Political Transformation, Media Change, and the City in the Holy Roman Empire from the Fifteenth to Seventeeth Centuries', in: Coy, Jason Philip, Marschke, Benjamin, Sabean, David Warren (eds.), *The Holy Roman Empire, Reconsidered*, New York: Berghahn, pp. 11–34

Holt, Paul (1927), 'Die militärische Einteilung der Reichsstadt Köln von 1583–1794', in: *Jahrbuch des Kölnischen Geschichtsvereins* 8/9, pp. 135–181

Holthöfer, Ernst (ed.) (1986), *Gesetzgebung in Europa im Spiegel alter Drucke. Rariora aus den Beständen des Max-Planck-Instituts für Europäische Rechtsgeschichte Frankfurt am Main*, Frankfurt am Main: Max-Planck-Institut für europäische Rechtsgeschichte

Holzborn, Timo (2003), *Die Geschichte der Gesetzespublikation – insbesondere von den Anfängen des Buchdrucks um 1450 bis zur Einführung von Gesetzesblättern im 19. Jahrhundert*, Berlin: Tenea

Honemann, Volker (2000), 'Vorformen des Einblattdruckes. Urkunden – Schrifttafeln – Textierte Tafelbilder – Anschläge – Einblatthandschriften', in: Honemann, Volker, Griese, Sabine, Eisermann, Falk, Ostermann, Marcus (eds.), *Einblattdrucke des 15. und frühen 16. Jahrhunderts*, Tübingen: Niemeyer, pp. 1–43

Honemann, Volker (2016), 'Neue Medien für die Stadt. Einblattdrucke, Flugblätter und Flugschriften 1450–1520', in: Fouquet, Gerhard, Hirschbiegel, Jan, Rabeler, Sven (eds.), *Residenzstädte der Vormoderne. Umrisse eines europäischen Phänomens*, Ostfildern: Thorbecke, pp. 349–370

Honemann, Volker, Eisermann, Falk, Griese, Sabine, Ostermann, Marcus (eds.) (2000), *Einblattdrucke des 15. und frühen 16. Jahrhunderts. Probleme, Perspektiven, Fallstudien*, Tübingen: Niemeyer

Honemann, Volker, Griese, Sabine, Eisermann, Falk (1999), 'Zu Wesen und Bedeutung des textierten Einblattdrucks im 15. und frühen 16. Jahrhundert', in: Keller, Hagen, Meier, Christel, Scharff, Thomas (eds.), *Schriftlichkeit und Lebenspraxis im Mittelalter. Erfassen, Bewahren und Verändern*, Munich: Wilhelm Fink Verlag, pp. 333–348

Imhof, Dirk (2014), *Jan Moretus and the Continuation of the Plantin Press. A bibliography of the works published and printed by Jan Moretus I in Antwerp (1589–1610)*, Leiden: Brill/De Graaf

Ing, Janet (1983), 'The Mainz Indulgences of 1454/5. A Review of Recent Scholarship', in: *The British Library Journal* 9, pp. 14–31

Irsigler, Franz (1980), 'Bettler, Dirnen und Henker im spätmittelalterlichen und frühneuzeitlichen Köln. Zur Analyse sozialer Randgruppen', in: *Geschichte in Köln* 7,1, pp. 32–64

Isenmann, Eberhard (1999), 'Die Reichsstadt in der Frühen Neuzeit', in: Schwerhoff, Gerd, Mölich, Georg (eds.), *Köln als Kommunikationszentrum. Studien zur frühneuzeitlichen Stadtgeschichte*, Cologne: Dumont, pp. 39–87

Isenmann, Eberhard (2010), 'The Notion of the Common Good, the Concept of Politics, and Practical Policies in Late Medieval and Early Modern German Cities', in: Lecuppre-Desjardin, Élodie, Bruaene, Anne-Laure van (eds.), *De Bono Communi. The Discourse and Practice of the Common Good in the European City (13th–16th c.)*, Turnhout: Brepols, pp. 107–148

Isenmann, Eberhard (2014), *Die Deutsche Stadt im Mittelalter 1150–1550*, 2nd ed., Cologne: Böhlau

Janssen, Geert (2011), 'Quo Vadis? Catholic Perceptions of Flight and the Revolt of the Low Countries, 1566–1609', in: *Renaissance Quaterly* 64,2, pp. 472–499

Janssen, Geert (2012), 'The Counter-Reformation of the Refugee: Exile and the Shaping of Catholic Militancy in the Dutch Revolt', in: *Journal of Ecclesiastical History* 63,4, pp. 671–692

Janssen, Geert (2014), *The Dutch Revolt and Catholic Exile in Reformation Europe*, Cambridge: Cambridge University Press

Jilka, Richard (1990), 'Aspekte des bürgerlichen Wachdienstes in Köln im 18. und 19. Jahrhundert', in: *Geschichte in Köln* 28,1, pp. 79–103

Juchhoff, Rudolf (1957), 'Cholinus, Maternus', in: *Neue Deutsche Biographie* 3, available online: https://www.deutsche-biographie.de/pnd119640619.html#ndbcontent

KAUFMANN, THOMAS (2019), *Die Mitte der Reformation. Eine Studie zu Buchdruck und Publizistik im deutschen Sprachgebiet, zu ihren Akteuren und deren Strategien, Inszenierungs- und Ausdrucksformen*, Tübingen: Mohr Siebeck

KELLENBENZ, HERMANN (1975), 'Wirtschaftsgeschichte Kölns im 16. und beginnenden 17. Jahrhundert', in: KELLENBENZ, HERMANN (ed.), *Zwei Jahrtausende Kölner Wirtschaft*, 2 vols, Cologne: Greven, I, pp. 321–427

KEMPKENS, DIETER (2014), 'Der Erfolg der Prognostica auf dem Buchmarkt in der Frühen Neuzeit', in: *Jahrbuch für Kommunikationsgeschichte* 16, pp. 5–27

KEUNECKE, Hans-Otto (1987), 'Jobst Gutknecht – Der Drucker des Nürnberger Rates', in: *Gutenberg-Jahrbuch* 62, pp. 146–157

KEUNECKE, HANS-OTTO (2015), 'Wirtschaftlicher Erfolg und Wohlstand bei deutschen Inkunabelndruckern. Ein Blick auf die Spitzengruppe', in: *Gutenberg-Jahrbuch* 90, pp. 64–82

KEUSSEN, HERMANN (1918), 'Regesten und Auszüge zur Geschichte der Universität Köln', in: *Mitteilungen aus dem Stadtarchiv von Köln* 36/37, pp. 1–546

KISSLING, PETER (2003), 'Reichsstädtische und territoriale Policeyen. Ein Vergleich der Reichsstadt und der Grafschaft Kempten im 16. Jahrhundert', in: BLICKLE, PETER, KISSLING, PETER, SCHMIDT, HEINRICH RICHARD (eds.), *Gute Policey als Politik im 16. Jahrhundert. Die Entstehung des öffentlichen Raumes in Oberdeutschland*, Frankfurt am Main: Klostermann, pp. 229–283

KOTKAS, TOOMAS (2014), *Royal Police Ordinances in Early Modern Sweden. The Emergence of Voluntaristic Understanding of Law*, Leiden: Brill

KRIEG, WALTER (1953), *Materialien zu einer Entwicklungsgeschichte der Bücher-Preise und des Autoren-Honorars vom 15. bis zum 20. Jahrhundert*, Vienna: Stubenrauch

KRISCHER, ANDRÉ (2011), 'Rituale und politische Öffentlichkeit in der Alten Stadt', in: SCHWERHOFF, GERD (ed.), *Stadt und Öffentlichkeit in der Frühen Neuzeit*, Cologne, Böhlau, pp. 125–157

KROPF, BLAISE (2003), 'Der Begriff aus der politischen Theorie – das Konzept aus der administrativen Praxis. Zum Entstehen der *police* im frühneuzeitlichen Frankreich', in: BLICKLE, PETER, KISSLING, PETER, SCHMIDT, HEINRICH RICHARD (eds.), *Gute Policey als Politik im 16. Jahrhundert. Die Entstehung des öffentlichen Raumes in Oberdeutschland*, Frankfurt am Main: Klostermann, pp. 491–514

KÜMIN, BEAT (2009), 'Political Culture in the Holy Roman Empire', in: *German History* 27, pp. 131–144

KÜMIN, BEAT, WÜRGLER, ANDREAS (1997), 'Petitions, Gravamina and the Early Modern State: Local Influence on Central Legislation in England and Germany (Hesse)', in: *Parliaments, Estates and Representation* 17,1, pp. 39–60

KÜNAST, HANS-JÖRG (1997), *'Getruckt zu Augspurg'. Buchdruck und Buchhandel in Augsburg zwischen 1468 und 1555*, Tübingen: Max Niemeyer Verlag

KYLE, CHRIS R. (2015), 'Monarch and Marketplace. Proclamations as News in Early Modern England', in: *Huntington Library Quarterly* 78,4, pp. 771–787

LAKE, PETER, PINCUS, STEVEN (2006), 'Rethinking the Public Sphere in Early Modern England', in: *Journal of British Studies* 45, pp. 270–292

LAMAL, NINA (2015), 'Commerce and Good Governance: The Broadsheet Ordinances in the Van der Meulen Archive', in: PETTEGREE, ANDREW (ed.), *Broadsheets. Single-Sheet Publishing in the First Age of Print*, Leiden: Brill, pp. 207–239

LANDWEHR, ACHIM (2000), *Policey im Alltag. Die Implementation frühneuzeitlicher Policeyordnungen in Leonberg*, Frankfurt am Main: Klostermann

LANDWEHR, ACHIM, SIMON, THOMAS (eds.) (2011), *Repertorium der Policeyordnungen der Frühen Neuzeit*. Vol. 4: *Baden und Württemberg*, Frankfurt am Main: Klostermann

LANG, THOMAS (2015) 'Simprecht Reinhart: Formschneider, Maler, Drucker, Bettmeister – Spuren eines Lebens im Schatten von Lucas Cranach d. Ä.', in: LÜCK, HEINER,

Bünz, Enno, Helten, Leonhard, Kohnle, Armin, Sack, Dorothée, Stephan, Hans-Georg (eds.), *Das ernestinische Wittenberg: Spuren Cranachs in Schloss und Stadt*, Petersberg: Imhof, pp. 93–138

Langensteiner, Matthias (2008), *Für Land und Lutherthum. Die Politik Herzog Christophs von Württemberg (1550–1568)*, Cologne: Böhlau

Lasch, Alexander (2010), '"Es sey das Fewer in der Stadt." Textpragmatische und -grammatische Überlegungen zu vormodernen Feuerordnungen', in: Ziegler, Arne (ed.), *Historische Textgrammatik und Historische Syntax des Deutschen: Traditionen, Innovationen, Perspektiven*, 2 vols, Berlin: De Gruyter, pp. 759–780

Laufs, Adolf, Schroeder, Klaus-Peter (2014), 'Landrecht', in: Cordes, Albrecht et al. (eds.), *Handwörterbuch zur deutschen Rechtsgeschichte* (HRG), 2nd ed, Vol. III, 19. Lfg., col. 552–559, HRGdigital: www.HRGdigital.de/HRG.landrecht

Le Bailly, Marie-Charlotte (2021), '"Na de publicatie van den niewe ordonnantie". The publication and printing of ordinances for the Court of Holland, 1462–1600', in: *History* (forthcoming).

Limbach, Saskia (2014), 'Propaganda im Druck – Politische Kommunikation beim 'Armen Konrad"', in: Rückert, Peter (ed.), *Der 'Arme Konrad' vor Gericht. Verhöre, Sprüche und Lieder in Württemberg 1514. Begleitbuch und Katalog zur Ausstellung des Landesarchivs Baden-Württemberg, Hauptstaatsarchiv Stuttgart*, Stuttgart: Kohlhammer, pp. 40–47

Limbach, Saskia (2016), 'Tracing Lost Broadsheet Ordinances Printed in Sixteenth-Century Cologne', in: Bruni, Flavia, Pettegree, Andrew (eds.), *Lost Books. Reconstructing the Print World of Pre-Industrial Europe*, Leiden: Brill, pp. 488–503

Limbach, Saskia (2019), 'Life and Production of Magdalena Morhart. A Successful Business Woman in Sixteenth-Century Germany', in: *Gutenberg-Jahrbuch* 94, pp. 151–172

Limbach, Saskia (2021), '"Let it be known". New perspectives on broadsheets and political communication at the time of Maximilian I', in: *troJa. Kolloquium und Jahrbuch für Renaissancemusikforschung* 18 (forthcoming)

Lorenz, Sönke (2010), 'Vom herrschaftlichen Rat zu den Landständen in Württemberg. Die Entwicklung vom 13. bis zum 16. Jahrhundert', in: Rückert, Peter, Lorenz, Sönke (eds.), *Auf dem Weg zur politischen Partizipation? Landstände und Herrschaft im deutschen Südwesten*, Stuttgart: Kohlhammer, pp. 1–28

Lundin, Matthew (2012), *Paper Memory. A Sixteenth-Century Townsman Writes His World*, Cambridge (MA): Harvard University Press

Lutter, Christina (2002), '"An das Volk von Venedig!" Propaganda Maximilians I. in Venedig', in: Hruza, Karel (ed.), *Propaganda, Kommunikation und Öffentlichkeit (11.–16. Jahrhundert)*, Wien: Verl. der Österr. Akad. der Wiss., pp. 235–254

Machill, Horst (ed.) (1974), *Handbuch des Buchhandels*. Vol. 1, Hamburg: Verlag für Buchmarktforschung

Mallinckrodt, Rebekka von (2005), *Struktur und kollektiver Eigensinn. Kölner Laienbruderschaften im Zeitalter der Konfessionalisierung*, Göttingen: Vandenhoeck & Ruprecht

Mathis, Franz (1992), *Die deutsche Wirtschaft im 16. Jahrhundert*, Munich: Oldenbourg

McLeod, Jane (2011), *Licensing Loyalty. Printers, Patrons, and the State in Early Modern France*, University Park (PA): Pennsylvania State University Press

Meester, Jan de (2016), 'To Kill Two Birds with One Stone. Keeping Immigrants in by Granting Free Burghership in: Early Modern Antwerp', in: Munck, Bert de, Davids, Karel (eds.), *Innovation and Creativity in Late Medieval and Early Modern European Cities*, London: Routledge, pp. 95–114

Methuen, Charlotte (1994), 'Securing the Reformation Through Education: The Duke's Scholarship System of Sixteenth-Century Württemberg', in: *The Sixteenth Century Journal* 25,4, pp. 841–851

Militzer, Klaus (ed.) (1996), *Stadtrat, Stadtrecht, Bürgerfreiheit. Ausstellung aus Anlass des 600. Jahrestages des Verbundbriefes vom 14. September 1396*, Cologne: Historisches Archiv der Stadt Köln

Militzer, Klaus (ed.) (2005), *Repertorium der Policeyordnungen der Frühen Neuzeit. Reichsstädte 2: Köln*, 2 vols, Frankfurt am Main: Klostermann

Milner, Stephen T. (2013), '"Fanno bandire, notificare, et expressamente comandare": Town Criers and the Information Economy of Renaissance Florence', in: *I Tatti Studies in the Italian Renaissance* 16, pp. 107–151

Mocker, Ute (1991), 'Quellen zur historischen Statistik des Herzogtums Württemberg vom 15./16. bis zum 18./19. Jahrhundert', in: Fischer, Wolfram, Kunz, Andreas (eds.), *Grundlagen der Historischen Statistik von Deutschland. Quellen, Methoden, Forschungsziele*, Opladen: Westdeutscher Verlag, pp. 126–147

Molitor, Stephan (ed.) (1995), *1495: Württemberg wird Herzogtum. Dokumente aus dem Hauptstaatsarchiv Stuttgart zu einem epochalen Ereignis. Begleitbuch zur Ausstellung des Hauptstaatsarchivs Stuttgart im Württembergischen Landesmuseum Stuttgart vom 20. Juli bis 3. Oktober 1995*, Stuttgart: Hauptstaatsarchiv Stuttgart

Müller, Jan-Dirk (2004), 'Publizistik unter Maximilian I. Zwischen Buchdruck und mündlicher Verkündung', in: Frevert, Ute, Braungart, Wolfgang (eds.), *Sprachen des Politischen. Medien und Medialität in der Geschichte*, Göttingen: Vandenhoeck & Ruprecht, pp. 95–122

Needham, Paul (2014), 'The Formats of Incunable Broadsides', in: Haug, Christine, Thiele, Rolf (eds.), *Buch-Bibliothek-Region. Wolfgang Schmitz zum 65. Geburtstag*, Wiesbaden: Harrassowitz, pp. 127–144

Ostermann, Marcus (2000), '"Vmb kurczweil vnd schiessens willen." Zu den gedruckten Schützenbriefen des 15. Jahrhunderts', in: Honemann, Volker, Griese, Sabine, Eisermann, Falk, Ostermann, Marcus (eds.), *Einblattdrucke des 15. und frühen 16. Jahrhunderts*, Tübingen: Niemeyer, pp. 397–443

Parker, Geoffrey (2013), *Global Crisis. War, Climate Change and Catastrophe in the Seventeenth Century*, New Haven (CT): Yale University Press

Patterson, Annabel M. (1984), *Censorship and Interpretation. The Conditions of Writing and Reading in Early Modern England*, Madison (WI): University of Wisconsin Press

Peacey, Jason (2004), *Politicians and Pamphleteers. Propaganda During the English Civil Wars and Interregnum*, Aldershot: Ashgate

Pettegree, Andrew (2005), *Reformation and the Culture of Persuasion*, Cambridge: Cambridge University Press

Pettegree, Andrew (2010), *The Book in the Renaissance*, New Haven (CT): Yale University Press

Pettegree, Andrew (2015), *Brand Luther*, New York: Penguin

Pettegree, Andrew (ed.) (2017a), *Broadsheets. Single-Sheet Publishing in the First Age of Print*, Leiden: Brill

Pettegree, Andrew (2017b), 'Broadsheets: Single-Sheet Publishing in the First Age of Print. Typology and Typography', in: Pettegree, Andrew (ed.) (2017a), *Broadsheets. Single-Sheet Publishing in the First Age of Print*, Leiden: Brill, pp. 3–32

Peuckert, Valérie (2011), 'Materne Cholinus, un imprimeur arlonais à Cologne (1525–1588)', in: *Le Bulletin de l'Institut Archéologique du Luxembourg* 1/2, pp. 30–33

Pitz, Ernst (2001), *Bürgereinigung und Städteeinigung. Studien zur Verfassungsgeschichte der Hansestädte und der deutschen Hanse*, Cologne: Böhlau

Quarthal, Franz (1991), 'Verfassung und Verwaltung in südwestdeutschen Städten der Frühen Neuzeit', in: Stolleis, Michael (ed.), *Recht, Verfassung und Verwaltung in der frühneuzeitlichen Stadt*, Cologne: Böhlau, pp. 217–239

Rautenberg, Ursula (1990), 'Der päpstliche Gesandte und Ablaßkommissar Raymundus Peraudi als Auftraggeber des Druckers Hermann Bungart – ein bisher unbeleuchtetes Kapitel Kölner Legendendrucke in der Frühneuzeit', in: Rickheit, Gert, Wichter, Sigurd (eds.), *Dialog. Festschrift für Siegfried Grosse*, Tübingen: Niemeyer, pp. 185–199

Rautenberg, Ursula (1996), *Überlieferung und Druck. Heiligenlegenden aus frühen Kölner Offizinen*, Tübingen, Max Niemeyer

Rautenberg, Ursula (2000), 'Warum Einblattdrucke einseitig bedruckt sind. Zum Zusammenhang von Druckverfahren und medialem Typus', in: Honemann, Volker, Griese, Sabine, Eisermann, Falk, Ostermann, Marcus (eds.), *Einblattdrucke des 15. und frühen 16. Jahrhunderts*, Tübingen: Niemeyer, pp. 129–142

Raven, James (2007), *The Business of Books. Booksellers and the English Book Trade, 1450 – 1850*, New Heaven (CT): Yale University Press

Raymond, Joad (1999), 'The Newspaper, Public Opinion, and the Public Sphere in the Seventeenth Century', in: Raymond, Joad (ed.), *News, Newspapers and Society in Early Modern Britain*, London/Portland (OR): Frank Cass, pp. 109–140

Raymond, Joad (2003), *Pamphlets and Pamphleteering in Early Modern Britain*, Cambridge: Cambridge University Press

Raymond, Joad (ed.) (2011), *Cheap Print in Britain and Ireland to 1660*, Oxford: Oxford University Press

Rees, Graham, Wakely, Maria (2009), *Publishing, Politics, and Culture. The King's Printers in the Age of James I and VI*, Oxford: Oxford University Press

Reit, Reinhold (1999), *Lohn und Leistung. Lohnformen im Gewerbe 1450–1900*, Stuttgart: Franz Steiner Verlag

Reske, Christoph (2015), *Die Buchdrucker des 16. und 17. Jahrhunderts im deutschen Sprachgebiet*, 2nd ed, Wiesbaden: Harrassowitz

Reuter, Wolfgang (1958), 'Zur Wirtschafts- und Sozialgeschichte des Buchdruckgewerbes im Rheinland bis 1800', in: *Archiv für Geschichte des Buchwesens* 1, pp. 642–736

Reyscher, August Ludwig (ed.) (1828–1851), *Vollständige, historisch und kritisch bearbeitete Sammlung der württembergischen Gese[t]ze*, 19 vols, Stuttgart/Tübingen: Cotta/Fues

Rial Costas, Benito (2017), 'Marketing a New Legal Code in Fifteenth-Century Castile: A Case Study of the Interactions Between Crown, Law and Printing', in: Bellingradt, Daniel et al. (eds), *Books in Motion in Early Modern Europe. Beyond Production, Circulation, and Consumption*, Cham: Palgrave Macmillan, pp. 87–108

Rospocher, Massimo (ed.) (2012), *Beyond the Public Sphere. Opinions, Publics, Spaces in Early Modern Europe*, Bologna/Berlin: Il Mulino/Duncker & Humblot

Rospocher, Massimo, Salman, Jeroen, Salmi, Hannu (eds.) (2019), *Crossing Borders, Crossing Cultures. Popular Print in Europe (1450–1900)*, Berlin: De Gruyter

Rox, Barbara (2012), *Schutz religiöser Gefühle im freiheitlichen Verfassungsstaat?* Tübingen: Mohr Siebeck

Rublack, Ulinka (1997), 'Frühneuzeitliche Staatlichkeit und lokale Herrschaftspraxis in Württemberg', in: *Zeitschrift für Historische Forschung* 24, pp. 347–376

Rudersdorf, Manfred (1992), 'Hessen', in: Schindling, Anton, Ziegler, Walter (eds.), *Die Territorien des Reiches im Zeitalter der Reformation und Konfessionalisierung.* Vol. 4: *Mittleres Deutschland*, Münster: Aschendorff, pp. 255–288

Ruff, Julius R. (2001), *Violence in Early Modern Europe 1500–1800*, Cambridge: Cambridge University Press

Ruland, Anton (1863), 'Zur Druckgeschichte des vom Fürstbischof Julius zu Würzburg herausgegebenen Breviarium secundum usum ecclesiae Herbipolensis von 1575', in: *Serapeum* 24, pp. 219–223

Salzberg, Rosa (2014), *The Ephemeral City. Cheap Print and Urban Culture in Renaissance Venice*, Manchester: Manchester University Press

Santoro, Marco (2013), *Die Geschichte des Buchhandels in Italien*, translated by Heribert Streicher, Wiesbaden: Harrassowitz

Sattler, Christian Friedrich (1769–1783), *Geschichte des Herzogthums Würtenberg unter der Regierung der Herzogen*, 13 vols, Tübingen: Reiß

Schaab, Meinrad, Schwarzmaier, Hansmartin, Taddey, Gerhard (eds.) (2000), *Handbuch der Baden-Württembergischen Geschichte* (Vol. 1,2), Stuttgart: Klett-Cotta

Schäfer, Gerhard (ed.) (1984), *Reformation in Württemberg. Ausstellung zur 450-Jahr-Feier der Evangelischen Landeskirche*, Stuttgart: Calwer Verlag

Schanze, Frieder (2000), 'Inkunabeln oder Postinkunabeln? Zur Problematik der "Inkunabelgrenze" am Beispiel von 5 Druckern und 111 Einblattdrucken', in: Honemann, Volker, Griese, Sabine, Eisermann, Falk, Ostermann, Marcus (eds.), *Einblattdrucke des 15. und frühen 16. Jahrhunderts*, Tübingen: Niemeyer, pp. 45–122

Scheck, Friedemann (2014), 'Herzog Ulrich und der "Arme Konrad"', in: Rückert, Peter (ed.), *Der 'Arme Konrad' vor Gericht. Verhöre, Sprüche und Lieder in Württemberg 1514. Begleitbuch und Katalog zur Ausstellung des Landesarchivs Baden-Württemberg, Hauptstaatsarchiv Stuttgart*, Stuttgart: Kohlhammer, pp. 68–75

Schennach, Martin P. (2008), 'Zuschreiben von Bedeutung: Publikation und Normintensität frühneuzeitlicher Gesetze', in: *Zeitschrift der Savigny-Stiftung für Rechtsgeschichte, Germanistische Abteilung* 125, pp. 133–180

Schennach, Martin P. (2010), *Gesetz und Herrschaft. Die Entstehung des Gesetzgebungsstaates am Beispiel Tirols*, Cologne: Böhlau

Schilling, Heinz (1972), *Niederländische Exulanten im 16. Jahrhundert. Ihre Stellung im Sozialgefüge und im religiösen Leben deutscher und englischer Städte*, Gütersloh: Mohn

Schilling, Heinz (2004), *Die Stadt in der frühen Neuzeit*, 2nd ed., Munich: Oldenbourg

Schilling, Lothar (2002), 'Gesetzgebung als Kommunikation. Zu symbolischen und expressiven Aspekten französischer "ordonnances de réformation" des 16. und frühen 17. Jahrhunderts', in: Neuhaus, Helmut, Stollberg-Rilinger, Barbara (eds.), *Menschen und Strukturen in der Geschichte Alteuropas. Festschrift für Johannes Kunisch zur Vollendung seines 65. Lebensjahres*, Berlin: Duncker & Humblot, pp. 133–165

Schlögl, Rudolf (ed.) (2004), *Interaktion und Herrschaft. Die Politik in der frühneuzeitlichen Stadt*, Konstanz: UVK Verlagsgesellschaft

Schlögl, Rudolf (2008), 'Politik beobachten. Öffentlichkeit und Medien in der Frühen Neuzeit', in: *Zeitschrift für Historische Forschung* 35,4, pp. 581–616

Schlögl, Rudolf (2014), *Anwesende und Abwesende. Grundriss für eine Gesellschaftsgeschichte der Frühen Neuzeit*, Konstanz: Konstanz University Press

Schlüter, Theodor C. (1993), 'Der Streitschriftenkrieg um den Reformationsversuch in den Jahren 1543–1547', in: Link, Hans-Georg (ed.), *450 Jahre Kölner Reformationsversuch. Zwischen Reform und Reformation*, Alfter: Stallberg, pp. 83–88

Schlüter, Theodor (2005), *Flug- und Streitschriften zur 'Kölner Reformation'. Die Publizistik um den Reformationsversuch des Kölner Erzbischofs und Kurfürsten Hermann von Wied (1515–1547)*, Wiesbaden: Harrassowitz

Schmelzeisen, Gustaf Klemens (1955), *Polizeiordnungen und Privatrecht*, Cologne: Böhlau

Schmitz, Wolfgang (2017), 'Beten und Lesen im Untergrund. Evangelischer Buchdruck in der katholischen Reichsstadt Köln bis zum Ende der kölnischen Reformation ca. 1547', in: Kaufmann, Thomas, Mittler, Elmar (eds.), *Reformation und Buch. Akteure und Strategien frühreformatorischer Druckerzeugnisse*, Wiesbaden: Harrassowitz, pp. 85–104

Schnitzler, Thomas (1992), 'Die Kölner Schützenfeste des 15. und 16. Jahrhunderts – Zum Sportfest in 'vormoderner Zeit'', in: *Jahrbuch des Kölnischen Geschichtsvereins* 63,1, pp. 127–142

Schnurr, Eva-Maria (2009a), *Religionskonflikt und Öffentlichkeit. Eine Mediengeschichte des Kölner Krieges (1582 bis 1590)*, Cologne: Böhlau

Schnurr, Eva-Maria (2009b), '"Jedem anbringer gleub ich so balt nit." Informationsbeschaffung und Mediennutzung des Kölner Bürgers Hermann Weinsberg während des Kölner Kriegs (1582 bis 1590)', in: *Geschichte in Köln* 56,1, pp. 171–206

Scholz (2020), *Borders and Freedom of Movement in the Holy Roman Empire*, Oxford: Oxford University Press

Schott, Theodor (1879), 'Zur Geschichte des Buchhandels in Tübingen', in: *Archiv für die Geschichte des Deutschen Buchhandels* 2, pp. 241–254

Schottenloher, Karl (1907), *Die Buchdruckertätigkeit Georg Erlingers in Bamberg von 1522 bis 1541*, Leipzig: R. Haupt

Schottenloher, Karl (1927a), 'Hans Wehrlich, genannt Hans von Erfurt, der Drucker des Wormser Edikts (1518–1532)', in: *Gutenberg-Jahrbuch* 2, pp. 53–67

Schottenloher, Karl (1927b), *Pfalzgraf Ottheinrich und das Buch. Ein Beitrag zur Geschichte der evangelischen Publizistik*, Münster: Verlag der Aschendorffschen Verlagsbuchhandlung

Schottenloher, Karl (1940), 'Silvan Otmar in Augsburg, der Drucker des Schwäbischen Bundes 1519–1535', in: *Gutenberg-Jahrbuch* 15, pp. 281–296

Schottenloher, Karl (1944/1949), 'Der Frühdruck im Dienste der öffentlichen Verwaltung', in: *Gutenberg-Jahrbuch* 24, pp. 138–148

Schwerhoff, Gerd (1991), *Köln im Kreuzverhör. Kriminalität, Herrschaft und Gesellschaft in einer frühneuzeitlichen Stadt*, Bonn: Bouvier

Schwerhoff, Gerd (1994), 'Die goldene Freiheit der Bürger. Zu den Bedeutungsebenen eines Grundwertes in der stadtkölnischen Geschichte (13.–17. Jahrhundert)', in: Schreiner, Klaus, Meier, Ulrich (eds.), *Stadtregiment und Bürgerfreiheit. Handlungsspielräume in deutschen und italienischen Städten des späten Mittelalters und der frühen Neuzeit*, Göttingen: Vandenhoeck & Ruprecht, pp. 84–119

Schwerhoff, Gerd (2004), 'Öffentliche Räume und politische Kultur in der frühneuzeitlichen Stadt. Eine Skizze am Beispiel der Reichsstadt Köln', in: Schlögl, Rudolf (ed.), *Interaktion und Herrschaft. Die Politik in der frühneuzeitlichen Stadt*, Konstanz: UVK Verlagsgesellschaft

Schwerhoff, Gerd (2005a), 'Die große Welt im kleinen Raum. Zur Ver-Ortung überlokaler Kommunikationsräume in der Frühen Neuzeit', in: Dürr, Renate, Schwerhoff, Gerd (eds.), *Kirchen, Märkte und Tavernen. Erfahrungs- und Handlungsräume in der Frühen Neuzeit*, Frankfurt am Main: Klostermann, pp. 367–375

Schwerhoff, Gerd (2005b), *Zungen wie Schwerter. Blasphemie in alteuropäischen Gesellschaften 1200–1650*, Konstanz: UVK Verlagsgesellschaft

Schwerhoff, Gerd (ed.) (2011), *Stadt und Öffentlichkeit in der Frühen Neuzeit*, Cologne, Böhlau

Schwerhoff, Gerd, Mölich, Georg (eds.) (1999), *Köln als Kommunikationszentrum. Studien zur frühneuzeitlichen Stadtgeschichte*, Cologne: DuMont

Schwerhoff, Gerd, Rau, Susanne (2004), 'Öffentliche Räume in der Frühen Neuzeit. Überlegungen zu Leitbegriffen und Themen eines Forschungsfeldes', in: Schwerhoff, Gerd, Rau, Susanne (eds.), *Zwischen Gotteshaus und Taverne. Öffentliche Räume in Spätmittelalter und früher Neuzeit*, Cologne: Böhlau, pp. 11–52

Scott, Tom (2002), *Society and Economy in Germany 1300–1600*, Basingstoke: Palgrave

Scott, Tom (2005a), *Town, Country, and Regions in Reformation Germany*, Leiden: Brill

Scott, Tom (2005b), 'From the Bundschuh to the Peasants' War: From Revolutionary Conspiracy to the Revolution of the Common Man', in: Scott, Tom (ed.), *Town, Country, and Regions in Reformation Germany*, Leiden: Brill, pp. 125–148

Scribner, Robert W. (1976), 'Why was there no Reformation in Cologne', in: *Bulletin of the Institute of Historical Research* 49, pp. 217–241

Scribner, Robert W. (1987), 'Police and the Territorial State in Sixteenth-Century Württemberg', in: Scott, Tom, Kouri, E. I. (eds.), *Politics and Society in Reformation Europe*, Basingstoke: Palgrave Macmillan, pp. 103–120

Seggern, Harm von (2009), 'Gedruckte Urkunden – Ein neues Propagandainstrument in der zweiten Hälfte des 15. Jahrhunderts?', in: Auge, Oliver, Werlich, Ralf-Gunnar, Zeilinger, Gabriel (eds.), *Fürsten an der Zeitenwende zwischen Gruppenbild und Individualität*, Thorbecke, pp. 129–144

Sehling, Emil et al. (eds.) (1902–2015), *Die evangelischen Kirchenordnungen des XVI. Jahrhunderts*, 21 vols, Leipzig/Tübingen: Reisland/Mohr Siebeck

Silver, Larry (2008), *Marketing Maximilian. The Visual Ideology of a Holy Roman Emperor*, Princeton (NJ): Princeton University Press

Sommer, Ingrid Karin (ed.) (1971), *Die Chronik des Stuttgarter Ratsherrn Sebastian Küng*, Stuttgart: Ernst Klett

Spufford, Margaret (1981), *Small Books and Pleasant Histories. Popular Fiction and Its Readership in Seventeenth-Century England*, London: Methuen

Stallybrass, Peter (2007), '"Little Jobs": Broadsides and the Printing Revolution', in: Alcorn Baron, Sabrina, Lindquist, Eric N., Shevlin, Eleanor F. (eds.), *Agent of Change: Print Culture Studies after Elizabeth L. Eisenstein*, Amherst/Boston (MA): University of Massachusetts Press, pp. 315–341

Steiff, Karl (1881), *Der erste Buchdruck in Tübingen (1498–1534)*, Tübingen: Laupp

Stollberg-Rilinger, Barbara, Neu, Tim, Brauner, Christina (eds.) (2013), *Alles nur symbolisch? Bilanz und Perspektiven der Erforschung symbolischer Kommunikation*, Cologne: Böhlau

Stollberg-Rilinger, Barbara, Neu, Tim (2013), 'Einleitung', in: Stollberg-Rilinger, Barbara, Neu, Tim, Brauner, Christina (eds.), *Alles nur symbolisch? Bilanz und Perspektiven der Erforschung symbolischer Kommunikation*, Cologne: Böhlau, pp. 11–32

Stolleis, Michael (2014), *History of Social Law in Germany*, translated by Thomas Dunlap, Berlin: Springer

Te Brake, Wayne (1998), *Shaping History. Ordinary People in European Politics, 1500–1700*, Berkeley (CA): University of California Press

Tischer, Anuschka (2012), *Offizielle Kriegsbegründungen in der Frühen Neuzeit. Herrscherkommunikation in Europa zwischen Souveränität und korporativem Selbstverständnis*, Berlin: Lit Verlag

Tlusty, Ann (2001), *Bacchus and Civic Order. The Culture of Drink in Early Modern Germany*, Charlottesville (VA): University Press of Virginia

Tlusty, Ann (2011), *The Martial Ethic in Early Modern Germany. Civic Duty and the Right of Arms*, Basingstoke: Palgrave Macmillan

Todd, Christopher (1991), *Political Bias, Censorship and the Dissolution of the 'Official' Press in Eighteenth-Century France*, New York: Edwin Mellen Press

Tolley, Bruce (1995), *Pastors and Parishioners in Württemberg during the late Reformation, 1581–1621*, Stanford (CA): Stanford University Press

Trugenberger, Volker (1994), '"Ob den portten drey hirschhorn in gelbem veld." Die württembergische Amtsstadt im 15. und 16. Jahrhundert', in: Treffeisen, Jürgen, Andermann, Kurt (eds.), *Landesherrliche Städte in Südwestdeutschland*, Sigmaringen: Thorbecke, pp. 131–156. Available online: http://hdl.handle.net/10900/46409

Volkmar, Christoph (2008), *Reform statt Reformation. Die Kirchenpolitik Herzog Georgs von Sachsen 1488–1525*, Tübingen: Mohr Siebeck

Volz, Hans (1963), 'Zur Geschichte des Wittenberger Buchdrucks, 1544–57', in: *Gutenberg-Jahrbuch* 38, pp. 113–119

Weber, Matthias (ed.) (2002), *Die Reichspolizeiordnungen von 1530, 1548 und 1577. Historische Einführung und Edition*, Frankfurt am Main: Klostermann

Weber, Wolfgang E.J. (2006), '"Bekennen und thun hiemit kunth und offentlich." Bemerkungen zur kommunikativen Funktion der Reichsabschiede des 16. Jahrhunderts', in: Lanzinner Maximilian, Strohmeyer, Arno (eds.), *Der Reichstag 1486–1613: Kommunikation, Wahrnehmung, Öffentlichkeit*, Göttingen: Vandenhoeck & Ruprecht, pp. 281–311

Wetzel Richard, Heitmeyer, Erika (eds.) (2013), *Johan Leisentrit's Geistliche Lieder und Psalmen, 1567. Hymnody of the Counter-Reformation in Germany*, Madison (NJ): Fairleigh Dickinson University Press

Whaley, Joachim (2012), *Germany and the Holy Roman Empire*, 2 vols, Oxford: Oxford University Press

Widmann, Hans, Kliemann, Horst, Wendt, Bernhard (eds.) (1965), *Der deutsche Buchhandel in Urkunden und Quellen*, 2 vols, Hamburg: Hauswedell

Widmann, Hans (1971a), 'Professor Philipp Apian als Drucker in Tübingen', in: *Gutenberg-Jahrbuch* 46, pp. 224–228

Widmann, Hans (1971b), *Tübingen als Verlagsstadt*, Tübingen: Mohr Siebeck

Winter, Christian (2014), 'Für gute Ordnung und Policey. Die Landesordnungen in der Frühen Neuzeit', in: Dingel, Irene, Kohnle, Armin (eds.), *Gute Ordnung. Ordnungsmodelle und Ordnungsvorstellungen in der Reformationszeit*, Leipzig: Evangelische Verlagsanstalt, pp. 87–107

Zanardi, Zita (ed.) (1996–2014), *Bononia Manifesta. Catalogo dei bandi, editti, costituzioni e provvedimenti diversi, stampati nel XVI secolo per Bologna e il suo Territorio*, Florence: Olschki

Zapnik, Jörg (ed.) (2016), *Repertorium der Policeyordnungen der pommerschen Städte bis zur Reichsgründung 1871*, Cologne: Böhlau

Zaret, David (2000), *Origins of Democratic Culture. Printing, Petitions, and the Public Sphere in Early-Modern England*, Princeton (NJ): Princeton University Press

Zaretzky, Otto (1912), 'Ein Quentelsches Rechnungsbuch aus der zweiten Hälfte des 16. Jahrhunderts', in: *Annalen des Historischen Vereins für den Niederrhein* 93, pp. 55–102

Unpublished work

DUNTZE, OLIVER (1999), *Die Kölner Offizin des Jaspar von Gennep*, Unpublished master's thesis, University of Cologne

KIM, LAUREN J. (2008), *French Royal Acts printed before 1601*, Unpublished thesis, University of St Andrews. Available online: http://hdl.handle.net/10023/463

ODENBREIT, JULIA (2014), *Einblattdrucke des 16. Jahrhunderts in Gedächtnisorganisationen. Erfassung und Erschließung*, Berlin: Institut für Bibliotheks- und Informationswissenschaft der Humboldt-Universität zu Berlin. Available online: https://edoc.hu-berlin.de/handle/18452/2764

SCHMITZ, WOLFGANG (1990), *Die Überlieferung deutscher Texte im Kölner Buchdruck des 15. und 16. Jahrhunderts*, Unpublished habilitation, University of Cologne. Available online: https://kups.ub.uni-koeln.de/1234/1/schmitz.pdf

WATSON, RÓISÍN (2015), *Lutheran Piety and Visual Culture in the Duchy of Württemberg, 1534–c.1700*, Unpublished thesis, University of St Andrews, 2015

WEDUWEN, ARTHUR DER (2018), *Selling the Republican Ideal. State Communication in the Dutch Golden Age*. Unpublished thesis, University of St Andrews, 2018

Appendix

Additional information on cited broadsheets issued by the rulers of Württemberg and Cologne in the sixteenth century

Note to the appendix

This appendix presents, for the first time, a comprehensive overview of broadsheet publications printed in Württemberg and Cologne in the sixteenth century.[1] Almost all of the items presented here were previously unknown to book historians. After I compiled this data, the USTC project team kindly agreed to integrate my records into the USTC online and provided me with the record numbers before publication.

For legal historians this appendix compliments the Policeyordnung volumes, listing many additional copies in the BL, DHM, KSM, USBK and WLB. It also provides information on the identified printers and corrects the volumes especially with regard to the dates of the records. The appendix provides links to over 270 digital copies, which were made available recently by the DHM, HStASt, WLB, USBK and HAStK.[2] As the latter only links to the collection and not the specific page, I have added the specific image number in the digitised collection to allow for easier navigation (e.g. the three copies of appendix no. 37 are images 66, 67 and 70 out of the total 168 images of Best. 90 (Handel): A 921, hence I added the information [66/168] etc. after the copies). In due time, the HAStK will digitise the microfilms of the edict collection (Best. 14 (Edikte)) and make them available online as well. The links provided offer access to the digital copies of the broadsheets, and they will be directly integrated into both the e-book and the future open access version of the book (planned for 2024). The appendix has been divided by geography and ordered by year of publication.

The main purpose of this appendix is not to provide a full bibliographical description of the editions, but to give information on the items cited in the study, including information on print runs, payments or lost editions, and emphasise

1 In the case of Cologne, it also includes seven pamphlet editions which were not recorded in the national bibliography *VD16*. The editons are nos. 163, 164, 241, 246, 247, 343, 359.

2 Both the DHM and the HAStK are currently implementing a new viewer. Hence some links may be momentarily unavailable or only accessible using Internet Explorer.

mistakes in earlier reference works. The USTC reference substitutes any ISTC or GW number for those publications listed as alleged incunabula.

Description:

a. author (in the standard form of the language of origin)
b. short-title including issue date (occasionally, a uniform title is used)
c. imprint (inferred information will be displayed with [], in the standard form of the language of origin)
d. references
e. copies, shelfmarks (where possible) and links to digital copies

References and copy information are displayed in abbreviated form:

Archives and libraries

BL	British Library London
DHM	Deutsches Historisches Museum Berlin
GNM	Germanisches Nationalmuseum Nürnberg
HAStK	Historisches Archiv der Stadt Köln
HStASt	Hauptstaatsarchiv Stuttgart
KSM	Kölnisches Stadtmuseum
USBK	Universitäts- und Stadtbibliothek Köln
WLB	Württembergische Landesbibliothek Stuttgart

Bibliographies and reference works

BC	Borchling, Conrad and Bruno Claussen (eds.) (1976), *Niederdeutsche Bibliographie. Gesamtverzeichnis der niederdeutschen Drucke bis zum Jahre 1800*, 3 vols, Utrecht: Hes Publishers
Policey K	Militzer, Klaus (ed.) (2005), *Repertorium der Policeyordnungen der Frühen Neuzeit. Reichsstädte 2: Köln*, 2 vols, Frankfurt am Main: Klostermann
Policey W	Landwehr, Achim and Thomas Simon (eds.) (2011), *Repertorium der Policeyordnungen der Frühen Neuzeit.* Vol. 4: *Baden und Württemberg*, Frankfurt am Main: Klostermann
Ratsedikte	Keussen, Hermann (1899): 'Inhaltsverzeichniss zu den Sammlungen der Rathsedikte 1493–1819', in: *Mittheilungen aus dem Stadtarchiv von Köln* 29, pp. 159–336
RB	Groten, Manfred and Manfred Huiskes (eds.) (1998–2003), *Beschlüsse des Rates der Stadt Köln, 1320–1550. Die Ratsmemoriale und ergänzende Überlieferung, 1320–1543*, 6 vols, Düsseldorf: Droste
Steiff	Steiff, Karl (1881), *Der erste Buchdruck in Tübingen (1498–1534)*, Tübingen: Laupp
USTC	Universal Short Title Catalogue, www.ustc.ac.uk

The spelling of sixteenth-century German was not standardised except to improve legibility. The contractions 'ā', 'ē', 'ī', 'ō', 'ū' were replaced with the correct nasal; abbreviations were resolved wherever possible.

Württemberg

1. **Württemberg, Ulrich, Herzog von,** 1511
Allen und ieglichen Churfürsten fürstenn gaistlichenn und weltlichen herrn - Einladung zu einem Rennen am 11 Mai 1512 (21.12.1511) ([Tübingen: Thomas Anshelm, 1511]).
Reference: Steiff 26; USTC 2507580
Copies: WLB, HBFC 2
http://digital.wlb-stuttgart.de/purl/bsz43482528X

2. **Württemberg, Ulrich, Herzog von,** 1514
Warhafftig underrichtung der uffrurn unnd hanndlungen sich im fürstenthumb Wirtemberg begeben ([16.08.]1514) ([Tübingen: Thomas Anshelm, 1514]).
Reference: Steiff 61; USTC 2507582
Copies: HStASt, A 45 Bü 9; WLB, HBFC 5
http://www.landesarchiv-bw.de/plink/?f=1-1211671-58
http://digital.wlb-stuttgart.de/purl/bsz476681200

3. **Württemberg, Ulrich, Herzog von,** 1514
Unser freuntlich un underthenig willig dienst zuvor hochwirdiger fürst - Begleitschreiben an die Bischöfe zur Unterrichtung ([16.08.]1514) ([Tübingen: Thomas Anshelm, 1514]).
Reference: Steiff 62a; USTC 2507583
Copies: HStASt, A 45 Bü 10
http://www.landesarchiv-bw.de/plink/?f=1-1211670-3
http://www.landesarchiv-bw.de/plink/?f=1-1211670-4
(with blank address on the back)
http://www.landesarchiv-bw.de/plink/?f=1-1211670-6
(addressed to Prince-Bishop Reinhard of Worms)

4. **Württemberg, Ulrich, Herzog von,** 1514
Ulrich (von gottes gnaden) lieber besunder und günstiger herr - Begleitschreiben an die Äbte zur Unterrichtung ([16.08.]1514) ([Tübingen: Thomas Anshelm, 1514]).

Reference: USTC 2507584
Copies: HStASt, A 45 Bü 10
http://www.landesarchiv-bw.de/plink/?f=1-1211670-10
http://www.landesarchiv-bw.de/plink/?f=1-1211670-12
http://www.landesarchiv-bw.de/plink/?f=1-1211670-13
http://www.landesarchiv-bw.de/plink/?f=1-1211670-15
http://www.landesarchiv-bw.de/plink/?f=1-1211670-16
http://www.landesarchiv-bw.de/plink/?f=1-1211670-17
http://www.landesarchiv-bw.de/plink/?f=1-1211670-19
http://www.landesarchiv-bw.de/plink/?f=1-1211670-21
http://www.landesarchiv-bw.de/plink/?f=1-1211670-235

5. **Württemberg, Ulrich, Herzog von,** 1514
Ulrich (von gottes gnaden) lieber besunder und günstiger herr - Begleitschreiben an die Reichsstädte zur Unterrichtung ([16.08.]1514) ([Tübingen: Thomas Anshelm, 1514]).
Reference: USTC 2507593
Copies: HStASt, A 45 Bü 10
http://www.landesarchiv-bw.de/plink/?f=1-1211670-63
http://www.landesarchiv-bw.de/plink/?f=1-1211670-64
http://www.landesarchiv-bw.de/plink/?f=1-1211670-65
http://www.landesarchiv-bw.de/plink/?f=1-1211670-66
http://www.landesarchiv-bw.de/plink/?f=1-1211670-67
http://www.landesarchiv-bw.de/plink/?f=1-1211670-68
http://www.landesarchiv-bw.de/plink/?f=1-1211670-70
http://www.landesarchiv-bw.de/plink/?f=1-1211670-72
http://www.landesarchiv-bw.de/plink/?f=1-1211670-73
http://www.landesarchiv-bw.de/plink/?f=1-1211670-74
http://www.landesarchiv-bw.de/plink/?f=1-1211670-75
http://www.landesarchiv-bw.de/plink/?f=1-1211670-76
http://www.landesarchiv-bw.de/plink/?f=1-1211670-77
http://www.landesarchiv-bw.de/plink/?f=1-1211670-79
http://www.landesarchiv-bw.de/plink/?f=1-1211670-80
http://www.landesarchiv-bw.de/plink/?f=1-1211670-81
http://www.landesarchiv-bw.de/plink/?f=1-1211670-82
http://www.landesarchiv-bw.de/plink/?f=1-1211670-83
http://www.landesarchiv-bw.de/plink/?f=1-1211670-84

6. **Württemberg, Ulrich, Herzog von,** 1514
Wir schicken euch auch hie mit zwu warhafftig underrichtungen - Begleitschreiben an die Amtleute zur Unterrichtung ([16.08.]1514) ([Tübingen: Thomas Anshelm, 1514]).

Reference: Steiff 62e; USTC 2507586
Copies: HStASt, A 45 Bü 10
http://www.landesarchiv-bw.de/plink/?f=1-1211670-86

7. **Württemberg, Ulrich, Herzog von,** 1514
Unser freuntlich und underthenig willig dienst zuvor hochgeborner fürst lieber oheim und gnediger herr - Begleitschreiben an die Fürsten zur Unterrichtung ([16.08.]1514) ([Tübingen: Thomas Anshelm, 1514]).
Reference: USTC 2507854
Copies: HStASt, A 45 Bü 10
http://www.landesarchiv-bw.de/plink/?f=1-1211670-27
(addressed to Duke Albrecht of Mecklenburg, unopened)
http://www.landesarchiv-bw.de/plink/?f=1-1211670-29
http://www.landesarchiv-bw.de/plink/?f=1-1211670-30

8. **Württemberg, Ulrich, Herzog von,** 1514
Ulrich (von gottes gnaden) wolgeborner lieber besunder und gnediger herr - Begleitschreiben an die Grafen zur Unterrichtung ([16.08.]1514) ([Tübingen: Thomas Anshelm, 1514]).
Reference: USTC 2507585
Copies: HStASt, A 45 Bü 10
http://www.landesarchiv-bw.de/plink/?f=1-1211670-32
http://www.landesarchiv-bw.de/plink/?f=1-1211670-33
http://www.landesarchiv-bw.de/plink/?f=1-1211670-34
http://www.landesarchiv-bw.de/plink/?f=1-1211670-35
http://www.landesarchiv-bw.de/plink/?f=1-1211670-36
http://www.landesarchiv-bw.de/plink/?f=1-1211670-37
http://www.landesarchiv-bw.de/plink/?f=1-1211670-38
http://www.landesarchiv-bw.de/plink/?f=1-1211670-39
http://www.landesarchiv-bw.de/plink/?f=1-1211670-40
http://www.landesarchiv-bw.de/plink/?f=1-1211670-41
http://www.landesarchiv-bw.de/plink/?f=1-1211670-42
http://www.landesarchiv-bw.de/plink/?f=1-1211670-43
http://www.landesarchiv-bw.de/plink/?f=1-1211670-44
http://www.landesarchiv-bw.de/plink/?f=1-1211670-45
http://www.landesarchiv-bw.de/plink/?f=1-1211670-46
http://www.landesarchiv-bw.de/plink/?f=1-1211670-47
http://www.landesarchiv-bw.de/plink/?f=1-1211670-48
http://www.landesarchiv-bw.de/plink/?f=1-1211670-49
http://www.landesarchiv-bw.de/plink/?f=1-1211670-50
(addressed to the Count of Wied)

9. **Württemberg, Ulrich, Herzog von,** 1514
Ulrich (von gottes gnaden) wolgeborner lieber besunder und gnediger herr - Begleitschreiben an die Freiherren zur Unterrichtung ([16.08.]1514) ([Tübingen: Thomas Anshelm, 1514]).
Reference: USTC 2509000
Copies: HStASt, A 45 Bü 10
http://www.landesarchiv-bw.de/plink/?f=1-1211670-54
(addressed to Freiherr zu Westerburg)
http://www.landesarchiv-bw.de/plink/?f=1-1211670-56
http://www.landesarchiv-bw.de/plink/?f=1-1211670-57
http://www.landesarchiv-bw.de/plink/?f=1-1211670-58
http://www.landesarchiv-bw.de/plink/?f=1-1211670-59
http://www.landesarchiv-bw.de/plink/?f=1-1211670-60
http://www.landesarchiv-bw.de/plink/?f=1-1211670-61

10. **Württemberg, Ulrich, Herzog von,** 1514
Ulrich (von gottes gnaden) liebe getreuen, wir haben uns entschlossen, das ieder underthon der ußgetretten kainen zůhaußen zubeherbergen,atzen,trencken noch im inn ainicherlai weg hilff zuthun ([19.08.]1514) ([Tübingen: Thomas Anshelm, 1514]).
Reference: USTC 2507587
Copies: HStASt, A 45 Bü 11; WLB, HBFC 6
http://digital.wlb-stuttgart.de/purl/bsz434851035

11. **Württemberg, Ulrich, Herzog von,** 1515
Ulrich (von gottes gnaden), das füro dhain Amptman unsers fürstenthumbs kain gewerb, wirtschafft noch uffkauff mit früchten oder anderm tryben soll (20.01.1515) ([s.l., s.n., 1515]).
Reference: Policey W 16; USTC 2507032
Copies: HStASt, A 39 Bü 1

12. **Württemberg, Ulrich, Herzog von,** 1515
Ulrich (von gottes gnaden), ersame getreuewer, ir wißt, das sich die welt mit den zwaien hochverbotten laßtern, Gotzlestern und Zutrinckens, vermaßen, hierin ain ordnung und straff den übertrettern fürgenomen (23.04.1515) ([Tübingen: Thomas Anshelm, 1515]).
Reference: Policey W 18; USTC 2507033
Copies: HStASt, A 39 Bü 12; HStASt, A 38 Bü 12; A 238 Bü 1

13. **Württemberg, Ferdinand, Statthalter in,** 1521
Ersamer lieber unnd guter freund, ir wißt, das sich die welt mit den zweien lastern Gotzlesterns und Zutrinckens zum ho[e]chsten beflecken und vermaligen, zu wolfart haben wir ain ordnung uffgesetzt, ir wo[e]

lt das volck an der Cantzel und sunft warnen (20.08.1521) ([s.l., s.n., 1521]).
Reference: Policey W 30; USTC 2507034
Copies: HStASt, A 39 Bü 1; HStASt, A 238 Bü 1; HStASt, A 251 Bd. 107

14. Karl V, Kaiser, 1521
Karl (von gottes gnaden) wo[e]llen dass du die lehenßpflicht thüest (00.00.1521) ([Tübingen: Thomas Anshelm, 1521]).
Reference: USTC 2507610
Copies: HStASt, A 251 Bd. 107; WLB, HBFC 52
http://digital.wlb-stuttgart.de/purl/bsz394511913

15. Karl V, Kaiser, 1521
Wjr Karl (von gottes gnaden) wo[e]llen das ir am dryzehenden tag des monats februarij euch inn Stutgarten verfüegen und ewre Lehen empfahen (07.01.1521) ([Ulm: Johann Grüner, 1521]).
Reference: USTC 2507641
Copies: WLB, HBFC 83; WLB, HBFC 123
http://digital.wlb-stuttgart.de/purl/bsz335340881

16. Württemberg, Ferdinand, Statthalter in, 1522
Wjr des Durchleüchtigsten: Großmechtigen - Mandat gegen Luther und seine Lehre (26.11.1522) ([Stuttgart: Hans Wehrlich, 1522]).
Reference: USTC 2507604
Copies: HStASt, A 63 Bü 2/6
http://www.landesarchiv-bw.de/plink/?f=1-1465134-16

17. Württemberg, Ferdinand, Statthalter in, 1533
Wir Ferdinand (von Gottes genaden) zu fürderug und gutem vom wege[n] der vischereyen auff dem Necker notdurfftige ordnungen (17.10.1533) ([Tübingen: Ulrich I Morhart, 1533]).
Reference: Steiff 154; USTC 2507637
Copies: WLB, HBFC 76
http://digital.wlb-stuttgart.de/purl/bsz444418636

18. Württemberg, Ulrich, Herzog von, 1534
WIr Ulrich von Gots Gnaden, Hertzog zu Tegk und Wirtenberg sein demnach des willens uns als ein gnediger Her und Landfurst zuhalten (01.05.1534) ([s.l., s.n., 1534]).
Reference: USTC 2507623
Copies: HStASt, A 84 Bü 29

19. **Württemberg, Ulrich, Herzog von,** 1534
Allen und jeden, den diser Brief furkomt - Ausschreiben, die vorgenommene Rekuperation und Eroberung des Herzogtums Württemberg betreffend ([Marburg: Franz Rhode, 1534]).
Reference: USTC 2507644
Copies: WLB, HBFC 17
http://digital.wlb-stuttgart.de/purl/bsz476688639

20. **Württemberg, Ulrich, Herzog von,** 1535
Von Gottes gnaden, wir Ulrich gebieten euch allen, die sich der feurbüchssen gebraucht haben innerhalb vier wochen nach dato dis mandats dieselbigen verkauffen und hinweg thun, deren nit mer gebrauchen (18.02.1535) ([Tübingen: Ulrich I Morhart, 1535]).
Reference: Policey W 63; USTC 2507020
Copies: HStASt, J 17 Bü 14

21. **Württemberg, Ulrich, Herzog von,** 1543
Von gottes gnaden, wir Ulrich gepieten, das ir euch Wiltpretschiessens und weidwerck treibens enthalten (31.05.1543) ([Tübingen: Ulrich I Morhart, 1543]).
Reference: Policey W 94; USTC 2507036
Copies: HStASt, A 251 Bd. 107; HStASt, A 39 Bü 1

22. **Württemberg, Ulrich, Herzog von,** 1544
Von gottes gnaden, wir Ulrich embieten unsern gruß. Als die Ro[e]). Kei. Maie. bedacht, das unsers glaubens erbfeind der Türck nicht abgewendt werde mo[e]g, so haben ho[e]chstgedachte Kei. Maie. für notwendig angesehen, das alle gleiche anlag und steür gebe (15.11.1544) ([Tübingen: Ulrich I Morhart, 1544]).
Reference: USTC 2507024
Copies: HStASt, A 238 Bü 1; HStASt, J 17 Bü 14

23. **Württemberg, Ulrich, Herzog von,** 1548
Von Gottes genaden, wir Urich fu[e]gen euch zuwissen, das die Ro[e] misch Kayserlich Maiestat ein Ordnung und Reformation gutter Pollicey beschlossen, die neben anderem des Gotslesterens und zutrinckens halben von wort zu wort also lutet (16.11.1548) ([Tübingen: Ulrich I Morhart, 1548]).
Reference: Policey W 103; USTC 2507577
Copies: HStASt, A 39 Bü 1; HStASt, A 38 Bü 12; HStASt, A 251 Bd. 107; WLB, HBFC 20
http://digital.wlb-stuttgart.de/purl/bsz435430149

24. **Württemberg, Christoph, Herzog von,** 1554
Von Gottes Gnaden, wir Christoff geben euch zu erkennendas niemand mer Früchten zukauffen, dann einer zu seinem ta[e]glichen Haußbrauch und Beckenhandwerck notturfftig were, Darzu keinem zugelassen mit seiner eigenen Wolle zuverlegen (27.03.1554) ([Tübingen: Ulrich I Morhart, 1554]).
Reference: Policey W 145; USTC 2507011
Copies: HStASt, A 58 Bü 1b; HStASt, A 251 Bd. 107

25. **Württemberg, Christoph, Herzog von,** 1554
Von Gottes genaden, wir Christoff gebieten euch, das fürohin kein boden jn unserm Fürstenthumb, der gutt zu a[e]ckern, wisen, ga[e]rten oder zu holtz geschlacht und gewechßnig, mehr zu Weingarten umgebrochen, außgereüt, gepflanzt oder gemacht werden soll (11.06.1554) ([Tübingen: Ulrich I Morhart, 1554]).
Reference: Policey W 148; USTC 2507039
Copies: HStASt, A 39 Bü 2; HStASt, A 238 Bü 1; HStASt, A 251 Bd. 107

26. **Württemberg, Christoph, Herzog von,** 1554
Von Gottes gnaden, wir Christoff haben auf jüngst gehaltnem Landtag volgende Satzungen verabschidet - Straff der Wildbretschützen (20.01.1554) ([Tübingen: Ulrich I Morhart, 1554]).
Reference: Policey W 144; USTC 2507579
Copies: HStASt, A 39 Bü 2; HStASt, A 238 Bü 1; HStASt, A 251 Bd. 107

27. **Württemberg, Ludwig, Herzog von,** 1572
Von Gottes gnaden wir Ludwig Hertzog zu Würtemberg bevelhen euch Amptleutten, verbrecher, so verbotten Gelt in unser Fürstenthumb fu[e]hren mo[e]chten, dieselbigen auffhalten (06.12.1572) ([Tübingen: Georg Gruppenbach, 1572]).
Reference: Policey W 212; USTC 2507000
Copies: HStASt, A 238 Bü 2; HStASt, A 39 Bü 3; HStASt, A 251 Bd. 108

Cologne

28. Köln – Rat, c.1500
Golt, Item der golt gulden xxxiii. alb. Item ein Rosen nobel xvii marck (Münztabelle) ([Köln: s.n., c.1500]).
Reference: Ratsedikte 12; USTC 2505631
Notes: Format: 28.0 × 20.5, Satzspiegel: 15.6 × 19.2
Copies: HAStK, Best. 14 (Edikte): 14, Nr. 2; USBK, SB1051
http://www.ub.uni-koeln.de/cdm/ref/collection/rheinmono/id/825325

29. Köln – Rat, c.1500
Golt, Item der golt gulden xxxiii. alb. Item ein Rosen nobel xvii marck (Münztabelle) ([Köln: s.n., c. 1500]).
Reference: Ratsedikte 13; USTC 2505632
Notes: Format: 32.3 × 27.5, Satzspiegel: 18.7 × 22.5
Copies: HAStK, Best. 14 (Edikte): 14, Nr. 3; USBK, SB1051

30. Köln – Rat, 1501
Den Eirsamen Vursichtigen wijsen Burgermeisteren und Rayde der Stede (Einladen zum Armbrust- und Büchsenschiessen, 16.11.1501) ([Köln: Johann II Koelhoff, 1501]).
Reference: BC 353; USTC 753283
Notes: Koelhoff received the astounding sum of 17 Gulden for the production, which suggests a very high print run, see chapter 4
Copies: HAStK; GNM, Inv. Nr. HB 2631 Kapsel 1379; Washington, National Gallery of Art, Rosenwald Collection, 1951.16.4.
https://www.bildindex.de/document/obj00171357?medium=mi08353f05
https://www.monasterium.net/mom/IlluminierteUrkunden/1501-10-16_Washington/charter

31. Köln – Rat, 1503
Nach dem der hoichwirdige in gode Herre Raymundus Peraudi Cardinaill und Legate (Ordnung für Prozession) ([Köln: Hermann Bungart, 1503]).
Reference: BC 372; USTC 753286
Copies: HAStK

32. Köln – Rat, 1503
In nomine domine Amen (Erklärung wegen der Appellation an den Römischen Stuhl gegen den Bannbrief des Erzbischofs) ([Köln: Hermann Bungart, 1503]).
Reference: BC 373; USTC 753287
Copies: Staatsbibliothek Berlin, Einbl. 1503-1 m; USBK; HAStK

33. Köln – Rat, 1505
Eynunge und frutnlich verstant van hundert Jaren tuschen deme hoechgeboren Fursten (Vertrag der Stadt Köln mit Hermann, Kurfürst von Köln) ([Köln: Hermann Bungart, 1505]).
Reference: BC 394; USTC 753291
Copies: Landesarchiv Nordrhein-Westfalen (Rheinland); USBK; HAStK

34. Köln – Rat, 1506
Ir Ereber lude, wie waill unde heren vam Raide myt Jren und den geschickden frunden (Münzordnung) ([Köln: Hermann Bungart, 1506]).
Reference: BC 403; Policy K 1359; USTC 753292
Copies: HAStK, Best. 14 (Edikte): 14, Nr. 10

35. Köln – Rat, 1510
Dyt is die Ordenunge die eyn werdich Raet der Stede Coelne up die gulden un Sylveren muntze (Münzordnung) ([Köln: Hermann Bungart, 1510]).
Reference: BC 467; Policey K 1372; USTC 753296
Copies: HAStK, Best. 14 (Edikte): 14, Nr. 8; GNM, Inv. Nr. HB 17044 Kapsel 1278
https://www.bildindex.de/document/obj00013165

36. Köln – Rat, 1510
Ordenunge wes dese herna geschrene [sic] pennynge an der marck (Münzordnung) ([Köln: Hermann Bungart, 1510]).
Reference: BC 486; USTC 753297
Copies: HAStK

37. Köln – Rat, 1511
Wir Burgermeystere und Rait der louelicher unser keyserlicher und des heilgin Richs srijer Stat Coelne doin kunt (Münzeinigung mit Erzbischof von Köln und Herzog von Jülich und Berg, 12.05.1511) ([Köln: Heinrich von Neuss, 1511]).
Reference: BC 498; Policey K 1386; Ratsedikte 21; USTC 753299

Copies: HAStK, Best. 90 (Handel): A 921, fol. 53; HAStK, Best. 90 (Handel): A 921, fol. 54; HAStK, Best. 90 (Handel): A 921, fol. 56
http://historischesarchivkoeln.de:8080/actaproweb/archive.xhtml?id=Vz++++++00098713hupp#Vz______00098713hupp [66/168]
http://historischesarchivkoeln.de:8080/actaproweb/archive.xhtml?id=Vz++++++00098713hupp#Vz______00098713hupp [67/168]
http://historischesarchivkoeln.de:8080/actaproweb/archive.xhtml?id=Vz++++++00098713hupp#Vz______00098713hupp [70/168]

38. Köln – Rat, 1511
Jr Eirber lude unse herren vam Raide willen uch niet verhalden dat sie zosampt iren frunden und den geschickten vytt allen Reeden (Münzeinigung, Montag nach Jubilate, 1511) ([Köln: Heinrich von Neuss, 1511]).
Reference: BC 499; Policey K 1382; Ratsedikte 21; USTC 753300
Copies: HAStK, Best. 14 (Edikte): 14, Nr. 9; HAStK, Best. 90 (Handel): A 921, fol. 55; USBK, SB1051; USBK, Einblattsammlung
http://historischesarchivkoeln.de:8080/actaproweb/archive.xhtml?id=Vz++++++00098713hupp#Vz______00098713hupp [68/168]
http://www.ub.uni-koeln.de/cdm/ref/collection/rheinmono/id/802652

39. Köln – Rat, 1513
Ordnung und verdrach eyns Eirsamen Raitz misamptversamelungen und geschyckten (Accisen-Ordnung, 01.03.1513) ([Köln: Heinrich von Neuss, 1513]).
Reference: BC 525; Policey K 1394; Ratsedikte 22; USTC 753356
Copies: HAStK, Best. 14 (Edikte): 8, Nr. 39

40. Köln – Rat, 1513
Item as eyn Eirber gemeynde van allen Ampten und gaffelen luyde eyns brieffs hiebevoir begert haet (Aufhebung der ausserordentlichen Accisen, 19.06.1513) ([Köln: Hermann Bungart, 1513]).
Reference: BC 526; Policey K 1420; USTC 753357
Copies: HAStK, Best. 30 (Verfassung und Verwaltung): V 107, fol. 272
http://historischesarchivkoeln.de:8080/actaproweb/archive.xhtml?id=Vz++++++00145607MHupElko#Vz______00145607MHupElko [289/643]

41. Köln – Rat, 1513
Ersame lieve frunde, as uch vor acht dagen vergehalden ist worden wie men uch op die bekentenisse der ghenre die unlangs mit urre alre wist willen unde bewesen na Scheffen oirdel ([Köln: Hermann Bungart, 1513]).
Reference: BC 528; Policey K 1391; Ratsedikte 3892; USTC 753358
Copies: HAStK, Best. 30 (Verfassung und Verwaltung): V 107, fol. 333 & fol. 581; HAStK, Best. 14 (Edikte): 8, Nr. 40; HAStK, Best. 14 (Edikte): 9, Nr. 129
http://historischesarchivkoeln.de:8080/actaproweb/archive.xhtml?id=Vz++++++00145607MHupElko#Vz______00145607MHupElko [348 & 588/643]

42. Köln – Rat, 1515
Dyt is die ordenunge, wie, wa und wan[n]e men dat uyßwendige broit herbynnen Coelne brengen vort veilehaven und v[e]kouffen sall (13.04.1515) ([Köln: s.n., 1515]).
Reference: BC 563; Policey K 1465; Ratsedikte 23; USTC 2506462
Copies: HAStK, Best. 90 (Handel): A 349, fol. 1, GNM, Inv. Nr. HB 15574, Kapsel 1228
http://historischesarchivkoeln.de:8080/actaproweb/archive.xhtml?id=Vz++++++00098015hupp#Vz______00098015hupp [3/69]

43. Köln – Rat, 1516
Wir Burgermeistere und Rait der loeblicher unser keyserlicher unnd des heilghen Reichs fryer Stat Colne (Münzmandat, 09.06.1516) ([Köln: Hermann Bungart, 1516]).
Reference: BC 582; Policey K 1474; Ratsedikte 24; USTC 753364
Copies: HAStK, Best. 14 (Edikte): 14, Nr. 11; HAStK, Best. 90 (Handel): A 921, fol. 63; USBK, SB1051; GNM, Inv. Nr. HB 15577 Kapsel 1278
http://historischesarchivkoeln.de:8080/actaproweb/archive.xhtml?id=Vz++++++00098713hupp#Vz______00098713hupp [77/168]
http://www.ub.uni-koeln.de/cdm/ref/collection/rheinmono/id/668229

44. Köln – Rat, 1517
Soe as eyn tzijt lanck her sich etliche yrthum und bebrechen gehalden hain tüschen dem dürchluchtigen hoichgeboren fursten unden gnedigen alreliefsten hernn heren Johan (Einigung mit Johann, Herzog von Jülich-Cleves-Berg, 04.02.1517) ([Köln: Hermann Bungart, 1517]).
Reference: BC 592 A; USTC 753306
Copies: HAStK

45. **Köln – Rat,** 1517
Dyt herna beschreven synt etlige artikulen die und'anderen vyss der ver Eynonge tusschen unsers hernn gnade van Guylge ind dem Berge Ind der Stat Coelne ([Köln: Hermann Bungart, 1517]).
Reference: BC 606; USTC 753367
Copies: HAStK

46. **Köln – Rat,** 1519
Ir eirber luyde, as unse herene vam Raide hiebefur Anno &c xviii. In octobri an uch unnd andere (Anleihe von 2000 Gulden) ([Köln: Hermann Bungart, 1519]).
Reference: BC 628; USTC 753370
Copies: USBK

47. **Köln – Rat,** 1521
Anno xc.xxi. Martis quintamartii berdragen uff allen Gaffelen tzo Jesen (Ersuchen für die abgegangenen Bevollmächtigten Ersatz zu wählen, 05.03.1521) ([Köln: Hermann Bungart, 1521]).
Reference: BC 689; USTC 753381
Copies: USBK

48. **Köln – Rat,** 1524
Münzordnung (Samstag nach Kiliani, 1524) ([Köln: s.n., 1524]).
Reference: USTC 2505630
Copies: USBK, SB1051
http://www.ub.uni-koeln.de/cdm/ref/collection/rheinmono/id/668437

49. **Köln – Rat,** 1525
Wir Burgermeistere und Rait der Steide Coelne doin kunt allermenigklich (Ordnung für den Verkauf fremden Brotes in der Stadt, 04.12.1525) ([Köln: Hermann Bungart, 1525]).
Reference: BC 804; Policey K 1637; USTC 753404
Copies: HAStK, Best. 14 (Edikte): 5, Nr. 120b

50. **Köln – Rat,** c.1525
Gotteslästerung ([Köln: s.n., c. 1525]).
Reference: Policey K 1579; Ratsedikte 3878; USTC 2506250
Copies: HAStK, Best. 14 (Edikte): 13, Nr. 110

51. **Köln – Rat,** 1525
Handelsordnung (26.08.1525) ([Köln: s.n., 1525]).
Reference: Policey K 1623; USTC 2506251
Copies: HAStK, Best. 90 (Handel): A 339a, fol. 46

52. **Köln – Rat,** 1527
Wyr Burgermeystere und Raidt der Stat Collne Doin kundt offentlich und warnen hoe myt (Erlass gegen die Hinterziehung der Accise für Mehl, Brot, Malz und Fleisch, 16.03.1527) ([Köln: s.n., 1527]).
Reference: BC 915; Policey K 1681; Ratsedikte 38; USTC 753414
Copies: HAStK, Best. 90 (Handel): A 349, fol. 6; HAStK, Best. 14 (Edikte): 8, Nr. 77
http://historischesarchivkoeln.de:8080/actaproweb/archive.xhtml?id=Vz++++++00098015hupp#Vz______00098015hupp [8/69]

53. **Köln – Rat,** 1527
Wyr Burgermeistere unnd Rait der Stat Coelne doin kunt allermeniglich myt diesen entgainwordigen brieff (Freies Geleit den Käufern und Verkäufern der Kölner Viehmärkte, 01.09.1527) ([Köln: s.n., 1527]).
Reference: BC 916; Policey K 1692; Ratsedikte 40; USTC 753415
Copies: HAStK, Best. 14 (Edikte): 8, Nr. 154; HAStK, USBK, Einblattsammlung

54. **Köln – Rat,** 1527
Münzordnung ([Köln: Johannes Soter, 1527]).
Reference: Policey K 1685; USTC 2505467
Copies: no copy known (inferred from manuscript notes on HAStK, Best. 14 Bd. 14, Nr. 16)

55. **Köln – Rat,** 1528
Wir Burgermeistere unnd Rait der Stat Coelne doin kunt alle die Provande und victualia, Fruchte, Wyn, Saltz, Herynck tzom veylen kouff brengen, geleyde hain (01.09.1528) ([Köln: s.n., 1528]).
Reference: Policey K 1723; Ratsedikte 42; USTC 2506404
Copies: HAStK, Best. 90 (Handel): A 550, fol. 1; HAStK, Best. 14 (Edikte): 8, Nr. 155; HAStK, Best. 14 (Edikte): 3, Nr. 182
http://historischesarchivkoeln.de:8080/actaproweb/archive.xhtml?id=Vz++++++00098246hupp#Vz______00098246hupp [3/161]

56. **Köln – Rat,** 1529
Verordnung betreffend Erbschaftswesen (06.06.1529) ([Köln: s.n., 1529]).
Reference: Policey K 1746; USTC 2506252
Copies: HAStK, Best. 50 (Köln und das Reich): 61/2, fol. 26; HAStK, Best. 50 (Köln und das Reich): 61/2, fol. 25

57. **Köln – Rat,** 1529
Wir Burgermeistere unnd Rait der Stat Coelne doin kunt alle die Provande und victualia als Fruchte un[n] Wyn, Saltz, Herynck tzom veylen kouff brengen, geleyde hain (01.09.1529) ([Köln: s.n., 1529]).
Reference: Policey K 1755; Ratsedikte 43; USTC 2506405
Copies: HAStK, Best. 90 (Handel): A 339, fol. 1a; HAStK, Best. 90 (Handel): A 335, fol. 1; HAStK, Best. 14 (Edikte): 8, Nr. 156; HAStK, Best. 90 (Handel): A 550, fol. 2
http://historischesarchivkoeln.de:8080/actaproweb/archive.xhtml?id=Vz++++++00098246hupp#Vz______00098246hupp [4/161]
http://historischesarchivkoeln.de:8080/actaproweb/archive.xhtml?id=Vz++++++00097996hupp#Vz______00097996hupp [2/231]
http://historischesarchivkoeln.de:8080/actaproweb/archive.xhtml?id=Vz++++++00097991hupp#Vz______00097991hupp [3/103]

58. **Köln – Rat,** c.1530
Wyr Burgermeistere und Raidt (Einfuhrverordnung für Brot) ([Köln: s.n., c.1530]).
Reference: Policey K 1763; USTC 2506253
Notes: possibly the ordinance produced in August 1526, RB, III, p. 330, no. 408
Copies: HAStK, Best. 90 (Handel): A 349, fol. 3
http://historischesarchivkoeln.de:8080/actaproweb/archive.xhtml?id=Vz++++++00098015hupp#Vz______00098015hupp [5/69]

59. **Köln – Rat,** 1531
Wir Burgermeister unnd Ratt der Satt [sic] Colne Thun allen unserenn burgerenn unnd Inwoneren, Geystlichen unnd werentlichen stands (Münzordnung, 01.09.1531) ([Köln: Eucharius Hirtzhorn, 1531]).
Reference: BC 1081; Policey K 1803; Ratsedikte 44; USTC 753440
Copies: HAStK, Best. 14 (Edikte): 14, Nr. 18

60. **Köln – Rat,** 1531
Wir Burgermeistere unnd Rait der Stat Coelne, doin kunt allermenniglich myt diesen entgainwordigen brieff (Marktverordnung betreffend Vieh- und Viktualieneinfuhr, 01.09.1531) ([Köln: s.n., 1531]).
Reference: Policey K 1802; Ratsedikte 45; USTC 2505539
Copies: HAStK, Best. 14 (Edikte): 8, Nr. 157; USBK, Einblattsammlung

61. **Köln – Rat,** 1532
Wir Burgermeister unnd Rait der Steide Cölne doin künt allerneniglich, So als sich etliche zeyt her der goult guldenn mit anderem goulde (Ordnung der Gulden und silbernen Münzen, 23.02.1532) ([Köln: Eucharius Hirtzhorn, 1532]).
Reference: BC 1081; Policey K 1822; Ratsedikte 46; USTC 753445
Notes: printed in at least 200 copies (see chapter 4)
Copies: HAStK, Best. 14 (Edikte): 14, Nr. 17; HAStK, Best. 14 (Edikte): 14, Nr. 5; USBK, Einblattsammlung; USBK, SB1051
http://www.ub.uni-koeln.de/cdm/ref/collection/rheinmono/id/670208

62. **Köln – Rat,** 1534
Item ein Goltgulden xxvii rader alb (Münzordnung und Valvation, 04.04.1534) ([Köln: Eucharius Hirtzhorn, 1534]).
Reference: BC 1194; Policey K 1853; Ratsedikte 48; USTC 753451
Copies: HAStK, Best. 14 (Edikte): 14, Nr. 19

63. **Köln – Rat,** c.1535
Wyr Burgermeistere und Rait der Stat Collen Thun hiermit allen und jeden unseren Burgeren (Münzordnung) ([Köln: s.n., c.1535]).
Reference: BC 1222; Policey K 1866; USTC 753457
Copies: HAStK, Best. 14 (Edikte): 14, Nr. 22a

64. **Köln – Rat,** 1537
Item ein Goltgulden xxvii rader alb (Valvationstabelle, 03.03.1537, zur Münzordnung vom 28.02.1537) ([Köln: s.n., 1537]).
Reference: BC 1263; Policey K 1882; USTC 753462
Copies: HAStK, Best. 14 (Edikte): 14, Nr. 21b

65. **Köln – Rat,** 1537
Wyr Burgermeistere und Rait der Stat Collen Thun allen und jeden unseren und unser Stat zu wissen (Münzverordnung, 24.02.1537) ([Köln: s.n., 1537]).
Reference: BC 1262 (wrong date!), Policey K 1881; Ratsedikte 50; USTC 2505627
Copies: HAStK, Best. 14 (Edikte): 14, Nr. 20; USBK, Einblattsammlung; USBK, SB1051
http://www.ub.uni-koeln.de/cdm/ref/collection/rheinmono/id/672145

66. **Köln – Rat,** 1543
Wir Burgermeistere und Rath der stat Cölln fögen allen unseren underthanen (Valvationsordnung goldener und silberner Münzen) ([Köln: s.n., 1543]).
Reference: BC 1391; Policey K 1934; USTC 753477
Copies: HAStK, Best. 14 (Edikte): 14, Nr. 23 [part I]; HAStK, Best. 14 (Edikte): 14, Nr. 24 [part II]

67. **Köln – Rat,** 1544
Wyr Burgermeistere und Rath der Stadt Co[e]lne thun kunth eynen jeden Hantierer so mit Fischwerck handelen unserer alter herbrachter Ordnung darnach zu halten (06.03.1544) ([Köln: s.n., 1544]).
Reference: Policey K 1944; Ratsedikte 56; USTC 2505644
Copies: HAStK, Best. 90 (Handel): A 321, fol. 20; HAStK, Best. 14 (Edikte): 16, Nr. 119
http://historischesarchivkoeln.de:8080/actaproweb/archive.xhtml?id=Vz++++++00097977hupp#Vz______00097977hupp [30/282]

68. **Köln – Rat,** 1544
Gotteslästerung (18.08.1544) ([Köln: s.n., 1544]).
Reference: Policey K 1952; Ratsedikte 57; USTC 2505645
Copies: HAStK, Best. 14 (Edikte): 3, Nr. 111; HAStK, Best. 14 (Edikte): 1, Nr. 102

69. **Köln – Rat,** 1544
Türkenkrieg, Kriegsdienst, bezüglich kaiserliches Mandat ([Köln: s.n., 1544]).
Reference: Policey K 1941; Ratsedikte 3881; USTC 2506257
Notes: printed in 100 copies (see chapter 4; RB, V, p. 212, no. 180)
Copies: HAStK, Best. 14 (Edikte): 9, Nr. 156

70. **Köln – Rat,** 1545
Schmähbücher und -abbildungen (02.10.1545) ([Köln: Jaspar von Gennep, 1545]).
Reference: Policey K 1963 (dated) & 2079 (not dated); Ratsedikte 3878; USTC 2506261
Copies: HAStK, Best. 14 (Edikte): 1, Nr. 129; HAStK, Best. 14 (Edikte): 13, Nr. 115

71. Köln – Rat, 1548
Zensurordnung (25.09.1548) ([Köln: s.n., 1548]).
Reference: Policey K 1993; USTC 2506264
Copies: HAStK, Best. 50 (Köln und das Reich): 107/2, fol. 11

72. Köln – Rat, 1549
Münzordnung mit Abbildung verbotener Münzen ([16.08.1549]) ([Köln: Jaspar von Gennep, 1549]).
Reference: Policey K 2007 (dated) & 2081 (undated); Ratsedikte 3889; USTC 2506290
Notes: Date inferred from contemporary manuscript copy, see Policey K 2007
Copies: HAStK, Best. 14 (Edikte): 14, Nr. 32; HAStK, Best. 90 (Handel): A 921, fol. 82; HAStK, Best. 90 (Handel): A 927, fol. 11; USBK, SB1051
http://historischesarchivkoeln.de:8080/actaproweb/archive.xhtml?id=Vz++++++00098713hupp#Vz______00098713hupp [97/168]
http://historischesarchivkoeln.de:8080/actaproweb/archive.xhtml?id=Vz++++++00098720hupp#Vz______00098720hupp [17/151]
http://www.ub.uni-koeln.de/cdm/ref/collection/rheinmono/id/825967

73. Köln – Rat, c.1550
Brotaccise ([Köln: s.n., c. 1550]).
Reference: Policey K 2026; USTC 2506267
Copies: HAStK, Best. 14 (Edikte): 3, Nr. 60

74. Köln – Rat, c.1550
Brotaccise ([Köln: s.n., c. 1550]).
Reference: Policey K 2025; USTC 2506266
Copies: HAStK, Best. 14 (Edikte): 3, Nr. 59

75. Köln – Rat, c.1550
Gebet gegen die Türken, Sonntags nach der Predigt zu verlesen ([Köln: s.n., c. 1550]).
Reference: Policey K 2032; Ratsedikte 61; USTC 2505649
Copies: HAStK, Best. 14 (Edikte): 3, Nr. 151

76. Köln – Rat, c.1550
Gotteslästerung ([Köln: Jaspar von Gennep, c. 1550]).
Reference: Ratsedikte 3878; USTC 2505650
Copies: HAStK, Best. 14 (Edikte): 13, Nr. 116

77. Köln – Rat, c.1550
Prozessionsordnung ([Köln: s.n., c. 1550]).
Reference: Policey K 2028; Ratsedikte 3879; USTC 2506268
Copies: HAStK, Best. 14 (Edikte): 16, Nr. 63; HAStK, Best. 14 (Edikte): 3, Nr. 115

78. Köln – Rat, c.1550
Ordnung eyna Ersamen Raths dieser Loblichen Stat Colne, wie, wo und wanne man das usswendige brot herbeynnen Coln brengen, veyl haben, un verkauffen sall ([Köln: s.n., c. 1550]).
Reference: Policey K 2036; Ratsedikte 3896; USTC 2506272
Copies: HAStK, Best. 90 (Handel): A 349, fol. 7; HAStK, Best. 14 (Edikte): 5, Nr. 121
http://historischesarchivkoeln.de:8080/actaproweb/archive.xhtml?id=Vz++++++00098015hupp#Vz______00098015hupp [9/69]

79. Köln – Rat, c.1550
Brotedikt ([Köln: Jaspar von Gennep, c. 1550]).
Reference: Policey K 2037; Ratsedikte 3896; USTC 2506278
Copies: HAStK, Best. 14 (Edikte): 5, Nr. 123

80. Köln – Rat, c.1550
Schifferordnung ([Köln: Jaspar von Gennep, c. 1550]).
Reference: Policey K 2062; USTC 2506281
Copies: HAStK, Best. 14 (Edikte): 7, Nr. 5; HAStK, Best. 14 (Edikte): 7, Nr. 4

81. Köln – Rat, c.1550
Pest: Formular zur Veranstaltung einer Prozession ([Köln: Jaspar von Gennep, c. 1550]).
Reference: Policey K 2063; Ratsedikte 3879; USTC 2506282
Copies: HAStK, Best. 14 (Edikte): 16, Nr. 62

82. Köln – Rat, c.1550
Guetlich gesynnen an allen pastoren und predicanten, uff der predig stoelen der gemeine Burgerschafft und anhoeren zu vermelden ([Köln: Jaspar von Gennep, c. 1550]).
Reference: Policey K 2064; Ratsedikte 3879; USTC 2506283
Copies: HAStK, Best. 14 (Edikte): 16, Nr. 64

83. Köln – Rat, c.1550
Türkenkrieg: Prozessionen zu veranstalten ([Köln: s.n., c. 1550]).
Reference: Policey K 2065; Ratsedikte 3880; USTC 2506284
Copies: HAStK, Best. 14 (Edikte): 16, Nr. 69

84. Köln – Rat, c.1550
Wie sich ein jeder in Rhumors, Lermens, Tumults, auff- oder Anlauffs, Item Brandts- oder ander Unglückszeiten und Geschrey verhalten soll ([Köln: s.n., c. 1550]).
Reference: Policey K 2067; Ratsedikte 3888; USTC 2506285
Copies: HAStK, Best. 14 (Edikte): 6, Nr. 135; HAStK, Best. 14 (Edikte): 6, Nr. 140; HAStK, Best. 14 (Edikte): 7, Nr. 223

85. Köln – Rat, c.1550
Trinkgefässe des Rates nach dem Gebrauch nicht stehen zu lassen ([Köln: s.n., c. 1550]).
Reference: Policey K 2070; Ratsedikte 3897; USTC 2506287
Copies: HAStK, Best. 14 (Edikte): 20, Nr. 1a

86. Köln – Rat, c.1550
Nachem die nachgesetzte Golt und Silbern Müntzen ußgebotten werden, so soll ezn jder hiemit gewarndt sein, so[e]lch Geltt vor geine Werschafft zuentpfangen nach ußzugeben (Münzordnung mit Abbildung verbotener Münzen ([Köln: Jaspar von Gennep, c. 1550])).
Reference: Policey K 2082 & 2972; Ratsedikte 3889; USTC 2506291
Copies: HAStK, Best. 14 (Edikte): 14, Nr. 33; HAStK, Best. 90 (Handel): A 927, fol. 12
http://historischesarchivkoeln.de:8080/actaproweb/archive.xhtml?id=Vz++++++00098720hupp#Vz______00098720hupp [18/151]

87. Köln – Rat, c.1550
Münzordnung mit Abbildung verbotener Münzen ([Köln: Jaspar von Gennep, c. 1550]).
Reference: Policey K 2085; Ratsedikte 84; USTC 2506293
Copies: HAStK, Best. 14 (Edikte): 14, Nr. 49

88. Köln – Rat, 1553
Wyr Bürgermeistere und Rath der Stadt Collen (Münzverordnung mit Abbildung eines Lütticher Thalers, 12.07.1553) ([Köln]: Jaspar von Gennep, [1553]).
Reference: Policey K 2292; Ratsedikte 69; USTC 2505626

Copies: HAStK, Best. 14 (Edikte): 14, Nr. 26 (handwritten note: 'publiziert d. 12 Julij Anno 53'); USBK, SB1051 (catalogue entry gives the wrong date 1552)
http://www.ub.uni-koeln.de/cdm/ref/collection/rheinmono/id/814405

89. **Köln – Rat,** 1553
Münzverordnung (01.07.1553) ([Köln: Jaspar von Gennep, 1553]).
Reference: Policey K 2291; Ratsedikte 68; USTC 2505655
Copies: HAStK, Best. 14 (Edikte): 14, Nr. 28

90. **Köln – Rat,** 1553
Wyr Bürgermeistere und Rath der Stat Collen doin kunth das alle ußwendigen jre broit zween dage in der wochen under unseren Statt Portzen zu veilem kauff brengen (25.09.1553) ([Köln: Jaspar von Gennep, 1553]).
Reference: Policey K 2296; Ratsedikte 70; USTC 2506406
Copies: HAStK, Best. 90 (Handel): A 349, fol. 8; HAStK, Best. 14 (Edikte): 5, Nr. 124
http://historischesarchivkoeln.de:8080/actaproweb/archive.xhtml?id=Vz++++++00098015hupp#Vz______00098015hupp [10/69]

91. **Köln – Rat,** 1554
Münzordnung ([Köln: Jaspar von Gennep, 1554]).
Reference: Policey K 2299; Ratsedikte 3891; USTC 2506294
Copies: HAStK, Best. 14 (Edikte): 14, Nr. 29

92. **Köln – Rat,** 1555
Münzverordnung und Tabelle (20.01.1555) ([Köln: Jaspar von Gennep, 1555]).
Reference: Policey K 2326; Ratsedikte 72; USTC 2505657
Copies: HAStK, Best. 14 (Edikte): 14, Nr. 30

93. **Köln – Rat,** 1555
Wiedertäufer (10.07.1555) ([Köln: Jaspar von Gennep, 1555]).
Reference: Policey K 2339; Ratsedikte 73; USTC 2505658
Copies: HAStK, Best. 14 (Edikte): 1, Nr. 166; HAStK, Best. 14 (Edikte): 18, Nr. 150

94. **Köln – Rat,** 1555
Schmähschriften, Gotteslästerung (04.12.1555) ([Köln: Jaspar von Gennep, 1555]).
Reference: Policey K 2354; Ratsedikte 76; USTC 2505661

Copies: HAStK, Best. 14 (Edikte): 13, Nr. 112; HAStK, Best. 14 (Edikte): 1, Nr. 128

95. Köln – Rat, 1557
Als nuhe eine zeither alle fruchten ... Demnach gebiete[n] wir ... allen ... so fru[e]chten zu veilhe[m] kauff brengen (12.04.1557) ([Köln: s.n., 1557]).
Reference: Policey K 2388; Ratsedikte 77; USTC 2506407
Copies: HAStK, Best. 90 (Handel): A 349, fol. 12; HAStK, Best. 14 (Edikte): 5, Nr. 109
http://historischesarchivkoeln.de:8080/actaproweb/archive.xhtml?id=Vz++++++00098015hupp#Vz______00098015hupp [15/69]

96. Köln – Rat, 1558
NAch dem das regiment der Stette, durch gutte Pollicei erhaltenn werden muß (Bettler, Leprosen, Säue, 17.10.1558) ([Köln: Jaspar von Gennep, 1558]).
Reference: Policey K 2430; Ratsedikte 78; USTC 2505546
Copies: HAStK, Best. 14 (Edikte): 17, Nr. 147; HAStK, Best. 14 (Edikte): 3, Nr. 144; USBK, Einblattsammlung

97. Köln – Rat, 1559
Wiedertäufer, Ketzer (10.09.1559) ([Köln: s.n., 1559]).
Reference: Policey K 2457 (wrong date); Ratsedikte 83; USTC 2505665
Copies: HAStK, Best. 14 (Edikte): 18, Nr. 152; HAStK, Best. 14 (Edikte): 1, Nr. 167.

98. Köln – Rat, 1559
WyR Burgermeistere un[n] Rath der Stat Co[e]llen doin kunt allen und jegklichen Ußwendigen, so einish Broit ... binnen unse Stat Co[e]llen zu feilhem kauff zu brengen gemeint seindt (00.00.1559) ([Köln: Jaspar von Gennep, 1559]).
Reference: Policey K 2438; Ratsedikte 3896; USTC 2506295
Copies: HAStK, Best. 90 (Handel): A 349, fol. 2; HAStK, Best. 90 (Handel): A 349, fol. 10; HAStK, Best. 90 (Handel): A 349, fol. 9; HAStK, Best. 14 (Edikte): 5, Nr. 122
http://historischesarchivkoeln.de:8080/actaproweb/archive.xhtml?id=Vz++++++00098015hupp#Vz______00098015hupp [4/69]
http://historischesarchivkoeln.de:8080/actaproweb/archive.xhtml?id=Vz++++++00098015hupp#Vz______00098015hupp [11/69]
http://historischesarchivkoeln.de:8080/actaproweb/archive.xhtml?id=Vz++++++00098015hupp#Vz______00098015hupp [12/69]

99. **Köln – Rat,** 1559
Verhaltensedikt (nach 29.11.1559) ([Köln: s.n., 1559]).
Reference: Policey K 2466; USTC 2506296
Copies: HAStK, Best. 50 (Köln und das Reich): 121/10, fol. 7

100. **Köln – Rat,** 1559
Edikt bezüglich Landfrieden (nach 29.11.1559) ([Köln: s.n., 1559]).
Reference: Policey K 2467; USTC 2506297
Copies: HAStK, Best. 50 (Köln und das Reich): 121/10, fol. 12

101. **Köln – Rat,** 1559
Edikt bezüglich Festnahme (nach 29.11.1559) ([Köln: s.n., 1559]).
Reference: Policey K 2468; USTC 2506298
Copies: HAStK, Best. 50 (Köln und das Reich): 121/10, fol. 9; HAStK, Best. 50 (Köln und das Reich): 121/10, fol. 8; HAStK, Best. 50 (Köln und das Reich): 121/10, fol. 6

102. **Köln – Rat,** 1559
WJR Bu[e]rgermeistere un[n] Rath der Stadt Co[e]lle[n] doin … kunth nemlich das alle ußwendige[n] ire Brote zween dage in der wochen … zu veilem kauff brengen (01.09.1559) ([Köln: Jaspar von Gennep, 1559]).
Reference: Policey K 2455; Ratsedikte 82; USTC 2506408
Copies: HAStK, Best. 90 (Handel): A 349, fol. 13; HAStK, Best. 14 (Edikte): 5, Nr. 124a
http://historischesarchivkoeln.de:8080/actaproweb/archive.xhtml?id=Vz++++++00098015hupp#Vz______00098015hupp [16/69]

103. **Köln – Rat,** 1560
Ordnung welcher gestalt die Ober unnd Niderle[n]dische Schiff leut, so des Reynstraums und Kranen dür der Stat Co[e]llen gebrauchen wollen, sich mit ab und anlege[n] auch Lossen und Laden halten sollen (06.03.1560) ([Köln: s.n., 1560]).
Reference: Policey K 2477; Ratsedikte 85; USTC 2506409
Copies: HAStK, Best. 90 (Handel): A 155, fol. 5; HAStK, Best. 14 (Edikte): 16, Nr. 251; HAStK, Best. 14 (Edikte): 16, Nr. 237; HAStK, Best. 14 (Edikte): 16, Nr. 218; DHM 1989/1041
http://historischesarchivkoeln.de:8080/actaproweb/archive.xhtml?id=Vz++++++00097788hupp#Vz______00097788hupp [8/129]

104. **Köln – Rat,** 1561
Taglohntaxen (23.08.1561) ([Köln: Jaspar von Gennep, 1561]).
Reference: Policey K 2509; Ratsedikte 87; USTC 2505667

Copies: HAStK, Best. 30 (Verfassung und Verwaltung): N 751, fol. 12; HAStK, Best. 14 (Edikte): 3, Nr. 184; HAStK, Best. 14 (Edikte): 1, Nr. 186 [part I]; HAStK, Best. 14 (Edikte): 1, Nr. 182 [part II]

105. Köln – Rat, 1562
Münzverordnung mit Abbildung verbotener Münzen ([Köln: Jaspar von Gennep, 1562]).
Reference: Policey K 2474; Ratsedikte 90; USTC 2505670
Copies: HAStK, Best. 14 (Edikte): 14, Nr. 41; HAStK, Best. 14 (Edikte): 14, Nr. 40

106. Köln – Rat, 1564
Wie Bürgermeistere und Rath der Statt Co[e]ln thun kunth allen (Münzverordnung mit Abbildung verbotener Münzen, 31.07.1564) (Köln: Jaspar von Gennep, [1564]).
Reference: Policey K 2569; Ratsedikte 97; USTC 2505624
Copies: HAStK, Best. 90 (Handel): A 927, fol. 1; HAStK, Best. 14 (Edikte): 14, Nr. 35; KSM
http://historischesarchivkoeln.de:8080/actaproweb/archive.xhtml?id=Vz++++++00098720hupp#Vz______00098720hupp [3/151] [part I]
http://historischesarchivkoeln.de:8080/actaproweb/archive.xhtml?id=Vz++++++00098720hupp#Vz______00098720hupp [5/151] [part II]
http://historischesarchivkoeln.de:8080/actaproweb/archive.xhtml?id=Vz++++++00098720hupp#Vz______00098720hupp [6/151] [part III]
http://historischesarchivkoeln.de:8080/actaproweb/archive.xhtml?id=Vz++++++00098720hupp#Vz______00098720hupp [7/151] [part IV]

107. Köln – Rat, 1564
Fischmarkt, Vorkauf von Lachs (25.02.1564) ([Köln: s.n., 1564]).
Reference: Policey K 2561; Ratsedikte 93; USTC 2505673
Copies: HAStK, Best. 14 (Edikte): 5, Nr. 188; HAStK, Best. 14 (Edikte): 3, Nr. 118

108. Köln – Rat, 1565
WJr Burgermeister unnd Rath der Stadt Co[e]ln (Münzverordnung bzw. Verbot gute Münzen auszuführen (07.03.1565) ([Köln: s.n., 1565]).
Reference: Policey K 2584; Ratsedikte 99; USTC 2505623

Copies: HAStK, Best. 14 (Edikte): 14, Nr. 43; HAStK, Best. 14 (Edikte): 3, Nr. 160; USBK, Einblattsammlung, USBK, SB1051 http://www.ub.uni-koeln.de/cdm/ref/collection/rheinmono/id/674076

109. Köln – Rat, 1565
Münzverordnung mit Abbildung von gangbaren und verbotenen Sorten (01.05.1565) (Köln: Gottfried Hirtzhorn d. J., [1565]).
Reference: Policey K 2598; Ratsedikte 100; USTC 2505677
Copies: HAStK, Best. 14 (Edikte): 14, Nr. 42 [part I]; HAStK, Best. 14 (Edikte): 14, Nr. 44 [part II]; HAStK, Best. 14 (Edikte): 14, Nr. 45 [part III]; HAStK, Best. 14 (Edikte): 14, Nr. 46 [part IV]; HAStK, Best. 14 (Edikte): 14, Nr. 47 [part V]

110. Köln – Rat, 1565
Unterrichtsordnung für Primärschulen (07.05.1565) ([Köln: s.n., 1565]).
Reference: Policey K 2599; Ratsedikte 101; USTC 2505678
Copies: HAStK, Best. 14 (Edikte): 6, Nr. 220

111. Köln – Rat, 1566
Wir Burgermeistere und Rath der Stadt Co[e]llen thun kundt die geschwechte geringe und des Reichs ordnung ungemeeß geschlagene Thaler (20.08.1566) ([Köln: s.n., 1566]).
Reference: Ratsedikte 104; USTC 2505455
Copies: KSM (used to be HAStK Best. 14 (Edikte): 14, Nr. 50)

https://www.bildindex.de/document/obj05205006?medium=mi00949e07

112. Köln – Rat, 1566
Wir Bürgermeistere unnd Rath der Stadt Coelln Thun kundt (Münzverordnung 21.05.1566) ([Köln: s.n., 1566]).
Reference: Policey K 2628; Ratsedikte 103; USTC 2505622
Copies: USBK, SB1051; HAStK, Best. 14 (Edikte): 14, Nr. 48

113. Köln – Rat, 1566
Marktverordnung für Vieh (01.09.1566) ([Köln: s.n., 1566]).
Reference: Policey K 2637; Ratsedikte 105; USTC 2505681
Copies: HAStK, Best. 14 (Edikte): 8, Nr. 158

114. Köln – Rat, 1567
Münzverordnung mit Abbildungen und Tabellen der neu geschlagenen Sorten (31.05.1567) ([Köln: s.n., 1567]).

Reference: Policey K 2656; Ratsedikte 107; USTC 2505683
Copies: HAStK, Best. 14 (Edikte): 14, Nr. 53

115. Köln – Rat, 1567
Marktverordnung für Vieh- und Victualieneinfuhr, Geleit (01.09.1567) ([Köln: s.n., 1567]).
Reference: Policey K 2665; Ratsedikte 108; USTC 2505684
Copies: HAStK, Best. 14 (Edikte): 8, Nr. 159; HAStK, Best. 14 (Edikte): 3, Nr. 181

116. Köln – Rat, 1568
Wie Buergermeistere unnd Rath der Statt Coellen (Accisenverordnung für fremdes Mehl und Brot, 06.08.1568) ([Köln: s.n., 1568]).
Reference: Policey K 2714; Ratsedikte 114; USTC 2505459
Copies: HAStK, Best. 14 (Edikte): 8, Nr. 78; HAStK, Best. 14 (Edikte): 1, Nr. 188; USBK, RH Kasten 1549

117. Köln – Rat, 1568
Wir Bürgermesitere unnd Rath der Statt Cöllen (Münzverordnung betreffend minderwertige Sorten, 09.08.1568) ([Köln: s.n., 1568]).
Reference: Policey K 2715; Ratsedikte 115; USTC 2505621
Copies: HAStK, Best. 14 (Edikte): 14, Nr. 52; USBK, SB1051
http://www.ub.uni-koeln.de/cdm/ref/collection/rheinmono/id/695730

118. Köln – Rat, 1568
Ordnung wie sich inwendige unnd ußwendige mit verkauffen unnd ingelden Wilpratz, fliegende und lauffende, vort Eyern, hönern, und anderem Federviehe uff dem Altenmarck und sonsr auch ander Krämer verhalten söllen (16.01.1568) ([Köln: s.n., 1568]).
Reference: Policey K 2681; Ratsedikte 109; USTC 2505685
Copies: HAStK, Best. 90 (Handel): A 550, fol. 46; HAStK, Best. 90 (Handel): A 549, fol. 31–34; HAStK, Best. 14 (Edikte): 5, Nr. 148
http://historischesarchivkoeln.de:8080/actaproweb/archive.xhtml?id=Vz++++++00098246hupp#Vz______00098246hupp [47/161]
http://historischesarchivkoeln.de:8080/actaproweb/archive.xhtml?id=Vz++++++00098245hupp#Vz______00098245hupp [33/48] [part I]
http://historischesarchivkoeln.de:8080/actaproweb/archive.xhtml?id=Vz++++++00098245hupp#Vz______00098245hupp [35/48] [part II]

119. Köln – Rat, 1568
Wir Bürgermeistere und Rath thun kundt unnd nit gestatten, sich infrembde Krigsbewerbüng, sonderlich die so wider die Kön. zu Hispanien zubegeben (09.07.1568) ([Köln: s.n., 1568]).
Reference: Policey K 2707; Ratsedikte 110; USTC 2505687
Copies: HAStK, Best. 14 (Edikte): 1, Nr. 110; Koninklijke Bibliotheek Den Haag KW 1056 K 1 [44]
https://resolver.kb.nl/resolve?urn=urn:gvn:KONB16:130357162

120. Köln – Rat, 1568
Kriegswerbung in fremde Dienste verboten (30.07.1568) ([Köln: s.n., 1568]).
Reference: Policey K 2712 & 2713; Ratsedikte 112; USTC 2505689
Copies: HAStK, Best. 14 (Edikte): 1, Nr. 112; HAStK, Best. 14 (Edikte): 11, Nr. 57

121. Köln – Rat, 1568
Marktverordnung für Vieh (01.09.1568) ([Köln: s.n., 1568]).
Reference: Policey K 2720; Ratsedikte 116; USTC 2505691
Copies: HAStK, Best. 14 (Edikte): 8, Nr. 160

122. Köln – Rat, 1568
Schweine auf den Gassen nicht zu dulden (03.11.1568) ([Köln: s.n., 1568]).
Reference: Policey K 2743; Ratsedikte 117; USTC 2505692
Copies: HAStK, Best. 14 (Edikte): 6, Nr. 265

123. Köln – Rat, 1569
Unse Herren vom Rath wollen hiermit alle und jegliche ingesessen abermals ernstlich gewarnt des Gotslaesteren (28.01.1569) ([Köln: s.n., 1569]).
Reference: Policey K 2759; Ratsedikte 118; USTC 2505542
Copies: HAStK, Best. 14 (Edikte): 13, Nr. 113; HAStK, Best. 14 (Edikte): 1, Nr. 100; USBK, Einblattsammlung

124. Köln – Rat, 1569
Demnach die gemeine drencken auff dem Heumarck, Newmarck, Weitmarck, und anderen zu nutz, In unnd Außwendigen, umb ihre Pferde darin zu drencken (Brunnen- und Tränkenverunreinigung 20.07.1569) ([Köln: s.n., 1569]).
Reference: Policey K 2772; Ratsedikte 120; USTC 2505548
Copies: HAStK, Best. 14 (Edikte): 13, Nr. 140; HAStK, Best. 14 (Edikte): 1, Nr. 59; USBK, Einblattsammlung

125. Köln – Rat, 1569
ALß ein Erbar Rath ... das alle frembde und außwendige ... binnen dreien tagen ... auß dieser Statt hinweg thun und sich weiters darin nicht finden lassen sollen (06.04.1569) ([Köln: s.n., 1569]).
Reference: Policey K 2764; Ratsedikte 119; USTC 2505693
Copies: HAStK, Best. 14 (Edikte): 12, Nr. 31; HAStK, Best. 14 (Edikte): 1, Nr. 17; DHM 1989/1043

126. Köln – Rat, 1569
Ein Erbar Rath dieser Statt Co[e]llen gebieten allen, das niemandes in das Feld noch an den Rein den Kolern und Karren entgegen lauffen oder gehen solle (Steinkohleverkauf, 12.10.1569) ([Köln: s.n., 1569]).
Reference: Policey K 2780; Ratsedikte 121; USTC 2505694
Copies: HAStK, Best. 90 (Handel): A 206, fol. 71; HAStK, Best. 14 (Edikte): 5, Nr. 224
http://historischesarchivkoeln.de:8080/actaproweb/archive.xhtml?id=Vz++++++00097847hupp#Vz______00097847hupp [77/142]

127. Köln – Rat, 1569
Schifferverordnung (21.11.1569) ([Köln: s.n., 1569]).
Reference: Policey K 2786; Ratsedikte 123; USTC 2505696
Copies: HAStK, Best. 14 (Edikte): 16, Nr. 238; HAStK, Best. 14 (Edikte): 16, Nr. 252; HAStK, Best. 90 (Handel): A 539, fol. 3
http://historischesarchivkoeln.de:8080/actaproweb/archive.xhtml?id=Vz++++++00098232hupp#Vz______00098232hupp [8/76]

128. Köln – Rat, 1570
Einfuhrverordnung für Brot und Mehl (13.11.1570) ([Köln: s.n., 1570]).
Reference: Policey K 2817; Ratsedikte 67; USTC 2505654
Copies: HAStK, Best. 14 (Edikte): 8, Nr. 79 (Policey K wrongly lists copies of No. 144)

129. Köln – Rat, c.1570
Marktverordnung: Wild-, Geflügel- und Victualientaxen ([Köln: s.n., c. 1570]).
Reference: Policey K 2027; Ratsedikte 125; USTC 2505699
Copies: HAStK, Best. 14 (Edikte): 3, Nr. 78

130. Köln – Rat, 1570
Fastenverordnung: Fleischverkauf und -essen betreffend (13.02.1570) ([Köln: s.n., 1570]).

Reference: Policey K 2798; Ratsedikte 127; USTC 2505701
Copies: HAStK, Best. 14 (Edikte): 16, Nr. 51 (Policey K 2798 does not list this printed copy)

131. Köln – Rat, 1571
Wir Burgermeistere und Rath der Statt Co[e]lln thun kundt, das ettliche außwendige heimlich ohn verrichtung der gepuerlicher Accinsen ire gutter herin schleiffen, das wir mit gegenwu[e]rtigem verbot dessen sich zuenthalten (22.08.1571) ([Köln: s.n., 1571]).
Reference: Policey K 2844; Ratsedikte 129; USTC 2505703
Copies: HAStK, Best. 90 (Handel): A 520, fol. 51; HAStK, Best. 14 (Edikte): 8, Nr. 41
http://historischesarchivkoeln.de:8080/actaproweb/archive.xhtml?id=Vz++++++00098210hupp#Vz______00098210hupp [48/67]

132. Köln – Rat, 1571
Marktverordnung für Vieh- und Victualieneinfuhr (01.09.1571) ([Köln: s.n., 1571]).
Reference: Policey K 2845; Ratsedikte 131; USTC 2505705
Copies: HAStK, Best. 14 (Edikte): 3, Nr. 179

133. Köln – Rat, 1571
Korneinfuhrverordnung Jülich (19.10.1571) ([Köln: s.n., 1571]).
Reference: Policey K 2853; Ratsedikte 132; USTC 2505706
Copies: HAStK, Best. 14 (Edikte): 3, Nr. 168; HAStK, Best. 14 (Edikte): 3, Nr. 167

134. Köln – Rat, 1571
Accisen (20.08.1571) ([Köln: s.n., 1571]).
Reference: Policey K 2843; USTC 2506301
Copies: HAStK, Best. 95 (Zunft): A 182, Nr. 209
http://historischesarchivkoeln.de:8080/actaproweb/archive.xhtml?id=Vz++++++00000530frehde#Vz______00000530frehde [108/295]

135. Köln – Rat, 1572
Unsere Herren vom Rathe gebiethe[n] allen Bu[e]rgern, das sie sich solchs von Korn und anderen getreide Bra[n]dwein mache[n]s hinfurther gentzlich enthalte[n] (13.01.1572) ([Köln: s.n., 1572]).
Reference: Policey K 2864; Ratsedikte 136; USTC 2505454
Copies: HAStK, Best. 14 (Edikte): 9, Nr. 1; HAStK, Best. 14 (Edikte): 1, Nr. 13; KSM

136. Köln – Rat, 1572
Specification der verbottenen außlendlischen unnd heimischen Müntzen (07.01.1572) ([Köln: s.n., 1572]).
Reference: Policey K 2862; USTC 2505620
Copies: USBK, SB1051 (slightly different edition of No. 141)
http://www.ub.uni-koeln.de/cdm/ref/collection/rheinmono/id/724840

137. Köln – Rat, 1572
Verkaufsverordnung für fremdes Brot (09.01.1572) ([Köln: s.n., 1572]).
Reference: Policey K 2863; Ratsedikte 135; USTC 2505709
Copies: HAStK, Best. 14 (Edikte): 5, Nr. 126

138. Köln – Rat, 1572
Münzverordnung nebst Tabelle der verbotenen und gangbaren Sorten (07.03.1572) ([Köln: s.n., 1572]).
Reference: Policey K 2867; Ratsedikte 138; USTC 2505710
Copies: HAStK, Best. 14 (Edikte): 14, Nr. 56; HAStK, Best. 14 (Edikte): 14, Nr. 54

139. Köln – Rat, 1572
Kriegswerbung von Fremden verboten (23.05.1572) ([Köln: s.n., 1572]).
Reference: Policey K 2878; Ratsedikte 139; USTC 2505711
Copies: HAStK, Best. 14 (Edikte): 11, Nr. 122; HAStK, Best. 14 (Edikte): 3, Nr. 169; HAStK, Best. 14 (Edikte): 3, Nr. 166; HAStK, Best. 14 (Edikte): 3, Nr. 165; HAStK, Best. 14 (Edikte): 1, Nr. 113

140. Köln – Rat, 1572
Als unsere herrn vom Rathe gepieten, das keiner beraubte gudere in diese Statt inprengen und das sich kein burger der Rheuter oder Landtzknechten, so un dieser Statt reiten, mit schmegewort annehmen oder mitwillen zufuegen (18.08.1572) ([Köln: s.n., 1572]).
Reference: Policey K 2885; Ratsedikte 140; USTC 2505712
Copies: HAStK, Best. 14 (Edikte): 1, Nr. 95; HAStK, Best. 14 (Edikte): 11, Nr. 32; HAStK, Best. 14 (Edikte): 1, Nr. 96; DHM Do 94/56
https://www.dhm.de/datenbank/dhm.php?seite=5&fld_0=HA940526

141. Köln – Rat, 1572
Wir Bu[e]rgermeistere und Rath des heiligen Reichs Stadt Co[e]llen thun allen und jeden undern Mitbu[e]rgeren hiermit zuwissen (Münzedikt, 07.01.1572) ([Köln: s.n., 1572]).
Reference: Policey K 2862; USTC 2506303

Copies: HAStK, Best. 90 (Handel): A 921, fol. 87
http://historischesarchivkoeln.de:8080/actaproweb/archive.xhtml?id=Vz++++++00098713hupp#Vz______00098713hupp [103/168]

142. Köln – Rat, 1572
Unsere Herren vom Rathe wollen nachgesetzte ordnung bej geldung uns verkauffung der Fisch nach gelegenheit dieser zeit unverbruchtlich gehalten (01.02.1572) ([Köln: s.n., 1572]).
Reference: Policey K 2865; Ratsedikte 137; USTC 2506410
Copies: HAStK, Best. 90 (Handel): A 323, fol. 8; HAStK, Best. 90 (Handel): A 323, fol. 9; HAStK, Best. 14 (Edikte): 5, Nr. 171; HAStK, Best. 14 (Edikte): 3, Nr. 77; DHM 1989/1045.1
http://historischesarchivkoeln.de:8080/actaproweb/archive.xhtml?id=Vz++++++00097979hupp#Vz______00097979hupp [11/87]
http://historischesarchivkoeln.de:8080/actaproweb/archive.xhtml?id=Vz++++++00097979hupp#Vz______00097979hupp [12/87]

143. Köln – Rat, 1573
Fischordnung ([Köln: s.n., 1573]).
Reference: USTC 2505476
Copies: no copy known (inferred from manuscript notes on DHM 1989/1045.1)

144. Köln – Rat, 1573
Wir Bürgermeister un[n] Rath der Stadt Coelln, doin kunth, das alle ußwendigen ire Broit zween dage in der wochen als Dienstags ung Freitags verkauffen sollen (27.07.1573) ([Köln: s.n., 1573]).
Reference: Policey K 2915; Ratsedikte 143; USTC 2505541
Copies: HAStK, Best. 90 (Handel): A 349, fol. 15; HAStK, Best. 14 (Edikte): 5, Nr. 125; HAStK, Best. 95 (Zunft): A 182, fol. 211; USBK, Einblattsammlung
http://historischesarchivkoeln.de:8080/actaproweb/archive.xhtml?id=Vz++++++00000530frehde#Vz______00000530frehde [109/295]
http://historischesarchivkoeln.de:8080/actaproweb/archive.xhtml?id=Vz++++++00098015hupp#Vz______00098015hupp [18/69]

145. Köln – Rat, 1573
Marktverordnung für einkommendes Vieh und Victualien Geleit (01.09.1573) ([Köln: s.n., 1573]).

Reference: Policey K 2921; Ratsedikte 144; USTC 2505715
Copies: HAStK, Best. 14 (Edikte): 8, Nr. 161; HAStK, Best. 14 (Edikte): 3, Nr. 178

146. Köln – Rat, 1573
Verordnung und Satzung der Keuffe von Christmeß bis an die vasten - Marktverordnung: Wild- und Geflügeltaxen (10.12.1573) ([Köln: s.n., 1573]).
Reference: Policey K 2932; Ratsedikte 146; USTC 2505717
Copies: HAStK, Best. 14 (Edikte): 5, Nr. 149

147. Köln – Rat, 1573
Kundt sei jedermenniglich ... das man ... das Niderlendisch gutte Saltz gefodden An de[n] Stapell und Rein ... uß messen, Daselbst und sunst in der Saltzgassen am aldem und Heumarck ... dasselbig alleyne und kein ander Saltz verkauffen solle (13.04.1573) ([Köln: s.n., 1573]).
Reference: Policey K 2905; USTC 2506304
Copies: HAStK, Best. 90 (Handel): A 398, fol. 5; HAStK, Best. 90 (Handel): A 398, fol. 6
http://historischesarchivkoeln.de:8080/actaproweb/archive.xhtml?id=Vz++++++00098073hupp#Vz______00098073hupp [8/29]
http://historischesarchivkoeln.de:8080/actaproweb/archive.xhtml?id=Vz++++++00098073hupp#Vz______00098073hupp [10/29]

148. Köln – Rat, 1573
Handelsordnung (18.09.1573) ([Köln: s.n., 1573]).
Reference: Policey K 2922; USTC 2506305
Copies: HAStK, Best. 90 (Handel): A 339a, fol. 47

149. Köln – Rat, 1574
Fuhrlohn von der Reingassen in die Statt Holtz, Wein und Steine zu fuehren (30.11.1574) ([Köln: s.n., 1574]).
Reference: Policey K 2956; Ratsedikte 147; USTC 2505718
Copies: HAStK, Best. 14 (Edikte): 7, Nr. 63

150. Köln – Rat, 1574
Fremdenverordnung: Verdächtige und Bettler festzunehmen (17.02.1574) ([Köln: s.n., 1574]).
Reference: Policey K 2935; Ratsedikte 149; USTC 2505720
Copies: HAStK, Best. 14 (Edikte): 1, Nr. 114

151. Köln – Rat, 1574
UNsere Herrn vom Rathe thun hiemit jedermenniglich zu wissen … das hinfurter alle gesaltzen Fischwerck als mit namen, Bollich, Reinfisch, Schollen, Wittingk … gleich den Gro[e]nenfischen mit dem gewichte und pfundt verkaufft werden solle (05.03.1574) ([Köln: s.n., 1574]).
Reference: Policey K 2937; Ratsedikte 150; USTC 2505721
Copies: HAStK, Best. 90 (Handel): A 321, fol. 46; HAStK, Best. 90 (Handel): A 321, fol. 47; HAStK, Best. 90 (Handel): A 321, fol. 48; HAStK, Best. 90 (Handel): A 510, fol. 9; HAStK, Best. 14 (Edikte): 5, Nr. 192; HAStK, Best. 14 (Edikte): 3, Nr. 74; DHM 1989/1046
http://historischesarchivkoeln.de:8080/actaproweb/archive.xhtml?id=Vz++++++00098198hupp#Vz______00098198hupp [9/422]
http://historischesarchivkoeln.de:8080/actaproweb/archive.xhtml?id=Vz++++++00097977hupp#Vz______00097977hupp [58/282]
http://historischesarchivkoeln.de:8080/actaproweb/archive.xhtml?id=Vz++++++00097977hupp#Vz______00097977hupp [59/282]
http://historischesarchivkoeln.de:8080/actaproweb/archive.xhtml?id=Vz++++++00097977hupp#Vz______00097977hupp [60/282]

152. Köln – Rat, 1574
Kundt sey Jedermenniglich daß außsonderer erlaubniß eins Erbaren Raths dieser deß heiligen Reichs Statt Co[e]lln ein offenbar Kauffhauß am Malzbüchel … darinnen allehandt Gu[e]tter zu feilem Kauff und verkauff geben (07.04.1574) ([Köln: s.n., 1574]).
Reference: Policey K 2940; USTC 2506306
Copies: HAStK, Best. 90 (Handel): A 424, fol. 17
http://historischesarchivkoeln.de:8080/actaproweb/archive.xhtml?id=Vz++++++00098104hupp#Vz______00098104hupp [21/138]

153. Köln – Rat, 1574
Fuhrlohn von der Saltzgassen, Haußkrahnen unnd Hasenpfortzen von Wein zu fuehren (30.11.1574) ([Köln: s.n., 1574]).
Reference: Policey K 2957; Ratsedikte 3931; USTC 2506307
Copies: HAStK, Best. 14 (Edikte): 7, Nr. 64

154. Köln – Rat, 1574

Fuhrlohn von der Dranckgassen, Mo[e]hlengassen und Marsilius Krahnen Holtz, Wein und Steine zu fuehren (30.11.1574) ([Köln: s.n., 1574]).

Reference: Policey K 2958; Ratsedikte 147; USTC 2506308

Copies: HAStK, Best. 14 (Edikte): 7, Nr. 65

155. Köln – Rat, 1574

Zu wissen sey jeidermenniglich, Demnach ein Erbar Rathe … wo[e]llen alle unnd jede Ochssen kauffleuthe ernstlich gewarnet haben, das sie sich des vorkauffs der Ochssen Kauffleuthen zwischen wegs nit abgelden, oder vorkauff mache[n] (02.09.1574) ([Köln: s.n., 1574]).

Reference: Policey K 2953; Ratsedikte 153; USTC 2506411

Copies: HAStK, Best. 90 (Handel): A 339, fol. 103; HAStK, Best. 14 (Edikte): 8, Nr. 199; HAStK, Best. 14 (Edikte): 3, Nr. 183 http://historischesarchivkoeln.de:8080/actaproweb/archive.xhtml?id=Vz++++++00097996hupp#Vz______00097996hupp [98/231]

156. Köln – Rat, 1574

Ordnung wie sich In unnd ußwendige mit verkauffen und ingelden Wilpratz fliegende und lauffende vort Eyern, Ho[e]nern und andern Feder viche … uff dem Altenmarck und sonst auch ander Krämer sich verhalten sollen (10.12.1574) ([Köln: s.n., 1574]).

Reference: Policey K 2960; Ratsedikte 154; USTC 2506412

Copies: HAStK, Best. 90 (Handel): A 549, fol. 44–47; HAStK, Best. 14 (Edikte): 5, Nr. 150 http://historischesarchivkoeln.de:8080/actaproweb/archive.xhtml?id=Vz++++++00098245hupp#Vz______00098245hupp [46/48] [part I] http://historischesarchivkoeln.de:8080/actaproweb/archive.xhtml?id=Vz++++++00098245hupp#Vz______00098245hupp [48/48] [part II]

157. Köln – Rat, 1574

Kundt und zuwissen sei Jedermenniglich … das in betzalung schuldiger wein Aczins von in und ußwendigen allerhandt ungepur gebraucht. Als haben darinnb unsere herrn vom Rathe die altie verdrege in ordnung zustellen bevhole[n] (03.05.[15]74) ([Köln: s.n., 1574]).

Reference: Policey K 2945; Ratsedikte 151; USTC 2506463

Copies: HAStK, Best. 90 (Handel): A 439, fol. 39; HAStK, Best. 90 (Handel): A 439, fol. 48; HAStK, Best. 90 (Handel): A 439, fol. 94;

HAStK, Best. 90 (Handel): A 439, fol. 95; HAStK, Best. 90 (Handel): A 439, fol. 244; HAStK, Best. 90 (Handel): A 437, fol. 36; HAStK, Best. 14 (Edikte): loses Blatt; HAStK, Best. 14 (Edikte): 9, Nr. 51; HAStK, Best. 14 (Edikte): 3, Nr. 39
http://historischesarchivkoeln.de:8080/actaproweb/archive.xhtml?id=Vz++++++00098121hupp#Vz______00098121hupp [42/245]
http://historischesarchivkoeln.de:8080/actaproweb/archive.xhtml?id=Vz++++++00098121hupp#Vz______00098121hupp [52/245]
http://historischesarchivkoeln.de:8080/actaproweb/archive.xhtml?id=Vz++++++00098121hupp#Vz______00098121hupp [98/245]
http://historischesarchivkoeln.de:8080/actaproweb/archive.xhtml?id=Vz++++++00098121hupp#Vz______00098121hupp [100/245]
http://historischesarchivkoeln.de:8080/actaproweb/archive.xhtml?id=Vz++++++00098121hupp#Vz______00098121hupp [242/245]
http://historischesarchivkoeln.de:8080/actaproweb/archive.xhtml?id=Vz++++++00098119hupp#Vz______00098119hupp [39/312]

158. Köln – Rat, 1575
Auff begeren eines Erbarn Raths. Soll der Herr Pastor nehsten Sondags … verkundigen (Brunnen und Viehtränken nicht verunreinigen, 03.08.1575) ([Köln: Maternus Cholinus, 1575]).
Reference: Policey K 3002; Ratsedikte 157; USTC 2505547
Notes: produced in 50–60 copies for which Cholinus received 1 Taler, see printer's invoice (fig. 4.3.)
Copies: HAStK, Best. 14 (Edikte): 13, Nr. 142; HAStK, Best. 14 (Edikte): 1, Nr. 63; USBK, Einblattsammlung

159. Köln – Rat, 1575
Auff begeren eins Erbaren Radts der Stadt Cöllen. SOllen die Herrn Pastoren … negst Sondag … verkundigen - Öffentliches Gebet für den verstorbenen Jung-Graf Carl Friedrich von Jülich angeordnet (00.03.1575) ([Köln: s.n., 1575]).
Reference: Policey K 2991; Ratsedikte 155; USTC 2505723
Copies: HAStK, Best. 14 (Edikte): 16, Nr. 73 ('jüngst verlauffen Monat Februaris)

160. Köln – Rat, 1575

Kundt unnd zu wissen sey iedermenniglich ... gebieten ... unsere Herrn allen ... dz sie ... ire Leinendoich ... in das Leinen kaufhauß uf dem Aldenmarckt furen (25.11.1575) ([Köln: Maternus Cholinus, 1575]).
Reference: Policey K 3008; Ratsedikte 163; USTC 2505730
Notes: produced in 50–60 copies for which Cholinus received 1 Taler, see printer's invoice (fig. 4.3.)
Copies: HAStK, Best. 90 (Handel): A 79, fol. 12; HAStK, Best. 90 (Handel): A 79, fol. 13; HAStK, Best. 90 (Handel): A 382, fol. 56; HAStK, Best. 14 (Edikte): 8, Nr. 42
http://historischesarchivkoeln.de:8080/actaproweb/archive.xhtml?id=Vz++++++00097700hupp#Vz______00097700hupp [15/95]
http://historischesarchivkoeln.de:8080/actaproweb/archive.xhtml?id=Vz++++++00097700hupp#Vz______00097700hupp [16/95]

161. Köln – Rat, c.1575

Ordnung auff dem Aldenmarckt belangende das Standtgelt und was die Brotwieger, Ko[e]ch, die Gewalterichters Diener und die vier Klocken auff die Ordnung und Roll schweren sollen ([Köln: s.n., c. 1575]).
Reference: Policey K 2968; USTC 2506309
Copies: HAStK, Best. 90 (Handel): A 356, fol. 7; HAStK, Best. 90 (Handel): A 549, fol. 41–43
http://historischesarchivkoeln.de:8080/actaproweb/archive.xhtml?id=Vz++++++00098245hupp#Vz______00098245hupp [42/48] [part I]
http://historischesarchivkoeln.de:8080/actaproweb/archive.xhtml?id=Vz++++++00098245hupp#Vz______00098245hupp [44/48] [part II]
http://historischesarchivkoeln.de:8080/actaproweb/archive.xhtml?id=Vz++++++00098025hupp#Vz______00098025hupp [9/47] [part I]

162. Köln – Rat, c.1575

Ordnung auff dem alten Mart belandende das Standtgelt und was die Brotweiger, Ko[e]ch, die Gewaltreichters Diener und die vier Klocken auff die ordnung und Roll schweren sollen ([Köln: s.n., c. 1575]).
Reference: Policey K 2968 (different edition); USTC 2506310
Copies: HAStK, Best. 90 (Handel): A 552, fol. 26
http://historischesarchivkoeln.de:8080/actaproweb/archive.xhtml?id=Vz++++++00098249hupp#Vz______00098249hupp [26/108]

163. Köln – Rat, c.1575
Ersetzte Ordnung der Beletter von 6 Fahnen ([Köln: s.n., c. 1575]).
Reference: Policey K 2975; Ratsedikte 3885; USTC 2506312
Notes: pamphlet
Copies: HAStK, Best. 14 (Edikte): 6, Nr. 66

164. Köln – Rat, c.1575
Articuln, so den Burgeren anfangks und generaliter sollen fürgehaltten werden ([Köln: s.n., c. 1575]).
Reference: Policey K 2976 (also wrongly listed as Policey K 2029); Ratsedikte 3884; USTC 2506313
Notes: pamphlet
Copies: HAStK, Best. 14 (Edikte): 6, Nr. 75

165. Köln – Rat, 1576
Uff begeren eins Erbaren Rhats der Statt Co[e]llen (Bettlerverordnung, 08.02.1576) ([Köln: Maternus Cholinus, 1576]).
Reference: Policey K 3014; Ratsedikte 166; USTC 2505544
Notes: produced in 50–60 copies for which Cholinus received 1 Taler, see printer's invoice (fig. 4.3.)
Copies: HAStK, Best. 295 (Geistliche Abteilung): Mappe 32, fol. 60; HAStK, Best. 14 (Edikte): 17, Nr. 149; HAStK, Best. 14 (Edikte): 1, Nr. 22; USBK, Einblattsammlung

166. Köln – Rat, 1576
Ordnung wie in Brandtznoethen, Wapengeschei und hendelen gegen den verbundtbrieff ein jeder Burger und Inwoner dieser Stadt sich halten, und auff watt Platzen die Burgerschafft sich versamblen solle (Brand- und Wehrordnung, 16.11.1576) ([Köln: Maternus Cholinus, 1576]).
Reference: Policey K 3036; Ratsedikte 172; USTC 2505571
Copies: HAStK, Best. Best. 30 (Verfassung und Verwaltung): N 20, fol. 1; HAStK, Best. 14 (Edikte): 6, Nr. 137; HAStK, Best. 14 (Edikte): 3, Nr. 58; USBK, Einblattsammlung; DHM Do 94/68

167. Köln – Rat, 1576
Krahnenverordnung (09.01.1576) ([Köln: Maternus Cholinus, 1576]).
Reference: Policey K 3011; Ratsedikte 164; USTC 2505731
Notes: produced in 50–60 copies for which Cholinus received 1 Taler, see printer's invoice (fig. 4.3.)
Copies: HAStK, Best. 14 (Edikte): 16, Nr. 219; HAStK, Best. 14 (Edikte): 3, Nr. 154; HAStK, Best. 14 (Edikte): 3, Nr. 104

168. **Köln – Rat,** 1576
Geleit für Niederländer beim Einbringen von Gütern und Proviant (30.03.1576) ([Köln: Maternus Cholinus, 1576]).
Reference: Policey K 3016; Ratsedikte 167; USTC 2505732
Notes: produced in 50–60 copies for which Cholinus received 1 Taler, see printer's invoice (fig. 4.3.)
Copies: HAStK, Best. 14 (Edikte): 3, Nr. 163; HAStK, Best. 14 (Edikte): 3, Nr. 87

169. **Köln – Rat,** 1576
Marktverordnung betreffend Einfuhr von Vieh (01.09.1576) ([Köln: Maternus Cholinus, 1576]).
Reference: Policey K 3030; Ratsedikte 169; USTC 2505733
Copies: HAStK, Best. 14 (Edikte): 8, Nr. 162

170. **Köln – Rat,** 1576
Zu wissen sey jedermenniglich, als unsere Herrn vom Rathe mit Ernste[m] bevelch dern hieunden abcontrafeiten Thaller fur Wertschafft keinen zu empfangen, noch ußzugeben oder einzuschleiffen (18.04.1576) ([Köln: Maternus Cholinus, 1576]).
Reference: Policey K 3019; USTC 2506315
Notes: produced in 50–60 copies for which Cholinus received 1 Taler, see printer's invoice (fig. 4.3.)
Copies: HAStK, Best. 90 (Handel): A 927, fol. 10
http://historischesarchivkoeln.de:8080/actaproweb/archive.xhtml?id=Vz++++++00098720hupp#Vz______00098720hupp [15/151]

171. **Köln – Rat,** 1576
Zu wissen sey allen, das keiner in oder fur dieser Statt kein Westphelisch, Lunenburgisch, Hessisch oder dergleichen Saltz groß noch mit fasseren klein verkaufen sollen (27.01.1576) ([Köln: Maternus Cholinus, 1576]).
Reference: Policey K 3016; Ratsedikte 167; USTC 2506413
Notes: produced in 50–60 copies for which Cholinus received 1 Taler, see printer's invoice (fig. 4.3.)
Copies: HAStK, Best. 90 (Handel): A 398, fol. 7; HAStK, Best. 90 (Handel): A 398, fol. 8; HAStK, Best. 90 (Handel): A 398, fol. 9; HAStK, Best. 14 (Edikte): 13, Nr. 187; HAStK, Best. 14 (Edikte): 3, Nr. 152
http://historischesarchivkoeln.de:8080/actaproweb/archive.xhtml?id=Vz++++++00098073hupp#Vz______00098073hupp [11/29]

http://historischesarchivkoeln.de:8080/actaproweb/archive.xhtml?id=Vz++++++00098073hupp#Vz______00098073hupp [12/29]
http://historischesarchivkoeln.de:8080/actaproweb/archive.xhtml?id=Vz++++++00098073hupp#Vz______00098073hupp [13/29]

172. Köln – Rat, 1577
Wir Burgermeister und Rhat des heiligen Reichs Statt Collen (Münzverordnung mit Abbildungen, 26.08.1577) ([Köln: Maternus Cholinus, 1577]).
Reference: Policey K 3062; Ratsedikte 177; USTC 2505615
Copies: HAStK, Best. 14 (Edikte): 14, Nr. 62; USBK, SB1051
http://www.ub.uni-koeln.de/cdm/ref/collection/rheinmono/id/671977

173. Köln – Rat, 1577
Wir Burgermeistere und Rathe der Statt Coelln (Münzverordnung mit Abbildungen, 27.05.1577) ([Köln: Maternus Cholinus, 1577]).
Reference: Policey K 3053; Ratsedikte 175; USTC 2505616
Copies: HAStK, Best. 14 (Edikte): 14, Nr. 61; USBK, SB1051
http://www.ub.uni-koeln.de/cdm/ref/collection/rheinmono/id/721263

174. Köln – Rat, 1577
Wir Burgermeistere und Rathe des Heil[igen] Reichs Statt Coelln (Münzverordnung betreffend die minderwertigen Münzen, 09.01.1577) ([Köln: Maternus Cholinus, 1577]).
Reference: Policey K 3044; Ratsedikte 173; USTC 2505618
Copies: HAStK, Best. 14 (Edikte): 14, Nr. 59; USBK, SB1051
http://www.ub.uni-koeln.de/cdm/ref/collection/rheinmono/id/700795

175. Köln – Rat, 1577
Münzverordnung mit Abbildungen (19.04.1577) ([Köln: Maternus Cholinus, 1577]).
Reference: Policey K 3051; Ratsedikte 174; USTC 2505736
Copies: HAStK, Best. 14 (Edikte): 14, Nr. 60

176. Köln – Rat, 1577
Münzverordnung betreffend gefälschte Sorten (05.08.1577) ([Köln: Maternus Cholinus, 1577]).
Reference: Policey K 3059; Ratsedikte 176; USTC 2505737
Copies: HAStK, Best. 14 (Edikte): 14, Nr. 63

177. Köln – Rat, 1577
Marktverordnung für Vieh und Proviant (01.09.1577) ([Köln: Maternus Cholinus, 1577]).
Reference: Policey K 3063; Ratsedikte 180; USTC 2505740
Copies: HAStK, Best. 14 (Edikte): 8, Nr. 165

178. Köln – Rat, 1578
Wir Burgermeister und Rathe deß H[eiligen] Reichs Statt Coeln, thun kundt (Münzverordnung mit Abbildung der verbotenen Sorten, 13.06.1578) ([Köln: Maternus Cholinus, 1578]).
Reference: Policey K 3077; Ratsedikte 190; USTC 2505611
Copies: HAStK, Best. 14 (Edikte): 14, Nr. 69; USBK, SB1051; USBK, Einblattsammlung
http://www.ub.uni-koeln.de/cdm/ref/collection/rheinmono/id/728366

179. Köln – Rat, 1578
Kundt sey Jedermenniglich, daß unsere Hern vom Rathe (Münzverordnung betreffend verbotene neue Thaler, 12.03.1578) ([Köln: Maternus Cholinus, 1578]).
Reference: Policey K 3081 ; Ratsedikte 188; USTC 2505612
Copies: HAStK, Best. 14 (Edikte): 14, Nr. 68; USBK, SB1051
http://www.ub.uni-koeln.de/cdm/ref/collection/rheinmono/id/705388

180. Köln – Rat, 1578
Wir Burgermeistere unnd Rhate der Statt Co[e]lln (Münzverordnung betreffend verbotene Sorten mit Abbildungen, 13.01.1578) ([Köln: Maternus Cholinus, 1578]).
Reference: Policey K 3076; Ratsedikte 184; USTC 2505613
Copies: HAStK, Best. 14 (Edikte): 14, Nr. 67; USBK, SB1051 (2 copies)
http://www.ub.uni-koeln.de/cdm/ref/collection/rheinmono/id/720529
http://www.ub.uni-koeln.de/cdm/ref/collection/rheinmono/id/727638

181. Köln – Rat, 1578
Kundt sey jedermenniglich, das unsere Herrn vom Rathe greiflich spüren (Münzverordnung betreffend die Scheidemünze, 01.01.1578) ([Köln: Maternus Cholinus, 1578]).
Reference: Policey K 3074; Ratsedikte 182; USTC 2505614
Copies: HAStK, Best. 14 (Edikte): 14, Nr. 65; USBK, SB1051

182. Köln – Rat, 1578
Münzverordnung mit Abbildungen verbotener Sorten (30.08.1578) ([Köln: Maternus Cholinus, 1578]).
Reference: Policey K 3095; Ratsedikte 179; USTC 2505739
Copies: HAStK, Best. 14 (Edikte): 14, Nr. 70

183. Köln – Rat, 1578
UNsere Hern vom Rade spuren in der that, das durch etliche Muntzwexler undoegliche heller zum Hern Berge oder woe dieselbe gemuntz heringebracht … solche heller … hie durch verbieten (22.01.1578) ([Köln: Maternus Cholinus, 1578]).
Reference: Policey K 3078; Ratsedikte 185; USTC 2505743
Copies: HAStK, Best. 90 (Handel): A 927, fol. 13; HAStK, Best. 14 (Edikte): 14, Nr. 66
http://historischesarchivkoeln.de:8080/actaproweb/archive.xhtml?id=Vz++++++00098720hupp#Vz______00098720hupp [19/151]

184. Köln – Rat, 1578
Rolle und Ordnung, was ein jeglich Stueck ahm Kran auß oder in zu Kranen zubezalen schueldig ist (Krahnenverordnung und Taxe, 28.01.1578) ([Köln: Maternus Cholinus, 1578]).
Reference: Policey K 3079; Ratsedikte 186; USTC 2505744
Copies: HAStK, Best. 14 (Edikte): 16, Nr. 220; DHM 1989/1047
https://www.dhm.de/datenbank/dhm.php?seite=5&fld_0=NN000662

185. Köln – Rat, 1578
Münzverordnung betreffend minderwerthige Bergische Groschen (12.02.1578) ([Köln: Maternus Cholinus, 1578]).
Reference: Policey K 3080; Ratsedikte 187; USTC 2505745
Copies: HAStK, Best. 14 (Edikte): 14, Nr. 64c

186. Köln – Rat, 1578
Sonntagsruhe und Feierabend (30.05.1578) ([Köln: Maternus Cholinus, 1578]).
Reference: Policey K 3085; Ratsedikte 189; USTC 2505746
Copies: HAStK, Best. 14 (Edikte): 17, Nr. 200; HAStK, Best. 14 (Edikte): 3, Nr. 88

187. Köln – Rat, 1578
Begräbnissverordnung (08.08.1578) ([Köln: Maternus Cholinus, 1578]).
Reference: Policey K 3090; Ratsedikte 191; USTC 2505747

Copies: HAStK, Best. 14 (Edikte): 16, Nr. 1; HAStK, Best. 14 (Edikte): 1, Nr. 35

188. Köln – Rat, 1578
Wiedertäufer, Ketzer, Buchdrucker (10.12.1578) ([Köln: Maternus Cholinus, 1578]).
Reference: Policey K 2052 & 3110; Ratsedikte 193; USTC 2505748
Copies: HAStK, Best. 7030 (Chroniken und Darstellungen): 187a, fol. 130r; HAStK, Best. 14 (Edikte): 18, Nr. 153; HAStK, Best. 14 (Edikte): 1, Nr. 169

189. Köln – Rat, 1578
Anzeigepflicht von Faßbindern (12.09.1578) ([Köln: Maternus Cholinus, 1578]).
Reference: Policey K 3097; USTC 2506316
Copies: HAStK, Best. 95 (Zunft): A 428, S. 187
http://historischesarchivkoeln.de:8080/actaproweb/archive.xhtml?id=Vz++++++00000885frehde#Vz______00000885frehde [87/222]

190. Köln – Rat, 1578
Kundt und zu wissen sey jedermenniglich, das keine Weine in, durch, oder auß der Stadt gefurt, es werden dan erstlich Kranmeisteren geliefferet (03.10.1578) ([Köln: Maternus Cholinus, 1578]).
Reference: Policey K 3099; Ratsedikte 192; USTC 2506414
Copies: HAStK, Best. 90 (Handel): A 539, fol. 4; HAStK, Best. 90 (Handel): A 439, fol. 117; HAStK, Best. 90 (Handel): A 155, fol. 8; HAStK, Best. 14 (Edikte): 9, Nr. 90
http://historischesarchivkoeln.de:8080/actaproweb/archive.xhtml?id=Vz++++++00098232hupp#Vz______00098232hupp [10/76]
http://historischesarchivkoeln.de:8080/actaproweb/archive.xhtml?id=Vz++++++00097788hupp#Vz______00097788hupp [12/129]
http://historischesarchivkoeln.de:8080/actaproweb/archive.xhtml?id=Vz++++++00098121hupp#Vz______00098121hupp [123/245]

191. Köln – Rat, 1579
Kundt sey jedermenniglich, demnach unsere Herrn vom Rathe mit zu thun und gutachten der Wein Aczinß halbert (27.03.1579) ([Köln: Maternus Cholinus, 1579]).
Reference: Policey K 3120; Ratsedikte 196; USTC 2505564

Copies: HAStK, Best. 90 (Handel): A 439, fol. 113; HAStK, Best. 90 (Handel): A 439, fol. 114; HAStK, Best. 14 (Edikte): 9, Nr. 52; HAStK, Best. 14 (Edikte): 3, Nr. 40; USBK, Einblattsammlung http://historischesarchivkoeln.de:8080/actaproweb/archive.xhtml?id=Vz++++++00098121hupp#Vz______00098121hupp [119/245]
http://historischesarchivkoeln.de:8080/actaproweb/archive.xhtml?id=Vz++++++00098121hupp#Vz______00098121hupp [120/245]

192. Köln – Rat, 1579
Strassenreinigung, Zusammenrotten verboten (30.03.1579) ([Köln: Maternus Cholinus, 1579]).
Reference: Policey K 3121; Ratsedikte 197; USTC 2505751
Copies: HAStK, Best. 14 (Edikte): 7, Nr. 224; HAStK, Best. 14 (Edikte): 1, Nr. 19

193. Köln – Rat, 1579
Münzverordnung mit Abbildungen verbotener Sorten (19.05.1579) ([Köln: Maternus Cholinus, 1579]).
Reference: Policey K 3125; Ratsedikte 198; USTC 2505752
Copies: HAStK, Best. 14 (Edikte): 14, Nr. 74

194. Köln – Rat, 1579
Qualifikationsverordnung (20.07.1579) ([Köln: Maternus Cholinus, 1579]).
Reference: Policey K 3134; Ratsedikte 199; USTC 2505753
Copies: HAStK, Best. 14 (Edikte): 12, Nr. 32

195. Köln – Rat, 1579
Marktverordnung betreffend Vieh und Proviant (01.09.1579) ([Köln: Maternus Cholinus, 1579]).
Reference: Policey K 3139; Ratsedikte 201; USTC 2505755
Copies: HAStK, Best. 14 (Edikte): 8, Nr. 166

196. Köln – Rat, 1579
Geleit für Niederländer (28.09.1579) ([Köln: Maternus Cholinus, 1579]).
Reference: Policey K 3140; USTC 2505756
Copies: HAStK, Best. 14 (Edikte): 8, Nr. 164;

197. Köln – Rat, 1579
Schiffladungsverordnung für Niederländer (09.10.1579) ([Köln: Maternus Cholinus, 1579]).

Reference: Policey K 3141; Ratsedikte 203; USTC 2505757
Copies: HAStK, Best. 14 (Edikte): 3, Nr. 253; HAStK, Best. 14 (Edikte): 3, Nr. 239; HAStK, Best. 14 (Edikte): 3, Nr. 103

198. Köln – Rat, 1579
Wollentuch betreffend gerechte Tücher und Teufelsfarbe (31.10.1579) ([Köln: Maternus Cholinus, 1579]).
Reference: Policey K 3142; Ratsedikte 204; USTC 2505758
Copies: HAStK, Best. 95 (Zunft): A 29, S. 113; HAStK, Best. 14 (Edikte): 7, Nr. 22; HAStK, Best. 14 (Edikte): 1, Nr. 165
http://historischesarchivkoeln.de:8080/actaproweb/archive.xhtml?id=Vz++++++00000261frehde#Vz______00000261frehde [103/348]

199. Köln – Rat, 1580
Kundt sey jedermenniglich, das unseren Herrn vom Rathe gewißlich furkommen, das Alter gueter Ordnung zu wider, wenig Kolen in die Maß geliebert, sondern in Stecken ungemessen verkaufft werden (Steinkohlen- und Holz-Verkaufsverordnung, 24.10.1580) ([Köln: Maternus Cholinus, 1580]).
Reference: Policey K 3163; Ratsedikte 210; USTC 2505461
Copies: HAStK, Best. 90 (Handel): A 206, fol. 82; HAStK, Best. 14 (Edikte): 5, Nr. 225; HAStK, Best. 14 (Edikte): 3, Nr. 100; USBK, RH Kasten 1567; DHM Do 94/57
http://historischesarchivkoeln.de:8080/actaproweb/archive.xhtml?id=Vz++++++00097847hupp#Vz______00097847hupp [88/142]
https://www.dhm.de/datenbank/dhm.php?seite=5&fld_0=HA940537

200. Köln – Rat, 1580
Auff begeren eins Erbaren Raths SOl der Herr Pastor nechst Sontag von der Cantzel, der Gemeinde verkündigen (Brandverordnung: Wasser an die Häuser zu stellen, 02.11.1580) ([Köln: Maternus Cholinus, 1580]).
Reference: Policey K 3166 (wrong date); Ratsedikte 212; USTC 2505562
Copies: HAStK, Best. 30 (Verfassung und Verwaltung): N 862, fol. 3; HAStK, Best. 14 (Edikte): 1, Nr. 5; USBK, Einblattsammlung; DHM 1989/1107

201. Köln – Rat, c.1580
Münzverordnung nebst Abbildung verbotener Sorten ([Köln: Maternus Cholinus, 1580]).
Reference: Policey K 2083; Ratsedikte 207; USTC 2505761

Copies: HAStK, Best. 14 (Edikte): 14, Nr. 36 (mit Münzen aus dem Jahre 1579)

202. Köln – Rat, 1580
Kundt und zuwissen sey allen Gaffeln, Personen, biß die sich geburlich qualificiert, kein gebot zuthun (15.01.1580) ([Köln: Maternus Cholinus, 1580]).
Reference: Policey K 3145; Ratsedikte 208; USTC 2505762
Copies: HAStK, Best. 14 (Edikte): 12, Nr. 33; HAStK, Best. 14 (Edikte): 1, Nr. 191; HAStK, Best. 14 (Edikte): 1, Nr. 75; HAStK, Best. 14 (Edikte): 1, Nr. 74; DHM 1989/1049
https://www.dhm.de/datenbank/dhm.php?seite=5&fld_0=NN000660

203. Köln – Rat, 1580
Pollerwerth-Bau (18.11.1580) ([Köln: Maternus Cholinus, 1580]).
Reference: Policey K 3167; Ratsedikte 213; USTC 2505763
Copies: HAStK, Best. 14 (Edikte): 16, Nr. 134; HAStK, Best. 14 (Edikte): 3, Nr. 119a

204. Köln – Rat, 1580
Kundt und zu wissen sey jedermenniglich, das unsere Herrn vom Rathe gepieten alle enthalten sollen, einige wahren oder Gu[e]ttere ohne Zeichen auß zu arbeiten oder tragen zu lassen (Acciseordnung, 18.03.1580) ([Köln: Maternus Cholinus, 1580]).
Reference: Policey K 3149; Ratsedikte 209; USTC 2506415
Copies: HAStK, Best. 90 (Handel): A 155, fol. 20; HAStK, Best. 90 (Handel): A 155, fol. 19; HAStK, Best. 90 (Handel): A 155, fol. 18; HAStK, Best. 90 (Handel): A 155, fol. 17; HAStK, Best. 90 (Handel): A 155, fol. 16; HAStK, Best. 14 (Edikte): 16, Nr. 268; HAStK, Best. 14 (Edikte): 3, Nr. 109
http://historischesarchivkoeln.de:8080/actaproweb/archive.xhtml?id=Vz++++++00097788hupp#Vz______00097788hupp [20/129]
http://historischesarchivkoeln.de:8080/actaproweb/archive.xhtml?id=Vz++++++00097788hupp#Vz______00097788hupp [22/129]
http://historischesarchivkoeln.de:8080/actaproweb/archive.xhtml?id=Vz++++++00097788hupp#Vz______00097788hupp [26/129]
http://historischesarchivkoeln.de:8080/actaproweb/archive.xhtml?id=Vz++++++00097788hupp#Vz______00097788hupp [27/129]

http://historischesarchivkoeln.de:8080/actaproweb/archive.xhtml?id=Vz++++++00097788hupp#Vz______00097788hupp [28/129]

205. Köln – Rat, 1581
Unsere Herrn vom Rathe wollen nachgesetzte Ordnung bey geldung vnd verkauffung der Fisch nach gelegenheit diser zeyt vnuerbrüchlich gehalten haben auff ernste straff der jhenigen so dargegen thun oder sträfflich befunden werden (12.02.1581) ([Köln: Maternus Cholinus, 1581]).
Reference: Policey K 3172; Ratsedikte 215; USTC 751478
Copies: HAStK, Best. 90 (Handel): A 323, fol. 10; HAStK, Best. 90 (Handel): A 323, fol. 11; HAStK, Best. 14 (Edikte): 5, Nr. 176; Bayerische Staatsbibliothek München, Res/Slg.Faust 11
http://historischesarchivkoeln.de:8080/actaproweb/archive.xhtml?id=Vz++++++00097979hupp#Vz______00097979hupp [13/87]
http://historischesarchivkoeln.de:8080/actaproweb/archive.xhtml?id=Vz++++++00097979hupp#Vz______00097979hupp [14/87]
http://bsbipad.bsb.lrz.de/nas/einblattdrucke/350000011_0_r.pdf

206. Köln – Rat, 1581
Fuhrlohn von der Saltzgassen, Haußkrahnen, Hasenpfort von Wein zu fuehren (28.06.1581) ([Köln: Maternus Cholinus, 1581]).
Reference: Policey K 3191; Ratsedikte 218; USTC 2505450
Copies: HAStK, Best. 90 (Handel): A 560, fol. 17; HAStK, Best. 14 (Edikte): 7, Nr. 68; KSM
http://historischesarchivkoeln.de:8080/actaproweb/archive.xhtml?id=Vz++++++00098258hupp#Vz______00098258hupp [23/195]

207. Köln – Rat, 1581
Nachdem der Hochwurdigster Fuerst unnd Herr, Her Gebhardt, Ertzbischoffen deß Ertzstiffts Coelln (Schiessspiel am Severinsthor, 01.08.1581) ([Köln: Maternus Cholinus, 1581]).
Reference: Policey K 3196; Ratsedikte 222; USTC 2505465
Copies: HAStK, Best. 14 (Edikte): 17, Nr. 3; USBK, Einblattsammlung; HAStK, Best. 30/N (Nachträge), A N/479, fol. 21; HAStK, Best. 30/N (Nachträge), A N/479, fol. 22
http://historischesarchivkoeln.de:8080/actaproweb/archive.xhtml?id=Vz++++++00132966Paprless#Vz______00132966Paprless [8/178]

http://historischesarchivkoeln.de:8080/actaproweb/archive.xhtml?id=Vz++++++00132966Paprless#Vz______00132966Paprless [9/178]

208. Köln – Rat, 1581
Wjr Burgermeistere und Rath deß heiligen Reichs freier Statt Cöln (Einladung zum Schießspiel, 17.03.1581) ([Köln: Maternus Cholinus, 1581]).
Reference: USTC 2507575
Copies: HAStK, Best. 30/N (Nachträge), A N/486, fol. 2 [part I], HAStK, Best. 30/N (Nachträge), A N/486, fol. 3 [part II]; HAStK, Best. 30/N, (Nachträge), A N/486, fol. 4 [part III], http://historischesarchivkoeln.de:8080/actaproweb/archive.xhtml?id=Vz++++++00132968Paprless#Vz______00132968Paprless [5, 6, 7 & 8 /27]

209. Köln – Rat, 1581
Als unsere Herrn vom Rathe bericht, daß durch und bey dem Klotzwerffen und schiessen auff dem Graben vil gefahr unnd muthwille zubesorgen (18.04.1581) ([Köln: Maternus Cholinus, 1581]).
Reference: Policey K 3178; Ratsedikte 216; USTC 2505561
Copies: HAStK, Best. 14 (Edikte): 13, Nr. 8; HAStK, Best. 14 (Edikte): 1, Nr. 107; USBK, Einblattsammlung; DHM 1989/1050

210. Köln – Rat, 1581
Kundt und zu wissen sey jedermenniglich, daß unsere Herrn vom Rathe (Münzverordnung betreffend geringer Sorten 20.01.1581) ([Köln: Maternus Cholinus, 1581]).
Reference: Policey K 3171; Ratsedikte 214; USTC 2505610
Copies: HAStK, Best. 14 (Edikte): 14, Nr. 76; USBK, SB1051 http://www.ub.uni-koeln.de/cdm/ref/collection/rheinmono/id/706936

211. Köln – Rat, 1581
Münzverordnung, minderwerthige Sorten betreffend (22.05.1581) ([Köln: Maternus Cholinus, 1581]).
Reference: Policey K 3183; Ratsedikte 217; USTC 2505764
Copies: HAStK, Best. 14 (Edikte): 14, Nr. 73

212. Köln – Rat, 1581
Münzverordnung mit Abbildungen verbotener Sorten (07.07.1581) ([Köln: Maternus Cholinus, 1581]).

Reference: Policey K 2080& 3192; Ratsedikte 219 & 3889; USTC 2505765
Copies: HAStK, Best. 14 (Edikte): 14, Nr. 77; HAStK, Best. 14 (Edikte): 14, Nr. 31, USBK SB1051
http://www.ub.uni-koeln.de/cdm/ref/collection/rheinmono/id/721450

213. Köln – Rat, 1581
Brandverordnung, Peter Vinkels-Feuer verboten; Wasser vor die Häuser zu stellen (21.07.1581) ([Köln: Maternus Cholinus, 1581]).
Reference: Policey K 3193; Ratsedikte 220; USTC 2505766
Copies: HAStK, Best. 30 (Verfassung und Verwaltung): N 20, fol. 18; HAStK, Best. 30 (Verfassung und Verwaltung): N 20, fol. 17; HAStK, Best. 14 (Edikte): 1, Nr. 7; HAStK, Best. 14 (Edikte): 6, Nr. 172; HAStK, Best. 14 (Edikte): 6, Nr. 139

214. Köln – Rat, 1581
Münzverordnung betreffend Verschlechterung (31.07.1581) ([Köln: Maternus Cholinus, 1581]).
Reference: Policey K 3195; Ratsedikte 221; USTC 2505767
Copies: HAStK, Best. 14 (Edikte): 14, Nr. 75

215. Köln – Rat, 1581
Poller Werth (01.09.1581) ([Köln: Maternus Cholinus, 1581]).
Reference: Policey K 3200; Ratsedikte 224; USTC 2505769
Copies: HAStK, Best. 14 (Edikte): 16, Nr. 135

216. Köln – Rat, 1581
Schiessen in der Stadt mit Büchsen verboten bei Tag und Nacht (06.09.1581) ([Köln: Maternus Cholinus, 1581]).
Reference: Policey K 3202; Ratsedikte 225; USTC 2505770
Copies: HAStK, Best. 14 (Edikte): 13, Nr. 11; HAStK, Best. 14 (Edikte): 1, Nr. 32

217. Köln – Rat, 1581
Vertrag und Ernewerung ettlicher Alten Statuten und Ordnung (08.09.1581) ([Köln: Maternus Cholinus, 1581]).
Reference: Policey K 3204; Ratsedikte 226; USTC 2505771
Copies: HAStK, Best. 14 (Edikte): 12, Nr. 6; HAStK, Best. 14 (Edikte): 3, Nr. 70; HAStK, Best. 30 (Verfassung und Verwaltung): N 376, fol. 1

218. Köln – Rat, 1581
Gaffelverordnung: Notare und Anwälte haben einer Gaffel beizutreten (13.09.1581) ([Köln: Maternus Cholinus, 1581]).
Reference: Policey K 3206; Ratsedikte 228; USTC 2505773
Copies: HAStK, Best. 30 (Verfassung und Verwaltung): V 66 III, S. 160–161; HAStK, Best. 30 (Verfassung und Verwaltung): G 133, fol. 19; HAStK, Best. 30 (Verfassung und Verwaltung): G 133, fol. 18; HAStK, Best. 30 (Verfassung und Verwaltung): G 133, fol. 17; HAStK, Best. 14 (Edikte): 12, Nr. 225; HAStK Best. 14 (Edikte): 12, Nr. 7

219. Köln – Rat, 1581
Schützenordnung (17.05.1581) ([Köln: Maternus Cholinus, 1581]).
Reference: Policey K 3182; USTC 2506319
Copies: HAStK, Best. 30 (Verfassung und Verwaltung): N 486, fol. 3

220. Köln – Rat, 1581
Beherbergungsverordnung (12.06.1581) ([Köln: Maternus Cholinus, 1581]).
Reference: Policey K 3185; USTC 2506321
Copies: HAStK, Reformationsakten 5, fol. 49; HAStK, Best. 14 (Edikte): 29, Nr. 3

221. Köln – Rat, 1581
Fuhrlohn von der Reingassen in der statt Holtz, Wein und Stein zu fuehren (28.06.1581) ([Köln: Maternus Cholinus, 1581]).
Reference: Policey K 3190; Ratsedikte 218; USTC 2506322
Copies: HAStK, Best. 14 (Edikte): 7, Nr. 67; HAStK, Best. 90 (Handel): A 560, fol. 16; HAStK, Best. 90 (Handel): A 560, fol. 15
http://historischesarchivkoeln.de:8080/actaproweb/archive.xhtml?id=Vz++++++00098258hupp#Vz______00098258hupp [21/195]
http://historischesarchivkoeln.de:8080/actaproweb/archive.xhtml?id=Vz++++++00098258hupp#Vz______00098258hupp [22/195]

222. Köln – Rat, 1581
Drackgaß, Muellengaß und Marsilius Kranen Holtz, wein und Stein zu fuehren (28.06.1581) ([Köln: Maternus Cholinus, 1581]).
Reference: Policey K 3189; Ratsedikte 218; USTC 2506323
Copies: HAStK, Best. 14 (Edikte): 7, Nr. 66

223. Köln – Rat, 1582
Wir Burgermeistere und Rath, vort alle Raethe, und die Vier un viertzige deß Heiligen Reichs freyer Stadt Coelln (Verwahrung des Rathes gegen verhetzende Patente des Kurfürsten 28.11.1582) ([Köln: Maternus Cholinus, 1582]).
Reference: Policey K 3252; Ratsedikte 241; USTC 2505572
Notes: Policey K 3252 does not list any of the printed copies
Copies: HAStK, Best. 14 (Edikte): loses Blatt; USBK, SB1051

224. Köln – Rat, 1582
Wir Burgermeistere unnd Rathe des Heil. Reichs freyer Statt Coelln (Münzverordnung betreffend schlechter Sorten 14.05.1582) ([Köln: Maternus Cholinus, 1582]).
Reference: Policey K 3227; Ratsedikte 235; USTC 2505608
Copies: HAStK, Best. 14 (Edikte): 14, Nr. 80; USBK, SB1051
http://www.ub.uni-koeln.de/cdm/ref/collection/rheinmono/id/708916

225. Köln – Rat, 1582
Zu wissen sey jedermenniglich, das eine newe Sort von Thaler, under deß Furstenthumbs Gerle gepre[n]g. Derowege[n] denselben fur wertschafft nicht auß zugeben (21.03.1582) ([Köln: Maternus Cholinus, 1582]).
Reference: Policey K 3222; Ratsedikte 232; USTC 2505609
Copies: HAStK, Best. 14 (Edikte): 14, Nr. 81; HAStK, Best. 90 (Handel): A 927, fol. 15; HAStK, Best. 14 (Edikte): 14, Nr. 77a; USBK, SB1051
http://historischesarchivkoeln.de:8080/actaproweb/archive.xhtml?id=Vz++++++00098720hupp#Vz______00098720hupp [22/151]
http://www.ub.uni-koeln.de/cdm/ref/collection/rheinmono/id/706939

226. Köln – Rat, 1582
Accisen-Hintergehung: Waren unter fremden Namen nicht abzunehmen (27.01.1582) ([Köln: Maternus Cholinus, 1582]).
Reference: Policey K 3215; Ratsedikte 229; USTC 2505774
Copies: HAStK, Best. 14 (Edikte): 8, Nr. 80; HAStK, Best. 14 (Edikte): 3, Nr. 41

227. Köln – Rat, 1582
Münzverordnung mit Tabelle der gangbaren Sorten (28.01.1582) ([Köln: Maternus Cholinus, 1582]).

Reference: Policey K 3216; Ratsedikte 230; USTC 2505775
Copies: HAStK, Best. 14 (Edikte): 14, Nr. 79

228. Köln – Rat, 1582
Kaiserliche oder päpstliche Mandate nicht ohne das Vorwissen des Rathes zu verkündigen (23.04.1582) ([Köln: Maternus Cholinus, 1582]).
Reference: Policey K 3225; Ratsedikte 233; USTC 2505777
Copies: HAStK, Best. 30 (Verfassung und Verwaltung): N 376, fol. 4; HAStK, Best. 30 (Verfassung und Verwaltung): N 376, fol. 3; HAStK, Best. 14 (Edikte): 12, Nr. 226; HAStK, Best. 14 (Edikte): 3, Nr. 71

229. Köln – Rat, 1582
Strassenverunreinigung durch Schutt verboten (06.06.1582) ([Köln: Maternus Cholinus, 1582]).
Reference: Policey K 3234; Ratsedikte 236; USTC 2505778
Copies: HAStK, Best. 14 (Edikte): 6, Nr. 277

230. Köln – Rat, 1582
Wachtsteuer (20.08.1582) ([Köln: Maternus Cholinus, 1582]).
Reference: Policey K 3246; Ratsedikte 238; USTC 2505779
Copies: HAStK, Best. 14 (Edikte): 9, Nr. 106

231. Köln – Rat, 1582
Zu wissen sey iedermenniglich, das unsern Herrn vom Rathe fu[e] rkommen das alle Burger vilberuhrten Hering fur auffrecht liefferbar Kauffmanns gutt un[n] also dur nießbare gutte Speiß halten sollen ohne argelist (05.03.1582) ([Köln: Maternus Cholinus, 1582]).
Reference: Policey K 3219; USTC 2506324
Copies: HAStK, Best. 90 (Handel): A 510, fol. 16
http://historischesarchivkoeln.de:8080/actaproweb/archive.xhtml?id=Vz++++++00098198hupp#Vz______00098198hupp [16/422]

232. Köln – Rat, 1582
Nachdem unsere Herrn vom Rathe dieser des heiligen Reichs freyer Statt Cölln vielen Außländischen die beywohnung gestattet ... Derwegen jenen un[n] andern außländisch[en] die unser Religion nit sein lenger nit vertrwen soll (06.08.1582) ([Köln: Maternus Cholinus, 1582]).
Reference: Policey K 3244; Ratsedikte 237; USTC 2506417
Copies: HAStK, Best. 14 (Edikte): 16, Nr. 101; HAStK, Best. 14 (Edikte): 12, Nr. 34; HAStK, Best. 14 (Edikte): 3, Nr. 66; HAStK,

Best. 14 (Edikte): 3, Nr. 15; HAStK, Best. 14 (Edikte): 1, Nr. 76; HAStK, Best. 14 (Edikte): 1, Nr. 77

233. Köln – Rat, 1582
Nachdem Graff Adolff von Neuwenar - Ketzerische Schriften und Predigten verboten (28.08.1582) ([Köln: Maternus Cholinus, 1582]).
Reference: Policey K 3247; Ratsedikte 239; USTC 2506418
Copies: HAStK, Best. 14 (Edikte): 6, Nr. 192

234. Köln – Rat, 1582
Diesen uhralten verdrag sal man zu allen halven Jaren uff den Gaffelen gleich na dem Verbundt brieff lesen. Dat man geine brieffe die van frembden Herrn, Edel off onedel kommen up den Gaffeln lesen sall (26.11.1582) ([Köln: Maternus Cholinus, 1582]).
Reference: Policey K 3251; Ratsedikte 240; USTC 2506419
Copies: HAStK, Best. 14 (Edikte): 12, Nr. 8; HAStK, Best. 14 (Edikte): 7, Nr. 87; HAStK, Best. 14 (Edikte): 3, Nr. 153; HAStK, Best. 14 (Edikte): 3, Nr. 14; HAStK, Best. 14 (Edikte): 1, Nr. 94

235. Köln – Rat, 1583
Kundt sey jedermenniglich, demnach unsere Herrn vom Rathe wie sie dan under anderen vorsorgunge auch die Kettewacht verordnet (23.08.1583) ([Köln: Maternus Cholinus, 1583]).
Reference: Policey K 3282; Ratsedikte 249; USTC 2505559
Copies: HAStK, Best. 14 (Edikte): 6, Nr. 119; HAStK, Best. 30 (Verfassung und Verwaltung): N 20, fol. 8; USBK, Einblattsammlung

236. Köln – Rat, 1583
Krahnenordnung (08.02.1583) ([Köln: Maternus Cholinus, 1583]).
Reference: Policey K 3262; Ratsedikte 244; USTC 2505781
Copies: HAStK, Best. 14 (Edikte): 3, Nr. 114

237. Köln – Rat, 1583
Beraubung von Schiffen (08.02.1583) ([Köln: Maternus Cholinus, 1583]).
Reference: Policey K 3262; Ratsedikte 245 & 246; USTC 2505782
Copies: HAStK, Best. 14 (Edikte): 1, Nr. 46; HAStK, Best. 14 (Edikte): 16, Nr. 274

238. Köln – Rat, 1583
Münzverordnung nebst Abbildungen verbotener Heller (09.03.1583) ([Köln: Maternus Cholinus, 1583]).

Reference: Policey K 3266; Ratsedikte 247; USTC 2505784
Copies: HAStK, Best. 14 (Edikte): 14, Nr. 78

239. Köln – Rat, 1583
Pulver ohne Wissen des Raths nicht in die Stadt zu bringen (26.04.1583) ([Köln: Maternus Cholinus, 1583]).
Reference: Ratsedikte 248; USTC 2505785
Copies: HAStK, Best. 14 (Edikte): 3, Nr. 121; HAStK, Best. 14 (Edikte): 1, Nr. 126

240. Köln – Rat, 1583
Raubgüter nicht einzubringen (07.09.1583) ([Köln: Maternus Cholinus, 1583]).
Reference: Ratsedikte 250; USTC 2505786
Copies: HAStK, Best. 14 (Edikte): 11, Nr. 35

241. Köln – Rat, 1583
Wacht Ordnung (00.10.1583) ([Köln: Maternus Cholinus, 1583]).
Reference: Policey K 3290; Ratsedikte 252; USTC 2505787
Notes: pamphlet
Copies: HAStK, Best. 14 (Edikte): 6, Nr. 67

242. Köln – Rat, 1583
Gregorianische Kalenderverbesserung (28.10.1583) ([Köln: Maternus Cholinus, 1583]).
Reference: Policey K 3296; Ratsedikte 253; USTC 2505788
Copies: HAStK, Best. 14 (Edikte): 5, Nr. 29
https://www.bildindex.de/document/obj05243132

243. Köln – Rat, 1583
Pforten-Wachtordnung für loses Gesindel und Bettler (07.12.1583) ([Köln: Maternus Cholinus, 1583]).
Reference: Policey K 3299; Ratsedikte 254; USTC 2505789
Copies: HAStK, Best. 14 (Edikte): 17, Nr. 81; HAStK, Best. 14 (Edikte): 11, Nr. 33; HAStK, Best. 14 (Edikte): 1, Nr. 23

244. Köln – Rat, 1583
Wachtordnung: Kriegsartikel für die Pforten (17.10.1583) ([Köln: Maternus Cholinus, 1583]).
Reference: Policey K 3291; Ratsedikte 3887; USTC 2506325
Copies: HAStK, Best. 30 (Verfassung und Verwaltung): N 20, fol. 9; HAStK, Best. 14 (Edikte): 6, Nr. 70

245. Köln – Rat, 1583

Edikt wider der Ketzerei (25.10.1583) ([Köln: Maternus Cholinus, 1583]).

Reference: Policey K 3294; USTC 2506326

Copies: HAStK, Reformationsakten 5, fol. 119a

246. Köln – Rat, 1583

Ordnung von Sechs Fahnen zu Wachen ([Köln: Maternus Cholinus, 1583]).

Reference: Policey K 3259 (also wrongly listed as Policey K 2030); Ratsedikte 3885; USTC 2506420

Notes: pamphlet

Copies: HAStK, Best. 33 (Militaria): A 45, fol. 144 f.; HAStK, Best. 33 (Militaria): A 45, fol. 142 f.; HAStK, Best. 14 (Edikte): 3, Nr. 133; HAStK, Best. 14 (Edikte): 6, Nr. 65

247. Köln – Rat, 1583

Nachdem ein Erbar Rath in erfahrung kommen, etliche Fürsten und Graven die Statt Co[e]lln begeben wo[e]llen, hat ein Rath nachfolgende Wachtordnung bey nächtlicher weil zuhalten ernstlich gebotten (29.01.1583) ([Köln: Maternus Cholinus, 1583]).

Reference: Policey K 3260; USTC 2506421

Notes: pamphlet

Copies: HAStK, Best. 33 (Militaria), A 53/Militaria, Bd. 46, fol. 61; HAStK, Best. 30 (Verfassung und Verwaltung): N 677, fol. 4 f.; HAStK, Best. 30 (Verfassung und Verwaltung): N 20, fol. 6 f.; HAStK, Best. 30 (Verfassung und Verwaltung): N 20, fol. 4 f.; HAStK, Best. 30 (Verfassung und Verwaltung): N 20, fol. 2 f.; HAStK, Best. 14 (Edikte): 6, Nr. 69; HAStK, Best. 14 (Edikte): 6, Nr. 68

http://historischesarchivkoeln.de:8080/actaproweb/archive.xhtml?id=Vz++++++00099408hupp#Vz______00099408hupp [65/440]

http://historischesarchivkoeln.de:8080/actaproweb/archive.xhtml?id=Vz++++++00099408hupp#Vz______00099408hupp [66/440]

248. Köln – Rat, 1583

Wir Burgermeistere un[n] Rathe thun hiemitt kundt, daß sich keinder inn dieser gefahrlicher zeitt in frembder herrn dienste usserhalb dieser Stadt begeben solle (25.09.1583) ([Köln: Maternus Cholinus, 1583]).

Reference: Policey K 3289; Ratsedikte 251; USTC 2506422
Copies: HAStK, Best. 14 (Edikte): 11, Nr. 59; HAStK, Best. 14 (Edikte): 1, Nr. 115

249. Köln – Rat, 1584
Der verordneten Schreiber ahn den Pfortten Befelch unnd Eydt (01.06.1584) ([Köln: Maternus Cholinus, 1584]).
Reference: Policey K 3329; USTC 2505477
Copies: HAStK, Best. 30 (Verfassung und Verwaltung): N 256; DHM 1989/1051
https://www.dhm.de/datenbank/dhm.php?seite=5&fld_0=NN000658

250. Köln – Rat, 1584
Wir Buergermeistere unnd Rathe des Heill[igen] Reichs Freyer Statt Colln (Münzverordnung mit Abbildungen der minderwertigen Sorten, 25.10.1584) ([Köln: Maternus Cholinus, 1584]).
Reference: Policey K 3344; Ratsedikte 265; USTC 2505606
Copies: HAStK, Best. 14 (Edikte): 14, Nr. 83; USBK, SB1051
http://www.ub.uni-koeln.de/cdm/ref/collection/rheinmono/id/709856

251. Köln – Rat, 1584
Wir Buergermeistere unnd Rathe des Heyl. Reichs Stadt Coelln (Münzverordnung mit Abbildungen minderwertiger Sorten, 28.05.1584) ([Köln: Maternus Cholinus, 1584]).
Reference: Policey K 3327; Ratsedikte 259; USTC 2505607
Copies: HAStK, Best. 14 (Edikte): 14, Nr. 82; USBK, SB1051
http://www.ub.uni-koeln.de/cdm/ref/collection/rheinmono/id/708966

252. Köln – Rat, 1584
Ruhestörung (02.01.1584) ([Köln: Maternus Cholinus, 1584]).
Reference: Policey K 3302; Ratsedikte 255; USTC 2505790
Copies: HAStK, Best. 14 (Edikte): 7, Nr. 225

253. Köln – Rat, 1584
Kundt und zu wissen sey, dz keiner an den Pfortzen oder ausserhalb der Statt einige Kriegs Oberster, Befelchshabere mitt schmehe oder boßhafften wortten zu belaidigen (23.01.1584) ([Köln: Maternus Cholinus, 1584]).
Reference: Policey K 3306; Ratsedikte 257; USTC 2505792
Copies: HAStK, Best. 14 (Edikte): 13, Nr. 117; DHM Do 94/58
https://www.dhm.de/datenbank/dhm.php?seite=5&fld_0=HA940535

254. Köln – Rat, 1584
Wallgrabenverordnung betreffend Baumfrevel und Viehweide (11.07.1584) ([Köln: Maternus Cholinus, 1584]).
Reference: Policey K 3331; Ratsedikte 261; USTC 2505793
Copies: HAStK, Best. 14 (Edikte): 6, Nr. 1

255. Köln – Rat, 1584
Judengeleit aufzusagen (12.07.1584) ([Köln: Maternus Cholinus, 1584]).
Reference: Policey K 3332; Ratsedikte 262; USTC 2505794
Copies: HAStK, Best. 14 (Edikte): 7, Nr. 272; HAStK, Best. 14 (Edikte): 3, Nr. 139

256. Köln – Rat, 1584
Marktordnung für Vieh (11.10.1584) ([Köln: Maternus Cholinus, 1584]).
Reference: Policey K 3341; Ratsedikte 263; USTC 2505795
Copies: HAStK, Best. 90 (Handel): A 339a, fol. 48; HAStK, Best. 14 (Edikte): 8, Nr. 239

257. Köln – Rat, 1584
Accise für Wein (12.10.1584) ([Köln: Maternus Cholinus, 1584]).
Reference: Policey K 3342; Ratsedikte 264; USTC 2505796
Copies: HAStK, Best. 14 (Edikte): 9, Nr. 84

258. Köln – Rat, 1584
Handelsverordnung (22.02.1584) ([Köln: Maternus Cholinus, 1584]).
Reference: Policey K 3310; USTC 2506327
Copies: HAStK, Best. 14 (Edikte): 11, Nr. 34

259. Köln – Rat, 1584
Kundt und zuwissen sey Jedermenniglich. Nach dem unsere Herrn vom Rathe … wegen der schu[e]ldiger Accinsen deß Brandtweins und Essigs … viele verkürtzung … furgenommen… als habenn … unsere Herren vom Rathe diese … Ordnung verdragen und beschlossen (13.04.1584) ([Köln: Maternus Cholinus, 1584]).
Reference: Policey K 3322; Ratsedikte 258; USTC 2506423
Copies: HAStK, Best. 90 (Handel): A 74, fol. 6; HAStK, Best. 90 (Handel): A 74, fol. 5; HAStK, Best. 14 (Edikte): 9, Nr. 2; HAStK, Best. 14 (Edikte): 3, Nr. 45; HAStK, Best. 14 (Edikte): 3, Nr. 10
http://historischesarchivkoeln.de:8080/actaproweb/archive.xhtml?id=Vz++++++00097693hupp#Vz______00097693hupp
[9 & 11/75]

260. Köln – Rat, 1584
Wir Bu[e]rgermeistere unnd Rath … Thun kundt … Das wir … den hundersten pfenning und andere geburniß … ein unnd bey zu brengen … beschlossen (01.06.1584) ([Köln: Maternus Cholinus, 1584]).
Reference: Policey K 3328; Ratsedikte 260; USTC 2506424
Copies: HAStK, Best. 90 (Handel): A 520, fol. 48; HAStK, Best. 14 (Edikte): 8, Nr. 43; HAStK, Best. 14 (Edikte): 3, Nr. 113; HAStK, Best. 14 (Edikte): 3, Nr. 96; HAStK, Best. 14 (Edikte): 3, Nr. 9 http://historischesarchivkoeln.de:8080/actaproweb/archive.xhtml?id=Vz++++++00098210hupp#Vz______00098210hupp [45/67]

261. Köln – Rat, 1585
Unsere Herrn vom Rathe spueren den groessen Mißbrauch, so Donnerstags und Freitags auff dem Marckt … und gepieten darumb … das deß Do[n]erstags auff dem Thumhoff keinem Fremden mit eintzigen noch mit Herden Ochsen zu gelden vergu[e]n[n]t (21.10.1585) ([Köln: Maternus Cholinus, 1585]).
Reference: Policey K 3374; Ratsedikte 272; USTC 2505545
Copies: HAStK, Best. 90 (Handel): A 339a, fol. 50; HAStK, Best. 14 (Edikte): 8, Nr. 210; HAStK, Best. 14 (Edikte): 3, Nr. 180; USBK, Einblattsammlung; DHM 1989/1054
https://www.dhm.de/datenbank/dhm.php?seite=5&fld_0=NN000655

262. Köln – Rat, 1585
Nachdem unsere Herrn vom Rathe bevelhen, das alle vor zwentzig Jahren angenommene Burgere, in Schrifften mit Namen und anzeige uberbringen sollen (Fremdenordnung, 29.05.1585) ([Köln: Maternus Cholinus, 1585]).
Reference: Policey K 3364; Ratsedikte 268; USTC 2505566
Copies: HAStK, Best. 30 (Verfassung und Verwaltung): N 404, fol. 1; HAStK, Best. 30 (Verfassung und Verwaltung): N 342, fol. 13–16; HAStK, Best. 14 (Edikte): 12, Nr. 35; HAStK, Best. 14 (Edikte): 1, Nr. 79; HAStK, Best. 14 (Edikte): 1, Nr. 78; USBK, Einblattsammlung; DHM 1989/1053
https://www.dhm.de/datenbank/dhm.php?seite=5&fld_0=NN000656

263. Köln – Rat, 1585
Nachdem wir Burgermeistere un Rath eine Wachtordnung publiciern lassen, wollen wir dieselbige von newes bestettigt haben (16.05.1585) ([Köln: Maternus Cholinus, 1585]).
Reference: Policey K 3361; Ratsedikte 266; USTC 2505797

Copies: HAStK, Best. 33 (Militaria), A 53/Militaria, Bd. 46, fol. 64; HAStK, Best. 14 (Edikte): 6, Nr. 71; HAStK, Best. 14 (Edikte): 1, Nr. 6; DHM 1989/1052
http://historischesarchivkoeln.de:8080/actaproweb/archive.xhtml?id=Vz++++++00099408hupp#Vz______00099408hupp
[67/440]

264. Köln – Rat, 1585
Wacht- und Fremdenordnung: tägliche Listen einzureichen (27.05.1585) ([Köln: Maternus Cholinus, 1585]).
Reference: Policey K 3362; Ratsedikte 267; USTC 2505798
Copies: HAStK, Best. 30 (Verfassung und Verwaltung): N 404, fol. 2; HAStK, Best. 30 (Verfassung und Verwaltung): N 342, fol. 12; HAStK, Best. 30 (Verfassung und Verwaltung): N 342, fol. 11; HAStK, Best. 14 (Edikte): 17, Nr. 82; HAStK, Best. 14 (Edikte): 3, Nr. 164

265. Köln – Rat, 1585
Sonntagsruhe: Hausirhandel verboten (09.08.1585) ([Köln: Maternus Cholinus, 1585]).
Reference: Policey K 3367; Ratsedikte 269; USTC 2505799
Copies: HAStK, Best. 14 (Edikte): 13, Nr. 105

266. Köln – Rat, 1585
Marktverordnung betreffend Vieh und Proviant (01.09.1585) ([Köln: Maternus Cholinus, 1585]).
Reference: Policey K 3371; Ratsedikte 270; USTC 2505800
Copies: HAStK, Best. 14 (Edikte): 8, Nr. 167

267. Köln – Rat, 1585
Nach vleißiger Deliberation … vermögh voriger … Edicten keine … verdechtige Leutte mehr auß dem Niderlanden hie in die Statt [zu lassen, auch nicht] die Wiedertheuffer und andere … verbandte Leute (18.09.1585) ([Köln: Maternus Cholinus, 1585]).
Reference: Policey K 3372; Ratsedikte 271; USTC 2506425
Copies: HAStK, Best. 33 (Militaria), A 53/Militaria, Bd. 46, fol. 65; HAStK, Best. 30 (Verfassung und Verwaltung): N 342, fol. 17; HAStK, Best. 14 (Edikte): 18, Nr. 155; HAStK, Best. 14 (Edikte): 12, Nr. 36; HAStK, Best. 14 (Edikte): 1, Nr. 172; HAStK, Best. 14 (Edikte): 1, Nr. 151
http://historischesarchivkoeln.de:8080/actaproweb/archive.xhtml?id=Vz++++++00099408hupp#Vz______00099408hupp
[68/440]

268. Köln – Rat, 1586
Rolle und Ordnung, was ein jeglich Stuck ahm Krain auß oder in zu Krainen zubetzalen schuldig ist (Krahnenverordnung und -Taxe, 05.11.1586) ([Köln: Maternus Cholinus, 1586]).
Reference: Policey K 3405; Ratsedikte 281; USTC 2505808
Copies: HAStK, Best. 14 (Edikte): 16, Nr. 221

269. Köln – Rat, 1586
Kaiserliche Verordnung Kölner Kaufleute zu Wasser und Land nicht zu belästigen (07.11.1586) ([Köln: Maternus Cholinus, 1586]).
Reference: Policey K 3406; Ratsedikte 278 & 282; USTC 2505809
Copies: HAStK, Best. 14 (Edikte): 3, Nr. 97, HAStK, Best. 14 (Edikte): 16, Nr. 132

270. Köln – Rat, 1586
Wachtverordnung betreffend Holz und Licht (26.11.1586) ([Köln: Maternus Cholinus, 1586]).
Reference: Policey K 3407; Ratsedikte 285; USTC 2505812
Copies: HAStK, Best. 14 (Edikte): 6, Nr. 72; HAStK, Best. 14 (Edikte): 1, Nr. 156

271. Köln – Rat, 1586
Pfortenordnung (26.04.1586) ([Köln: Maternus Cholinus, 1586]).
Reference: Policey K 3385; USTC 2506328
Copies: HAStK, Best. 30 (Verfassung und Verwaltung): N 20, fol. 10

272. Köln – Rat, 1586
Unsere Herrn vom Rathe gebieten, das man auff den Gaffeln keine frembde oder auch jhenige von Neuß, den Außlegern, oder auch ander verbotten Kriegsbewerbung sich beygefügt gehabt, auff noch ahnnemen, vilweniger beeyden (08.10.1586) ([Köln: Maternus Cholinus, 1586]).
Reference: Policey K 3402; Ratsedikte 280; USTC 2506426
Copies: HAStK, Best. 14 (Edikte): 12, Nr. 37; HAStK, Best. 14 (Edikte): 1, Nr. 118; HAStK, Best. 14 (Edikte): 1, unfoliiert zwischen fol. 8 und 12

273. Köln – Rat, 1587
Rolle und Ordnung was ein jeglich Stueck ahm Kran auß oder in zu Kranen zuzalen schueldig ist (28.01.1587) ([Köln: Maternus Cholinus, 1587]).
Reference: Policey K 3419; Ratsedikte 288; USTC 2505462
Copies: HAStK, Best. 14 (Edikte): 16, Nr. 222; USBK, RH Kasten 1570

274. Köln – Rat, 1587
Fuhrlohn von der Rheingassen in der Statt Holtz, Wein und Stein zu fuehren (00.00.1587) ([Köln: Maternus Cholinus, 1587]).
Reference: Policey K 3415; Ratsedikte 286; USTC 2505813
Copies: HAStK, Best. 14 (Edikte): 7, Nr. 69

275. Köln – Rat, 1587
Münzverordnung nebst Abbildungen verbotener Sorten (23.11.1587) ([Köln: Maternus Cholinus, 1587]).
Reference: Policey K 3451; Ratsedikte 287; USTC 2505814
Copies: HAStK, Best. 14 (Edikte): 14, Nr. 85

276. Köln – Rat, 1587
Accise-Freiheit der Geistlichen (24.04.1587) ([Köln: Maternus Cholinus, 1587]).
Reference: Policey K 3435; Ratsedikte 292; USTC 2505816
Copies: HAStK, Best. 14 (Edikte): 29, Nr. 4; HAStK, Best. 14 (Edikte): 8, Nr. 82

277. Köln – Rat, 1587
Fuhrlohntaxe für Holz (25.04.1587) ([Köln: Maternus Cholinus, 1587]).
Reference: Policey K 3436; Ratsedikte 293; USTC 2505817
Copies: HAStK, Best. 14 (Edikte): 7, Nr. 70

278. Köln – Rat, 1587
Postverordnung (Henott) (22.05.1587) ([Köln: Maternus Cholinus, 1587]).
Reference: Policey K 3438; Ratsedikte 295; USTC 2505818
Copies: HAStK, Best. 14 (Edikte): 13, Nr. 178; HAStK, Best. 14 (Edikte): 3, Nr. 119b

279. Köln – Rat, 1587
Schuttabladen in der Stadt verboten (29.07.1587) ([Köln: Maternus Cholinus, 1587]).
Reference: Policey K 3442; Ratsedikte 297; USTC 2505820
Copies: HAStK, Best. 14 (Edikte): 6, Nr. 278; HAStK, Best. 14 (Edikte): 3, Nr. 161; HAStK, Best. 14 (Edikte): 1, Nr. 106

280. Köln – Rat, 1587
Accise von Früchten (28.05.1587) ([Köln: Maternus Cholinus, 1587]).
Reference: Policey K 3445; Ratsedikte 298; USTC 2505821
Copies: HAStK, Best. 30 (Verfassung und Verwaltung): N 27, fol. 102; HAStK, Best. 14 (Edikte): 8, Nr. 83

281. Köln – Rat, 1587
Rheinmühlenordnung (28.08.1587) ([Köln: Maternus Cholinus, 1587]).
Reference: Policey K 3445; Ratsedikte 299; USTC 2505822
Copies: HAStK, Best. 14 (Edikte): 3, Nr. 138 (Policey K wrongly lists more copies in this collection and does not differentiate between this edition and the edition above)

282. Köln – Rat, 1587
Marktverordnung für Vieh und Proviant (01.09.1587) ([Köln: Maternus Cholinus, 1587]).
Reference: Policey K 3446; Ratsedikte 300; USTC 2505823
Copies: HAStK, Best. 14 (Edikte): 8, Nr. 168

283. Köln – Rat, 1587
Münzverordnung betreffend Münzsteigerung (28.09.1587) ([Köln: Maternus Cholinus, 1587]).
Reference: Policey K 3447; Ratsedikte 301; USTC 2505824
Copies: HAStK, Best. 14 (Edikte): 14, Nr. 84

284. Köln – Rat, 1587
Münzverordnung mit Abbildungen verbotener Sorten (00.10.1587) ([Köln: Maternus Cholinus, 1587]).
Reference: Ratsedikte 302; USTC 2505825
Copies: HAStK, Best. 14 (Edikte): 14, Nr. 90; HAStK, Best. 14 (Edikte): 14, Nr. 85a

285. Köln – Rat, 1587
Von der Tag und Pforten Wacht (00.00.1587) ([Köln: Maternus Cholinus, 1587]).
Reference: Policey K 3416; Ratsedikte 3886; USTC 2506329
Copies: HAStK, Best. 30 (Verfassung und Verwaltung): N 20, fol. 13; HAStK, Best. 30 (Verfassung und Verwaltung): N 20, fol. 12; HAStK, Best. 30 (Verfassung und Verwaltung): N 20, fol. 11; HAStK, Best. 14 (Edikte): 6, Nr. 76

286. Köln – Rat, 1587
Zuwissen sei Jedermenniglich, das Unsere Herrn vom Rathe … gepieten, daß keiner … sich gelu[e]sten lasse einich Maltz auff einiche Mull ohn erlaubnuß oder auch auff beide Maltzmullen fu[e]hren zulassen (23.02.1587) ([Köln: Maternus Cholinus, 1587]).
Reference: Policey K 3424; Ratsedikte 290; USTC 2506427

Copies: HAStK, Best. 90 (Handel): A 349, fol. 16; HAStK, Best. 14 (Edikte): 8, Nr. 81; HAStK, Best. 14 (Edikte): 3, Nr. 42
http://historischesarchivkoeln.de:8080/actaproweb/archive.xhtml?id=Vz++++++00098015hupp#Vz______00098015hupp [19/69]

287. Köln – Rat, 1587
Wir Bu[e]rgermeistere und Rathe des heiligen Reichs Freyer Statt Co[e]llen thun hiermit … zuwissen … das einem jeden … so sein Korn oder andere Früchten hierhin geführt … durch unsere … Schreibern ein Zeichen nemen wu[e]rde (05.10.1587) ([Köln: Maternus Cholinus, 1587]).
Reference: Policey K 3449; Ratsedikte 303; USTC 2506428
Copies: HAStK, Best. 90 (Handel): A 349, fol. 17; HAStK, Best. 14 (Edikte): 5, Nr. 62b; HAStK, Best. 14 (Edikte): 3, Nr. 90
http://historischesarchivkoeln.de:8080/actaproweb/archive.xhtml?id=Vz++++++00098015hupp#Vz______00098015hupp [20/69]

288. Köln – Rat, 1587
Ordnung wie eß mit den weinen und anderen dro[e]gen gu[e]etteren so am Rein nidergelacht, gehalten werden soll (16.04.1587) ([Köln: Maternus Cholinus, 1587]).
Reference: Policey K 3434; Ratsedikte 291; USTC 2506460
Copies: HAStK, Best. 14 (Edikte): 3, Nr. 105; HAStK, Best. 14 (Edikte): 16, Nr. 149; HAStK, Best. 90 (Handel): A 155, fol. 21; Best. 90 (Handel): A 316, fol. 48
http://historischesarchivkoeln.de:8080/actaproweb/archive.xhtml?id=Vz++++++00097788hupp#Vz______00097788hupp [30/129]
http://historischesarchivkoeln.de:8080/actaproweb/archive.xhtml?id=Vz++++++00097970hupp#Vz______00097970hupp [52/155]

289. Köln – Rat, 1588
Zu wissen sey Jedermenniglich, das unsere Herrn vom Rathe sich der alter Rollen von den Apotheken erinnert (Visitation von Apotheken, 23.05.1588) ([Köln: Maternus Cholinus, 1588]).
Reference: Policey K 3471; Ratsedikte 305; USTC 2505563
Copies: HAStK, Best. 30 (Verfassung und Verwaltung): N 47, fol. 22; HAStK, Best. 30 (Verfassung und Verwaltung): N 47, fol. 21; HAStK, Best. 30 (Verfassung und Verwaltung): N 47, fol. 20;

HAStK, Best. 30 (Verfassung und Verwaltung): N 47, fol. 19; HAStK, Best. 14 (Edikte): 3, Nr. 48; Best. 14 (Edikte): 13, Nr. 45; USBK, Einblattsammlung

290. Köln – Rat, 1588
Verkaufsordnung für fremdes Brot (14.05.1588) ([Köln: Maternus Cholinus, 1588]).
Reference: Policey K 3470; Ratsedikte 304; USTC 2505826
Copies: HAStK, Best. 14 (Edikte): 5, Nr. 127; HAStK, Best. 14 (Edikte): 3, Nr. 61

291. Köln – Rat, 1588
Schiffslandungsverordnung für Niederländer; Krahnenverordnung (09.12.1588) ([Köln: s.n., 1588]).
Reference: Policey K 3484; Ratsedikte 307; USTC 2505827
Copies: HAStK, Best. 14 (Edikte): 16, Nr. 254; HAStK Best. 14 (Edikte): 16, Nr. 240

292. Köln – Rat, 1588
Wir Bürgermeister und Rathe … thun … allen … zuwissen, daß keiner sich gelüsten lassen … solle in oder ausserhalb den Veldt Lägern von den Kriegßleuthen geraubte güttere zukauffen unnd anhero zubrengen (07.09.1588) ([Köln: Maternus Cholinus, 1588]).
Reference: Policey K 3479; Ratsedikte 306; USTC 2506429
Copies: HAStK, Best. 14 (Edikte): 1, Nr. 98; HAStK, Best. 14 (Edikte): 1, Nr. 99; DHM Do 94/59 https://www.dhm.de/datenbank/dhm.php?seite=5&fld_0=HA940533

293. Köln – Rat, 1589
Wir Bu[e]rgermeistere un[n] Raht … gebieten herdurch ernstlich daß ein ieglicher seine Vercke[n] … an den Wa[e]llen in seinen Sta[e]llen oder andern unverweißlichen ortern halten… unnd in due Statt oder auff die Gassen nicht kommen lassen (25.08.1589) ([Köln: s.n., 1589]).
Reference: Policey K 3510; Ratsedikte 318; USTC 2505453
Copies: HAStK, Best. 14 (Edikte): 6, Nr. 266; HAStK, Best. 14 (Edikte): 1, Nr. 152a; KSM; USBK, Einblattsammlung

294. Köln – Rat, 1589
Kundt sey iedermenniglich, daß unsere Herrn vom Rathe fu[e]rkommen (Münzverordnung betreffend Beschneidung, 21.06.1589) ([Köln: s.n., 1589]).

Reference: Policey K 3497; Ratsedikte 312; USTC 2505605
Copies: HAStK, Best. 14 (Edikte): 14, Nr. 87; USBK, SB1051
http://www.ub.uni-koeln.de/cdm/ref/collection/rheinmono/id/711710

295. Köln – Rat, 1589
Kundt sey, daß unsere Herrn vom Rahte nach fu[e]rhin gehabter Probation (Münzordnung, 08.11.1589) [Köln: s.n., 1589]).
Reference: Policey K 3520 & 3519; Ratsedikte 384; USTC 2505828
Copies: HAStK, Best. 90 (Handel): A 927, fol. 16; HAStK, Best. 14 (Edikte): 14, Nr. 89; USBK, SB1051
http://historischesarchivkoeln.de:8080/actaproweb/archive.xhtml?id=Vz++++++00098720hupp#Vz______00098720hupp [23/151]
http://www.ub.uni-koeln.de/cdm/ref/collection/rheinmono/id/711150

296. Köln – Rat, 1589
Münzverordnung mit Abbildung eines verbotenen Metzer-Blank (11.01.1589) ([Köln: s.n., 1589]).
Reference: Policey K 3487; Ratsedikte 309; USTC 2505829
Copies: HAStK, Best. 14 (Edikte): 14, Nr. 86

297. Köln – Rat, 1589
Holzordnung: Forstfrevel (20.01.1589) ([Köln: s.n., 1589]).
Reference: Policey K 3489; Ratsedikte 310; USTC 2505830
Copies: HAStK, Best. 14 (Edikte): 13, Nr. 165; HAStK, Best. 14 (Edikte): 3, Nr. 101

298. Köln – Rat, 1589
Strassenverunreinigung durch Schuttabladung verboten (03.07.1589) ([Köln: s.n., 1589]).
Reference: Policey K 3500; Ratsedikte 314; USTC 2505832
Copies: HAStK, Best. 14 (Edikte): 6, Nr. 279; HAStK, Best. 14 (Edikte): 1, Nr. 62

299. Köln – Rat, 1589
Werftverordnung für Schiffer (25.08.1589) ([Köln: s.n., 1589]).
Reference: Policey K 3511; Ratsedikte 317; USTC 2505834
Copies: HAStK, Best. 14 (Edikte): 16, Nr. 223

300. Köln – Rat, 1589
Wachtordnung (19.07.1589) ([Köln: s.n., 1589]).
Reference: Policey K 3502; USTC 2506330
Copies: HAStK, Best. 30 (Verfassung und Verwaltung): N 776, fol. 1; HAStK, Best. 30 (Verfassung und Verwaltung): N 342, fol. 28

301. Köln – Rat, 1589
Wir Bu[e]rger Meister und Rath des heiligen Reichs freyer Statt Co[e]lln thun … kundt … daß uns der hunderste Pfennig von allen dru[e]gen und andern Kauffmans Waren, so allhier in Co[e]lln verkaufft getrewlich inzubringen gebu[e]ren thue (10.03.1589) ([Köln: s.n., 1589]).
Reference: Policey K 3493; Ratsedikte 311; USTC 2506430
Copies: HAStK, Best. 14 (Edikte): 3, Nr. 150; HAStK, Best. 14 (Edikte): 3, Nr. 95; HAStK, Best. 14 (Edikte): 3, Nr. 94; HAStK, Best. 14 (Edikte): 3, Nr. 32; HAStK, Best. 14 (Edikte): 3, Nr. 31; HAStK, Best. 90 (Handel): A 520, fol. 56&57; DHM Do 2009/303
http://historischesarchivkoeln.de:8080/actaproweb/archive.xhtml?id=Vz++++++00098210hupp#Vz______00098210hupp [54/67] [part I]
http://historischesarchivkoeln.de:8080/actaproweb/archive.xhtml?id=Vz++++++00098210hupp#Vz______00098210hupp [50/67] [part II]
https://www.dhm.de/datenbank/dhm.php?seite=5&fld_0=NN003152 [part I]

302. Köln – Rat, 1589
Wir Bu[e]rgermeister un[n] Rath des heilige[n] Ro[e]mischen Reichs Freyer Statt Co[e]lln thun kundt ... Folgt obgedachter werht, satz und valor der Gulden und Silbern Müntz, wie dieslb nach dem 14. Octobris eingenommen werden solle (12.08.1589) ([Köln: s.n., 1589]).
Reference: Policey K 3505; Ratsedikte 315; USTC 2506431
Copies: HAStK, Best. 90 (Handel): A 921, fol. 97; HAStK, Best. 14 (Edikte): 14, Nr. 87a
http://historischesarchivkoeln.de:8080/actaproweb/archive.xhtml?id=Vz++++++00098713hupp#Vz______00098713hupp [117/168]

303. Köln – Rat, 1589
Wir Bu[e]rgermeistere unnd Rathe des Heil[igen] Reichs Freyer Statt Co[e]lln … gebieten … daß kein Bu[e]rger … gelüsten lassen sollen einige Fruchten aussenhalb unserer Statt … an sich zubringen (06.12.1589) ([Köln: s.n., 1589]).

Reference: Policey K 3523; Ratsedikte 319; USTC 2506432
Copies: HAStK, Best. 90 (Handel): A 349, fol. 18; HAStK, Best. 14 (Edikte): 5, Nr. 64
http://historischesarchivkoeln.de:8080/actaproweb/archive.xhtml?id=Vz++++++00098015hupp#Vz______00098015hupp [21/69]

304. Köln – Rat, 1590
Kundt sey Jedermenniglich, dß unsere Herrn vom Rathe den grossen bedrog durch Inprengung deß vilfeltigen frembden Brots (Broteinfuhrordnung, 03.08.1590) ([Köln: s.n., 1590]).
Reference: Policey K 3560; Ratsedikte 327; USTC 2505538
Copies: HAStK, Best. 14 (Edikte): 5, Nr. 129; HAStK, Best. 14 (Edikte): 3, Nr. 62; USBK, Einblattsammlung

305. Köln – Rat, 1590
Zuwissen sey Jedermenniglich, daß unsere Herrn vom Rathe die unden unden gesetzte, als newe Müntzsorten auffziehen (Münzordnung mit Abbildungen verbotener Sorten, 29.08.1590) ([Köln: s.n., 1590]).
Reference: Policey K 3563; Ratsedikte 328; USTC 2505602
Copies: HAStK, Best. 14 (Edikte): 14, Nr. 94; HAStK, Best. 14 (Edikte): 14, Nr. 93a; USBK, SB1051
http://www.ub.uni-koeln.de/cdm/ref/collection/rheinmono/id/717336

306. Köln – Rat, 1590
Kundt und zuwissen sey menniglich, alß unsere Herrn vom Rathe (Münzordnung mit Abbildungen verbotener Sorten, 21.05.1590) ([Köln: s.n., 1590]).
Reference: Policey K 3549; Ratsedikte 325; USTC 2505603
Copies: HAStK, Best. 14 (Edikte): 14, Nr. 92; USBK, SB1051
http://www.ub.uni-koeln.de/cdm/ref/collection/rheinmono/id/715461

307. Köln – Rat, 1590
Wir Burgermeister, und Rhaet. des Heiligen Reichs freier Statt Coelln (Münzverordnung, 11.05.1590) ([Köln: s.n., 1590]).
Reference: Policey K 3548; Ratsedikte 324; USTC 2505604
Copies: HAStK, Best. 14 (Edikte): 14, Nr. 91; USBK, SB1051
http://www.ub.uni-koeln.de/cdm/ref/collection/rheinmono/id/712534

308. Köln – Rat, 1590
Münzverordnung und Tabelle (14.07.1590) ([Köln: s.n., 1590]).
Reference: Policey K 3556; Ratsedikte 326; USTC 2505839
Copies: HAStK, Best. 14 (Edikte): 14, Nr. 93

309. Köln – Rat, 1590
Marktverordnung Vieh und Proviant (01.09.1590) ([Köln: s.n., 1590]).
Reference: Policey K 3564; Ratsedikte 329; USTC 2505840
Copies: HAStK, Best. 14 (Edikte): 8, Nr. 169

310. Köln – Rat, 1591
Kundt und zuwissen sey allen Burgern und Ingesessenen (Wachtordnung, 09.10.1591) ([Köln: s.n., 1591]).
Reference: Policey K; 3582 Ratsedikte 331; USTC 2505452
Copies: HAStK, Best. 14 (Edikte): 6, Nr. 73; KSM

311. Köln – Rat, 1591
Fastenverordnung betreffend Fleischverkauf und -essen (15.03.1591) ([Köln: s.n., 1591]).
Reference: Policey K 3570; Ratsedikte 330; USTC 2505841
Copies: HAStK, Best. 90 (Handel): A 335a, fol. 51; HAStK, Best. 14 (Edikte): 16, Nr. 52

312. Köln – Rat, 1592
Gebetsverordnung beim Tod des Herzogs v. Jülich (31.01.1592) ([Köln: s.n., 1592]).
Reference: Policey K 3589; Ratsedikte 334; USTC 2505843
Copies: HAStK, Best. 14 (Edikte): 16, Nr. 70

313. Köln – Rat, 1592
Brunnen und Tränken der Pferde nicht zu verunreinigen durch Waschen der Schweine (10.08.1592) ([Köln: s.n., 1592]).
Reference: Policey K 3601; Ratsedikte 336; USTC 2505844
Copies: HAStK, Best. 14 (Edikte): 13, Nr. 143; HAStK, Best. 14 (Edikte): 1, Nr. 60

314. Köln – Rat, 1592
Wir Bu[e]rgermeistere und Rathe gebieten, daß ein jedweder der Abgestorbenen abfall anzeigen sollen (09.09.1592) ([Köln: s.n., 1592]).
Reference: Policey K 3604; Ratsedikte 337; USTC 2505845
Copies: HAStK, Best. 30 (Verfassung und Verwaltung): N 230, fol. 2; HAStK, Best. 30 (Verfassung und Verwaltung): N 49, fol. 18; HAStK, Best. 14 (Edikte): 16, Nr. 2; HAStK, Best. 14 (Edikte): 3, Nr. 123; HAStK, Best. 14 (Edikte): 3, Nr. 122; HAStK, Best. 14

(Edikte): 1, Nr. 39; HAStK, Best. 14 (Edikte): 1, Nr. 38; HAStK, Best. 14 (Edikte): 1, Nr. 37; HAStK, Best. 14 (Edikte): 1, Nr. 36; DHM 1989/1055
https://www.dhm.de/datenbank/dhm.php?seite=5&fld_0=NN000654

315. Köln – Rat, 1592
Marktverordnung für Vieh; Vorkauf vor der Stadt verboten (09.10.1592) ([Köln: s.n., 1592]).
Reference: Policey K 3609; Ratsedikte 338; USTC 2505846
Copies: HAStK, Best. 90 (Handel): A 339a, fol. 52; HAStK, Best. 14 (Edikte): 8, Nr. 200; HAStK, Best. 14 (Edikte): 3, Nr. 157

316. Köln – Rat, 1592
Wir Bu[e]rgermeistere unnd Rahte ... gebieten ... Kauff unnd Schiffleuthen hiemit ... daß sie ... ankom[m]ende waaren un[n] Gu[e] tere, wie breuchlich im Kauffhauß angeben und durch unsere beeydte Dienere ... auffarbeiten lassen und die schuldige gebu[e]r bezalen ... sollen (20.04.1592) ([Köln: s.n., 1592]).
Reference: Policey K 3597; USTC 2506331
Copies: HAStK, Best. 90 (Handel): A 510, fol. 17
http://historischesarchivkoeln.de:8080/actaproweb/archive.xhtml?id=Vz++++++00098198hupp#Vz______00098198hupp [17/422]

317. Köln – Rat, 1592
Kundt sey jedermenniglich, daß nach angeho[e]rter klag etlicher Bu[e] rger, so mit Saltz handtieren, der Saltzdiener ihre belohnung gesteigert (Salzverkaufsordnung, 28.02.(1592) ([Köln: s.n., 1592]).
Reference: Policey K 3592; Ratsedikte 335; USTC 2506433
Copies: HAStK, Best. 90 (Handel): A 398, fol. 12 (handwritten note: 'Anno 92'); HAStK, Best. 90 (Handel): A 398, fol. 13; HAStK, Best. 90 (Handel): A 398, fol. 20; HAStK, Best. 14 (Edikte): 13, Nr. 188
http://historischesarchivkoeln.de:8080/actaproweb/archive.xhtml?id=Vz++++++00098073hupp#Vz______00098073hupp [17/29]
http://historischesarchivkoeln.de:8080/actaproweb/archive.xhtml?id=Vz++++++00098073hupp#Vz______00098073hupp [20/29]
http://historischesarchivkoeln.de:8080/actaproweb/archive.xhtml?id=Vz++++++00098073hupp#Vz______00098073hupp [13/29]

318. Köln – Rat, 1593
Zuwissen sey Jedermenniglichen ... Das die Raderpfennigen vill zu hohe uber den werdt außbracht ... Derwegen ... dieselbe Pfenningen in diesem Craiß zuverbieten (22.10.1593) ([Köln: s.n., 1593]).

Reference: Policey K 3640; Ratsedikte 342; USTC 2505601
Copies: HAStK, Best. 90 (Handel): A 921, fol. 103; HAStK, Best. 14 (Edikte): 14, Nr. 98; USBK, SB1051
http://historischesarchivkoeln.de:8080/actaproweb/archive.xhtml?id=Vz++++++00098713hupp#Vz______00098713hupp [124/168]
http://www.ub.uni-koeln.de/cdm/ref/collection/rheinmono/id/717767

319. Köln – Rat, 1593
Kriegswerbung in fremde Dienste verboten (22.03.1593) ([Köln: s.n., 1593]).
Reference: Policey K 3623; Ratsedikte 339; USTC 2505847
Copies: HAStK, Best. 14 (Edikte): 11, Nr. 60

320. Köln – Rat, 1593
Kunt und zu wissen sey Jedermenniglich … (Viehhandelsordnung, 08.10.1593) ([Köln: s.n., 1593]).
Reference: Policey K 3638; Ratsedikte 341; USTC 2505848
Copies: HAStK, Best. 14 (Edikte): 8, Nr. 240; HAStK, Best. 14 (Edikte): 3, Nr. 173 f.; HAStK, Best. 14 (Edikte): 3, Nr. 37 f.; HAStK, Best. 14 (Edikte): 3, Nr. 7 f.; DHM Do 94/60
https://www.dhm.de/datenbank/dhm.php?seite=5&fld_0=HA940536

321. Köln – Rat, 1593
Fuhrlohn was von der Mu[e]llengassen in die Statt Wein auff zu fu[e]ren, zu zahlen schuldig sey (26.04.1593) ([Köln: s.n., 1593]).
Reference: Policey K 3628; USTC 2506333
Copies: HAStK, Best. 14 (Edikte): 29, Nr. 6; HAStK, Best. 90 (Handel): A 560, fol. 18
http://historischesarchivkoeln.de:8080/actaproweb/archive.xhtml?id=Vz++++++00098258hupp#Vz______00098258hupp [24/195]

322. Köln – Rat, 1593
Wir Bu[e]rgermeistere un[n] Raht … gebieten … allen … so einige Ochsen, Khue oder Rinderfellen … allhier binnen geschlagt auß dieser Statt zu fu[e]hren wollen, daß sie erstlich in unserm Kauffhauß Gu[e]rtzenich bey den … Accinß Meisteren die gerechte gebuernuß … bezahlen (30.08.1593) ([Köln: s.n., 1593]).
Reference: Policey K 3633; USTC 2506335
Copies: HAStK, Best. 90 (Handel): A 521, fol. 6; HAStK, Best. 90 (Handel): A 532, fol. 51; HAStK, Best. 90 (Handel): A 372, fol. 11

http://historischesarchivkoeln.de:8080/actaproweb/archive.xhtml?id=Vz++++++00098223hupp#Vz______00098223hupp [53/96]
http://historischesarchivkoeln.de:8080/actaproweb/archive.xhtml?id=Vz++++++00098211hupp#Vz______00098211hupp [8/104]
http://historischesarchivkoeln.de:8080/actaproweb/archive.xhtml?id=Vz++++++00098043hupp#Vz______00098043hupp [13/213]

323. Köln – Rat, 1593
Eines Erbaren Rhats des heiligen Reichs freyer Statt Co[e]lln Rolle un Ordnung wie es in der Wolku[e]chen gehalten sol werden (08.09.1593) ([Köln: s.n., 1593]).
Reference: Policey K 3634; Ratsedikte 340; USTC 2506434
Copies: HAStK, Best. 90 (Handel): A 466/1, fol. 34 & 35; HAStK, Best. 14 (Edikte): 8, Nr. 36; HAStK, Best. 14 (Edikte): 3, Nr. 141; HAStK, Best. 14 (Edikte): 3, Nr. 140
http://historischesarchivkoeln.de:8080/actaproweb/archive.xhtml?id=Vz++++++00098153hupp#Vz______00098153hupp [46/70] [part I]
http://historischesarchivkoeln.de:8080/actaproweb/archive.xhtml?id=Vz++++++00098153hupp#Vz______00098153hupp [48/70] [part II]

324. Köln – Rat, 1593
Kundt und zu wissen sey jedermenniglich, demnach und als unsere Herrn vom Rathe gebieten, das niemand mit fruchten gehen umb einigen kauff zumachen, dann sie sollen auf die vorgerurte platzen und stenden kommen (27.12.1593) ([Köln: s.n., 1593]).
Reference: Policey K 3643 (also wrongly listed as Policey K 1940); Ratsedikte 343; USTC 2506435
Copies: HAStK, Best. 90 (Handel): A 349, fol. 19; HAStK, Best. 14 (Edikte): 5, Nr. 63; HAStK, Best. 14 (Edikte): 3, Nr. 72
http://historischesarchivkoeln.de:8080/actaproweb/archive.xhtml?id=Vz++++++00098015hupp#Vz______00098015hupp [22/69]

325. Köln – Rat, 1594
Demnach hiebevorn neben anderen befelch und Edicten, sonderlich in dero mit zuthnn aller Rhäte und vier und viertzigen auffgerichter Wachordnung (22.06.1594) ([Köln: s.n., 1594]).

Reference: Policey K 3666; Ratsedikte 350; USTC 2505481
Copies: HAStK, Best. 33 (Militaria): A 64, fol. 73; HAStK, Best. 14 (Edikte): 6, Nr. 74; HAStK, Best. 14 (Edikte): 12, Nr. 39; HAStK, Best. 14 (Edikte): 1, Nr. 4; HAStK, Best. 14 (Edikte): 1, Nr. 3; HAStK, Best. 30 (Verfassung und Verwaltung): N 20, fol. 14

326. Köln – Rat, 1594
KUndt und zuwissen sey Jedermenniglich, daß ein Erbar Rath dieser deß Heill[igen] Reichs Freyer Statt Coelln (Spazieren gehen und Schwatzen in der Domkirche verboten, 07.01.1594) ([Köln: s.n., 1594]).
Reference: Policey K 3655; Ratsedikte 345; USTC 2505567
Copies: HAStK, Best. 14 (Edikte): 16, Nr. 49; HAStK, Best. 14 (Edikte): 1, Nr. 58; HAStK, Best. 14 (Edikte): 1, Nr. 57; USBK, Einblattsammlung

327. Köln – Rat, c.1594
Prozession bezüglich Türkenkrieg angeordnet (00.00.1594) ([Köln: s.n., c. 1594]).
Reference: Policey K 3646; Ratsedikte 344; Policey K 3530; USTC 2505849
Copies: HAStK, Best. 14 (Edikte): 11, Nr. 105; HAStK, Best. 14 (Edikte): 1, Nr. 140

328. Köln – Rat, 1594
Schnapsverkauf in Kameretten, Tanzschulen und ‚Leckerbisscher' verboten (28.01.1594) ([Köln: s.n., 1594]).
Reference: Policey K 3657; Ratsedikte 346; USTC 2505850
Copies: HAStK, Best. 14 (Edikte): 17, Nr. 13; HAStK, Best. 14 (Edikte): 1, Nr. 48; HAStK, Best. 14 (Edikte): 1, Nr. 47

329. Köln – Rat, 1594
Türkenkrieg: Prozessionen und Gebete angeordnet (04.03.1594) ([Köln: s.n., 1594]).
Reference: Policey K 3659; Ratsedikte 348; USTC 2505852
Copies: HAStK, Best. 14 (Edikte): 16, Nr. 71; HAStK, Best. 14 (Edikte): 11, Nr. 106

330. Köln – Rat, 1594
Marktverordnung: aufzutreibendes Vieh (18.08.1594) ([Köln: s.n., 1594]).
Reference: Policey K 1951 (wrong date); Ratsedikte 352; USTC 2505854

Copies: HAStK, Best. 14 (Edikte): 3, Nr. 175; HAStK, Best. 14 (Edikte): 8, Nr. 201; HAStK, Best. 14 (Edikte): 3, Nr. 33–34

331. Köln – Rat, 1594
Marktverordnung: Vieh und Proviant: Geleit (01.09.1594) ([Köln: s.n., 1594]).
Reference: Policey K 3672; Ratsedikte 353; USTC 2505855
Copies: HAStK, Best. 14 (Edikte): 8, Nr. 170; HAStK, Best. 14 (Edikte): 3, Nr. 23

332. Köln – Rat, 1594
Marktverordnung: Früchteeinfuhr (07.09.1594) ([Köln: s.n., 1594]).
Reference: Policey K 3673; Ratsedikte 354; USTC 2505856
Copies: HAStK, Best. 14 (Edikte): 5, Nr. 62; HAStK, Best. 14 (Edikte): 3, Nr. 91

333. Köln – Rat, 1594
Branntweinverkauf verboten (28.01.1594) ([Köln: s.n., 1594]).
Reference: Policey K 1942 (wrong date); USTC 2506258
Copies: HAStK, Best. 14 (Edikte): 3, Nr. 145

334. Köln – Rat, 1594
WJr Bu[e]rgermeistere un[n] Rahte ... thun kundt ... allen Schradern, Arbeitern unnd andern ... daß sie sich keiner Weinsorten auffzuladen undernemmen sollen, die nicht zuvor mit ... Wachszeichen ... versiegelt seyn (16.11.1594) ([Köln: s.n., 1594]).
Reference: Policey K 3678; USTC 2506336
Copies: HAStK, Best. 90 (Handel): A 445, fol. 45; HAStK, Best. 90 (Handel): A 439, fol. 169; HAStK, Best. 90 (Handel): A 437, fol. 66; HAStK, Best. 90 (Handel): A 437, fol. 65
http://historischesarchivkoeln.de:8080/actaproweb/archive.xhtml?id=Vz++++++00098121hupp#Vz______00098121hupp [169/245]
http://historischesarchivkoeln.de:8080/actaproweb/archive.xhtml?id=Vz++++++00098129hupp#Vz______00098129hupp [47/55]
http://historischesarchivkoeln.de:8080/actaproweb/archive.xhtml?id=Vz++++++00098119hupp#Vz______00098119hupp [69/312]
http://historischesarchivkoeln.de:8080/actaproweb/archive.xhtml?id=Vz++++++00098119hupp#Vz______00098119hupp [70/312]

335. Köln – Rat, 1594

Zuwissen sey Jedermenniglich … daß alsolche botter so auß dem Reich von Aachen, von der Maaß … sollen zur Wagen … im grossen Kauffhauß gefu[e]hrt und daselbst gewiegen werden (15.07.1594) ([Köln: s.n., 1594]).

Reference: Policey K 3646 & 3668 (also wrongly listed as Policey K 1950); Ratsedikte 351; USTC 2506436

Copies: HAStK, Best. 90 (Handel): A 549, fol. 35; HAStK, Best. 14 (Edikte): 5, Nr. 171; HAStK, Best. 14 (Edikte): 3, Nr. 81 http://historischesarchivkoeln.de:8080/actaproweb/archive.xhtml?id=Vz++++++00098245hupp#Vz______00098245hupp [36/48]

336. Köln – Rat, 1595

Kurtze Ordnung oder bericht, wessen sich die abgenommene Soldaten bey der Tag Wacht, solle verhalten (24.03.1595) ([Köln: s.n., 1595]).

Reference: Policey K 3693; Ratsedikte 358; USTC 2505480

Copies: HAStK, Best. 14 (Edikte): 3, Nr. 110; HAStK, Best. 30 (Verfassung und Verwaltung): N 20, fol. 15

337. Köln – Rat, 1595

Wiedertäufer (30.06.1595) ([Köln: s.n., 1595]).

Reference: Policey K 3708; Ratsedikte 361; USTC 2505862

Copies: HAStK, Best. 14 (Edikte): 1, Nr. 172; HAStK, Best. 14 (Edikte): 18, Nr. 156; HAStK, Best. 14 (Edikte): 1, Nr. 171

338. Köln – Rat, 1595

Marktverordnung: Vieh, Proviant (01.09.1595) ([Köln: s.n., 1595]).

Reference: Policey K 3715; Ratsedikte 364; USTC 2505864

Copies: HAStK, Best. 14 (Edikte): 8, Nr. 171

339. Köln – Rat, 1595

Demnach ein Erbar Raht (Kontribution: Protest, diese im Bereich der Stadt beizutreiben, 04.10.1595) ([Köln: s.n., 1595]).

Reference: Policey K 3718; Ratsedikte 365; USTC 2505865

Copies: HAStK, Best. 14 (Edikte): 6, Nr. 193

340. Köln – Rat, 1595

ALs unß Bu[e]rgermeistere unnd Rhat des heiligen Reichs Freyer Statt Co[e]lln … wollen wir … allen Underka[e]uffen am Pferdtmarckt geboten haben (Marktverordnung, [07.08.]1595) ([Köln: s.n., 1595]).

Reference: Policey K 3711; Ratsedikte 363; USTC 2506437

Copies: HAStK, Best. 90 (Handel): A 393, fol. 9 (handwritten note: 'ahm 7. tage Augusti'); HAStK, Best. 14 (Edikte): 8, Nr. 94; DHM Do 94/61 (handwritten note: 'ahm 7. tage des Monats Augusti') http://historischesarchivkoeln.de:8080/actaproweb/archive.xhtml?id=Vz++++++00098067hupp#Vz______00098067hupp [11/17] https://www.dhm.de/datenbank/dhm.php?seite=5&fld_0=HA940529

341. Köln – Rat, 1595
WJr Bu[e]rgermeistere unnd Rahte … wollen … hiemit angezogenes Edict von den Kornfru[e]chten … erweidert soviel erlautert und declarirt haben (04.10.1595) ([Köln: s.n., 1595]).
Reference: Policey K 3717; Ratsedikte 366; USTC 2506438
Copies: HAStK, Best. 90 (Handel): A 349, fol. 23; HAStK, Best. 14 (Edikte): 3, Nr. 73
http://historischesarchivkoeln.de:8080/actaproweb/archive.xhtml?id=Vz++++++00098015hupp#Vz______00098015hupp [26/69]

342. Köln – Rat, 1596
WJr Bu[e]rgermeistere und Raht dieser deß Heil. Reichs freyer Statt Coelln (Schmähschriften sowie Beschädigung und Verhöhnung der Rathsedikte, 16.09.1596) ([Köln: s.n., 1596]).
Reference: Policey K 3756; Ratsedikte 380; USTC 2505543
Copies: HAStK, Best. 14 (Edikte): 13, Nr. 118; HAStK, Best. 14 (Edikte): 1, Nr. 131; USBK, Einblattsammlung

343. Köln – Rat, 1596
Marktverordnung: Vieh-Unterkäuferordnung (00.00.1596) ([Köln: s.n., 1596]).
Reference: Policey K 3725; Ratsedikte 367; USTC 2505866
Notes: pamphlet
Copies: HAStK, Best. 90 (Handel): A 339a, fol. 73–80; HAStK, Best. 14 (Edikte): 8, Nr. 249

344. Köln – Rat, 1596
Wirtschaftsverordnung: Besuch der Tavernen auf dem andern Rheinufer an Sonn- und Festtagen verboten (10.06.1596) ([Köln: s.n., 1596]).
Reference: Policey K 1971 (wrong date) Policey K 3741; Ratsedikte 372; USTC 2505870
Copies: HAStK, Best. 14 (Edikte): 17, Nr. 10; HAStK, Best. 14 (Edikte): 1, Nr. 67; HAStK, Best. 14 (Edikte): 1, Nr. 66; HAStK, Best. 14 (Edikte): 3, Nr. 136

345. Köln – Rat, 1596
Öffentliches Gebet um bessere Witterung (19.06.1596) ([Köln: s.n., 1596]).
Reference: Policey K 3744; Ratsedikte 373; USTC 2505871
Copies: HAStK, Best. 295 (Geistliche Abteilung): Mappe 32, fol. 65; HAStK, Best. 14 (Edikte): 16, Nr. 72

346. Köln – Rat, 1596
Wir Bu[e]rgermeistere und Rhat ... thun zuwissen ... das die Steinmetzer, Zimmerleut und Leyendecker ... jhren Taglohn gesteigert, mehr gefordert ... so gebieten wir ... Arbeitsleuten ... mehr nit geben, dan hierin albereidt gemeldet (02.08.1596) ([Köln: s.n., 1596]).
Reference: Policey K 1972 (wrong date!); Policey K 3749; Ratsedikte 376; USTC 2505872
Copies: HAStK, Best. 14 (Edikte): 5, Nr. 4; DHM 1989/1056 https://www.dhm.de/datenbank/dhm.php?seite=5&fld_0=NN000653

347. Köln – Rat, 1596
Marktverordnung: Vieh und Proviant (01.09.1596) ([Köln: s.n., 1596]).
Reference: Policey K 3754; Ratsedikte 379; USTC 2505875
Copies: HAStK, Best. 14 (Edikte): 8, Nr. 172

348. Köln – Rat, 1596
Belohnung der Sechzehen am Fisch Kauffhauß (08.04.1596) ([Köln: s.n., 1596]).
Reference: Policey K 3734; USTC 2506337
Copies: HAStK, Best. 90 (Handel): A 514, fol. 11 http://historischesarchivkoeln.de:8080/actaproweb/archive.xhtml?id=Vz++++++00098203hupp#Vz______00098203hupp [13/246]

349. Köln – Rat, 1596
Vieheschreiber eidt (Amtseid, 27.09.1596) ([Köln: s.n., 1596]).
Reference: Policey K 3760; USTC 2506339
Copies: HAStK, Best. 90 (Handel): A 339a, fol. 86f; HAStK, Best. 90 (Handel): A 339a, fol. 69f

350. Köln – Rat, 1596
Ordnung der Gro[e]ner Fisch, wie die am Fischmarckt zuverkauffen (01.03.1596) ([Köln: s.n., 1596]).
Reference: Policey K 3730; Ratsedikte 370; USTC 2506439

Copies: HAStK, Best. 90 (Handel): A 323, fol. 25; HAStK, Best. 14 (Edikte): 5, Nr. 178
http://historischesarchivkoeln.de:8080/actaproweb/archive.xhtml?id=Vz++++++00097979hupp#Vz______00097979hupp [27/87]

351. Köln – Rat, 1596
WJr Bu[e]rgermeister unnd Rhat deß heil[igen] Reichs freyer Statt Co[e]lln ... Ordnung der gro[e]ner fisch, wie die ahm fischmarck und sonst von den Außwendigen vermög des Edicts zuverkauffen (01.07.1596) ([Köln: s.n., 1596]).
Reference: Policey K 3746; Ratsedikte 374; USTC 2506440
Copies: HAStK, Best. 90 (Handel): A 323, fol. 26; HAStK, Best. 14 (Edikte): 5, Nr. 179
http://historischesarchivkoeln.de:8080/actaproweb/archive.xhtml?id=Vz++++++00097979hupp#Vz______00097979hupp [29/87]

352. Köln – Rat, 1596
Wir Bu[e]rgermeistere und Raht des heyl[igen] Reichs freyer Statt Co[e]lln ... verwarnen ... euch ... daß vortniehe keiner understehe mit Documenten ... zu Wesel, Rhurort ... verfertigt sein eingeladen ... Saltz zu qualificiren (02.08.1596) ([Köln: s.n., 1596]).
Reference: Policey K 3750; Ratsedikte 375; USTC 2506441
Copies: HAStK, Best. 14 (Edikte): 13, Nr. 189; HAStK, Best. 90 (Handel): A 398, fol. 14; HAStK, Best. 90 (Handel): A 398, fol. 15
http://historischesarchivkoeln.de:8080/actaproweb/archive.xhtml?id=Vz++++++00098073hupp#Vz______00098073hupp [21/29]
http://historischesarchivkoeln.de:8080/actaproweb/archive.xhtml?id=Vz++++++00098073hupp#Vz______00098073hupp [22/29]

353. Köln – Rat, 1596
Kundt und zuwissen sey Jedermenniglich, Nach dem ... alle Vor und Ma[e]yka[e]uff ... verbotten ... den zugegen ... auff dem Viehmarckt ... unordnung geu[e]bt worden ... So ... hiemit abermaln obgemelte ... ordnungen erweitert (27.09.1596) ([Köln: s.n., 1596]).
Reference: Policey K 3759; Ratsedikte 381; USTC 2506442
Copies: HAStK, Best. 90 (Handel): A 339, fol. 132; HAStK, Best. 14 (Edikte): 8, Nr. 202; HAStK, Best. 14 (Edikte): 3, Nr. 177; HAStK, Best. 14 (Edikte): 3, Nr. 176; HAStK, Best. 14 (Edikte): 3, Nr. 6; HAStK, Best. 14 (Edikte): 3, Nr. 5; DHM Do 94/63

http://historischesarchivkoeln.de:8080/actaproweb/archive.xhtml?id=Vz++++++00097996hupp#Vz______00097996hupp [127/231]
https://www.dhm.de/datenbank/dhm.php?seite=5&fld_0=HA940528

354. Köln – Rat, 1596
Demnach wir Burgermeistere und Rhat dieser deß heil[igen] Reichs freyer Statt Co[e]lln bevelch, das all, so sich hinfurter der Mackelerey zu undernehmen bedacht, sich bey der Rentkammer ahn statt der Accinßmesiter ahngeben (02.12.1596) ([Köln: s.n., 1596]).
Reference: Policey K 3763; Ratsedikte 382; USTC 2506443
Copies: HAStK, Best. 90 (Handel): A 520, fol. 55; HAStK, Best. 14 (Edikte): 7, Nr. 49
http://historischesarchivkoeln.de:8080/actaproweb/archive.xhtml?id=Vz++++++00098210hupp#Vz______00098210hupp [52/67]

355. Köln – Rat, 1597
Registration bey anstehender Raths Chur auff allen Gaffeln zu publicieren - Ratswahl betreffend (02.06.1597) ([Köln: s.n., 1597]).
Reference: Policey K 3782 & 3784; Ratsedikte 387 & 389; USTC 2505435
Copies: HAStK, Best. 14 (Edikte): 3, Nr. 149; HAStK, Best. 14 (Edikte): 1, Nr. 91; HAStK, Best. 14 (Edikte): 12, Nr. 17; USBK, Einblattsammlung

356. Köln – Rat, 1597
WJr Bürgermeistere und Rhat dieser deß heiligen Reichs freyer Statt Co[e]lln thun kundt … Als … Gott … Pest unnd … Kranckheiten entzu[e]nden lassen … verordnen hiermit (06.01.1597) ([Köln: s.n., 1597]).
Reference: Policey K 3767; Ratsedikte 383; USTC 2505451
Copies: KSM

357. Köln – Rat, 1597
WJr Bu[e]rgermeistere und Raht des H[eiligen] Reichs freyer Statt Co[e]lln, fu[e]gen allen … hiemit zu wissen, daß … vil falscher Rosennobelen … außgegeben … derwegen … solche untu[e]glige Rosennobeln … abreissen zulassen (28.11.1597). ([Köln: s.n., 1597]).
Reference: Policey K 3795; Ratsedikte 392; USTC 2505600
Copies: HAStK, Best. 90 (Handel): A 927, fol. 17; HAStK, Best. 14 (Edikte): 14, Nr. 95; USBK, SB1051

http://historischesarchivkoeln.de:8080/actaproweb/archive.xhtml?id=Vz++++++00098720hupp#Vz______00098720hupp [24/151]
http://www.ub.uni-koeln.de/cdm/ref/collection/rheinmono/id/718456

358. Köln – Rat, 1597
WJr Bürgermeistere und Rhat ... thun allen ... hiermit kundt ... daß keiner unser Underthanen sich in außwenidge Bestallung oder gemeine Kriegdienst einlassen (16.03.1597) ([Köln: s.n., 1597]).
Reference: Policey K 3771; Ratsedikte 386; USTC 2505878
Copies: HAStK, Best. 14 (Edikte): 11, Nr. 123; HAStK, Best. 14 (Edikte): 11, Nr. 107; DHM Do 94/64
https://www.dhm.de/datenbank/dhm.php?seite=5&fld_0=HA940532

359. Köln – Rat, 1597
Begräbnisordnung und Taxe (11.06.1597) ([Köln: s.n., 1597]).
Reference: Policey K 3783; Ratsedikte 388; USTC 2505879
Notes: pamphlet
Copies: HAStK, Best. 30 (Verfassung und Verwaltung): N 230, fol. 3; HAStK, Best. 14 (Edikte): 16, Nr. 4; HAStK, Best. 14 (Edikte): 1, Nr. 40–42

360. Köln – Rat, 1597
Wir Bu[e]rgermeistere und Raht ... bekennen ... Das wir allen ... die in unsere Statt Proviande und Victualia ... und andere Wahr zu vielem kauff brengen ... gleide ... gegeben haben (01.09.1597) ([Köln: s.n., 1597]).
Reference: Policey K 3791; Ratsedikte 390; USTC 2505880
Copies: HAStK, Best. 14 (Edikte): 8, Nr. 173; DHM Do 94/65
https://www.dhm.de/datenbank/dhm.php?seite=5&fld_0=HA940531

361. Köln – Rat, 1597
Marktverordnung: Vieh (20.10.1597) ([Köln: s.n., 1597]).
Reference: Policey K 3792; Ratsedikte 391; USTC 2505881
Copies: HAStK, Best. 90 (Handel): A 339a, fol. 63 f.; HAStK, Best. 14 (Edikte): 8, Nr. 241; HAStK, Best. 14 (Edikte): 3, Nr. 156

362. Köln – Rat, 1598
Schifflandungsverordnung, Krahnenverordnung (12.03.1598) ([Köln: s.n., 1598]).
Reference: Policey K 3798; Ratsedikte 393; USTC 2505882
Copies: HAStK, Best. 14 (Edikte): 16, Nr. 241; HAStK, Best. 14 (Edikte): 3, Nr. 112

363. Köln – Rat, 1598
Steinkohlen: Verkaufsordnung (08.07.1598) ([Köln: s.n., 1598]).
Reference: Policey K 3804; Ratsedikte 396; USTC 2505884
Copies: HAStK, Best. 14 (Edikte): 5, Nr. 226; HAStK, Best. 14 (Edikte): 1, Nr. 184

364. Köln – Rat, 1598
Marktverordnung: Vieh und Proviant (01.09.1598) ([Köln: s.n., 1598]).
Reference: Policey K 3809; Ratsedikte 398; USTC 2505886
Copies: HAStK, Best. 14 (Edikte): 8, Nr. 174

365. Köln – Rat, 1598
Wachtordnung (02.09.1598) ([Köln: s.n., 1598]).
Reference: Policey K 3810; USTC 2506341
Copies: HAStK, Best. 30 (Verfassung und Verwaltung): N 404, fol. 4; HAStK, Best. 30 (Verfassung und Verwaltung): N 404, fol. 3

366. Köln – Rat, 1598
WJr Bu[e]rgermeister und Rhat deß Heil[igen] Reichs freyer Statt Co[e]lln … thun kundt ... Ordnung der gro[e]ner Fisch, wie die am Fischmarckt und sonst von den Außwendigen vermo[e]g des Edicts zuverkauffen (29.05.1598) ([Köln: s.n., 1598]).
Reference: Policey K 3802; Ratsedikte 394; USTC 2506444
Copies: HAStK, Best. 90 (Handel): A 323, fol. 27; HAStK, Best. 14 (Edikte): 5, Nr. 180; HAStK, Best. 14 (Edikte): 3, Nr. 79
http://historischesarchivkoeln.de:8080/actaproweb/archive.xhtml?id=Vz++++++00097979hupp#Vz______00097979hupp [30/87]

367. Köln – Rat, 1599
Marktverordnung: Vieh und Proviant (01.09.1599) ([Köln: s.n., 1599]).
Reference: Policey K 3829; Ratsedikte 399; USTC 2505887
Copies: HAStK, Best. 14 (Edikte): 8, Nr. 175

368. Köln – Rat, 1599
Marktverordnung: Vorkauf (02.07.1599) ([Köln: s.n., 1599]).
Reference: Policey K 3824; Ratsedikte 400; USTC 2505888

Copies: HAStK, Best. 14 (Edikte): 5, Nr. 163; HAStK, Best. 14 (Edikte): 3, Nr. 47

369. Köln – Rat, 1599
Untersuchung des Bachlaufes angeordnet (10.09.1599) ([Köln: s.n., 1599]).
Reference: Policey K 3830; Ratsedikte 402; USTC 2505889
Copies: HAStK, Best. 14 (Edikte): 8, Nr. 135; HAStK, Best. 14 (Edikte): 1, Nr. 2; HAStK, Best. 14 (Edikte): 1, Nr. 1

370. Köln – Rat, 1599
Seidenspinnerei wieder aufzuruchten (20.12.1599) ([Köln: s.n., 1599]).
Reference: Policey K 3841; Ratsedikte 403; USTC 2505890
Copies: HAStK, Best. 95 (Zunft): A 459, Nr. 10 & 11; HAStK, Best. 95 (Zunft): A 462, Nr. 346; HAStK, Best. 14 (Edikte): 7, Nr. 18; HAStK, Best. 14 (Edikte): 3, Nr. 130; HAStK, Best. 14 (Edikte): 3, Nr. 129
15&17/86]
http://historischesarchivkoeln.de:8080/actaproweb/archive.xhtml?id=Vz++++++00000941frehde#Vz______00000941frehde [174/304]

371. Köln – Rat, 1599
WJr Burgermeistere und Raht (Hundertpfennig, 07.06.1599) ([Köln: s.n., 1599]).
Reference: USTC 2506275
Copies: HAStK, Best. 90 (Handel): A 520, fol. 57–59
http://historischesarchivkoeln.de:8080/actaproweb/archive.xhtml?id=Vz++++++00098210hupp#Vz______00098210hupp [55/67] [part I]
http://historischesarchivkoeln.de:8080/actaproweb/archive.xhtml?id=Vz++++++00098210hupp#Vz______00098210hupp [57/67] [part II]

372. Köln – Rat, 1599
Befelch des Raths, dem die Herrn Coronellen, Lieutenanten, Hauptleuth und Befehlchhabere der Fahnen sollen gelieben unnd dem gemeeß sich erzeigen (Wachtordnung, 28.07.1599) ([Köln: s.n., 1599]).
Reference: Policey K 3826; USTC 2506342
Copies: HAStK, Best. 30 (Verfassung und Verwaltung): N 20, fol. 19; HAStK, Best. 14 (Edikte): 29, Nr. 7

373. Köln – Rat, 1599

WJr Burgermeistere und Rath deß Heyl[igen] Reichs freier Statt Co[e]lln thun kundt ... Folgt Ordnung der gro[e]ner Fisch, wie die am Fischmarck und sonst von den Außwendigen vermo[e]g des Edicts zuverkauffen (12.07.1599) ([Köln: s.n., 1599]).

Reference: Policey K 2004 (wrong date!); Policey K 3825; Ratsedikte 401; USTC 2506445

Copies: HAStK, Best. 90 (Handel): A 323, fol. 28; HAStK, Best. 90 (Handel): A 323, fol. 29; HAStK, Best. 14 (Edikte): 5, Nr. 177; HAStK, Best. 14 (Edikte): 3, Nr. 80

http://historischesarchivkoeln.de:8080/actaproweb/archive.xhtml?id=Vz++++++00097979hupp#Vz______00097979hupp [32/87]

http://historischesarchivkoeln.de:8080/actaproweb/archive.xhtml?id=Vz++++++00097979hupp#Vz______00097979hupp [34/87]

374. Köln – Rat, 1600

WJr Bu[e]rgerma[e]istere und Raht dieser deß Heyligen Reichs freyer Stadt Co[e]lln Thun kundt ... Daß Wir allen ... die in unsere Statt Proviandt und Victualia ... zu feylem kauff bringen ... geleyde geben haben (01.09.1600) ([Köln: s.n., 1600]).

Reference: Policey K 3880; Ratsedikte 415; USTC 2505557

Copies: HAStK Best. 90 (Handel): A 335, fol. 10; HAStK Best. 90 (Handel): N 11, fol. 10; HAStK Best. 90 (Handel): A 550, fol. 82; HAStK Best. 14 (Edikte): 8, Nr. 178; HAStK Best. 14 (Edikte): 8, Nr. 177; HAStK Best. 14 (Edikte): 8, Nr. 176; HAStK Best. 90 (Handel): A 339, fol. 133; USBK, Einblattsammlung

http://historischesarchivkoeln.de:8080/actaproweb/archive.xhtml?id=Vz++++++00098246hupp#Vz______00098246hupp [88/161]

http://historischesarchivkoeln.de:8080/actaproweb/archive.xhtml?id=Vz++++++00097996hupp#Vz______00097996hupp [129/231]

http://historischesarchivkoeln.de:8080/actaproweb/archive.xhtml?id=Vz++++++00097991hupp#Vz______00097991hupp [14/103]

375. Köln – Rat, 1600

WJr Bu[e]rgermeistere unnd Raht dieser des Heiligen Reichs freyer Statt Co[e]lln ... wollen ... einem jedweder, der sich des Saltzhandels gebraucht ... hiermit gewarnt haben ... sich der alter Ordnung ... gemeeß zuverhalten (10.01.1600) ([Köln: s.n., 1600]).

Reference: Policey K 3860; Ratsedikte 407; USTC 2505892

Copies: HAStK Best. 90 (Handel): A 150, fol. 22; HAStK Best. 90 (Handel): A 398, fol. 16; HAStK Best. 90 (Handel): A 398, fol. 17; HAStK Best. 14 (Edikte): 4, Nr. 26; HAStK Best. 14 (Edikte): 20, Nr. 13; HAStK Best. 14 (Edikte): 13, Nr. 191; HAStK Best. 14 (Edikte): 13, Nr. 190; HAStK Best. 14 (Edikte): 3, Nr. 124
http://historischesarchivkoeln.de:8080/actaproweb/archive.xhtml?id=Vz++++++00098073hupp#Vz______00098073hupp [23/29]
http://historischesarchivkoeln.de:8080/actaproweb/archive.xhtml?id=Vz++++++00098073hupp#Vz______00098073hupp [25/29]
http://historischesarchivkoeln.de:8080/actaproweb/archive.xhtml?id=Vz++++++00097788hupp#Vz______00097788hupp [34/129]

376. Köln – Rat, 1600
Wiedertäufer und Vertriebene aus Vreden und Honnoff nicht aufzunehmen (21.01.1600) ([Köln: s.n., 1600]).
Reference: Policey K 3861; Ratsedikte 408; USTC 2505893
Copies: HAStK, Best. 14 (Edikte): 18, Nr. 157; HAStK Best. 14 (Edikte): 1, Nr. 173

377. Köln – Rat, 1600
WJr Bu[e]rgermeistere und Rath … gebieten … allen, daß sie keinem Dienstbotten … Kisten, Kasten und Truhen in jhre Häuser unnd verwarsamb auffnehmen (02.02.1600) ([Köln: s.n., 1600]).
Reference: Policey K 3863 (wrong date); Ratsedikte 409; USTC 2505894
Copies: HAStK, Best. 14 (Edikte): 1, Nr. 55; HAStK Best. 14 (Edikte): 1, Nr. 56; HAStK Best. 14 (Edikte): 3, Nr. 20; HAStK Best. 14 (Edikte): 6, Nr. 238; DHM Do 94/66

378. Köln – Rat, 1600
Seidenhandel und -Farben (15.03.1600) ([Köln: s.n., 1600]).
Reference: Policey K 3865; Ratsedikte 410; USTC 2505895
Copies: HAStK, Best. 14 (Edikte): 7, Nr. 17; HAStK Best. 14 (Edikte): 3, Nr. 126; HAStK Best. 14 (Edikte): 3, Nr. 125

379. Köln – Rat, 1600
KUndt und zu wissen sey Jedermenniglich, das unsere Herrn vom Rathe … befehlen lassen, auff den Gaffelheusern und in jhre gesellschafft, keine außwendigen Leuthe … Annemen (14.06.[1]600) ([Köln: s.n., 1600]).
Reference: Policey K 3873; Ratsedikte 411; USTC 2505896

Copies: HAStK, Best. 14 (Edikte): 12, Nr. 40; HAStK Best. 14 (Edikte): 3, Nr. 50; HAStK Best. 14 (Edikte): 1, Nr. 81; DHM Do 94/67
https://www.dhm.de/datenbank/dhm.php?seite=5&fld_0=HA940527

380. Köln – Rat, 1600
WJr Bu[e]rgermeistere und Rath ... Folgt Ordnung der gro[e]ner Fische, wie die vermu[e]g dieses Edicts zuverkauffen (30.08.1600) ([Köln: s.n., 1600]).
Reference: Policey K 3879; Ratsedikte 414; USTC 2505898
Copies: HAStK Best. 14 (Edikte): 5, Nr. 181

381. Köln – Rat, 1600
Marktverordnung (Vieh, 29.09.1600) ([Köln: s.n., 1600]).
Reference: Policey K 3881; Ratsedikte 416; USTC 2505899
Copies: HAStK Best. 14 (Edikte): 8, Nr. 203; HAStK Best. 14 (Edikte): 3, Nr. 172; HAStK Best. 14 (Edikte): 3, Nr. 171; HAStK Best. 14 (Edikte): 3, Nr. 108

382. Köln – Rat, 1600
Marktverordnung: Holzver- und -vorkauf (13.11.1600) ([Köln: s.n., 1600]).
Reference: Policey K 3885; Ratsedikte 417; USTC 2505900
Copies: HAStK, Best. 14 (Edikte): 5, Nr. 237; HAStK Best. 14 (Edikte): 3, Nr. 102; HAStK Best. 14 (Edikte): 3, Nr. 21

383. Köln – Rat, 1600
Fuhrlohn, was von der Dranckgassen, in die Statt Wein, Holtz und Stein auff zu fu[e]hren, zu zahlen schuldig seye (13.11.1600) ([Köln: s.n., 1600]).
Reference: Policey K 3886; USTC 2506347
Copies: HAStK, Best. 90 (Handel): A 560, fol. 22; HAStK Best. 14 (Edikte): 7, Nr. 73
http://historischesarchivkoeln.de:8080/actaproweb/archive.xhtml?id=Vz++++++00098258hupp#Vz______00098258hupp [31/195]

384. Köln – Rat, 1600
Fuhrlohn, was von der Rheingassen in die Statt Wein, Holtz und Stein auff zu fu[e]hren zu zahlen schuldig seye (13.11.1600) ([Köln: s.n., 1600]).
Reference: Policey K 3887; USTC 2506348

Copies: HAStK Best. 14 (Edikte): 7, Nr. 71; HAStK Best. 90 (Handel): A 560, fol. 23; HAStK Best. 90 (Handel): A 560, fol. 21 http://historischesarchivkoeln.de:8080/actaproweb/archive.xhtml?id=Vz++++++00098258hupp#Vz______00098258hupp [30/195]
http://historischesarchivkoeln.de:8080/actaproweb/archive.xhtml?id=Vz++++++00098258hupp#Vz______00098258hupp [32/195]

385. Köln – Rat, 1600
Fuhrlohn, was von der Muellengassen in die Statt Wein, Holtz und Stein auff zu fu[e]hren zu zahlen schuldig seye (13.11.1600) ([Köln: s.n., 1600]).
Reference: Policey K 3888; USTC 2506349
Copies: HAStK, Best. 14 (Edikte): 7, Nr. 72

Index